Worlds of History

A Comparative Reader

Volume One: To 1550

Kevin Reilly
Raritan Valley College

Bedford/St. Martin's
Boston • New York

To My Teachers: Eugene Meehan, Traian Stoianovich, Donald Weinstein, and the memory of Warren Susman

For Bedford/St. Martin's
History Editor: Katherine E. Kurzman
Developmental Editor: Charisse Kiino
Production Editors: Tony Perriello and Stasia Zomkowski
Production Supervisor: Catherine Hetmansky
Marketing Manager: Charles Cavaliere
Editorial Assistants: Becky Anderson, Molly Kalkstein, and Chip Turner
Production Assistant: Helaine Denenberg
Copyeditor: Marie Salter
Text Design: George McLean
Cover Design: Ann Gallager
Cover Art: Firdawsu's Shahnama, c. 1370 (*Jamshid Teaching the Crafts*). Topkapi Palace Museum, Istanbul, Turkey. *A Mason and a Carpenter.* The British Library, London, United Kingdom
Composition: Pine Tree Composition, Inc.
Printing and Binding: Haddon Craftsmen, Inc.

President: Charles H. Christensen
Editorial Director: Joan E. Feinberg
Director of Editing, Design, and Production: Marcia Cohen
Managing Editor: Elizabeth M. Schaaf

Library of Congress Catalog Card Number: 98-87546

Manufactured in the United States of America.

4 3
f e

For information, write: Bedford/St. Martin's, 75 Arlington Street, Boston, MA 02116 (617-426-7440)

ISBN: 0-312-15789-4 (Volume 1)
0-312-15788-6 (Volume 2)

Acknowledgments

Al-Muttaqi, excerpts from *Kanz al'Umman* from Bernard Lewis, ed., *Islam from the Prophet Muhammad to the Capture of Constantinople,* Volume I. Copyright © 1974. Reprinted with the permission of HarperCollins Publishers, Inc.

Anonymous, "Chandyoga Upanishad" from *The Upanishads,* translated by Juan Mascaro. Copyright © 1965 by Juan Mascaro. Reprinted with the permission of Penguin Books, Ltd.

Preface

Worlds of History is designed to meet a need that marks a new stage in the maturation of world history as an introductory course. In 1982 when the World History Association was founded, there were just three college textbooks and one reader devoted to the topic. In those early years, defining the subject matter of world history, creating a canon of sources, and distinguishing world history from other fields of history were our top priorities.

In recent years, as world history has matured in content and importance, becoming *the* introductory course in the college history curriculum, our attentions have turned to how and what students learn. We teach subject matter, but we must also teach certain skills — what the Romans called "habits of mind." This book is meant to address both these needs, conferring knowledge and critical thinking skills. These invaluable skills (for example, how to approach historical evidence, argument, and interpretation) inform how students think about the past, present, and future, and will serve them well throughout their lives.

Meant for the introductory world history course, Volume One of this two-volume reader contains ninety primary and secondary source selections that answer the question "What is essential for students to learn?", in terms of content and thinking skills. Fourteen chapters, organized chronologically, should correspond to general survey texts and to most instructors' syllabi. Understanding that some variation might exist, I have included a correlation chart in the new instructor's manual (*Editor's Notes to Accompany* WORLDS OF HISTORY) that matches each reading in this text with related chapters in sixteen of the most widely used survey texts. By dividing *Worlds of History* into two volumes, I hope to accommodate those instructors whose world history survey courses are divided into two terms, with a break at around 1500. In response to recent arguments that human history should be presented in the larger context of the history of the Earth, pre-history begins Volume One.

TOPICAL ORGANIZATION

After thirty years of teaching, I am convinced that students are generally more interested in topics than eras, and that an appreciation of period and process can be taught by focusing on topics. Some of the topics in this volume have precise chronological parameters (e.g., the First

Crusade or the Spanish conquest of Mexico) and form the basis of a single chapter; other topics, such as gender or ecology and technology, are relevant to every period and provide a basis for comparison across long stretches of time. Chapter 2 asks students to compare gender roles at two stages of human history — the Neolithic and the urban. Chapter 9 contrasts ideas of love and marriage in a single era and across many continents by examining medieval European, Chinese, Japanese, and Muslim societies.

Different periodization also calls for different analytical skills; in general, brief periods require more focused analysis and longer periods broader synthesis. Thus, Chapter 10 on the First Crusade provides an opportunity for students to examine the construction of a fairly tight narrative. Chapter 11 on technology, ecology, and science spans a millennium of developments and events, and helps students evaluate grand syntheses. As a result, students are exposed to a variety of dimensions of human history and gain experience in thinking about history's breadth and depth.

Readings can function as discrete entities while at the same time relate clearly to each other, offering numerous opportunities for analysis, evaluation, and synthesis. As a collection of fourteen topical chapters, this comparative anthology works incrementally — through fascinating, varied, and relevant readings — to direct student learning and to encourage intellectual development.

COMPARATIVE APPROACH

History demands careful comparison. In *Worlds of History,* the connections among readings in a single chapter encourage students to compare one reading with another. On a more basic level, the recognition of similarities and differences helps students make useful connections that are at the root of all critical thinking. Each chapter is constructed around a general, directed comparison. In some, students are asked to compare cultures and civilizations; in others, two sides of an encounter; in still others, two periods or two interpretations. Clearly, world history involves more than comparison, but careful analysis, well-chosen examples, and discerning judgments are vital beginnings.

THINKING HISTORICALLY

In recent years, world historians have begun to show great interest in pedagogical issues. Carnegie Mellon University and Northeastern University, among others, have developed courses and materials that attempt to delineate steps in the learning process, to benefit future historians and future students. Such attempts reflect the growing national interest in general education, the academy's attention to "critical thinking skills," and the wide acceptance of world history as valuable basic training in cultural literacy and global awareness. This book continues that effort.

Each chapter in *Worlds of History* teaches a particular historical thinking skill; further, these skills are organized in a sequence from the easiest to the most difficult, so that a student's capacity to manipulate knowledge — to analyze, synthesize, and interpret — builds one step at a time. Among the skills included are distinguishing evidence and interpretation, examining sources for points of view, evaluating interpretations, and understanding how and why historical debates change.

To emphasize both skill building and content, each chapter and every reading have a dual introduction. The first, "Historical Context," concerns subject matter, while the second, "Thinking Historically," focuses on skill acquisition and mastery. The two parts, while related, have been separated to allow instructors maximum flexibility. Each chapter concludes with "Reflections," a section that summarizes or extends the chapters' lessons. Visual images and maps are included. A companion instructor's manual provides the rationale for the selection and organization of the readings; it also highlights some teaching strategies and provides information about ancillary resources, including films and Internet sites.

Not all instructors will agree that these are the most important skills on which to focus. Regardless, my pedagogical choices were guided by the readings and topics of each chapter, as well as by their success in my own classroom. I would be grateful for classroom feedback on these learning exercises and for suggestions for other skills to emphasize in future editions. Please post your remarks and suggestions on the Bedford/St. Martin's Web site at www.bedfordstmartins.com.

ACKNOWLEDGMENTS

A book like this cannot be written without the help and advice, even if sometimes unheeded, of a vast army of colleagues and professionals. I count myself enormously fortunate to have met and known such a large group of gifted and generous scholars and teachers in my years with the World History Association. Among them, I would like to thank those who were reviewers and questionnaire respondents for this book: Helen E. Anderson, University of Indianapolis; Charlotte Beahan, Murray State University; Norman R. Bennett, Boston University; Robert Berry, Salisbury State University; Fritz Blackwell, Washington State University; Jurgen Buchenen, Wingate University; Nancy Clark, California Polytechnic State University, San Luis Obispo; Ralph Croizier, University of Victoria; Ross E. Dunn, San Diego State University; Martha L. Edwards, Truman State University; Mark Finlay, Armstrong Atlantic State University; Lorraine Gesick, University of Nebraska–Omaha; Samuel Goldberger, Capital Community Technical College; Ed Haynes, Winthrop University; Karen Jolly, University of Hawaii at Manoa; Newton Key, Eastern Illinois University; Sharon McGee, Thomas More College; Marian P. Nelson, University of Nebraska–Omaha; Joseph M. Norton, Dutchess Community College; Donathon Olliff, Auburn University; Patricia O'Neill, Central Oregon Community College; William G. Palmer, Marshall University; Maarten L. Pereboom, Salisbury State University; Vera Blinn Reber, Shippensburg State University; Sarah E. Sharbach, Salisbury State University; Marc J. Stern, Bentley College; Ronald J. Weber, University of Texas at El Paso; Sally West, Truman State University; and Ken Wolf, Murray State University.

Other friends and colleagues contributed selections, suggestions, and advice for the book in other ways. Among them, I would like to thank the following: Michael Adas, Rutgers University; Jerry Bentley, University of Hawaii; David Berry, Essex County Community College; Catherine Clay, Shippensburg University; Roger Cranse, Norwich University; Philip Curtin, Johns Hopkins University; Steve Gosch, University of Wisconsin at Eau Claire; Gregory Guzman, Bradley University; Brock Haussamen, Raritan Valley College; Sarah Hughes, Shippensburg University; Allen Howard, Rutgers University; Karen Jolly, University of Hawaii; Maghan Keita, Villanova University; Pat Manning, Northeastern University; William H. McNeill, University of Chicago; John Mears, Southern Methodist University; Gyan Prakash, Princeton University; Heidi Roupp, Aspen High School; Richard Rosen, Drexel University; Robert Rosen, University of California at Los Angeles; John Russell-Wood, Johns Hopkins University; Lynda Shaffer, Tufts University; Anthony Snyder, Brookdale Community College; Leften Stavrianos, University of California at San Diego; Peter Stearns, Carnegie Mellon University; Robert Tignor, Princeton University; Mary Evelyn Tucker, Bucknell University; Judith Zinsser, Miami University; and John Voll, University of New Hampshire.

I also want to thank the people at Bedford/St. Martin's, especially Charles Christensen, President, and Joan Feinberg, Editorial Director, who inherited the third edition of *Readings in World Civilization* almost at the moment it was published, for not being satisfied with only a fourth edition of a proven success but encouraging me to transform the book for a new generation of students. Katherine Kurzman, History Editor, put together a superb team headed by Charisse Kiino, Developmental Editor, whose thoroughness, intelligence, and good humor lightened the load while lighting the way. Editorial Assistants Chip

Turner, Molly Kalkstein, and Becky Anderson provided invaluable support. The production team, headed by Elizabeth Schaaf, Managing Editor, proved a model of "just-in-time" publishing. Tony Perriello and Stasia Zomkowski, Production Editors, and Marie Salter, Copyeditor, queried widely and well, and polished my pedestrian prose. Donna Dennison, Art Director, coordinated the cover design. Carole Frohlich, Photo Researcher, and Ann Gallager, Cover Designer, tracked down illustrations and designed the beautiful covers.

While writing this book, memories of my own introduction to history and critical thinking have come flooding back to me. I was blessed at Rutgers in the 1960s with teachers I still aspire to emulate. Eugene Meehan taught me that learning could be both hard work and fun. Traian Stoianovich, who introduced me to the work of his own teacher, Fernand Braudel, demonstrated a vision of history that was boundless, and demanded only originality from this graduate student. Donald Weinstein taught me to listen to students as if they were Stradivarii. And Warren Susman filled a room with more life than I ever knew existed. I dedicate this book to them.

Finally, I want to thank my own institution, Raritan Valley College, for nurturing my career, allowing me to teach whatever I wanted, and entrusting me with some of the best students one could encounter anywhere. I could not ask for anything more. Except, of course, a loving wife like Pearl.

Introduction

You have here fourteen lessons in world history, each of which deals with a particular historical period from human origins to the 1500s. (The second volume covers the last five hundred years.) Each lesson concerns a topic and an historical period. Some of the topics are as narrow and specific as the First Crusade and the Mongols while others are as broad and general as technology and ecology and cities. In some cases you will read about a long period of time, while in others you will examine a short period of time in greater depth.

Besides learning about each historical period and particular topics, you will also be coached to think systematically in a particular way. I call these exercises "Thinking Historically" because they are habits of mind that I associate with my own study of history. They are intended not to turn you into historians necessarily, but to help you in all your college courses and throughout the rest of your lives. Let me give you a couple of examples. The first chapter leads you to construct time lines, clearly something that historians do. But the value of the exercise is that in constructing time lines, you become more perceptive about time, the passage of time, measuring time, the time between events — all of which are useful throughout life. Similarly, a number of chapters help you in various ways to distinguish between fact and opinion, an ability as necessary at work, on a jury, in the voting booth, or in a discussion with friends as it is for the historian.

World history is nothing less than everything ever done or imagined, so we are not going to cover it all. In a famous novel, *Ulysses,* by James Joyce, the author imagines the thoughts and actions of a few friends on a single day in Dublin, June 16, 1904. The book runs almost a thousand pages. There were a lot more than a few people in Dublin on that particular day, a lot more places than Dublin in the world, and countless more days than that one in world history. So we will be forced to choose places and times. Our choices will include some particular days, like the day in 1519 that Cortés and Montezuma met, but most of the time our attention will be directed toward much longer periods. And while we will "visit" particular places like Mexico City in 1519, we will normally look at more than one place at a time. We will do this by employing a comparative approach. Comparisons can be enormously useful in studying world history. When we compare London and Cairo, Greece and India, Rome and China, Christians and Buddhists, and Spaniards and Aztecs, we learn about the general and the specific at the same time. My hope is that by comparing some of the various *worlds* of history, an understanding of world history will emerge.

Contents

5. Empire and Officialdom: Bureaucracy, Law, and Individuality *123*

Two thousand years ago the Chinese Han dynasty and the Roman Empire spanned across Eurasia. But they governed their vast realms according to different principles and with different personnel. Biographical studies reveal much about the role of individuals in different empires.

6. Tribal to Universal Religion *163*

Two religious traditions transformed themselves into universal religions at about the same time in two different parts of Asia as each became part of a more connected world. Their holy books reveal the changes as well as the desire to hold on to the tried and true.

7. Missionaries, Monasteries, and Conversions *192*

Christian evangelists in the Roman Empire and Buddhist missionaries in Asia both offered other-wordly salvation to people used to civic, family, and practical rites. How did they succeed? Were their successes based on similar strategies or needs? What can we know about the ideas of those they converted and failed to convert?

8. Medieval Civilizations *233*

Three great civilizations spanned Eurasia between 500 and 1500. Of the three, China and Islam were the strongest, Europe the weakest. But their differences can be best understood by looking separately at the social structure, economy, politics, and culture of each.

49. J. J. SAUNDERS, Civilization of Medieval Islam 251
50. ICHISADA MIYAZAKI, The Chinese Civil Service Exam System 261
51. LIU TSUNG-YUAN, Camel Kuo the Gardener 269
52. Rules for the Fan Lineage's Charitable Estate 271
Reflections 273

9. Love and Marriage 275

Love and marriage make the world go 'round today, but not a thousand years ago. Love meant different things in China, Japan, Europe, and the Islamic world. By reading what they said about love, you can make the comparison yourself.

HISTORICAL CONTEXT: Medieval Societies and Cultures, 1000–1200 C.E. 275

THINKING HISTORICALLY: Developing Comparisons from Sources 275

53. LI CH'ING-CHAO, A Wife's Collection 276
54. MURASAKI SHIKIBU, From *The Tale of Genji* 283
55. SEI SHONAGON, From *The Pillow Book* 291
56. OMAR KHAYYÁM, From *The Rubáiyát* 298
57. ANDREAS CAPELLANUS, From *The Art of Courtly Love* 304
Reflections 310

10. The First Crusade 311

No war looks the same to both sides. Despite their mutual support of a "just" or "holy" war, the Christians and Muslims viewed each other over an enormous gulf. Your challenge is to tell a story both would recognize.

HISTORICAL CONTEXT: Muslims, Christians, and Jews during the First Crusade, 1095–1099 C.E. 311

THINKING HISTORICALLY: Analyzing and Writing Narrative 311

58. AMIN MAALOUF, From *The Crusades Through Arab Eyes* 312
59. ANNA COMNENA, From *The Alexiad* 323
Map of Crusader Routes 324
60. WILLIAM OF TYRE, Peter the Hermit 328
61. ROBERT THE MONK, Pope Urban II's Call to the First Crusade 331

62. Chronicle of Solomon bar Simson 334
63. COUNT STEPHEN OF BLOIS, Letter from Antioch 340
64. RAYMOND OF ST. GILES, COUNT OF TOULOUSE, The Capture of Jerusalem by the Crusaders 342
Reflections 346

11. Technology, Ecology, and Science 347

The most important changes since the Middle Ages have been technological. Did these changes originate in Europe or South Asia? In comparing two interpretations, can pictures offer clues?

HISTORICAL CONTEXT: Europe, Asia, and Africa, 500–1500 C.E. 347

THINKING HISTORICALLY: Recognizing and Explaining Major Changes and Using Pictorial Evidence 348

65. LYNN WHITE JR., The Historical Roots of Our Ecological Crisis 349
66. *Life of Boniface:* Converting the Hessians 360
67. Image from a Cistercian Manuscript, Twelfth Century 362
68. Image from a Calendar, Fifteenth Century 364
69. FAN KUAN, Image of a Chinese Landscape 366
70. WEN ZHENGMING, Image of Chinese Nature to Depict Human Strength 368
71. LYNDA SHAFFER, Southernization 370
Reflections 383

12. "Barbarians" and Mongols 386

In the thirteenth century, the Mongols created the largest empire the world had ever known. Did they bring peace, as they claimed, or unrelieved terror as those they conquered complained? How do you judge the past?

HISTORICAL CONTEXT: Mongol Eurasia, 1200–1350 C.E. 386

THINKING HISTORICALLY: Making Moral Judgments about History 387

72. GREGORY GUZMAN, Were the Barbarians a Negative or Positive Factor in Ancient and Medieval History? 388

1

Origins and History

HISTORICAL CONTEXT

Natural History and Human History, 5 Billion–5 Thousand Years Ago

The subject of history is change. The context of history is place and time. While the "place" of world history is the entire planet, the "time" can vary considerably.

In this chapter, you will read abbreviated world histories that focus on time periods long past. We begin with the largest canvas possible: the history of the Earth. Next we examine the history of life on Earth, then the history of human life. The first three selections are not world histories in the conventional sense; that is, they are not histories of human activity. Rather, they are histories of the world and of important changes in the world.

The final two selections are histories of human activity, though, again, of time periods long past. The selection by Fowler addresses the earliest stage of human activity: hunting and gathering. It points to a particular activity — weaving — that was not previously associated with our hunting-gathering ancestors. Prior to this discovery, it was believed that weaving first appeared in humankind's next development stage, the invention of agriculture. The last selection by Wilford concerns the span of history since the beginnings of agriculture. Here, too, recent research may force us to revise our thinking: Agriculture may have begun earlier in the Americas than has previously been thought.

This chapter covers vast spans of time for two reasons: First, it is always humbling to realize, in the grand scheme of things, how briefly we humans have lived and acted upon our planet. Second, we are forced to wonder what we might miss when we study, as we do in most history courses, only the last five or ten thousand years of planetary history. After reading these selections, you might ask, what is the proper subject of world history?

THINKING HISTORICALLY

Making Time Lines

Historians try to date events not because the dates have any meaning in and of themselves, but in order to compare two or more events. If we had only a single date, it would tell us nothing. It is always in comparing and gaining perspective that true insight comes. By comparing dates, we can determine whether events occurred simultaneously, whether two events were near or far in time, and whether change was gradual or fast.

To make these judgments, we need to date as many events as possible and then chart the events on something that will clearly show their relationships in time. In the first selection, Carl Sagan uses a calendar and a clock to show the relationships of certain events in the history of the Earth. More frequently, historians use time lines to chart change. Time lines function as chronological yardsticks or rulers, with events being placed at appropriate intervals based on the "measure" used; for example, days, weeks, or years.

Time lines, as useful as they are, are specific to the span of time they measure. There can be no single time line for world history. Time lines are tools constructed to answer particular questions. Throughout the chapter, I ask you to create time lines of your own.

1

CARL SAGAN

From *The Dragons of Eden: Speculations on the Origins of Human Intelligence*

The astronomer Carl Sagan was one of the great popularizers of science in the twentieth century. In this selection from one of his many books, he finds a simple way to demonstrate the vastness of Earth's history. He plots the history of the planet on a calendar for a single year and, in this framework, he notes that the first humans appeared

Carl Sagan, *The Dragons of Eden: Speculations on the Origins of Human Intelligence* (New York: Random House, 1977), 13–17.

at 10:30 P.M. on New Year's Eve. What does this approach show you about the relationship between the history of the Earth and the history of humankind?

Thinking Historically

Transfer some of the important dates of Sagan's calendar to a time line. Draw a 12-inch line horizontally on a piece of paper, marking inch designations. The Big Bang is at the left end (0), and today is at the right end (12). Your world history course will deal only with the last hour on Sagan's log of events for December 31. Where would that be on your time line? Where would you place your own life on this time line? Where would you place the life of one of your grandparents? What is the major disadvantage of a time line drawn to this scale? What is its advantage?

The world is very old, and human beings are very young. Significant events in our personal lives are measured in years or less; our lifetimes in decades; our family genealogies in centuries; and all of recorded history in millennia. But we have been preceded by an awesome vista of time, extending for prodigious periods into the past, about which we know little — both because there are no written records and because we have real difficulty in grasping the immensity of the intervals involved.

Yet we are able to date events in the remote past. Geological stratification and radioactive dating provide information on archaeological, paleontological, and geological events; and astrophysical theory provides data on the ages of planetary surfaces, stars, and the Milky Way Galaxy, as well as an estimate of the time that has elapsed since that extraordinary event called the Big Bang — an explosion that involved all of the matter and energy in the present universe. The Big Bang may be the beginning of the universe, or it may be a discontinuity in which information about the earlier history of the universe was destroyed. But it is certainly the earliest event about which we have any record.

The most instructive way I know to express this cosmic chronology is to imagine the fifteen-billion-year lifetime of the universe (or at least its present incarnation since the Big Bang) compressed into the span of a single year. Then every billion years of Earth history would correspond to about twenty-four days of our cosmic year, and one second of that year to 475 real revolutions of the Earth about the sun. [Following] I present the cosmic chronology in three forms: a list of some representative pre-December dates; a calendar for the month of December; and a closer look at the late evening of New Year's Eve. On this scale, the events of our history books — even books that make significant efforts to deprovincialize the present — are so compressed that it is necessary to give a second-by-second recounting of the last seconds of the cosmic year. Even then, we find events listed as contemporary that we have been taught to consider as widely separated in time. In the history of life, an equally rich tapestry must have been woven in other periods — for example, between 10:02 and 10:03 on the morning of April 6th or September 16th. But we have detailed records only for the very end of the cosmic year.

The chronology corresponds to the best evidence now available. But some of it is rather shaky. No one would be astounded if, for example, it turns out that plants colonized the land in the Ordovician rather than the Silurian Period; or that segmented worms appeared earlier in the Precambrian Period than indicated. Also, in the chronology of the last ten seconds of the cosmic year, it was obviously impossible for me to include all significant events; I hope I may be excused for not having explicitly mentioned advances in art, music, and literature or the historically significant American, French, Russian, and Chinese revolutions.

The construction of such tables and calendars is inevitably humbling. It is disconcerting to find that in such a cosmic year the Earth does not condense out of interstellar matter until early September; dinosaurs emerge on Christmas Eve; flowers arise on December 28th; and men and women originate at 10:30 P.M. on New Year's Eve. All of recorded history occupies the last ten seconds of December 31; and the time from the waning of the Middle Ages to the present occupies little more than one second. But because I have arranged it that way, the first cosmic year has just ended. And despite the insignificance of the instant we have so far occupied in cosmic time, it is clear that what happens on and near Earth at the beginning of the second cosmic year will depend very much on the scientific wisdom and the distinctly human sensitivity of mankind.

Pre-December Dates

Big Bang	January 1
Origin of the Milky Way Galaxy	May 1
Origin of the solar system	September 9
Formation of the Earth	September 14
Origin of life on Earth	~September 25
Formation of the oldest rocks known on Earth	October 2
Date of oldest fossils (bacteria and blue-green algae)	October 9
Invention of sex (by microorganisms)	~November 1
Oldest fossil photosynthetic plants	November 12
Eukaryotes (first cells with nuclei) flourish	November 15

~ = *approximately*

Cosmic Calendar / December

SUNDAY	MONDAY	TUESDAY	WEDNESDAY	THURSDAY	FRIDAY	SATURDAY
	1 Significant oxygen atmosphere begins to develop on Earth.	2	3	4	5 Extensive vulcanism and channel formation on Mars.	6
7	8	9	10	11	12	13
14	15	16 First worms.	17 Precambrian ends. Paleozoic Era and Cambrian Period begin. Invertebrates flourish.	18 First oceanic plankton. Trilobites flourish.	19 Ordovician Period. First fish. First vertebrates.	20 Silurian Period. First vascular plants. Plants begin colonization of land.
21 Devonian Period begins. First insects. Animals begin colonization of land.	22 First amphibians. First winged insects.	23 Carboniferous Period. First trees. First reptiles.	24 Permian Period begins. First dinosaurs.	25 Paleozoic Era ends. Mesozoic Era begins.	26 Triassic Period. First mammals.	27 Jurassic Period. First birds.
28 Cretaceous Period. First flowers. Dinosaurs become extinct.	29 Mesozoic Era ends. Cenozoic Era and Tertiary Period begin. First cetaceans. First primates.	30 Early evolution of frontal lobes in the brains of primates. First hominids. Giant mammals flourish.	31 End of the Pliocene Period. Quaternary (Pleistocene and Holocene) Period. First humans.			

December 31

Origin of *Proconsul* and *Ramapithecus,* probable ancestors of apes and men	~1:30 P.M.
First humans	~10:30 P.M.
Widespread use of stone tools	11:00 P.M.
Domestication of fire by Peking man	11:46 P.M.
Beginning of most recent glacial period	11:56 P.M.
Seafarers settle Australia	11:58 P.M.
Extensive cave painting in Europe	11:59 P.M.
Invention of agriculture	11:59:20 P.M.
Neolithic civilization; first cities	11:59:35 P.M.
First dynasties in Sumer, Ebla, and Egypt; development of astronomy	11:59:50 P.M.
Invention of the alphabet; Akkadian Empire	11:59:51 P.M.
Hammurabic legal codes in Babylon; Middle Kingdom in Egypt	11:59:52 P.M.
Bronze metallurgy; Mycenaean culture; Trojan War; Olmec culture; invention of the compass	11:59:53 P.M.
Iron metallurgy; First Assyrian Empire; Kingdom of Israel; founding of Carthage by Phoenicia	11:59:54 P.M.
Asokan India; Ch'in Dynasty China; Periclean Athens; birth of Buddha	11:59:55 P.M.
Euclidean geometry; Archimedean physics; Ptolemaic astronomy; Roman Empire; birth of Christ	11:59:56 P.M.
Zero and decimals invented in Indian arithmetic; Rome falls; Moslem conquests	11:59:57 P.M.
Mayan civilization; Sung Dynasty China; Byzantine Empire; Mongol invasion; Crusades	11:59:58 P.M.
Renaissance in Europe; voyages of discovery from Europe and from Ming Dynasty China; emergence of the experimental method in science	11:59:59 P.M.

~ = *approximately*

2

JOHN NOBLE WILFORD

Three Fossil Discoveries Clarify the Murky Origins of Life

This article from the *New York Times* was written to inform readers about current developments in science. What current developments does the author report? What is the significance of the date for the first multicellular life forms? What was the "Cambrian Explosion" of life forms?

Thinking Historically

After you read the article, note the importance of the dates that are mentioned: 4.6 billion years ago, 3.8 billion years ago, 1.7 billion years ago, and 543 million years ago.

Create a time line by running a line across the bottom of a notebook page and marking off ten equal sections. On the far left, label the first notch 5 billion years ago, the next 4.5 billion years ago, and so on until you reach 0.5 billion years ago. At the far right, the last notch, write "today." Next, note on your time line the dates mentioned in the article — to simplify matters, you might round them off to increments of 0.5 billion years.

Now recall what these dates mean. Think of each date as a turning point in the history of life on Earth. Write a one-paragraph history of life on Earth that includes these dates. Illustrate your history by drawing a graph — using your time line as the basis — to show the increase in life forms during the last five billion years. Could you argue that your paragraph and graph constitute a "world history"?

Last, note how often scientists and universities from various parts of the world are mentioned in the article. Try to find these locations on a world map. What does the participation of these different people tell you about science today?

Life, as far as scientists can tell, gained a foothold on earth almost as soon as possible, then took an exceedingly long time rising above its

---

John Noble Wilford, "Three Fossil Discoveries Clarify the Murky Origins of Life," *New York Times*, Oct. 31, 1995, C1–C7.

simple origins, and finally, 530 million years ago, erupted in a springtime of riotous proliferation. In an astonishingly brief time, insects, earthworms, corals, sponges, mollusks, and animals with rudimentary backbones — all the major body plans of today — made their first appearance in what is known as the Cambrian Explosion.

But there are many yawning gaps in this early history of life, and so scientists welcomed reports last week of three discoveries. The reports offered important refinements in the timing of three events that have puzzled scientists trying to reconstruct the mysterious first steps in the emergence of life. The events are the introduction of large multicellular organisms, the existence of some flat jellyfish-like organisms as possible predecessors of Cambrian life, and the emergence of chordates, the core group of vertebrates that would eventually include humans.

Dr. Steven M. Stanley, a paleontologist at Johns Hopkins University in Baltimore, said the findings were the latest manifestation of a "really exciting and most important activity in the field, the development of much better chronologies that constrain our views of what actually happened."

In the beginning, 4.6 billion years ago, the planet was covered with molten rock and bombarded steadily by swarms of meteorites. Not until the surface cooled down about 4 billion years ago could there be life, the first evidence for which are 3.8 billion-year-old fossils of a kind of blue-green algae similar to pond scum. These were simple organisms with single cells lacking nuclei. It was apparently another 2 billion years before more complex cells with nuclei evolved. Until recently, little evidence existed for multicellular organisms before a billion years ago.

Now, digging in sediments in northern China near Jixian, Chinese geologists say they have gathered evidence suggesting a much earlier emergence of more complex life than previously thought. They found more than 300 fossils of leaflike multicellular plants that lived on the sea floor 1.7 billion years ago. These were described as resembling longfengshanids, which lived 700 million years later and were assumed to be the earliest reliably dated multicellular organisms.

The Chinese scientists acknowledged the discovery in Michigan of an even older spaghetti-shaped organism, but suggested that it and other early fossils "are not confidently interpreted" as multicellular plants.

Writing in the current issue of the journal *Science,* Dr. Zhu Shixing and Dr. Chen Huineng of the Chinese Academy of Geological Sciences in Tianjin said the newly discovered fossils "imply that megascopic multicellular organisms originated 1.7 billion years ago or earlier." As such, they added, the new data "have implications for the understanding of the evolution and other related aspects of Precambrian life."

Another discovery may solve the mystery of what has been called a "broken link" in the poorly understood evolutionary chain prior to the Cambrian Explosion.

For half a century, scientists have not known what to make of creatures resembling jellyfish that were found in ancient sediments of the Ediacara Hills of southern Australia and subsequently in fossil beds elsewhere in the world. Were these plants or animals? Precursors of later life or a failed experiment in biological innovation that came to a dead end? The problem was determining exactly when they lived and if, as it once seemed, they died out before the Cambrian Explosion and thus could not be directly ancestral to any of the new life forms.

Applying more precise dating technologies to Ediacaran fossils from the deserts of Namibia in southern Africa, geologists at the Massachusetts Institute of Technology and Harvard University determined that the youngest organisms had indeed survived into the early period of the Cambrian, 543 million years ago. The team, led by Dr. John Grotzinger of M.I.T., reported the results in *Science*.

"If Grotzinger and company are correct, that's excellent news," Dr. Simon Conway Morris, a paleontologist at Cambridge University in England, was quoted as saying in an accompanying article in the journal.

Scientists said the new evidence left open the possibility that there was after all no broken link in the evolutionary chain and that Ediacaran organisms could have played a role in the development of a multitude of flora and fauna that characterize the Cambrian period and are the predecessors of life on earth today.

Dr. Samuel Bowring, an M.I.T. geologist on the research team, said, "What this shows is that evolution likely proceeded smoothly as opposed to having a period of evolution followed by an extinction, which would open ecological niches allowing other life forms to develop."

The dating was done on grains of the mineral zircon found in trace amounts in volcanic ash. By analyzing the decay rates of uranium into lead, the geologists obtained dates for the fossil-bearing sediments that they say are accurate to within plus or minus one million years, a refinement previously unattainable on samples that old.

"Five to ten years ago, being able to date something to within five million years was a major achievement," Dr. Bowring said. "The more precisely we can resolve time, the more sophisticated the evolutionary questions we can address."

Dr. Stanley of Johns Hopkins suggested that the Ediacaran fossil record might have been deceptive. Evidence for these soft-bodied organisms from the sea floors was found in such profusion in sediments just before the Cambrian period because nothing was scavenging on them at that time. Then the fossils seemed to disappear. Was this the sign of a true extinction, or merely an absence of fossil remains of that particular life? With the greater diversity of life in the Cambrian, he said, there could have been many scavengers munching on the Ediacara organisms before they had a chance to become fossils.

The most abundant remains of animal life originating in the Cambrian period are found in the Burgess Shale, fossil beds in the Canadian Rockies that have been the main source of knowledge about this time. But for the last decade, paleontologists have been mining an important new source at Chengjiang in the Chinese province of Yunnan, which was the site of the third discovery reported last week.

An international team of scientists described finding what may be the earliest known representative of the Chordate, the branch of the animal kingdom that includes vertebrates and two lesser known allied forms of life. Previous generations of scientists had thought that chordates evolved in the later Ordovician geological period. Later evolution, they liked to think, could imply advanced and special status to the branch of life leading to humans.

In a report in the journal *Nature,* Dr. Lars Ramskold, a paleontologist at the University of Uppsala in Sweden, and colleagues said they had identified 525-million-year-old fossils of a strange, fishlike creature, which they have named Yunnanozoon lividum. One of the characteristics linking the specimen to chordates is its notochord, the precursor of a spinal column.

The researchers said Yunnanozoon appeared to belong to the division of chordates known as cephalochordates, which are closely related to backboned animals, including humans, but not of them. Current representatives of the group include amphioxus, a shy marine creature.

The identification of the new specimen as a chordate will be controversial, scientists said. The only other possible chordate from the Cambrian period, the Pikaia from the Burgess Shale, has not been described in a sufficiently detailed report and so has yet to be accorded full scientific standing. But the discoverers of the Chengjiang fossil said that the presence of one division of chordates in the Cambrian period indicated that the entire branch probably existed then as well.

In a commentary accompanying the chordate report, Dr. Stephen Jay Gould, a Harvard paleontologist and evolutionary biologist, said the "unambiguously identified chordate from the still earlier Chengjiang fauna now seals the fate" of previous efforts to assert the specialness of human ancestry by separating it from the herd of new Cambrian animal forms.

"So much for chordate uniqueness marked by slightly later evolution," he wrote. "As for our place in the history of life, we are of it, not above it."

3

MARY KILBOURNE MATOSSIAN

From Hominids to Human Beings

This selection is part of a chapter from a recent world history book. How is the subject of this chapter different from the previous article? How is this time period different?

What, according to the author, happened in East Africa around 15 million years ago? What happened as a long-term result of this change around 4.5 million years ago? What happened about 2.5 million years ago? 200,000 years ago? 35,000 years ago? 27,000 years ago?

Thinking Historically

What happens if you try to place the dates in this selection on the time line you drew for the previous article?

Draw a time line specific to this selection. Mark the left-most notch "5 million years ago," then add ten equally spaced notches, ending with "today" on the far right. Label notches in increments of 0.5 million years. Now plot the major dates referred to in the article, indicating to what the dates refer.

If you were to extend this time line to include 15 million years ago — using the same incremental scale — how many pages more would you need? If you wanted to include the dates mentioned in this chapter's first selection by Carl Sagan, how many pages more would you need?

To understand the geography of this selection, locate the Great Rift Valley on a topographic map, which will show the rift in relief.

Anthropologists have named us *Homo sapiens sapiens,* the clever, clever hominid. Over a century ago certain scientists abandoned the Western creation myth and began to seek human origins in nature among the primates (apes and monkeys). If apes and people had many resemblances, what kind of creatures linked the two species? When and where did this linking happen?

The discoveries of physical anthropologists and geneticists have indeed established that we belong to the primate family. The line of hominids (bipedal apes, apes who walk on two legs) differentiated from that

---

Mary Kilbourne Matossian, "From Hominids to Human Beings," in *Shaping World History* (Armonk, NY: M. E. Sharpe, 1997), 9–14.

of other apes about five million years ago. We share with chimpanzees and bonabos (pygmy chimpanzees) between 98 percent and 99 percent of our structural genes. Who can watch primates in a zoo without experiencing a shock of recognition?

In December 1992 in Ethiopia, Tim White, an anthropologist from the University of California at Berkeley, and his team discovered the earliest hominid yet known. They announced their discovery in September 1994. Anthropologists believe that the bones discovered are almost 4.5 million years old. These hominids walked upright, were four feet tall, and lived in a woodland setting. Their skull capacity was about one third that of ours. They lived very close to the time of separation between hominids and apes estimated by geneticists — five million years ago.

In August 1995 Maeve Leakey and her team discovered in Kenya similar hominids that were 4.1 million years old. These hominids are estimated to have weighed between 101 and 121 pounds. This is the most recent of a long sequence of discoveries. It now seems likely that hominids differentiated from apes in northeast Africa, in or near the Great Rift Valley of Ethiopia, Kenya, and Tanzania. Hominids had habitually upright posture and walked on two legs. They lived mainly on the ground, not in trees. These attributes appeared long before their brain expanded and they began to make tools.

About fifteen million years ago the environment in East Africa was changing. The earth's crust was splitting apart in places, while highland domes of up to nine thousand feet formed in Ethiopia and Kenya. These domes blocked the west-to-east airflow and threw the land to the east into rain shadow. Lacking moisture, the continuous forests in the east fragmented into patches of forest, woodland, and shrubland. About twelve million years ago the Great Rift Valley, running north to south, appeared in East Africa.

This development had two major biological consequences. First, the Great Rift Valley was an east-west barrier to the migration of animal populations. Second, although the apes in the dense jungle on the west side of the valley were already adapted to a humid climate and thus were not forced to adjust to a new environment, in the east a rich mosaic of ecological conditions emerged. Biologists believe that mosaic environments drive evolutionary innovation, since competing successfully in such an environment requires new adaptations. The hominids — bipedal apes — developed in such a place. This is the first example of the influence of climatic change on prehistory.

According to Peter Rodman and Henry McHenry, on the east side of the Great Rift Valley, where woodlands were scattered, a bipedal ape had an advantage. It could move more easily from one grove of food-bearing trees to a more distant grove. An ape who walked habitually on two legs was more energy-efficient than an ape who walked on four. Upright posture was also more efficient for cooling the body in the daytime heat. Other anatomical changes made it easier for hominids to stride and to run. The beginning of brain expansion in hominids began in Africa around 2.5 million years ago with *Homo habilis* and was associated with the appearance of the earliest stone tools. By 1.8 million years ago a more advanced hominid, *Homo erectus,* was making sharp-edged tools. The process involved knocking one rock against another, chipping off a sharp flake from the "core" stone and using the flake as a knife. Hominids could use this knife to cut through the hides of most animals and get to the meat quickly. Evidence shows that with this innovation hominid meat eating soon increased.

There was probably a positive feedback loop between the expansion of the hominid brain and meat eating. The hominid brain is three times as big as that of an ape of similar body size. Meat is an excellent source of protein and, because of its fat content, is high in calories; this helps to support the larger brain. At the same time the growth of the brain in relation to body weight favored the improvement of human hunting skills and higher meat consumption. In hominid females, the pelvic opening widened to compensate for the increased brain size of the hominid infant. However, that was not enough, and any greater widening would reduce bipedal mobility. A solution to the problem of increased hominid brain size was the natural selection of those hominids that produced children born "too early," with brain size only one third that of an adult. These infants are slow to mature and so depend on their parents for a longer period. This extends the time that parents can transmit culture (patterns of behavior) to their offspring. In contrast, baby apes are born with a brain one half the size of that of an adult ape. They mature more quickly than hominids do, but have fewer years of dependency to learn from their parents.

What sort of culture did prehistoric humans transmit? Cultural anthropologists who have studied the way of life of foragers (hunter-gatherers) today say that the usual size of a human band is twenty-five persons, including children and adults. A larger unit, the dialectical tribe, includes about five hundred persons. Foragers use only temporary camps and move about on their range. Since longevity was usually only twenty-five to thirty years, many children were raised by relatives, their parents being dead. The band, not the nuclear family, was the principal social unit. A band acquires food cooperatively, by hunting and gathering, and shares it. Adults teach their children, who are born self-centered, to become sensitive to the needs of others and to share food.

Is such sharing, social behavior unique to humans? Frans de Waal, a researcher at the Yerkes Primate Research Center in Atlanta, Georgia, discovered that chimpanzee groups consist of caring, sharing individuals who form self-policing networks. He believes that the roots of morality may be far older than we are. A chimpanzee seems to realize that social disorder is a threat to its individual well-being. When rivals embrace, signaling an end to their fight, the whole colony may break into loud, joyous celebration.

However, chimpanzees share food and other treasures only when it is to their advantage. They cheat when they can get away with it by hiding a private stock of food. When cheating, they try to deceive other members of the group. Fortunately, they live in groups of less than a hundred, so they can watch each other and identify the cheaters. Older chimpanzees deny food to young cheaters by excluding them from sharing in the next windfall.

It appears that both our moral and immoral tendencies are part of the natural order. Both "good" and "evil" are aspects of our adaptive and competitive strategies. We can imagine that human goodness developed out of the need to adjust to a cooperative group. By belonging to such a group an individual had a major advantage in the struggle to survive and reproduce.

No more can we think of stone-tool making and sharing behavior as unique to our species. Nor are we unique in our capacity for tactical deception and savagery. Rather, we have a place in a natural mammalian continuum.

The only behavior unique to humans appears to be the ability to communicate quickly with a large number of phonemes (discrete sounds). We can make fifty phonemes; apes can make only twelve. Humans can speak more quickly and articulately than any other species. The placement of our vocal organs makes this possible.

When did our ancestors acquire spoken language involving more than twelve phonemes? Some anthropologists think it was as far back as 2.5 million years ago (the time of *Homo habilis*). Most agree that complex spoken language goes back at least thirty-five thousand years to the time of the cave paintings in Europe. They think that language evolved as a means of social interaction, allowing individuals to prevent fights or settle them more easily.

Recent discoveries in the Pavlov Hills of the Czech Republic indicate that ceramics and weaving go back twenty-seven thousand years — to before the beginning of settled life. These skills were probably the innovations of women, because women could make pots and weave while they took care of children.

When did people exactly like us, anatomically speaking, appear? Many anthropologists think that our species (*Homo sapiens sapiens*) differentiated around two hundred thousand years ago in either south or northeast Africa. From northeast Africa people spread across the earth. They went to the Near East, Europe, China, Southeast Asia, Australia, the Pacific Islands, and the Americas.

Lucky humans settled on lands suited to agriculture. Only they could look forward to sustained population growth and civilization.

They were especially lucky if the relationship between land and water in their region was favorable for water transportation, as the cost of moving bulk goods by water for a given distance was one eighth to one twentieth that of moving them by land. Waterborne commerce may have been just as fundamental as the development of farming for the birth of civilization.

4

BRENDA FOWLER

Find Suggests Weaving Preceded Settled Life

In the previous selection, the author mentions the discovery in the Czech Republic of ceramics and weaving that date back twenty-seven thousand years. This selection is a news report of that find.

The discovery is especially important because weaving and ceramics have always been thought of as Neolithic (literally "new stone") inventions. The Neolithic Age began with the domestication of plants, the beginning of farming or agriculture, a little more than ten thousand years ago.

How was it possible for this society of hunters and gatherers (a Paleolithic, or old Stone Age society) to discover weaving and ceramics? How, according to the author, does this discovery change our idea of hunting-gathering society?

Because this early invention of weaving and ceramics was apparently lost and then reinvented in agricultural society, how does the discovery change our association of weaving and ceramics with agriculture? Can historical "firsts" sometimes be misleading?

Thinking Historically

Create a time line that will show the important dates in this selection, notably twenty-seven thousand years ago and the beginnings of agriculture ten thousand years ago. You might choose to span your time line from fifty thousand years ago to the present. Compare this to

---

Brenda Fowler, "Find Suggests Weaving Preceded Settled Life," *New York Times,* May 9, 1995, C1.

your previous time line. Does it offer a different perspective on some of the same events?

Some 27,000 years ago, an innovative group of hunters and gatherers were in the habit of setting up their summer base camps near a river along the Pavlov Hills in what is now the southeastern Czech Republic. They mixed the fine soil with water and molded it into human and animal figurines and fired them, creating the oldest known fired ceramics. They took the two-and-a-half-million-year-old technology of flaking stone tools a step further by grinding them into smoothly polished pendants and rings, the earliest known examples of ground stone technology in Europe.

And now, at a meeting here last week of the Society for American Archeology, scientists announced that this same group, contemporaries of the earliest cave painters of France and northern Spain, has left the oldest evidence of weaving in the world. The site has yielded clay fragments bearing impressions of textiles or basketry, which according to Dr. James M. Adovasio of Mercyhurst College in Erie, Pennsylvania, and Dr. Olga Soffer of the University of Illinois at Urbana, push back the known origin of these technologies at least 7,000 years, to 27,000 years ago.

It also validates a suggestion long offered by some archeologists that the origin of textile technology by far predates the Neolithic period of plant and animal domestication to which it had traditionally been assigned. Archeologists tended to believe that people did not weave until they abandoned the migratory hunting and gathering way of life and settled into permanent agricultural villages with domesticated plants and animals, a process that was getting under way in many parts of the world by around 8000 B.C. and is known as the Neolithic. Once they were sedentary, the story went, they could develop such technologies as ceramics and weaving.

"I think this will really blow the socks off the Neolithic people because they always think they've got the first of everything," Dr. Soffer said in an interview. "We have this association of fabric and ceramics and ground stone technology with the Neolithic although we've known about ceramics from these people at Pavlov for a while, but it was written in Czech or German and it didn't make an impact."

Some scholars of the Upper Paleolithic, which in that part of the world stretches from about 40,000 to 12,000 years ago, had predicted that textiles might have been around at that time. "It's not very unexpected but it's very important," said Dr. Anthony Marks, an archeologist at Southern Methodist University in Dallas.

Textile specialists, especially, were encouraged by the discovery.

"It indicates how important textile structures are," said Dr. John Peter Wild, an archeologist at the University of Manchester in England. "You're way ahead of metals. The only technologies you have to compare it with in sheer brilliance of execution are stone implements. This is the organic technology that matches it."

Previously, the earliest known basketry dated to no earlier than around 13,000 years ago and the oldest piece of woven cloth was a 9,000-year-old specimen from Cayonu in southern Turkey. The oldest known twisted fibers, which could have been woven into basketry or textiles, were found in Israel and date to about 19,300 years ago.

Because baskets and textiles are made of organic materials, they perish rapidly once deposited, Dr. Adovasio said in an interview. Not surprisingly, the absence of hard evidence for textiles in the Paleolithic molded the theories on the origins and development of weaving technology.

The evidence presented last week consists of four small fragments of fired clay bearing negative impressions of a textile or finely twined basket, Dr. Soffer said. Along with hundreds of thousands of other artifacts at the rich site, they were excavated in 1954 by Dr. Bohuslav Klima, a Moravian archeologist. In the summer of 1990, Dr. Soffer, sorting through about 3,000 clay fragments in an effort to categorize them stylistically, noticed four pieces, about the size of a quarter, with markings on their concave sides.

She photographed them, with the notation "plant fibers?" and the next year showed them to her colleague, Dr. Adovasio, who, she said, went "absolutely ballistic."

Three radiocarbon dates of ashes at the site ranged from 24,870 to 26,980 years ago, and Dr. Soffer said the fragments could date from anytime between. She said she was entirely confident of the dating because there was no evidence at the site of any human occupation at all after 24,870 years ago, so the pieces could not have come from any other layers deposited later.

Analyzing magnified, high resolution photographs of the fragments, Dr. Adovasio determined that two fragments bore two different weaves and two bore indistinct parallel impressions that might be from warps, the vertical threads of a weave. He could see the alignment of the plant fibrils in the photographs so he knew the fibers were made of plant material, or bast, and not sinew, which can also be woven. Among the plants that could have provided bast were the yew and alder trees or the milkweed and nettle, the researchers said.

The archeologists did not know whether the impressions were made intentionally or accidentally. Many of the fragments were found in ash deposits. Analysis of all four showed that they had been fired at 600 to 800 degrees Fahrenheit, which is consistent with a simple kiln or a bonfire, or even a dwelling burning down, Dr. Soffer said. One possibility is that the woven item was unintentionally pressed into wet clay near a hearth — perhaps by walking on it — and subsequently fired.

Because the fragments are so small and no selvage, or defined edge, is apparent on them, Dr. Adovasio could not determine what they came from. He said the mesh would have been similar to that in a potato sack and might have come from a bag, mat, clothing, or a basket. While it would have been possible to make the pieces without some sort of loom, it would have been far easier using one, he said, even if that meant only tying one end of the warp around a tree and the other around one's waist.

"This demonstrates an amazing investment of energy," he said.

Dr. Elizabeth J. W. Barber, a prehistoric textile scholar at Occidental College in Los Angeles, noted that plain, or true weave, involved passing a weft, or horizontal, thread over one warp thread, under the next warp thread, over the next, and so on. If a nonflexible stick is woven through the warp like this, then the process can be mechanized halfway. Raising the stick lifts up every other thread of the warp (or whichever warp threads are required for the desired weave) and the weft thread can be speedily pulled through. For the following pass, the position of the separated warp threads must be reversed and that is where a heddle, which individually holds the warp threads of the second group and attaches them to a bar, comes in.

The type of weave in the Pavlov clay fragments is "twining"; though it too can produce a cloth, it cannot be mechanized because the parallel weft threads cross each other. Dr. Barber said twining produced a more stable weave because the weft threads twisted around each other and prevented sliding.

"When you see them switching from twining over to the true weave or plain weave by around 7000 B.C., then they've figured out mechanization," she said. "They've given up stability of weave for speed of production."

Dr. Adovasio noted that twining itself was already a relatively advanced form of weaving technology. He suggested twining might even be as much as 40,000 years old.

"If they're making this, then they're making cordage," said David Hyland, an archeologist at Gannon University in Erie, Pennsylvania. Cordage, essentially plant fibers twisted together, includes string and rope.

"And if they can make this, they can make anything in the way of a net, trap, or snare," said Dr. Adovasio, who believes that because of the scarcity of evidence, prehistorians had underestimated the importance of woven materials in early peoples' lives. Conversely, he said, because of their relative abundance, stone tools have been overemphasized in archeologists' interpretations of prehistoric economies.

"I don't buy a lot of the gender studies stuff," began Dr. Adovasio. "But mostly men have done the analysis of Paleolithic sites and they have in their minds the macho hunter of extinct megafauna. Guys who hunt woolly mammoths are not supposed to be making these."

The model of the Paleolithic men going off with spears to hunt while the women stayed home and gathered plants around the camp may be too simple, he said.

"Maybe they killed one mammoth every 10 years and never stopped talking about it," Dr. Soffer said.

At the Pavlov and nearby Dolni Vestonice sites, for example, Dr. Klima unearthed far more bones of smaller animals than of mammoths. While the former may have been hunted with spears, it is more likely that nets were used to capture small animals like rabbits, the archeologists said.

"This tool," noted Dr. Hyland, of cloth, "represents a much greater level of success where used for hunting than lithic tools."

Dr. Adovasio, who has been working with textiles for more than 25 years, said he hoped the discovery would inspire archeologists to learn more about how textiles and basketry decayed and to pay more attention to the possibility that textiles or their impressions are preserved on sites.

One mystery is what became of the apparently advanced technologies of these Central European hunters and gatherers after 22,000 years ago, when, as the weather gradually turned colder, the archeological record of their presence in the Pavlov Hills suddenly ceased.

"You've got the huge Scandinavian ice sheet coming down from the north and glaciers coming from the Alps and you get this no-man's land and people get out of there," Dr. Soffer said.

She suspects that some went east and some southeast. But except for a few random fired ceramics and bits of net or cord in eastern Europe, the technologies themselves remain silent for the next 7,000 to 10,000 years. When they resurface, the skills the Pavlov people employed so fancifully have been converted to practical purpose. The technique of stone grinding, instead of being used in decorative items alone, is now applied to making hoes and axes. Fired clay turns up not in figurines but in cooking and storage vessels.

"It had never dawned on these people that they could make a pot," Dr. Soffer noted.

Textiles and basketry, too, anchor themselves firmly into the technological landscape.

"It's like who invented the first flying machine? Leonardo da Vinci," Dr. Soffer said. "But Boeing didn't start making them until this century. There has to be a social and economic context for new technology. If you don't have the context, then it won't really go anywhere."

5

JOHN NOBLE WILFORD

The Seeds of History: A Find in Mexico

This article from the *New York Times* informs us of new discoveries concerning the development of agriculture in Mexico (or the Americas in general). What old idea about the agricultural revolution does this modify? How was the agricultural revolution in the Americas different from that in the Middle East?

Thinking Historically

Construct a time line that shows the important dates in the domestication of plants throughout the world. Choose a beginning date that will allow you to show at least the last ten thousand years so you can show the entire agricultural or Neolithic Age. Compare this to your other time lines. Place it on one of the earlier ones. Is either more "true," or just more "useful"?

An analysis of squash seeds from a Mexican cave has cast new light on the beginnings of agriculture in pre-Columbian America. It showed that ancient Americans began domesticating a few plants at least 4,000 years earlier than previously thought. But then they took a much longer time to become full-fledged farmers than did people in the Middle East, the first agriculturalists.

Using an improved radiocarbon dating technique, Dr. Bruce D. Smith, director of the archeobiology program at the National Museum of Natural History in Washington, determined that the squash seeds, of the size and shape of domesticated types, were 8,000 to 10,000 years old. Similar research had previously produced evidence of domesticated squash, corn, and beans in Mexico no earlier than 5,000 years ago, and nothing found elsewhere in the Americas has proved to be older.

Since the more recent date still stands for cultivated staples like corn and beans, archeologists said the new findings suggest that ancient Americans may have domesticated some wild squash for gourds and high-protein seeds, but for several thousand years they remained essen-

---

John Noble Wilford, "The Seeds of History: A Find in Mexico," *New York Times*, May 9, 1997, A9.

tially hunters and gatherers. It may not have been until about 4,700 ago in Mexico that they were established as true farmers, planting and harvesting corn and beans as well as squash instead of just gathering wild plants.

By contrast, in the Fertile Crescent of the ancient Middle East, a well-watered area that arcs across northern Syria and extends from the Euphrates and Tigris Rivers on the east to the Nile River on the west, people were domesticating wheat, barley, and other plants more than 10,000 years ago; in less than a thousand years they were true farmers, settled in villages. The ancient Chinese made a similarly rapid transition after first domesticating plants 7,500 years ago.

Dr. Smith reported the surprisingly early dates for domesticated squash in an article that is being published in today's issue of the journal *Science.* An accompanying article said the research was forcing ethnobotanists and archeobiologists to rethink the definition of a farmer in early civilizations.

Dr. Gayle J. Fritz, an archeobotanist at Washington University in St. Louis, said the earlier dates for the domesticated squash appeared to be firm and "highly significant."

But she questioned whether the squash was cultivated as a food or only for gourds, to be used as cups or fishing floats. The squash, *Cucurbita pepo,* is the same species that includes modern pumpkins and summer squash. But this newly domesticated variety was small and hard like a baseball, with little to recommend it as a food except for its seeds.

For this reason, Dr. Fritz said the new date for domesticated squash perhaps should not be regarded as the beginning of the transition to agriculture. Instead, these people were hunters and gatherers who grew a few crops like gourds.

"They weren't on any fast-track to becoming farmers," she said.

Dr. Smith said in an interview yesterday that the research might require archeologists to revise their "conceptual framework that always divides early people as either hunter-gatherers or agriculturalists."

Nearly all of the evidence for early American agriculture comes from five caves in Mexico, first excavated by Dr. Kent Flannery of the University of Michigan and Dr. Richard MacNeish, an independent American archeologist. In recent years, analysis of plant fragments from four of the caves yielded relatively young ages for domestication, no more than 5,000 years old.

Dr. Smith then re-examined samples collected in the fifth cave, called Guilá Naquitz, near Oaxaca in southeastern Mexico. The corn and beans in the other caves might be relatively young, but the squash seeds from this cave ranged form 8,000 and 10,000 years old, according to a reliable carbon 14 dating technique called accelerator mass spectrometry. . . .

REFLECTIONS

The great variety of possible time lines reminds us that history can focus on different time periods. Any history must make some judgment about how things have changed over time, and these changes can be measured only within an appropriate framework. Consider, for instance, what type of time line you would use if you wanted to compare the publication dates of each selection in this chapter. And, again, what time line would you use to plot your life as well as your parents' and grandparents' lives?

Thinking of time in a linear way can be quite useful, but there are many things a time line cannot do. It does not, for instance, establish a definitive relationship between two events except within the context of time. Assume time relationships to be coincidental unless there is reason to believe otherwise. The fact that one event occurred before another cannot, by itself, establish causation. Determining cause and effect is a complex process that begins with knowledge of when things happened.

Recognize, too, that a linear way of thinking about time is not the only way. Time might also be thought of as recurring cycles, a vast continuum. Seasons, holidays, even birthdays bring us back to familiar times: They become our touchstones. Recurring dreams, images, feelings, and smells can make the past the present, if only for a moment. Ecstatic experiences eliminate time entirely — time does fly when you're having fun.

Culturally speaking, linear time is a Western (European and American) concept. In ancient India, by contrast, philosophers imagined time as an endless series of cycles rather than a straight line. If you envisioned time as a cycle, how would you chart it? If you thought of time as a never-ending cycle, would history matter?

2

Women and the Origins of Patriarchy

HISTORICAL CONTEXT

Gathering, Agricultural, and Urban Societies, 20,000–3000 B.C.E.

The inequalities in education, income, leisure, and political power that exist between men and women in most of the world today have a long history. Our question in this chapter is, how long? Some critics attribute these inequalities to a system of patriarchy, by which they mean a general complex of male domination that pervades ideas, institutions, and personal expectations throughout society. We ask here if this patriarchy has a historical dimension, a historical beginning, middle, and presumably an end. As you read the selections in this chapter, pay particular attention to the lives of women.

The selections in this chapter span the three types of societies known to human history: hunting and gathering (the earliest human lifestyle), agricultural and pastoral (beginning about ten thousand years ago), and urban (beginning about five thousand years ago). Thus, we can speak of the agricultural revolution (8000 B.C.E.) and the urban revolution (3000 B.C.E.) as two of the most important changes in human history. These events drastically transformed the way people earned a living and led to increased populations, greater productivity, and radically changed life styles. Each of these stages of human development brought to the fore unique methods of working, living, and thinking.

We know, for instance, that human populations increased greatly with each of these revolutions in human technology. We know that as people became permanently settled in agricultural villages and then cities, economic and social differences between groups of people became more marked. Class differences became more distinct. Did differences between men and women increase as well? Specifically, did patriarchy originate as part of the transition from agricultural to urban society?

THINKING HISTORICALLY

Distinguishing Dates from Stages

To answer the previous question, you must think about the changing roles of women in history and determine whether urban society is a distinct stage of history. Thinking of historical stages is different from thinking of isolated dates or even time lines. Once historians have dated and placed events on a time line, they are able to see overlap and concurrence. Simultaneous events appear at the same point on the same line, highlighting potential similarities between societies. For instance, the development of the first cities along three important river valleys — the Tigris-Euphrates, the Nile, and the Indus — occurred approximately five thousand years ago (3000 B.C.E.). The discovery that all three of these areas produced cities (and the elements of city life — specialization, social classes, kingship, priests, writing, etc. — at the same time) leads us to a more useful sense of time. We can speak of an urban revolution, or an "urban stage" of history that recognizes the similarity between regions, peoples, and processes. If a number of the world's major societies undergo a process of city building at the same time, and if that process is not reversed but rather repeated elsewhere, we can think of that stage as an almost inevitable part of the historical process.

Even if all societies did not go through the same urbanization process five thousand years ago, we can still recognize that similarities occur in the development of city or urban societies regardless of when they were formed. We recognize that there is an urban stage of history that is distinct from our time lines. So, for instance, when we notice that some American societies became urbanized around 1000 B.C.E. and some European societies did not become urbanized for another thousand years, it does not matter, because we have recognized the process.

When we recognize a pattern, we are able to think of history in stages, which allows history to become more meaningful and intelligible to us. It is no longer just "one damn date after another." Rather, history takes on a direction and, sometimes it seems, even a goal.

The problem with stage theories of history, however, is that they are abstractions of actual historical events. They provide a nice plot, but because of their search for similarity and order, often they risk ignoring the facts. History does *not* have a goal, most historians would caution. It is difficult enough to discern direction. In this chapter, consider whether the stage theory helps or hinders our understanding of the history of women.

6

MARJORIE SHOSTAK

From *Nisa: The Life and Words of a !Kung Woman*

Marjorie Shostak, a writer and photographer, interviewed Nisa, a woman of the hunting-gathering !Kung people of the Kalahari Desert of Southern Africa. (The exclamation point at the beginning of !Kung is used to indicate one of the clicking sounds used in their language.) From these interviews, which took place between 1969 and 1971, Shostak compiled Nisa's story in Nisa's own words.

As you read Nisa's account of her childhood and early adulthood, consider in what ways it is similar to, and in what ways different from, that of a young woman growing up today in modern society. If Nisa is typical of women in her society, do !Kung women have more or less authority, prestige, or power than women in your own society?

Finally, what does Nisa's story tell us about women in hunting-gathering society?

Thinking Historically

Keep in mind that Nisa is a late twentieth-century woman. If you were to put her on a time line of the last fifteen thousand years, you would have hunting-gathering society on the first third of the line, agricultural society on the middle third, and urban society on the last third, with Nisa all the way on the right — just where you would place yourself. This seeming incongruity is how a time line differs from a comparison of "stages" of history. When we think of stages of history, we are abstracting the human past in a way that vastly oversimplifies what happened but allows us to draw important conclusions. We know hunting and gathering did not end ten thousand years ago when agriculture first began. Hunters and gatherers still live in the world today — in places like the Arctic, the Amazon, and the Kalahari. That is why we use Nisa's account, which we are lucky to have. We can have no vivid first-person accounts from those ancient hunters and gatherers — they are dead, and writing was not invented until the first cities developed five thousand years ago. So we generalize from

---

Marjorie Shostak, *Nisa: The Life and Words of a !Kung Woman* (Cambridge: Harvard University Press, 1981), 51, 56–59, 61–62, 89–90, 132–38.

Nisa's experience because we know that in some ways her life is like that of our hunting-gathering ancestors. But there are ways in which it is not. At the very least, the hunters and gatherers in the world today have been pushed by agriculturalists and city people into the most remote parts of the globe — like the Kalahari desert.

Using a contemporary of ours, like Nisa, as a kind of representative of our most distant ancestors is clearly a very strange thing to do. Why does it work? What precautions should we take?

I remember when my mother was pregnant with Kumsa. I was still small and I asked, "Mommy, that baby inside you . . . when that baby is born, will it come out from your belly button? Will the baby grow and grow until Daddy breaks open your stomach with a knife and takes my little sibling out?" She said, "No, it won't come out that way. When you give birth, a baby comes from here," and she pointed to her genitals. Then she said, "And after he is born, you can carry your little sibling around." I said, "Yes, I'll carry him!" . . .

After Kumsa was born, I sometimes just played by myself. I'd take the big kaross and lie down in it. I'd think, "Oh, I'm a child playing all alone. Where could I possibly go by myself?" Then I'd sit up and say, "Mommy, take my little brother from your kaross and let me play with him." But whenever she did, I hit him and made him cry. Even though he was still a little baby, I hit him. Then my mother would say, "You still want to nurse, but I won't let you. When Kumsa wants to, I'll let him. But whenever you want to, I'll cover my breasts with my hand and you'll feel ashamed." . . .

Another day, my mother was lying down asleep with Kumsa, and I quietly sneaked up on them. I took Kumsa away from her, put him down on the other side of the hut, and came back and lay down beside her. While she slept, I took her nipple, put it in my mouth, and began to nurse. I nursed and nursed and nursed. Maybe she thought it was my little brother. But he was still lying where I left him, while I stole his milk. I had already begun to feel wonderfully full when she woke up. She saw me and cried, "Where . . . tell me . . . what did you do with Kumsa? Where is he?" At that moment, he started to cry. I said, "He's over there."

She grabbed me and pushed me, hard, away from her. I lay there and cried. She went to Kumsa, picked him up, and laid him down beside her. She insulted me, cursing my genitals, "Have you gone crazy? Nisa-Big-Genitals, what's the matter with you? What craziness grabbed you that you took Kumsa, put him somewhere else, then lay down and nursed? Nisa-Big-Genitals! You must be crazy! I thought it was Kumsa nursing!" I lay there, crying. Then I said, "I've already nursed. I'm full. Let your baby nurse now. Go, feed him. I'm going to play." I got up and went and played. Later, I came back and stayed with my mother and her son. We stayed around together the rest of the day.

Later, when my father came back from the bush, she said, "Do you see what kind of mind your daughter has? Go, hit her! Hit her after you hear what she's done. Your daughter almost killed Kumsa! This tiny little baby, this tiny little thing, she took from beside me and dropped somewhere else. I was lying down, holding him, and fell asleep. That's when she took him from me and left him by himself. She came back, lay down, and started to nurse. Now, hit your daughter!"

I lied, "What? She's lying! Me . . . Daddy, I didn't nurse. I didn't take Kumsa and leave him by himself. Truly, I didn't. She's tricking you. She's lying. I didn't nurse. I don't even want her milk anymore." My father said, "If I ever hear of this again, I'll beat you! Don't ever do something like that again!" I said, "Yes, he's my little brother, isn't he? My brother, my little baby brother, and I *love* him. I won't do that again. He can nurse all by himself. Daddy, even if you're not here, I won't steal mommy's breasts. They belong to my brother." . . .

This was also when I used to steal food, although it only happened once in a while. Some days I wouldn't steal anything and would just stay around playing, without doing any mischief. But other times, when they left me in the village, I'd steal and ruin their things. That's what they said when they yelled at me and hit me. They said I had no sense.

It happened over all types of food: sweet nin berries or klaru bulbs, other times it was mongongo nuts. I'd think, "Uhn, uhn, they won't give me any of that. But if I steal it, they'll hit me." Sometimes, before my mother went gathering, she'd leave food inside a leather pouch and hang it high on one of the branches inside the hut. If it was klaru, she'd peel off the skins before putting them inside.

But as soon as she left, I'd steal whatever was left in the bag. I'd find the biggest bulbs and take them. I'd hang the bag back on the branch and go sit somewhere to eat. When my mother came back, she'd say, "Oh! Nisa was in here and stole all the bulbs!" She'd hit me and yell, "Don't steal! What's the matter with you that inside you there is so much stealing? Stop taking things! Why are you so full of something like that?" . . .

I started to cry. Mother broke off a branch and hit me, "Don't steal! Can't you understand! I tell you, but you don't listen. Don't your ears hear when I talk to you?" I said, "Uhn, uhn. Mommy's been making me feel bad for too long now. I'm going to stay with Grandma. Mommy keeps saying I steal things and hits me so that my skin hurts. I'm going to go stay with Grandma. I'll go where she goes and sleep beside her wherever she sleeps. And when she goes out digging klaru, I'll eat what she brings back."

But when I went to my grandmother, she said, "No, I can't take care of you this time. If you stay with me, you'll be hungry. I'm old and only go gathering one day in many. Most mornings I just stay around. We'll sit together and hunger will kill you. Now, go back and sit beside your mother and father." I said, "No, Daddy will hit. Mommy will hit me. My skin hurts from being hit. I want to stay with you."

I lived with her for a while. But I was still full of tears. I just cried and cried and cried. I sat with her and no matter if the sun was setting or was high in the sky, I just cried. One month, when the nearly full moon rose just after sunset, I want back to my mother's hut. I said, "Mommy, you hate me. You always hit me. I'm going to stay on with Grandma. You hate me and hit me until I can't stand it any more. I'm tired."

Another time when I went to my grandmother, we lived in another village, nearby. While I was there, my father said to my mother, "Go, go bring Nisa back. Get her so she can be with me. What did she do that you chased her away from here?" When I was told they wanted me to come back I said, "No, I won't go back. I'm not going to do what he said. I don't want to live with Mother. I want to stay with Grandma; my skin still hurts. Today, yes, this very day here, I'm going to just continue to sleep beside Grandma."

So, I stayed with her. Then, one day she said, "I'm going to take you back to your mother and father." She took me to them, saying, "Today, I'm giving Nisa back to you. But isn't there someone here who will take good care of her? You don't just hit and hit a child like this one. She likes food and likes to eat. All of you are lazy. You've just left her so she hasn't grown well. If there were still plenty of food around, I'd continue to take care of her. She'd just continue to grow up beside me. Only after she had grown up, would she leave. Because all of you have killed this child with hunger. With your own fingers you've beaten her, beaten her as though she weren't a Zhun/twa. She was always crying. Look at her now, how small she still is." But my mother said, "No, listen to me. You little granddaughter . . . whenever she saw food with her eyes, she'd just start crying."

Oh, but my heart was happy! Grandmother was scolding Mother! I held so much happiness in my heart that I laughed and laughed. But when Grandmother went home and left me there I cried and cried. My father yelled at me, but he didn't hit me. His anger usually came out only from his mouth. "You're so senseless! Don't you realize that after you left, everything felt less important? We wanted you to be with us. Yes, even your mother wanted you and missed you. Today, everything will be all right when you stay with us. Your mother will take you where she goes; the two of you will do things together and go gathering together. Why do you refuse to leave your grandmother now?"

But I cried and cried. I didn't want to leave her. "Mommy, let me go back and stay with Grandma, let me follow after her." But my father said,

"That's enough. No more talk like that. There's nothing here that will hit you. Now, be quiet." And I was quiet. After that, when my father dug klaru bulbs, I ate them, and when he dug chon bulbs, I ate them. I ate everything they gave me, and I wasn't yelled at any more. . . .

I used to watch my father when he left the village early in the morning, his quiver on his shoulder. He'd usually be gone all day. If he shot something, when he came back, he'd say, "Eh, I went out to the bush this morning and first I saw an animal, a giraffe. But I didn't track it well. Then I saw an eland and struck it with my arrow. Let's wait until tomorrow before we go find it." The next day we'd fill our ostrich eggshell containers with water and everyone would go to where the animal had died.

One time, my father went hunting with some other men and they took dogs with them. First they saw a baby wildebeest and killed it. Then, they went after the mother wildebeest and killed that too. They also killed a warthog.

As they were coming back, I saw them and shouted out, "Ho, ho, Daddy's bringing home meat! Daddy's coming home with meat!" My mother said, "You're talking nonsense. Your father hasn't even come home yet." Then she turned to where I was looking and said, "Eh-hey, daughter! Your father certainly has killed something. He *is* coming with meat."

I remember another time when my father's younger brother traveled from far away to come and live with us. The day before he arrived he killed an eland. He left it in the bush and continued on to our village. When he arrived, only mother and I were there. He greeted us and asked where his brother was. Mother said, "Eh, he went to look at some tracks he had seen near a porcupine hole. He'll be back when the sun sets." We sat together the rest of the day. When the sun was low in the sky, my father came back. My uncle said, "Yesterday, as I was coming here, there was an eland — perhaps it was just a small one — but I spent a long time tracking it and finally killed it in the thicket beyond the dry water pan. Why don't we get the meat and bring it back to the village?" We packed some things, left others hanging in the trees, and went to where the eland had died. It was a huge animal with plenty of fat. We lived there while they skinned the animal and the meat into strips to dry. A few days later we started home, the men carrying the meat on sticks and the women carrying it in their karosses.

At first my mother carried me on her shoulder. After a long way, she set me down and I started to cry. She was angry, "You're a big girl. You know how to walk." It was true that I was fairly big by then, but I still wanted to be carried. My older brother said, "Stop yelling at her, she's already crying," and he picked me up and carried me. After a long time walking, he also put me down. Eventually, we arrived back at the village.

We lived, eating meat; lived and lived. Then, it was finished. . . .

When adults talked to me, I listened. When I was still a young girl with no breasts, they told me that when a young woman grows up, her parents give her a husband and she continues to grow up next to him.

When they first talked to me about it, I said, "What kind of thing am I that I should take a husband? When I grow up, I won't marry. I'll just lie by myself. If I married, what would I be doing it for?"

My father said, "You don't know what you're saying. I, I am your father and am old; your mother is old, too. When you marry, you will gather food and give it to your husband to eat. He also will do things for you. If you refuse, who will give you food? Who will give you things to wear?"

I said, "There's no question about it, I won't take a husband. Why should I? As I am now, I'm still a child and won't marry." I said to my mother, "You say you have a man for me to marry? Why don't you take him and set him beside Daddy? You marry him and let them be co-husbands. What have I done that you're telling me I should marry?"

My mother said, "Nonsense. When I tell you I'm going to give you a husband, why do you say you want me to marry him? Why are you talking to me like this?"

I said, "Because I'm only a child. When I grow up and you tell me to take a husband, I'll agree. But I haven't passed through my childhood yet and I won't marry!" . . .

When I still had no breasts, when my genitals still weren't developed, when my chest was without anything on it, that was when a man named Bo came from a distant area and people started talking about marriage. Was I not almost a young woman?

One day, my parents and his parents began building our marriage hut. The day we were married, they carried me to it and set me down inside. I cried and cried and cried. Later, I ran back to my parents' hut, lay down beside my little brother, and slept, a deep sleep like death.

The next night, Nukha, an older woman, took me into the hut and stayed with me. She lay down between Bo and myself, because young girls who are still children are afraid of their husbands. So, it is our custom for an older woman to come into the young girl's hut to teach her not to be afraid. The woman is supposed to help the girl learn to like her husband. Once the couple is living nicely together and getting along, the older woman leaves them beside each other.

That's what Nukha was supposed to do. Even the people who saw her come into the hut with me thought she would lay me down and that once I fell asleep, she would leave and go home to her husband.

But Nukha had within her clever deceit. My heart refused Bo because I was a child, but Nukha, she liked him. That was why, when she laid me down in the hut with my husband, she was also laying me down with her lover. She put me in front and Bo was behind. We stayed like that for a very long time. As soon as I was asleep, they started to make love. But as Bo made love to Nukha, they knocked into me. I kept waking up as they bumped me, again and again.

I thought, "I'm just a child. I don't understand about such things. What are people doing when they move around like that? How come Nukha took me into my marriage hut and laid me down beside my husband, but when I started to cry, she changed places with me and lay down next to him? Is he hers? How come he belongs to her yet Mommy and Daddy said I should marry him?"

I lay there, thinking my thoughts. Before dawn broke, Nukha got up and went back to her husband. I lay there, sleeping, and when it started getting light, I went back to my mother's hut.

The next night, when darkness sat, Nukha came for me again. I cried, "He's your man! Yesterday you took me and brought me inside the hut, but after we all lay there, he was with you! Why are you now bringing me to someone who is yours?" She said, "That's not true, he's not mine. He's *your* husband. Now, go to your hut and sit there. Later, we'll lie down."

She brought me to the hut, but once inside, I cried and cried and cried. I was still crying when Nukha lay down with us. After we had been lying there for a very long time, Bo started to make love to her again. I thought, "What is this? What am I? Am I supposed to watch this? Don't they see me? Do they think I'm only a baby?" Later, I got up and told them I had to urinate. I passed by them and went to lie down in mother's hut and stayed there until morning broke.

That day, I went gathering with my mother and father. As we were collecting mongongo nuts and klaru roots, my mother said, "Nisa, as you are, you're already a young woman. Yet, when you go into your marriage hut to lie down, you get up, come back, and lie down with me. Do you think I have married you? No, I'm the one who gave birth to you. Now, take this man as your husband, this strong man who will get food, for you and for me to eat. Is your father the only one who can find food? A husband kills things and gives them to you; a husband works on things that become your things; a husband gets meat that is food for you to eat. Now, you have a husband, Bo; he has married you."

I said, "Mommy, let me stay with you. When night sits, let me sleep next to you. What have you done to me that I'm only a child, yet the first husband you give me belongs to Nukha?" My mother said, "Why are you saying that? Nukha's husband is not your husband. Her husband sits elsewhere, in another hut."

I said, "Well . . . the other night when she took me and put me into the hut, she laid me down in front of her; Bo slept behind. But later, they woke me up, moving around the way they did. It was the same last night. Again, I slept in front and Bo behind and again, they kept bumping into me. I'm not sure exactly what they were doing, but that's why tonight, when night sits, I want to stay with you and sleep next to you. Don't take me over there again."

My mother said, "Yo! My daughter! They were moving about?" I said. "Mm. They woke me while I was sleeping. That's why I got up and came back to you." She said, "Yo! How horny that Bo is! He's screwing Nukha! You are going to leave that man, that's the only thing I will agree to now."

My father said, "I don't like what you've told us. You're only a child, Nisa, and adults are the ones responsible for arranging your marriage. But when an adult gives a husband and that husband makes love to someone else, then that adult hasn't done well. I understand what you have told us and I say that Bo has deceived me. Therefore, when Nukha comes for you tonight, I will refuse to let you go. I will say, 'My daughter won't go into her marriage hut because you, Nukha, you have already taken him for a husband.' "

We continued to talk on our way back. When we arrived at the village, I sat down with my parents. Bo walked over to our marriage hut, then Nukha went over to him. I sat and watched as they talked. I thought, "Those two, they were screwing! That's why they kept bumping into me!"

I sat with Mother and Father while we ate. When evening came, Nukha walked over to us. "Nisa, come, let me take you to your hut." I said, "I won't go." She said, "Get up. Let me take you over there. It's your hut. How come you're already married but today you won't make your hut your home?"

That's when my mother, drinking anger, went over to Nukha and said, "As I'm standing here, I want you to tell me something. Nisa is a child who fears her husband. Yet, when you took her to her hut, you and her husband had sex together. Don't you know her husband should be trying to help bring her up? But that isn't something either of you are thinking about!"

Nukha didn't say anything, but the fire in my mother's words burned. My mother began to yell, cursing her, "Horny, that's what you are! You're no longer going to take Nisa to her husband. And, if you ever have sex with him again, I'll crack your face open. You horny woman! You'd screw your own father!"

That's when my father said, "No, don't do all the talking. You're a woman yet, how come you didn't ask me? I am a man and I will do the talking now. You, you just listen to what I say. Nisa is my child. I also gave birth to her. Now, you are are a woman and will be quiet because I am a man."

Then he said, "Nukha, I'm going to tell you something. I am Gau and today I'm going to pull my talk from inside myself and give it to you. We came together here for this marriage, but now something very bad has happened, something I do not agree to at all. Nisa is no longer going to go from here, where I am sitting, to that hut over there, that hut which you have already made your own. She is no longer going to look for anything for herself near that hut."

He continued, "Because, when I agree to give a man to my daughter, then he is only for my daughter. Nisa is a child and her husband isn't there for two to share. So go, take that man, he's already yours. Today my daughter will sit with me; she will sit here and sleep here. Tomorrow I will take her and we will move away. What you have already done to this marriage is the way it will remain."

Nukha didn't say anything. She left and went to the hut without me. Bo said, "Where's Nisa? Why are you empty, returning here alone?" Nukha said, "Nisa's father refused to let her go. She told him that you had made love to me and that's what he just now told me. I don't know what to do about this, but I won't go back to their hut again." Bo said, "I have no use for that kind of talk. Get the girl and come back with her." She said, "I'm not going to Gau's hut. We're finished with that talk now. And when I say I'm finished, I'm saying I won't go back there again."

She left and walked over to her own hut. When her husband saw her, he said, "So, you and Bo are lovers! Nisa said that when you took her to Bo, the two of you . . . how exactly *did* Bo reward you for your help?" But Nukha said, "No, I don't like Bo and he's not my lover. Nisa is just a child and it is just a child's talk she is talking."

Bo walked over to us. He tried to talk but my father said, "You, be quiet. I'm the one who's going to talk about this." So Bo didn't say anything more, and my father talked until it was finished.

The next morning, very early, my father, mother, and aunt packed our things and we all left. We slept in the mongongo groves that night and traveled on until we reached another water hole where we continued to live.

We lived and lived and nothing more happened for a while. After a long time had passed, Bo strung together some trade beads made of wood, put them into a sack with food, and traveled the long distance to the water hole where we were living.

It was late afternoon; the sun had almost left the sky. I had been out gathering with my mother, and we were coming back from the bush. We arrived in the village and my mother saw them, "Eh-hey, Bo's over there. What's he doing here? I long ago refused him. I didn't ask him to come back. I wonder what he thinks he's going to take away from here?"

We put down our gatherings and sat. We greeted Bo and his relatives—his mother, his aunt, Nukha, and Nukha's mother. Bo's mother said, "We have come because we want to take Nisa back with us." Bo said, "I'm again asking for your child. I want to take her back with me."

My father said, "No, I only just took her from you. That was the end. I won't take her and then give her again. Maybe you didn't hear me the first time? I already told you that I refused. Bo is Nukha's husband and my daughter won't be with him again. An adult woman does not make love to the man who marries Nisa."

Then he said, "Today, Nisa will just continue to live with us. Some day, another man will come and marry her. If she stays healthy and her eyes stand strong, if God doesn't kill her and she doesn't die, if God stands beside her and helps, then we will find another man to give to her."

That night, when darkness set, we all slept. I slept beside mother. When morning broke, Bo took Nukha, her mother, and the others and they left. I stayed behind. They were gone, finally gone.

We continued to stay at that water hole, eating things, doing things, and just living. No one talked further about giving me another husband, and we just lived and lived and lived.

7

ELISE BOULDING

Women and the Agricultural Revolution

Because women were the foragers or gatherers in hunting-gathering society (while men were normally the hunters), women were the likely developers of agriculture. The earliest form of agriculture was horticulture, a simple process of planting seeds with a digging stick and tending the plants in a garden. Elise Boulding imagines how the planting of wild einkorn, a wheatlike grain of the ancient Middle East, must have transformed the lives of men and women about ten thousand years ago. How might this early agriculture or horticulture have contributed to women's power or prestige?

Thinking Historically

Boulding draws a distinction between the early horticultural stage of agriculture and the later agriculture that depended on animal-drawn plows. How might this later stage of agriculture have changed the roles of men and women?

If Boulding is correct, is agriculture one stage for the history of women, or are there two stages? In terms of the history of food, does agriculture comprise one or two stages? Does our idea of stages of history depend on what we are studying?

There is some disagreement about whether the domestication of animals or plants came first. In fact, both were probably happening at the same time. There is evidence from campfire remains as long ago as 20,000 B.C. that women had discovered the food value of einkorn, a kind of wild wheat that grows all through the fertile crescent.[1] An enterprising Oklahoma agronomist, Professor Jack Harlan of the University of Oklahoma, noticed several years ago, on an expedition to eastern Turkey, how thick these stands of wild einkorn grew. He tried harvesting some, and once he had resorted to a nine-thousand-year-old

[1] The Tigris-Euphrates river valley, so called because it forms a crescent of highly fertile land between the Persian Gulf and the uplands near the Mediterranean Sea. [Ed.]

Elise Boulding, *The Underside of History: A View of Women Through Time* (Boulder, CO: Westview Press, 1976), 114–17, 118–19.

flint sickle blade set in a new wooden handle (he tried to use his bare hands first, with disastrous results), he was able to come away with an excellent harvest. After weighing what he had reaped, he estimated that a single good stand of einkorn would feed a family for a whole year. He also found that the grains had 50 percent more protein than the wheat we use now in North America for bread flour. Einkorn grains are found everywhere on the ancient home-base sites of the fertile crescent, either as roasted hulls in cooking hearths, or as imprints in the mud-and-straw walls of the earliest preagriculture huts.

It would be inevitable that grains from sheaves of einkorn carried in from a distant field would drop in well-trodden soil just outside the home base, or perhaps in a nearby pile of refuse. When the band returned the following year to this campsite — perhaps a favorite one, since not all campsites were revisited — there would be a fine stand of einkorn waiting for them right at their doorstep. We might say that the plants taught the women how to cultivate them. Planting, however, was quite a step beyond just leaving some stalks at the site where they were picked, to seed themselves for the next year. There was less reason for deliberate planting as long as bands were primarily nomadic and there was plenty of game to follow. But in time there was a premium on campsites that would have abundant grain and fruit and nuts nearby, and then there was point in scattering extra grain on the ground near the campsite for the next year. Because of the construction of the seed, einkorn easily plants itself, so it was a good plant for initiating humans into agriculture.

Gradually, bands lengthened their stays at their more productive home bases, harvesting what had been "planted" more or less intentionally, and letting the few sheep they had raised from infancy graze on nearby hills. One year there would be such a fine stand of wheat at their favorite home base, and so many sheep ambling about, that a band would decide just to stay for a while, not to move on that year.

If any one band of nomads could have anticipated what lay in store for humankind as a result of that fateful decision (made separately by thousands of little bands over the next ten thousand years), would they after all have moved on? While it may have been a relief not to be on the move, they in fact exchanged a life of relative ease, with enough to eat and few possessions, for a life of hard work, enough to eat, and economic surplus. As [archeologist V. Gordon] Childe says, "a mild acquisitiveness could now take its place among human desires."

Successful nomads have a much easier life than do farmers. Among the !Kung bushmen today, the men hunt about four days a week and the women only need to work two-and-a-half days at gathering to feed their families amply for a week. (At that, meat is a luxury item, and most of the nourishment comes from nuts and roots.) The rest of their time is leisure, to be enjoyed in visiting, creating and carrying out rituals, and just "being."

The First Settlements

For better or worse, the women and the men settled down. They settled in the caves of Belt and Hotu to a prosperous life of farming and herding on the Caspian. They settled in Eynan, Jericho, Jarmo, Beidha, Catal Huyuk, Hacilar, Arpachiyah, and Kherokitia in Cyprus, and in uncounted villages that no archaeologist's shovel has touched. These places were home-base sites first, some going back thousands of years. By 10,000 B.C. Eynan had fifty houses, small stone domes, seven meters in diameter, around a central area with storage pits. This was probably preagricultural, still a hunting and gathering band, but a settled one. The village covered two thousand square meters. Each hut had a hearth, and child and infant burials were found under some of the floors. Three successive layers of fifty stone houses have been found at the same site, so it must have been a remarkably stable site for a settlement.

What was life like, once bands settled down? This was almost from the start a woman's world. She would mark out the fields for planting, because she knew where the grain grew best, and would probably work in the fields together with the other women of the band. There would not be separate fields at first, but as the former nomads shifted from each sleeping in individual huts to building houses for family groups of mother, father, and children, a separate family feeling must have developed and women may have divided the fields by family groups.

Their fire-hardened pointed digging sticks, formerly used in gathering, now became a multipurpose implement for planting and cultivating the soil. At harvest time everyone, including the children, would help bring in the grain. The women also continued to gather fruit and nuts, again with the help of the children. The children watched the sheep and goats, but the women did the milking and cheese making. Ethnologists who have studied both foraging and agricultural societies comment on the change in the way of life for children that comes with agriculture. Whereas in foraging societies they have no responsibilities beyond feeding themselves and learning the hunting and foraging skills they will need, and therefore they have much leisure, it is very common in agricultural societies to put children to work at the age of three, chasing birds from the food plots. Older children watch the animals, and keep them out of the planted areas.

The agriculture practiced by these first women farmers and their children, producing enough food for subsistence only, must be distinguished from that agriculture which developed out of subsistence farming and which produced surpluses and fed nonfarming populations in towns. The first type is commonly called horticulture and is carried out with hand tools only. The second is agriculture proper, and involves intensive cultivation with the use of plow and (where necessary) irrigation. In areas like the hilly flanks of the fertile crescent in the Middle East, horticulture moved fairly rapidly into agriculture as it spread to the fertile plains. As we shall see, trading centers grew into towns and cities needing food from the countryside. Women and children could not unaided produce the necessary surpluses, and by the time the digging stick had turned into an animal-drawn plow, they were no longer the primary workers of the fields.

The simpler form of farming continued in areas where the soil was less fertile, and particularly in the tropical forest areas of Africa. Here soils were quickly exhausted, and each year the village women would enlist the men in helping to clear new fields which were then burned over in the slash-and-burn pattern which helped reconstitute the soils for planting again. The slash-and-burn pattern of horticulture has continued into this century, since it is a highly adaptive technique for meager tropical soils. Where the simple horticultural methods continued to be used, women continued as the primary farmers, always with their children as helpers. In a few of these societies women continued also in the positions of power; these are usually the tribes labeled by ethnologists as matrilocal. Not many tribes have survived into the twentieth century with a matrilocal pattern, however, though traces of matrilineal descent reckoning are not infrequent.

The first women farmers in the Zagreb foothills were very busy. Not only did they tend the fields and do the other chores mentioned above, they also probably built the round stone or mud-brick houses in the first villages. The frequency with which women construct shelters in foraging societies has already been cited.

Women also began to spend more time on making tools and containers. No longer needing to hold the family possessions down to what they could carry, women could luxuriate in being able to choose larger and heavier grinding stones that crushed grain more efficiently. They could make containers to hold food stores that would never have to go on the road. They ground fine stone bowls, made rough baskets, and in the process of lining their baskets with mud accidentally discovered that a mudlined basket placed in the hearth would come out hardened — the first pottery. [Archeologist] Sonja Cole suggests that pottery was invented in Khartoum in Africa about 8000 B.C., spreading northwest to the Mediterranean, but the same process probably happened over and over again as people became more sedentary.

The evidence from food remains in these early villages, 10,000 to 6000 B.C., indicates that men were still hunting, to supplement the agriculture and modest domestic herds. This means that they were not around very much. When they were, they probably shared in some of the home-base tasks.

Evidence from some of the earliest village layouts suggests that adults lived in individual huts, women keeping the children with them.

Marriage agreements apparently did not at first entail shared living quarters. As the agricultural productivity of the women increased, and the shift was made to dwellings for family units, husband-wife interaction probably became more frequent and family living patterns more complex.

With the accumulation of property, decisions about how it was to be allocated had to be made. The nature of these agreements is hardly to be found in the archaeological record, so we must extrapolate from what we know of the "purest" matrilineal tribes of the recent past.

The senior woman of a family and her daughters and sons formed the property-holding unit for the family. The senior woman's *brother* would be the administrator of the properties. His power, whether over property or in political decision making, would be derivative from his status as brother (usually but not always the oldest) to the senior woman in a family. This role of the brother, so important in present-day matrilineal societies, may not have been very important in the period we are now considering, between 12,000 and 8000 B.C.

8

GERDA LERNER

The Urban Revolution: Origins of Patriarchy

Often called "the rise of civilization," the urban revolution ushered in many changes five thousand years ago. The city societies or city-states that developed in Mesopotamia, Egypt, and the Indus River Valley after 3000 B.C.E. gave rise to the first kings, temples, priests, and social classes, as well as to writing, laws, metallurgy, warfare, markets, and private property. With the city-state came patriarchy, the assertion of male power, and the subordination of women — the signs of which were clear in Sumer and Mesopotamia. Assemblies of men or kings ruled both cities. Mesopotamian law codes favored men: Women could be divorced, punished, or sold into slavery for adultery, while men could not. Laws also required that women wear veils, restricted women's freedom of movement, and treated women as the property of fathers or husbands.

Gerda Lerner, *The Creation of Patriarchy* (Oxford: Oxford University Press, 1986), 141–45.

As we might suspect, the cultural signs of the ancient urban civilizations were also predominantly male. Kings in ancient Egypt were worshiped as gods. Cities worshiped Sky Father Gods. One Egyptian myth of creation describes the great god Ra emerging from the waters of Nun and creating the Egyptian universe from his own body. A Mesopotamian creation story, the *Enuma Elish,* recounts a primordial battle between the male god Marduk and the mother goddess Tiamat: Marduk splits Tiamat's heart with his arrow and then cracks her dead body in half like a shellfish, her hollowed-out form becoming heaven and earth.

In this selection from modern historian Gerda Lerner's *The Creation of Patriarchy,* the author gives considerable attention to the way in which religious ideas changed as city-based states replaced the world of small Neolithic villages. At the beginning of the selection, Lerner notes the impact of urban social classes and patriarchy. Because cities legislated the rule of the rich and powerful classes above the poor and slaves, there were periods in which some women — the wives and daughters of wealthy and powerful men — benefited at the expense of other women. Eventually, though, city law curtailed the freedom of all women, rich and poor. Despite these restrictions, some women continued to play a role in popular religion. What was that role? How important do you think it was?

What do you think of the author's comparison of Ishtar and the Virgin Mary? Does this comparison suggest that Christianity was more patriarchal? Do we live in a patriarchy today? What would suggest a modern patriarchy? What would suggest its absence?

Thinking Historically

Any stage theory of history depends on a series of broad generalizations. We might distinguish two here. First, Lerner suggests that cities, archaic states, kings, gods, militarism, and patriarchy are all related, that they appeared at about the same time as part of the same process of change. Notice how Lerner links some of these elements, one to the other. Do you find some of these couplings more persuasive than others?

Second, notice the absence of specific dates in this selection. The kinds of evidence Lerner uses here cannot be dated very precisely. She uses phrases like "the first half of the third millennium B.C.," which would mean between 3000 and 2500 B.C.E. Such indefinite spans make drawing a time line difficult, but try it. Mark off ten thousand years ago (8000 B.C.E.) for the agricultural revolution and five thousand years ago (3000 B.C.E.) for the urban revolution. Where on this time line would you place the origins of patriarchy? Where would you place the substitution of Sky Father Gods for Earth Mother God-

desses? Try to indicate on the time line the period in which people in Mesopotamia worshiped Ishtar. Lerner provides no dates, but she is clearly writing about the period after 3000 B.C.E. — Ishtar was a Mesopotamian goddess. Notice the time lag between the imposition of patriarchial laws and the slower process of replacing goddesses with gods. How does Lerner account for this time lag?

Do you think religion would be slower to change than law or social custom? Could the worship of Ishtar have been representative of an earlier, more agricultural, religious tradition?

. . . In Mesopotamian societies the institutionalization of patriarchy created sharply defined boundaries between women of different classes, although the development of the new gender definitions and of the customs associated with them proceeded unevenly. The state, during the process of the establishment of written law codes, increased the property rights of upper-class women, while it circumscribed their sexual rights and finally totally eroded them. The lifelong dependency of women on fathers and husbands became so firmly established in law and custom as to be considered "natural" and god-given. In the case of lower-class women, their labor power served either their families or those who owned their families' services. Their sexual and reproductive capacities were commodified, traded, leased, or sold in the interest of male family members. Women of all classes had traditionally been excluded from military power and were, by the turn of the first millennium B.C., excluded from formal education, insofar as it had become institutionalized.

Yet, even then, powerful women in powerful roles lived on in cultic service, in religious representation, and in symbols. There was a considerable time lag between the subordination of women in patriarchal society and the declassing of the goddesses. As we trace below changes in the position of male and female god figures in the pantheon of the gods in a period of over a thousand years, we should keep in mind that the power of the goddesses and their priestesses in daily life and in popular religion continued in force, even as the supreme goddesses were dethroned. It is remarkable that in societies which had subordinated women economically, educationally, and legally, the spiritual and metaphysical power of goddesses remained active and strong.

We have some indication of what practical religion was like from archaeological artifacts and from temple hymns and prayers. In Mesopotamian societies the feeding of and service to the gods was considered essential to the survival of the community. This service was performed by male and female temple servants. For important decisions of state, in warfare, and for important personal decisions one would consult an oracle or a diviner, who might be either a man or a woman. In personal distress, sickness, or misfortune the afflicted person would seek the help of his or her household-god and, if this was of no avail, would appeal to any one of a number of gods or goddesses who had particular qualities needed to cure the affliction. If the appeal were to a goddess, the sick person also required the intercession and good services of a priestess of the particular goddess. There were, of course, also male gods who could benefit one in case of illness, and these would usually be served by a male priest.

For example, in Babylonia a sick man or woman would approach the Ishtar temple in a spirit of humility on the assumption that the sickness was a result of his or her transgression. The petitioner would bring appropriate offerings: food, a young animal for sacrifice, oil, and wine. For the goddess Ishtar such offerings quite frequently included images of a vulva, the symbol of her fertility, fashioned out of precious lapis lazuli stone. The afflicted person would prostrate himself before the priestess and recite some appropriate hymns and prayers. A typical prayer contained the following lines:

> Gracious Ishtar, who rules over the universe,
> Heroic Ishtar, who creates humankind,
> who walks before the cattle, who loves the shepherd . . .
> You give justice to the distressed, the suffering you give
> them justice.
> Without you the river will not open,
> the river which brings us life will not be closed,
> without you the canal will not open,
> the canal from which the scattered drink,
> will not be closed . . . Ishtar, merciful lady . . .
> hear me and grant me mercy.

Mesopotamian men or women, in distress or sickness, humbled themselves before a goddess-figure and her priestly servant. In words reflecting the attitude of slave toward master, they praised and worshiped the goddess's power. Thus, another hymn to Ishtar addresses her as "mistress of the battle field, who pulls down the mountains"; "Majestic one, lioness among the gods, who conquers the angry gods, strongest among rulers, who leads kings by the lead; you who open the wombs of women . . . mighty Ishtar, how great is your strength!" Heaping praise upon praise, the petitioner continued:

> Where you cast your glance, the dead awaken, the sick arise;
> The bewildered, beholding your face, find the right way.
> I appeal to you, miserable and distraught,
> tortured by pain, your servant,
> be merciful and hear my prayer! . . .
> I await you, my mistress; my soul turns toward you.
> I beseech you: Relieve my plight.
> Absolve me of my guilt, my wickedness, my sin,
> forget my misdeeds, accept my plea!

We should note that the petitioners regarded the goddess as all-powerful. In the symbol of the goddess's vulva, fashioned of precious stone and offered up in her praise, they celebrated the sacredness of female sexuality and its mysterious life-giving force, which included the power to heal. And in the very prayers appealing to the goddess's mercy, they praised her as mistress of the battlefield, more powerful than kings, more powerful than other gods. Their prayers to the gods similarly extolled the god's virtues and listed his powers in superlatives. My point here is that men and women offering such prayers when in distress must have thought of women, just as they thought of men, as capable of metaphysical power and as potential mediators between the gods and human beings. That is a mental image quite different from that of Christians, for example, who in a later time would pray to the Virgin Mary to intercede with God in their behalf. The power of the Virgin lies in her ability to appeal to God's mercy; it derives from her motherhood and the miracle of her immaculate conception. She has no power for herself, and the very sources of her power to intercede separate her irrevocably from other women. The goddess Ishtar and other goddesses like her had power in their own right. It was the kind of power men had, derived from military exploits and the ability to impose her will on the gods or to influence them. And yet Ishtar was female, endowed with a sexuality like that of ordinary women. One cannot help but wonder at the contradiction between the power of the goddesses and the increasing societal constraints upon the lives of most women in Ancient Mesopotamia.

Unlike the changes in the social and economic status of women, which have received only tangential and scattered attention in Ancient Mesopotamian studies, the transition from polytheism to monotheism and its attendant shift in emphasis from powerful goddesses to a single male god have been the subject of a vast literature. The topic has been approached from the vantage point of theology, archaeology, anthropology, and literature. Historical and artistic artifacts have been interpreted with the tools of their respective disciplines; linguistic and philosophical studies have added to the richness of interpretation. With Freud and Jung and Erich Fromm, psychiatry and psychology have been added as analytic tools, focusing our attention on myth, symbols, and archetypes. And recently a number of feminist scholars from various disciplines have discussed the period and the subject from yet another vantage point, one which is critical of patriarchal assumptions.

Such a richness and diversity of sources and interpretations makes it impossible to discuss and critique them all within the confines of this volume. I will therefore focus, as I have done throughout, on a few analytic questions and discuss in detail a few models which, I believe, illustrate larger patterns.

Methodologically, the most problematic question is the relation between changes in society and changes in religious beliefs and myths. The archaeologist, art historian, and historian can record, document, and observe such changes, but their causes and their meaning cannot be given with any kind of certainty. Different systems of interpretation offer varying answers, none of which is totally satisfying. In the present case it seems to me most important to record and survey the historical evidence and to offer a coherent explanation, which I admit is somewhat speculative. So are all the other explanations including, above all, the patriarchal tradition.

I am assuming that Mesopotamian religion responded to and reflected social conditions in the various societies. Mental constructs cannot be created from a void; they always reflect events and concepts of historic human beings in society. Thus, the existence of an assembly of the gods in "The Epic of Gilgamesh" has been interpreted as indicating the existence of village assemblies in pre-state Mesopotamian society. Similarly, the explanation in the Sumerian Atrahasis myth that the gods created men in order that men might serve them and relieve them of hard work can be regarded as a reflection of social conditions in the Sumerian city-states of the first half of the third millennium B.C., in which large numbers of people worked on irrigation projects and in agricultural labor centered on the temples. The relation between myth and reality is not usually that direct, but we can assume that no people could invent the concept of an assembly of the gods if they had not at some time experienced and known a like institution on earth. While we cannot say with certainty that certain political and economic changes "caused" changes in religious beliefs and myths, we cannot help but notice a pattern in the changes of religious beliefs in a number of societies, following upon or concurrent with certain societal changes.

My thesis is that, just as the development of plow agriculture, coinciding with increasing militarism, brought major changes in kinship and in gender relations, so did the development of strong kingships and of archaic states bring changes in religious beliefs and symbols. The observable pattern is: first, the demotion of the Mother-Goddess figure and the ascendance and later dominance of her male consort/son; then his merging with a storm-god into a male Creator-God, who heads the pantheon of gods and goddesses. Wherever such changes occur, the power of creation and of fertility is transfered from the Goddess to the God.

REFLECTIONS

An historical stage is a specific example of a larger process that historians call *periodization*. Dividing history into periods is one way historians make the past comprehensible. Without periodization, history would be a vast, unwieldly continuum, lacking points of reference, forms, intelligibility, and meaning.

One of the earliest forms of historical periodization — years of reign — was a natural system of record keeping in the ancient cities dominated by kings. Each kingdom had its own list of kings, and each marked the current date by numbering the years of the king's reign. Some ancient societies periodized their history according to the years of rule of local officials or priesthoods. In the ancient Roman Republic, time was figured according to the terms of the elected consuls. The ancient Greeks used four-year periods called Olympiads, beginning with the first Olympic games in 776 B.C.

The ancient Greeks did not use "B.C.," of course. The periodization of world history into B.C. ("before Christ") and A.D. (*anno Domini,* "the Year of Our Lord" or "after Christ") did not come until the sixth century A.D., when a Christian monk named Dionysius Exiguus hit upon a way to center Christ as the major turning point in history. We use a variant of this system in this text, when designating events "B.C.E." for "before the common era" or "C.E." for "of the common era." This translation of "B.C." and "A.D." avoids the Christian bias of the older system but preserves its simplicity. The Christian system has been used worldwide to delineate time and coordinate different dynastic calendars for more than two thousand years.

All systems of periodization implicitly claim to designate important transitions in the past. The periodization of Dionysius inscribed the Christian belief that Christ's life, death, and resurrection fundamentally changed world history: Because Christ died to atone for the sins of humankind, only those who lived after Christ's sacrifice could be saved when they died. Few other systems of periodization made such a sweeping claim, though, of course, most people today — even many non-Christians — use it because of its convenience. Muslims count the years from a year one A.H. (*anno Hegire,* designating the year of the prophet Muhammad's escape from Mecca to Medina) in 622 A.D. of the Christian calendar, and Jews date the years from a Biblical year one, but these methods do not mark important "before" and "after" periods.

Millennia, centuries, and decades are useful periods for societies that count in tens and (after the spread of Indian numerals) use the zero. While such multiples are only mathematical, some historians use them for rough periodization, to distinguish between the 1950s and the 1960s or between the eighteenth and nineteenth centuries, for example, as if there were a genuine and important transition between one period and the other. If asked why they do this, such historians might say that things do not change overnight at the end of the decade or century and that overall one period is different from another. Sometimes historians "stretch" the boundaries of centuries or decades in order to account for earlier or later changes. For example, some historians speak of "the long nineteenth century," embracing the period from the French Revolution in 1789 to the First World War in 1914, on the grounds that peoples' lives were transformed in 1789 rather than in 1800 and in 1914 rather than in 1900. Similarly, the "sixties," as a term for American society and culture during the Vietnam War era, often means the period from about 1963 to about 1975, since Civil Rights and antiwar activity became significant a few years after the beginning of the decade and the war continued until 1975.

Characterizing and defining a decade or century in chronological terms is only one method of periodization, however. Processes can also be periodized. In this chapter we have periodized world history by process. All of world history can be divided into three periods — hunting/gathering, agricultural/pastoral, and urban. These are overlapping and continuing periods, and we can date only the beginning of the agricultural/pastoral and the urban periods, at about ten thousand and five thousand years ago, respectively. None of these periods has ended, as there are still hunters and gatherers and many farmers and pastoralists in the world. Still, the periodization is useful, because both the agricultural/pastoral revolution and the urban revolution brought about widespread and permanent changes.

We have also tried to locate patriarchy in an historical period, suggesting that it was a product of the urban revolution. This is to say that patriarchy did not exist in hunting/gathering or agricultural/pastoral societies. We have not attempted to periodize changes in patriarchy over the course of the last five thousand years, but we could investigate this as well. Many people would say that patriarchy has been declining in recent decades. Is this a valid view, or is it a view specific to North America? If patriarchy is a product of cities and if the world is becoming more urban, can patriarchy be declining globally? What forces do you see bringing a decline or end to patriarchy?

To periodize something like the history of patriarchy would require a good deal of knowledge about the history of male and female relations over the course of the last five thousand years. That is a tall order for anyone. But you can get a sense of how the historian goes about periodizing and a feeling for its value if you periodize something you know a lot about. You might start, for instance, with your own life. Think of the most important change or changes in your life. How have these changes divided your life into certain periods? Outline your autobiography by marking these periods as parts or chapters of the story of your life so far. As you review these periods of your life, recognize how periodization must be grounded in reality. Defining these periods may help you understand yourself better.

To gain a sense of how periodization is imposed on reality, imagine how a parent or good friend would periodize your life. How would you periodize your life ten or twenty years from now? How would you have done it five years ago?

3

The Urban Revolution and "Civilization"

HISTORICAL CONTEXT

Mesopotamia and Egypt, 3500–1000 B.C.E.

The urban revolution that began approximately five thousand years ago produced a vast complex of new inventions, institutions, and ideas in cities that dominated surrounding farms and pastures. The first selection in this chapter surveys the wide range of innovations in these earliest civilizations.

The term "civilization" has to be used cautiously. Especially when the idea of civilization is used as a part of a stage theory of human history, there is a tendency to assume that technological advancement is the same as moral advancement. For instance, it was quite common a hundred years ago for scholars to describe ancient history as the progression from "savagery" to "barbarism" to "civilization." More recently, critics of modern civilization have sometimes taken the opposite tack, arguing as the poet T. S. Eliot did that modern cities are the source of "syphilization."

It would be a shame to throw out the word "civilization" because it has been written more often with an axe than with a stylus. The fact remains that the ancient cities created new forms of life for better or worse that were radically different from the world of agricultural villages. If we discard the word "civilization" as too overburdened with prejudice, we will have to find another one to describe that complex of changes. The term "civilization" has the advantage of coming from the Latin root word for city, *civitas,* from which we also get *civic, civilian,* and *citizen.* But, as the first selection argues, cities also created social classes, institutionalized inequalities, and calls to arms; most civilizations created soldiers as well as civilians.

The earliest cities, the small city-states on the Tigris and Euphrates in ancient Sumer included King Gilgamesh's Uruk, which is recounted in the second reading. Later cities, like Hammurabi's Babylon, united Sumerian city-states and upriver pastoral kingdoms into giant empires. The third reading presents selections from Hammurabi's law code.

The ancient Egyptian empire depended less on cities than on the power of the king or pharaoh, but life along the Nile was magnified in the pharaoh's residence city and in his future home in the City of the Dead. In the last selection, we visit one of its residents.

As you read these selections, consider the overall transformation of the urban revolution in both Mesopotamia and Egypt. Note also the differences between Mesopotamian and Egyptian civilizations.

THINKING HISTORICALLY

Distinguishing Primary and Secondary Sources

For some historians, the "age of cities" is the beginning of history because it was in this age that writing began. The period before city building and the creation of writing systems thus is often called "prehistory."

Our knowledge of ancient cities is enormously enhanced by ancient writings. Writings from the period being studied are called primary sources. These would include literature, law codes, inscriptions, indeed virtually anything from the time and place being studied. Secondary sources are different in one major way: They are written after the fact. History books or historical interpretations are secondary sources. They are secondary in that they rely on primary sources for information. Historians read, study, and interpret primary sources to compose secondary sources. In this chapter you will read one secondary source and three primary sources to help you learn ways to discern sources and extrapolate information from them.

9

KEVIN REILLY

Cities and Civilization

This selection from a college textbook is an obvious secondary source. You know it is a secondary source because it was written long after the events described by a modern historian — me.

From my perspective, this selection does two things. First, it explores the wide range of changes brought about by the urban revolution, from particulars like writing and money and metallurgy to abstractions like social class, visual acuity, and anonymity. After you read the selection, you might make a list of all of the inventions and new phenomena of cities. You will likely be surprised by the great number of ideas, institutions, and activities that originated in the first cities. You might also find it interesting to place pluses and minuses next to the items on your list to help you determine whether "civilization" (city life) was, on balance, beneficial or harmful.

Second, the selection compares the "civilizations" of Mesopotamia and Egypt. What, according to the selection, are the chief differences between Mesopotamian and Egyptian civilization, and what accounts for these differences?

Thinking Historically

To get a feel for the differences between a primary source and a secondary source (like this one), try to determine what primary sources might lead to some of these interpretations. Choose a sentence or two that appears specific enough to be based on a primary source. What kind of source could lead to such an interpretation? Conversely, find interpretations in this selection that *could not* possibly derive from a primary source and ask yourself, why not?

The Urban Revolution: Civilization and Class

The full-scale urban revolution occurred not in the rain-watered lands that first turned some villages into cities, but in the potentially more

---

Kevin Reilly, *The West and the World: A History of Civilization*, 2nd ed. (New York: Harper & Row, 1989), 48–54, 56, 58, 60.

productive river valleys of Mesopotamia around 3500 B.C. Situated along the Tigris and Euphrates rivers, large villages like Eridu, Erech, Lagash, Kish, and later Ur and Babylon built irrigation systems that increased farm production enormously. Settlements like these were able to support five thousand, even ten thousand people, and still allow something like 10 percent of the inhabitants to work full-time at nonfarming occupations.

A change of this scale was a revolution, certainly the most important revolution in human living since the invention of agriculture five thousand years earlier. The urban revolution was prepared by a whole series of technological inventions in agricultural society. Between 6000 and 3000 B.C. people not only learned how to harness the power of oxen and the wind with the plow, the wheeled cart, and the sailboat; they also discovered the physical properties of metals, learned how to smelt copper and bronze, and began to work out a calendar based on the movements of the sun. River valleys like those of the Tigris and Euphrates were muddy swamps that had to be drained and irrigated to take advantage of the rich soil deposits. The dry land had literally to be built by teams of organized workers.

Therefore, cities required an organizational revolution that was every bit as important as the technological one. This was accomplished under the direction of the new class of rulers and managers — probably from the grasslands — who often treated the emerging cities as a conquered province. The work of irrigation itself allowed the rulers ample opportunity to coerce the inhabitants of these new cities. Rain knows no social distinctions. Irrigated water must be controlled and channeled.

It is no wonder then that the first cities gave us our first kings and our first class societies. Almost everywhere that cities spread (or were again invented) after 3000 B.C. — along the Nile of Egypt, on the Indus River in Pakistan, or in Turkey and China, and later in Middle America — the king is usually described as the founder of cities. Almost everywhere these kings were able to endow their control with religious sanction. In Egypt and America the king was god. In Mesopotamia a new class of priests carried out the needs of the king's religion of control.

In some cities the new priesthood would appoint the king. In others, the priests were merely his lieutenants. When they were most loyal, their religion served to deify the king. The teachings of the new class of Mesopotamian priests, for instance, were that their god had created the people solely to work for the king and make his life easier. But even when the priesthood attempted to wrest some of the king's power from him, the priests taught the people to accept the divided society, which benefited king and priesthood as providers of a natural god-given order. The priesthood, after all, was responsible for measuring time, bounding space, and predicting seasonal events. The mastery of people was easy for those who controlled time and space.

The priesthood was only one of the new classes that insured the respectability of the warrior-chieftain turned king. Other palace intellectuals — scribes (or writers), doctors, magicians, and diviners — also struggled to maintain the king's prestige and manage his kingdom. This new class was rewarded, as were the priests, with leisure, status, and magnificent buildings, all of which further exalted the majesty of the king and his city.

Beneath the king, the priesthood, and the new class of intellectuals-managers was another new class charged with maintaining the king's law and order. Soldiers and police were also inventions of the first cities. Like the surrounding city wall, the king's military guard served a double function: they provided defense from outside attack and an obstacle to internal rebellion.

That these were the most important classes of city society can be seen from the physical remains of the first cities. The archeologist's spade has uncovered the monumental buildings of these classes in virtually all of the first cities. The palace, the temple, and the citadel (or fort) are, indeed, the monuments that distinguish cities from villages. Further, the size of these buildings and the permanency of their construction (compared with the small, cheaply built homes of the farmers) attest to the fundamental class divisions of city society.

Civilization: Security and Variety

The most obvious achievements of the first civilizations are the monuments — the pyramids, temples, palaces, statues, and treasures — that were created for the new ruling class of kings, nobles, priests, and their officials. But civilized life is much more than the capacity to create monuments.

Civilized life is secure life. At the most basic level this means security from the sudden destruction that village communities might suffer. Civilized life gives the feeling of permanence. It offers regularity, stability, order, even routine. Plans can be made. Expectations can be realized. People can be expected to act predictably, according to the rules.

The first cities were able to attain stability with walls that shielded the inhabitants from nomads and armies, with the first codes of law that defined human relationships, with police and officials that enforced the laws, and with institutions that functioned beyond the lives of their particular members. City life offered considerably more permanence and security than village life.

Civilization involves more than security, however. A city that provided only order would be more like a prison than a civilization. The first cities provided something that the best-ordered villages lacked. They provided far greater variety: more races and ethnic groups were speaking more languages, engaged in more occupations, and living a greater variety of life-styles. The abundance of choice, the opportunities for new sensations, new experiences, knowledge — these have always been the appeals of city life. The opportunities for growth and enrichment were far greater than the possibilities of plow and pasture life.

Security plus variety equals creativity. At least the possibility of a more creative, expressive life was available in the protected, semipermanent city enclosures that drew, like magnets, foreign traders and diplomats, new ideas about gods and nature, strange foods and customs, and the magicians, ministers, and mercenaries of the king's court. Civilization is the enriched life that this dynamic urban setting permitted and the human creativity and opportunity that it encouraged. At the very least, cities made even the most common slave think and feel a greater range of things than the tightly knit, clanish agricultural village allowed. That was (and still is) the root of innovation and creativity — of civilization itself.

The variety of people and the complexity of city life required new and more general means of communication. The villager knew everyone personally. Cities brought together people who often did not even speak the same language. Not only law codes but written language itself became a way to bridge the many gaps of human variety. Cities invented writing so that strangers could communicate, and so that those communications could become permanent — remembered publicly, officially recorded. [Writer and philosopher Ralph Waldo] Emerson was right when he said that the city lives by memory, but it was the official memory that enabled the city to carry on its business or religion beyond the lifetime of the village elders. Written symbols that everyone could recognize became the basis of laws, invention, education, taxes, accounting, contracts, and obligations. In short, writing and records made it possible for each generation to begin on the shoulders of its ancestors. Village life and knowledge often seemed to start from scratch. Thus, cities cultivated not only memory and the past, but hope and the future as well. City civilizations invented not only history and record keeping but also prophecy and social planning.

Writing was one city invention that made more general communication possible. Money was another. Money made it possible to deal with anyone just as an agreed-upon public language did. Unnecessary in the village climate of mutual obligations, money was essential in the city society of strangers. Such general media of communication as writing and money vastly increased the number of things that could be said and thought, bought and sold. As a consequence, city life was more impersonal than village life, but also more dynamic and more exciting.

The "Eye" and "I"

[Communication theorist] Marshall McLuhan has written that "civilization gave the barbarian an eye for an ear." We might add that civilization also gave an "I" for an "us." City life made the "eye" and the "I" more important than they had been in the village. The invention of writing made knowledge more visual. The eye had to be trained to recognize the minute differences in letters and words. Eyes took in a greater abundance of detail: laws, prices, the strange cloak of the foreigner, the odd type of shoes made by the new craftsworker from who-knows-where, the colors of the fruit and vegetable market, elaborate painting in the temple, as well as the written word. In the village one learned by listening. In the city seeing was believing. In the new city courts of law an "eyewitness account" was believed to be more reliable than "hearsay evidence." In some villages even today, the heard and the spoken are thought more reliable than the written and the seen. In the city, even spoken language took on the uniformity and absence of emotion that is unavoidable in the written word. Perhaps emotions themselves became less violent. "Civilized" is always used to mean emotional restraint, control of the more violent passions, and a greater understanding, even tolerance, of the different and foreign.

Perhaps empathy (the capacity to put yourself in someone else's shoes) increased in cities — so full of so many different others that had to be understood. When a Turkish villager was recently asked, "What would you do if you were president of your country?" he stammered: "My God! How can you ask such a thing? How can I . . . I cannot . . . president of Turkey . . . master of the whole world?" He was completely unable to imagine himself as president. It was as removed from his experience as if he were master of the world. Similarly, a Lebanese villager who was asked what he would do if he were editor of a newspaper accused the interviewer of ridiculing him, and frantically waved the interviewer on to another question. Such a life was beyond his comprehension. It was too foreign to imagine. The very variety of city life must have increased the capacity of the lowest commoner to imagine, empathize, sympathize, and criticize.

The oral culture of the village reinforced the accepted by saying and singing it almost monotonously. The elders, the storytellers, and the minstrels must have had prodigious memories. But their stories changed only gradually and slightly. The spoken word was sacred. To say it differently was to change the truth. The written culture of cities taught "point of *view*." An urban individual did not have to remember everything. That was done permanently on paper. Knowledge became a recognition of different interpretations and the capacity to look up things. The awareness of variety meant the possibility of criticism, analysis, and an ever-newer synthesis. It is no wonder that the technical and scientific knowledge of cities increased at a geometric rate compared with the knowledge of villages. The multiplication of knowledge was implicit in the city's demand to recognize difference and variety. Civilization has come to mean that ever-expanding body of knowledge and skill. Its finest achievements have been that knowledge, its writing, and its visual art. The city and civilization (like the child) are to be seen and not heard.

It may seem strange to say that the impersonal life of cities contributed greatly to the development of personality — the "I" as well as the "eye." Village life was in a sense much more personal. Everything was taken personally. Villagers deal with each other not as "the blacksmith," "the baker," "that guy who owes me a goat," or "that no-good bum." They do not even "deal" with each other. They know each other by name and family. They love, hate, support, and murder each other because of who they are, because of personal feelings, because of personal and family responsibility. They have full, varied relationships with each member of the village. They do not merely buy salt from this person, talk about the weather with this other person, and discuss personal matters with only this other person. They share too much with each other to divide up their relationships in that way.

City life is a life of separated, partial relationships. In a city you do not know about the butcher's life, wife, kids, and problems. You do not care. You are in a hurry. You have too many other things to do. You might discuss the weather — but while he's cutting. You came to buy meat. Many urban relationships are like that. There are many business, trading, or "dealing" relationships because there are simply too many people to know them all as relatives.

The impersonality of city life is a shame in a way. (It makes it easier to get mugged by someone who does not even hate you.) But the luxurious variety of impersonal relationships (at least some of the time) provide the freedom for the individual personality to emerge. Maybe that is why people have often dreamed of leaving family and friends (usually for a city) in the hope of "finding themselves." Certainly, the camaraderie and community of village life had a darker side of surveillance and conformity. When everything was known about everyone, it was difficult for the individual to find his or her individuality. Family ties and village custom were often obstacles to asserting self-identity. The city offered its inhabitants a huge variety of possible relationships and personal identities. The urban inhabitant was freer than his village cousin to choose friends, lovers, associates, occupation, housing, and life-style. The city was full of choices that the village could not afford or condone. The village probably provided more security in being like everyone else and doing what was expected. But the city provided the variety of possibilities that could allow the individual to follow the "inner self" and cultivate inner gardens.

The class divisions of city society made it difficult for commoners to achieve an effective or creative individuality. But the wealthy and powerful — especially the king — were able to develop models of individuality and personality that were revolutionary. No one before had ever achieved such a sense of the self, and the model of the king's power and freedom became a goal for the rest of the society. The luxury, leisure, and opportunity of the king was a revolutionary force. In contrast to a village elder, the king could do whatever he wanted. Recognizing that, more and more city inhabitants asked, "Why can't we?" City revolutions have continually extended class privilege and opportunities ever since.

Once a society has achieved a level of abundance, once it can offer the technological means, the educational opportunities, the creative outlets necessary for everyone to lead meaningful, happy, healthy lives, then classes may be a hindrance. Class divisions were, however, a definite stimulus to productivity and creativity in the early city civilizations. The democratic villagers preferred stability to improvement. As a result, their horizons were severely limited. They died early, lived precipitously, and suffered without much hope. The rulers of the first cities discovered the possibilities of leisure, creation, and the good life. They invented heaven and utopia — first for themselves. Only very gradually has the invention of civilization, of human potential, sifted down to those beneath the ruling class. In many cases, luxury, leisure, freedom, and opportunity are still the monopolies of the elite. But once the powerful have exploited the poor enough to establish their own paradise on earth and their own immortality after death, the poor also have broader horizons and plans.

Mesopotamian and Egyptian Civilizations: A Tale of Two Rivers

Experts disagree as to whether Mesopotamian or Egyptian civilization is older. Mesopotamian influence in Egypt was considerable enough to suggest slightly earlier origins, but both had evolved distinct civilizations by 3000 B.C. Indeed, the difference between the two civilizations attests to the existence of multiple routes to civilized life. In both cases, river valleys provided the necessary water and silt for an agricultural surplus large enough to support classes of specialists who did not have to farm. But the differing nature of the rivers had much to do with the different types of civilization that evolved.

The Egyptians were blessed with the easier and more reliable of the two rivers. The Nile overflowed its banks predictably every year on the parched ground in the summer after August 15, well after the harvest had been gathered, depositing its rich sediment, and withdrawing by early October, leaving little salt or marsh, in time for the sowing of winter crops. Later sowings for summer crops required only simple canals that tapped the river upstream and the natural drainage of the Nile Valley. Further, transportation on the Nile was simplified by the fact that the prevailing winds blew from the north, while the river flowed from the south, making navigation a matter of using sails upstream and dispensing with them coming downstream.

The Euphrates offered none of these advantages as it cut its way through Mesopotamia. The Euphrates flowed high above the flood plain (unlike the neighboring Tigris) so that its waters could be used, but it flooded suddenly and without warning in the late spring, after the summer crops had been sown and before the winter crops could be harvested. Thus, the flooding of the Euphrates offered no natural irrigation. Its waters were needed at other times, and its flooding was destructive. Canals were necessary to drain off water for irrigation when the river was low, and these canals had to be adequately blocked, and the banks reinforced, when the river flooded. Further, since the Euphrates was not as easily navigable as the Nile, the main canals had to serve as major transportation arteries as well.

In Mesopotamia the flood was the enemy. The Mesopotamian deities who ruled the waters, Nin-Girsu and Tiamat, were feared. The forces of nature were often evil. Life was a struggle. In Egypt, on the other hand, life was viewed as a cooperation with nature. Even the Egyptian god of the flood, Hapi, was a helpful deity, who provided the people's daily bread. Egyptian priests and philosophers were much more at ease with their world than were their Mesopotamian counterparts. And, partly because of their different experiences with their rivers, the Mesopotamians developed a civilization based on cities, while the Egyptians did not. From the first Sumerian city-states on the lower Euphrates to the later northern Mesopotamian capital of Babylon, civilization was the product and expression of city life. Egyptian civilization, in contrast, was the creation of the pharaoh's court rather than of cities. Beyond the court, which was moved from one location to another, Egypt remained a country of peasant villages.

A prime reason for Egypt's lack of urbanization was the ease of farming on the banks of the Nile. Canal irrigation was a relatively simple process that did not demand much organization. Small market towns were sufficient for the needs of the countryside. They housed artisans, shopkeepers, the priests of the local temple, and the agents of the pharaoh, but they never swelled with a large middle class and never developed large-scale industry or commerce.

In Sumer, and later in Mesopotamia, the enormous task of fighting the Euphrates required a complex social organization with immediate local needs. Only communal labor could build and maintain the network of subsidiary canals for irrigation and drainage. Constant supervision was necessary to keep the canals free of silt, to remove salt deposits, to maintain the riverbanks at flood-time, and to prevent any farmer from monopolizing the water in periods of drought. Life on the Euphrates required cooperative work and responsibility that never ceased. It encouraged absolute, administrative control over an area larger than the village, and it fostered participation and loyalty to an irrigated area smaller than the imperial state. The city-state was the political answer to the economic problems of Sumer and Mesopotamia.

The religious practices in the Euphrates Valley reflected and supported city organization. Residents of each local area worshiped the local god while recognizing the existence of other local gods in a larger Sumerian, and eventually Mesopotamian, pantheon of gods. The priests of the local temple supervised canal work, the collection of taxes, and the storage of written records, as well as the proper maintenance of religious rituals. Thus, religious loyalty reinforced civic loyalty. Peasant and middle-class Sumerians thought of themselves as citizens of their particular city, worshipers of their particular city god, subjects of their particular god's earthly representative, but not as Sumerian nationals. By contrast, the Egyptian peasant was always an Egyptian, a subject of the pharaoh, but never a citizen.

The local, civic orientation of Mesopotamian cities can be seen in the physical structure of the capital city of Sumer, the city of Ur. Like other cities on the Euphrates, Ur was surrounded by a wall. It was dominated by the temple of Nannar, the moon-god who owned the city, and the palace complex beneath the temple. The residential areas were situated outside of the sacred Temenos, or temple compound, but within the walls, between the river and the main canal. The well-excavated remains of Ur of the seventeenth century B.C. show a residential street plan that looks like many Middle Eastern cities of today. A highly congested area of winding alleys and broad streets sheltered one- and two-story houses of merchants, shopkeepers, tradespeople, and occasional priests and scribes that suggest a large, relatively prosperous middle class. Most houses were built around a central courtyard that offered shade throughout the day, with mud-brick, often even plastered, outside walls that protected a number of interior rooms from the sun and the eyes of the tax inspector. The remains of seventeenth-century Ur show both the variety and the density of modern city life. There are specialized districts throughout the city. Certain trades have their special quarters: a bakers' square, probably special areas for the dyers, tanners, potters, and metalworkers. But life is mixed together as well. Subsidiary gods have temples outside the Temenos. Small and large houses are jumbled next to each other. There seems to be a slum area near the Temenos, but there are small houses for workers, tenant farmers, and the poor throughout the city. And no shop or urban professional is more than a short walking distance away. The entire size of the walled city was an oval that extended three-quarters of a mile long and a half a mile wide.

A well-excavated Egyptian city from roughly the same period (the fourteenth century B.C.) offers some striking contrasts. Akhetaton, or Tell el Amarna, Pharaoh Akhenaton's capital on the Nile, was not enclosed by walls or canals. It merely straggled down the eastern bank of the Nile for five miles and faded into the desert. Without the need for extensive irrigation or protection, Tell el Amarna shows little of the crowded, vital density of Ur. Its layout lacks any sense of urgency. The North Palace of the pharaoh is a mile and a half north of the temple complex and offices, which are three and a half miles from the official pleasure garden. The palaces of the court nobility and the large residences of the court's officials front one of the two main roads that parallel the river, or they are situated at random. There is plenty of physical space (and social space) between these and the bunched villages of workers' houses. The remains suggest very little in the way of a middle class or a merchant or professional class beyond the pharaoh's specialists and retainers. Life for the wealthy was, judging from the housing, more luxurious than at Ur, but for the majority of the population, city life was less rich. In many ways, the pharaoh's court at Tell el Amarna was not a city at all.

10

From *The Epic of Gilgamesh*

This selection is a primary source for the study of ancient Mesopotamia — the land between the two great rivers, the Tigris and Euphrates. It is also the earliest written story in any language.

Gilgamesh was an ancient king of Sumer, who lived about 2700 B.C.E. Since *The Epic* comes from a thousand years later, we can assume Sumerians told this story about King Gilgamesh for some time before it was written down. In Sumer, writing was initially used by temple priests to keep track of property and taxes. Soon, however, writing was used to preserve stories and to celebrate kings. *The Epic of Gilgamesh* is one of the earliest examples of such literature.

The Epic of Gilgamesh, trans. N. K. Sanders (London: Penguin Books, 1972), 61–69, 108–13.

The more you know about the Sumerian people, the more information you will be able to mine from your source. In the previous secondary selection, you read some historical background that will help you make sense of this story. Look in *The Epic* for evidence of the urban revolution discussed in the previous selection. What is the meaning of the story of the taming of Enkidu by the harlot? Does Enkidu also tame Gilgamesh? What two worlds do Enkidu and Gilgamesh represent?

Do the authors or listeners of *The Epic* think city life is better than life in the country? What according to *The Epic* are the advantages of the city? What are its problems?

What does the story of the flood tell you about life in ancient Mesopotamia? Would you expect the ancient Egyptians to tell a similar story?

Thinking Historically

Reading a primary source differs markedly from reading a secondary source. Primary sources were not written with you or me in mind. It is safe to say that the author of *The Epic of Gilgamesh* never even imagined our existence. For this reason, primary sources are a bit difficult to access. Reading a primary source usually requires some intensive work. You have to keep asking yourself, why was this story told? How would a story like this help or teach people at that time? That is, you have to put yourself in the original context of the story, both in terms of teller and listener.

Primary sources offer us a piece of the past. No historian is in your way explaining things. With your unique perspective, you have an advantage over the intended audience: You can ask questions about the source that the author and intended audience never imagined or, possibly, would not have dared ask.

Ask a question for which this primary source can provide an answer, then find the answer. Next write an abbreviated secondary source in a sentence or two.

Prologue: Gilgamesh King in Uruk

I will proclaim to the world the deeds of Gilgamesh. This was the man to whom all things were known; this was the king who knew the countries of the world. He was wise, he saw mysteries and knew secret things, he brought us a tale of the days before the flood. He went on a long journey, was weary, worn-out with labor; returning he rested, he engraved on a stone the whole story.

When the gods created Gilgamesh they gave him a perfect body. Shamash the glorious sun endowed him with beauty, Adad the god of the storm endowed him with courage, the great gods made his beauty perfect, surpassing all others, terrifying like a great wild bull. Two thirds they made him god and one third man.

In Uruk he built walls, a great rampart, and the temple of blessed Eanna for the god of the firmament Anu, and for Ishtar the goddess of love. Look at it still today: the outer wall where the cornice runs, it shines with the brilliance of copper; and the inner wall, it has no equal. Touch the threshold; it is ancient. Approach Eanna the dwelling of Ishtar, our lady of love and war, the like of which no latter-day king, no man alive can equal. Climb upon the wall of Uruk; walk along it, I say; regard the foundation terrace and examine the masonry; is it not burnt brick and good? The seven sages laid the foundations.

The Coming of Enkidu

Gilgamesh went abroad in the world, but he met with none who could withstand his arms till he came to Uruk. But the men of Uruk muttered in their houses, "Gilgamesh sounds the tocsin for his amusement, his arrogance has no bounds by day or night. No son is left with his father, for Gilgamesh takes from all, even the children; yet the king should be a shepherd to his people. His lust leaves no virgin to her lover, neither the warrior's daughter nor the wife of the noble; yet this is the shepherd of the city, wise, comely, and resolute."

The gods heard their lament, the gods of heaven cried to the Lord of Uruk, to Anu the god of Uruk: "A goddess made him, strong as a savage bull, none can withstand his arms. No son is left with his father, for Gilgamesh takes them all; and is this the king, the shepherd of his people? His lust leaves no virgin to her lover, neither the warrior's daughter nor the wife of the noble." When Anu had heard their lamentation the gods cried to Aruru, the goddess of creation, "You made him, O Aruru, now create his equal; let it be as like him as his own reflection, his second self, stormy head for stormy heart. Let them contend together and leave Uruk in quiet."

So the goddess conceived an image in her mind, and it was of the stuff of Anu of the firmament. She dipped her hands in water and pinched off clay, she let it fall in the wilderness, and noble Enkidu was created. There was virtue in him of the god of war, of Ninurta himself. His body was rough; he had long hair like a woman's; it waved like the hair of Nisaba, the goddess of corn. His body was covered with matted hair like Samuqan's, the god of cattle. He was innocent of mankind; he knew nothing of cultivated land.

Enkidu ate grass in the hills with the gazelle and lurked with wild beasts at the water-holes; he had joy of the water with the herds of wild game. But there was a trapper who met him one day face to face at the drinking-hole, for the wild game had entered his territory. On three days he met him face to face, and the trapper was frozen with fear. He went back to his house with the game that he had caught, and he was dumb, benumbed with terror. His face was altered like that of one who has made a long journey. With awe in his heart he spoke to his father: "Father, there is a man, unlike any other, who comes down from the hills. He is the strongest in the world, he is like an immortal from heaven. He ranges over the hills with wild beasts and eats grass; he ranges through your land and comes down to the wells. I am afraid and dare not go near him. He fills in the pits which I dig and tears up my traps set for the game; he helps the beasts to escape and now they slip through my fingers."

His father opened his mouth and said to the trapper, "My son, in Uruk lives Gilgamesh; no one has ever prevailed against him, he is strong as a star from heaven. Go to Uruk, find Gilgamesh, extol the strength of this wild man. Ask him to give you a harlot, a wanton from the temple of love; return with her, and let her woman's power overpower this man. When next he comes down to drink at the wells she will be there, stripped naked; and when he sees her beckoning he will embrace her, and then the wild beasts will reject him."

So the trapper set out on his journey to Uruk and addressed himself to Gilgamesh saying, "A man unlike any other is roaming now in the pastures; he is as strong as a star from heaven and I am afraid to approach him. He helps the wild game to escape; he fills in my pits and pulls up my traps." Gilgamesh said, "Trapper, go back, take with you a harlot, a child of pleasure. At the drinking-hole she will strip, and when he sees her beckoning he will embrace her and the game of the wilderness will surely reject him."

Now the trapper returned, taking the harlot with him. After a three days' journey they came to the drinking-hole, and there they sat down; the harlot and the trapper sat facing one another and waited for the game to come. For the first day and for the second day the two sat waiting, but on the third day the herds came; they came down to drink and Enkidu was with them. The small wild creatures of the plains were glad of the water, and Enkidu with them, who ate grass with the gazelle and was born in the hills; and she saw him; the savage man, come from far-off in the hills. The trapper spoke to her: "There he is. Now, woman, make your breasts bare, have no shame, do not delay but welcome his love. Let him see you naked, let him possess your body. When he comes near uncover yourself and lie with him; teach him, the savage man, your woman's art, for when he murmurs love to you the wild beasts that shared his life in the hills will reject him."

She was not ashamed to take him, she made herself naked and welcomed his eagerness; as he lay on her murmuring love she taught him the woman's art. For six days and seven nights they lay together, for Enkidu had forgotten his home in the hills; but when he was satisfied he went back to the wild beasts. Then, when the gazelle saw him, they bolted away; when the wild creatures saw him they fled. Enkidu would have followed, but his body was bound as though with a cord, his knees gave way when he started to run, his swiftness was gone. And now the wild creatures had all fled away; Enkidu was grown weak, for wisdom was in him, and the thoughts of a man were in his heart. So he returned and sat down at the woman's feet, and listened intently to what she said. "You are wise, Enkidu, and now you have become like a god. Why do you want to run wild with the beasts in the hills? Come with me. I will take you to strong-walled Uruk, to the blessed temple of Ishtar and of Anu, of love and of heaven: there Gilgamesh lives, who is very strong, and like a wild bull he lords it over men."

When she had spoken Enkidu was pleased; he longed for a comrade, for one who would understand his heart. "Come, woman, and take me to that holy temple, to the house of Anu and of Ishtar, and to the place where Gilgamesh lords it over people. I will challenge him boldly, I will cry out aloud in Uruk, 'I am the strongest here, I have come to change the old order, I am he who was born in the hills, I am he who is strongest of all.'"

She said, "Let us go, and let him see your face. I know very well where Gilgamesh is in great Uruk. O Enkidu, there all the people are dressed in their gorgeous robes, every day is holiday, the young men and the girls are wonderful to see. How sweet they smell! All the great ones are roused from their beds. O Enkidu, you who love life, I will show you Gilgamesh, a man of many moods; you shall look at him well in his radiant manhood. His body is perfect in strength and maturity; he never rests by night or day. He is stronger than you, so leave your boasting. Shamash the glorious sun has given favors to Gilgamesh, and Anu of the heavens, and Enlil, and Ea the wise has given him deep understanding. I tell you, even before you have left the wilderness, Gilgamesh will know in his dreams that you are coming."

Now Gilgamesh got up to tell his dream to his mother, Ninsun, one of the wise gods. "Mother, last night I had a dream. I was full of joy, the young heroes were round me and I walked through the night under the stars of the firmament, and one, a meteor of the stuff of Anu, fell down from heaven. I tried to lift it but it proved too heavy. All the people of Uruk came round to see it, the common people jostled and the nobles thronged to kiss its feet; and to me its attraction was like the love of woman. They helped me, I braced my forehead and I raised it with thongs and brought it to you, and you yourself pronounced it my brother."

Then Ninsun, who is well-beloved and wise, said to Gilgamesh, "This star of heaven which descended like a meteor from the sky; which you tried to lift, but found too heavy, when you tried to move it it would not budge, and so you brought it to my feet; I made it for you, a goad and spur, and you were drawn as though to a woman. This is the strong comrade, the one who brings help to his friend in his need. He is the strongest of wild creatures, the stuff of Anu; born in the grasslands and the wild hills reared him; when you see him you will be glad; you will love him as a woman and he will never forsake you. This is the meaning of the dream."

Gilgamesh said, "Mother, I dreamed a second dream. In the streets of strong-walled Uruk there lay an axe; the shape of it was strange and the people thronged round. I saw it and was glad. I bent down, deeply drawn towards it; I loved it like a woman and wore it at my side." Ninsun answered, "That axe, which you saw, which drew you so powerfully like love of a woman, that is the comrade whom I give you, and he will come in his strength like one of the host of heaven. He is the brave companion who rescues his friend in necessity." Gilgamesh said to his mother, "A friend, a counsellor has come to me from Enlil, and now I shall befriend and counsel him." So Gilgamesh told his dreams; and the harlot retold them to Enkidu.

And now she said to Enkidu, "When I look at you you have become like a god. Why do you yearn to run wild again with the beasts in the hills? Get up from the ground, the bed of a shepherd." He listened to her words with care. It was good advice that she gave. She divided her clothing in two and with the one half she clothed him and with the other herself; and holding his hand she led him like a child to the sheepfolds, into the shepherds' tents. There all the shepherds crowded round to see him, they put down bread in front of him, but Enkidu could only suck the milk of wild animals. He fumbled and gaped, at a loss what to do or how he should eat the bread and drink the strong wine. Then the woman said, "Enkidu, eat bread, it is the staff of life; drink the wine, it is the custom of the land." So he ate till he was full and drank strong wine, seven goblets. He became merry, his heart exulted and his face shone. He rubbed down the matted hair of his body and anointed himself with oil. Enkidu had become a man; but when he had put on man's clothing he appeared like a bridegroom. He took arms to hunt the lion so that the shepherds could rest at night. He caught wolves and lions and the herdsmen lay down in peace; for Enkidu was their watchman, that strong man who had no rival.

He was merry living with the shepherds, till one day lifting his eyes he saw a man approaching. He said to the harlot, "Woman, fetch that man here. Why has he come? I wish to know his name." She went and called the man saying, "Sir, where are you going on this weary journey?" The man answered, saying to Enkidu, "Gilgamesh has gone into the marriage-house and shut out the people. He does strange things in Uruk, the city of great streets. At the roll of the drum work begins for the men, and work for the women. Gilgamesh the king is about to celebrate marriage with the Queen of Love, and he still demands to be first with the bride, the king to be first and the husband to follow, for that was ordained by the gods from his birth, from the time the umbilical cord was cut. But now the drums roll for the choice of the bride and the city groans." At these words Enkidu turned white in the face. "I will go to the place where Gilgamesh lords it over the people, I will challenge him boldly, and I will cry aloud in Uruk, 'I have come to change the old order, for I am the strongest here.'"

Now Enkidu strode in front and the woman followed behind. He entered Uruk, that great market, and all the folk thronged round him where he stood in the street in strong-walled Uruk. The people jostled; speaking of him they said, "He is the spit of Gilgamesh." "He is shorter." "He is bigger of bone." "This is the one who was reared on the milk of wild beasts. His is the greatest strength." The men rejoiced: "Now Gilgamesh has met his match. This great one, this hero whose beauty is like a god, he is a match even for Gilgamesh."

In Uruk the bridal bed was made, fit for the goddess of love. The bride waited for the bridegroom, but in the night Gilgamesh got up and came to the house. Then Enkidu stepped out, he stood in the street and blocked the way. Mighty Gilgamesh came on and Enkidu met him at the gate. He put out his foot and prevented Gilgamesh from entering the house, so they grappled, holding each other like bulls. They broke the doorposts and the walls shook, they snorted like bulls locked together. They shattered the doorposts and the walls shook. Gilgamesh bent his knee with his foot planted on the ground and with a turn Enkidu was thrown. Then immediately his fury died. When Enkidu was thrown he said to Gilgamesh, "There is not another like you in the world. Ninsun, who is as strong as a wild ox in the byre, she was the mother who bore you, and now you are raised above all men, and Enlil has given you the kingship, for your strength surpasses the strength of men." So Enkidu and Gilgamesh embraced and their friendship was sealed.

The Story of the Flood

"You know the city Shurrupak, it stands on the banks of Euphrates? That city grew old and the gods that were in it were old. There was Anu, lord of the firmament, their father, and warrior Enlil their counsellor, Ninurta the helper, and Ennugi watcher over canals; and with them also was Ea. In those days the world teemed, the people multiplied, the world bellowed like a wild bull, and the great god was aroused by the clamour. Enlil heard the clamour and he said to the gods in council, 'The uproar of mankind is intolerable and sleep is no longer possible by reason of the babel.' So the gods agreed to exterminate mankind. Enlil did this, but Ea because of his oath warned me in a dream. He whispered their words to my house of reeds, 'Reed-house, reed-house! Wall, O wall, hearken reed-house, wall reflect; O man of Shurrupak, son of Ubara-Tutu; tear down your house and build a boat, abandon possessions and look for life, despise worldly goods and save your soul alive. Tear down your house, I say, and build a boat. These are the measurements of the barque as you shall build her: let her beam equal her length, let her deck be roofed like the vault that covers the abyss; then take up into the boat the seed of all living creatures.'

"When I had understood I said to my lord, 'Behold, what you have commanded I will honour and perform, but how shall I answer the people, the city, the elders?' The Ea opened his mouth and said to me, his servant, 'Tell them this: I have learnt that Enlil is wrathful against me, I dare no longer walk in his land nor live in his city; I will go down to the Gulf to dwell with Ea my lord. But on you he will rain down abundance, rare fish and shy wild-fowl, a rich harvest-tide. In the evening the rider of the storm will bring you wheat in torrents.'

"In the first light of dawn all my household gathered round me, the children brought pitch and the men whatever was necessary. On the fifth day I laid the keel and the ribs, then I made fast the planking. The ground-space was one acre, each side of the deck measured one hundred and twenty cubits, making a square. I built six decks below, seven in all, I divided them into nine sections with bulkheads between. I drove in wedges where needed, I saw to the punt-poles, and laid in supplies. The carriers brought oil in baskets, I poured pitch into the furnace and asphalt and oil; more oil was consumed in caulking, and more again the master of the boat took into his stores. I slaughtered bullocks for the people and every day I killed sheep. I gave the shipwrights wine to drink as though it were river water, raw wine and red wine and oil and white wine. There was feasting then as there is at the time of the New Year's festival; I myself anointed my head. On the seventh day the boat was complete.

"Then was the launching full of difficulty; there was shifting of ballast above and below till two thirds was submerged. I loaded into her all that I had of gold and of living things, my family, my kin, the beast of the field both wild and tame, and all the craftsmen. I sent them on board, for the time that Shamash had ordained was already fulfilled when he said 'In the evening, when the rider of the storm sends down the destroying rain, enter the boat and batten her down.' The time was fulfilled, the evening came, the rider of the storm sent down the rain. I looked out at the weather and it was terrible, so I too boarded the boat and battened her down. All was now complete, the battening and the caulking; so I handed the tiller to Puzur-Amurri the steersman, with the navigation and the care of the whole boat.

"With the first light of dawn a black cloud came from the horizon; it thundered within where Adad, lord of the storm was riding. In front over hill and plain Shullat and Hanish, heralds of the storm, led on. Then the gods of the abyss rose up; Nergal pulled out the dams of the nether waters, Ninurta the war-lord threw down the dykes, and the seven judges of hell, the Annunaki, raised their torches, lighting the land with their livid flame. A stupor of despair went up to heaven when the god of the storm turned daylight to darkness, when he smashed the land like a cup. One whole day the tempest raged, gathering fury as it went, it poured over the people like the tides of battle; a man could not see his brother nor the people be seen from heaven. Even the gods were terrified at the flood, they fled to the highest heaven, the firmament of Anu; they crouched against the walls, cowering like curs. Then Ishtar the sweet-voiced Queen of Heaven cried out like a woman in travail: 'Alas the days of old are turned to dust because I commanded evil; why did I command this evil in the council of all the gods? I commanded wars to destroy the people, but are they not my people, for I brought them forth? Now like the spawn of fish they float in the ocean.' The great gods of heaven and of hell wept, they covered their mouths.

"For six days and six nights the winds blew, torrent and tempest and flood overwhelmed the world, tempest and flood raged together like warring hosts. When the seventh day dawned the storm from the south subsided, the sea grew calm, the flood was stilled; I looked at the face of the world and there was silence, all mankind was turned to clay. The surface of the sea stretched as flat as a roof-top; I opened a hatch and the light fell on my face. Then I bowed low, I sat down and I wept, the tears streamed down my face, for on every side was the waste of water. I looked for land in vain, but fourteen leagues distant there appeared a mountain, and there the boat grounded; on the mountain of Nisir the boat held fast, she held fast and did not budge. One day she held, and a second day on the mountain of Nisir she held fast and did not budge. A third day, and a fourth day she held fast on the mountain and did not budge; a fifth day and a sixth day she held fast on the mountain. When the seventh day dawned I loosed a dove and let her go. She flew away, but finding no resting-place she returned. Then I loosed a swallow, and she flew away but finding no resting-place she returned. I loosed a raven, she saw that the waters had retreated, she ate, she flew around, she cawed, and she did not come back. Then I threw everything open to the four winds, I made a sacrifice and poured out a libation on the mountain top. Seven and again seven cauldrons I set up on their stands, I heaped up wood and cane and cedar and myrtle. When the gods smelled the sweet savour, they gathered like flies over the sacrifice. Then, at last, Isthar also came, she lifted her necklace with the jewels of heaven that once Anu had made to please her. 'O you gods here present, by the lapis lazuli round my neck I shall remember these days as I remember the jewels of my throat; these last days I shall not forget. Let all the gods gather round the sacrifice, except Enlil. He shall not approach this offering, for without reflection he brought the flood; he consigned my people to destruction.'

"When Enlil had come, when he saw the boat, he was wrath and swelled with anger at the gods, the host of heaven, 'Has any of these mortals escaped? Not one was to have survived the destruction.' Then the god of the wells and canals Ninurta opened his mouth and said to the warrior Enlil, 'Who is there of the gods that devise without Ea? It is Ea alone who knows all things.' Then Ea opened his mouth and spoke to warrior Enlil, 'Wisest of gods, hero Enlil, how could you so senselessly bring down the flood?

Lay upon the sinner his sin,
Lay upon the transgressor his transgression,
Punish him a little when he breaks loose,
Do not drive him too hard or he perishes;
Would that a lion had ravaged mankind
Rather than the flood,
Would that a wolf had ravaged mankind
Rather than the flood,
Would that famine had wasted the world
Rather than the flood,
Would that pestilence had wasted mankind
Rather than the flood.

It was not I that revealed the secret of the gods; the wise man learned it in a dream. Now take your counsel what shall be done with him.'

"Then Enlil went up into the boat, he took me by the hand and my wife and made us enter the boat and kneel down on either side, he standing between us. He touched our foreheads to bless us saying, 'In time past Utnapishtim was a mortal man; henceforth he and his wife shall live in the distance at the mouth of the rivers.' Thus it was that the gods took me and placed me here to live in the distance, at the mouth of the rivers."

11

From Hammurabi's Code

King Hammurabi of Babylon conquered the entire area of Mesopotamia (including Sumer) between 1793 and 1750 B.C.E. His law code provides us with a rare insight into the daily life of ancient urban society.

Law codes give us an idea of a people's sense of justice and notions of proper punishment. This selection includes only parts of Hammurabi's Code, so we cannot conclude that if something is not mentioned here it was not a matter of legal concern. We can, however, deduce much about Babylonian society from the laws mentioned in this essay.

What do these laws tell us about class divisions or social distinctions in Babylonian society? What can we learn from these laws about the roles of women and men? Which laws or punishments seem unusual today? What does that difference suggest to you about ancient Babylon compared to modern society?

Thinking Historically

As a primary source, law codes are extremely useful. They zero in on a society's main concerns, revealing minutiae of daily life in great detail. But, for a number of reasons, law codes cannot be viewed as a precise reflection of society.

We cannot assume, for instance, that all of Hammurabi's laws were strictly followed or enforced, nor can we assume that for our own society. If there were a law against something, we can safely assume that some people obeyed it and some people did not. (That is, if no one engaged in the behavior, there would be no need for the law.) Therefore, law codes suggest a broad range of behaviors in a society. Is there any way you could tell — from the information in the law code itself — if any of these laws were ignored, unnecessary, or not enforced? Can you think of a law (federal, state, or local) that does not give an accurate picture of today's society?

While laws tell us something about the concerns of the society that produces them, we cannot presume that all members of society share the same concerns. Recall that, especially in ancient society, laws were written by the literate, powerful few. What evidence do you see of the upper-class composition of Babylonian law in this code?

"Hammurabi's Code," from C. H. Johns, *Babylonian and Assyrian Laws, Contracts and Letters* [Library of Ancient Inscriptions] (New York: Charles Scribner's Sons, 1904), 33–35.

Finally, if an ancient law seems similar to our own, we cannot assume that the law reflects motives, intents, or goals similar to our own laws. Laws must be considered within the context of the society in which they were created. Notice, for instance, the laws in Hammurabi's Code that may seem, by our standards, intended to protect women. On closer examination, what appears to be their goal?

Theft

6. If a man has stolen goods from a temple, or house, he shall be put to death; and he that has received the stolen property from him shall be put to death.

8. If a patrician has stolen ox, sheep, ass, pig, or ship, whether from a temple, or a house, he shall pay thirtyfold. If he be a plebeian, he shall return tenfold. If the thief cannot pay, he shall be put to death.

14. If a man has stolen a child, he shall be put to death.

15. If a man has induced either a male or female slave from the house of a patrician, or plebeian, to leave the city, he shall be put to death.

21. If a man has broken into a house he shall be killed before the breach and buried there.

22. If a man has committed highway robbery and has been caught, that man shall be put to death.

23. If the highwayman has not been caught, the man that has been robbed shall state on oath what he has lost and the city or district governor in whose territory or district the robbery took place shall restore to him what he has lost.

128. If a man has taken a wife and has not executed a marriage-contract, that woman is not a wife.

129. If a man's wife be caught lying with another, they shall be strangled and cast into the water. If the wife's husband would save his wife, the king can save his servant.

130. If a man has ravished another's betrothed wife, who is a virgin, while still living in her father's house, and has been caught in the act, that man shall be put to death; the woman shall go free.

131. If a man's wife has been accused by her husband, and has not been caught lying with another, she shall swear her innocence, and return to her house.

138. If a man has divorced his wife, who has not borne him children, he shall pay over to her as much money as was given for her bride-price and the marriage-portion which she brought from her father's house, and so shall divorce her.

139. If there was no bride-price, he shall give her one mina of silver, as a price of divorce.

140. If he be a plebeian, he shall give her one-third of a mina of silver.

148. If a man has married a wife and a disease has seized her, if he is determined to marry a second wife, he shall marry her. He shall not divorce the wife whom the disease has seized. In the home they made together she shall dwell, and he shall maintain her as long as she lives.

149. If that woman was not pleased to stay in her husband's house, he shall pay over to her the marriage-portion which she brought from her father's house, and she shall go away.

153. If a man's wife, for the sake of another, has caused her husband to be killed, that woman shall be impaled.

154. If a man has committed incest with his daughter, that man shall be banished from the city.

155. If a man has betrothed a maiden to his son and his son has known her, and afterward the man has lain in her bosom, and been caught, that man shall be strangled and she shall be cast into the water.

156. If a man has betrothed a maiden to his son, and his son has not known her, and that man has lain in her bosom, he shall pay her half a mina of silver, and shall pay over to her whatever she brought from her father's house, and the husband of her choice shall marry her.

186. If a man has taken a young child to be his son, and after he has taken him, the child discovers his own parents, he shall return to his father's house.

188, 189. If a craftsman has taken a child to bring up and has taught him his handicraft, he shall not be reclaimed. If he has not taught him his handicraft that foster child shall return to his father's house.

Assault

195. If a son has struck his father, his hands shall be cut off.

196. If a man has knocked out the eye of a patrician, his eye shall be knocked out.

197. If he has broken the limb of a patrician, his limb shall be broken.

198. If he has knocked out the eye of a plebeian or has broken the limb of a plebeian's servant, he shall pay one mina of silver.

199. If he has knocked out the eye of a patrician's servant, or broken the limb of a patrician's servant, he shall pay half his value.

200. If a patrician has knocked out the tooth of a man that is his equal, his tooth shall be knocked out.

201. If he has knocked out the tooth of a plebeian, he shall pay one-third of a mina of silver.

Liability

229. If a builder has built a house for a man, and has not made his work sound, and the house he built has fallen, and caused the death of its owner, that builder shall be put to death.

230. If it is the owner's son that is killed, the builder's son shall be put to death.

231. If it is the slave of the owner that is killed, the builder shall give slave for slave to the owner of the house.

232. If he has caused the loss of goods, he shall render back whatever he has destroyed. Moreover, because he did not make sound the house he built, and it fell, at his own cost he shall rebuild the house that fell.

237. If a man has hired a boat and a boatman, and loaded it with corn, wool, oil, or dates, or whatever it be, and the boatman has been careless, and sunk the boat, or lost what is in it, the boatman shall restore the boat which he sank, and whatever he lost that was in it.

238. If a boatman has sunk a man's boat, and has floated it again, he shall pay half its value in silver.

251. If a man's ox be a gorer, and has revealed its evil propensity as a gorer, and he has not blunted its horn, or shut up the ox, and then that ox has gored a free man, and caused his death, the owner shall pay half a mina of silver.

252. If it be a slave that has been killed, he shall pay one-third of a mina of silver.

12

Setne Khamwas and Naneferkaptah

This primary source is an ancient Egyptian story about the efforts of Prince Khamwas to steal a magical book from the tomb of a Prince Naneferkaptah, who lived long before. The historical Setne Khamwas,

---

"Setne Khamwas and Naneferkaptah" (Setne I), in Miriam Lichtheim, *Ancient Egyptian Literature,* Volume III; *The Late Period* (Berkeley: University of California Press, 1980), 127–38.

the fourth son of King Ramses II (r. 1304–1237 B.C.E.), was an avid restorer of ancient monuments and chief priest of the God Ptah, the patron god of crafts and the old capital of Memphis. The identity of the ancient Naneferkaptah is lost in legend. The papyrus that is translated here was written a thousand years after Prince Khamwas died.

What does the story tell you about the lives of princes in ancient Egypt? What does it suggest about Egyptian ideas of death, the afterlife, and history?

Notice the importance of words and books for Khamwas and Naneferkaptah. What is the intent and meaning of passages in the story that suggest that words, writing, or books have magical properties? What do you think is the moral of the story?

Thinking Historically

Like *The Epic of Gilgamesh,* this story is meant to instruct and entertain rather than to describe life in the ancient world. But like *The Epic,* it offers us an opportunity to mine a wealth of detail about the world that produced it. We learn, for instance, something about Egyptian royal marriage that reveals a range of behavior much as a law code would. Write a few sentences (little secondary accounts) that accurately describe aspects of ancient Egyptian behavior based on information revealed by the story.

You might notice here and in *The Epic* the teller's use of repetitive passages. What effect does this device have? Why do you think it was done?

The lost beginning may be reconstructed as follows:

Prince Khamwas, son of King Ramses II and high priest of Ptah at Memphis, was a very learned scribe and magician who spent his time in the study of ancient monuments and books. One day he was told of the existence of a book of magic written by the god Thoth himself and kept in the tomb of a prince named Naneferkaptah (Na-nefer-ka-ptah), who had lived in the distant past and was buried somewhere in the vast necropolis of Memphis. After a long search, Prince Khamwas, accompanied by his foster brother Inaros, found the tomb of Naneferkaptah and entered it. He saw the magic book, which radiated a strong light, and tried to seize it. But the spirits of Naneferkaptah and of his wife Ahwere rose up to defend their cherished possession.

Ahwere and her son Merib were not buried in this Memphite tomb but rather in distant Coptos, where they had lost the lives. But the spirit of Ahwere was with her husband at this critical moment, and she now stood before Prince Khamwas and told him how her husband had acquired the magic book and how they had all paid for it with their lives. She begins her story by relating that she and Naneferkaptah had been brother and sister and the only children of a Pharaoh named Mernebptah. They had loved each other very much and had wanted to marry. But Pharaoh wished to marry his son to the daughter of a general and his daughter to the son of a general. In her anguish Ahwere had asked the steward of Pharaoh's palace to plead with Pharaoh in her behalf. The steward had done so and Pharaoh had become silent and distressed. To the steward's question, why he was distressed, Pharaoh answered:

(Here begins the story on page 3 of the papyrus)

"It is you who distress me. If it so happens that I have only two children, is it right to marry the one to the other? I will marry Naneferkaptah to the daughter of a general, and I will marry Ahwere to the son of another general, so that our family may increase!"

When the time came for the banquet to be set before Pharaoh, they came for me and took me to the banquet. But my heart was very sad and I did not have my former looks. Pharaoh said to me: "Ahwere, was it you who sent to me with those foolish words, 'Let me marry [Naneferkaptah, my] elder [brother]'?"

I said to him: "Let me marry the son of a general, and let him marry the daughter of another general, so that our family may increase!" I laughed and Pharaoh laughed.[1]

[When the steward of the palace came] Pharaoh [said to him]: "Steward, let Ahwere be taken to the house of Naneferkaptah tonight, and let all sorts of beautiful things be taken with her."

I was taken as a wife to the house of Naneferkaptah [that night, and Pharaoh] sent me a present of silver and gold, and all Pharaoh's household sent me presents. Naneferkaptah made holiday with me, and he entertained all Pharaoh's household. He slept with me that night and found me [pleasing. He slept with] me again and again, and we loved each other.

When my time of purification came I made no more purification.[2] It was reported to Pharaoh, and his heart was very happy. Pharaoh had many things taken [out of the treasury] and sent me presents of silver, gold, and royal linen, all very beautiful. When my time of bearing came, I bore this boy who is before you, who was named Merib. He was entered in the register of the House of Life.[3]

[1] By her pert quotation of the king's own words Ahwere won the king over, so that he permitted her to marry her brother.

[2] I.e., her menstruation period had failed to come.

[3] If that is the correct rendering it implies that members of the royal house were registered in the House of Life.

[It so happened that] my brother Naneferkaptah [had no] occupation on earth but walking on the desert of Memphis, reading the writings that were in the tombs of the Pharaohs and on the stelae of the scribes of the House of Life and the writings that were on [the other monuments, for his zeal] concerning writings was very great.

After this there was a procession in honor of Ptah, and Naneferkaptah went into the temple to worship. As he was walking behind the procession, reading the writings on the shrines of the gods, [an old priest saw] him and laughed. Naneferkaptah said to him: "Why are you laughing at me?" He said: "I am not laughing at you. I am laughing because you are reading writings that have no [importance for anyone]. If you desire to read writings, come to me and I will have you taken to the place where that book is that Thoth wrote with his own hand, when he came down following the other gods. Two spells are written in it. When you [recite the first spell you will] charm the sky, the earth, the netherworld, the mountains, and the waters. You will discover what all the birds of the sky and all the reptiles are saying. You will see the fish of the deep [though there are twenty-one divine cubits of water] over [them]. When you recite the second spell, it will happen that, whether you are in the netherworld or in your form on earth, you will see Pre appearing in the sky with his Ennead, and the Moon in its form of rising."

[Naneferkaptah said to him]: "As he (the king) lives, tell me a good thing that you desire, so that I may do it for you, and you send me to the place where this book is!"

The priest said to Naneferkaptah: "If you wish to be sent [to the place where this book is] you must give me a hundred pieces of silver for my burial, and you must endow me with two priestly stipends tax free."

Naneferkaptah called a servant and had the hundred pieces of silver given to the priest. He added the two stipends and had [the priest] endowed with them [tax free].

The priest said to Naneferkaptah: "The book in question is in the middle of the water of Coptos in a box of iron. In the box of iron is a box of [copper. In the box of copper is] a box of juniper wood. In the box of juniper wood is a box of ivory and ebony. In the box of ivory and ebony is a [box of silver. In the box of silver] is a box of gold, and in it is the book. [There are six miles of] serpents, scorpions, and all kinds of reptiles around the box in which the book is, and there is [an eternal serpent around] this same box."

When the priest had thus spoken to Naneferkaptah, he did not know where on earth he was. He came out of the temple, he told [me everything that had happened to him]. He [said] to me: "I will go to Coptos, I will bring this book, hastening back to the north again." But

I chided the priest, saying: "May Neith curse you for having told him these [dreadful things! You have brought] me combat, you have brought me strife. The region of Thebes, I now find it [abhorrent]." I did what I could with Naneferkaptah to prevent him from going to Coptos; he did not listen to me. He went to [Pharaoh and told] Pharaoh everything that the priest had said to him.

Pharaoh said to him: "What is that [you want]?" He said to him: "Let the ship of Pharaoh be given to me with its equipment. I will take Ahwere [and her boy Merib] to the south with me, I will bring this book without delay."

The ship of Pharaoh was given [him] with its equipment. We boarded it, we set sail, we arrived [at Coptos]. It [was announced] to the priests of Isis of Coptos and the chief priest of Isis. They came down to meet us, hastening to meet Naneferkaptah, and their wives came down to meet me. [We went up from the shore and went into] the temple of Isis and Harpocrates. Naneferkaptah sent for an ox, a goose, and wine. He made burnt offering and libation before Isis of Coptos and Harpocrates. We were taken to a very beautiful house [filled with all good things].

Naneferkaptah spent four days making holiday with the priests of Isis of Coptos, and the wives of the priests of Isis made holiday with me. When the morning of our fifth day came, Naneferkaptah had [much] pure [wax brought] to him. He made a boat filled with its rowers and sailors. He recited a spell to them, he made them live, he gave them breath, he put them on the water. He filled the ship of Pharaoh with sand, [he tied it to the other boat]. He [went] on board, and I sat above the water of Coptos, saying: "I shall learn what happens to him."

He said to the rowers: "Row me to the place where the book is!" [They rowed him by night] as by day. In three days he reached it. He cast sand before him, and a gap formed in the river. He found six miles of serpents, scorpions, and all kinds of reptiles around [the place where the book was]. He found an eternal serpent around this same box. He recited a spell to the six miles of serpents, scorpions, and all kinds of reptiles that were around the box, and did not let them come up. [He went to the place where] the eternal serpent was. He fought it and killed it. It came to life again and resumed its shape. He fought it again, a second time, and killed it; it came to life again. He [fought it again, a third] time, cut it in two pieces, and put sand between one piece and the other. [It died] and no longer resumed its shape.

Naneferkaptah went to the place where the box was. [He found it was a box of] iron. He opened it and found a box of copper. He opened it and found a box of juniper wood. He opened it and found a box of ivory and ebony. [He opened it and found a box of] silver. He opened it and found a box of gold. He opened it and found the book in it. He brought the book up out of the box of gold.

He recited a spell from it; [he charmed the sky, the earth, the netherworld, the] mountains, the waters. He discovered what all the birds of the sky and the fish of the deep and the beasts of the deserts were saying. He recited another spell; he saw [Pre appearing in the sky with his Ennead], and the Moon rising, and the stars in their forms. He saw the fish of the deep, though there were twenty-one divine cubits of water over them. He recited a spell to the [water; he made it resume its form].

[He went on] board, he said to the rowers: "Row me back to the place [I came] from." They rowed him by night as by day. He reached me at the place where I was; [he found me sitting] above the water of Coptos, not having drunk nor eaten, not having done anything on earth, and looking like a person who has reached the Good House.[4]

I said to Naneferkaptah ["Welcome back! Let me] see this book for which we have taken these [great] pains!" He put the book into my hand. I recited one spell from it; I charmed the sky, the earth, the netherworld, the mountains, the waters. I discovered what all the birds of the sky and the fish of the deep and the beasts were saying. I recited another spell; I saw Pre appearing in the sky with his Ennead. I saw the Moon rising, and all the stars of the sky in their forms. I saw the fish of the deep, though there were twenty-one divine cubits of water over them.

As I could not write — I mean, compared with Naneferkaptah, my brother, who was a good scribe and very wise man — he had a sheet of new papyrus brought to him. He wrote on it every word that was in the book before him. He soaked it in beer, he dissolved it in water. When he knew it had dissolved, he drank it and knew what had been in it.

We returned to Coptos the same day and made holiday before Isis of Coptos and Harpocrates. We went on board, we traveled north, we reached a point six miles north of Coptos.

Now Thoth had found out everything that had happened to Naneferkaptah regarding the book, and Thoth hastened to report it to Pre, saying: "Learn of my right and my case against Naneferkaptah, the son of Pharaoh Mernebptah! He went to my storehouse; he plundered it; he seized my box with my document. He killed my guardian who was watching over it!" He was told: "He is yours together with every person belonging to him." They sent a divine power from heaven, saying: "Do not allow Naneferkaptah and any person belonging to him to get to Memphis safely!"

[4] The house of embalming; i.e., she looked like a dead person.

At a certain moment the boy Merib came out from under the awning of Pharaoh's ship, fell into the water, and drowned. All the people on board cried out. Naneferkaptah came out from his tent, recited a spell to him, and made him rise up, though there were twenty-one divine cubits of water over him. He recited a spell to him and made him relate to him everything that had happened to him, and the nature of the accusation that Thoth had made before Pre.

We returned to Coptos with him. We had him taken to the Good House. We had him tended, we had him embalmed like a prince and important person. We laid him to rest in his coffin in the desert of Coptos. Naneferkaptah, my brother, said: "Let us go north, let us not delay, lest Pharaoh hear the things that have happened to us and his heart become sad because of them." We went on board, we went north without delay.

Six miles north of Coptos, at the place where the boy Merib had fallen into the river, I came out from under the awning of Pharaoh's ship, fell into the river, and drowned. All the people on board cried out and told Naneferkaptah. He came out from the tent of Pharaoh's ship, recited a spell to me, and made me rise up, though there were twenty-one divine cubits of water over me. He had me brought up, recited a spell to me, and made me relate to him everything that had happened to me, and the nature of the accusation that Thoth had made before Pre.

He returned to Coptos with me. He had me taken to the Good House. He had me tended, he had me embalmed in the manner of a prince and very important person. He laid me to rest in the tomb in which the boy Merib was resting. He went on board, he went north without delay.

Six miles north of Coptos, at the place where we had fallen into the river, he spoke to his heart saying: "Could I go to Coptos and dwell there also? If I go to Memphis now and Pharaoh asks me about his children, what shall I say to him? Can I say to him, 'I took your children to the region of Thebes; I killed them and stayed alive, and I have come to Memphis yet alive'?"

He sent for a scarf of royal linen belonging to him, and made it into a bandage; he bound the book, placed it on his body, and made it fast. Naneferkaptah came out from under the awning of Pharaoh's ship, fell into the water, and drowned. All the people on board cried out, saying: "Great woe, said woe! Will he return, the good scribe, the learned man whose like has not been?"

Pharaoh's ship sailed north, no man on earth knowing where Naneferkaptah was. They reached Memphis and sent word to Pharaoh. Pharaoh came down to meet Pharaoh's ship; he wore mourning and all the people of Memphis wore mourning, including the priests of Ptah, the chief priest of Ptah, the council, and all Pharaoh's household. Then they saw Naneferkaptah holding on to the rudders of Pharaoh's ship through his craft of a good scribe. They brought him up and saw the book on his body.

Pharaoh said: "Let this book that is on his body be hidden." Then said the council of Pharaoh and the priests of Ptah and the chief priest of Ptah to Pharaoh: "Our great lord — O may he have the lifetime of Pre — Naneferkaptah was a good scribe and a very learned man!" Pharaoh had them give him entry into the Good House on the sixteenth day, wrapping on the thirty-fifth, burial on the seventieth day. And they laid him to rest in his coffin in his resting place.

These are the evil things that befell us on account of this book of which you say, "Let it be given to me." You have no claim to it, whereas our lives on earth were taken on account of it!

Setne Takes the Book

Setne said to Ahwere: "Let me have this book that I see between you and Naneferkaptah, or else I will take it by force!" Naneferkaptah rose from the bier and said: "Are you Setne, to whom this woman has told these dire things and you have not accepted them? The said book, will you be able to seize it through the power of a good scribe, or through skill in playing draughts with me? Let the two of us play draughts for it!" Said Setne, "I am ready."

They put before them the game board with its pieces, and they both played. Naneferkaptah won one game from Setne. He recited a spell to him, struck his head with the game-box that was before him, and made him sink into the ground as far as his legs. He did the same with the second game. He won it from Setne, and made him sink into the ground as far as his phallus. He did the same with the third game, and made him sink into the ground as far as his ears. After this Setne was in great straits at the hands of Naneferkaptah.

Setne called to his foster-brother Inaros, saying: "Hasten up to the earth and tell Pharaoh everything that has happened to me; and bring the amulets of my father Ptah and my books of sorcery." He hastened up to the earth and told Pharaoh everything that had happened to Setne. Pharaoh said: "Take him the amulets of his father Ptah and his books of sorcery." Inaros hastened down into the tomb. He put the amulets on the body of Setne, and he jumped up in that very moment. Setne stretched out his hand for the book and seized it. Then, as Setne came up from the tomb, light went before him, darkness went behind him, and Ahwere wept after him, saying: "Hail, O darkness! Farewell, O light! Everything that was in the tomb has departed!" Naneferkaptah said to Ahwere: "Let your heart not grieve. I will make him bring this book back here, with a forked stick in his hand and a lighted brazier on his head!"[5]

Setne came up from the tomb and made it fast behind him, as it had been. Setne went before Pharaoh and related to him the things that had happened to him on account of the book. Pharaoh said to Setne: "Take this book back to the tomb of Naneferkaptah like a wise man, or else he will make you take it back with a forked stick in your hand and a lighted brazier on your head." Setne did not listen to him. Then Setne had no occupation on earth but to unroll the book and read from it to everyone.

Setne and Tabubu

After this it happened one day that Setne was strolling in the forecourt of the temple of Ptah. Then he saw [a woman] who was very beautiful, there being no other woman like her in appearance. She was beautiful and wore many golden jewels, and maid servants walked behind her as well as two men servants belonging to her household. The moment Setne saw her, he did not know where on earth he was. He called his man servant, saying: "Hasten to the place where this woman is, and find out what her position is." The man servant hastened to the place where the woman was. He called to the maid servant who was following her and asked her, saying, "What woman is this?" She told him: "It is Tabubu, the daughter of the prophet of Bastet, mistress of Ankhtawi. She has come here to worship Ptah, the great god."

The servant returned to Setne and related to him every word she had said to him. Setne said to the servant: "Go, say to the maid, 'It is Setne Khamwas, the son of Pharaoh Usermare, who has sent me to say, "I will give you ten pieces of gold — spend an hour with me. Or do you have a complaint of wrongdoing? I will have it settled for you. I will have you taken to a hidden place where no one on earth shall find you."'"

The servant returned to the place where Tabubu was. He called her maid and told her. She cried out as if what he said was an insult. Tabubu said to the servant: "Stop talking to this foolish maid; come and speak with me." The servant hastened to where Tabubu was and said to her: "I will give you ten pieces of gold; spend an hour with Setne Khamwas, the son of Pharaoh Usermare. If you have a complaint of wrongdoing, he will have it settled for you. He will take you to a hidden place where no one on earth shall find you."

[5] These must have been symbols of repentance.

Tabubu said: "Go, tell Setne, 'I am of priestly rank, I am not a low person. If you desire to do what you wish with me, you must come to Bubastis, to my house. It is furnished with everything, and you shall do what you wish with me, without anyone on earth finding me and without my acting like a low woman of the street.'"

The servant returned to Setne and told him everything she had said to him. He said, "That suits (me)!" Everyone around Setne was indignant.

Setne had a boat brought to him. He went on board and hastened to Bubastis. When he came to the west of the suburb he found a very lofty house that had a wall around it, a garden on its north, and a seat at its door. Setne asked, "Whose house is this?" They told him, "It is the house of Tabubu." Setne went inside the wall. While he turned his face to the storehouse in the garden they announced him to Tabubu. She came down, took Setne's hand, and said to him: "By the welfare of the house of the prophet of Bastet, mistress of Ankhtawi, which you have reached, it will please me greatly if you will take the trouble to come up with me."

Setne walked up the stairs of the house with Tabubu. He found the upper story of the house swept and adorned, its floor adorned with real lapis-lazuli and real turquoise. Many couches were in it, spread with royal linen, and many golden cups were on the table. A golden cup was filled with wine and put into Setne's hand. She said to him, "May it please you to eat something. He said to her, "I could not do that." Incense was put on the brazier; ointment was brought to him of the kind provided for Pharaoh. Setne made holiday with Tabubu, never having seen anyone like her.

Setne said to Tabubu: "Let us accomplish what we have come here for." She said to him: "You will return to your house in which you live. I am of priestly rank; I am not a low person. If you desire to do what you wish with me you must make for me a deed of maintenance and of compensation in money for everything, all goods belonging to you." He said to her: "Send for the schoolteacher." He was brought at once. He made for her a deed of maintenance and of compensation in money for everything, all goods belonging to him.

At this moment one came to announce to Setne, "Your children are below." He said, "Let them be brought up." Tabubu rose and put on a garment of royal linen. Setne saw all her limbs through it, and his desire became even greater than it had been before. Setne said: "Tabubu, let me accomplish what I have come here for!" She said to him: "You will return to your house in which you live. I am of priestly rank; I am not a low person. If you desire to do what you wish with me, you must make your children subscribe to my deed. Do not leave them to contend with my children over your property." He had his children brought and made them subscribe to the deed.

Setne said to Tabubu: "Let me accomplish what I have come for!" She said to him: "You will return to your house in which you live. I am of priestly rank; I am not a low person. If you desire to do what you wish with me, you must have your children killed. Do not leave them to contend with my children over your property." Setne said: "Let the abomination that came into your head be done to them." She had his children killed before him. She had them thrown down from the window to the dogs and cats. They ate their flesh, and he heard them as he drank with Tabubu.

Setne said to Tabubu: "Let us accomplish what we have come here for! All the things that you have said, I have done them all for you." She said to him: "Come now to this storehouse." Setne went to the storehouse. He lay down on a couch of ivory and ebony, his wish about to be fulfilled. Tabubu lay down beside Setne. He stretched out his hand to touch her, and she opened her mouth wide in a loud cry. Setne awoke in a state of great heat, his phallus in a . . . , and there were no clothes on him at all.

At this moment Setne saw a noble person borne in a litter, with many men running beside him, and he had the likeness of Pharaoh. Setne was about to rise but could not rise for shame because he had no clothes on. Pharaoh said: "Setne, what is this state that you are in?" He said: "It is Naneferkaptah who has done it all to me!" Pharaoh said: "Go to Memphis; your children want you; they stand in their rank before Pharaoh." Setne said to Pharaoh: "My great lord — O may he have the lifetime of Pre — how can I go to Memphis with no clothes on me at all?" Pharaoh called to a servant who was standing by and made him give clothes to Setne. Pharaoh said: "Setne, go to Memphis; your children are alive; they stand in their rank before Pharaoh."

Setne Returns the Book

When Setne came to Memphis he embraced his children, for he found them alive. Pharaoh said to Setne: "Was it a state of drunkenness you were in before?" Setne related everything that had happened with Tabubu and Naneferkaptah. Pharaoh said: "Setne, I did what I could with you before, saying, 'They will kill you if you do not take this book back to the place you took it from.' You have not listened to me until now. Take this book back to Naneferkaptah, with a forked stick in your hand and a lighted brazier on your head."

When Setne came out from before Pharaoh, there was a forked stick in his hand and a lighted brazier on his head. He went down into the tomb in which Naneferkaptah was. Ahwere said to him: "Setne, it is the great god Ptah who has brought you back safely." Naneferkaptah laughed, saying, "It is what I told you before." Setne greeted Naneferkaptah, and he found one could say that Pre was in the whole tomb. Ahwere and Naneferkaptah greeted Setne warmly.

Setne said: "Naneferkaptah, is there any matter which is shameful?"[6] Naneferkaptah said: "Setne, you know that Ahwere and her son Merib are in Coptos; here in this tomb they are through the craft of a good scribe. Let it be asked of you to undertake the task of going to Coptos and [bringing them] of here."

When Setne had come up from the tomb, he went before Pharaoh and related to Pharaoh everything that Naneferkaptah had said to him. Pharaoh said: "Setne, go to Coptos, bring Ahwere and her son Merib." He said to Pharaoh: "Let the ship of Pharaoh and its equipment be given to me."

The ship of Pharaoh and its equipment were given to him. He went on board, he set sail, he reached Coptos without delay. It was announced to the priests of Isis of Coptos, and the chief priest of Isis. They came down to meet him, they conducted him to the shore.

He went up from it, he went into the temple of Isis of Coptos and Harpocrates. He sent for an ox, a goose, and wine, and made burnt offering and libation before Isis of Coptos and Harpocrates. He went to the desert of Coptos with the priests of Isis and the chief priest of Isis. They spent three days and three nights searching in all the tombs on the desert of Coptos, turning over the stelae of the scribes of the House of Life, and reading the inscriptions on them. They did not find the resting place in which Ahwere and her son were.

When Naneferkaptah found that they did not find the resting place of Ahwere and her son Merib, he rose up as an old man, a very aged priest, and came to meet Setne. When Setne saw him he said to the old man: "You have the appearance of a man of great age. Do you know the resting place in which Ahwere and her son Merib are?" The old man said to Setne: "My great-grandfather said to my grandfather, 'The resting place of Ahwere and her son Merib is at the south corner of the house of the [chief of police].'"

Setne said to the old man: "Perhaps there is some wrong that the chief of police did to you, on account of which you are trying to have his house torn down?" The old man said to Setne: "Have a watch set over me, and let the house of the chief of police be demolished. If they do not find Ahwere and her son Merib under the south corner of his house, let punishment be done to me."

They set a watch over the old man, and they found the resting place of Ahwere and her son Merib under the south corner of the house of the chief of police. Setne let the two noble persons enter into Pharaoh's ship. He had the house of the chief of police built as it had been before. Naneferkaptah let Setne learn the fact that it was he who had come to

[6] I.e., "Is there anything wrong that I could set right for you?"

Coptos, to let them find the resting place in which Ahwere and her son Merib were. Setne went on board Pharaoh's ship. He went north and without delay he reached Memphis with all the people who were with him. When it was announced before Pharaoh, he came down to meet the ship of Pharaoh. He let the noble persons enter into the tomb in which Naneferkaptah was. He had it closed over them all together.

Colophon

This is the complete text, a tale of Setne Khamwas and Naneferkaptah, and his wife Ahwere and her son Merib. It was copied by ——— in year 15, first month of winter.

REFLECTIONS

The difference between primary and secondary sources is in one sense quite obvious. Primary sources derive *from* the period. Secondary sources are written *about* the period. A secondary source puts forth *one* interpretation, whereas primary sources can be interpreted in many ways. In this chapter, only the first selection is a secondary source; the other three selections are clearly primary sources.

Still, the difference between primary and secondary sources is not always so clear. I mentioned that *The Epic of Gilgamesh* was written sometime after the events it purports to describe. Actually, the version you read came from tablets dating from about 700 B.C.E., almost two thousand years after the events of the story. Since *The Epic* presents itself as the story of the ancient king, we might regard it as a history. It would be comparable to a history written today about the period of Christ. No one would call a modern history of the period of Christ a primary source.

Nevertheless, for us *The Epic* is a primary source because we are not making a distinction between the world of 2700 B.C.E. and the world of 700 B.C.E. We do not believe that the story changed much over those two thousand years and, even if it had, in this chapter we were looking at the urban age as a long time period of thousands of years. In other words, even at 700 B.C.E., *The Epic* was *from* the ancient world.

Further, stylistic elements in *The Epic* and in Setne Khamwas reveal they are myths rather than historical accounts, and myths are primary sources for the beliefs and values of their time. We mentioned the repetitive phrasing in Setne Khamwas. What other elements in the structure or style of these works warns the reader that a myth is being told rather than an accurate historical account?

4

Identity in Caste versus Territorial Societies

HISTORICAL CONTEXT

Greece and India, 1000–300 B.C.E.

Both India and Greece developed ancient city-based civilizations within a thousand years of the urban revolution. In India that civilization was concentrated on the Indus River valley in what is today Pakistan. In Greece the Minoan civilization on the island of Crete was followed by the Mycenaean civilization on the mainland. But both ancient Indian and ancient Greek civilizations had disappeared when new peoples from the grasslands of Eurasia settled in both areas between 1500 and 1000 B.C.E. Called by later generations the Aryans in India and the Dorians in Greece, these pastoral peoples came with horses, different customs, and new technologies. The Aryans came with chariots (as had the early Mycenaeans), while the Dorians, somewhat later, brought iron tools and weapons.

Despite the similar origins of the newcomers and the similar urban experience of the lands in which they settled, Aryan India and Dorian Greece developed in significantly different ways. As William H. McNeill writes in the first selection, by the year 500 B.C.E. Indian and Greek civilizations had found entirely different ways of organizing and administering their societies. And these differences had profound effects on the subsequent history of Indian and European society.

THINKING HISTORICALLY

Interpreting Primary Sources in Light of a Secondary Source

In Chapter 3, we distinguished between primary and secondary sources. Similarly, we begin here with a secondary source, or an interpretation. We then turn, as we did in the last chapter, to a series of primary sources.

But while our focus in the last chapter was mainly to recognize and distinguish primary from secondary sources, here we are concerned more explicitly with the relationship of the primary sources to the secondary interpretation — how one affects our reading of the other.

In this chapter, the primary sources were chosen to illustrate points made in the introductory interpretation. This provides an opportunity to understand the interpretation in some detail and with some degree of subtlety. The primary sources do not give you enough material to argue that McNeill is right or wrong, but you will be able to flesh out some of the meaning of his interpretation. You might also reflect more generally on the relationship of sources and interpretations. You will be asked how particular sources support or even contradict the interpretation. You will consider the relevance of sources for other interpretations, and you will imagine what sort of sources you might seek for evidence.

13

WILLIAM H. McNEILL

Greek and Indian Civilization

William H. McNeill is one of the leading world historians in the United States. In this selection from his college textbook, *A World History,* he compares the different ways in which Indian and Greek civilizations of the classical age (by around 500 B.C.E.) organized themselves. He distinguishes between Indian *caste* and Greek *territorial sovereignty.* These concepts are complex but useful to distinguish between two of the basic ways societies organize and identify themselves. As you read, try to define what each term means. McNeill argues that caste and territorial sovereignty had enormously different effects on the subsequent development of Indian and European society. What were some of these different effects?

Thinking Historically

As you read this secondary source or historical interpretation, consider what sort of primary sources might have led McNeill to this

---

William H. McNeill, *A World History,* 2nd ed. (New York: Oxford University Press, 1971), 78–83, 88, 90, 95, 99–100.

view or support his interpretation. Notice especially that in the first half of the selection, McNeill mentions specific ancient Indian writings: These are obvious primary sources for his interpretation. Not having read McNeill's primary sources, can you imagine what in them would lead to this interpretation?

Less of McNeill's interpretation of Greece is included in this selection and, consequently, there is no mention of primary sources. In this chapter, you will read a number of Greek primary sources, but at this point can you speculate about what types of sources would demonstrate the Greek idea of territorial sovereignty?

Keep in mind that caste and territorial sovereignty are modern terms not known or used by the ancients; therefore, you will not find them in the primary sources that follow. What words might the ancient Indians or Greeks have used to denote these concepts?

Caste

A modern caste is a group of persons who will eat with one another and intermarry, while excluding others from these two intimacies. In addition, members of any particular caste must bear some distinguishing mark, so that everyone will know who belongs and who does not belong to it. Definite rules for how to behave in the presence of members of other castes also become necessary in situations where such contacts are frequent. When an entire society comes to be organized on these principles, any group of strangers or intruders automatically becomes another caste, for the exclusive habits of the rest of the population inevitably thrust the newcomers in upon themselves when it comes to eating and marrying. A large caste may easily break into smaller groupings as a result of some dispute, or through mere geographical separation over a period of time. New castes can form around new occupations. Wanderers and displaced individuals who find a new niche in society are automatically compelled to eat together and marry one another by the caste-bound habits of their neighbors.

How or when Indian society came to be organized along these lines remains unclear. Perhaps the Indus civilization itself was built upon something like the caste principle. Or perhaps the antipathy between Aryan invaders and the dark-skinned people whom they attacked lay at the root of the caste system of later India. But whatever the origins of caste, three features of Indian thought and feeling were mobilized to sustain the caste principle in later times. One of these was the idea of ceremonial purity. Fear of contaminating oneself by contact with a member of a lower, "unclean" caste gave Brahmans and others near the top of the pyramid strong reasons for limiting their association with low-caste persons.

From the other end of the scale, too, the poor and humble had strong reasons for clinging to caste. All but the most miserable and marginal could look down upon somebody, a not unimportant psychological feature of the system. In addition, the humbler castes were often groups that had only recently emerged from primitive forest life. They naturally sought to maintain their peculiar customs and habits, even in the context of urban or mixed village life, where men of different backgrounds and different castes lived side by side. Other civilized societies usually persuaded or compelled newcomers to surrender their peculiar ways, and assimilated them in the course of a few generations to the civilized population as a whole. In India, on the contrary, such groups were able to retain their separate identities indefinitely by preserving their own peculiar customs within the caste framework, generation after generation.

The third factor sustaining the caste principle was theoretical: the doctrine of reincarnation and of "varna." The latter declared that all men were naturally divided into four castes: the Brahmans who prayed, the Kshatriyas who fought, the Vaisyas who worked, and the Sudras who performed unclean tasks. Official doctrine classified the first three castes as Aryan, the last as non-Aryan, and put much stress on caste rank, from Brahmans at the top to Sudras at the bottom. Reality never corresponded even remotely to this theory. There were hundreds if not thousands of castes in India, rather than the four recognized in Brahmanical teaching. But apparent injustices and anomalies disappeared when the doctrine of reincarnation was combined with the doctrine of varna. The idea of reincarnation, indeed, gave logical explanation and justification to the system by explaining caste as a divinely established institution, hereditary from father to son, and designed to reward and punish souls for their actions in former lives. This undoubtedly helped to stabilize the confused reality. A man of unblemished life, born into the lowest caste, could hope for rebirth higher up the ladder. Conversely, a man of high caste who failed to conform to proper standards could expect rebirth in a lower caste. A man even risked reincarnation as a worm or beetle, if his misbehavior deserved such a punishment.

Clearly, the caste system as observed today did not exist in ancient India. Yet modern castes are the outgrowth of patterns of social organization that are as old as the oldest records. Early Buddhist stories, for instance, reveal many episodes turning upon caste distinctions, and passages in the *Rig Veda* and other ancient writings imply caste-like practices and attitudes. By 500 B.C. we can at least be sure that the seeds from which the modern caste organization of society grew had already sprouted luxuriantly on Indian soil.

Caste lessened the significance of political, territorial administration. Everyone identified himself first and foremost with his caste. But a caste ordinarily lacked both definite internal administration and distinct territorial boundaries. Instead, members of a particular caste mingled with men of other castes, observing the necessary precautions to prevent contamination of one by the other. No king or ruler could command the undivided loyalty of people who felt themselves to belong to a caste rather than to a state. Indeed, to all ordinary caste members, rulers, officials, soldiers, and tax collectors were likely to seem mere troublesome outsiders, to be neglected whenever possible and obeyed only as far as necessary. The fragile character of most Indian states resulted in large part from this fact. A striking absence of information about war and government is characteristic of all early Indian history; and this, too, presumably reflects Indian peoples' characteristic emotional disengagement from the state and from politics. . . .

The Vedas and Brahmanas

Our knowledge of Aryan religion derives from the Vedas. The Vedas, used as handbooks of religious ritual, consist of songs that were recited aloud during sacrifices, together with other passages instructing the priests what to do during the ceremony. In course of time, the language of the Vedas became more or less unintelligible, even to priests. A great effort was thereupon made to preserve details of accent and pronunciation, by insisting on exact memorization of texts from master to pupil across the generations. Every jot and tittle of the inherited verses was felt to matter, since a misplaced line or mispronounced word could nullify a whole sacrifice and might even provoke divine displeasure.

Preoccupation with correctness of detail speedily shifted emphasis from the gods of the Aryan pantheon to the act of worship and invocation itself. Aryan priests may also have learned about magical powers claimed by priests of the Indus civilization. At any rate, some Brahmans began to argue that by performing rituals correctly they could actually compel the gods to grant what was asked of them. Indeed, proper sacrifice and invocation created the world of gods and men anew, and stabilized afresh the critical relation between natural and supernatural reality. In such a view, the importance and personalities of the separate gods shrank to triviality, while the power and skill of the priesthood was greatly magnified. These extravagent priestly claims were freely put forward in texts called Brahmanas. These were cast in the form of commentaries on the Vedas, purportedly explaining what the older texts really meant, but often changing meanings in the process.

The Upanishads and Mysticism

Priestly claims to exercise authority over gods and men were never widely accepted in ancient India. Chiefs and warriors might be a bit wary of priestly magic, but they were not eager to cede to the priests the primacy claimed by the Brahmanas. Humbler ranks of society also objected to priestly presumption. This is proved by the fact that a rival type of piety took hold in India and soon came to constitute the most distinctive element in the whole religious tradition of the land. Another body of oral literature, the Upanishads, constitutes our evidence of this religious development. The Upanishads are not systematic treatises nor do they agree in all details. Yet they do express a general consensus on important points.

First of all, the Upanishads conceive the end of religious life in a radically new way. Instead of seeking riches, health, and long life, a wise and holy man strives merely to escape the endless round of rebirth. Success allows his soul to dissolve into the All from whence it had come, triumphantly transcending the suffering, pain, and imperfection of existence.

In the second place, holiness and release from the cycle of rebirths were attained not by obedience to priests nor by observance of ceremonies. The truly holy man had no need of intermediaries and, for that matter, no need of gods. Instead, by a process of self-discipline, meditation, asceticism, and withdrawal from the ordinary concerns of daily life, the successful religious athlete might attain a mystic vision of Truth — a vision which left the seer purged and happy. The nature and content of the mystic vision could never be expressed in words. It revealed Truth by achieving an identity between the individual soul and the Soul of the universe. Such an experience, surpassing human understanding and ordinary language, constituted a foretaste of the ultimate bliss of self-annihilation in the All, which was the final goal of wise and holy life. . . .

While India worked its way toward the definition of a new and distinctive civilization on one flank of the ancient Middle East, on its other flank another new civilization was also emerging: the Greek. The principal stages of early Greek history closely resemble what we know or can surmise about Indian development. But the end product differed fundamentally. The Greeks put political organization into territorial states above all other bases of human association, and attempted to explain the world and man not in terms of mystic illumination but through laws of nature. Thus despite a similar start, when fierce "tamers of horses" — like those of whom Homer[1] later sang — over-

[1] Greek poet c. 800 B.C.E.; author of *The Iliad* and *The Odyssey*. [Ed.]

ran priest-led agricultural societies, the Indian and Greek styles of civilization diverged strikingly by 500 B.C. . . .

The self-governing city-states created by Greeks on the coast of Asia Minor had . . . great . . . importance in world history. For by inventing the city-state or *polis* (hence our word "politics"), the Greeks of Ionia established the prototype from which the whole Western world derived its penchant for political organization into territorially defined sovereign units, i.e. into states. The supremacy of territoriality over all other forms of human association is neither natural nor inevitable, as the Indian caste principle may remind us. . . .

Dominance of the Polis in Greek Culture

So powerful and compelling was the psychological pull of the polis that almost every aspect of Greek cultural activity was speedily caught up in and — as it were — digested by the new master institution of Greek civilization. Religion, art, literature, philosophy, took shape or acquired a new accent through their relationship with the all-engulfing object of the citizens' affection. . . .

Despite the general success of the polis ordering of things, a few individuals fretted over the logical inconsistencies of Greek religion and traditional world view. As trade developed, opportunities to learn about the wisdom of the East multiplied. Inquiring Greeks soon discovered that among the priestly experts of the Middle East there was no agreement about such fundamental questions as how the world was created or why the planets periodically checked their forward movement through the heavens and went backward for a while before resuming their former motion. It was in Ionia that men first confronted this sort of question systematically enough to bother recording their views. These, the first philosophers, sought to explain the phenomena of the world by imaginative exercise of their power of reason. Finding conflicting and unsupported stories about the gods to be unsatisfactory, they took the drastic step of omitting the gods entirely, and boldly substituted natural law instead as the ruling force of the universe. To be sure, the Ionian philosophers did not agree among themselves when they sought to describe how the laws of nature worked, and their naive efforts to explain an ever wider range of phenomena did not meet with much success.

Nevertheless, their attempts at using speculative reason to explain the nature of things marked a major turning point in human intellectual development. The Ionian concept of a universe ruled not by the whim of some divine personality but by an impersonal and unchangeable law has never since been forgotten. Throughout the subsequent history of European and Middle Eastern thought, this distinctively Greek view of the nature of things stood in persistent and fruitful tension with the older, Middle Eastern theistic explanation of the universe. Particular thinkers, reluctant to abandon either position entirely, have sought to reconcile the omnipotence of the divine will with the unchangeability of natural law by means of the most various arguments. Since, however, the two views are as logically incompatible with one another as were the myths from which the Ionian philosophers started, no formulation or reconciliation ever attained lasting and universal consent. Men always had to start over again to reshape for themselves a more satisfactory metaphysic and theology. Here, therefore, lay a growing point for all subsequent European thought which has not yet been exhausted.

Indeed, the recent successes of natural science seem to have vindicated the Ionian concept of natural law in ways and with a complexity that would have utterly amazed Thales (d. *c.* 546 B.C.) or any of his successors, who merely voiced what turned out to be amazingly lucky guesses. How did they do it? It seems plausible to suggest that the Ionians hit upon the notion of natural law by simply projecting the tight little world of the polis upon the universe. For it was a fact that the polis was regulated by law, not by the personal will or whim of a ruler. If such invisible abstractions could govern human behavior and confine it to certain roughly predictable paths of action, why could not similar laws control the natural world? To such a question, it appears, the Ionians gave an affirmative answer, and in doing so gave a distinctive cast to all subsequent Greek and European thought.

Limitations of the Polis

It would be a mistake to leave the impression that all facets of Greek life fitted smoothly and easily into the polis frame. The busy public world left scant room for the inwardness of personal experience. Striving for purification, for salvation, for holiness, which found such ample expression in the Indian cultural setting, was almost excluded. Yet the Greeks were not immune from such impulses. Through the ancient mystery religions, as well as through such an association as the "Order" founded by Pythagoras, the famous mathematician and mystic (d. *c.* 507 B.C.), they sought to meet these needs. But when such efforts took organized form, a fundamental incompatibility between the claims of the polis to the unqualified loyalty of every citizen and the pursuit of personal holiness quickly became apparent. This was illustrated by the stormy history of the Pythagorean Order. Either the organized seekers after holiness captured the polis, as happened for a while in the city of Croton in southern Italy, or the magistrates of the polis persecuted the Order, as happened in Pythagoras' old age. There seemed no workable ground of compromise in this, the earliest recorded instance of conflict between church and state in Western history.

The fundamental difference between Greek and Indian institutions as shaped by about 500 B.C. was made apparent by this episode. The loose federation of cultures allowed by the caste principle in India experienced no difficulty at all in accommodating organized seekers after holiness such as the communities of Buddhist monks. By contrast, the exclusive claim upon the citizens' time, effort, and affection which had been staked out by the Greek polis allowed no sort of corporate rival.

Enormous energies were tapped by the polis. A wider segment of the total population was engaged in cultural and political action than had been possible in any earlier civilized society, and the brilliant flowering of classical Greek civilization was the consequence. Yet the very intensity of the political tie excluded ranges of activity and sensitivity that were not compatible with a territorial organization of human groupings, and sowed seeds of civil strife between the Greek cities which soon proved disastrous. But every achievement involves a surrender of alternatives: it is merely that the Greek achievement, by its very magnitude, casts an unusually clear light upon what it also excluded.

14

From the Rig-Veda: Sacrifice as Creation

As McNeill discusses in the previous selection, the Vedas are the writings of the ancient Brahman priests in India. They cover a wide variety of religious subjects and concerns: ritual, sacrifice, hymns, healing, incantations, allegories, philosophy, and the problems of everyday life. In general, the earliest Vedas (like the Rig-Veda) are more concerned with the specifics of ritual and sacrifice, reflecting the needs and instructions of the priests during the Aryan conquest. The last of the Vedas (like the Upanishads) are in general more philosophical — less concerned with ritual and more speculative.

"Rg Veda," 10.90, in *Sources of Indian Tradition,* 2nd ed., ed. and rev. Ainslie T. Embree (New York: Columbia University Press, 1988), 18–19.

This selection is from the Rig-Veda. What happened when Purusha was sacrificed? What is the meaning of this first sacrifice? How does this story support the role of priests?

Thinking Historically

Consider how this primary source supports the division of Indian society into castes, as McNeill discusses in the previous selection. The castes are mentioned in only one paragraph. What are the four castes mentioned in that paragraph? Notice the alternate name for one of them. In addition to the names of the castes, what information does this paragraph provide concerning the functions and relative importance of each caste?

Reread the paragraph prior to the one mentioning castes and notice how the naming of the castes fits into the larger point of this story about the sacrifice of Purusha. How does this story suggest that the people who wrote the Rig-Veda thought the division of society into four castes was pretty basic? Can you deduce from this source which of the four castes was most likely the originator of the story? Does this support anything else that McNeill said in his interpretation?

Thousand-headed Purusha, thousand-eyed, thousand-footed — he, having pervaded the earth on all sides, still extends ten fingers beyond it.

Purusha alone is all this — whatever has been and whatever is going to be. Further, he is the lord of immortality and also of what grows on account of food.

Such is his greatness; greater, indeed, than this is Purusha. All creatures constitute but one-quarter of him, his three-quarters are the immortal in the heaven.

With his three-quarters did Purusha rise up; one-quarter of him again remains here. With it did he variously spread out on all sides over what eats and what eats not.

From him was Virāj born, from Virāj the evolved Purusha. He, being born, projected himself behind the earth as also before it.

When the gods performed the sacrifice with Purusha as the oblation, then the spring was its clarified butter, the summer the sacrificial fuel, and the autumn the oblation.

The sacrificial victim, namely, Purusha, born at the very beginning, they sprinkled with sacred water upon the sacrificial grass. With him as oblation, the gods performed the sacrifice, and also the Sādhyas [a class of semidivine beings] and the rishis [ancient seers].

From that wholly offered sacrificial oblation were born the verses [ṛc] and the sacred chants; from it were born the meters [*chandas*]; the sacrificial formula was born from it.

From it horses were born and also those animals who have double rows [i.e., upper and lower] of teeth; cows were born from it, from it were born goats and sheep.

When they divided Purusha, in how many different portions did they arrange him? What became of his mouth, what of his two arms? What were his two thighs and his two feet called?

His mouth became the brāhman; his two arms were made into the rajanya; his two thighs the vaishyas; from his two feet the shūdra was born.

The moon was born from the mind, from the eye the sun was born; from the mouth Indra and Agni, from the breath [*prāna*] the wind [*vāyu*] was born.

From the navel was the atmosphere created, from the head the heaven issued forth; from the two feet was born the earth and the quarters (the cardinal directions) from the ear. Thus did they fashion the worlds.

Seven were the enclosing sticks in this sacrifice, thrice seven were the fire-sticks made when the gods, performing the sacrifice, bound down Purusha, the sacrificial victim.

With this sacrificial oblation did the gods offer the sacrifice. These were the first norms [*dharma*] of sacrifice. These greatnesses reached to the sky wherein live the ancient Sādhyas and gods.

15

From the Upanishads: Karma and Reincarnation

The idea of karma (cause and effect, appropriate consequences) can be found in the earliest Upanishads. Karma meant that the fruits of any thoughts or actions would inevitably be fulfilled. Good karma

---

Brihad Aranyaka, IV:4:5–6, in *The Thirteen Principle Upanishads,* ed. and trans. R. E. Hume (Bombay: Oxford University Press, 1954), 140–41. *Chandogya,* V:10:7, in Hume, quoted in *The Hindu Tradition: Readings in Oriental Thought,* ed. Ainslee T. Embree (New York: Vintage, 1966, copyright renewed 1994), 62–63.

would be enhanced; bad karma would lead to more bad karma. The universe was a system of complete justice in which all people got what they deserved. The idea that the soul might be reborn in another body may have been an even older idea, but in the Upanishads it combined easily with the idea of karma. That a good soul was reborn in a higher life, or a bad soul in a lower, was perhaps a more material, less subtle, version of the justice of karma. The idea of reincarnation, or the transmigration of souls, united justice with caste.

What effect would these ideas have on people? In what ways would these ideas aid people in gaining a sense of power over their lives? How might these ideas be tools of control? What does "morality" mean in this tradition?

Thinking Historically

How does the idea of karma presented in this primary source support McNeill's interpretation of the importance of the caste system in India? Would the idea of reincarnation make caste organization stronger or weaker?

Reread the selection by McNeill. Does this Upanishad support McNeill's belief that the Upanishads were a radical departure from the earlier Vedas?

According as one acts, according as one conducts himself, so does he become. The doer of good becomes good. The doer of evil becomes evil. One becomes virtuous by virtuous action, bad by bad action.

But people say: "A person is made not of acts, but of desires only." In reply to this I say: As is his desire, such is his resolve; as is his resolve, such the action he performs; what action *(karma)* he performs, that he procures for himself.

On this point there is this verse: —

Where one's mind is attached — the inner self
Goes thereto with action, being attached to it alone.

Obtaining the end of his action,
Whatever he does in this world,
He comes again from that world
To this world of action.

— So the man who desires.

Now the man who does not desire. — He who is without desire, who is freed from desire, whose desire is satisfied, whose desire is the Soul — his breaths do not depart. Being very Brahman, he goes to Brahman.

Accordingly, those who are of pleasant conduct here — the prospect is, indeed, that they will enter a pleasant womb, either the womb of a Brahman, or the womb of a Kshatriya, or the womb of a Vaishya. But those who are of stinking conduct here — the prospect is, indeed, that they will enter a stinking womb, either the womb of a dog, or the womb of a swine, or the womb of an outcaste (*candāla*).

16

From the Upanishads: Brahman and Atman

In this selection *Brahman* does not refer to priests or to a god ministered by priests. Brahman is all divinity, and all is Brahman. Even the individual soul or *atman* can be one with the universal Brahman. How would ideas like these challenge the caste system?

Thinking Historically

McNeill suggests that the Upanishads expressed a religious vision in opposition to the religion of priests, sacrifice, and caste. Would this selection from the Upanishads be a better example of that interpretation than the previous selection?

Great is the Gayatri, the most sacred verse of the Vedas; but how much greater is the Infinity of Brahman! A quarter of his being is this whole vast universe: the other three quarters are his heaven of Immortality. (3.12.5)

There is a Light that shines beyond all things on earth, beyond us all, beyond the heavens, beyond the highest, the very highest heavens. This is the Light that shines in our heart. (3.13.7)

All this universe is in the truth Brahman. He is the beginning and end and life of all. As such, in silence, give unto him adoration.

Chandogya Upanishad, in *The Upanishads*, trans. Juan Mascaro (Harmondsworth: Penguin Press, 1965), 113–14.

Man in truth is made of faith. As his faith is in this life, so he becomes in the beyond: with faith and vision let him work.

There is a Spirit that is mind and life, light and truth and vast spaces. He contains all works and desires and all perfumes and all tastes. He enfolds the whole universe, and in silence is loving to all.

This is the Spirit that is in my heart, smaller than a grain of rice, or a grain of barley, or a grain of mustard-seed, or a grain of canary-seed, or the kernel of a grain of canary-seed. This is the Spirit that is in my heart, greater than the earth, greater than the sky, greater than heaven itself, greater than all these worlds.

He contains all works and desires and all perfumes and all tastes. He enfolds the whole universe and in silence is loving to all. This is the Spirit that is in my heart, this is Brahman.

To him I shall come when I go beyond this life. And to him will come he who has faith and doubts not. Thus said Sandilya, thus said Sandilya. (3.14)

17

From the Bhagavad Gita: Caste and Self

The Bhagavad Gita is the best-known work in Hindu religious literature. It is part of a larger epic called the *Mahabharata,* a story of two feuding families that may have had its origins in the Aryan invasion of 1500 B.C.E. The Bhagavad Gita is a philosophical interlude that interrupts the story just before the great battle between the two families. It poses some fundamental questions about the nature of life, death, and proper religious behavior. It begins as the leader of one of the battling armies, Arjuna, asks why he should fight his friends and relatives on the other side. The answer comes from none other than the god Krishna, who has taken the form of Arjuna's charioteer.

What is Krishna's answer? What will happen to the people Arjuna kills? What will happen to Arjuna? What would happen to Arjuna if he refused to fight the battle? What does this selection tell you about Hindu ideas of life, death, and the self?

Bhagavad Gita, trans. Barbara Stoler Miller (New York: Bantam Books, 1986), 31–34, 52, 86–87.

Thinking Historically

In some ways this work is a reconciliation of the conflict in the Upanishads between caste and *atman*. Doing the *dharma*, or duty of caste, is seen as a liberating act. Would the acceptance of this story support or challenge the caste system? Does this primary source support McNeill's interpretation of Indian society?

Lord Krishna

You grieve for those beyond grief,
and you speak words of insight;
but learned men do not grieve
for the dead or the living.

Never have I not existed,
nor you, nor these kings;
and never in the future
shall we cease to exist.

Just as the embodied self
enters childhood, youth, and old age,
so does it enter another body;
this does not confound a steadfast man.

Contacts with matter make us feel
heat and cold, pleasure and pain.
Arjuna, you must learn to endure
fleeting things — they come and go!

When these cannot torment a man,
when suffering and joy are equal
for him and he has courage,
he is fit for immortality.

Nothing of nonbeing comes to be,
nor does being cease to exist;
the boundary between these two
is seen by men who see reality.

Indestructible is the presence
that pervades all this;
no one can destroy
this unchanging reality.

Our bodies are known to end,
but the embodied self is enduring,
indestructible, and immeasurable;
therefore, Arjuna, fight the battle!

He who thinks this self a killer
and he who thinks it killed,
both fail to understand;
it does not kill, nor is it killed.

It is not born,
it does not die;
having been,
it will never not be;
unborn, enduring,
constant, and primordial,
it is not killed
when the body is killed.

Arjuna, when a man knows the self
to be indestructible, enduring, unborn,
unchanging, how does he kill
or cause anyone to kill?

As a man discards
worn-out clothes
to put on new
and different ones,
so the embodied self
discards
its worn-out bodies
to take on other new ones.

Weapons do not cut it,
fire does not burn it,
waters do not wet it,
wind does not wither it.

It cannot be cut or burned;
it cannot be wet or withered;
it is enduring, all-pervasive,
fixed, immovable, and timeless.

It is called unmanifest,
inconceivable, and immutable;
since you know that to be so,
you should not grieve!

If you think of its birth
and death as ever-recurring,
then too, Great Warrior,
you have no cause to grieve!

Death is certain for anyone born,
and birth is certain for the dead;
since the cycle is inevitable,
you have no cause to grieve!

Creatures are unmanifest in origin,
manifest in the midst of life,
and unmanifest again in the end.
Since this is so, why do you lament!

Rarely someone
sees it,
rarely another
speaks it,
rarely anyone
hears it —
even hearing it,
no one really knows it.

The self embodied in the body
of every being is indestructible;
you have no cause to grieve
for all these creatures, Arjuna!

Look to your own duty;
do not tremble before it;
nothing is better for a warrior
than a battle of sacred duty.

The doors of heaven open
for warriors who rejoice
to have a battle like this
thrust on them by chance.

If you fail to wage this war
of sacred duty,
you will abandon your own duty
and fame only to gain evil.

People will tell
of your undying shame,
and for a man of honor
shame is worse than death.

In this next passage from the Bhagavad-Gita, Krishna reveals a deeper meaning to his message to Arjuna. Not only must Arjuna act like a warrior because that is his caste, but he must also act without regard to the consequences of his action. What does Krishna seem to mean by this? How does one do "nothing at all even when he engages in action"?

Abandoning attachment to fruits
of action, always content, independent,
he does nothing at all
even when he engages in action.

He incurs no guilt if he has no hope,
restrains his thought and himself,
abandons possessions,
and performs actions with his body only.

Content with whatever comes by chance,
beyond dualities, free from envy,
impartial to failure and success,
he is not bound even when he acts.

When a man is unattached and free,
his reason deep in knowledge,
acting only in sacrifice,
his action is wholly dissolved.

When devoted men sacrifice
to other deities with faith,
they sacrifice to me, Arjuna,
however aberrant the rites.

I am the enjoyer
and the lord of all sacrifices;
they do not know me in reality,
and so they fail.

Votaries of the gods go to the gods,
ancestor-worshippers go to the ancestors,
those who propitiate ghosts go to them,
and my worshippers go to me.

The leaf or flower or fruit or water
that he offers with devotion,
I take from the man of self-restraint
in response to his devotion.

Whatever you do — what you take,
what you offer, what you give,
what penances you perform —
do as an offering to me, Arjuna!

You will be freed from the bonds of action,
from the fruit of fortune and misfortune;
armed with the discipline of renunciation,
your self liberated, you will join me.

I am impartial to all creatures,
and no one is hateful or dear to me;
but men devoted to me are in me,
and I am within them.

If he is devoted solely to me,
even a violent criminal
must be deemed a man of virtue,
for his resolve is right.

His spirit quickens to sacred duty,
and he finds eternal peace;
Arjuna, know that no one
devoted to me is lost.

If they rely on me, Arjuna,
women, commoners, men of low rank,
even men born in the womb of evil,
reach the highest way.

How easy it is then for holy priests
and devoted royal sages —
in this transient world of sorrow,
devote yourself to me!

Keep me in your mind and devotion,
sacrifice to me, bow to me,
discipline yourself toward me,
and you will reach me!

18

ARISTOTLE

From *The Athenian Constitution:* Territorial Sovereignty

The process of establishing political authority based on the territorial state was not achieved at one particular moment in history. Much of Greek history (indeed much of world history since the Greeks) witnessed the struggle of territorial authority over family, blood, and kinship ties.

The process of replacing kinship and tribal alliances with a territorial "politics of place" can, however, be seen in the constitutional reforms attributed to the Athenian noble Cleisthenes in 508 B.C.E. Cleisthenes was not a democrat; his reform of Athenian politics was probably intended to win popular support for himself in his struggle with other noble families. But the inadvertent results of his reforms were to establish the necessary basis for democracy: a territorial state in which commoners as citizens had a stake in government. A description of those reforms is contained in a document called "The Athenian Constitution," discovered in Egypt only a hundred years ago and thought to have been written by the philosopher Aristotle (384–322 B.C.E.) around 330 B.C.E.

Modern scholars doubt that Cleisthenes created the demes (local neighborhoods) that were the basis of his reforms. Some existed earlier. But by making the demes the root of political organization, he undoubtedly undercut the power of dominant families. As demes were given real authority, power shifted from relatives to residents. Also, as Cleisthenes expanded the number of citizens, the deme structure became more "deme-ocratic."

Notice how the constitutional reform combined a sense of local, residential identity with citizenship in a larger city-state by tying city, country, and coastal demes together in each new "tribe." Why were these new tribes less "tribal" than the old ones? What would be the modern equivalent of these new tribes? Was democracy possible without a shift from kinship to territorial or civic identity? Was it inevitable?

Aristotle, "The Athenian Constitution," in *Aristotle, Politics, and the Athenian Constitution,* trans. John Warrington (London: David Campbell Publishers, 1959).

Thinking Historically

Territorial sovereignty is something we take for granted. It means the law of the land. Regardless of the beliefs of our parents or ancestors, we obey the law of the territory. In the United States, we are bound to observe the law of the nation and the law of the state and municipal ordinances. We do not take our own family law with us when we move from one town or state or country to another. When we go to Japan, we are bound by Japanese law, even if we are not Japanese. In the modern world, sovereignty, ultimate authority, is tied to territory. Because this is so obvious to us in modern society, it is difficult to imagine it as something that was not always the case.

Historians have to acknowledge that things they and their societies take for granted may not have always existed; rather, they have developed throughout history. McNeill's interpretation of the essential difference between India and Greece makes such a leap. Many people have pointed out the unique Athenian invention of democracy. But McNeill recognized that the Athenians invented democracy because they had already invented something more fundamental — territorial sovereignty, politics, government, citizenship. Why is a document like "The Athenian Constitution" more likely to support than lead to McNeill's interpretation? Why would the Indian documents be more likely, ironically, to prompt McNeill's insights about Greece?

. . . The overthrow of the Peisistratid tyranny left the city split into two actions under Isagoras and Cleisthenes respectively. The former, a son of Tisander, had supported the tyrants; the latter was an Alcmaeonid. Cleisthenes, defeated in the political clubs, won over the people by offering citizen rights to the masses. Thereupon Isagoras, who had fallen behind in the race for power, once more invoked the help of his friend Cleomenes and persuaded him to exorcise the pollution; that is, to expel the Alcmaeonidae, who were believed still to be accursed. Cleisthenes accordingly withdrew from Attica with a small band of adherents, while Cleomenes proceeded to drive out seven hundred Athenian families. The Spartan next attempted to dissolve the Council and to set up Isagoras with three hundred of his supporters as the sovereign authority. The Council, however, resisted; the populace flew to arms; and Cleomenes with Isagoras and all their forces took refuge in the Acropolis, to which the people laid siege and blockaded them for two days. On the third day it was agreed that Cleomenes and his followers should withdraw. Cleisthenes and his fellow exiles were recalled.

The people were now in control, and Cleisthenes, their leader, was recognized as head of the popular party. This was not surprising; for the Alcmaeonidae were largely responsible for the overthrow of the tyrants, with whom they had been in conflict during most of their rule.

. . . The people, therefore, had every grounds for confidence in Cleisthenes. Accordingly, three years after the destruction of the tyranny, in the archonship of Isagoras, he used his influence as leader of the popular party to carry out a number of reforms. (A) He divided the population into ten tribes instead of the old four. His purpose here was to intermix the members of the tribes so that more persons might have civic rights; and hence the advice "not to notice the tribes" which was tendered to those who would examine the lists of the clans. (B) He increased the membership of the Council from 400 to 500, each tribe now contributing fifty instead of one hundred as before. His reason for not organizing the people into *twelve* tribes was to avoid the necessity of using the existing division into trittyes, which would have meant failing to regroup the population on a satisfactory basis. (C) He divided the country into thirty portions — ten urban and suburban, ten coastal, and ten inland — each containing a certain number of demes. These portions he called trittyes, and assigned three of them by lot to each tribe in such a way that each should have one portion in each of the three localities just mentioned. Furthermore, those who lived in any given deme were to be reckoned fellow demesmen. This arrangement was intended to protect new citizens from being shown up as such by the habitual use of family names. Men were to be officially described by the names of their demes; and it is thus that Athenians still speak of one another. Demes had now supplanted the old naucraries,[1] and Cleisthenes therefore appointed Demarchs whose duties were identical with those of the former Naucrari. He named some of the demes from their localities, and others from their supposed founders; for certain areas no longer corresponded to named localities. On the other hand, he allowed everyone to retain his family and clan and religious rites according to ancestral custom. He also gave the ten tribes names which the Delphic oracle had chosen out of one hundred selected national heroes.

[1] Forty-eight subdivisions of the old four tribes, each responsible for one galley of the Athenian navy. [Ed.]

19

THUCYDIDES

The Funeral Oration of Pericles

The most famous statement of Greek loyalty to the city-state is the following account of the funeral speech of the Athenian statesman Pericles in the classic *History of the Peloponnesian War* by the ancient historian Thucydides. The speech eulogized the Athenian soldiers who had died in the war against Sparta in 431 B.C.E.

Notice the high value placed on loyalty to Athens and service to the state. Here is the origin of patriotism. Pericles also insists that Athens is a democratic city-state. Notice his praise of Athenian freedom as well as public service. Could there be a conflict between personal freedom and public service? If so, how would Pericles resolve such a conflict? You might also notice that Pericles is praising Athenian citizen-soldiers who died defending not their home but the empire. Could there be a conflict between Athenian democracy and the ambitious empire?

Thinking Historically

Are the sentiments that Pericles expresses a consequence of territorial sovereignty? Could such sentiments be expressed in defense of caste? Notice how Pericles speaks of ancestors, family, and parents. Do his words suggest any potential conflict between family ties and loyalty to the state? How is Pericles able to convince his audience of the priority of the state over kinship ties? How does this primary source provide evidence for McNeill's interpretation?

Most of those who have spoken here before me have commended the lawgiver who added this oration to our other funeral customs; it seemed to them a worthy thing that such an honour should be given at their burial to the dead who have fallen on the field of battle. But I should have preferred that, when men's deeds have been brave, they should be honoured in deed only, and with such an honour as this public funeral, which you are now witnessing. Then the reputation of many would not have been imperilled on the eloquence or want of eloquence

---

The History of Thucydides, Book II, trans. Benjamin Jowett (New York: Tandy-Thomas, 1909).

of one, and their virtues believed or not as he spoke well or ill. For it is difficult to say neither too little nor too much; and even moderation is apt not to give the impression of truthfulness. The friend of the dead who knows the facts is likely to think that the words of the speaker fall short of his knowledge and of his wishes; another who is not so well informed, when he hears of anything which surpasses his own powers, will be envious and will suspect exaggeration. Mankind are tolerant of the praises of others as long as each hearer thinks that he can do as well or nearly as well himself, but, when the speaker rises above him, jealousy is aroused and he begins to be incredulous. However, since our ancestors have set the seal of their approval upon the practice, I must obey, and to the utmost of my power shall endeavour to satisfy the wishes and beliefs of all who hear me.

I will speak first of our ancestors, for it is right and seemly that now, when we are lamenting the dead, a tribute should be paid to their memory. There has never been a time when they did not inhabit this land, which by their valour they have handed down from generation to generation, and we have received from them a free state. But if they were worthy of praise, still more were our fathers, who added to their inheritance, and after many a struggle transmitted to us their sons this great empire. And we ourselves assembled here today, who are still most of us in the vigour of life, have carried the work of improvement further, and have richly endowed our city with all things, so that she is sufficient for herself both in peace and war. Of the military exploits by which our various possessions were acquired, or of the energy with which we or our fathers drove back the tide of war, Hellenic or Barbarian [non-Greek], I will not speak: for the tale would be long and is familiar to you. But before I praise the dead, I should like to point out by what principles of action we rose to power, and under what institutions and through what manner of life our empire became great. For I conceive that such thoughts are not unsuited to the occasion, and that this numerous assembly of citizens and strangers may profitably listen to them.

Our form of government does not enter into rivalry with the institutions of others. We do not copy our neighbours, but are an example to them. It is true that we are called a democracy, for the administration is in the hands of the many and not of the few. But while the law secures equal justice to all alike in their private disputes, the claim of excellence is also recognised; and when a citizen is in any way distinguished, he is preferred to the public service, not as a matter of privilege, but as the reward of merit. Neither is poverty a bar, but a man may benefit his country whatever be the obscurity of his condition. There is no exclusiveness in our public life, and in our private intercourse we are not suspicious of one another, nor angry with our neighbour if he does what he likes; we do not put on sour looks at him which, though harmless, are not pleasant. While we are thus unconstrained in our private intercourse, a spirit of reverence pervades our public acts; we are prevented from doing wrong by respect for the authorities and for the laws, having an especial regard to those which are ordained for the protection of the injured as well as to those unwritten laws which bring upon the transgressor of them the reprobation of the general sentiment.

And we have not forgotten to provide for our weary spirits many relaxations from toil; we have regular games and sacrifices throughout the year; our homes are beautiful and elegant; and the delight which we daily feel in all these things helps to banish melancholy. Because of the greatness of our city the fruits of the whole earth flow in upon us; so that we enjoy the goods of other countries as freely as of our own.

Then, again, our military training is in many respects superior to that of our adversaries. Our city is thrown open to the world, and we never expel a foreigner or prevent him from seeing or learning anything of which the secret if revealed to an enemy might profit him. We rely not upon management or trickery, but upon our own hearts and hands. And in the matter of education, whereas they from early youth are always undergoing laborious exercises which are to make them brave, we live at ease, and yet are equally ready to face the perils which they face. And here is the proof. The Lacedaemonians come into Attica not by themselves, but with their whole confederacy following; we go alone into a neighbour's country; and although our opponents are fighting for their homes and we on a foreign soil, we have seldom any difficulty in overcoming them. Our enemies have never yet felt our united strength; the care of a navy divides our attention, and on land we are obliged to send our own citizens everywhere. But they, if they meet and defeat a part of our army, are as proud as if they had routed us all, and when defeated they pretend to have been vanquished by us all.

If then we prefer to meet danger with a light heart but without laborious training, and with a courage which is gained by habit and not enforced by law, are we not greatly the gainers? Since we do not anticipate the pain, although, when the hour comes, we can be as brave as those who never allow themselves to rest; and thus too our city is equally admirable in peace and in war. For we are lovers of the beautiful, yet simple in our tastes, and we cultivate the mind without loss of manliness. Wealth we employ, not for talk and ostentation, but when there is a real use for it. To avow poverty with us is no disgrace; the true disgrace is in doing nothing to avoid it. An Athenian citizen does not neglect the state because he takes care of his own household; and even those of us who are engaged in business have a very fair idea of politics. We alone regard a man who takes no interest in public affairs, not as a harmless, but as a useless character; and if few of us are originators, we are all sound judges of policy. The great impediment to action is, in our opinion, not discussion, but the want of that knowledge which is gained by discussion preparatory to action. For we have a peculiar power of thinking before we act and of acting too, whereas other men are courageous from ignorance but hesitate upon reflection. And they are surely to be esteemed the bravest spirits who, having the clearest sense both of the pains and pleasures of life, do not on that account shrink from danger. In doing good, again, we are unlike others; we make our friends by conferring, not by receiving favours. Now he who confers a favour is the firmer friend, because he would fain by kindness keep alive the memory of an obligation; but the recipient is colder in his feelings, because he knows that in requiting another's generosity he will not be winning gratitude but only paying a debt. We alone do good to our neighbours, not upon a calculation of interest, but in the confidence of freedom and in a frank and fearless spirit.

To sum up: I say that Athens is the school of Hellas, and that the individual Athenian in his own person seems to have the power of adapting himself to the most varied forms of action with the utmost versatility and grace. This is no passing and idle word, but truth and fact; and the assertion is verified by the position to which these qualities have raised the state. For in the hour of trial Athens alone among her contemporaries is superior to the report of her. No enemy who comes against her is indignant at the reverses which he sustains at the hands of such a city; no subject complains that his masters are unworthy of him. And we shall assuredly not be without witnesses; there are mighty monuments of our power which will make us the wonder of this and of succeeding ages; we shall not need the praises of Homer or of any other panegyrist whose poetry may please for the moment, although his representation of the facts will not bear the light of day. For we have compelled every land and every sea to open a path for our valour, and have everywhere planted eternal memorials of our friendship and of our enmity. Such is the city of whose sake these men nobly fought and died; they could not bear the thought that she might be taken from them; and every one of us who survive should gladly toil on her behalf.

I have dwelt upon the greatness of Athens because I want to show you that we are contending for a higher prize than those who enjoy none of these privileges, and to establish by manifest proof the merit of these men whom I am now commemorating. Their loftiest praise has been already spoken. For in magnifying the city I have magnified them, and men like them whose virtues made her glorious. And of how few Hellenes can it be said as of them, that their deeds when weighed in the balance have been found equal to their fame! Methinks that a death such as theirs has been given the true measure of a man's worth; it may be the first revelation of his virtues, but is at any rate their final seal. For even those who come short in other ways may justly plead the valour with which they have fought for their country; they have blotted out the evil with the good, and have benefited the state more by their public services than they have injured her by their private actions. None of these men were enervated by wealth or hesitated to resign for pleasures of life, none of them put off the evil day in the hope, natural to poverty, that a man, though poor, may one day become rich. But, deeming that the punishment of their enemies was sweeter than any of these things, and that they could fall in no nobler cause, they determined at the hazard of their lives to be honourably avenged, and to leave the rest. They resigned to hope their unknown chance of happiness; but in the fact of death they resolved to rely upon themselves alone. And when the moment came they were minded to resist and suffer, rather than to fly and save their lives; they ran away from the word of dishonour, but on the battlefield their feet stood fast, and in an instant, at the height of their fortune, they passed away from the scene, not of their fear, but of their glory.

Such was the end of these men; they were worthy of Athens, and the living need not desire to have a more heroic spirit, although they may pray for a less fatal issue. The value of such a spirit is not to be expressed in words. Any one can discourse to you forever about the advantages of a brave defence, which you know already. But instead of listening to him I would have you day by day fix your eyes upon the greatness of Athens, until you become filled with the love of her; and when you are impressed by the spectacle of her glory, reflect that this empire has been acquired by men who knew their duty and had the courage to do it, who in the hour of conflict had the fear of dishonour always present to them, and who, if ever they failed in an enterprise, would not allow their virtues to be lost to their country, but freely gave their lives to her as the fairest offering which they could present at her feast. The sacrifice which they collectively made was individually repaid to them; for they received again each one of himself a praise which grows not old, and the noblest of all sepulchres — I speak not of that in which their remains are laid, but of that in which their glory survives, and is proclaimed always and on every fitting occasion both in word and deed. For the whole earth is the sepulchre of famous men; not only are they commemorated by columns and inscriptions in their own country, but in foreign lands there dwells also an unwritten memorial of them, graven not on stone but in the hearts of men. Make them your examples, and, esteeming courage to be freedom and freedom to be happiness, do not weigh too nicely the perils of war. The unfortunate who has no hope of a change for the better has less reason to throw away his life than the prosperous who, if he survives, is always liable to a change for the worse, and to whom any accidental fall makes the most serious difference. To a man of spirit, cowardice and disaster coming together are far more bitter than death striking him unperceived at a time when he is full of courage and animated by the general hope.

Wherefore I do not now commiserate the parents of the dead who stand here; I would rather comfort them. You know that your life has been passed amid manifold vicissitudes; and that they may be deemed fortunate who have gained most honour, whether an honourable death like theirs, or an honourable sorrow like yours, and whose days have been so ordered that the term of their happiness is likewise the term of their life. I know how hard it is to make you feel this, when the good fortune of others will too often remind you of the gladness which once lightened your hearts. And sorrow is felt at the want of those blessings, not which a man never knew, but which were a part of his life before they were taken from him. Some of you are of an age at which they may hope to have other children, and they ought to bear their sorrow better; not only will the children who may hereafter be born make them forget their own lost ones, but the city will be doubly a gainer. She will not be left desolate, and she will be safer. For a man's counsel cannot have equal weight or worth, when he alone has no children to risk in the general danger. To those of you who have passed their prime, I say: Congratulate yourselves that you have been happy during the greater part of your days; remember that your life of sorrow will not last long, and be comforted by the glory of those who are gone. For the love of honour alone is ever young, and not riches, as some say, but honour is the delight of men when they are old and useless.

To you who are the sons and brothers of the departed, I see that the struggle to emulate them will be an arduous one. For all men praise the dead, and, however pre-eminent your virtue may be, hardly will you be thought, I do not say to equal, but even to approach them. The living have their rivals and detractors, but when a man is out of the way, the honour and good-will which he receives is unalloyed. And, if I am to speak of womanly virtues to those of you who will henceforth be widows, let me sum them up in one short admonition: To a woman not to show more weakness than is natural to her sex is a great glory, and not to be talked about for good or for evil among men.

I have paid the required tribute, in obedience to the law, making use of such fitting words as I had. The tribute of deeds has been paid in part; for the dead have been honourably interred, and it remains only that their children should be maintained at the public charge until they are grown up; this is the solid prize with which, as with a garland, Athens crowns her sons living and dead, after a struggle like theirs. For where the rewards of virtue are greatest, there the noblest citizens are enlisted in the service of the state. And now, when you have duly lamented, everyone his own dead, you may depart.

20

PLATO

From *The Republic*

This selection is from one of the world's most famous books of philosophy. Two events dominated the early life of Plato (428–348 B.C.E.), turning him away from the public life he was expected to lead. Plato was born in the shadow of the Peloponnesian War, which ended with the defeat of Athens in his twenty-third year. The postwar governments, especially the democracy that condemned his teacher Socrates in 399 B.C.E., turned him away from the political arena to a life of contemplation.

Plato's philosophical books, called dialogues because of the way they develop ideas from discussion and debate, follow Plato's teacher Socrates around the city-state of Athens. Often they begin, like *The Republic,* with a view of Socrates and other Athenian citizens enjoying the public spaces and festivals of the city. Notice in this introduction how territorial sovereignty creates public space and public activities.

Thinking Historically

Plato was neither a democrat nor politically active. Nevertheless, his life and his philosophy exemplify a commitment to the world of what McNeill calls "territorial sovereignty."

A primary source can support a particular interpretation by espousing it, as Plato espouses the benefits of living in a territorial state or thinking about government. But a source can also provide internal evidence for an interpretation of the society from which it comes. What clues can you find in Plato's text that would indicate that his life and the lives of the people around him are shaped by the city-state?

Chapter 1

SOCRATES. I walked down to the Piraeus yesterday with Glaucon, the son of Ariston, to make my prayers to the goddess. As this was the first celebration of her festival, I wished also to see how the ceremony would be conducted. The Thracians, I thought, made as fine a show in

Plato, *The Republic of Plato,* trans. F. M. Cornford (London: Oxford University Press, 1941), 2–3, 177–79, 227–35.

the procession as our own people, though they did well enough. The prayers and the spectacle were over, and we were leaving to go back to the city, when from some way off Polemarchus, the son of Cephalus, caught sight of us starting homewards and sent his slave running to ask us to wait for him. The boy caught my garment from behind and gave me the message.

I turned around and asked where his master was.

There, he answered; coming up behind. Please wait.

Very well, said Glaucon; we will.

A minute later Polemarchus joined us, with Glaucon's brother, Adeimantus, and Niceratus, the son of Nicias, and some others who must have been at the procession.

Socrates, said Polemarchus, I do believe you are starting back to town and leaving us.

You have guessed right, I answered.

Well, he said, you see what a large party we are?

I do.

Unless you are more than a match for us, then, you must stay here.

Isn't there another alternative? said I; we might convince you that you must let us go.

How will you convince us, if we refuse to listen?

We cannot, said Glaucon.

Well, we shall refuse; make up your minds to that.

Here Adeimantus interposed: Don't you even know that in the evening there is going to be a torch-race on horseback in honour of the goddess?

On horseback! I exclaimed; that is something new. How will they do it? Are the riders going to race with torches and hand them on to one another?

Just so, said Polemarchus. Besides, there will be a festival lasting all night, which will be worth seeing. We will go out after dinner and look on. We shall find plenty of young men there and we can have a talk. So please stay, and don't disappoint us.

It looks as if we had better stay, said Glaucon.

Well, said I, if you think so, we will.

Accordingly, we went home with Polemarchus.

At the home of Polemarchus, the participants meet a number of other old friends. After the usual greetings and gossip, the discussion begins in response to Socrates' question, what is justice?

Each of the participants poses an idea of justice that Socrates challenges. Then Socrates outlines an ideal state that would be based on absolute justice. In the following selection he is asked how this ideal could ever come about.

Aside from the specifics of Socrates' argument, notice the way in which public issues, for Socrates, are passionate personal concerns.

Chapter 18

But really, Socrates, Glaucon continued, if you are allowed to go on like this, I am afraid you will forget all about the question you thrust aside some time ago; whether a society so constituted can ever come into existence, and if so, how. No doubt, if it did exist, all manner of good things would come about. I can even add some that you have passed over. Men who acknowledged one another as fathers, sons, or brothers and always used those names among themselves would never desert one another; so they would fight with unequalled bravery. And if their womenfolk went out with them to war, either in the ranks or drawn up in the rear to intimidate the enemy and act as a reserve in case of need, I am sure all this would make them invincible. At home, too, I can see many advantages you have not mentioned. But, since I admit that our commonwealth would have all these merits and any number more, if once it came into existence, you need not describe it in further detail. All we have now to do is to convince ourselves that it can be brought into being and how.

This is a very sudden onslaught, said I; you have no mercy on my shilly-shallying. Perhaps you do not realize that, after I have barely escaped the first two waves, the third, which you are now bringing down upon me, is the most formidable of all. When you have seen what it is like and heard my reply, you will be ready to excuse the very natural fears which made me shrink from putting forward such a paradox for discussion.

The more you talk like that, he said, the less we shall be willing to let you off from telling us how this constitution can come into existence; so you had better waste no more time.

Well, said I, let me begin by reminding you that what brought us to this point was our inquiry into the nature of justice and injustice.

True; but what of that?

Merely this: suppose we do find out what justice is, are we going to demand that a man who is just shall have a character which exactly corresponds in every respect to the ideal of justice? Or shall we be satisfied if he comes as near to the ideal as possible and has in him a larger measure of that quality than the rest of the world?

That will satisfy me.

If so, when we set out to discover the essential nature of justice and injustice and what a perfectly just and a perfectly unjust man would be like, supposing them to exist, our purpose was to use them as ideal patterns: we were to observe the degree of happiness or unhappiness that each exhibited, and to draw the necessary inference that our own destiny would be like that of the one we most resembled. We did not set out to show that these ideals could exist in fact.

That is true.

Then suppose a painter had drawn an ideally beautiful figure complete to the last touch, would you think any the worse of him, if he could not show that a person as beautiful as that could exist?

No, I should not.

Well, we have been constructing in discourse the pattern of an ideal state. Is our theory any the worse, if we cannot prove it possible that a state so organized should be actually founded?

Surely not.

That, then, is the truth of the matter. But if, for your satisfaction, I am to do my best to show under what conditions our ideal would have the best chance of being realized, I must ask you once more to admit that the same principle applies here. Can theory ever be fully realized in practice? Is it not in the nature of things that action should come less close to truth than thought? People may not think so; but do you agree or not?

I do.

Then you must not insist upon my showing that this construction we have traced in thought could be reproduced in fact down to the last detail. You must admit that we shall have found a way to meet your demand for realization, if we can discover how a state might he constituted in the closest accordance with our description. Will not that content you? It would be enough for me.

And for me too.

Then our next attempt, it seems, must be to point out what defect in the working of existing states prevents them from being so organized, and what is the least change that would effect a transformation into this type of government — a single change if possible, or perhaps two; at any rate let us make the changes as few and insignificant as may be.

By all means.

Well, there is one change which, as I believe we can show, would bring about this revolution — not a small change, certainly, nor an easy one, but possible.

What is it?

I have now to confront what we called the third and greatest wave. But I must state my paradox, even though the wave should break in laughter over my head and drown me in ignominy. Now mark what I am going to say.

Go on.

Unless either philosophers become kings in their countries or those who are now called kings and rulers come to be sufficiently inspired with a genuine desire for wisdom; unless, that is to say, political power and philosophy meet together, while the many natures who now go their several ways in the one or the other direction are forcibly debarred from doing so, there can be no rest from troubles, my dear Glaucon, for states, nor yet, as I believe, for all mankind; nor can this commonwealth which we have imagined ever till then see the light of day and grow to its full stature. This it was that I have so long hung back from saying; I knew what a paradox it would be, because it is hard to see that there is no other way of happiness either for the state or for the individual.

Socrates, exclaimed Glaucon, after delivering yourself of such a pronouncement as that, you must expect a whole multitude of by no means contemptible assailants to fling off their coats, snatch up the handiest weapon, and make a rush at you, breathing fire and slaughter. If you cannot find arguments to beat them off and make your escape, you will learn what it means to be the target of scorn and derision.

Well, it was you who got me into this trouble.

Yes, and a good thing too. However, I will not leave you in the lurch. You shall have my friendly encouragement for what it is worth; and perhaps you may find me more complaisant than some would be in answering your questions. With such backing you must try to convince the unbelievers.

I will, now that I have such a powerful ally.

In arguing that philosophers should be kings, Plato (or Socrates) was parting ways with the democratic tradition of Athens. Like other conservative Athenians, he seems to have believed that democracy degenerated into mob rule. The root of this antidemocratic philosophy was the belief that the mass of people were horribly ignorant and only the rare philosopher had true understanding. Plato expressed this idea in one of the most famous passages in the history of philosophy: the parable of the cave.

Next, said I, here is a parable to illustrate the degrees in which our nature may be enlightened or unenlightened. Imagine the condition of men living in a sort of cavernous chamber underground, with an entrance open to the light and a long passage all down the cave. Here they have been from childhood, chained by the leg and also by the neck, so that they cannot move and can see only what is in front of them, because the chains will not let them turn their heads. At some distance higher up is the light of a fire burning behind them; and between the prisoners and the fire is a track with a parapet built along it, like the screen at a puppet-show, which hides the performers while they show their puppets over the top.

I see, said he.

Now behind this parapet imagine persons carrying along various artificial objects, including figures of men and animals in wood or stone or other materials, which project above the parapet. Naturally, some of these persons will be talking, others silent.

It is a strange picture, he said, and a strange sort of prisoners.

Like ourselves, I replied; for in the first place prisoners so confined would have seen nothing of themselves or of one another, except the shadows thrown by the firelight on the wall of the Cave facing them, would they?

Not if all their lives they had been prevented from moving their heads.

And they would have seen as little of the objects carried past.

Of course.

Now, if they could talk to one another, would they not suppose that their words referred only to those passing shadows which they saw?

Necessarily.

And suppose their prison had an echo from the wall facing them? When one of the people crossing behind them spoke, they could only suppose that the sound came from the shadow passing before their eyes.

No doubt.

In every way, then, such prisoners would recognize as reality nothing but the shadows of those artificial objects.

Inevitably.

Now consider what would happen if their release from the chains and the healing of their unwisdom should come about in this way. Suppose one of them was set free and forced suddenly to stand up, turn his head, and walk with eyes lifted to the light; all these movements would be painful, and he would be too dazzled to make out the objects whose shadows he had been used to see. What do you think he would say, if someone told him that what he had formerly seen was meaningless illusion, but now, being somewhat nearer to reality and turned towards more real objects, he was getting a truer view? Suppose further that he were shown the various objects being carried by and were made to say, in reply to questions, what each of them was. Would he not be perplexed and believe the objects now shown him to be not so real as what he formerly saw?

Yes, not nearly so real.

And if he were forced to look at the firelight itself, would not his eyes ache, so that he would try to escape and turn back to the things which he could see distinctly, convinced that they really were clearer than these other objects now being shown to him?

Yes.

And suppose someone were to drag him away forcibly up the steep and rugged ascent and not let him go until he had hauled him out into the sunlight, would he not suffer pain and vexation at such treatment, and, when he had come out into the light, find his eyes so full of its radiance that he could not see a single one of the things that he was now told were real?

Certainly he would not see them all at once.

He would need, then, to grow accustomed before he could see things in that upper world. At first it would be easiest to make out shadows, and then the images of men and things reflected in water, and later on the things themselves. After that, it would be easier to watch the heavenly bodies and the sky itself by night, looking at the light of the moon and stars rather than the Sun and the Sun's light in the daytime.

Yes, surely.

Last of all, he would be able to look at the Sun and contemplate its nature, not as it appears when reflected in water or any alien medium, but as it is in itself in its own domain.

No doubt.

And now he would begin to draw the conclusion that it is the Sun that produces the seasons and the course of the year and controls everything in the visible world, and moreover is in a way the cause of all that he and his companions used to see.

Clearly he would come at last to that conclusion.

Then if he called to mind his fellow prisoners and what passed for wisdom in his former dwelling-place, he would surely think himself happy in the change and be sorry for them. They may have had a practice of honouring and commending one another, with prizes for the man who had the keenest eye for the passing shadows and the best memory for the order in which they followed or accompanied one another, so that he could make a good guess as to which was going to come next. Would our released prisoner be likely to covet those prizes or to envy the men exalted to honour and power in the Cave? Would he not feel like Homer's Achilles, that he would far sooner "be on earth as a hired servant in the house of a landless man" or endure anything rather than go back to his old beliefs and live in the old way?

Yes, he would prefer any fate to such a life.

Now imagine what would happen if he went down again to take his former seat in the Cave. Coming suddenly out of the sunlight, his eyes would be filled with darkness. He might be required once more to deliver his opinion on those shadows, in competition with the prisoners who had never been released, while his eyesight was still dim and unsteady; and it might take some time to become used to the darkness. They would laugh at him and say that he had gone up only to come back with his sight ruined; it was worth no one's while even to attempt the ascent. If they could lay hands on the man who was trying to set them free and lead them up, they would kill him.

Yes, they would.

Every feature in this parable, my dear Glaucon, is meant to fit our earlier analysis. The prison dwelling corresponds to the region revealed to us through the sense of sight, and the firelight within it to the power of the Sun. The ascent to see the things in the upper world you may take as standing for the upward journey of the soul into the region of the intelligible; then you will be in possession of what I surmise, since that is what you wish to be told. Heaven knows whether it is true; but this, at any rate, is how it appears to me. In the world of knowledge, the last thing to be perceived and only with great difficulty is the essential Form of Goodness. Once it is perceived, the conclusion must follow that, for all things, this is the cause of whatever is right and good; in the visible world it gives birth to light and to the lord of light, while it is itself sovereign in the intelligible world and the parent of intelligence and truth. Without having had a vision of this Form no one can act with wisdom, either in his own life or in matters of state.

So far as I can understand, I share your belief.

Then you may also agree that it is no wonder if those who have reached their height are reluctant to manage the affairs of men. Their souls long to spend all their time in that upper world — naturally enough, if here once more our parable holds true. Nor, again, is it at all strange that one who comes from the contemplation of divine things to the miseries of human life should appear awkward and ridiculous when, with eyes still dazed and not yet accustomed to the darkness, he is compelled, in a law court or elsewhere, to dispute about the shadows of justice or the images that cast those shadows, and to wrangle over the notions of what is right in the minds of men who have never beheld Justice itself.

It is not at all strange.

No; a sensible man will remember that the eyes may be confused in two ways — by a change from light to darkness or from darkness to light; and he will recognize that the same thing happens to the soul. When he sees it troubled and unable to discern anything clearly, instead of laughing thoughtlessly, he will ask whether, coming from a brighter existence, its unaccustomed vision is obscured by the darkness, in which case he will think its condition enviable and its life a happy one; or whether, emerging from the depths of ignorance, it is dazzled by excess of light. If so, he will rather feel sorry for it; or, if he were inclined to laugh, that would be less ridiculous than to laugh at the soul which has come down from the light.

That is a fair statement.

If this is true, then, we must conclude that education is not what it is said to be by some, who profess to put knowledge into a soul which does not possess it, as if they could put sight into blind eyes. On the contrary, our own account signifies that the soul of every man does possess the power of learning the truth and the organ to see it with; and that, just as one might have to turn the whole body round in order that the eye should see light instead of darkness, so the entire soul must be turned away from this changing world, until its eye can bear to contemplate reality and that supreme splendour which we have called the Good. Hence there may well be an art whose aim would be to effect this very thing, the conversion of the soul, in the readiest way; not to put the power of sight into the soul's eye, which already has it, but to ensure that, instead of looking in the wrong direction, it is turned the way it ought to be.

Yes, it may well be so.

It looks, then, as though wisdom were different from those ordinary virtues, as they are called, which are not far removed from bodily qualities, in that they can be produced by habituation and exercise in a soul which has not possessed them from the first. Wisdom, it seems, is certainly the virtue of some diviner faculty, which never loses its power, though its use for good or harm depends on the direction towards which it is turned. You must have noticed in dishonest men with a reputation for sagacity the shrewd glance of a narrow intelligence piercing the objects to which it is directed. There is nothing wrong with their power of vision, but it has been forced into the service of evil, so that the keener its sight, the more harm it works.

Quite true.

And yet if the growth of a nature like this had been pruned from earliest childhood, cleared of those clinging overgrowths which come of gluttony and all luxurious pleasure and, like leaden weights charged with affinity to this mortal world, hang upon the soul, bending its vision downwards; if, freed from these, the soul were turned round towards true reality, then this same power in these very men would see the truth as keenly as the objects it is turned to now.

Yes, very likely.

Is it not also likely, or indeed certain after what has been said, that a state can never be properly governed either by the uneducated who know nothing of truth or by men who are allowed to spend all their days in the pursuit of culture? The ignorant have no single mark before their eyes at which they must aim in all the conduct of their own lives and of affairs of state; and the others will not engage in action if they can help it, dreaming that, while still alive, they have been translated to the Islands of the Blest.

Quite true.

It is for us, then, as founders of a commonwealth, to bring compulsion to bear on the noblest natures. They must be made to climb the ascent to the vision of Goodness, which we called the highest object of knowledge; and, when they have looked upon it long enough, they must not be allowed, as they now are, to remain on the heights, refusing to come down again to the prisoners or to take any part in their labours and rewards, however much or little these may be worth.

Shall we not be doing them an injustice, if we force on them a worse life than they might have?

You have forgotten again, my friend, that the law is not concerned to make any one class specially happy, but to ensure the welfare of the commonwealth as a whole. By persuasion or constraint it will unite the citizens in harmony, making them share whatever benefits each class can contribute to the common good; and its purpose in forming men of that spirit was not that each should be left to go his own way, but that they should be instrumental in binding the community into one.

True, I had forgotten.

You will see, then, Glaucon, that there will be no real injustice in compelling our philosophers to watch over and care for the other citizens. We can fairly tell them that their compeers in other states may quite reasonably refuse to collaborate: there they have sprung up, like a self-sown plant, in despite of their country's institutions; no one has fostered their growth, and they cannot be expected to show gratitude for a care they have never received. "But," we shall say, "it is not so with you. We have brought you into existence for your country's sake as well as for your own, to be like leaders and king-bees in a hive; you have been better and more thoroughly educated than those others and hence you are more capable of playing your part both as men of thought and as men of action. You must go down, then, each in his turn, to live with the rest and let your eyes grow accustomed to the darkness. You will then see a thousand times better than those who live there always; you will recognize every image for what it is and know what it represents, because you have seen justice, beauty, and goodness in their reality; and so you and we shall find life in our commonwealth no mere dream, as it is in most existing states, where men live fighting one another about shadows and quarrelling for power, as if that were a great prize; whereas in truth government can be at its best and free from dissension only where the destined rulers are least desirous of holding office."

Quite true.

Then will our pupils refuse to listen and to take their turns at sharing in the work of the community, though they may live together for most of their time in a purer air?

No; it is a fair demand, and they are fair-minded men. No doubt, unlike any ruler of the present day, they will think of holding power as an unavoidable necessity.

Yes, my friend; for the truth is that you can have a well-governed society only if you can discover for your future rulers a better way of life than being in office; then only will power be in the hands of men who are rich, not in gold, but in the wealth that brings happiness, a good and wise life. All goes wrong when, starved for lack of anything good in their own lives, men turn to public affairs hoping to snatch from thence the happiness they hunger for. They set about fighting for power, and this internecine conflict ruins them and their country. The life of true philosophy is the only one that looks down upon offices of state; and access to power must be confined to men who are not in love with it; otherwise rivals will start fighting. So whom else can you compel to undertake the guardianship of the commonwealth, if not those who, besides understanding best the principles of government, enjoy a nobler life than the politician's and look for rewards of a different kind?

There is indeed no other choice.

REFLECTIONS

While Plato opposed democracy, he did not oppose territorial sovereignty or its effects, such as personal involvement in public policy and politics. You might reread Plato and underline the sections where participation in politics is assumed to be a proper activity. This assumption was widespread in ancient Greece, but it hardly existed in India.

Compare Plato's investigation of politics with Arjuna's in the Bhagavad-Gita. Can you imagine Arjuna asking any of the questions that Plato asked? You might try to imagine a conversation between Plato and Arjuna. How accurately would they understand each other's assumptions? Would Plato's distrust of democracy elicit some sympathy from Arjuna?

We might expect democrats like Aristotle, Thucydides, and Pericles to be even more at odds with the caste-based politics of the Bhagavad-Gita. Nevertheless, there might be some points of agreement as well. Both Pericles and the author of the Bhagavad-Gita, for instance, approve of killing and dying, but they do so for very different reasons. Try to define what those reasons are. What do they tell us about the differences between their two societies?

5

Empire and Officialdom: Bureaucracy, Law, and Individuality

HISTORICAL CONTEXT

China and Rome, 300 B.C.E.–300 C.E.

Between 200 B.C.E. and 200 C.E., both China and Rome conquered expansive territories that made them the two leading empires of the world. China was unified by the Qin (Ch'in) dynasty, from which its name derives, around 221 B.C.E. Its successor, the Han dynasty (202 B.C.E.–220 C.E.) expanded China's boundaries almost to the point where they are today. Similarly, between 218 B.C.E. and 117 C.E. Rome expanded from a modest territory that included most of modern Italy to one that spanned across almost all of Europe: England and Portugal to the west, Western Asia from Turkey to Iran, and the entire region surrounding the Mediterranean Sea, including North Africa and Egypt. In this four-hundred-year period each of these empires controlled between one and a half and two million square miles and about sixty million people.

Governing such vast realms posed problems greater than those faced by earlier empires. To control such large areas, the Chinese and Romans adopted solutions that were in some ways similar and in other ways quite different. Chinese governance was more centralized and more bureaucratic than Roman. Chinese bureaucracy meant even-handed, professional administration as well as red tape. Roman rule relied more on law, the army, and private regional administrators who sometimes were more intent on personal gain than justice.

Empires are steamrollers; they crush idiosyncrasy. In governing extensive territories and millions of people, bureaucratic and legal considerations often outweigh individual needs. Empires need standard measures, uniform decisions, predictable outcomes, and individual compliance. At the same time, large numbers of people can prosper under a government that keeps the peace or makes decisions that are responsible, reliable, and fair. Some individuals have lives or fortunes enhanced by the forces an empire can command — for example, a merchant who can transport goods unmolested over thousands of miles, a provincial governor who rules with the backing of an emperor-god.

In this chapter, we examine some of the ways in which these first huge administrative empires in world history affected the lives of certain individuals. For both China and Rome, an emperor and an official are given attention. This enables us to see the governance of an empire at two important levels. We can gauge the effectiveness of emperors and their ability to communicate to implement policy through officialdom. We can also compare the differing effects of Chinese and Roman administration. While our study of individuals is necessarily limited to the influential few who have left their mark — rulers and writers — in reading their biographies, we glimpse the lives they ruled.

THINKING HISTORICALLY

Using Biography in History

This chapter includes excerpts from biographies and autobiographies. To acquire a deep and nuanced understanding of the life of a particular individual, it is important to study self-written works or biographies by contemporaries or by modern historians. In all these sources, of course, there are bound to be distortions, exaggerations, and lapses, especially in autobiographies. Even if one is truthful, who can resist the temptation to accentuate the positive? Who can remember everything he or she has done, said, or heard?

Although it is important to pay attention to the merits or vices of the individuals studied in this chapter, our main purpose in reading the accounts of their lives is to understand what it was like to be an emperor or an official of a vast empire. We do this in order to estimate the room for individual action or decision making in such huge administrative machines. Were they mere cogs in the wheel or ineffective figureheads? Or were they powerful players and authoritarian rulers?

Our efforts, however, still suggest a series of questions of historical method that you should keep in mind as you read the following accounts. What is the relationships between biography and history, between one life and all people? How representative is any single life? How reliable is the telling? How reliable is the teller?

Do not neglect the skills you have learned in previous chapters. You might choose to begin this chapter by distinguishing primary from secondary sources. Observe how your reading of secondary sources affects your reading of primary source material and vice versa.

21

PATRICIA BUCKLEY EBREY

The Creation of the Bureaucratic Empire

As the title suggests, this selection from *The Cambridge Illustrated History of China* explains the origins of bureaucracy in the unification of China by the First Emperor. Was bureaucracy (in the sense of routine, formal procedures carried out by government officials) the inevitable result of unification, or did the First Emperor choose to create it? How did the First Emperor's subjects respond to centralization of power? Did the Han dynasty emperors change or continue the First Emperor's policies? What groups in China opposed centralization and bureaucracy, and why? Who benefited?

Thinking Historically

Notice how Ebrey, the modern historian, tells the story of the First Emperor's life and influence. You might call paragraphs 4 through 9 a mini-biography. Why, in this case, are history and biography almost the same, and what does that say about the power of an individual?

Ebrey follows King Zheng's lead and calls him the "First Emperor." Does that title make his acts seem less his own and more those of his office (in other words, less a part of his personal biography)?

Notice also how Ebrey tells the story of the First Emperor's deeds. She refers at different points to "King Zheng," the "First Emperor" and "the government." Does this suggest a slight difference in meaning?

Historians have the choice of writing in an active voice ("He *did* such and such") or a passive voice ("Such and such *was done*.") Notice how Ebrey uses both methods while writing about King Zheng. Is one method more personal or more biographical?

To write a convincing life story, biographers like to get into the minds of their subjects. Since the minds of others are difficult to understand and impossible to know completely, historians — like courtroom lawyers — are usually cautious when describing mental states, preferring instead simply to describe what happened. Notice the few times in which Ebrey refers to what was going on in the First Emperor's mind. What sort of evidence might she have for such descriptions?

Patricia Buckley Ebrey, *The Cambridge Illustrated History of China* (Cambridge: Cambridge University Press, 1996), 60–61, 63–65.

With Qin's victories over all of its rivals, China became a great agrarian empire. The centralized bureaucratic monarchy, the form of government that was to characterize most of the rest of Chinese history, was created by the Qin (ruled in all of China 221–206 B.C.) and entrenched during the much longer Han dynasty (202 B.C.–A.D. 220). It was in this period too that the geographic scope of China proper — the region in which Chinese were to become the dominant ethnic group — was staked out as the government extended overlordship across vast regions as far south as Vietnam. The ideology of the new state incorporated elements of Legalist, Daoist, and Confucian[1] origin, but the officials who administered the state came to be identified more and more with Confucian learning, giving them a degree of independence from the throne. Over time local elites were drawn both to Confucian learning and to government service, and the Han government came very much to depend on cooperation between local officials and the local elites.

Unification by Qin

Qin, the westernmost of the Zhou[2] states, had begun as a royal domain assigned the task of raising horses and defending against the barbarians. After the Zhou royal house fled the Wei River valley to resettle at Luoyang in 770 B.C., Qin was able to expand its territory and become the main power in the west. Not as urban or as culturally advanced as the eastern states, Qin seemed in early and mid Zhou times a rough and crude place, not that far removed from the Rong, Qiang, and Di tribes along its frontiers with which it regularly fought.

To help them strengthen their state, the Qin rulers of late Zhou times recruited advisors, strategists, and diplomats from the territories of their rivals. Lord Shang arrived in Qin in 361 B.C. and soon launched a series of Legalist measures intended to strengthen the power of the ruler. . . . By the third century B.C., the people of Qin had become exceptionally law-abiding, agricultural production had been increased, and direct taxation was bringing substantial revenues to the king's coffers. On visiting Qin in about 264 B.C., the Confucian philosopher Xunzi reported that the people stood in deep awe of their officials and the officials were serious and sincere, free from the tendency to form cliques.

[1] The three primary schools of philosophy in China (see Chap. 7). The Confucian school, in emphasizing respect for the elderly and those in authority, tended to support government, but it could be critical of governments that were not proper role models. [Ed.]

[2] The Zhou (pronounced "Joe") dynasty governed from 1050–256 B.C.E. [Ed.]

The man who was to preside over the unification of China, King Zheng, came to the throne in 247 B.C., as a boy of nine. With the aid of two key ministers, Lü Buwei and Li Si, he led Qin to one military victory after another. In the final decade, from 230 to 221 B.C., Qin conquered the states of Han, Zhao, Wei, Chu, Yan, and Qi. Finally ruling "All-Under-Heaven," King Zheng took a new title for himself, First Emperor (*Shi huangdi*). "Emperor" (*huangdi*) was a term he coined by combining two words for "august" and "lord," words that until then had been used for the legendary sage rulers of China's remote past.

Later Chinese historians did not celebrate the First Emperor as one of the greatest conquerors of all time (as one suspects Greek or Roman historians would have), but rather castigated him as a cruel, arbitrary, impetuous, suspicious, and superstitious megalomaniac. The First Emperor was determined not only to amalgamate China into a single state, but to impose uniformity on it. Maintaining local forms of currency, weights and measures, or writing scripts was made an act of treason. The old states and their noble houses were abolished; the country was divided into thirty-six commanderies, each in turn divided into counties. The government dispatched officials to administer these new units and controlled them by a mass of regulations, reporting requirements, and penalties for inadequate performance. To guard against the possibility of local leaders organizing rebellions, private possession of arms was made illegal and hundreds of thousands of prominent or wealthy families from the conquered states were ordered to move to the capital, Xianyang (near Xi'an in Shaanxi province). As a result of the First Emperor's thoroughness, China lost much of its heritage, including local traditions of all sorts.

Criticism of the government was not tolerated by the First Emperor, who wanted the government to control knowledge. Education was to be provided only by officials and solely for the purpose of training future officials. After his advisor Li Si complained that scholars used records of the past to denigrate the emperor's policies and undermine popular support, all writings other than useful manuals on topics like agriculture, medicine, or divination were ordered to be collected for burning. Recalcitrant scholars were also suppressed — tradition holds that 460 were buried alive in a common grave as a warning against defiance of the emperor's orders.

Ordinary people also suffered harsh treatment. Reporting crimes was rewarded, and the lawbreakers, once convicted, were punished severely by execution, hard labour, or mutilation (ranging from cutting off the whiskers to the nose or the left foot). Even perfectly law-abiding people were subject to onerous labour service, and both conscripted and penal labour were used for the building of palaces, roads, canals, imperial tombs, and fortifications. Several hundred thousand subjects were conscripted to build a huge new palace complex in 212 B.C. Even more were drafted to construct the Great Wall. Earlier states had built ramparts of rammed earth along their borders. Qin knocked down those that separated the old states and connected those along the northern frontier to make a vast defensive system to protect against incursions from the nomads to the north.

The First Emperor's successes were due in no small measure to his determination to manage every detail of his government himself. He set quotas for the weight of documents he would read and dispose of each day, not resting until he had finished his paperwork. He made several tours of the country to inspect his new realm and awe his subjects. At sacred places he erected stone tablets inscribed with accounts of his exploits; his empire, he declared in one, extended in all directions, so that "Wherever human life is found, all acknowledge its sovereignty."

After surviving three assassination attempts the First Emperor became obsessed with avoiding death and devoted his energies to discovering the secrets of immortality. He sent a delegation of young men and women out to sea to search for Peng Lai, a mythical land of immortality. Historical accounts of the vast sums and huge labour contingents he expended on the secret construction of his tomb have been verified by archaeological excavations. Three pits discovered about half a mile from the emperor's tomb (not itself yet excavated) contain thousands of life-size terracotta figures of armed soldiers and horses, lined up to protect the emperor.

The Han Government

The institutions Qin had fashioned to concentrate power in the hands of the monarch made the stability of the government dependent on the strength and character of the occupant of the throne. When the First Emperor died in 210 B.C., the Qin imperial structure fell apart. The legitimate heir was promptly murdered by his younger brother and uprisings soon followed. In 209 B.C. a group of conscripted peasants delayed by rain decided to become outlaws rather than face death for arriving late for their frontier service. To their surprise they soon found thousands of malcontents eager to join them. Similar revolts of people eager to escape the burden of Qin labour and military service broke out elsewhere. In 208 B.C. the Second Emperor killed his minister Li Si; in 207 B.C. he was assassinated by the new chief minister, who was in turn murdered by the successor he placed on the throne. Meanwhile, Qin generals were defecting and former nobles of the late Zhou states took to raising armies. The eventual victor was Liu Bang, known in history as Gaozu (r. 202–195 B.C.), a man of modest background who had served the Qin as a minor local functionary, in charge of a postal relay station. In 206 B.C. he took the title King of Han and in 202 B.C. defeated his main rival, the brilliant aristocratic general Xiang Yu. Gaozu made his capital at Chang'an, only a few miles from the site of the Qin capital, which had been burnt to the ground during the rebellion.

At the time Qin was overthrown, most people apparently associated centralization with tyranny and believed the Han government should parcel out domains as the early Zhou had. Gaozu thus began by rewarding his old comrades with large territories to govern as vassal states, an action he soon recognized as a mistake, since dispersed power proved a danger to the emperor. Thus the challenge for the early Han government was to develop a form of centralized power that could secure order and dynastic stability without undue harshness, one that, in more Chinese terms, combined military strength (*wu*) with the morally centered civil arts (*wen*).

The Han dynasty retained Qin's principal weapon against the old aristocracy, namely direct administration of localities by officials appointed by the court for their merit, not their birth, and subject to dismissal, transfer, and discipline. Han prefects and magistrates had broad responsibilities and powers: they judged lawsuits, collected and dispatched taxes, performed ceremonies of the state-sponsored religion, commanded troops, decided when and how to undertake public works like flood control, kept an eye on the local economy and local education, and selected subordinates from the local population. Those successful as local administrators could be promoted to serve at court as the head of a ministry or as a counsellor to the emperor.

The key figure in the strengthening of the Han governmental apparatus was Wudi (r. 141–87 B.C.), emperor for over fifty years. After coming to the throne as a vigorous young man of fifteen, Wudi set about curbing the power of princes and other lords; he confiscated the domains of over half of them on whatever pretext he could find. Moreover he decreed that domains would have to be divided among all the lord's heirs, thus guaranteeing that they would diminish in size with each passing generation. He curbed the power of great merchants as well, in the process gaining new sources of revenue through his state monopolies and commercial taxes. In foreign relations he was especially aggressive, reversing earlier conciliatory policies. . . . In the cultural realm he imposed his authority as well. He instituted imperial rituals as grand as the empire he ruled. He lured the finest writers and scholars to his court and at the same time suppressed rival cultural centres, including some princely courts. . . .

22

SIMA QIAN

The Annals of Qin

This section is taken from one of the great ancient histories of China. Sima Qian (145–86 B.C.E.), like generations of Simas before him, was Grand Historian of China. Usually, the official historians flattered the emperor, but Sima Qian had the courage to criticize his own emperor, Wudi, who had punished Sima Qian with castration for defending a general who had surrendered. In this selection he writes of the First Emperor, beginning with the period shortly after unification.

What evidence do you see of bureaucratic organization before the First Emperor? What appear to be the main reasons why the First Emperor wants to centralize authority? What kind of power is exercised by the various officials mentioned in the history? To what extent are the changes that the First Emperor decrees his own ideas? To what extent were these changes probably routine for earlier kings of Qin or kings of other Chinese states? How does the king of Qin distinguish himself from the king of Zhou, the previous dynasty?

Thinking Historically

Ancient historical writers relied on biography more than modern historians do. An important goal of history in the ancient world was to retell the stories of famous men as object lessons of proper or improper behavior. What object lesson do you think Sima Qian is trying to make? What lesson do you take from the story?

If everything that Sima Qian reports about the First Emperor were true, how would you change Ebrey's history of him in the previous selection?

. . . Chief Minister Wang Wan, Imperial Secretary Feng Jie, Superintendent of Trials Li Si, and others all said: "In days of old the territory of the Five Emperors was 1,000 *li*[1] square, and beyond this was the territory of the feudal princes and of the barbarians. Some of the feudal princes came to court and some did not, for the Son of Heaven was unable to exercise control. Now Your Majesty has raised a righteous

[1] One *li* is about a third of a mile. [Ed.]

Sima Qian, *Historial Records,* trans. Raymond Dawson (Oxford: Oxford University Press, 1994), 63–68.

army to punish the oppressors and bring peace and order to all under Heaven, so that everywhere within the seas has become our provinces and districts and the laws and ordinances have as a result become unified. This is something which has never once existed from remote antiquity onwards, and which the Five Emperors did not attain. Your servants have carefully discussed this with the scholars of broad learning and, as in antiquity there was the Heavenly August, the Earthly August, and the Supreme August, and the Supreme August was the most highly honoured, so your servants, risking death, submit a venerable title, and propose that the King should become "the Supreme August." His commands should be "edicts," his orders should be "decrees," and the Son of Heaven should refer to himself as "the mysterious one." The King said: "Omit the word 'supreme' and write 'august' and pick out the title of 'emperor' used from remote antiquity, so that the title will be 'August Emperor.' The rest shall be as you suggest." And an edict was issued saying that it should be done. King Zhuangxiang was to be posthumously honoured as "the Supreme August on High."

The following edict was issued: "We have heard that in high antiquity there were titles but no posthumous names. In middle antiquity there were titles, but when people died they were provided with posthumous names in accordance with their conduct. If this is so, then it is a case of the son passing judgement on the father and the subject passing judgement on the ruler. This is quite pointless, and We will not adopt this practice in such matters. Henceforward the law on posthumous names is abolished. We are the First August Emperor and later generations will be numbered in accordance with this system, Second Generation, Third Generation, right down to Ten Thousandth Generation,[2] and this tradition will continue without end."

To continue the succession of the Five Powers[3] the First Emperor considered that, as Zhou had got the Power of Fire and Qin was replacing the Zhou power, it should adopt what fire does not overcome, so it was precisely at this moment that the Power of Water started. The beginning of the year was changed, and the court celebrations all started at the beginning of the tenth month. In all garments, flags, and pennants, black was made predominant. And as far as number was con-

2 One of the most ironic moments in history, since Second Generation had been on the throne for only a few years when the whole edifice came tumbling down.

3 According to this theory, the Five Powers (sometimes known as Five Elements, but in the Chinese *wu de,* using the *de* which is often translated as 'virtue') were each in turn associated with a new dynasty. . . . There was much speculation concerning this doctrine, and differences of opinion as to which power should be associated with which historical period. There was also an elaborate system of correspondences between powers, colours, numbers, and so on. The colour black and number six, which are referred to in the text, were associated with the Power of Water.

cerned they took six as the basis of calculation, so that tallies and law caps were 6 inches, carriages were 6 feet wide, 6 feet equalled a "pace," and imperial carriages had six horses. The Yellow River was renamed "the Powerful Water" to inaugurate the Power of Water. Repression was intensive and matters were all decided by the law, for only through harsh treatment and the abandonment of humanness, kindness, harmony, and righteousness could he accord with the destiny of the Five Powers. And so the law was made rigorous, and for a long time no amnesty was declared.

The Chief Minister Wang Wan and others said: "The states are newly defeated and the territories of Yan, Qi, and Chu are distant, so if we do not establish kings for them there will be no means of bringing order to them. We beg to set up your sons in authority, but it is up to the Supreme One alone to favour us with his agreement." The First Emperor handed down their suggestion to the ministers, and they all thought this would be expedient. But the Superintendent of Trials Li Si advised: "Only after an extremely large number of sons and younger brothers and people of the same surname had been enfeoffed by King Wen and King Wu did they win the adherence of the distant, and then they attacked and smote each other and behaved like enemies. And when the feudal states wrought vengeance on each other more and more, the Zhou Son of Heaven was incapable of preventing them. Now all within the seas has been unified thanks to Your Majesty's divine power, and everywhere has been turned into provinces and districts. And if your sons and the successful officials are richly rewarded from the public revenues, that will be quite sufficient to secure easy control. If there is no dissension throughout the Empire, then this is the technique for securing tranquillity. To establish feudal states would not be expedient." The First Emperor said: "It is because of the existence of marquises and kings that all under Heaven has shared in suffering from unceasing hostilities. When, thanks to the ancestral temples, all under Heaven has for the first time been brought to order, if states are reintroduced, this will mean the establishment of armies, and it would surely be difficult to seek peace in those places. The advice of the Superintendent of Trials is right."

So the Empire was divided into thirty-six provinces, and a governor and army commander and an inspector were established for each. The people were renamed "the black-headed people," and there were great celebrations. The weapons from all under Heaven were gathered in and collected together at Xianyang and were melted down to make bells and stands and twelve statues of men made of metal, each 1,000 piculs in weight,[4] to be set up in the courts and palaces. All weights and mea-

[4] A huge weight, since a picul is what a man can carry.

sures were placed under a unified system, and the axle length of carriages was standardized. For writings they standardized the characters.[5]

The land to the east stretched as far as the sea and Chaoxian, to the west as far as Lintao and Qiangzhong, to the south as far as the land where the doors face north, and in the north they constructed defences along the Yellow River to form the frontier, and along the Yin Mountains as far as Liaodong. One hundred and twenty thousand powerful and wealthy households from all under Heaven were transferred to Xianyang. All the temples together with Zhangtai and Shanglin were to the south of the Wei. Every time Qin destroyed a feudal state, a replica of its palaces and mansions was produced and it was created on the slope north of Xianyang, overlooking the Wei to the south, while eastwards from Yongmen as far as the Jing and Wei there was a series of mansions, connecting walkways, and pavilions. The beautiful women, bells, and drums[6] which they had obtained from the various states were installed there to fill them.

In the twenty-seventh year the First Emperor toured Longxi and Beidi, went out via Jitou Mountain and passed Huizhong. Then he built the Xin palace south of the Wei, and subsequently it was renamed the Temple of the Apex, to represent the Apex of Heaven. From the Temple of the Apex a roadway went through to Mount Li, and the front hall of the Ganquan palace was built, and they built a walled roadway from Xianyang to connect with it. This year one degree of promotion was bestowed and express roads were constructed.

In the twenty-eighth year the First Emperor travelled eastwards through his provinces and districts and ascended Mount Zouyi. He set up a stone tablet, and after discussion with the various Confucian scholars of Lu an inscription was carved on the stone extolling the virtue of Qin. They also discussed the matter of the *feng* and *shan* sacrifices[7] and the sacrifices to mountains and rivers. So next he ascended Mount Tai, set up a stone tablet, and made the *feng* sacrifice. As he descended and there was a violent onset of wind and rain, he rested under a tree, which was consequently enfeoffed as fifth-rank grandee.[8] He made the *shan* sacrifice at Liangfu. The stone tablet that he had set up was inscribed with the following words:

[5] In this version of the reforms the text speaks of the standardization of the script rather than of bureaucratic practice. The standardization of the axle length of carriages may appear bizarre or possibly a concession to numerology, but it may have seemed prudent to have wheel-ruts a standard size, especially in [the soft soil of] loess country.

[6] Possession of harems and the means of providing musical entertainment were the prizes of conquest which symbolized the unification. This is a clear statement of the commonly expressed view that the main purpose of political power was to ensure that one enjoyed all the pleasures of life.

[7] Important sacrifices performed by emperors when they felt their authority was secure.

[8] A ranking of nobility. [Ed.]

When the August Emperor came to the throne, he created regulations and made the laws intelligent, and his subjects cherished his instructions.

In the twenty-sixth year of his rule, he for the first time unified all under Heaven, and there were none who did not submit.

In person he made tours of the black-headed people in distant places, climbed this Mount Tai, and gazed all around at the eastern limits.

His servants who were in attendance concentrated on following his footsteps, looked upon his deeds as the foundation and source of their own conduct, and reverently celebrated his achievements and virtue.

As the Way of good government circulates, all creation obtains its proper place, and everything has its laws and patterns.

His great righteousness shines forth with its blessings, to be handed down to later generations, and they are to receive it with compliance and not make changes in it.

The August Emperor is personally sage, and has brought peace to all under Heaven, and has been tireless in government.

Rising early and retiring late, he has instituted long-lasting benefits, and has brought especial glory to instructions and precepts.

His maxims and rules spread all around, and far and near everything has been properly organized, and everyone receives the benefits of his sagely ambitions.

Noble and base have been divided off and made clear, and men and women conform in accordance with propriety, and carefully fulfil their duties.

Private and public are made manifest and distinguished, and nothing is not pure and clean, for the benefit of our heirs and successors.

His influence will last to all eternity, and the decrees he bequeaths will be revered, and his grave admonitions will be inherited for ever. . . .

23

SIMA QIAN

The Builder of the Great Wall

Here the Grand Historian tells a story of Meng Tian, the official of the First Emperor who built the Great Wall, a vast defensive system along the northern frontier meant to protect China from the nomads to the north. The story offers a full cast of officials, noble heads of feudal families, and princes. How important are the various ministers, generals, officials, and scholars to the court and emperor? Did the bureaucracy protect officials from court intrigue or private vengeance? If not, why do you suppose someone like Meng Tian or his brother Meng Yi would work there?

Thinking Historically

This selection is titled "The Builder of the Great Wall," but how much of the story does the building of this massive project occupy? Compare the treatment of the subject with that in the previous two selections. Is there anything Sima Qian mentions about Meng Tian's life that you would include in a discussion of the building of the Great Wall? What other things would you like to know about him if you were writing such a history?

This story has two endings — one added by Sima Qian in the first person in the last paragraph. How does Sima Qian's last paragraph offer a different moral lesson than the prior ending?

As for Meng Tian, his forebears were men of Qi. Tian's paternal grandfather, Meng Ao, came from Qi to serve King Zhaoxiang of Qin, and attained the office of senior minister. In the first year of King Zhuangxiang of Qin, Meng Ao became general of Qin, made an assault on Hann and took Chenggao and Xingyang, and established the Sanchuan province. In the second year Meng Ao attacked Zhao and took thirty-seven cities. In the third year of the First Emperor, Meng Ao attacked Hann and took thirteen cities. In the fifth year Meng Ao attacked Wei, took twenty cities, and established Dong province. In the seventh year of the First Emperor, Meng Ao died. Ao's son was called Wu and Wu's son was called Tian. Tian at one time kept legal records

---

Sima Qian, *Historical Records,* trans. Raymond Dawson (Oxford: Oxford University Press, 1994), 55–61.

and was in charge of the relevant literature. In the twenty-third year of the First Emperor, Meng Wu became an assistant general of Qin and, together with Wang Jian, made an attack on Chu and inflicted a major defeat upon it and killed Xiang Yan. In the twenty-fourth year Meng Wu attacked Chu and took the King of Chu prisoner. Meng Tian's younger brother was Meng Yi.

In the twenty-sixth year of the First Emperor, Meng Tian was able to become a general of Qin on account of the long-term service given by his family. He attacked Qi and inflicted a major defeat upon it, and was appointed Prefect of the Capital. When Qin had unified all under Heaven, Meng Tian was consequently given command of a host of 300,000 to go north and drive out the Rong and Di barbarians and take over the territory to the south of the Yellow River.[1] He built the Great Wall, taking advantage of the lie of the land and making use of the passes. It started from Lintao and went as far as Liaodong, extending more than 10,000 *li*.[2] Crossing the Yellow River, it followed the Yang Mountains and wriggled northwards. His army was exposed to the elements in the field for more than ten years when they were stationed in Shang province, and at this time Meng Tian filled the Xiongnu with terror.

The First Emperor held the Meng family in the highest esteem. Having confidence in them and so entrusting them with responsibility, he regarded them as men of quality. He allowed Meng Yi to be on terms of close intimacy, and he reached the position of senior minister. When he went out, he took him with him in his carriage, and within the palace he was constantly in the imperial presence. Tian was given responsibility for matters outside the capital, but Yi was constantly made to take part in internal planning. They were reputed to be loyal and trustworthy, so that none even of the general or leading ministers dared to take issue with them in these matters.

Zhao Gao[3] was a distant connection of the various Zhaos. He had several brothers, and all of them were born in the hidden part of the palace. His mother had been condemned to death, and her descendants were to be of low station for generations to come. When the King of Qin[4] heard that Zhao Gao was forceful and well acquainted with the law, he promoted him and made him Director of Palace Coach-houses. Thereupon Gao privately served Prince Huhai and gave him instruction in judicial decisions. When Zhao Gao committed a major crime, the

1 Area south of the river when it takes an east-west course in what is now Inner Mongolia.

2 One *li* is about a third of a mile. [Ed.]

3 The Zhao surname was that of the royal family of the state of that name.

4 By this time he had already become First Emperor, so this usage and the next are both anachronistic.

King of Qin ordered Meng Yi to try him at law. Yi did not dare to show partiality, so he condemned Gao to death and removed him from the register of officials, but because of Gao's estimable performance in the conduct of affairs, the Emperor pardoned him and restored his office and rank.

The First Emperor intended to travel throughout the Empire and go via Jiuyuan directly to Ganquan, so he made Meng Tian open up a road from Jiuyuan straight to Ganquan, hollowing out mountains and filling in valleys for 1,800 *li.* The road had not yet been completed when the First Emperor in the winter of the thirty-seventh year went forth on his journey and travelled to Kuaiji. Going along the sea coast, he went north to Langye. When he fell ill on the way, he made Meng Yi return to offer prayers to the mountains and streams. He had not yet got back when the First Emperor passed away on reaching Shaqiu. It was kept a secret, and none of the officials knew. At this time Chief Minister Li Si, Prince Huhai, and Director of Palace Coach-houses Zhao Gao were in constant attendance. Gao had regularly obtained favours from Huhai and wanted him to be set on the throne. He was also resentful that when Meng Yi had tried him at law he had not been in favour of letting him off. Consequently he felt like doing him harm, and so he secretly plotted together with Chief Minister Li Si and Prince Huhai to establish Huhai as crown prince. When the Crown Prince had been established, messengers were sent to bestow death on Prince Fusu and Meng Tian because of their alleged crimes. Even after Fusu was dead, Meng Tian felt suspicious and requested confirmation of it. The messengers handed Meng Tian over to the law officers and replaced him.

The messengers returned and made their report, and when Huhai heard that Fusa was dead he intended to free Meng Tian. But Zhao Gao, fearing that the Meng family would again be treated with honour and be employed on affairs, felt resentful about this.

So when Meng Yi got back, Zhao Gao, making his plans on the pretext of loyalty towards Huhai, intended on this account to wipe out the Meng family. "Your servant hears that the previous Emperor had long intended to promote a man of quality and set up a crown prince," he therefore said, "but Meng Yi had remonstrated and said that this would be improper. But if he was aware that you were a man of quality and yet insisted that you should not be set up, this would be acting disloyally and deluding one's sovereign. In your servant's foolish opinion, the best thing would be to put him to death." Paying heed, Huhai had Meng Yi put in bonds at Dai. (Previously he had taken Meng Tian prisoner at Yangzhou.) When the announcement of mourning reached Xianyang and the funeral had taken place, the Crown Prince was set up as Second Generation Emperor and Zhao Gao, being admitted to terms of close intimacy, slandered the Meng family day and night, seeking out their crimes and mistakes so as to recommend their impeachment.

Ziying came forward to remonstrate, saying: "I hear that in ancient times King Qian of Zhao killed his good minister Li Mu and employed Yan Ju, and King Xi of Yan secretly employed the stratagems of Jing Ke and ignored the pact with Qin, and King Jian of Qi killed loyal ministers from ancient families which had given long-standing service and made use of the counsels of Hou Sheng. Each of these three rulers lost their states through changing ancient ways so that disaster befell them. Now the Meng family are important officials and counsellors of Qin and yet our sovereign intends to get rid of them all in a single morning, but your servant humbly considers this to be improper. Your servant hears that it is impossible for one who plans frivolously to govern a state and it is impossible for one who exercises wisdom on his own to preserve his ruler. If you put to death loyal servants and set up people who have nothing to do with integrity, then within the palace this will cause all your servants to lose confidence in each other, and in the field it will cause the purposes of your fighting men to lose their cohesion. Your servant humbly considers this to be improper."

Huhai did not take any notice, but dispatched the imperial scribe Qu Gong to ride relay and go to Dai and instruct Meng Yi as follows: "You, minister, made things difficult when our previous sovereign wanted to set up a crown prince. Now the Chief Minister considers that you are disloyal, and that your whole clan is implicated in the crime. But in the kindness of Our heart We bestow death[5] upon you, minister, which is surely extremely gracious. It is for you to give this your consideration!" . . .

Second Generation also dispatched messengers to go to Yangzhou, with the following instructions for Meng Tian: "Your errors, my lord, have become numerous, and your younger brother Yi bears a great burden of guilt, so the law has caught up with you." "From my grandfather right down to his sons and grandsons," said Meng Tian, "their achievements and trustworthiness have been built up in Qin over three generations. Now your servant has been in command of more than 300,000 soldiers, and although he personally is a prisoner, his influence is sufficient to instigate a revolt. But as one who safeguards righteousness although he is aware he is bound to die, he does not dare to disgrace the teachings of his forebears, and in this way he does not forget his former sovereign. In former times when King Cheng of Zhou was first set on the throne and had not yet left his swaddling clothes, Dan Duke of Zhou carried the King on his back to go to court, and ultimately restored order in all under Heaven. When King Cheng had an illness and was in extreme danger, Duke Dan personally cut his fingernails and sank the parings in the Yellow River. 'The King does not yet

[5] I.e., give opportunity to commit suicide, instead of being executed.

possess understanding, and it is I who handle affairs,' he said. 'If there is a crime-engendered disaster, I accept the unfortunate consequences of it.' Accordingly he made an account and stored it away in the repository of records, and he may be said to have behaved with good faith. When the time came when the King was able to govern the country, there was a malicious official who said: 'Dan Duke of Zhou has long intended to make a rebellion, and if the King is not prepared, there is bound to be a major crisis.' The King was consequently furious and Dan Duke of Zhou ran away and fled to Chu. When King Cheng looked in the repository of records, he got hold of the account of the sinking, and so he said, with tears streaming down his face: 'Who said that Dan Duke of Zhou intended to make a rebellion?' He killed the one who had said this and restored Dan Duke of Zhou. Thus the *Book of Zhou* says: 'One must put them in threes and fives.'[6] Now for generations my family has avoided duplicity, so if our affairs are finally in such straits, this is bound to be due to the methods of a wicked minister rebelliously stirring up trouble. That King Cheng made a mistake, but when he restored the situation, he ultimately flourished; but Jie killed Guan Longfeng and Zhou killed Prince Bi Gan, and they did not repent, and when they died their country was destroyed. Your servant therefore says that errors can be remedied and remonstrance can be understood. To examine into threes and fives is the method of supreme sages. All in all, your servant's words have not been for the purpose of seeking to escape from blame. He is about to die because he is making a remonstrance, and he wishes Your Majesty would think about following the Way for the sake of the myriad people." "Your servants have received an imperial decree to carry out the law on you, general," said the messengers, "and they do not dare to report your words to the Supreme One." Meng Tian sighed deeply. "For what am I being blamed by Heaven," he cried, "that I should die although I have avoided error?" After a good long while he solemnly said: "There is a crime for which I certainly ought to die. I built a wall stretching more than 10,000 *li* from Lintao as far as Liaodong, and so in the course of this I surely could not avoid cutting through the earth's arteries. This then is my crime." And so he swallowed poison and killed himself.

The Grand Historiographer says: "I have been to the northern border and returned via the direct road. On my journey I observed the ramparts of the Great Wall which Meng Tian built for Qin. He hollowed out the mountains and filled in the valleys and opened up a direct road. To be sure, he showed little concern for the efforts of the people. Qin had only just destroyed the feudal states and the hearts of

[6] I.e., one must sort people out. No such quotation is to be found in this section of the *Book of Documents*.

the people of all under Heaven had not yet been restored to order, and the wounded had not yet been healed; but Tian, although he had become a famous general, did not use this occasion to remonstrate strongly and remedy the distresses of the people, minister to the old and enable the orphans to survive, and strive to cultivate harmony among the masses. Instead he embarked on great enterprises to pander to imperial ambition, so was it not therefore reasonable that both he and his brother should suffer the death penalty? Why in that case should cutting the arteries of the earth be made a crime?"

24

NICHOLAS PURCELL

Rome: The Arts of Government

The evolution of Rome to empire was somewhat different from that of China. In China, the state of Qin formed a unified state by suppressing the independent power of local kings, princes, and nobility. In other words, the First Emperor and the emperors of the Han dynasty brought an end to feudalism.

Conversely, before Rome became an empire, it was a *republic:* a unified state, not a series of competing feudal powers. The Roman republic inherited Greek ideas of territorial sovereignty and popular government. But as Roman military power spread beyond Italy, a republican form of government became more and more untenable. Governors had to be sent to conquered provinces, soldiers had to be recruited, and taxes had to be collected from non-Romans. The authority of popular institutions of government was eclipsed first by the aristocratic senate and then by warring generals, the dictator Caesar (47–44 B.C.E.), and finally Octavian, Caesar's nephew and adopted successor, who after 27 B.C.E. declared himself Augustus (Revered) and Imperator (Emperor).

Thus, for at least one hundred years before Rome officially became an empire, it governed vast territories of conquered and allied peoples.

Nicholas Purcell, "The Arts of Government," in *The Oxford History of the Classical World: The Roman World,* ed. John Boardman, Jasper Griffin, and Oswyn Murray (Oxford: Oxford University Press, 1988), 154, 155, 156, 170–74, 175–77.

The way in which it ruled these subjects after Augustus had been honed by generations of provincial governors and did not change significantly.

Purcell, a modern historian, argues that Roman procedures for administering the empire were developed piecemeal to fit the circumstances. Instead of a trained professional bureaucracy, the Romans relied on law and the military to keep order and peace. The power of the central government, and of the emperor, was as great as that of the Chinese emperor, but Roman officials were more like independent contractors than civil servants.

What is the evidence for Roman administration being less bureaucratic than that of China? Was the Roman Empire less centralized than China or merely less bureaucratic? What, according to Purcell, held the Roman Empire together in the absence of an efficient and far-reaching bureaucracy?

Thinking Historically

This is an institutional history, a history of Roman government. As such, the personal stories of individual administrators offer relevant information, but there is no need to tell their life stories. Indeed, unlike emperors, there are simply too many officials to attempt to recount the details of their lives.

Notice how few proper names are included in these pages. Would you like more information on particular administrators? If Rome were less bureaucratic, would we need to know more, or fewer, individual stories? And what does that say about the power of one person in such a government?

. . . "And it came to pass in those days, that there went out a decree from Caesar Augustus, that all the world should be enrolled to be taxed" (Luke 2:1). The evangelist wants to emphasize the centrality in world history of the coming of the Messiah, and accordingly links the birth of Christ to the moment when the power of Rome seemed at its most universal. For him, as often for us, the power of Rome is most potently expressed by reference to its administrative activity. St. Luke, however, was wrong. We know now that no such decree commanded a universal registration of the Roman world, at this time or any other; he exaggerated Roman omnipotence on the basis of the experience of a single province. It remains extremely easy for us too to misunderstand the scope, practice, and effects of Rome's governmental procedures. We mistake patterns of decision-making for policies and take hierarchical sequences of posts for career-structures. When we find the taking of minutes or the accumulation of archives, we immediately see a bureaucracy. Virtuosity in the public service is confused with professionalism. Recent work has been able to show well how far Rome's administration failed, or could be corrupted or subverted, or simply had no effect but oppression on thousands of provincials. There have been fewer examinations of the way in which the arts of government at which the Romans thought themselves that they excelled actually worked — imposing civilization and peace, leniency to the defeated, and war to the last with the proud (Virgil, *Aeneid* 6. 852–3). . . .

Roman theories of government were not elaborate; the practice too was simple. Two broad categories cover almost all the activities of Roman rule: settling disputes between communities or individuals, and assembling men, goods, or money — jurisdiction and exaction. Antiquity recognized three main types of authority: magistrate, soldier, and master of a household; and all governmental activity in the Roman Empire can be linked with one of these. The first, deriving from the Greek city, covers both the immemorial officers of the city-state which Rome had been and the magistrates of the hundreds of essentially self-governing cities which made up nearly all the Roman Empire. In a *polis* magistrates ran the military; at Rome the usual citizen militia became under the Empire a permanent, institutionally separate army, whose officers played an ever greater part in government culminating in the militarization of the third century. Finally, in a slave-owning society the type of authority exercised within the household was naturally recognizably different, and also came to be of considerable importance in government. . . . [I]t was always through activities which we would hesitate to call governmental that Roman rule was most effectively maintained: through the involvement of the upper classes in public religion, spectacles, impressive patronage of architecture, philosophy, literature, painting; and in civil benefactions all over the Empire. The civilizing and beneficial effects of this should be remembered as we move on to find the actual administrative and executive structure of the Empire erratic and illiberal.

Rome had from the earliest times enjoyed very close contacts with the Greek world, and had, like most ancient cities, a tripartite political structure of magistrates, council (the Senate), and popular assembly. The importance of the last for our purpose is that its early power produced the uniquely Roman and constitutionally vital concept of *imperium*. The Roman people conferred upon its chosen magistrates the right to command it and the sanctions against disobedience — ever more strictly circumscribed — of corporal and capital punishment of its members. . . .

This is why Rome long retained the habit of dealing with her subjects with the respect deserved by the free, and why Roman rule so long remained indirect. To the end of antiquity most of the cities of the Empire and their territories were ruled by local magistrates many of whose domestic executive actions were taken as if they were independent; indeed they often needed to be reminded that there were limits to the licence they were allowed. Similarly Rome also long tolerated local kings and dynasts, and the survival of these dependent kingdoms and free cities contributed much to the fuzzy informality of the power structure of the Empire before the age of the Antonines.[1] . . .

The search for bureaucracy in the Roman world is vain. We should now look a little more closely at the concern with jurisdiction and exaction which Roman administrators really did have. Then, in conclusion, we can consider in general terms the nature of the governmental process and attempt to discover what really held the empire together.

Because Roman officials spent so much time in jurisdiction it was natural that Roman law should become more complicated and more sophisticated. The natural rule that jurisdiction gravitates to the highest available authority operated to increase the workload of governors, the great prefects at Rome, and the Emperor himself, and to hasten the adoption of Roman law. Even in the reign of Augustus,[2] Strabo[3] can already write that Crete, despite its own venerable legal tradition, had come, like all the provinces, to use the laws of Rome (10.4.22). And the bitterest realism about conditions in the Roman Empire cannot overlook the advantages of the existence of a legal framework to imperial rule, which the Hellenistic kingdoms had lacked, and which offered the Empire's subjects at least the theoretical possibility of redress and restrained the arbitrariness of Rome's rule. Law too grew at Rome with the problems first of city and then of Empire, and legal expertise came to provide an entry to the governing class. Professional legal practice was eventually one of the activities which gave many provincials a place in government, and Roman law was one of the most tenacious legacies of imperial rule — its greatest codification was the product of the eastern Empire under Justinian. There is not space here to recount the gradual evolution of Roman law, but the long accumulation of legal interpretations and precedents in the annual edicts of the praetors,[4] which, when codified by Hadrian,[5] formed the foundation of the legal system, and the role of the Emperor as a source of law and patron of the great jurists of the late second and early third centuries need

[1] 96–192 C.E., period of Roman imperial peace and prosperity; emperors included Trajan (r. 98–117), Hadrian (r. 117–138), and Marcus Aurelius (r. 161–180). [Ed.]

[2] Founder of Roman Empire, first of Julio-Claudian line of emperors; ruled as emperor from 27 B.C.E. to 14 C.E. [Ed.]

[3] Greek geographer and historian (63 B.C.E.–21 C.E.). [Ed.]

[4] Roman officials concerned with jurisdiction (law and administration); originally military; magistrates. [Ed.]

[5] Roman emperor (r. 117–138 C.E.). [Ed.]

stressing. For our purposes, however, two connected things are important. First, at Rome there was no question of the separation of judiciary and legislature which is so important a liberal principle to modern political thinkers. The law at Rome was on the whole the creation of judges, not lawgivers. The second point follows from this: legal measures show the same variety, casualness, and lack of generality which we find in Roman administrative decisions, and indeed it is difficult to separate the two. There is no proper ancient equivalent of statute law. The result was that the law was not always sufficiently universal, and the underprivileged might well not reap its benefits. Jewish nationalist writers, for example, compare the hypocrisy of Rome to the ambiguous associations of the unclean pig: "Just as a pig lies down and sticks out its trotters as though to say 'I am clean' [because they are cloven], so the evil empire robs and oppresses while pretending to execute justice."

For the burdens of Roman rule on the Empire were heavy and hated, and much of Roman government was devoted to ensuring their efficacy. The collection of tribute, direct and indirect tax, rents, levies in kind, recruits, protection money, requisitioning, and so on in total amounted to a very heavy oppression, even if the amount of tax formally due was not by comparative standards very high. Roman officials from the highest to the most menial were involved with these matters, and finance was a serious administrative concern. Augustus' great catalogue of his achievements is called in full *Res Gestae et Impensae* ("His Deeds and Expenditure"). And this is undoubtedly the view that most provincials had of the way the Empire worked. A prophecy of Rome's fall concentrated on both the exactions of the ruling power and the — less often discussed but equally odious — drain of manpower to Italy via the slave trade: "the wealth that Rome has received from tributary Asia threefold shall Asia receive again from Rome, which will pay in full the price of its insolent pride. And for each of those who labour in the land of the Italians twenty Italians shall toil in Asia as needy slaves" (*Oracula Sibyllina* 3.350 f.). Given this hostility to the harsh realities of the Empire, and given the amateur nature of Roman government, how was stability achieved?

Communications have been described as the nervous system of the body politic. Compared with what had gone before and what followed the rule of Rome, the frequency of movement and the security of roads and harbours was most impressive (though banditry never completely disappeared even from Italy). The imperial posting system, a creation of Augustus refined over the following centuries, became so huge, authoritative, and elaborate that it represented one of the heaviest burdens on the provincials whose food, animals, and dwellings were constantly being requisitioned for passing officials, as inscriptions from a wide range of places and times bear eloquent witness. But there can be no doubt that the roads and harbours of the Empire were one of the most necessary organs of Roman rule.

The transmission, retrieval, and storage of information is a still more basic ingredient of the stability, durability, and effectiveness of government. [German sociologist] Max Weber called documents the bureaucrat's tools of production. The Roman Empire has won a reputation for bureaucratic sophistication. So what of its documents? . . .

The documents were stored in archive rooms, some of which are known archaeologically. But although papers were kept, there were no filing cabinets, card indexes, reference numbers, registration forms. Collections of documents were made by pasting them together in chronological or — by no means as often as convenience would dictate — in alphabetical order. The codex, the presentation of documents as a book, was occasionally used, but the cartulary, a choice of really important documents for frequent reference, was unknown. Papers were preserved in archives, but it was well known that in most conditions papyrus did not keep well. Why did these things not matter? Because retrieval of documents from the archive was not a particularly urgent consideration in its formation. The tax assessment notice, the letter from the commanding officer, the tax receipt, the birth registration were used only once, in the process of checking a particular tax collection, or implementing a decision. Access to the document *might* be required a second time, but probably only a tiny fraction of all documents was ever looked at twice. The consultation of a document was a serious matter: "for which reason, pious and benevolent Caesar, order that I be given a copy from your *commentarii* as your father intended" says a petitioner to Hadrian. Administrative processes were a favour, a privilege, a wonder, which is why on documents like this, where only what does credit to the purchaser of the inscription appears, what seem to us to be banal details of this kind are recorded in full. So this one actually preserves Hadrian's orders to his secretaries: "Stasimus, Dapenis, publish the decision or opinion from the recorded version (*edite ex forma*)." Authentication was a serious problem, never entirely solved, which helped prevent reliance on documentary authority. The *sardonychus* or imperial signet-ring gave its name to a Palatine department[6] . . . , but there were often rumours that it had fallen into unauthorized hands. The Emperors used codes, but only rather simple ones. One of the principal reasons for the abuse of the public post system was that there was no reliable way of ensuring that only a limited number of people possessed authentic licences to demand hospitality and service. Distribution was another problem. It is very hard for us to imagine how difficult, despite the efficiency of communications, the

[6] Department of the palace administration of the Caesars (emperors). [Ed.]

systematic exchange of documentary information was. A letter of Trajan to Pliny[7] making an important administrative point need never have been known in next door Asia, let alone Germania Inferior. This is perhaps one reason why Pliny's heirs actually published his correspondence. This difficulty no doubt helped to discourage the formation of any monolithic imperial administrative structure.

Documents, once stored, were of surprisingly little use. Governmental acts could not afford to depend on such an unreliable basis. The archives represented continuity and stability, and were not for regular use. The truth appears well from the story of the disastrous fire of A.D. 192 at Rome, when the central imperial archives of the Palatine were completely destroyed. . . . There is no hint that Roman government was disrupted; but the event was taken as a token that the authority of Rome, embodied in these documents, would weaken. The omen is not so far removed from the association of Rome's universal rule with a census registration at the beginning of the Gospel of St. Luke. . . .

25

PLUTARCH

Cicero

Plutarch (46–120 C.E.) was one of the ancient world's most famous biographers. Cicero (106–43 B.C.E.) was a Roman statesman, considered Rome's greatest orator. In this selection Plutarch relates Cicero's early career as a Roman official in Sicily from 75 B.C.E. to 70 B.C.E.

Why would a Roman like Cicero take an official position in a place like Sicily? How would he expect it to advance his career? By Plutarch's account, was Cicero a good public official? What seems to be Cicero's source of power and authority: his office, his family, or his friends?

Thinking Historically

At the beginning of his work, Plutarch notes that he aims to write biography, not history. He picks and chooses incidents from his subjects' lives that best reveal their moral outlooks and inner thoughts,

[7] Pliny was an official for the emperor Trajan (r. 98–117 C.E.). The two kept up an extensive correspondence, an example of which is included in selection 37 (see Chap. 7). [Ed.]

Plutarch, *Fall of the Roman Republic,* trans. Rex Warner (London: Penguin, 1958), 316–19.

even if in doing so he must ignore their historical significance. How does Plutarch give the reader a feeling for Cicero's inner life? Compare Plutarch's biography of Cicero with Sima Qian's biography of Meng Tian. How are their goals and styles similar and different?

. . . He was appointed quaestor[1] at a time when there was a shortage of grain: Sicily was the province allotted to him, and at first he made himself unpopular with the Sicilians by forcing them to send grain to Rome. Later, however, when they had had experience of his careful management of affairs, his justice, and his kindly nature, they honoured him more than any governor they had ever had. It happened too that a number of young men from Rome, all from well-known and distinguished families, came up for trial before the praetor[2] in charge of Sicily on charges of indiscipline or cowardice in the war. Cicero undertook their defence and did it brilliantly, securing their acquittal. Afterwards, when he was on his way to Rome and, as the result of these successes, was feeling particularly proud of himself, he had, as he informs us, an amusing experience. In Campania he happened to meet a well-known man and one whom he considered a friend of his. Imagining that he had filled the whole of Rome with the fame and glory of his achievements, he asked this man: "What are people in Rome saying about what I've done? What do they think of it?" To which the reply was: "But, Cicero, you must tell me where you've been all this time." At the moment, he tells us, he was thoroughly discouraged by this. He saw that all the news about him had been swallowed up in the city like a drop of water in the ocean with no visible effect at all on his reputation. But afterwards he thought things over and saw that this glory for which he was contending was something infinite, that there was no fixed point at which one could say "now I have arrived"; and so he introduced some moderation into his ambitious thoughts. It remains true, however, that throughout his life he was always far too fond of praise and too concerned about what people thought of him; and this very often had a disturbing effect on policies of his which were in themselves excellent.

Now that he was beginning to go in for politics more seriously he came to the conclusion that it was a disgraceful thing that, while a craftsman who uses inanimate tools and inanimate materials still knows what each of these is called, where it can be found, and what it can do, the statesman, who uses men as his instruments for public ac-

[1] A specialist financial official. [Ed.]

[2] Roman official concerned with jurisdiction (law and administration); originally military; magistrates. [Ed.]

tion, should be slack and indifferent where knowledge of his fellow-citizens is concerned. He therefore trained himself not only to memorize names, but also to know in what part of the city every important person lived, where he had his country houses, who were his friends and who his neighbours. And so, whatever road in Italy Cicero happened to be travelling on, it was easy for him to name and to point out the estates and villas of his friends. His fortune was sufficient for his expenses, but was still small, so that people were surprised and admired him when he took no fees or gifts for his services as an advocate — particularly so at the time when he took on the case for the prosecution against Verres.[3] Verres had been, as praetor, governor of Sicily and was prosecuted by the Sicilians for his numerous misdeeds. Cicero secured his conviction not by the speech he made but, in a sense, by the speech which he did not make. For the praetors in charge of the courts in Rome were doing what they could for Verres and by various methods of postponement had had the case adjourned until the last possible day on which it could be heard. It therefore seemed obvious to them that, since one day wouldn't be long enough for the speeches of the advocates, the trial could not possibly be concluded. But Cicero stood up and said that there was no need of speeches; he merely called his witnesses and examined them and then asked the jury to cast their votes. There are still on record, however, a number of witty sayings of his in connection with this trial. For instance, when an ex-slave called Caecilius, who was suspected of Jewish practices, wanted to push himself forward instead of the Sicilian witnesses and to make a speech against Verres himself Cicero said: "What has a Jew got to do with a pig?" — "verres" being the Roman word for a castrated boar. And when Verres attacked Cicero and said that he was not a robust character, Cicero replied: "Surely this is the sort of language you ought to be using to your sons at home"; Verres having a grown-up son who had the reputation of being little better than a male prostitute. Then there was the remark he made to the orator Hortensius. Hortensius had not dared to speak for Verres at the trial proper, but when it came to the assessment of the fine he was induced to appear for him and received in reward a sphinx made of ivory. In the course of his speech Cicero made some oblique reference to him, and Hortensius interjected: "I am afraid I am not an expert at solving riddles"; to which Cicero replied: "Really? In spite of having the sphinx in your house?"

When Verres was convicted Cicero assessed the fine at 750,000 denarii, and because of this was suspected of having been bribed to make the fine a low one. However, the Sicilians were certainly grateful to him and when he was aedile[4] they sent him all sorts of livestock and farm pro-

[3] A corrupt governor in Sicily in 74–71 B.C.E.; see the next selection. [Ed.]
[4] A municipal officer in Rome concerned with buildings, police, and public welfare. [Ed.]

duce from their islands. He used this generosity of theirs only in order to lower the prices of food in Rome, making no profit out of it for himself.

He had a fine country estate at Arpinum, a farm near Naples, and another near Pompeii, neither of them very large. The dowry of his wife Terentia came to 100,000 denarii, and he also received a legacy which brought him 90,000. This was enough to enable him to live in easy circumstances, though on a modest scale, with the Greek and Roman men of letters with whom he associated. He rarely, if ever, had a regular meal before sunset, not so much because he was too busy as because he suffered from a weak digestion. He was indeed very particular and even fussy about his health in general and used to have massages at regular intervals and go for a fixed number of walks. By looking after himself in this way he managed to maintain a state of health which was free from illness and strong enough to support much hard work and many calls upon his energy. The house that used to belong to his father he made over to his brother and lived himself near the Palatine hill, so that those who came to visit him in the morning should not have the trouble of a long walk. And the visitors who came to his house every day were no fewer than those who went to call on Crassus because of his wealth or on Pompey because of his power in the army, these two being the greatest and most sought-after men in Rome. Pompey, in fact, used himself to call on Cicero, and owed much of his power and reputation to Cicero's help in politics. . . .

26

CICERO

Against Verres

Cicero wrote and published his legal arguments even when he did not present them in court. This is a tiny selection from his extensive brief against Verres, a corrupt Roman governor in Sicily.

What does Cicero reveal about the life of a provincial governor in the Roman Empire? If we can accept what Cicero says about himself

---

Cicero, "Against Verres" (II, 5), from *On Government,* trans. Michael Grant (London: Penguin, 1993), 29–31, 32–34, 45–46, 82–85.

as well as his accusations against Verres, how good, and how corrupt, could a Roman governor be? What could a governor do on his own authority? What were the constraints on improper administration or corruption?

What does this account suggest about the differences in political administration and decision making in Rome and China? Could a Chinese governor do the sort of things that Cicero accuses Verres of doing? Could you imagine Meng Tian in the role of either Verres or Cicero?

Thinking Historically

A prosecuting attorney's account of the life of the accused is a kind of mini-biography — though obviously presented in the most damning way possible. Cicero adds here as contrast an account of his own political life, a mini-autobiography — all noble thoughts and actions. Can you see signs of bias in these two accounts? If you were a judge or member of a jury, you would hear the other side of the story. Without that other side, is there anything you can believe from Cicero's account? At a minimum, what sorts of things could he not get away with inventing? Can you imagine any possible defenses Verres would have to some of these charges?

If you were writing a biography of Cicero, you would want to consult "Against Verres" and other writings for information. Do you see any evidence that Plutarch read it? Based on your reading of this small section from "Against Verres," would you suggest any changes in the previous selection to Plutarch?

. . . At the height of the summer, governors of Sicily are accustomed to move around. This is because they feel that the best season for inspecting their province is the time when the grain is on the threshing-floor. For that is when the workers are all gathered together, so that the size of the slave households can be reliably estimated, and the sort of work they are doing can be most easily seen. Yet at this time of year, when all other governors travel about, this novel type of commander, Verres, instead remained stationary, and had a camp set up for him at the city of Syracuse, and indeed in its most agreeable section. Precisely at the entrance of the harbour, where the gulf turns in from the sea-coast towards the city, he pitched a series of pavilions; they were constructed of fine linen, stretched on poles. Moving out of the governor's residence — the former palace of King Hiero[1] — he established himself on

[1] Hiero II, king of Syracuse (270–215 B.C.E.).

this new site so completely that, throughout all this time, it was impossible for anyone to catch a glimpse of him in the outside world.

Moreover, the only people allowed into this new dwelling of his were people whose job it was to share, or minister to, his sensualities. Here flocked all the women with whom he had had relations (and the number of them, at Syracuse, is past belief). Here assembled, also, the people whom Verres deemed worthy to be his friends — worthy, that is to say, to share the life of revelry in which he indulged. And Verres's son, too, by now a grown man, spent his time with men and women of the same type. His own character might incline him to be different from his father. But habit and upbringing made him his father's true son, all the same. . . .

Dressed in a purple Greek cloak and a tunic down to the ankles, Verres spent all this period having a good time with his women. However, while he was thus engaged, the absence of the chief magistrate from the Forum, the lack of any legal decisions and hearings, caused no one to feel in any way offended or displeased. Where Verres was staying, on the coast, there resounded a constant din of female voices and vocalists. In the Forum, on the other hand, laws and lawsuits had ceased to exist. But nobody minded. Men did not worry at all because, with Verres away, the law and the courts were suspended. On the contrary, his absence, they felt, was sparing them violence and brutality, and the savage, unprovoked plundering of their possessions. . . .

Next came his behavior when he had become a grown man. . . . I shall . . . only refer . . . to two recent matters, which will enable you to form your own idea about the rest of what was happening.

One was an entirely notorious fact, known to all the world: so well known that, during the consulships of Lucius Licinius Lucullus and Marcus Aurelius Cotta, every plainest rustic, from any country town, who came to Rome on legal business was aware of it. This fact that everyone learnt was that every single decision which Verres pronounced as city praetor had been made on the prompting of the prostitute Chelidon, and according to her wishes. A second matter that everyone knew about was this. Verres had, by this time, left the city, in his military commander's cloak. He had already offered his vows relating to his period of office and the welfare of the state. And yet time after time he got himself carried back to the city in a litter after darkness had fallen, in order to commit adultery with a woman who had a husband; though she was also available to everyone else. It was a proceeding entirely opposed to morality, to the auspices, to every principle of religion and human behaviour.

Heavens above, what different attitudes men have from one another, and what different intentions! Take my own case. If it is not true that I, when assuming the offices with which the Roman people has up to now honoured me, have felt the most solemn obligation to carry out my duties with the utmost conscientiousness, then, gentlemen, I will feel obliged, voluntarily, to sacrifice all the goodwill that you and our country have been kind enough to lavish upon my plans and hopes for the future! When I was elected quaestor,[2] I felt that the post had not only been conferred on me, but was a solemn trust committed into my hands. When I was carrying out the duties of my quaestorship in Sicily, I was convinced that all men's eyes were turned upon myself, and myself alone. It seemed to me that my own person, and my office, were set upon a stage, acting before an audience which was nothing less than the whole of the world. And so I denied myself all the amenities which are permitted to the incumbents of such offices, not only for the gratification of out-of-the-way tastes but even to satisfy the most orthodox and indispensable requirements. . . .

In return for the labour and worry . . . I shall be the recipient of certain privileges. I shall have the right to speak early in the Senate. I shall be entitled to wear a purple-bordered toga, and sit in a curule chair.[3] I shall be permitted a portrait bust, as my memorial for later generations. And yet, over and above all these things, gentlemen — as I hope for the favour of all the gods in heaven — I must assure you of something else. Certainly, I am very happy that the Roman people has honoured me with this post. And yet my happiness is overtaken by a feeling of consuming anxiety. What I am anxious about is that men should not just think that I was given this office because it had to go to one or another of the candidates. What I want is that they should believe that the people came to a correct decision, and that the appointment went to the right man.

But, in contrast, Verres, consider yourself. I do not propose to talk about the circumstances of your election as praetor. But think of the moment when your election was announced, when the crier declared that you had been invested with this high office, by the votes of the entire Assembly, its senior and junior sections alike. I cannot see how, on that occasion, the very sound of the crier's voice could have failed to inspire you with a feeling that a share in the government of your country had been entrusted into your hands — so that for this one, forthcoming, year at least you would have to keep away from the houses of prostitutes! . . .

Let me now tell you, also, of Verres's novel scheme for extracting loot — which he was the first man ever to devise. The normal practice had been that all communities should make provision for their own fleet's costs, comprising food and pay and all other such expenditure. This was done by supplying their commander with the necessary sum. Let us bear in mind that he, for his part, was never likely to venture to

[2] A comparatively junior rung on the official ladder.

[3] An ivory folding seat, reserved for senior, "curule" officials.

incur the danger that he would be charged with misappropriation by people in Rome. For it was his obligation to submit accounts to his fellow-citizens. Thus his conduct of his duties at all times involved not only work but personal risk. This, I repeat, was the invariable practice, not only in Sicily but in every other of our provinces as well. Indeed, it even applied to the pay and expenses of our Italian allies, and of the Latins too, during the period when we used to employ them as auxiliary troops.

Verres, however, was the first man, ever since our imperial rule began, to have ordered that all these funds should be counted out by the provincial communities, to himself in person, and looked after by individuals who were his own nominees. Now, why you chose to introduce this innovation, changing a custom that was so longstanding and universal, must be perfectly clear to all. It must be clear enough, too, why, although it would have been so manifestly convenient to leave the handling of the money in other hands, you nevertheless preferred to do nothing of the kind; and why you were willing to take over, personally, a function which was not only tiresome and troublesome but made you the object of suspicions of the most disagreeable nature.

Other schemes for making money, too, were set on foot by Verres. In this connection you should note, gentlemen, how many opportunities of the kind the naval situation alone supplied, quite apart from anything else. For cities were only too ready to pay Verres to exempt them from the requirement of providing sailors. Enlisted men could secure discharge for a fee. Then the pay they would have been due to receive would be diverted by Verres to himself, while at the same time he would fail to hand over to all the rest the pay to which they were entitled. . . .

Concerning the torments inflicted on other Roman citizens I prefer just to offer a general, comprehensive description, rather than considering them one by one. While Verres was governor, the prison built at Syracuse by the cruel despot Dionysius I, and known as the Stone Quarries, was the place where Roman citizens had to live. If the thought or sight of any of them caused Verres displeasure, the man was immediately thrown into the Quarries. I can see, gentlemen, that this makes you all very angry.

. . . Verres, how you could have had the nerve to use that place of confinement for foreign malefactors and criminals and pirates and enemies of Rome to incarcerate Roman citizens, in substantial numbers. It is remarkable that the prospect of your future trial never occurred to you, nor the thought of a gathering such as this, at which such a mass of listeners are staring at you with censorious, hostile gaze. How strange that the greatness of the Roman people never entered your mind or presented itself to your imagination, not to speak, as I said, of this great concourse that you might have to face. That you would never again have to appear before their eyes, never re-enter the Forum of the Roman nation, never again be obliged to submit to the authority of our laws and our courts, was surely more than you could have hoped for. . . .

If it had been some monarch, or foreign people or nation, that had treated Roman citizens in this way, we should surely be taking official measures to punish those responsible, and dispatch our armies against them. For we could not possibly have endured such a disgraceful slur upon the honour of Rome without exacting vengeance and punishment. Remember all those important wars upon which our ancestors embarked, because Roman citizens were said to have been insulted, Roman ship-masters placed under arrest, Roman traders subjected to robbery. Yet I, on this occasion, am not complaining because these merchants were arrested, I am not declaring it unendurable that they were robbed. My accusation is that, after their ships and slaves and trading goods had been taken away from them, they were hurled into prison, and in that prison, although Roman citizens, they were killed.

My theme, then, is the brutal execution of that multitude of Roman citizens. And I am speaking about it in Rome itself, before this vast gathering of Romans. I am speaking to a jury composed of senators, members of the most eminent body in the state. I am speaking in the Forum of our Roman people. Yet, if my audience were Scythians instead, what I am saying would move even their barbarian hearts. For so magnificent is our empire, so greatly is the name of Rome respected among all the nations of the world, that it is not felt permissible for any man whatsoever to treat our citizens with such savagery. . . .

27

SUETONIUS

Augustus

Suetonius, born about 70 C.E. in Algeria, taught literature in Rome, practiced law, and served as secretary to the emperors Trajan (r. 98–117) and Hadrian (r. 117–138) before he died around 140 C.E. He is best known for his work *The Twelve Caesars*, which is virtually the only remaining of his approximately sixteen books.

Suetonius, *The Twelve Caesars*, trans. Robert Graves, rev. Michael Grant (London: Penguin, 1979), 55–58, 62–63, 65–66, 68–69.

"Augustus" is the second of the twelve biographies included in that collection, coming after that of Julius Caesar (100–44 B.C.E.), the great-uncle of Augustus (63 B.C.E.–14 C.E.). Although Rome had already conquered much of its empire by the time of Julius Caesar's death in 44 B.C.E., it is the period after 27 B.C.E. — when Octavian took the name Augustus — that marks the end of the Roman republic and the beginning of the Roman Empire.

In this selection, what signs do you see of Roman administration of its empire? How did Augustus change the way provinces were governed? What sort of administrative machinery was in place at the time of his death?

Thinking Historically

Suetonius's *The Twelve Caesars* was the first biography to come down to us from ancient Rome. It is unclear whether Suetonius chose biography to distinguish his work from that of his contemporary — the great Roman historian Tacitus (55–117 C.E.) — but we do know that he chose a topical biographical format different from the chronological approach popularized by Plutarch. What advantage or disadvantage do you see to this topical approach? In what other ways is Suetonius's style of biography different from those of Plutarch and Sima Qian? Whose do you prefer, and why?

. . . This information is given by others; it is not derived from Augustus' own memoirs, which merely record that he came of a rich old equestrian family, and that his father had been the first Octavius to enter the Senate. Mark Antony wrote scornfully that Augustus's great-grandfather had been only a freedman, a rope-maker from the neighbourhood of Thurii; and his grandfather, a money-changer. This is as much information as I have managed to glean about the paternal ancestors of Augustus.

I cannot believe that Gaius Octavius, his father, was also a money-changer who distributed bribes among the voters in the Campus and undertook other electioneering services. He was certainly born rich; from the start of his life a man of wealth and repute, brought up in sufficient affluence to achieve office without having to engage in such practices; and proved a capable administrator. After his praetorship, he became governor of Macedonia, and the Senate commissioned him to pass through Thurii on his way there and disperse a group of outlawed slaves who, having fought under Spartacus and Catiline, were now holding possession of the district. He governed Macedonia courageously and justly, winning a big battle in Thrace, mainly against the

Bessians; and letters survive from Cicero reproaching his brother Quintus, then proconsular govenor of Asia, for inefficiency, and advising him to make Octavius his model in all diplomatic dealings with allies.

Gaius died suddenly on his return to Rome, before he could stand as a candidate for the consulship. He left three children: Octavia the Elder, Octavia the Younger, and Augustus. The mother of Octavia the Elder was Ancharia; the other two were his children by Atia, daughter of Marcus Atius Balbus and Julius Caesar's sister Julia. Balbus's family originated in Aricia, and could boast of many ancestral busts of senators; his mother was also closely related to Pompey the Great. Balbus served first as praetor, and then with a Commission of Twenty appointed under the Julian Law to divide estates in Campania among the commons. Mark Antony likewise tried to belittle Augustus's maternal line by alleging that his great-grandfather Balbus had been born in Africa, and kept first a perfumery and then a bakehouse at Aricia. Cassius of Parma similarly sneers at Augustus as the grandson of a baker and a money-changer, writing in one of his letters: "Your mother's flour came from a miserable Arician bakery, and the coin-stained hands of a money-changer from Nerulum kneaded it."

Augustus was born just before sunrise on 23 September, while Cicero and Gaius Antonius were Consuls, at Ox Heads, in the Palatine district; a shrine to him, built soon after his death, marks the spot. . . .

In the country mansion, near Velitrae, which belonged to Augustus's grandfather, a small room, not unlike a butler's pantry, is still sown and described as Augustus's nursery; the local people firmly believe that he was also born there. Religious scruples forbid anyone to enter except for some necessary reason, and after purification. It had long been believed that casual visitors would be overcome by a sudden awful terror; and recently this was proved true when, one night, a new owner of the mansion, either from ignorance or because he wanted to test the truth of the belief, went to sleep in the room. A few hours later he was hurled out of bed by a supernatural agency and found lying half-dead against the door, bedclothes and all.

. . . He adopted the surname Caesar to comply with the will of his mother's uncle, the Dictator; and then the title Augustus after a motion to that effect had been introduced by Munatius Plancus. Some senators wished him to be called Romulus, as the second founder of the city; but Plancus had his way. He argued that "Augustus" was both a more original and a more honourable title, since sanctuaries and all places consecrated by the augurs are known as "august" — the word being either an enlarged form of *auctus,* implying the "increase" of dignity thus given such places, or a product of the phrase *avium gestus gustusve,* "the behaviour and feeding of birds," which the augurs observed. Plancus supported his point by a quotation from Ennius's *Annals:*

"When glorious Rome had founded been, by augury august."

At the age of four Augustus[1] lost his father. At twelve he delivered a funeral oration in honour of his grandmother Julia, Julius Caesar's sister. At sixteen, having now come of age, he was awarded military decorations when Caesar celebrated his African triumph, though he had been too young for overseas service. Caesar then went to fight Pompey's sons in Spain; Augustus followed with a very small escort, along roads held by the enemy, after a shipwreck, too, and in a state of semi-convalescence from a serious illness. This action delighted Caesar, who, moreover, soon formed a high estimate of Augustus's character quite apart from the energetic manner in which he had made the journey.

Having recovered possession of the Spanish provinces, Caesar planned a war against the Dacians and Parthians, and sent Augustus ahead to Apollonia, in Illyria, where he spent his time studying Greek literature. News then came that Caesar had been assassinated, after naming him his heir, and Augustus was tempted, for awhile, to put himself under the protection of the troops quartered near by. However, deciding that this would be rash and premature, he returned to Rome and there entered upon his inheritance, despite his mother's doubts and the active opposition of his step-father, Marcius Philippus the ex-Consul. Augustus now levied armies, and governed the Empire: first with Antony and Lepidus as his colleagues; next, for nearly twelve years, with Antony alone; finally by himself for another forty-four years.

After this brief outline of Augustus's life, I shall fill in its various phases; but the story will be more readable and understandable if, instead of keeping chronological order, I use subject headings. . . .

Augustus introduced many reforms into the Army, besides reviving certain obsolete practices, and exacted the strictest discipline. He grudged even his generals home-leave to visit their wives, and granted this only during the winter. When a Roman knight cut off the thumbs of his two young sons to incapacitate them for Army service, Augustus had him and his property publicly auctioned; but, realizing that a group of tax-collectors were bidding for the man, knocked him down to an imperial freedman — with instructions that he should be sent away and allowed a free existence in some country place. He gave the entire Tenth Legion an ignominious discharge because of their insolent behaviour, and when some other legions also demanded their discharge in a similarly riotous manner, he disbanded them, withholding the bounty

[1] He is generally known as Octavian until 27 B.C.E., when he was given the title Augustus.

which they would have earned had they continued loyal. If a cohort broke in battle, Augustus ordered the survivors to draw lots, then executed every tenth man, and fed the remainder on barley bread instead of the customary wheat ration. Centurions found absent from their posts were sentenced to death, like other ranks, and any lesser dereliction of duty earned them one of several degrading punishments — such as being made to stand all day long in front of general headquarters, sometimes wearing tunics without sword-belts, sometimes carrying ten-foot poles, or even sods of turf. . . .

Under the Triumvirate, many of Augustus's acts won him the hatred of the people. Once, for instance, while addressing a soldier's assembly at which a crowd of civilians were also present, he saw a Roman knight named Pinarius transcribing his speech; and had him stabbed there and then as taking too close an interest in the proceedings. Again, a spiteful comment by Tedius Afer, Consul-elect, on some act of Augustus's, provoked him to such frightful threats that Afer committed suicide by jumping from a height. There was also the case of Quintus Gallius the praetor who, while paying Augustus his respects, clutched a set of writing-tablets underneath his robe. Augustus suspected that he had a sword, but dared not have him searched on the spot, for fear of being mistaken; so presently ordered an officer's party to drag him away from the tribunal. Gallius was tortured as if he were a slave; and though he confessed to nothing, Augustus himself tore out his eyes and sentenced him to death. In his own account of the incident, however, Augustus records that Gallius asked for an audience, attacked him unexpectedly, and was removed to prison; that, being then banished from Italy, he disappeared on the way to his place of exile, but whether he was shipwrecked or ambushed by bandits, nobody knew. . . .

Twice Augustus seriously thought of restoring the Republican system: immediately after the fall of Antony, when he remembered that Antony had often accused him of being the one obstacle to such a change; and again when he could not shake off an exhausting illness. He then actually summoned the chief Officers of State, with the rest of the Senate, to his house and gave them a faithful account of the military and financial state of the Empire. On reconsideration, however, he decided that to divide the responsibilities of government among several hands would be to jeopardize not only his own life, but national security; so he did not do so. The results were almost as good as his intentions, which he expressed from time to time and even published in an edict: "May I be privileged to build firm and lasting foundations for the Government of the State. May I also achieve the reward to which I aspire: that of being known as the author of the best possible Constitution, and of carrying with me, when I die, the hope that these foundations which I have established for the State will abide secure." And, indeed, he achieved this success, having taken great trouble to prevent his political system from causing any individual distress. . . .

Augustus's will, composed on 3 April of the previous year, while Lucius Plancus and Gaius Silius were consuls, occupied two notebooks, written partly in his own hand, partly in those of his freedmen Polybius and Hilarion. The Vestal Virgins[2] to whose safe-keeping he had entrusted these documents now produced them, as well as three rolls, also sealed by him. All were opened and read in the House. It proved that he had appointed Tiberius and Livia heirs to the bulk of his estate, directing that Tiberius should take two-thirds and adopt the name "Augustus," while Livia took the remaining third and adopted the name "Augusta." The heirs in the second degree were to be Tiberius's son Drusus, entitled to one-third of the reversion; and Germanicus, with his three sons, jointly entitled to the remainder. Many of Augustus's relatives and friends figured among the heirs in the third degree. He also left a bequest of 400,000 gold pieces to the Roman commons in general; 35,000 to the two tribes with which he had family connexions; ten to every Praetorian guardsmen; five to every member of the city cohorts; three to every legionary soldier. These legacies were to be paid on the nail, because he had always kept enough cash for the purpose. There were other minor bequests, some as large as 200 gold pieces, which were not to be settled until a year after his death because:

> . . . my heirs will not receive more than 1,500,000 gold pieces; for, although my friends have bequeathed me some 14,000,000 in the last twenty years, nearly the whole of this sum, besides what came to me from my father, from my adoptive father, and from others, has been used for the benefit of the State.

He had given orders that "should anything happen" to his daughter Julia, or his grand-daughter of the same name, their bodies must be excluded from the Mausoleum. One of the three sealed rolls contained directions for his own funeral; another, a record of his reign, which he wished to have engraved on bronze and posted at the entrance to the Mausoleum; the third, a statement of how many serving troops were stationed in different parts of the Empire, what money reserves were held by the Public Treasury and the Privy Purse, and what revenues were due for collection. He also supplied the names of freedmen and slave-secretaries who could furnish details, under all these heads, on demand.

2 Normally six in number, they served the goddess Vesta in her temple beside the forum. They served for thirty years during which time they were expected to remain virgins.

REFLECTIONS

The legacies of empire in both Rome and China have been considerable. While the Roman Empire was overrun by successive waves of nomadic peoples from the fourth to the eighth centuries, the eventual Christianization of those peoples in Europe was accompanied by the introduction of the Roman language (Latin), the refurbishing of Roman roads, and the revival of Roman law and legal principles. Latin-based languages and Roman-based law are employed today not only in Europe but in regions throughout the world. You might check a world language map to discover the number of countries in which a Latin language is spoken.

The most obvious legacy of the Chinese Empire is its continuation, with only brief interruptions, down to the twentieth century. The unique longevity of the Chinese Empire can be attributed to a lasting legacy: the strikingly early development of bureaucracy. The noted historian of China, Herrlee G. Creel, put the matter succinctly in *The Origins of Statecraft in China:*[1]

> . . . Certainly it is true that "modern bureaucracy" is in some respects unique, but the government of China very early resembled governments of our own day to a degree that is little appreciated. In the first century B.C., when it was already one of the largest states that the world has known, China had a centralized administration staffed by a professional bureaucracy drawn from all strata of the society. Of the men who held the highest office, that of Imperial Chancellor, during the second and first centuries B.C., at least twenty-two percent came from poor or humble families. In comparison, it has been calculated that only eighteen percent of the men who held the highest offices in the United States between 1789 and 1953 came from lower class families. China had a general pension system for higher civil servants beginning in A.D. 1; general pension systems for the British and American civil services date from 1810 and 1920 respectively.
>
> Already in the first century B.C. the Chinese bureaucracy was selected and promoted, in considerable degree, on the basis of such objective techniques as civil service examination and merit rating. In the West the first written civil service examination was apparently given in Berlin in 1693, and the systematic practice of the annual merit rating of officials was started in Britain after World War I. [German sociologist] Max Weber wrote that the Chinese "introduced, for the first time in the world, the use of qualifying examinations and certification of

[1] Herrlee G. Creel, *The Origins of Statecraft in China*, vol. I, *The Western Chou Empire* (Chicago: The University of Chicago Press, 1970), 7–8, 25–26.

the conduct of officials. . . . From the point of view of formal structure, this carried bureaucratic objectivity to the highest degree possible."

Control by elaborate written rules is a characteristic of modern bureaucracy that is generally emphasized. Such control was an outstanding feature of Chinese administration from a very early time. [Historian] Karl Bünger points out that whereas in the Roman Empire there was little development of law regulating the administration of the government, China very early had a body of such law "of astonishing completeness" such as did not appear in Europe until a late date. "Red tape" is an ancient institution in China.

We also think of bureaucratic government, with reason, as being increasingly involved with the amassing of statistics and reports. By the first century B.C. the gathering of statistics had grown into a major enterprise of the Chinese government. A whole army of officials, from the local to the national level, was engaged in collecting, recording, and checking figures of many sorts. We still have detailed data from the census of the Empire taken in A.D. 2. Roman census procedures were haphazard compared with those of China; in the West the systematic enumeration of the population of whole nations did not begin until modern times. [Historian] Hans Bielenstein writes that in China "statistical material has been kept from incomparably earlier times than in any other country."

The Imperial Chancellor sat at the center of this information network. In his office he had figures on land and population, maps of the Empire, and reports on harvests, banditry, and finances from the provinces. He prepared the budget and was required to keep the various departments within their allotted sums. The Roman Empire, on the other hand, operated without a budget until the end of the third century A.D., while the earliest budget in England is said to date from the thirteenth century. . . .

Creel goes on to argue that the later European adoption of bureaucracies and civil service examinations were not just reinventions of the same wheel. Such European innovations in the seventeenth and eighteenth centuries, he argues, were based explicitly on Chinese models.

. . . The "Great Elector," Frederick William (1620–1688), who "laid the cornerstone of the Prussian bureaucratic state," took a great personal interest in China and at one point hoped to establish direct relations with the country. He purchased a very considerable number of books in Chinese and patronized scholars who studied Chinese and published on China. . . .

One of the Privy Councillors of Frederick III, Samuel Pufendorf, made repeated reference to the Chinese civil service examinations in a work, first published in 1672, that was widely read and frequently reprinted. Pufendorf contrasted Western methods of selecting men for office with the technique of examination used by the Chinese. . . .

It was in Berlin in 1693, five years after Pufendorf had joined the government there, that what appear to be the first written civil service examinations ever given in Europe were administered. It would be difficult to suppose that the Chinese example had nothing to do with this event. It seems reasonably clear that here again the institution of examination had been diffused from China, this time in a form much closer to the original. . . .

Notice how Creel uses biographical information regarding Prussian rulers and Samuel Pufendorf in order to make his point. What other biographical information about these or other historical figures would you want to know in order to evaluate Creel's argument?

Creel also uses Chinese biographical information in an interesting way. In a previous selection he says that at least 22 percent of the men who held the highest office — Imperial Chancellor — in the first and second centuries B.C.E. came from poor or humble families. He points out that this figure comes from biographical data. But biographical data is not available for half the people who became Imperial Chancellor between 200 B.C.E. and 1 C.E. Would the half for whom there is no biographical information be more likely to come from rich or poor families? If their biographies were included, would the share of poor and humble families likely be higher or lower than 22 percent?

The gathering and comparison of many biographies to find common elements has recently been made manageable by the ease of computer searches. Judging from Creel's use of biography, what would be the advantages and disadvantages of collective biographies? What sort of biographies might be so numerous that we would need a computer to scan for repetitive elements?

6

Tribal to Universal Religion

HISTORICAL CONTEXT

Hindu-Buddhist and Judeo-Christian Traditions, 1000 B.C.E.–100 C.E.

From 1000 B.C.E. to 100 C.E. two major religious traditions, one centered in the Middle East and the other in northern India, split into at least four major religious traditions, so large that today they are embraced by a majority of the inhabitants of the world. Each of the two original traditions, Hinduism and Judaism, were in 1000 B.C.E. highly restricted in membership. Neither sought converts but ministered to their own, members of tribe and castes. This chapter explores how these two essentially inward-looking religions created universal religions, open to all. It is a story not only of the emergence of Christianity and Buddhism but also of the development of modern Judaic and Hindu religions, often called Rabbinical Judaism and devotional Hinduism.

Remarkably, both of these traditions moved from tribal to universal religions; even more remarkable are the commonalities, given their different routes along that path. While Hinduism cultivated a psychological approach to spiritual enlightenment out of a priestly religion of obligation, Judaism developed an abiding faith in historical providence from a disastrous history.

As you read the selections in this chapter, notice over the course of the first millennium B.C.E. how the dynamic in both core religions led to the creation of new faiths and the reform of the old. Notice also the fundamentally different ways these two great religious traditions changed. Finally, observe how the later offspring religions, Buddhism and Christianity, preached ideas that were already current, but not dominant, in the "parental" religious traditions.

THINKING HISTORICALLY

Detecting Change in Primary Sources

Understanding how religions change or evolve is especially difficult because of the tendency of religious adherents to emphasize the timelessness of their truths. Fortunately, religious commitment and belief does not require a denial of historical change. Indeed, many adherents have found strength in all manifestations of the sacred—the specific and historical as well as the universal and eternal.

Whether motives are primarily religious or secular, however, the historical study of religion offers a useful window on understanding large-scale changes in human behavior. Since religious traditions tend to conserve, repeat, and enshrine, change is more gradual than in many other aspects of human thought and behavior: fashion, say, or technology. Thus, when religions develop radically new ideas or institutions, we can learn much about human resistance and innovation by studying the circumstances.

Because religions typically prefer conservation over innovation, changes are often grafted on to old formulations. Historians who want to understand when and how change occurred must sometimes discover and unmask new ideas and ways of doing things that have been assimilated into the tradition. We will ask you to look for signs of this process of adapting and updating religious ideas.

28

Svetasvatara Upanishad

In Chapter 4 are selections from the Hindu Vedas and Upanishads that serve as an introduction to some of the basic ideas in Hinduism: the belief that animals and human castes were created out of the primal sacrifice of the god Purusha in the Vedas, the complementary ideas of karma and reincarnation in the Upanishads, and, lastly, the identification of Brahman and *atman* (self and God) also in the Upanishads.

Svetasvatara Upanishad in *The Upanishads: The Breath of the Eternal*, trans. Swami Prabhavananda and Frederick Manchester (Hollywood: The Vedanta Society of Southern California, 1948; New York: Mentor Books, 1957), 118–21.

We might look at the same selections again to understand the changing nature of Hinduism from the earliest Vedas to the latest Upanishads. For example, we see in selection 14 the interest of the Aryan invaders of India in defining and justifying caste differences and the supremacy of the Brahman priests as masters of sacrifice, prayers, rituals, and sacred hymns.

The authors of the Upanishads were less interested in sacrifice and priestly rituals and more absorbed by philosophical questions. Thus, selection 15 on karma and reincarnation spells out the idea of justice and a philosophy of nature that reflects the interests of a later settled society. Finally, selection 16 on the identity of Brahman and *atman* reflects an even more meditative Upanishad that virtually ignores the role of priests. This meditative tradition may have existed in early Hinduism, but there is far more evidence of its expression in the Upanishads (after 800 B.C.E.) than in the earlier Vedas.

The *Svetasvatara* Upanishad selection included here reflects an additional step along the path from the religion of priests, sacrifice, and caste obligation to individualized spirituality. Here the idea of the transmigration of souls from one body to another in an endless cycle of reincarnations — an idea that developed after the Vedas — is challenged by the idea that the individual who seeks Brahman might break out of the wheel of life. How would this idea of escaping reincarnation diminish the power of Brahman priests? How does it minimize the importance of caste and karma?

Thinking Historically

Recognizing changes in the Hindu tradition is more difficult than in the Judaic tradition. The literature of Judaism is full of historical references: names of historical figures and even dates. Hindu sacred literature, as you can tell from this brief introduction, shows virtually no interest in historical names and dates. Because time in India was conceived as cyclical, rather than linear, and the cycles of the Indian time scheme were immense, determining the exact time an event occurred was less important in Hindu thought than understanding its eternal meaning.

Consequently, our analysis of the changes in Hinduism is more logical than chronological. We can therefore speak of a long-term historical process even though we cannot date each step.

The oldest of the thirteen universally recognized Upanishads, all of which were composed between 800 and 400 B.C.E., are the Brihadaranyaka (from which selection 15 on karma and reincarnation is taken) and the Chandogya (from which selection 16 on *atman* and Brahman is taken). The *Svetasvatara* is one of the last of the thirteen, composed closer to 400 B.C.E. What is the idea of time suggested by this Upanishad?

This vast universe is a wheel. Upon it are all creatures that are subject to birth, death, and rebirth. Round and round it turns, and never stops. It is the wheel of Brahman. As long as the individual self thinks it is separate from Brahman, it revolves upon the wheel in bondage to the laws of birth, death, and rebirth. But when through the grace of Brahman it realizes its identity with him, it revolves upon the wheel no longer. It achieves immortality.

He who is realized by transcending the world of cause and effect, in deep contemplation, is expressly declared by the scriptures to be the Supreme Brahman. He is the substance, all else the shadow. He is the imperishable. The knowers of Brahman know him as the one reality behind all that seems. For this reason they are devoted to him. Absorbed in him, they attain freedom from the wheel of birth, death, and rebirth.

The Lord supports this universe, which is made up of the perishable and the imperishable, the manifest and the unmanifest. The individual soul, forgetful of the Lord, attaches itself to pleasure and thus is bound. When it comes to the Lord, it is freed from all its fetters.

Mind and matter, master and servant — both have existed from beginningless time. The Maya which unites them has also existed from beginningless time. When all three — mind, matter, and Maya — are known as one with Brahman, then is it realized that the Self is infinite and has no part in action. Then is it revealed that the Self is all.

Matter is perishable. The Lord, the destroyer of ignorance, is imperishable, immortal. He is the one God, the Lord of the perishable and of all souls. By meditating on him, by uniting oneself with him, by identifying oneself with him, one ceases to be ignorant.

Know God, and all fetters will be loosed. Ignorance will vanish. Birth, death, and rebirth will be no more. Meditate upon him and transcend physical consciousness. Thus will you reach union with the lord of the universe. Thus will you become identified with him who is One without a second. In him all your desires will find fulfillment.

The truth is that you are always united with the Lord. But you must *know* this. Nothing further is there to know. Meditate, and you will realize that mind, matter, and Maya (the power which unites mind and matter) are but three aspects of Brahman, the one reality.

Fire, though present in the firesticks, is not perceived until one stick is rubbed against another. The Self is like that fire: it is realized in the body by meditation on the sacred syllable OM.[1]

Let your body be the stick that is rubbed, the sacred syllable OM the stick that is rubbed against it. Thus shall you realize God, who is hidden within the body as fire is hidden within the wood.

[1] Sacred symbol for God and the sound chanted in meditation. [Ed.]

Like oil in sesame seeds, butter in cream, water in the river bed, fire in tinder, the Self dwells within the soul. Realize him through truthfulness and meditation.

Like butter in cream is the Self in everything. Knowledge of the Self is gained through meditation. The Self is Brahman. By Brahman is all ignorance destroyed.

To realize God, first control the outgoing senses and harness the mind. Then meditate upon the light in the heart of the fire — meditate, that is, upon pure consciousness as distinct from the ordinary consciousness of the intellect. Thus the Self, the Inner Reality, may be seen behind physical appearance.

Control your mind so that the Ultimate Reality, the self-luminous Lord, may be revealed. Strive earnestly for eternal bliss.

With the help of the mind and the intellect, keep the senses from attaching themselves to objects of pleasure. They will then be purified by the light of the Inner Reality, and that light will be revealed.

The wise control their minds, and unite their hearts with the infinite, the omniscient, the all-pervading Lord. Only discriminating souls practice spiritual disciplines. Great is the glory of the self-luminous being, the Inner Reality.

Hear, all ye children of immortal bliss, also ye gods who dwell in the high heavens: Follow only in the footsteps of the illumined ones, and by continuous meditation merge both mind and intellect in the eternal Brahman. The glorious Lord will be revealed to you.

Control the vital force. Set fire to the Self within by the practice of meditation. Be drunk with the wine of divine love. Thus shall you reach perfection.

Be devoted to the eternal Brahman. Unite the light within you with the light of Brahman. Thus will the source of ignorance be destroyed, and you will rise above karma.

Sit upright, holding the chest, throat, and head erect. Turn the senses and the mind inward to the lotus of the heart. Meditate on Brahman with the help of the syllable OM. Cross the fearful currents of the ocean of worldliness by means of the raft of Brahman — the sacred syllable OM.

With earnest effort hold the senses in check. Controlling the breath, regulate the vital activities. As a charioteer holds back his restive horses, so does a persevering aspirant hold back his mind.

Retire to a solitary place, such as a mountain cave or a sacred spot. The place must be protected from the wind and rain, and it must have a smooth, clean floor, free from pebbles and dust. It must not be damp, and it must be free from disturbing noises. It must be pleasing to the eye and quieting to the mind. Seated there, practice meditation and other spiritual exercises.

As you practice meditation, you may see in vision forms resembling snow, crystals, smoke, fire, lightning, fireflies, the sun, the moon. These are signs that you are on your way to the revelation of Brahman.

As you become absorbed in meditation, you will realize that the Self is separate from the body and for this reason will not be affected by disease, old age, or death.

29

Buddhism: Gotama's Discovery

Gotama Siddhartha (c. 563–c. 483 B.C.E.), known to history as the Buddha, was the son of a Hindu Kshatriya prince in northern India. This selection tells a traditional story about his youth. Because his father was warned by "Brahman soothsayers" that young Gotama would leave his home to live among the seekers in the forest, his father kept the boy distracted in the palace, the sufferings of people outside hidden from him. This selection begins when the prince or *raja* finally agrees to let Gotama tour outside the palace.

What does Gotama discover? What seems to be the meaning of these discoveries for him? How is his subsequent thought or behavior similar to that of other Hindus in the era? How is the message of this story similar to the lessons of the Upanishads, especially the *Svetasvatara* Upanishad?

Thinking Historically

None of the stories we have of the Buddha was written during his lifetime. For some four hundred years, stories of the Buddha were passed by word of mouth before they were put into writing. Can you see any signs in this story that it was memorized and told orally? When the stories were finally written, some were no doubt more faithful to the Buddha's actual words and experience than others. What elements in this story would most likely reflect the historical experience of Gotama? What parts of the story would most likely be added later by people who worshiped the Buddha?

"The Life of Gotama the Buddha," trans. E. H. Brewster, in Clarence H. Hamilton, *Buddhism* (1926; reprint, New York: Routledge, 1952).

Now the young lord Gotama, when many days had passed by, bade his charioteer make ready the state carriages, saying: "Get ready the carriages, good charioteer, and let us go through the park to inspect the pleasaunce." "Yes, my lord," replied the charioteer, and harnessed the state carriages and sent word to Gotama: "The carriages are ready, my lord; do now what you deem fit." Then Gotama mounted a state carriage and drove out in state into the park.

Now the young lord saw, as he was driving to the park, an aged man as bent as a roof gable, decrepit, leaning on a staff, tottering as he walked, afflicted and long past his prime. And seeing him Gotama said: "That man, good charioteer, what has he done, that his hair is not like that of other men, nor his body?"

"He is what is called an aged man, my lord."

"But why is he called aged?"

"He is called aged, my lord, because he has not much longer to live."

"But then, good charioteer, am I too subject to old age, one who has not got past old age?"

"You, my lord, and we too, we all are of a kind to grow old; we have not got past old age."

"Why then, good charioteer, enough of the park for today. Drive me back hence to my rooms."

"Yea, my lord," answered the charioteer, and drove him back. And he, going to his rooms, sat brooding sorrowful and depressed, thinking, "Shame then verily be upon this thing called birth, since to one born old age shows itself like that!"

Thereupon the rāja sent for the charioteer and asked him: "Well, good charioteer, did the boy take pleasure in the park? Was he pleased with it?"

"No, my lord, he was not."

"What then did he see on his drive?"

(And the Charioteer told the rāja all.)

Then the rāja thought thus: We must not have Gotama declining to rule. We must not have him going forth from the house into the homeless state. We must not let what the brāhman soothsayers spoke of come true.

So, that these things might not come to pass, he let the youth be still more surrounded by sensuous pleasures. And thus Gotama continued to live admidst the pleasures of sense.

Now after many days had passed by, the young lord again bade his charioteer make ready and drove forth as once before. . . .

And Gotama saw, as he was driving to the park, a sick man, suffering and very ill, fallen and weltering in his own water, by some being lifted up, by others being dressed. Seeing this, Gotama asked: "That man, good charioteer, what has he done that his eyes are not like others' eyes, nor his voice like the voice of other men?"

"He is what is called ill, my lord."

"But what is meant by ill?"

"It means, my lord, that he will hardly recover from his illness."

"But am I too, then, good charioteer, subject to fall ill; have I not got out of reach of illness?"

"You, my lord, and we too, we are all subject to fall ill; we have not got beyond the reach of illness."

"Why then, good charioteer, enough of the park for today. Drive me back hence to my rooms." "Yea, my lord," answered the charioteer, and drove him back. And he, going to his rooms, sat brooding sorrowful and depressed, thinking: Shame then verily be upon this thing called birth, since to one born decay shows itself like that, disease shows itself like that.

Thereupon the rāja sent for the charioteer and asked him: "Well, good charioteer, did the young lord take pleasure in the park and was he pleased with it?"

"No, my lord, he was not."

"What did he see then on his drive?"

(And the charioteer told the rāja all.)

Then the rāja thought thus: We must not have Gotama declining to rule; we must not have him going forth from the house to the homeless state; we must not let what the brāhman soothsayers spoke of come true.

So, that these things might not come to pass, he let the young man be still more abundantly surrounded by sensuous pleasures. And thus Gotama continued to live admidst the pleasures of sense.

Now once again, after many days . . . the young lord Gotama . . . drove forth.

And he saw, as he was driving to the park, a great concourse of people clad in garments of different colours constructing a funeral pyre. And seeing this he asked his charioteer: "Why now are all those people come together in garments of different colours, and making that pile?"

"It is because someone, my lord, has ended his days."

"Then drive the carriage close to him who has ended his days."

"Yea, my lord," answered the charioteer, and did so. And Gotama saw the corpse of him who had ended his days and asked: "What, good charioteer, is ending one's days?"

"It means, my lord, that neither mother, nor father, nor other kinsfolk will now see him, nor will he see them."

"But am I too then subject to death, have I not got beyond reach of death? Will neither the rāja, nor the ranee, nor any other of my kin see me more, or shall I again see them?"

"You, my lord, and we too, we are all subject to death; we have not passed beyond the reach of death. Neither the rāja, nor the ranee, nor any other of your kin will see you any more, nor will you see them."

"Why then, good charioteer, enough of the park for today. Drive me back hence to my rooms."

"Yea, my lord," replied the charioteer, and drove him back.

And he, going to his rooms, sat brooding sorrowful and depressed, thinking: Shame verily be upon this thing called birth, since to one born the decay of life, since disease, since death shows itself like that!

Thereupon the rāja questioned the charioteer as before and as before let Gotama be still more surrounded by sensuous enjoyment. And thus he continued to live amidst the pleasures of sense.

Now once again, after many days . . . the lord Gotama . . . drove forth.

And he saw, as he was driving to the park, a shaven-headed man, a recluse, wearing the yellow robe. And seeing him he asked the charioteer, "That man, good charioteer, what has he done that his head is unlike other men's heads and his clothes too are unlike those of others?"

"That is what they call a recluse, because, my lord, he is one who has gone forth."

"What is that, 'to have gone forth'?"

"To have gone forth, my lord, means being thorough in the religious life, thorough in the peaceful life, thorough in good action, thorough in meritorious conduct, thorough in harmlessness, thorough in kindness to all creatures."

"Excellent indeed, friend charioteer, is what they call a recluse, since so thorough is his conduct in all those respects, wherefore drive me up to that forthgone man."

"Yea, my lord," replied the charioteer and drove up to the recluse. Then Gotama addressed him, saying, "You master, what have you done that your head is not as other men's heads, nor your clothes as those of other men?"

"I, my lord, am one who has gone forth."

"What, master, does that mean?"

"It means, my lord, being thorough in the religious life, thorough in the peaceful life, thorough in good actions, thorough in meritorious conduct, thorough in harmlessness, thorough in kindness to all creatures."

"Excellently indeed, master, are you said to have gone forth since so thorough is your conduct in all those respects." Then the lord Gotama bade his charioteer, saying: "Come then, good charioteer, do you take the carriage and drive it back hence to my rooms. But I will even here cut off my hair, and don the yellow robe, and go forth from the house into the homeless state."

"Yea, my lord," replied the charioteer, and drove back. But the prince Gotama, there and then cutting off his hair and donning the yellow robe, went forth from the house into the homeless state.

Now at Kapilavatthu, the rāja's seat, a great number of persons, some eighty-four thousand souls, heard of what prince Gotama had done and thought: Surely this is no ordinary religious rule, this is no common going forth, in that prince Gotama himself has had his head shaved and has donned the yellow robe and has gone forth from the house into the homeless state. If prince Gotama has done this, why then should not we also? And they all had their heads shaved and donned the yellow robes; and in imitation of the Bodhisat [Buddha] they went forth from the house into the homeless state. So the Bodhisat went forth from the house into the homeless state. So the Bodhisat went up on his rounds through the villages, towns and cities accompanied by that multitude.

Now there arose in the mind of Gotama the Bodhisat, when he was meditating in seclusion, this thought: That indeed is not suitable for me that I should live beset. 'Twere better were I to dwell alone, far from the crowd.

So after a time he dwelt alone, away from the crowd. Those eighty-four thousand recluses went one way, and the Bodhisat went another way.

Now there arose in the mind of Gotama the Bodhisat, when he had gone to his place and was meditating in seclusion, this thought: Verily, this world had fallen upon trouble — one is born, and grows old, and dies, and falls from one state, and springs up in another. And from the suffering, moreover, no one knows of any way to escape, even from decay and death. O, when shall a way of escape from this suffering be made known — from decay and from death?

30

The Buddha's First Sermon

This is said to be the Buddha's first sermon, delivered shortly after he achieved enlightenment. It contains the essence of Buddhist thought: the four noble truths, the eightfold path, and the middle way. The middle way is the course between the extremes of the pursuit of pleasure and the pursuit of pain. It is defined by an eightfold path, eight steps to a peaceful mind. The four noble truths might be summarized as the following:

1. **Life is sorrow.**
2. **Sorrow is the result of selfish desire.**

The Buddhist Tradition in India, China and Japan, ed. William Theodore de Bary (New York: Random House, 1969), 16–17.

3. Selfish desire can be destroyed.
4. It can be destroyed by following the eightfold path.

What do these ideas mean? What was considered the value of a "middle way"? In what ways did the eightfold path offer a spiritual discipline? What answers did the four noble truths provide?

Thinking Historically

How is the tone and style of this selection different from "Gotama's Discovery"? Would these events occur before or after the "discovery"? Nevertheless, why is it likely that this story was created earlier than the previous one and is probably closer to the actual words and experience of the Buddha?

Thus I have heard. Once the Lord was at Vrānasī, at the deer park called Iwipatana. There he addressed the five monks:

There are two ends not to be served by a wanderer. What are these two? The pursuit of desires and of the pleasure which springs from desire, which is base, common, leading to rebirth, ignoble, and unprofitable; and the pursuit of pain and hardship, which is grievous, ignoble, and unprofitable. The Middle Way of the Tathāgata avoids both these ends. It is enlightened, it brings clear vision, it makes for wisdom, and leads to peace, insight, enlightenment, and Nirvāna. What is the Middle Way? . . . It is the Noble Eightfold Path — Right Views, Right Resolve, Right Speech, Right Conduct, Right Livelihood, Right Effort, Right Mindfulness, and Right Concentration. This is the Middle Way. . . .

And this is the Noble Truth of Sorrow. Birth is sorrow, age is sorrow, disease is sorrow, death is sorrow; contact with the unpleasant is sorrow, separation from the pleasant is sorrow, every wish unfulfilled is sorrow — in short all the five components of individuality are sorrow.

And this is the Noble Truth of the Arising of Sorrow. It arises from craving, which leads to rebirth, which brings delight and passion, and seeks pleasure now here, now there — the craving for sensual pleasure, the craving for continued life, the craving for power.

And this is the Noble Truth of the Stopping of Sorrow. It is the complete stopping of that craving, so that no passion remains, leaving it, being emancipated from it, being released from it, giving no place to it.

And this is the Noble Truth of the Way which Leads to the Stopping of Sorrow. It is the Noble Eightfold Path — Right Views, Right Resolve, Right Speech, Right Conduct, Right Livelihood, Right Effort, Right Mindfulness, and Right Concentration.

31

Buddhism and Caste

This story, part of the Buddhist canon that was written between one and four hundred years after his death, tells of a confrontation between the Buddha and Brahmans, members of the Hindu priestly caste. This encounter would have been common. Why would it be important? How would you expect most Brahmans to react to the Buddha's opposition to caste? Would some Brahmans be persuaded by the Buddha's arguments? How and why would the appeal of Buddhism be more universal than Hinduism?

Thinking Historically

Notice the mention of Greece and the dialogue style of this selection. If, as some scholars have suggested, there may be Greek influence here, which Greek writer would they be referring to? How might this Greek influence help us find an approximate date for this writing?

Once when the Lord was staying at Sāvatthī there were five hundred brāhmans from various countries in the city . . . and they thought: "This ascetic Gautama preaches that all four classes are pure. Who can refute him?"

At that time there was a young brāhman named Assalāyana in the city . . . a youth of sixteen, thoroughly versed in the Vedas . . . and in all brāhmanic learning. "He can do it!" thought the brāhmans, and so they asked him to try; but he answered, "The ascetic Gautama teaches a doctrine of his own, and such teachers are hard to refute. I can't do it!" They asked him a second time . . . and again he refused; and they asked him a third time, pointing out that he ought not to admit defeat without giving battle. This time he agreed, and so, surrounded by a crowd of brāhmans, he went to the Lord, and, after greeting him, sat down and said:

"Brāhmans maintain that only they are the highest class, and the others are below them. They are white, the others black; only they are pure, and not the others. Only they are the true sons of Brahmā, born

---

The Buddhist Tradition in India, China and Japan, ed. William Theodore de Bary (New York: Random House, 1969), 49–51.

from his mouth, born of Brahmā, creations of Brahmā, heirs of Brahmā. Now what does the worthy Gautama say to that?"

"Do the brāhmans really maintain this, Assalāyana, when they're born of women just like anyone else, of brāhman women who have their periods and conceive, give birth and nurse their children, just like any other women?"

"For all you say, this is what they think. . . . "

"Have you ever heard that in the lands of the Greeks and Kambojas and other peoples on the borders there are only two classes, masters and slaves, and a master can become a slave and vice versa?"

"Yes, I've heard so."

"And what strength or support does that fact give to the brāhmans' claim?"

"Nevertheless, that is what they think."

"Again if a man is a murderer, a thief, or an adulterer, or commits other grave sins, when his body breaks up on death does he pass on to purgatory if he's a kshatriya,[1] vaishya,[2] or shūdra,[3] but not if he's a brāhman?"

"No, Gautama. In such a case the same fate is in store for all men, whatever their class."

"And if he avoids grave sin, will he go to heaven if he's a brāhman, but not if he's a man of the lower classes?"

"No, Gautama. In such a case the same reward awaits all men, whatever their class."

"And is a brāhman capable of developing a mind of love without hate or ill-will, but not a man of the other classes?"

"No, Gautama. All four classes are capable of doing so."

"Can only a brāhman go down to a river and wash away dust and dirt, and not men of the other classes?"

"No, Gautama, all four classes can."

"Now suppose a king were to gather together a hundred men of different classes and to order the brāhmans and kshatriyas to take kindling wood of sāl, pine, lotus, or sandal, and light fires, while the low-class folk did the same with common wood. What do you think would happen? Would the fires of the high-born men blaze up brightly . . . and those of the humble fail?"

"No, Gautama. It would be alike with high and lowly. . . . Every fire would blaze with the same bright flame." . . .

"Suppose there are two young brāhman brothers, one a scholar and the other uneducated. Which of them would be served first at memorial feasts, festivals, and sacrifices, or when entertained as guests?"

[1] Warrior. [Ed.]

[2] Free peasant, artisan, or producer. [Ed.]

[3] Serf. [Ed.]

"The scholar, of course; for what great benefit would accrue from entertaining the uneducated one?"

"But suppose the scholar is ill-behaved and wicked, while the uneducated one is well-behaved and virtuous?"

"Then the uneducated one would be served first, for what great benefit would accrue from entertaining an ill-behaved and wicked man?"

"First, Assalāyana, you based your claim on birth, then you gave up birth for learning, and finally you have come round to my way of thinking, that all four classes are equally pure!"

At this Assalāyana sat silent . . . his shoulders hunched, his eyes cast down, thoughtful in mind, and with no answer at hand.

32

The Bible: History, Laws, and Psalms

Just as the caste-based Hinduism of ancient Aryan tribes gave rise to universal Buddhism after 500 B.C.E., so did the Judaism of the tribe of Abraham give birth to universalist Christianity. Judaism was already an ancient religion by the time of Jesus. It traced its roots back (perhaps two thousand years) to Abraham himself who, according to tradition, made a contract (or covenant) with God to worship him and him alone. This God promised Abraham and his descendants prosperity and many heirs. In return Abraham and his male descendants would be circumcised as a sign of their loyalty.

This commitment to one god, and one god only, was to mark the ancient Jews as unique. No other people in the ancient world were monotheistic. The people of Mesopotamia, Egypt, India, and the Mediterranean accepted various ancestral and natural gods. Only the Egyptians for a brief moment (around 1300 B.C.E.) preached the singularity of god, in this case the sun god Aton, but that was soon renounced. Since such a belief was unusual, the descendants of Abraham had difficulty accepting it. In their wanderings throughout the

Gen. 1:1–2:25, 17:1–17:14; Exod. 19:1–20:18; Lev. 1:1–1:9; Ps. 23:1–23:6; Amos 5:21–5:24. All biblical selections are from the King James Version.

land of the Tigris and Euphrates Rivers, from Abraham's native Ur to Egypt, the Jews came into contact with many different religious beliefs; some were even tempted by foreign gods. However by around 1300 B.C.E., Abraham's descendants escaped Egyptian domination, crossed the Red Sea, and with the help of Moses renewed their covenant with God in the Ten Commandments. Even then, stories were told of Jews who worshiped the Golden Calf and other idols and of the displeasure of the God of Abraham. "I am a jealous God," he told his people. "Thou shall not take other gods before you." In fact, seven hundred years later, the prophet Jeremiah (628–526 B.C.E.) chastised the people for worshiping Baal as well as Yahweh, the God of Abraham.

Such is the story told in the books of the Bible, written after the Jews settled in Jerusalem and the surrounding area sometime after 1000 B.C.E. They wrote of their history since the time of Abraham, even their version of the ages before the patriarch, stretching back to the beginning of the world. And in the heady days of Jewish kingdoms, Kings Saul, David, and Solomon ruled large parts of what is today Israel, Palestine, and Jordan by about 900 B.C.E. The book we know as the Bible included these histories, the laws of the two Jewish kingdoms Judah and Israel, and various other writings (songs, psalms, and philosophy).

As you read these first selections from the Bible (Genesis, Exodus, Leviticus, and Psalms), note how they are similar to, and different from, the Vedas and Upanishads of Hinduism. How, for instance, is the story of the beginning of the world different from the sacrifice of Purusha? Why is an understanding of history more important to the Jews than it was to the Hindus? Compare the role of morality in the religion of Jews and Hindus. In what sense is the morality of Judaism universal and that of Hinduism caste based? How is the Judaic emphasis on morality also different from Buddhist ideas?

Thinking Historically

Since the books of the Hebrew Bible were composed over a long period of time, from about 900 B.C.E. to about 165 B.C.E., we might expect to see changes in emphasis, especially since this period was such a tumultuous one in Jewish history. The immediate descendants of Abraham were a nomadic pastoral people — shepherds, Psalm 23 reminds us, though this beautiful psalm attributed to King David was written in an urban, monarchal stage of Jewish history. Leviticus, too, echoes an earlier pastoral life where animal sacrifice, and the worship by shepherds generally, was still practiced.

When did morality replace sacrifice as the sign of respect to the God of Abraham? Was it around 1300 B.C.E., the traditional date for the reception by Moses of the Ten Commandments? Or is the existence of Leviticus, perhaps five hundred years later, a sign that sacrifice was still practiced? The sentiments of Amos (783–743 B.C.E.) suggest a later rejection not only of animal sacrifice but also of moral obedience that was not truly felt.

When did monotheism (the belief in one god) become unequivocal, unquestioned? Since this was a new idea, there must have been a time when it wasn't held. Some scholars see signs of an earlier polytheism (belief in many gods) in the book of Genesis itself. Certainly the beginning of Genesis is no-nonsense monotheism, majestically so: "In the beginning God created the heaven and the earth." But scholars have pointed out that this opening precedes another story of origin beginning at Chapter 2, Verse 4, that not only tells the story over again, but does so without the intense declarative monotheism. They date this document at about 850 B.C.E. and the section from 1:1 to 2:3 at about 650 B.C.E. What evidence do you see in this second, older Genesis (after 2:4) of remnants of an older polytheism?

Finally, notice there is no heaven here — no afterlife. God promised Abraham land and prosperity. Even today, a belief in personal immortality is more accepted by Christians than Jews. Still, we will explore the development of that idea in Judaism in the second century B.C.E.

Genesis

Chapter 1

1 In the beginning God created the heaven and the earth. 2 And the
earth was without form, and void; and darkness was upon the face of
the deep. And the Spirit of God moved upon the face of the waters.
3 And God said, Let there be light: and there was light. 4 And God saw
the light, and it was good: and God divided the light from the darkness.
5 And God called the light Day, and the darkness he called Night. And
the evening and the morning were the first day.

6 And God said, Let there be a firmament in the midst of the waters, and let it divide the waters. 7 And God made the firmament, and
divided the waters which were under the firmament from the waters
which were above the firmament: and it was so. 8 And God called the
firmament Heaven. And the evening and the morning were the second day.

9 And God said, Let the waters under the heaven be gathered together unto one place, and let the dry land appear: and it was so. 10 And
God called the dry land Earth; and the gathering together of the water
called he Seas: and God saw it was good. 11 And God said, Let the earth

bring forth grass, the herb yielding seed, and the fruit tree yielding fruit after his kind, whose seed is in itself, upon the earth: and it was so. 12 And the earth brought forth grass, and herb yielding seed after his kind, and the tree yielding fruit, whose seed was in itself, after his kind: and God saw it was good. 13 And the evening and the morning were the third day.

14 And God said, Let there be lights in the firmament of the heaven to divide the day from the night; and let them be for signs, and for seasons, and for days, and years: 15 And let them be for lights in the firmament of the heaven to give light upon the earth: and it was so. 16 And God made two great lights; the greater light to rule the day, and the lesser light to rule the night: he made the stars also. 17 And God set them in the firmament of the heaven to give light upon the earth, 18 And to rule over the day and over the night, and to divide the light from the darkness: and God saw that it was good. 19 And the evening and the morning were the fourth day.

20 And God said, Let the waters bring forth abundantly the moving creatures that hath life, and fowl that may fly above the earth in the open firmament of heaven. 21 And God created great whales, and every living creature that moveth, which the waters brought forth abundantly, after their kind, and every winged fowl after his kind: and God saw that it was good. 22 And God blessed them, saying, Be fruitful, and multiply, and fill the waters in the seas, and let fowl multiply in the earth. 23 And the evening and the morning were the fifth day.

24 And God said, Let the earth bring forth the living creature after his kind, cattle, and creeping thing, and beast of the earth after his kind: and it was so. 25 And God made the beast of the earth after his kind, and cattle after their kind, and every thing that creepeth upon the earth after his kind: and God saw that it was good.

26 And God said, Let us make man in our image, after our likeness: and let them have dominion over the fish of the sea, and over the fowl of the air, and over the cattle, and over all the earth, and over every creeping thing that creepeth upon the earth. 27 So God created man in his own image, in the image of God created he him: male and female created he them. 28 And God blessed them, and God said unto them, Be fruitful, and multiply, and replenish the earth, and subdue it: and have dominion over the fish of the sea, and over the fowl of the air, and over every living thing that moveth upon the earth.

29 And God said, Behold, I have given you every herb bearing seed, which is upon the face of all the earth, and every tree, in which is the fruit of a tree yielding seed; to you it shall be for meat. 30 And to every beast of the earth, and to every fowl of the air, and to every thing that creepeth upon the earth, wherein there is life, I have given every green herb for meat: and it was so. 31 And God saw every thing that he had made, and, behold, it was very good. And the evening and the morning were the sixth day.

Chapter 2

1 Thus the heavens and the earth were finished, and all the host of them. 2 And on the seventh day God ended his work which he had made; and he rested on the seventh day from all his work which he had made. 3 And God blessed the seventh day, and sanctified it: because that in it he had rested from all this work which God created and made.

4 These are the generations of the heavens and of the earth when they were created, in the day that the Lord God made the earth and the heavens. 5 And every plant of the field before it was in the earth, and every herb of the field before it grew: for the Lord God had not caused it to rain upon the earth, and there was not a man to till the ground. 6 But there went up a mist from the earth, and watered the whole face of the ground. 7 And the Lord God formed man of the dust of the ground, and breathed into his nostrils the breath of life; and man became a living soul.

8 And the Lord God planted a garden eastward in Eden; and there he put the man whom he had formed. 9 And out of the ground made the Lord God to grow every tree that is pleasant to the sight, and good for food; and the tree of life also in the midst of the garden, and the tree of knowledge of good and evil. 10 And a river went out of Eden to water the garden; and from thence it was parted, and became into four heads. 11 The name of the first is Pison: that is it which compasseth the whole land of Havilah, where there is gold; 12 And the gold of the land is good: there is bdellium and the onyx stone. 13 And the name of the second river is Gihon: the same is it that compasseth the whole land of Ethiopia. 14 And the name of the third river is Hiddekel: that is it which goeth toward the east of Assyria. And the fourth river is Euphrates. 15 And the Lord God took the man, and put him into the garden of Eden to dress it and to keep it. 16 And the Lord God commanded the man, saying, Of every tree of the garden thou mayest freely eat: 17 But of the tree of the knowledge of good and evil, thou shalt not eat of it: for in the day that thou eatest thereof thou shalt surely die.

18 And the Lord God said, It is not good that the man should be alone; I will make him a help meet for him. 19 And out of the ground the Lord God formed every beast of the field, and every fowl of the air; and brought them unto Adam to see what he would call them: and whatsoever Adam called every living creature, that was the name thereof. 20 And Adam gave names to all cattle, and to the fowl of the air, and to every beast of the field; but for Adam there was not found a help meet for him. 21 And the Lord God caused a deep sleep to fall upon Adam, and he slept; and he took one of his ribs, and closed up the flesh instead thereof. 22 And the rib, which the Lord God had taken from man, made he a woman, and brought her unto the man. 23 And Adam said, This is now bone of my bones, and flesh of my flesh: she shall be called Woman, because she was taken out of man. 24 There-

fore shall a man leave his father and his mother, and shall cleave unto his wife: and they shall be one flesh. 25 And they were both naked, the man and his wife, and were not ashamed.

Chapter 17

1 And when Abram was ninety years old and nine, the Lord appeared to Abram, and said unto him, I am the Almighty God; walk before me, and be thou perfect. 2 And I will make my covenant between me and thee, and will multiply thee exceedingly. 3 And Abram fell on his face: and God talked with him, saying, 4 As for me, behold, my covenant is with thee, and thou shalt be a father of many nations. 5 Neither shall thy name any more be called Abram, but thy name shall be Abraham; for a father of many nations I have made thee. 6 And I will make thee exceeding fruitful, and I will make nations of thee, and kings shall come out of thee. 7 And I will establish my covenant between me and thee and thy seed after thee in their generations, for an everlasting covenant, to be a God unto thee and to thy seed after thee. 8 And I will give unto thee, and to thy seed after thee, the land wherein thou art a stranger, all the land of Canaan, for an everlasting possession; and I will be their God. 9 And God said unto Abraham. Thou shalt keep my covenant therefore, thou, and thy seed after thee in their generations. 10 This is my covenant, which he shall keep, between me and you and thy seed after thee; Every man child among you shall be circumcised. 11 And ye shall circumcise the flesh of your foreskin; and it shall be a token of the covenant betwixt me and you. 12 And he that is eight days old shall be circumcised among you, every man child in your generations, he that is born in the house, or bought with money of any stranger, which is not of thy seed. 13 He that is born in thy house, and he that is bought with thy money, must needs be circumcised: and my covenant shall be in your flesh for an everlasting covenant. 14 And the uncircumcised man child whose flesh of his foreskin is not circumcised, that soul shall be cut off from his people; he hath broken my covenant.

Exodus

Chapter 19

1 In the third month, when the children of Israel were gone forth out of the land of Egypt, the same day came they into the wilderness of Sinai. 2 For they were departed from Rephidim, and were come to the desert of Sinai, and had pitched in the wilderness; and there Israel camped before the mount. 3 And Moses went up unto God, and the Lord called

unto him out of the mountain, saying, Thus shalt thou say to the house of Jacob, and tell the children of Israel; 4 Ye have seen what I did unto the Egyptians, and how I bare you on eagles' wings, and brought you unto myself. 5 Now therefore, if ye will obey my voice indeed, and keep my covenant, then ye shall be a peculiar treasure unto me above all people: for all the earth is mine: 6 And ye shall be unto me a kingdom of priests, and a holy nation. These are the words which thou shalt speak unto the children of Israel.

7 And Moses came and called for the elders of the people, and laid before their faces all these words which the Lord commanded him. 8 And all the people answered together, and said, All that the Lord hath spoken we will do. And Moses returned the words of the people unto the Lord.
9 And the Lord said unto Moses, Lo, I come unto thee in a thick cloud, that the people may hear when I speak with thee, and believe thee for ever. And Moses told the words of the people unto the Lord.

Chapter 20

1 And God spake all these words, saying,

2 I am the Lord thy God, which have brought thee out of the land of Egypt, out of the house of bondage. 3 Thou shalt have no other gods before me.

4 Thou shalt not make unto thee any graven image, or any likeness of any thing that is in heaven above, or that is in the earth beneath, or that is in the water under the earth: 5 Thou shalt not bow down thyself to them, nor serve them: for I the Lord thy God am a jealous God, visiting the iniquity of the fathers upon the children unto the third and fourth generation of them that hate me; 6 And showing mercy unto thousands of them that love me, and keep my commandments.

7 Thou shalt not take the name of the Lord thy God in vain: for the Lord will not hold him guiltless that taketh his name in vain.

8 Remember the sabbath day, to keep it holy. 9 Six days shalt thou labor, and do all thy work: 10 But the seventh day is the sabbath of the Lord thy God: in it thou shalt not do any work, thou, nor thy son, nor thy daughter, nor thy manservant, nor thy maidservant, nor thy cattle, nor thy stranger that is within thy gates: 11 For in six days the Lord made heaven and earth, the sea, and all that in them is, and rested the seventh day: wherefore the Lord blessed the sabbath day, and hallowed it.

12 Honor thy father and thy mother: that thy days may be long upon the land which the Lord thy God giveth thee.

13 Thou shalt not kill.

14 Thou shalt not commit adultery.

15 Thou shalt not steal.

16 Thou shalt not bear false witness against thy neighbor.

17 Thou shalt not covet thy neighbor's house; thou shalt not covet thy neighbor's wife, nor his manservant, nor his maidservant, nor his ox, nor his ass, nor any thing that is thy neighbor's.

18 And all the people saw the thunderings, and the lightnings, and the noise of the trumpet, and the mountain smoking: and when the people saw it, they removed, and stood afar off.

Leviticus

Chapter 1

1 And the Lord called unto Moses, and spake unto him out of the tabernacle of the congregation, saying, 2 Speak unto the children of Israel, and
say unto them, If any man of you bring an offering unto the Lord, ye shall
bring your offering of the cattle, even of the herd, and of the flock.
3 If his offering be a burnt sacrifice of the herd, let him offer a male
without blemish: he shall offer it of his own voluntary will at the door of
the tabernacle of the congregation before the Lord. 4 And he shall put his
hand upon the head of the burnt offering; and it shall be accepted for him
to make atonement for him. 5 And he shall kill the bullock before the
Lord: and the priests, Aaron's sons, shall bring the blood, and sprinkle
the blood round about upon the altar that is by the door of the tabernacle
of the congregation. 6 And he shall flay the burnt offering, and cut it into
his pieces. 7 And the sons of Aaron the priest shall put fire upon the altar,
and lay the wood in order upon the fire: 8 And the priests, Aaron's sons,
shall lay the parts, the head, and the fat, in order upon the wood that is
on the fire which is upon the altar: 9 But his inwards and his legs shall he
wash in water: and the priest shall burn all on the altar, to be a burnt sacrifice, an offering made by fire, of a sweet savor unto the Lord.

Psalm 23

1 The Lord is my shepherd; I shall not want.

2 He maketh me to lie down in green pastures: He leadeth me beside the still waters.

3 He restoreth my soul: He leadeth me in the paths of righteousness for his name's sake.

4 Yea, though I walk through the valley of the shadow of death, I will fear no evil: for thou art with me; Thy rod and thy staff they comfort me.

5 Thou preparest a table before me in the presence of mine enemies: Thou anointest my head with oil; my cup runneth over.

6 Surely goodness and mercy shall follow me all the days of my life:
And I will dwell in the house of the Lord for ever.

Amos

Chapter 5

21 I hate, I despise your feast days, and I will not delight in your solemn assemblies.

22 Though you offer me burnt offerings and your meat offerings, I will not accept them: neither will I regard the peace offerings of your fat beasts.

23 Take thou away from me the noise of thy songs; for I will not hear the melody of thy viols.

24 But let judgment run down as waters, and righteousness as a mighty stream.

33

The Hebrew Bible: Prophets and Apocalypse

The golden days of Jewish kings were not to last. Powerful empires rose up to challenge and dominate the Jews: the Assyrians in 800 B.C.E., the Babylonians around 600 B.C.E., then the Medes, the Persians, the armies of Alexander the Great, his successor states — ruled by his generals and their descendants — and then the Romans after 64 B.C.E. The Babylonians were among the worst of the invaders. They conquered Jerusalem, destroyed the temple, and brought Jews as hostages to Babylon. In 538 B.C.E. Cyrus, king of the Persians, allowed Jews to return to Jerusalem and even rebuild the temple. But the Jews never regained their kingdom or independence (except for brief periods), and the Greek Seleucid rulers after Alexander proved to be intolerant of non-Greek forms of worship.

Ironically, it was during this period of conquest and dispersal that Judaism began to develop the elements of a universal religion. The Babylonian destruction of the temple and population transfer made

Dan. 12:1–12:13 King James.

the religion of Yahweh less dependent on place. Virtually all religions of the ancient world were bound to a particular place, usually the sacred temple where the god was thought to reside. Judaism remained a religion of the descendants of Abraham and his son Israel, and the period after 600 B.C.E. was one of intense cultivation of that identity. But much of the Hebrew Bible was composed in exile, as a way of recalling a common history, reaffirming a common identity, predicting a common future. The prophets foresaw a brighter future or explained how the violation of the covenant had brought God's wrath on the people. In exile in Babylon, the Psalms mourned the loss of Jerusalem. "By the rivers of Babylon. . . . we wept. . . . How shall we sing the Lord's song in a strange land?" Psalms 137:1–4. But in Babylon, the children of Israel found their God transcended worldly boundaries. "I am the Lord and there is none else. I form the light and create darkness," Isaiah (550–539 B.C.E.) wrote.

One of the great prophets of the exile and the postexile period was Daniel, described as one of the young men who was brought to Babylon by Nebuchadnezzar, conqueror of Jerusalem in 586 B.C.E. The Book of Daniel begins by recounting that conquest. In Babylon Nebuchadnezzar asked Daniel to reveal the meaning of a dream. Daniel told the king that a dream in which a large statue with a gold head, silver chest, bronze thighs, iron legs, and feet of clay is destroyed is a symbol of Nebuchadnezzar's golden kingdom and future kingdoms that will come after him. But, Daniel reveals, the destruction of the statue means that after the kings of clay, the world itself will come to an end.

Daniel is the first to predict this apocalyptic end to history and the first to envision personal immortality. Previous prophets had predicted a new independent kingdom of Judah or they had predicted God's punishment of his people, but Daniel predicted that God would come down to reign on earth forever, judging the living and the dead for all eternity. These ideas — an end to history, the Last Judgment, the Kingdom of God, eternal life or damnation — became more important later in Christianity than in Judaism, where these notions never entered the mainstream. But their appearance in Daniel shows the way in which Judaic ideas became more universal over the course of the first millennium B.C.E. Why would Daniel's ideas open the Judaic tradition to non-Jews or people not descended from Abraham? How would Daniel's prophecy affect his contemporaries? How would it affect you?

Thinking Historically

When did the idea of an afterlife enter Judaism? To answer this question we have to date the Book of Daniel, which is a bit more complex than it would seem. As mentioned, the book is presented as the prophecy of a Daniel who was taken from Jerusalem to Babylon around 586 B.C.E. If there was such a Daniel and he was a prophet, the version we have shows signs of continual updating. In the initial prophecy for Nebuchadnezzar and in similar instances reported throughout the Book of Daniel, the author predicts the string of empires that determined the fate of the Jews from the Babylonian to the Median to the Persian to the Greek under Alexander to the Seleucid (Alexander's successors). This is the meaning of the gold, silver, bronze, iron, clay sequence. In each case, the prophecy is vague (and sometimes inaccurate) when referring to the Babylonian period but very specific and exact about the period of iron and clay (the Selecuids). When Daniel speaks of the signs of the last days, his veiled references clearly refer to events during the reign of the Seleucid ruler Antiochus IV. He distinctly sees the desecration of the temple by Antiochus as the key event that will bring about God's eternal kingdom. Antiochus, who ruled from 175 to 163 B.C.E., pressured the Jews to accept Greek gods. In 168 B.C.E. he polluted the temple by slaughtering pigs on the altar and then erecting a statue of the Greek god Zeus — the event that Daniel predicts will bring on God's last judgment.

What would be the purpose of putting this prophecy in the writings of someone who had lived hundreds of years earlier? How does the age of Daniel's message give it added impact? When and why would the author of the Book of Daniel have predicted that the end of the world would occur 1290 days after an event in 168 B.C.E.? When and why would he have written "blessed are those who wait 1335 days"?

Daniel

Chapter 12

1 And at that time shall Michael stand up, the great prince which standeth for the children of thy people: and there shall be a time of trouble, such as never was since there was a nation even to that same time: and at that time thy people shall be delivered, every one that shall be found written in the book. 2 And many of them that sleep in the dust of the earth shall awake, some to everlasting life, and some to shame and everlasting contempt. 3 And they that be wise shall shine as the brightness of the firmament; and they that turn many to righteousness, as the stars forever and ever. 4 But thou, O Daniel, shut up the words, and seal the book, even to the time of the end: many shall run to and fro, and knowledge shall be increased.

5 Then I Daniel looked, and, behold, there stood other two, the one on this side of the bank of the river, and the other on that side of the bank of the river. 6 And one said to the man clothed in linen, which was upon the waters of the river, How long shall it be to the end of these wonders? 7 And I heard the man clothed in linen, which was upon the waters of the river, when he held up his right hand and his left hand unto heaven, and swore by him that liveth for ever, that it shall be for a time, times, and a half; and when he shall have accomplished to scatter the power of the holy people, all of these things shall be finished.

8 And I heard, but I understood not: then said I, O my Lord, what shall be the end of these things? 9 And he said, Go thy way, Daniel: for the words are closed up and sealed till the time of the end. 10 Many shall be purified, and made white, and tried; but the wicked shall do wickedly: and none of the wicked shall understand; but the wise shall understand.

11 And from the time that the daily sacrifice shall be taken away, and the abomination that maketh desolate set up, there shall be a thousand two hundred and ninety days. 12 Blessed is he that waiteth, and cometh to the thousand three hundred and five and thirty days. 13 But go thou thy way till the end be: for thou shalt rest, and stand in thy lot at the end of the days.

34

Christianity: Jesus According to Matthew

The related ideas first enunciated in Daniel — the coming end of the world or the Kingdom of God, the Last Judgment, individual immortality or life after death — were to become central to the branch of Judaism that produced Christianity. Along with Judaic monotheism and the insistence of the prophets (like Amos) on internalized morality, the idea of personal responsibility and eternal salvation or damnation gave Christianity an appeal that would eventually reach far beyond the children of Abraham.

Matt. 24:1–24:41 King James.

In this selection from the Gospel of Matthew, the evangelist recounts Jesus speaking of the apocalypse. There is a note of urgency here. Jesus tells his listeners that when they "see the abomination of desolation," they shall flee. Like Daniel, Jesus speaks of the signs that the end is at hand. He then tells his listeners "this generation shall not pass till all these things be fulfilled." (24:34)

In the same chapter, sometimes in the same paragraph, however, Matthew recounts Jesus telling his listeners that there is plenty of time before the end. There will be wars and rumors of wars, famines, earthquakes, false prophets. "And this gospel of the kingdom shall be preached in all the world for a witness unto all nations; and then shall the end come" (24:14).

What accounts for this apparent contradiction? If you were in the audience listening to Jesus, what idea would motivate you more — the fact that the end of the world is rapidly approaching or that it is generations away? If you were taking notes for the daily newspaper, which message would get the headline? If you were writing a history of Jesus for future generations, which message would you emphasize?

Thinking Historically

Matthew was writing about forty years after Jesus died. If he had been among those who heard Jesus speak, he took a long time to write it down. It is more likely that the author of this gospel is a generation evangelist, drawing on an earlier source, now lost. He may have had access to an earlier eyewitness account, or to a collection of sayings of Jesus. If he did have an earlier source, how would we determine what was in it?

We know that Matthew updated the words of Jesus for the benefit of those Christians living after 70 C.E. Notice, for example, Matthew's reference to Daniel in 24:15: Jesus tells his listeners that when they see the abomination of the temple of which Daniel spoke, they should flee into the mountains to prepare for the end. But we know today that Daniel was speaking of the desecration of the temple by Antiochus IV in 168 B.C.E. Matthew, unaware of the historical context of Daniel and writing after the Roman destruction of the temple in 70 C.E., believed that Roman destruction was the event Daniel was predicting. So Matthew updates the message of Jesus for future generations by including the temple desecration for the readers of his gospel ("whoso readeth understand"). This is one of the ways we know that Matthew was written after 70 C.E. Jesus would not have referred to an event which was for his audience forty years into the future, and expect his audience to understand his reference. So we know that Matthew added material that would update the message of Jesus for future generations. The question is how much did Matthew add to or alter

Jesus' message? Which parts of this selection would most likely have been updated by Matthew? Which quotations of Jesus were apt to need updating?

Matthew

Chapter 24

1 And Jesus went out, and departed from the temple: and his disciples
came to him for to show him the buildings of the temple. 2 And Jesus
said unto them, See ye not all these things? verily I say unto You,
There shall not be left here one stone upon another, that shall not be
thrown down. 3 And as he sat upon the Mount of Olives, the disciples
came unto him privately, saying, Tell us, when shall these things be?
and what shall be the sign of thy coming, and of the end of the world?
4 And Jesus answered and said unto them, Take heed that no man deceive you. 5 For many shall come in my name, saying, I am Christ;
and shall deceive many. 6 And ye shall hear of wars and rumors of
wars: see that ye be not troubled: for all these things must come to
pass, but the end is not yet. 7 For nation shall rise against nation, and
kingdom against kingdom: and there shall be famines, and pestilences,
and earthquakes, in divers places. 8 All these are the beginning of sorrows. 9 Then shall they deliver you up to be afflicted, and shall kill
you: and ye shall be hated of all nations for my name's sake. 10 And
then shall many be offended, and shall betray one another, and shall
hate one another. 11 And many false prophets shall rise, and shall deceive many. 12 And because iniquity shall abound, the love of many
shall wax cold. 13 But he that shall endure unto the end, the same
shall be saved. 14 And this gospel of the kingdom shall be preached
in all the world for a witness unto all nations; and then shall the end
come.

15 When ye therefore shall see the abomination of desolation, spoken of by Daniel the prophet, stand in the holy place (whoso readeth,
let him understand), 16 Then let them which be in Judea flee into the
mountains: 17 Let him which is on the housetop not come down to
take any thing out of his house: 18 Neither let him which is in the field
return back to take his clothes. 19 And woe unto them that are with
child, and to them that give suck in those days! 20 But pray ye that
your flight be not in the winter, neither on the sabbath day: 21 For then
shall be great tribulation, such as was not since the beginning of the
world to this time, no, nor ever shall be. 22 And except those days
should be shortened, there should no flesh be saved: but for the elect's
sake those days shall be shortened. 23 Then if any man shall say unto
you, Lo, here is Christ, or there; believe it not. 24 For there shall arise

false Christs, and false prophets, and shall show great signs and wonders; insomuch that, if it were possible, they shall deceive the very elect. 25 Behold, I have told you before. 26 Wherefore if they shall say unto you, Behold, he is in the desert; go not forth: behold he is in the secret chambers; believe it not. 27 For as the lightning cometh out of the east, and shineth even unto the west; so shall also the coming of the Son of man be. 28 For wheresoever the carcass is, there will the eagles be gathered together.

29 Immediately after the tribulation of those days shall the sun be darkened, and the moon shall not give her light, and the stars shall fall from heaven, and the powers of the heavens shall be shaken: 30 And then shall appear the sign of the Son of man in heaven: and then shall all the tribes of the earth mourn, and they shall see the Son of man coming in the clouds of heaven with power and great glory. 31 And he shall send his angels with a great sound of a trumpet, and they shall gather together his elect from the four winds, from one end of heaven to the other. 32 Now learn a parable of the fig tree; When his branch is yet tender, and putteth forth leaves, ye know that summer is nigh: 33 So likewise ye, when ye shall see all these things, know that it is near, even at the doors. 34 Verily I say unto you, This generation shall not pass, till all these things be fulfilled. 35 Heaven and earth shall pass away, but my words shall not pass away.

36 But of that day and hour knoweth no man, no, not the angels of heaven, but my Father only. 37 But as the days of Noe [Noah] were, so shall also the coming of the Son of man be. 38 For as in the days that were before the flood they were eating and drinking, marrying and giving in marriage, until the day that Noe entered into the ark, 39 And knew not until the flood came, and took them all away; so shall also the coming of the Son of man be. 40 Then shall two be in the field; the one shall be taken, and the other left. 41 Two women shall be grinding at the mill; the one shall be taken, and the other left.

REFLECTIONS

We have seen how Hinduism became Buddhism and how Judaism became Christianity, but neither Hinduism nor Judaism ended two thousand years ago. In fact, both "parental" religions underwent profound changes as well. Both became more universal, less dependent on particular places or people, and less limited to caste, region, or tribe.

We saw in the Upanishads how, around 500 B.C.E., Hinduism became almost monotheistic in its worship of Brahman. Similarly, about three hundred years later, Hindu devotional cults that centered on two of the other deities of the Hindu pantheon (Vishnu — especially in his incarnation as Krishna — and Shiva) developed. Reread the last eight stanzas of selection 17 from the Bhagavad Gita (written about 200 B.C.E.) to see how the worship of Vishnu/Krishna became enormously appealing to masses of Indian people.

At about the time of Jesus, Judaism also underwent a transformation that has continued until this day. A process that began with the destruction of the first temple and the captivity in Babylon in the sixth century B.C.E. — the development of a Judaism independent of a particular temple or place — was revived after the Romans destroyed the second temple in 70 C.E. The Roman conquest created a much greater diaspora (migration or dispersal) of Jews throughout the world than what the Babylonian conquest had spawned. Among new exiles throughout the world, Judaism became a religion of rabbis (teachers) rather than of temple priests. So great was this transformation of Judaism that one might argue, with Alan Segal in *Rebecca's Children,* that "the time of Jesus marks the birth of not one but two great religions in the West, Judaism and Christianity. . . . So great is the contrast between previous Jewish religious systems and rabbinism."[1]

And yet neither Judaism nor Hinduism became missionary religions; neither sought converts aggressively. Christianity and Buddhism did, however, and that is the subject of the next chapter.

[1] Alan F. Segal, *Rebecca's Children: Judaism and Christianity in the Roman World* (Cambridge: Harvard University Press, 1986), 1.

7

Missionaries, Monasteries, and Conversions

HISTORICAL CONTEXT

Expansion of Salvation Religions, 500 B.C.E.–600 C.E.

From their beginnings, Christianity and Buddhism were less tribal and more universal than their parental religions, Judaism and Hinduism. The messages of Jesus and Gotama emphasized personal religious experience over the dictates of caste, ancestry, and formal law. As such, their ideas *could* have appealed beyond Jews and Hindus, but even at the deaths of their founders, they did not. Both religions had to undergo further changes to loosen them from their parental ties. These changes were accomplished through the writings and work of St. Paul and the development of the doctrine of Mahayana Buddhism.

Paul almost single-handedly separated Jesus from his Jewish roots, making it possible for non-Jews to accept Jesus not as a Jewish teacher or even Messiah (king) but as the Son of God who was sacrificed for the sins of humankind. Paul's insistence that you did not have to be Jewish (in ancestry, religious observances, or dietary practices) to be Christian opened the faith (Paul's word) to the larger world. Belief in Christ as Savior was sufficient for eternal salvation.

At about the same time, Mahayana Buddhists taught of a Buddha who was more than a teacher and spiritual guide whom one could imitate or follow. They taught that the Buddha was a savior, responsive to prayer and worship. In fact, not only the Buddha but many saints, called Bodhisattvas, who had delayed their own entry into Nirvana to help others, would respond to prayer and devotion. For most ordinary people, Mahayana Buddhism was more accessible than the rigorous orthodox Buddhism that insisted on every individual becoming a monk (at least for a time) and living a life of poverty and meditation. Nevertheless, even orthodox Buddhism (called Theravada) won converts to its rigorous ways, especially in Southeast Asia, while Mahayana Buddhism swept north from India through China.

The formulation of these new faiths, by Paul and the Mahayana Buddhists, was only a first step toward the successful conversion of the Roman and Chinese Empires as well as many peoples in between. Christian and Buddhist believers and missionaries met enormous resistance in their advocacy of these universal faiths. They had to offer a faith that was open to all people and also had to convince people that they needed it. And while people in the ancient world were accustomed to including a new god when needed, they were not used to discarding the old ones, as the Christians demanded. In consequence, missionaries often found their efforts unappreciated and misunderstood. In some cases, their efforts to convert others resulted in a backlash of resentment, and they were forced to renounce their own beliefs or die for them.

In light of these difficulties, the readings in this chapter ask us to think about how it was possible for such minor religions two thousand years ago to convert millions of subjects in the Roman and Chinese Empires within the next few hundred years. Further, these countless conversions force us to consider how the two religions were similar and what was happening throughout Eurasia that explained their successes.

THINKING HISTORICALLY

Examining Sources for Opposing Views

This chapter will build on the work you have done on reading and interpreting primary sources. All of the selections in this chapter are primary sources. While they are not all written by missionaries or evangelists, each expresses a particular religious or philosophical belief, usually in opposition to another view. It is often difficult to know what view is being opposed because the authors of these selections are not motivated or able to give their opponents a fair hearing. When religions have become dominant, they have often succeeded in erasing any expression of the opposing views.

Because historians want to understand the totality of the past, not just the points of view that eventually prevailed, they have to examine the sources critically to find out what they were arguing against. This chapter suggests various strategies that will enable you to accomplish this.

35

ST. PAUL

From Letter to the Galatians

In his early years, Paul was a devout Jew, raised in the Greek- and Aramaic-speaking Jewish communities around Damascus, Syria. Offended by Jews who adopted Greek culture in place of the laws of Moses, he reserved a special distaste for the Jewish followers of Jesus and joined in the Jewish persecution of them.

As Paul told the story, one day, around the year 35 C.E., he was on the road to Damascus when he heard the voice of Jesus in the heavens ask: "Why do you persecute me?" Blinded and confused, he was taken into Damascus, where after three days of care by one of the persecuted, he regained his sight. After a period of reflection in the desert, he returned to Damascus to preach the faith he had earlier persecuted.

Around 37–38 C.E., Paul was forced to flee Damascus. He went to Jerusalem where he met Peter, the leader of the Twelve Apostles, and James, who, though not an apostle, as brother of Jesus played a dominant role in the Jerusalem group of Jewish followers of Jesus. The agent of their meeting was a Greek-speaking Jew named Barnabas, who had already been converting non-Jews to Jesus.

The group of Jewish followers of Jesus in Jerusalem continued to worship as Jews, attending the temple in Jerusalem, obeying Jewish law, following traditions, circumcising their sons, and observing dietary law. The only difference was that they believed Jesus was the Messiah, or king, and they believed that after his death and resurrection Jesus would return to rule. They also felt a special responsibility as the apostles and family of Jesus to supervise the developing Jewish sect of Jesus worshipers. That is why Paul came to them.

But they were wary of Paul's work for a number of reasons. Unlike them, Paul had not known Jesus. They believed he also misinterpreted the message of Jesus. For them, Jesus was the son of David who would return as King of the Jews, not the Son of God. Their preparation was centered at the temple in Jerusalem, supported by age-old Mosaic requirements. Jesus would return to the circumcised, those who followed Jewish law, dietary rules, and religious observances. The old Paul understood those sentiments, but the newly converted Paul believed that the crucifixion and resurrection had changed all

Gal. 1:1–2:20, 6:11–18 New English Bible.

that. For him, Jesus was the Son of God. Jesus had come to the Jews but he had come to save all of mankind.

Paul returned to his native Tarsus around 38 C.E. For the next ten years, he traveled throughout Syria and Cilicia (in what is today southern Turkey), converting Jewish synagogues to Jesus and founding new religious communities that included both Jewish and non-Jewish Christians (a word first used to refer to one of these mixed meetings in Antioch).

Around 49 C.E., the conflicting expectations of the Jewish followers of Jesus in Jerusalem and of the Greek Christian communities led by Paul and Barnabas came to a head. James sent Jewish emissaries to Antioch to challenge their practice of accepting noncircumcised, non-Jewish followers of Jesus and questioned the authority of Paul, who had converted many of their former members. To settle the matter, Paul and Barnabas traveled to Jerusalem. After discussion, they agreed that Paul could convert non-Jews while giving the apostle Peter authority over the conversion of Jews.

But Paul's letter to the Galatians suggests the agreement had broken down. Peter had come to Galatia followed by others sent by James, and the Galatians were not sure who to believe. There even seems to be some difference of opinion among those sent by James from Jerusalem.

How did Paul's letter to the Galatians meet this crisis? What is the essence of the gospel that Paul urges the Galatians to accept? What is Paul's attitude toward Mosaic Law?

Thinking Historically

Understanding the viewpoint of the Jewish followers of Jesus in Jerusalem through the writing of their antagonist is especially difficult because Paul was an effective propagandist; further, his letters have survived, and his side prevailed. If there ever were letters between James and Peter or from the Jerusalem apostles to the Galatians, they have disappeared. But how can we use the evidence we do have — Paul's letter — to better understand the attitudes of the apostles in Jerusalem?

Judging from Paul's response, what are the charges that James and the apostles might have leveled against him?

One of the problems in understanding the two sides to any controversy is that there are rarely only two sides. Not everyone on a side feels the same way, and people's views change. Often, seemingly casual phrasing in primary sources reveals much. Notice how Paul's description of his first meeting in Jerusalem (1:18–19) suggests his disappointment at not seeing the other apostles and hints at their disapproval by their absence. None of this is said, but certainly Paul

would have wanted to meet the apostles and certainly his arrival would have been important to them.

Positions also change in the spirit of compromise. Look at Paul's account of his second meeting in Jerusalem, probably in the famine year of 49 C.E. If the apostles had previously insisted that all followers of Jesus be circumcised and obey Jewish law, what compromises might have been made?

Finally, try to decipher some of the opposing and changing views in Paul's account of Peter's visit to Galatia. How did Peter's attitude toward Jewish dietary laws change in Galatia? What was the impact of the visit of James's other representatives on the attitudes of Peter and even Barnabas? Why were these such difficult issues for Peter and Barnabas?

Chapter 1

1 From Paul, an apostle, not by human appointment or human commission, but by commission from Jesus Christ and from God the Father who raised him from the dead. 2 I and the group of friends now with me send greetings to the Christian congregations of Galatia.

3 Grace and peace to you from God the Father and our Lord Jesus Christ, 4 who sacrificed himself for our sins, to rescue us out of this present age of wickedness, as our God and Father willed: 5 to whom be glory for ever and ever. Amen.

6 I am astonished to find you turning so quickly away from him who called you by grace, and following a different gospel. 7 Not that it is in fact another gospel; only there are persons who unsettle your minds by trying to distort the gospel of Christ. 8 But if anyone, if we ourselves or an angel from heaven, should preach a gospel at variance with the gospel we preached to you, he shall be held outcast. 9 I now repeat what I have said before: if anyone preaches a gospel at variance with the gospel which you received, let him be outcast!

10 Does my language now sound as if I were canvassing for men's support? Whose support do I want but God's alone? Do you think I am currying favour with men? If I still sought men's favour, I should be no servant of Christ.

11 I must make it clear to you, my friends, that the gospel you heard me preach is no human invention. 12 I did not take it over from any man; no man taught it me; I received it through a revelation of Jesus Christ.

13 You have heard what my manner of life was when I was still a practising Jew: how savagely I persecuted the church of God, and tried to destroy it; 14 and how in the practice of our national religion I was outstripping many of my Jewish contemporaries in my boundless devo-

tion to the traditions of my ancestors. 15 But then in his good pleasure God, who had set me apart from birth and called me through his grace, 16 chose to reveal his Son to me and through me, in order that I might proclaim him among the Gentiles. When that happened, without consulting any human being, 17 without going up to Jerusalem to see those who were apostles before me, I went off at once to Arabia, and afterwards returned to Damascus.

18 Three years later I did go up to Jerusalem to get to know Cephas [Peter]. I stayed with him for a fortnight, 19 without seeing any other of the apostles, except James the Lord's brother. 20 What I write is plain truth; before God I am not lying.

21 Next I went to the regions of Syria and Cilicia, 22 and remained unknown by sight to Christ's congregations in Judaea. 23 They only heard it said, "Our former persecutor is preaching the good news of the faith which once he tried to destroy"; 24 and they praised God for me.

Chapter 2

1 Next, fourteen years later, I went again to Jerusalem with Barnabas, taking Titus with us. 2 I went up because it had been revealed by God that I should do so. I laid before them — but at a private interview with the men of repute — the gospel which I am accustomed to preach to the Gentiles, to make sure that the race I had run, and was running, should not be run in vain. 3 Yet even my companion Titus, Greek though he is, was not compelled to be circumcised. 4 That course was urged only as a concession to certain sham-Christians, interlopers who had stolen in to spy upon the liberty we enjoy in the fellowship of Christ Jesus. These men wanted to bring us into bondage, 5 but not for one moment did I yield to their dictation; I was determined that the full truth of the Gospel should be maintained for you.

6 But as for the men of high reputation (not that their importance matters to me: God does not recognize these personal distinctions) — these men of repute, I say, did not prolong the consultation, 7 but on the contrary acknowledged that I had been entrusted with the Gospel for Gentiles as surely as Peter had been entrusted with the Gospel for Jews. 8 For God whose action made Peter an apostle to the Jews, also made me an apostle to the Gentiles.

9 Recognizing, then, the favour thus bestowed upon me, those reputed pillars of our society, James, Cephas, and John, accepted Barnabas and myself as partners, and shook hands upon it, agreeing that we should go to the Gentiles while they went to the Jews. 10 All they asked was that we should keep their poor in mind, which was the very thing I made it my business to do.

11 But when Cephas came to Antioch, I opposed him to his face, because he was clearly in the wrong. 12 For until certain persons came from James he was taking his meals with gentile Christians; but when they came he drew back and began to hold aloof, because he was afraid of the advocates of circumcision. 13 The other Jewish Christians showed the same lack of principle; even Barnabas was carried away and played false like the rest. 14 But when I saw that their conduct did not square with the truth of the Gospel, I said to Cephas, before the whole congregation, "If you, a Jew born and bred, live like a Gentile, and not like a Jew, how can you insist that Gentiles must live like Jews?"

15 We ourselves are Jews by birth, not Gentiles and sinners. 16 But we know that no man is ever justified by doing what the law demands, but only through faith in Christ Jesus; so we too have put our faith in Jesus Christ, in order that we might be justified through this faith, and not through deeds dictated by law; for by such deeds, Scripture says, no mortal man shall be justified.

17 If now, in seeking to be justified in Christ, we ourselves no less than the Gentiles turn out to be sinners against the law, does that mean that Christ is an abettor of sin? No, never! 18 No, if I start building up again a system which I have pulled down, then it is that I show myself up as a transgressor of the law. 19 For through the law I died to law — to live for God. 20 I have been crucified with Christ: the life I now live is not my life, but the life which Christ lives in me; and my present bodily life is lived by faith in the Son of God, who loved me and sacrificed himself for me. . . .

Chapter 6

. . . 11 "You see these big letters? I am now writing to you in my own hand. 12 It is all those who want to make a fair outward and bodily show who are trying to force circumcision upon you; their sole object is to escape persecution for the cross of Christ. 13 For even those who do receive circumcision are not thoroughgoing observers of the law: they only want you to be circumcised in order to boast of your having submitted to that outward rite. 14 But God forbid that I should boast of anything but the cross of our Lord Jesus Christ, through which the world is crucified to me and I to the world! 15 Circumcision is nothing; uncircumcision is nothing; the only thing that counts is new creation! 16 Whoever they are who take this principle for their guide, peace and mercy be upon them, and upon the whole Israel of God!

17 In future let no one make trouble for me, for I bear the marks of Jesus branded on my body.

18 The grace of our Lord Jesus Christ be with your spirit, my brothers. Amen.

36

From The Acts of the Apostles

The Acts of the Apostles in the Bible's New Testament is a history of the early Christian church. Tradition holds that the author is Luke, the Greek Gentile (non-Jewish) physician who accompanied Paul on his travels and also wrote the Gospel of Luke. (Note the author's inclusion of himself by switching to "we" in Acts 16: 11–17). However, Acts was first published about 105 C.E., making authorship by a contemporary of Paul unlikely. Further, Acts 15 gives a different account from Galatians of the conference in Jerusalem around 49 C.E. and glosses over the conflict between Paul and James. Notice the differences between these two accounts. What might account for the differences developing between the years 49 and 105 C.E.?

Regardless of when Acts was written, it provides a richly textured rendition of Paul's travels and of early Christian conversions and works, enabling us to consider how Christianity spread so effectively in the first century. From the evidence here, how was Paul successful in winning converts and aiding the growth of the new religion? Does Paul appear to be more effective with Jews or Greeks? What appears to be the role of Jewish synagogues in the development of the early church? Why did Christianity win so many converts so quickly?

Thinking Historically

Because Acts is a history rather than an evangelical letter written in the heat of some dispute, we get a more detailed and objective view of some of the groups who opposed Paul and the early Christians than we do in Galatians. Who are these various groups that spoke against Paul and the Christians, and what is the basis of their opposition? Which of these opponents would be less likely to convert to Christianity, and why?

While Acts allows us to see some of those who refused the message of Christianity, it is not immediately clear who it opposes. An exami-

---

Acts 15–20 New English Bible.

nation of the differing dates can help. In 49 C.E., Christianity was still very Jewish. Paul wanted to change that, but even he argued, negotiated, and compromised with Jerusalem. By 105 C.E., Jerusalem's Jewish community, including the Jewish Christians, has been virtually destroyed, its temple in ruins, the people dead or dispersed. The message of Christian communities throughout the Mediterranean was no longer Jewish. They had little to gain by association with the Jewish community the Romans had destroyed, and it was politically advantageous to ingratiate themselves with the Romans. Some historians of anti-Semitism have seen the beginning of Christian hatred of Jews in these conditions and in Acts. What signs of anti-Jewish feeling do you detect in this selection? Does the author give a more sympathetic treatment of non-Christian Greeks than non-Christian Jews? How does he make the Jerusalem disciples less Jewish and the opposition to Christianity more Jewish than was suggested by Paul's letter?

Chapter 15

1 Now certain persons who had come down from Judea began to teach the brotherhood that those who were not circumcised in accordance with Mosaic practice could not be saved. 2 That brought them into fierce dissension and controversy with Paul and Barnabas. And so it was arranged that these two and some others from Antioch should go up to Jerusalem to see the apostles and elders about this question.

3 They were sent on their way by the congregation, and travelled through Phoenicia and Samaria, telling the full story of the conversion of the Gentiles. The news caused great rejoicing among all the Christians there.

4 When they reached Jerusalem they were welcomed by the church and the apostles and elders, and reported all that God had helped them to do. 5 Then some of the Pharisaic party who had become believers came forward and said, "They must be circumcised and told to keep the Law of Moses."

6 The apostles and elders held a meeting to look into this matter; 7 and, after a long debate, Peter rose and addressed them. "My friends," he said, "in the early days, as you yourselves know, God made his choice among you and ordained that from my lips the Gentiles should hear and believe the message of the Gospel. 8 And God, who can read men's minds, showed his approval of them by giving the Holy Spirit to them, as he did to us. 9 He made no difference between them and us; for he purified their hearts by faith. 10 Then why do you now provoke God by laying on the shoulders of these converts a yoke which neither we nor our fathers were able to bear?" No, we believe

that it is by the grace of the Lord Jesus that we are saved, and so are
they."

12 At that the whole company fell silent and listened to Barnabas
and Paul as they told of all the signs and miracles that God had worked
among the Gentiles through them.

13 When they had finished speaking, James summed up: "My
friends," he said, "listen to me. 14 Simeon [Peter] has told how it first
happened that God took notice of the Gentiles, to choose from among
them a people to bear his name; 15 and this agrees with the words of
the prophets, as Scripture has it:

> 16 Thereafter I will return and rebuild the fallen house of David;
> Even from its ruins I will rebuild it, and set it up again,
> 17 That they may seek the Lord — all the rest of mankind,
> And the Gentiles, whom I have claimed for my own.
> 18 Thus says the Lord, whose work it is,
> Made known long ago.

19 "My judgement therefore is that we should impose no irksome
restrictions on those of the Gentiles who are turning to God, 20 but instruct them by letter to abstain from things polluted by contact with
idols, from fornication, from anything that has been strangled, and
from blood. 21 Moses, after all, has never lacked spokesmen in every
town for generations past; he is read in the synagogues Sabbath by
Sabbath."

22 Then the apostles and elders, with the agreement of the whole
church, resolved to choose representatives and send them to Antioch
with Paul and Barnabas. They chose two leading men in the community, Judas Barsabbas and Silas, 23 and gave them this letter to deliver:

"We, the apostles and elders, send greetings as brothers to our
brothers of gentile origin in Antioch, Syria, and Cilicia. 24 Forasmuch
as we have heard that some of our number, without any instructions
from us, have disturbed you with their talk and unsettled your minds,
25 we have resolved unanimously to send to you our chosen representatives with our well-beloved Barnabas and Paul, 26 who have devoted
themselves to the cause of our Lord Jesus Christ. 27 We are therefore
sending Judas and Silas, who will themselves confirm this by word of
mouth. 28 It is the decision of the Holy Spirit, and our decision, to lay
no further burden upon you beyond these essentials: 29 you are to abstain from meat that has been offered to idols, from blood, from anything that has been strangled, and from fornication. If you keep yourselves free from these things you will be doing right. Farewell."

30 So they were sent off on their journey and travelled down to Antioch, where they called the congregation together, and delivered the
letter. 31 When it was read, they all rejoiced at the encouragement it
brought. 32 Judas and Silas, who were prophets themselves, said much

to encourage and strengthen the members, 33 and, after spending some time there, were dismissed with the good wishes of the brethren, to return to those who had sent them. 35 But Paul and Barnabas stayed on at Antioch, and there, along with many others, they taught and preached the word of the Lord.

36 After a while Paul said to Barnabas, "Ought we not to go back now to see how our brothers are faring in the various towns where we proclaimed the word of the Lord?" 37 Barnabas wanted to take John Mark with them; 38 but Paul judged that the man who had deserted them in Pamphylia and had not gone on to share in their work was not the man to take with them now. 39 The dispute was so sharp that they parted company. Barnabas took Mark with him and sailed for Cyprus, 40 while Paul chose Silas. He started on his journey, commended by the brothers to the grace of the Lord, 41 and travelled through Syria and Cilicia bringing new strength to the congregations.

Chapter 16

1 He went on to Derbe and to Lystra, and there he found a disciple named Timothy, the son of a Jewish Christian mother and a Greek father. 2 He was well spoken of by the Christians at Lystra and Iconium, 3 and Paul wanted to have him in his company when he left the place. So he took him and circumcised him, out of consideration for the Jews who lived in those parts; for they all knew that his father was a Greek. 4 As they made their way from town to town they handed on the decisions taken by the apostles and elders in Jerusalem and enjoined their observance. 5 And so, day by day, the congregations grew stronger in faith and increased in numbers.

6 They travelled through the Phrygian and Galatian region, because they were prevented by the Holy Spirit from delivering the message in the province of Asia; 7 and when they approached the Mysian border they tried to enter Bithynia; but the Spirit of Jesus would not allow them, 8 so they skirted Mysia and reached the coast at Troas. 9 During the night a vision came to Paul: a Macedonian stood there appealing to him and saying, "Come across to Macedonia and help us." 10 After he had seen this vision we at once set about getting a passage to Macedonia, concluding that God had called us to bring them the good news.

11 So we sailed from Troas and made a straight run to Samothrace, the next day to Neapolis, 12 and from there to Philippi, a city of the first rank in that district of Macedonia, and a Roman colony. Here we stayed for some days, 13 and on the Sabbath day we went outside the city gate by the river-side, where we thought there would be a place of

prayer, and sat down and talked to the women who had gathered there. 14 One of them named Lydia, a dealer in purple fabric from the city of Thyatira, who was a worshipper of God, was listening, and the Lord opened her heart to respond to what Paul said. 15 She was baptized, and her household with her, and then she said to us, "If you have judged me to be a believer in the Lord, I beg you to come and stay in my house." And she insisted on our going.

"Once, when we were on our way to the place of prayer, we met a slave-girl who was possessed by an oracular spirit and brought large profits to her owners by telling fortunes. 17 She followed Paul and the rest of us, shouting, "These men are servants of the Supreme God, and are declaring to you a way of salvation." 18 She did this day after day, until Paul could bear it no longer. Rounding on the spirit he said, "I command you in the name of Jesus Christ to come out of her," and it went out there and then.

19 When the girl's owners saw that their hope of gain had gone, they seized Paul and Silas and dragged them to the city authorities in the main square; 20 and bringing them before the magistrates, they said, "These men are causing a disturbance in our city; 21 they are Jews; they are advocating customs which it is illegal for us Romans to adopt and follow." 22 The mob joined in the attack; and the magistrates tore off the prisoners' clothes and ordered them to be flogged. 23 After giving them a severe beating they flung them into prison and ordered the jailer to keep them under close guard. 24 In view of these orders, he put them in the inner prison and secured their feet in the stocks.

25 About midnight Paul and Silas, at their prayers, were singing praises to God, and the other prisoners were listening, 26 when suddenly there was such a violent earthquake that the foundations of the jail were shaken; all the doors burst open and all the prisoners found their fetters unfastened. 27 The jailer woke up to see the prison doors wide open, and assuming that the prisoners had escaped, drew his sword intending to kill himself. 28 But Paul shouted, "Do yourself no harm; we are all here." 29 The jailer called for lights, rushed in and threw himself down before Paul and Silas, trembling with fear. 30 He then escorted them out and said, "Masters, what must I do to be saved?" 31 They said, "Put your trust in the Lord Jesus, and you will be saved, you and your household." 32 Then they spoke the word of the Lord to him and to everyone in his house. 33 At that late hour of the night he took them and washed their wounds; and immediately afterwards he and his whole family were baptized. 34 He brought them into his house, set out a meal, and rejoiced with his whole household in his new-found faith in God.

35 When daylight came the magistrates sent their officers with instructions to release the men. 36 The jailer reported the message to

Paul: "The magistrates have sent word that you are to be released. So now you may go free, and blessings on your journey." 37 But Paul said to the officers: "They gave us a public flogging, though we are Roman citizens and have not been found guilty; they threw us into prison, and are they now to smuggle us out privately? No indeed! Let them come in person and escort us out." 38 The officers reported his words. The magistrates were alarmed to hear that they were Roman citizens, 39 and came and apologized to them. Then they escorted them out and requested them to go away from the city. 40 On leaving the prison, they went to Lydia's house, where they met their fellow-Christians, and spoke words of encouragement to them; then they departed.

Chapter 17

1 They now travelled by way of Amphipolis and Apollonia and came to Thessalonica, where there was a Jewish synagogue. 2 Following his usual practice Paul went to their meetings; and for the next three Sabbaths he argued with them, quoting texts of Scripture which he expounded and applied to show that the Messiah had to suffer and rise from the dead. "And this Jesus," he said, "whom I am proclaiming to you, is the Messiah." 4 Some of them were convinced and joined Paul and Silas; so did a great number of godfearing Greeks and a good many influential women.

5 But the Jews in their jealousy recruited some low fellows from the dregs of the populace, roused the rabble, and had the city in an uproar. They mobbed Jason's house, with the intention of bringing Paul and Silas before the town assembly. 6 Failing to find them, they dragged Jason himself and some members of the congregation before the magistrates, shouting, "The men who have made trouble all over the world have now come here; 7 and Jason has harboured them. They all flout the Emperor's laws, and assert that there is a rival king, Jesus." 8 These words caused a great commotion in the mob, which affected the magistrates also. 9 They bound over Jason and the others, and let them go.

10 As soon as darkness fell, the members of the congregation sent Paul and Silas off to Beroea. On arrival, they made their way to the synagogue. 11 The Jews here were more liberal-minded than those at Thessalonica: they received the message with great eagerness, studying the scriptures every day to see whether it was as they said. 12 Many of them therefore became believers, and so did a fair number of Greeks, women of standing as well as men. 13 But when the Thessalonian Jews learned that the word of God had now been proclaimed by Paul in Beroea, they came on there to stir up trouble and rouse the rabble.

14 Thereupon the members of the congregation sent Paul off at once to
go down to the coast, while Silas and Timothy both stayed behind.
15 Paul's escort brought him as far as Athens, and came away with instructions for Silas and Timothy to rejoin him with all speed.

16 Now while Paul was waiting for them at Athens he was exasper-
ated to see how the city was full of idols. 17 So he argued in the synagogue with the Jews and gentile worshippers, and also in the city
square every day with casual passers-by. 18 And some of the Epicurean
and Stoic philosophers joined issue with him. Some said, "What can
this charlatan be trying to say?"; others, "He would appear to be a
propagandist for foreign deities" — this because he was preaching
about Jesus and Resurrection. 19 So they took him and brought him
before the Court of Areopagus and said, "May we know what this new
doctrine is that you propound? 20 You are introducing ideas that
sound strange to us, and we should like to know what they mean."
21 (Now the Athenians in general and the foreigners there had no time
for anything but talking or hearing about the latest novelty.)

22 Then Paul stood up before the Court of Areopagus and said:
"Men of Athens, I see that in everything that concerns religion you are
uncommonly scrupulous. 23 For as I was going round looking at the
objects of your worship, I noticed among other things an altar bearing
the inscription 'To an Unknown God.' What you worship but do not
know — this is what I now proclaim.

24 "The God who created the world and everything in it, and who
is Lord of heaven and earth, does not live in shrines made by men. 25 It
is not because he lacks anything that he accepts service at men's hands,
for he is himself the universal giver of life and breath and all else. 26 He
created every race of men of one stock, to inhabit the whole earth's surface. He fixed the epochs of their history and the limits of their territory. 27 They were to seek God, and, it might be, touch and find him;
though indeed he is not far from each one of us, 28 for in him we live
and move, in him we exist; as some of your own poets have said, 'We
are also his offspring.' 29 As God's offspring, then, we ought not to
suppose that the deity is like an image in gold or silver or stone, shaped
by human craftsmanship and design. 30 As for the times of ignorance,
God has overlooked them; but now he commands mankind, all men
everywhere, to repent, 31 because he has fixed the day on which he will
have the world judged, and justly judged, by a man of his choosing; of
this he has given assurance to all by raising him from the dead."

32 When they heard about the raising of the dead, some scoffed;
and others said, "We will hear you on this subject some other time."
33 And so Paul left the assembly. 34 However, some men joined him
and became believers, including Dionysius, a member of the Court of
Areopagus; also a woman named Damaris, and others besides.

Chapter 18

1 After this he left Athens and went to Corinth. 2 There he fell in with
a Jew named Aquila, a native of Pontus, and his wife Priscilla; he had
recently arrived from Italy because Claudius had issued an edict that all
Jews should leave Rome. Paul approached them 3 and, because he was
of the same trade, he made his home with them, and they carried on
business together; they were tent-makers. 4 He also held discussions in
the synagogue Sabbath by Sabbath, trying to convince both Jews and
pagans.

5 Then Silas and Timothy came down from Macedonia, and Paul
devoted himself entirely to preaching, affirming before the Jews that the
Messiah was Jesus. 6 But when they opposed him and resorted to
abuse, he shook out the skirts of his cloak and said to them, "Your
blood be on your own heads! My conscience is clear; now I shall go to
the Gentiles." 7 With that he left, and went to the house of a worshipper of God named Titius Justus, who lived next door to the synagogue.
8 Crispus, who held office in the synagogue, now became a believer in
the Lord, with all his household; and a number of Corinthians listened
and believed, and were baptized. 9 One night in a vision the Lord said
to Paul, "Have no fear: go on with your preaching and do not be si-
lenced, 10 for I am with you and no one shall attempt to do you harm;
and there are many in this city who are my people." 11 So he settled
down for eighteen months, teaching the word of God among them.

37

Pliny Consults the Emperor Trajan

The inhabitants of an average city of the ancient Mediterranean worshiped dozens of gods, though usually one was thought to be a special guardian of the populace, a protector of the state, an embodiment of its territorial sovereignty. Cities of the Roman Empire added deities and cults from conquered and distant territories, creating a bewildering array. General toleration prevailed. No one cared which gods an

---

Pliny, Letters 10:96–97, from *Pliny Secundus: Letters and Panegyricus,* Loeb Classical Library, vol. II, trans. Betty Radice (Cambridge: Harvard University Press, 1959), 285, 287, 289, 291, 293.

individual worshiped. Only Rome, as the capital of the empire, might require worship of a state god, including at times, the emperor himself. But aside from this matter of loyalty to the state, one's religious convictions were one's own affair.

Christians ran afoul of the law and practice not only by refusing the demonstration of loyalty to the state but also by aggressively denying the validity of all other gods — an attitude the Romans defined as atheism, which, though not illegal, was distasteful to many.

Like the Jews, Christians were alternately persecuted and ignored. Roman oppression broke out when Nero blamed Christians for the great fire in Rome in 64 C.E. but then abated under the moderate rule of Trajan.

A brief correspondence between Pliny, serving as governor of Bithynia (in modern Turkey), and the Emperor Trajan from about the year 111 C.E. has survived, throwing light on official Roman policy toward Christians of that era. What does Pliny's letter to Trajan tell you about official Roman policy? What do you think of Trajan's answer?

Thinking Historically

Pliny is enforcing policy while at the same time personally repelled by the Christians. Try to distinguish these elements in Pliny's mind. What does he see as their legal guilt, and what does he find personally repelling? How do you explain Pliny's confusion about whether he should punish former Christians? What does Pliny know about the Christians?

Pliny mentions that some of the accused Christians admitted that they had been Christians but were no longer. Do you think some Christians left the religion under Roman pressure or persecution, or do you think they just said they had?

Pliny to the Emperor Trajan

It is my custom to refer all my difficulties to you, Sir, for no one is better able to resolve my doubts and to inform my ignorance.

I have never been present at an examination of Christians. Consequently, I do not know the nature or the extent of the punishments usually meted out to them, nor the grounds for starting an investigation and how far it should be pressed. Nor am I at all sure whether any distinction should be made between them on the grounds of age, or if young people and adults should be treated alike; whether a pardon ought to be granted to anyone retracting his beliefs, or if he has once professed Christianity, he shall gain nothing by renouncing it; and whether it is the mere name of Christian which is punishable, even if innocent of crime, or rather the crimes associated with the name.

For the moment this is the line I have taken with all persons brought before me on the charge of being Christians. I have asked them in person if they are Christians, and if they admit it, I repeat the question a second and third time, with a warning of the punishment awaiting them. If they persist, I order them to be led away for execution; for, whatever the nature of their admission, I am convinced that their stubbornness and unshakeable obstinacy ought not to go unpunished. There have been others similarly fanatical who are Roman citizens. I have entered them on the list of persons to be sent to Rome for trial.

Now that I have begun to deal with this problem, as so often happens, the charges are becoming more widespread and increasing in variety. An anonymous pamphlet has been circulated which contains the names of a number of accused persons. Among these I considered that I should dismiss any who denied that they were or ever had been Christians when they had repeated after me a formula of invocation to the gods and had made offerings of wine and incense to your statue (which I had ordered to be brought into court for this purpose along with the images of the gods), and furthermore had reviled the name of Christ: none of which things, I understand, any genuine Christian can be induced to do.

Others, whose names were given to me by an informer, first admitted the charge and then denied it; they said that they had ceased to be Christians two or more years previously, and some of them even twenty years ago. They all did reverence to your statue and the images of the gods in the same way as the others, and reviled the name of Christ. They also declared that the sum total of their guilt or error amounted to no more than this: they had met regularly before dawn on a fixed day to chant verses alternately among themselves in honour of Christ as if to a god, and also to bind themselves by oath, not for any criminal purpose, but to abstain from theft, robbery and adultery, to commit no breach of trust and not to deny a deposit when called upon to restore it. After this ceremony it had been their custom to disperse and reassemble later to take food of an ordinary, harmless kind; but they had in fact given up this practice since my edict, issued on your instructions, which banned all political societies. This made me decide it was all the more necessary to extract the truth by torture from two slave-women, whom they call deaconesses. I found nothing but a degenerate sort of cult carried to extravagant lengths.

I have therefore postponed any further examination and hastened to consult you. The question seems to me to be worthy of your consideration, especially in view of the number of persons endangered; for a great many individuals of every age and class, both men and women, are being brought to trial, and this is likely to continue. It is not only the towns, but villages and rural districts too which are infected through contact with this wretched cult. I think though that it is still possible for it to be checked and directed to better ends, for there is no doubt that people have begun to throng the temples which had been almost entirely deserted for a long time; the sacred rites which had been allowed to lapse are being performed again, and flesh of sacrificial victims is on sale everywhere, though up till recently scarcely anyone could be found to buy it. It is easy to infer from this that a great many people could be reformed if they were given an opportunity to repent.

Trajan to Pliny

You have followed the right course of procedure, my dear Pliny, in your examination of the cases of persons charged with being Christians, for it is impossible to lay down a general rule to a fixed formula. These people must not be hunted out; if they are brought before you and the charge against them is proved, they must be punished, but in the case of anyone who denies that he is a Christian, and makes it clear that he is not by offering prayers to our gods, he is to be pardoned as a result of his repentance however suspect his past conduct may be. But pamphlets circulated anonymously must play no part in any accusation. They create the worst sort of precedent and are quite out of keeping with the spirit of our age.

38

EUSEBIUS

From *The Life of Constantine*

If Christianity were persecuted by Roman officials and emperors, and if Christians were despised by the thoughtful and powerful elite of Roman society, how then did Christianity ever succeed? As the historian Ramsay MacMullen put it: "How did it ever happen that the church could grow at such a rate, so as actually to predominate in occasional little towns or districts by the turn of the second century

---

The Library of Nicene and Post-Nicene Fathers, ed. P. Schaff and H. Wace, vol. I, *Church History, Life of Constantine, Oration in Praise of Constantine,* (New York: The Christian Literature Company, 1890), 489–91.

[100 C.E.] and, by the turn of the fourth [300 C.E.], to have attained a population of, let us say, five million [in an empire of about 60 million]?"[1]

Part of the answer lies in the location of these Christians. They were more concentrated in urban than rural areas (the Latin word *pagan* meant "rural" before it meant "unchristian") and managed to gain significant advocates among the powerful elite.

No more powerful spokesman could be found than a Roman emperor, and so a short answer to the question of how Christianity succeeded must be "the Emperor Constantine" (288–337 C.E.). The emperor's historian Eusebius (260–339 C.E.) recognized both the importance of the emperor and the role of the empire in the success of Christianity in winning the Roman Empire:

> At the same time one universal power, the Roman Empire arose and flourished, while the enduring and implacable hatred of nation against nation was now removed; and as the knowledge of one god and one way of religion and salvation, even the doctrine of Christ, was made known to all mankind; so at the same time the entire dominion of the Roman Empire being invested in a single sovereign, profound peace reigned throughout the world. And thus, by the express appointment of the same God, two roots of blessing, the Roman Empire and the doctrine of Christian piety, sprang up together for the benefit of men.[2]

Eusebius wanted to believe that the victory of Christianity was implicit from the beginning of the Roman Empire. In his *History of the Church,* for instance, he says that at the time of the trial of Jesus, Pontius Pilate convinced the Emperor Tiberius to deify Jesus, but the Roman Senate prevented it. Further, Eusebius argues that Roman persecution of Christians was rare rather than frequent: Nero and Domitian the exceptions, Trajan more the rule.

Eusebius may have been more accurate in the broad sense. Universal religion and universal empire did go together, but the empire and Christianity were three hundred years old before the union occurred.

In his *Life of Constantine,* Eusebius, who knew the emperor, tells a story that must have circulated at the time to explain Constantine's support of Christianity (granting toleration to Christians and restoring Church lands as well as personal declarations of faith).

What do you think of Eusebius's explanation for Constantine's acceptance of Christianity? What does Constantine's reasoning say about how people of his day chose their religious beliefs and loyalties?

[1] Ramsay MacMullen, *Christianizing the Roman Empire,* A.D. 100–400 (New Haven: Yale University Press, 1984), 32. [Ed.]

[2] Eusebius, *Oration in Praise of Constantine,* xv, 4. [Ed.]

How would the conversion of the emperor encourage others to become Christians? What, if anything, might have slowed the advance of Christianity after 312 C.E.?

Thinking Historically

This story helps us to understand what Romans and Christians knew of each other in 312 C.E. Specifically, what did Constantine seem to know about Christianity before he converted? How might you expect his conversion to change his behavior?

Being convinced, however, that he needed some more powerful aid than his military forces could afford him,[3] on account of the wicked and magical enchantments which were so diligently practiced by the tyrant [Maxentius], he sought Divine assistance, deeming the possession of arms and a numerous soldiery of secondary importance, but believing the cooperating power of Deity invincible and not to be shaken. He considered, therefore, on what God he might rely for protection and assistance. While engaged in this enquiry, the thought occurred to him, that, of the many emperors who had preceded him, those who had rested their hopes in a multitude of gods, and served them with sacrifices and offerings, had in the first place been deceived by flattering predictions, and oracles which promised them all prosperity, and at last had met with an unhappy end, while not one of their gods had stood by to warn them of the impending wrath of heaven; while one alone who had pursued an entirely opposite course, who had condemned their error, and honored the Supreme God during his whole life, had found him to be the Saviour and Protector of his empire, and the Giver of every good thing. Reflecting on this, and well weighing the fact that they who had trusted in many gods had also fallen by manifold forms of death, without leaving behind them either family or offspring, stock, name, or memorial among men: while the God of his father had given to him, on the other hand, manifestations of his power and very many tokens: and considering farther that those who had already taken arms against the tyrant, and had marched to the battle-field under the protection of a multitude of gods, had met with a dishonorable end (for one of them had shamefully retreated from the contest without a blow, and the other, being slain in the midst of his own troops, became, as it were, the mere sport of death); reviewing, I say, all these considerations, he judged it to be folly indeed to join in the idle worship of those

[3] In 312 C.E., Constantine, who ruled Gaul and Britain, was about to invade Italy and try to gain the throne of the western empire by defeating Maxentius, who ruled Rome.

who were no gods, and after such convincing evidence, to err from the truth; and therefore felt it incumbent on him to honor his father's God alone.

Accordingly he called on Him with earnest prayer and supplications that he would reveal to him who He was, and stretch forth His right hand to help him in his present difficulties. And while he was thus praying with fervent entreaty, a most marvelous sign appeared to him from heaven, the account of which it might have been hard to believe had it been related by any other person. But since the victorious emperor himself long afterwards declared it to the writer of this history, when he was honored with his acquaintance and society, and confirmed his statement by an oath, who could hesitate to accredit the relation, especially since the testimony of after-time has established its truth? He said that about noon, when the day was already beginning to decline, he saw with his own eyes the trophy of a cross of light in the heavens, above the sun, and bearing the inscription, CONQUER BY THIS. At this sight he himself was struck with amazement, and his whole army also, which followed him on this expedition, and witnessed the miracle.

He said, moreover, that he doubted within himself what the import of this apparition could be. And while he continued to ponder and reason on its meaning, night suddenly came on; then in his sleep the Christ of God appeared to him with the same sign which he had seen in the heavens, and commanded him to make a likeness of that sign which he had seen in the heavens, and to use it as a safeguard in all engagements with his enemies.

At the dawn of day he arose, and communicated the marvel to his friends: and then, calling together the workers in gold and precious stones, he sat in the midst of them, and described to them the figure of the sign he had seen, bidding them represent it in gold and precious stones. And this representation I myself have had an opportunity of seeing.

Now it was made in the following manner. A long spear, overlaid with gold, formed the figure of the cross by means of a transverse bar laid over it. On the top of the whole was fixed a wreath of gold and precious stones; and within this, the symbol of the Saviour's name, two letters indicating the name of Christ by means of its initial characters, the letter *P* being intersected by *X* in its centre; and these letters the emperor was in the habit of wearing on his helmet at a later period. From the cross-bar of the spear was suspended a cloth, a royal piece, covered with a profuse embroidery of most brilliant precious stones; and which, being also richly interlaced with gold, presented an indescribable degree of beauty to the beholder. This banner was of a square form, and the upright staff, whose lower section was of great length, bore a golden half-length portrait of the pious emperor and his children on its upper part, beneath the trophy of the cross, and immediately above the embroidered banner.

The emperor constantly made use of this sign of salvation as a safeguard against every adverse and hostile power, and commanded that others similar to it should be carried at the head of all his armies.

These things were done shortly afterwards. But at the time above specified, being struck with amazement at the extraordinary vision, and resolving to worship no other God save Him who had appeared to him, he sent for those who were acquainted with the mysteries of His doctrines, and enquired who that God was, and what was intended by the sign of the vision he had seen.

They affirmed that He was God, the only begotten Son of the one and only God: that the sign which had appeared was the symbol of immortality, and the trophy of that victory over death which He had gained in time past when sojourning on earth. They taught him also the causes of His advent, and explained to him the true account of His incarnation. Thus he was instructed in these matters, and was impressed with wonder at the divine manifestation which had been presented to his sight. Comparing, therefore, the heavenly vision with the interpretation given, he found his judgment confirmed; and, in the persuasion that the knowledge of these things had been imparted to him by Divine teaching, he determined thenceforth to devote himself to the reading of the inspired writings.

39

Mahayana Buddhism

Salvation Buddhism developed more gradually than Pauline Christianity, and it took longer to sweep across China than Christianity took to convert Rome, but the effect was much the same.

The Buddha died five hundred years before Jesus. In the centuries after his death, Buddhist monks established monasteries, hospitals, and schools throughout India and Southeast Asia. These *Theravada,*

Aṣṭasāhasrikā Prajñāpāramitā, 22.402–3 and Pañcaviṃśatisāhasrikā Prajñāpāramitā, in *The Buddhist Tradition in India, China and Japan*, ed. William Theodore de Bary (New York: Random House, 1969), 40–41, 81–82.

or orthodox Buddhists, lived very much as the Buddha had. They believed the Buddha had been a wise guide — a model to follow in achieving Nirvana and passing on to eternal peace — but he was not a god (any more than everyone was).

Around the first and second centuries C.E., a new form of Buddhism developed in India that its adherents called *Mahayana* ("the Greater Vehicle") because it attracted more devotees than did Theravada orthodoxy, which the Mahayana Buddhists disparagingly called *Hinayana* ("the Lesser Vehicle"). What made Mahayana a more popular religion was its conception of the Buddha as a god who could be worshiped, who would answer prayers and offer salvation.

In the first centuries following Buddha's death, there were no statues or images of him. Instead, he was represented by a footprint or the empty throne of his father's palace. In the first century C.E., statues of the Buddha began to appear, and he became the object of worship in temples.

With the elevation of the Buddha to a god came a whole cast of saints — Bodhisattvas who achieved such holiness and love that they delayed their entry to Nirvana in order to help the rest of humanity in its quest.

The first of the following two passages from Mahayana texts describes the compassion of a Bodhisattva in saving all. The second compares the resolve of a Bodhisattva with the selfishness of Theravada "private buddhas" who achieve full enlightenment themselves but do not share their knowledge with others. Why would Mahayana Buddhism be a "greater vehicle" than Theravada Buddhism? Would Mahayana doctrines appeal more to you? Do you think they would appeal more to most people?

Thinking Historically

Both of these passages are written from the Mahayana point of view. Inevitably, this means that even the vocabulary suits the Mahayana position (for example, the use of *Hinayana* versus *Theravada*). What evidence do you see in these passages of a Mahayana monopoly of the good words? How might a Theravada Buddhist react to these passages? What do you think the Buddha would say?

I

The bodhisattva is endowed with wisdom of a kind whereby he looks on all beings as though victims going to the slaughter. And immense compassion grips him. His divine eye sees . . . innumerable beings, and he is filled with great distress at what he sees, for many bear the burden of past deeds which will be punished in purgatory, others will have unfortunate rebirths which will divide them from the Buddha and his teachings, others must soon be slain, others are caught in the net of false doctrine, others cannot find the path [of salvation], while others have gained a favorable rebirth only to lose it again.

So he pours out his love and compassion upon all those beings, and attends to them, thinking, "I shall become the savior of all beings, and set them free from their sufferings."

II

"What do you think, Shāriputra? Do any of the disciples and private buddhas ever think, 'After we have gained full enlightenment we will bring innumerable beings . . . to complete Nirvāna'?"

"Certainly not, Lord!"

"But," said the Lord, "the bodhisattva [has this resolve]. . . . A firefly . . . doesn't imagine that its glow will light up all India or shine all over it, and so the disciples and private buddhas don't think that they should lead all beings to Nirvāna . . . after they have gained full enlightenment. But the disc of the sun, when it has risen, lights up all India and shines all over it. Similarly the bodhisattva . . . when he has gained full enlightenment, brings countless beings to Nirvāna.

40

CONFUCIUS

From *The Analects*

Confucianism was the dominant philosophy, if not religion, that Indian Buddhist monks had to reckon with when trying to convert the Chinese. Confucianism was a much more formidable force in China than was paganism in Rome, if only because it was a single belief (rather than competing cults), and its principles were widely shared across China.

The Analects of Confucius, trans. Arthur Waley (London: George Allen & Unwin, 1958), 84, 88–89, 91–92, 94–96, 102–03, 105, 110, 121, 123, 126–27, 130–34, 141, 147–48, 155, 162, 166–68, 173–74, 190–91, 197–98, 200.

Confucius (c. 551–479 B.C.E.) was roughly a contemporary of the Buddha. As with the Buddha, the ideas that are called Confucian were gathered after Confucius's death by his followers. Nevertheless, they remained fairly constant throughout Chinese history, so we can reasonably assume that the followers of the Buddha would have faced ideas very much like these.

How would you characterize the Confucian tradition? Would you call it religious? Conservative? Democratic? Innovative? Explain your choice or choices.

Thinking Historically

One way to characterize a religious or cultural tradition is to ask yourself what they are *not* saying or to try to imagine who might disagree, and why. This exercise is useful because statements of principles like these often come across as so high-minded that we can only agree. But step back, after reading these statements, and try to determine what is not said, who might disagree, or what might bother at least some Chinese who heard these pronouncements two thousand years ago.

On Education

II,15 The Master said, "'He who learns but does not think, is lost.' He who thinks but does not learn is in great danger."

II,17 The Master said, "Yu, shall I teach you what knowledge is? When you know a thing, to recognize that you know it, and when you do not know a thing, to recognize that you do not know it. That is knowledge."

VII,1 The Master said, "I have 'transmitted what was taught to me without making up anything of my own.' I have been faithful to and loved the Ancients. In these respects, I make bold to think, not even our old P'eng can have excelled me."

VII,2 The Master said, "I have listened in silence and noted what was said. I have never grown tired of learning nor wearied of teaching others what I have learnt. These at least are merits which I can confidently claim."

XIII,9 When the Master was going to Wei, Jan Ch'iu drove him. The Master said, "What a dense population!" Jan Ch'iu said, "When the people have multiplied, what next should be done for them?" The Master said, "Enrich them." Jan Ch'iu said, "When one has enriched them, what next should be done for them?" The Master said, "Instruct them."

XV,35 The Master said, "When it comes to Goodness one need not avoid competing with one's teacher."

On Goodness

I,3 The Master said, "'Clever talk and a pretentious manner' are seldom found in the Good."

I,6 The Master said, "A young man's duty is to behave well to his parents at home and to his elders abroad, to be cautious in giving promises and punctual in keeping them, to have kindly feelings towards everyone, but seek the intimacy of the Good. If, when all that is done, he has any energy to spare, then let him study the polite arts."

IV,3,4 Of the adage, "Only a Good Man knows how to like people, knows how to dislike them," the Master said, "He whose heart is in the smallest degree set upon Goodness will dislike no one."

VII,15 The Master said, "He who seeks only coarse food to eat, water to drink and bent arm for pillow, will without looking for it find happiness to boot. Any thought of accepting wealth and rank by means that I know to be wrong is as remote from me as the clouds that float above."

XII,2 Jan Yung asked about Goodness. The Master said, "Behave when away from home as though you were in the presence of an important guest. Deal with the common people as though you were officiating at an important sacrifice. Do not do to others what you would not like yourself. Then there will be no feelings of opposition to you, whether it is the affairs of a State that you are handling or the affairs of a Family."

XV,23 Tzu-kung asked saying, "Is there any single saying that one can act upon all day and every day?" The Master said, "Perhaps the saying about consideration: 'Never do to others what you would not like them to do to you.'"

On the Gentleman

II,13 Tzu-kung asked about the true gentleman. The Master said, "He does not preach what he practices till he has practiced what he preaches."

III,7 The Master said, "Gentlemen never compete. You will say that in archery they do so. But even then they bow and make way for one another when they are going up the archery-ground, when they are coming down and at the subsequent drinking bout. Thus even when competing, they still remain gentlemen."

IV,5 "Wealth and rank are what every man desires; but if they can only be retained to the detriment of the Way he professes, he must relinquish them. Poverty and obscurity are what every man detests; but if they can only be avoided to the detriment of the Way he professes, he must accept them. The gentleman who ever parts company with Goodness does not fulfill that name. Never for a moment does a gentleman quit the way of Goodness. He is never so harried but that he cleaves to this; never so tottering but that he cleaves to this."

IV,16 The Master said, "A gentleman takes as much trouble to discover what is right as lesser men take to discover what will pay."

VI,25 The Master said, "A gentleman who is widely versed in letters and at the same time knows how to submit his learning to the restraints of ritual is not likely, I think, to go far wrong."

VIII,2 . . . The Master said, "When gentlemen deal generously with their own kin, the common people are incited to Goodness. When old dependents are not discarded, the common people will not be fickle."

IX,13 The Master wanted to settle among the Nine Wild Tribes of the East. Someone said, "I am afraid you would find it hard to put up with their lack of refinement." The Master said, "Were a true gentleman to settle among them there would soon be no trouble about lack of refinement."

XII,16 The Master said, "The gentleman calls attention to the good points in others; he does not call attention to their defects. The small man does just the reverse of this."

XV,18 The Master said, "A gentleman is distressed by his own lack of capacity; he is never distressed at the failure of others to recognize his merits."

XV,20 The Master said, "'The demands that a gentleman makes are upon himself; those that a small man makes are upon others.'"

XV,21 The Master said, "A gentleman is proud, but not quarrelsome, allies himself with individuals, but not with parties."

X,6 A gentleman does not wear facings of purple or mauve, nor in undress does he use pink or roan. In hot weather he wears an unlined gown of fine thread loosely woven, but puts on an outside garment before going out-of-doors. With a black robe he wears black lambskin; with a robe of undyed silk, fawn. With a yellow robe, fox fur. On his undress robe the fur cuffs are long; but the right is shorter than the left. His bedclothes must be half as long again as a man's height. The thicker kinds of fox and badger are for home wear. Except when in mourning, he wears all his girdle-ornaments. Apart from his Court apron, all his skirts are wider at the bottom than at the waist. Lambskin dyed black and a hat of dark-dyed silk must not be worn when making visits of condolence. At the Announcement of the New Moon he must go to Court in full Court dress.

On Filial Piety

II,5 Meng I Tzu asked about the treatment of parents. The Master said, "Never disobey!" When Fan Ch'ih was driving his carriage for him, the

Master said, "Meng asked me about the treatment of parents and I said, 'Never disobey!'" Fan Ch'ih said, "In what sense did you mean it?" The Master said, "While they are alive, serve them according to ritual. When they die, bury them according to ritual and sacrifice to them according to ritual."

II,7 Tzu-yu asked about the treatment of parents. The Master said, "'Filial sons' nowadays are people who see to it that their parents get enough to eat. But even dogs and horses are cared for to that extent. If there is no feeling of respect, wherein lies the difference?"

On Ritual and Music

III,3 The Master said, "A man who is not Good, what can he have to do with ritual? A man who is not Good, what can he have to do with music?"

III,4 Lin Fang asked for some main principles in connexion with ritual. The Master said, "A very big question. In ritual at large it is a safe rule always to be too sparing rather than too lavish; and in the particular case of mourning-rites, they should be dictated by grief rather than by fear."

VIII,2 The Master said, "Courtesy not bounded by the prescriptions of ritual becomes tiresome. Caution not bounded by the prescriptions of ritual becomes timidity, daring becomes turbulence, inflexibility becomes harshness."

VIII,8 The Master said, "Let a man be first incited by the *Songs,* then given a firm footing by the study of ritual, and finally perfected by music."

On Government by Moral Force

I,5 The Master said, "A country of a thousand war-chariots cannot be administered unless the ruler attends strictly to business, punctually observes his promises, is economical in expenditure, shows affection toward his subjects in general, and uses the labour of the peasantry only at the proper times of year."

II,3 The Master said, "Govern the people by regulations, keep order among them by chastisements, and they will flee from you, and lose all self-respect. Govern them by moral force, keep order among them by ritual and they will keep their self-respect and come to you of their own accord."

XII,11 Duke Ching of Ch'i asked Master K'ung about government, Master K'ung replied saying, "Let the prince be a prince, the minister a minister, the father a father and the son a son." The Duke said, "How true! For indeed when the prince is not a prince, the minister not a minister, the father not a father, the son not a son, one may have a dish of millet in front of one and yet not know if one will live to eat it."

XII,19 Chi L'ang-tzu asked Master K'ung about government, saying, "Suppose I were to slay those who have not the Way in order to help on those who have the Way, what would you think of it?" Master K'ung replied saying, "You are there to rule, not to slay. If you desire what is good, the people will at once be good. The essence of the gentleman is that of wind; the essence of small people is that of grass. And when a wind passes over the grass, it cannot choose but bend."

XIII,6 The Master said, "If the ruler himself is upright, all will go well even though he does not give orders. But if he himself is not upright, even though he gives orders, they will not be obeyed."

XIII,10 The Master said, "If only someone were to make use of me, even for a single year, I could do a great deal; and in three years I could finish off the whole work."

XIII,11 The Master said, "'Only if the right sort of people had charge of a country for a hundred years would it become really possible to stop cruelty and do away with slaughter.' How true the saying is!"

On Public Opinion

II,19 Duke Ai asked, "What can I do in order to get the support of the common people?" Master K'ung replied, "If you 'raise up the straight and set them on top of the crooked,' the commoners will support you. But if you raise the crooked and set them on top of the straight, the commoners will not support you."

II,20 Chi L'ang-tzu asked whether there were any form of encouragement by which he could induce the common people to be respectful and loyal. The Master said, "Approach them with dignity, and they will respect you. Show piety towards your parents and kindness toward your children, and they will be loyal to you. Promote those who are worthy, train those who are incompetent; that is the best form of encouragement."

XII,7 Tzu-kung asked about government. The Master said, "Sufficient food, sufficient weapons, and the confidence of the common people." Tzu-kung said, "Suppose you had no choice but to dispense with one of these three, which would you forgo?" The Master said, "Weapons." Tzu-kung said, "Suppose you were forced to dispense with one of the two that were left, which would you forgo?" The Master said, "Food. For from of old death has been the lot of all men; but a people that no longer trusts its rulers is lost indeed."

On Religion

III,11 Someone asked for an explanation of the Ancestral Sacrifice. The Master said, "I do not know. Anyone who knew the explanation could deal with all things under Heaven as easily as I lay this here"; and he laid his finger upon the palm of his hand.

V,12 Tzu-kung said, "Our Master's views concerning culture and the outward insignia of goodness, we are permitted to hear; but about Man's nature and the ways of Heaven he will not tell us anything at all."

VII,20 The Master never talked of prodigies, feats of strength, disorders or spirits.

VII,34 When the Master was very ill, Tzu-lu asked leave to perform the Rite of Expiation. The Master said, "Is there such a thing?" Tzu-lu answered saying, "There is. In one of the Dirges it says, 'We performed rites of expiation for you, calling upon the sky-spirits above and the earth-spirits below.'" The Master said, "My expiation began long ago!"

XI,11 Tzu-lu asked how one should serve ghosts and spirits. The Master said, "Till you have learnt to serve men, how can you serve ghosts?" Tzu-lu then ventured upon a question about the dead. The Master said, "Till you know about the living, how are you to know about the dead?"

41

LAO TZU

From the *Tao Te Ching*

When Indian missionaries brought Buddhism to China, they initially met strong resistance from Confucianism. Selection 43 will reveal some of the points of disagreement between Buddhism and Confucianism.

Eventually the Buddhists were successful by using the language of a very different Chinese philosophical tradition, Taoism. Lao Tzu

---

The Way and Its Power: A Study of the Tao Te Ching, trans. Arthur Waley (London: George Allen & Unwin, 1934), 141, 143, 145–46, 151–52, 155–56, 165–66.

may or may not have been an actual contemporary of Confucius, but the *Tao Te Ching* was written around the sixth century B.C.E. and Taoism remained an alternative vision to the dominant Confucianism. In what ways are the ideas expressed in the *Tao Te Ching* different from those of Confucianism? Might a person easily follow both Confucianism and Taoism, or would these philosophies appeal to different people? Compared to Confucianism, are the Taoist ideas more "religious"? Which set of ideas do you find more appealing? Why?

Thinking Historically

What would a Confucian say about the ideas expressed here?

> There was an important Mahayana Buddhist philosopher named Nargajuna in the first to second centuries C.E. who took the Buddhist position against striving or desire to a new level. Nargajuna believed that our everyday experiences were mere illusion. We are, he said, like the Buddhist monk who looks into his rice bowl and thinks he sees flies, when there are none. We see things that don't exist. In fact, nothing exists. The world is empty. We merely fill it up with our own perceptions. If we were able to get beyond our reliance on our ever-changing perceptions, we would recognize that only emptiness exists, only emptiness is real.

If you were a follower of Nargajuna, what would you think of Taoism?

Chapter I

The Way is like an empty vessel
That yet may be drawn from
Without ever needing to be filled.
It is bottomless; the very progenitor of all things in the world.
In it all sharpness is blunted,
All tangles untied,
All glare tempered,
All dust smoothed.
It is like a deep pool that never dries.
Was it too the child of something else? We cannot tell.
But as a substanceless image it existed before the Ancestor.

Chapter II

Stretch a bow to the very full,
And you will wish you had stopped in time;
Temper a sword-edge to its very sharpest,
And you will find it soon grows dull.
When bronze and jade fill your hall
It can no longer be guarded.
Wealth and place breed insolence
That brings ruin in its train.
When your work is done, then withdraw!
Such is Heaven's Way.

Chapter III

We put thirty spokes together and call it a wheel;
But it is on the space where there is nothing that the utility of the wheel depends.
We turn clay to make a vessel;
But it is on the space where there is nothing that the utility of the vessel depends.
We pierce doors and windows to make a house;
And it is on these spaces where there is nothing that the utility of the house depends.
Therefore just as we take advantage of what is, we should recognize the utility of what is not.

Chapter IV

Banish wisdom, discard knowledge,
And the people will be benefited a hundredfold.
Banish human kindness, discard morality,
And the people will be dutiful and compassionate.
Banish skill, discard profit,
And thieves and robbers will disappear.

42

Buddhism in China: From *The Disposition of Error*

The Disposition of Error **is a Buddhist guide for converting the Chinese. While the author and date are uncertain, this kind of tract was common under the Southern Dynasties (420–589 C.E.). The author uses a frequently asked questions (FAQ) format that enables us to see what the Chinese — mainly Confucian — objections were to Buddhism, as well as what they considered good Buddhist answers.**

What were the main Chinese objections to Buddhism? Why were Buddhist ideas of death such a stumbling block for Chinese Confucians? Were Confucian ideas about care of the body and hair only superficial concerns, or did they reflect basic differences between Confucianism and Buddhism?

Thinking Historically

How does Mou Tzu, the Buddhist monk, answer Confucian objections with quotes from the Confucian classics? How does he use the ideas of Lao Tzu or Taoism to answer the objections? Would this be a good guide to answering the objections of Chinese Taoists?

Why Is Buddhism Not Mentioned in the Chinese Classics?

The questioner said: If the way of the Buddha is the greatest and most venerable of ways, why did Yao, Shun, the Duke of Chou, and Confucius not practice it? In the seven Classics one sees no mention of it. You, sir, are fond of the *Book of Odes* and the *Book of History,* and you take pleasure in rites and music. Why, then, do you love the way of the Buddha and rejoice in outlandish arts? Can they exceed the Classics and commentaries and beautify the accomplishments of the sages? Permit me the liberty, sir, of advising you to reject them.

Mou Tzu said: All written works need not necessarily be the words of Confucius, and all medicine does not necessarily consist of the formulae of [the famous physician] P'ien-ch'üeh. What accords

---

Hung-ming chi, in Taishō daizōkyō, LII, 1–7, quoted in William Theodore de Bary, ed., *The Buddhist Tradition in India, China and Japan* (New York: Random House, 1969), 132–37.

with principle is to be followed, what heals the sick is good. The gentleman-scholar draws widely on all forms of good, and thereby benefits his character. Tzu-kung [a disciple of Confucius] said, "Did the Master have a permanent teacher?" Yao served Yin Shou, Shun served Wu-ch'eng, the Duke of Chou learned from Lü Wang, and Confucius learned from Lao Tzu. And none of these teachers is mentioned in the seven Classics. Although these four teachers were sages, to compare them to the Buddha would be like comparing a white deer to a unicorn, or a swallow to a phoenix. Yao, Shun, the Duke of Chou, and Confucius learned even from such teachers as these. How much less, then, may one reject the Buddha, whose distinguishing marks are extraordinary and whose superhuman powers know no bounds! How may one reject him and refuse to learn from him? The records and teachings of the Five Classics do not contain everything. Even if the Buddha is not mentioned in them, what occasion is there for suspicion?

Why Do Buddhist Monks Do Injury to Their Bodies?

The questioner said: The *Classic of Filial Piety* says, "Our torso, limbs, hair, and skin we receive from our fathers and mothers. We dare not do them injury." When Tseng Tzu was about to die, he bared his hands and feet.[1] But now the monks shave their heads. How this violates the sayings of the sages and is out of keeping with the way of the filially pious! . . .

Mou Tzu said: . . . Confucius has said, "He with whom one may follow a course is not necessarily he with whom one may weigh its merits." This is what is meant by doing what is best at the time. Furthermore, the *Classic of Filial Piety* says, "The kings of yore possessed the ultimate virtue and the essential Way." T'ai-po cut his hair short and tattooed his body, thus following of his own accord the customs of Wu and Yüeh and going against the spirit of the "torso, limbs, hair, and skin" passage.[2] And yet Confucius praised him, saying that his might well be called the ultimate virtue.

[1] To show he had preserved them intact from all harm.

[2] Uncle of King Wen of the Chou who retired to the barbarian land of Wu and cut his hair and tattooed his body in barbarian fashion, thus yielding his claim to the throne to King Wen.

Why Do Monks Not Marry?

The questioner said: Now of felicities there is none greater than the continuation of one's line, of unfilial conduct there is none worse than childlessness. The monks forsake wife and children, reject property and wealth. Some do not marry all their lives. How opposed this conduct is to felicity and filial piety! . . .

Mou Tzu said: . . . Wives, children, and property are the luxuries of the world, but simple living and inaction are the wonders of the Way. Lao Tzu has said, "Of reputation and life, which is dearer? Of life and property, which is worth more?" . . . Hsü Yu and Ch'ao-fu dwelt in a tree. Po I and Shu Ch'i starved in Shou-yang, but Confucius praised their worth, saying, "They sought to act in accordance with humanity and they succeeded in acting so." One does not hear of their being ill-spoken of because they were childless and propertyless. The monk practices the Way and substitutes that for the pleasures of disporting himself in the world. He accumulates goodness and wisdom in exchange for the joys of wife and children.

Death and Rebirth

The questioner said: The Buddhists say that after a man dies he will be reborn. I do not believe in the truth of these words. . . .

Mou Tzu said: . . . The spirit never perishes. Only the body decays. The body is like the roots and leaves of the five grains, the spirit is like the seeds and kernels of the five grains. When the roots and leaves come forth they inevitably die. But do the seeds and kernels perish? Only the body of one who has achieved the Way perishes. . . .

Someone said: If one follows the Way one dies. If one does not follow the Way one dies. What difference is there?

Mou Tzu said: You are the sort of person who, having not a single day of goodness, yet seeks a lifetime of fame. If one has the Way, even if one dies one's soul goes to an abode of happiness. If one does not have the Way, when one is dead one's soul suffers misfortune.

Why Should a Chinese Allow Himself to Be Influenced by Indian Ways?

The questioner said: Confucius said, "The barbarians with a ruler are not so good as the Chinese without one." Mencius criticized Ch'en Hsiang for rejecting his own education to adopt the ways of [the foreign teacher] Hsü Hsing, saying, "I have heard of using what is Chinese to change what is barbarian, but I have never heard of using what is barbarian to change what is Chinese." You, sir, at the age of twenty learned the way of Yao, Shun, Confucius, and the Duke of Chou. But now you have rejected them, and instead have taken up the arts of the barbarians. Is this not a great error?

Mou Tzu said: . . . What Confucius said was meant to rectify the way of the world, and what Mencius said was meant to deplore one-sidedness. Of old, when Confucius was thinking of taking residence among the nine barbarian nations, he said, "If a gentleman-scholar dwells in their midst, what baseness can there be among them?" . . . The Commentary says, "The north polar star is in the center of heaven and to the north of man." From this one can see that the land of China is not necessarily situated under the center of heaven. According to the Buddhist scriptures, above, below, and all around, all beings containing blood belong to the Buddha-clan. Therefore I revere and study these scriptures. Why should I reject the Way of Yao, Shun, Confucius, and the Duke of Chou? Gold and jade do not harm each other, crystal and amber do not cheapen each other. You say that another is in error when it is you yourself who err.

Why Must a Monk Renounce Worldly Pleasures?

The questioner said: Of those who live in the world, there is none who does not love wealth and position and hate poverty and baseness, none who does not enjoy pleasure and idleness and shrink from labor and fatigue. . . . But now the monks wear red cloth, they eat one meal a day, they bottle up the six emotions, and thus they live out their lives. What value is there in such an existence?

Mou Tzu said: Wealth and rank are what man desires, but if he cannot obtain them in a moral way, he should not enjoy them. Poverty and meanness are what man hates, but if he can only avoid them by departing from the Way, he should not avoid them. Lao Tzu has said, "The five colors make men's eyes blind, the five sounds make men's ears deaf, the five flavors dull the palate, chasing about and hunting make men's minds mad, possessions difficult to acquire bring men's conduct to an impasse. The sage acts for his belly, not for his eyes." Can these words possibly be vain? Liu-hsia Hui would not exchange his way of life for the rank of the three highest princes of the realm. Tuan-kan Mu would not exchange his for the wealth of Prince Wen of Wei. . . . All of them followed their ideas, and cared for nothing more. Is there no value in such an existence?

Why Does Mou Tzu Support His Contentions from Secular Rather Than Buddhist Literature?

The questioner said: You, sir, say that the scriptures are like the rivers and the sea, their phrases like brocade and embroidery. Why, then, do you not draw on the Buddhist scriptures to answer my question? Why instead do you refer to the books of *Odes* and *History,* joining together things that are different to make them appear the same?

Mou Tzu said: . . . I have quoted those things, sir, which I knew you would understand. Had I preached the words of the Buddhist scriptures or discussed the essence of non-action, it would have been like speaking to a blind man of the five colors or playing the five sounds to a deaf man.

Does Buddhism Have No Recipe for Immortality?

The questioner said: The Taoists say that Yao, Shun, the Duke of Chou, and Confucius and his seventy-two disciples did not die, but became immortals. The Buddhists say that men must all die, and that none can escape. What does this mean?

Mou Tzu said: Talk of immortality is superstitious and unfounded; it is not the word of the sages. Lao Tzu says, "Even Heaven and earth cannot be eternal. How much the less can man!" Confucius says, "The wise man leaves the world, but humanity and filial piety last forever." I have observed the six arts and examined the commentaries and records. According to them, Yao died, Shun had his [death place at] Mount Ts'ang-wu, Yü has his tomb on K'uai-chi, Po I and Shu Ch'i have their grave in Shou-yang. King Wen died before he could chastise Chou, King Wu died without waiting for King Ch'eng to grow up. We read of the Duke of Chou that he was reburied, and of Confucius that [shortly before his death] he dreamed of two pillars. [As for the disciples of Confucius], Po-yü died before his father, of Tzu Lu it is said that his flesh was chopped up and pickled.

43

The Introduction of Buddhism into Japan: From *The Chronicles of Japan*

The *Chronicles of Japan (Nihongi)* is one of the oldest primary sources for Japanese history. Written in Chinese in 720 C.E. by Japanese in the court of the reigning Yamato family, it is a valuable source of information about Japan in the sixth century.

The following two selections, the first from the year 538 and the second from 584, concern the introduction of Buddhism. How was Buddhism first introduced into Japan? What seems to have been the initial appeal of the new religion? How was the fate of the new religion determined? What seems to have happened between 538 and 584?

Thinking Historically

Religions spread and win converts in two ways: by convincing people and by changing tenets. How had the Buddhism that was apparently introduced by the Korean king into Japan in 538 C.E. changed from the time of the Buddha? Did Buddhist doctrine change further between 538 and 584, or did it simply become more "convincing?"

[552 C.E.] Winter, 10th month. King Syong of Paekche[1] sent [two envoys] with a present to the Emperor of an image of [the Buddha] in gold and copper, several flags and umbrellas, and a number of volumes of Sutras. Separately he presented a memorial in which he lauded the merit of diffusing abroad religious worship, saying: — "This doctrine is amongst all doctrines the most excellent. But it is hard to explain, and hard to comprehend. Even the Duke of Chou and Confucius had not attained to a knowledge of it. This doctrine can create religious merit and retribution [karma] without measure and without bounds, and so lead on to a full appreciation of the highest wisdom. Imagine a man in possession of treasures to his heart's content, so that he might satisfy all his wishes in proportion as he used them. Thus it is with the treasure of this wonderful doctrine. Every prayer is fulfilled and naught is wanting. Moreover, from distant India it has extended hither to the three [king-

[1] Paekche was one of the three main Korean kingdoms.

Nihongi: Chronicles of Japan from the Earliest Times, vol. 2, trans. W. G. Aston (New York: Oxford University Press, 1997), 65–67, 101–02.

doms of Korea], where there are none who do not receive it with reverence as it is preached to them.

"Thy servant, therefore, Syong, King of Paekche, has humbly dispatched a retainer to transmit it to the Imperial Country [of Japan], and to diffuse it abroad throughout the home provinces, so as to fulfil the recorded saying of Buddha: 'My law shall spread to the East.'"

This day the Emperor, having heard to the end, leaped for joy, and gave command to the envoys, saying: — "Never from former days until now have we had the opportunity of listening to so wonderful a doctrine. We are unable, however, to decide of ourselves." Accordingly he inquired of his ministers one after another, saying: — "The countenance of this Buddha which has been presented by the Western frontier state is of a severe dignity, such as we have never at all seen before. Ought it to be worshipped or not?" The Oho-omi [chief of the Soga clan] addressed the Emperor, saying: — "All the Western frontier lands without exception do it worship. Shall [our land of] Yamato alone refuse to do so?" [The chiefs of the Mononobe and Nakatomi clans] addressed the Emperor jointly, saying: — "Those who have ruled the Empire in this our state have always made it their care to worship in spring, summer, autumn, and winter the 180 [Shinto] gods of heaven and earth, and the gods of the land and of grain. If just at this time we were to worship in their stead foreign deities, it may be feared that we should incur the wrath of our national gods."

The Emperor said: — "Let [the image] be given to [the Oho-omi], who has shown his willingness to take it, and, as an experiment, make him to worship it."

The Oho-omi knelt down and received it with joy. He enthroned it in his house at Oharida, where he diligently carried out the rites of retirement from the world, and on that score purified his house at Mukuhara and made it a temple. After this a pestilence was rife in the land, from which the people died prematurely. As time went on it became worse and worse, and there was no remedy. [The chiefs of the Mononobe and Nakatomi clans] addressed the Emperor jointly, saying: — "It was because thy servants' advice on a former day was not approved that the people are dying thus of disease. If thou dost now retrace thy steps before matters have gone too far, joy will surely be the result! It will be well promptly to fling it away, and diligently to seek happiness in the future."

The Emperor said: — "Let it be done as you advise." Accordingly officials took the image of Buddha and abandoned it to the current of the Canal of Naniha. They also set fire to the Temple, and burnt it so that nothing was left. Hereupon, there being in the heavens neither clouds nor wind, a sudden conflagration consumed the Great Hall (of the Palace).

[584 C.E.] Autumn, 9th month. [A man] who had come from Paekche had a stone image of [the Bodhisattva] and an image of Buddha. This year [a Soga clansman named] Mumako Sukune, having asked for these two Buddhist images, sent [three retainers] in all directions to search out persons who practised Buddhism. Upon this he only found in the province of Harima a man [of Korean origin], who from a Buddhist priest had become a layman again. So the Oho-omi made him teacher, and caused him to receive [three young women] into religion . . . Mumako Sukune, still in accordance with the Law of Buddha, reverenced the three nuns, and gave orders to provide them with food and clothing. He erected a Buddhist temple on the east side of his dwelling, in which he enshrined the stone image of [the Bodhisattva]. He insisted on the three nuns holding a general meeting to partake of [a vegetarian meal]. At this time [the father of one of the nuns] found a Buddhist relic on [top of] the food, and presented it to Mumako Sukune. Mumako Sukune, by way of experiment, took the relic, and placing it on the middle of a block of iron, beat it with an iron sledgehammer, which he flourished aloft. The block and the sledgehammer were shattered to atoms, but the relic could not be crushed. Then the relic was cast into water, where it floated on the water or sank as one desired. In consequence of this, Mumako Sukune held faith in Buddhism and practised it unremittingly. [He] built another Buddhist temple at his house in Ishikaha. From this arose the beginning of Buddhism.

REFLECTIONS

Most of the selections in this chapter were written by religious thinkers — evangelists and missionaries — who hoped to change people's minds. They assumed that proper behavior will follow right ideas, but — unlike priests or administrators who concentrate on behavior — they are primarily concerned with instilling beliefs.

This emphasis on the intellectual side of human life, on believing and thinking as opposed to doing and being, raises a number of questions. First, one might ask: How effective was intellectual argument in converting populations who were largely illiterate and uneducated? When one observes how many conversions — even among those reported in these readings — resulted not from persuasive preaching but from fear or wonder in the wake of miracles or magic spells, what did conversion mean to the converted? Did the Japanese who adopted the Buddha because he seemed to bring prosperity behave differently from their parents who rejected the Buddha because he brought disaster? Did the jailer of Paul (Acts 16) change his life when an earthquake convinced him that Paul's god was superior to the Roman gods? And what of the millions who adopted the religion of the emperor?

Historians today are skeptical of the claim made in the path-breaking study *Conversion*[1] (1933) by Arthur Darby Nock that Christianity required a personal transformation, a rebirth, and that was part of its appeal. More typical today is the attitude of the historian Ramsay MacMullen[2] that regardless of upbringing or education, human beings display a wide range of religious temperaments "from the very 'cool' to the very 'hot' (p. 15). Perhaps the majority of people in any society are cooly circumspect rather than heatedly intense when it comes to matters of the supernatural. No doubt some lives are transformed, but probably many are not.

It should not surprise us, then, that despite the enormous achievement of the Christians and Buddhists studied here and the continued importance of those two religions globally, both Christian Rome and Buddhist China were reconverted to a large degree within centuries of their success. Christianity continued to spread through Western Rome, from Ireland to Constantinople. But the former Roman provinces of the Middle East and North Africa — including such "hot" Christian cities as Antioch and Carthage, which had attracted more than their share of martyrs and monastics — converted again to a new religion, Islam, that from 622 to 750 created an empire stretching from Spain to China.

Since Buddhism, unlike Christianity, had never demanded exclusive loyalty, its monasteries and temples continued to prosper in China as Confucian scholars won back the allegiance of the ruling elite. But the Confucian revival, called neo-Confucianism by later historians, was heavily influenced by Buddhism. Christianity and Buddhism had not only won empires, they had also prepared the way for their successors.

Are you yourself swayed more by ideas of fear and wonder? Do you think your responses are more typical of people in modern society than the ancient world? Is modern society more "cool" to religion?

[1] A. D. Nock, *Conversion: The Old and the New in Religion from Alexander the Great to Augustine of Hippo* (Oxford: Oxford University Press, 1933).

[2] Ramsay MacMullen, *Christianizing the Roman Empire,* A.D. *100–400* (New Haven: Yale University Press, 1984).

8

Medieval Civilizations

HISTORICAL CONTEXT

European, Islamic, and Chinese Societies, 600–1300 C.E.

In the centuries after 200 C.E., an influx of nomadic peoples from the grasslands of Eurasia into the Roman and Han Chinese Empires brought an end to the classical civilizations. In their wake, three distinct civilizations developed: European Christian, Islamic (after 622 C.E.), and Chinese. Of the three, the Chinese was most like its preceding classical civilization; in some ways the Sui dynasty (589–618) revived the institutions of the Han. The greatest change occurred in Western Europe, especially the former urban areas of the Roman Empire, some of which virtually disappeared. The area from Byzantium to the Indus River was radically transformed by the rise of Islam, but a foreign observer might have been struck more by the continuity of urban growth and material progress than by the change of faith in Western Asia from the classical to Muslim period.

In any case, these three worlds of Eurasia in the Middle Ages were vastly different from each other. The goal of this chapter is to explore some of those differences.

THINKING HISTORICALLY

Distinguishing Social, Economic, Political, and Cultural Aspects

Comparing civilizations is a daunting undertaking; there are so many variables one must keep in mind. Consequently, when historians compare civilizations, or any social system, they first break them down into parts. Most commonly, historians distinguish between the political, economic, social, and cultural features of a system. The political refers to how a society or civilization is governed, the economic to how it supports itself, the social to how it organizes population groups, including families, and the cultural to how it explains and represents itself, including its religion.

In this chapter, you are asked to be systematic in distinguishing among these features for each of the three main civilizations. We will break them down to compare each part — for example, European and Chinese politics, Muslim and Chinese culture — but also to see how the parts of each civilization make a whole: for example, how Chinese politics and Chinese culture fit together.

44

Feudalism: An Oath of Homage and Fealty

This primary source is from France, selected to illustrate one of the important institutions of Europe in the Middle Ages: feudalism. This document details the mutual obligation between a feudal lord and his vassal. In this case, the feudal lord is a religious institution, the monastery of St. Mary of Grasse. Acting for the monastery and its lands is the abbot, Leo. The vassal who holds the properties of the monastery as a fief, and in return pledges homage and fealty, is Bernard Atton, viscount of Carcassonne. The year is 1110.

What exactly does the viscount of Carcassonne promise to do? What is Leo the abbot's responsibility on behalf of the monastery? How new or old does this agreement appear to be? What else does this document tell you about the relationship of lords and vassals in European feudalism?

Thinking Historically

Using the distinctions suggested in the chapter introduction, how would you characterize this agreement? In short, is it an economic, political, social, or cultural agreement? Because it obviously has more than one of these elements, how might you argue for each of the four characterizations?

"Charter of Homage and Fealty of the Viscount of Carcassone, 1110," in D. C. Munro, *Translations and Reprints from the Original Sources of European History*, vol. IV, bk. 3 (Philadelphia: University of Pennsylvania Press, 1897), 18–20.

What would be the closest equivalent to this sort of agreement today? Would you characterize the modern equivalent as economic, political, social, or cultural?

In the name of the Lord, I, Bernard Atton, Viscount of Carcassonne, in the presence of my sons, Roger and Trencavel, and of Peter Roger of Barbazan, and William Hugo, and Raymond Mantellini, and Peter de Vietry, nobles, and of many other honorable men, who had come to the monastery of St. Mary of Grasse, to the honor of the festival of the august St. Mary; since lord Leo, abbot of the said monastery, has asked me, in the presence of all those above mentioned, to acknowledge to him the fealty and homage for the castles, manors, and places which the patrons, my ancestors, held from him and his predecessors and from the said monastery as a fief, and which I ought to hold as they held, I have made to the lord abbot Leo acknowledgment and homage as I ought to do.

Therefore, let all present and to come know that I the said Bernard Atton, lord and viscount of Carcassonne, acknowledge verily to thee my lord Leo, by the grace of God, abbot of St. Mary of Grasse, and to thy successors that I hold and ought to hold as a fief, in Carcassonne, the following: . . . Moreover, I acknowledge that I hold from thee and from the said monastery as a fief the castle of Termes in Narbonne; and in Minerve the castle of Ventaion, and the manors of Cassanolles, and of Ferral and Aiohars; and in Le Rogès, the little village of Longville; for each and all of which I make homage and fealty with hands and with mouth to thee my said lord abbot Leo and to thy successors, and I swear upon these four gospels of God that I will always be a faithful vassal to thee and to thy successors and to St. Mary of Grasse in all things in which a vassal is required to be faithful to his lord, and I will defend thee, my lord, and all thy successors, and the said monastery and the monks present and to come and the castles and manors and all your men and their possessions against all malefactors and invaders, at my request and that of my successors at my own cost; and I will give to thee power over all the castles and manors above described, in peace and in war, whenever they shall be claimed by thee or by thy successors.

Moreover I acknowledge that, as a recognition of the above fiefs, I and my successors ought to come to the said monastery, at our own expense, as often as a new abbot shall have been made, and there do homage and return to him the power over all the fiefs described above. And when the abbot shall mount his horse I and my heirs, viscounts of Carcassonne, and our successors ought to hold the stirrup for the honor of the dominion of St. Mary of Grasse; and to him and all who come with him, to as many as two hundred beasts, we should make the abbot's purveyance in the borough of St. Michael of Carcassonne, the first time he enters Carcassonne, with the best fish and meat and with eggs and cheese, honorably according to his will, and pay the expense of the shoeing of the horses, and for straw and fodder as the season shall require.

And if I or my sons or their successors do not observe to thee or to thy successors each and all the things declared above, and should come against these things, we wish that all the aforesaid fiefs should by that very fact be handed over to thee and to the said monastery of St. Mary of Grasse and to thy successors.

I, therefore, the aforesaid lord Leo, by the grace of God, abbot of St. Mary of Grasse, receive thy homage and fealty for all the fiefs of castles and manors and places which are described above; in the way and with the agreements and understandings written above; and likewise I concede to thee and thy heirs and their successors, the viscounts of Carcassonne, all the castles and manors and places aforesaid, as a fief, along with this present charter, divided through the alphabet. And I promise to thee and thy heirs and successors, viscounts of Carcassonne, under the religion of my order, that I will be good and faithful lord concerning all those things described above.

Moreover, I, the aforesaid viscount, acknowledge that the little villages of [twelve are listed] with the farmhouse of Mathus and the chateaux of Villalauro and Claromont, with the little villages of St. Stephen of Surlac, and of Upper and Lower Agrifolio, ought to belong to the said monastery, and whoever holds anything there holds from the same monastery, as we have seen and have heard read in the privileges and charters of the monastery, and as was there written.

Made in the year of the Incarnation of the Lord 1110, in the reign of Louis. Seal of [the witnesses named in paragraph one, Bernard Atton and abbot Leo] who has accepted this acknowledgment of the homage of the said viscount.

And I, the monk John, have written this charter at the command of the said lord Bernard Atton, viscount of Carcassonne and of his sons, on the day and year given above, in the presence and witness of all those named above.

45

Manorialism: Duties of a Villein

***Manorialism* is another term used to describe medieval European civilization. It concerns the life around the manor houses that were the centers of life in the countryside. Manors were owned by feudal lords whose income derived, at least in good part, from the work of free peasants and dependent serfs *(villeins)*.**

This document, from England in 1307, delineates the duties required of a villein, John of Cayworth, to the lord of the manor, Battle Abbey. What duties does the abbey require of John of Cayworth? What does he get in return? In what ways is this document similar to the previous one? In what ways is it different?

Thinking Historically

How is the social status of John of Cayworth different from that of Bernard Atton in the previous selection? What would you imagine about the differences in their economic welfare?

What would be the modern equivalent of this document? Would you call that modern equivalent economic, political, social, or cultural? Which word best characterizes this document?

They say that John of Cayworth holds one house and thirty acres of land, and he owes 2 *s.*[1] a year at Easter and Michaelmas, and he owes one cock and two hens at Christmas worth 4 *s.*

And he ought to harrow for two days at the sowing at Lent with one man and his own horse and harrow, the value of the work is 4 *d.*;[2] and he receives from the lord on each day three meals worth 3 *d.*; and the lord will thus lose 1 *d.;* and so this harrowing is worth nothing to the service of the lord.

And he ought to carry the manure of the lord for two days with one cart using his own two oxen, the work to value 8 *s.*, and he receives

[1] Shilling, a British measure of money traditionally worth 1/20 of a pound (now 1/10). [Ed.]

[2] Pence, smallest measure of British currency traditionally worth 1/12 of a shilling (now 1/10). "d" comes from Roman *denarius.* [Ed.]

"Services Due from a Villein, 1307," ed. S. R. Scargill-Bird, Customals of Battle Abbey (The Camden Society, 1887), 19–23.

from the lord three meals of the above value each day; and so the work is worth 3 *d.* clear.

And he should find one man for two days to mow the meadow of the lord, who can mow an estimated one acre and a half: the value of mowing one acre is 6 *d.*; and the total is 9 *d.*; and he receives for each day three meals of the above value, and thus the mowing is worth 4 *d.* clear.

And he ought to collect and carry that same hay which he has mowed, the value of the work is 3 *d.* And he has from the lord two meals to one man worth 1½ *d.*; thus the work is worth 1½ *d.* clear.

And he ought to carry the hay of the lord for one day with one cart and three animals of his own, the price of the work is 6 *d.*; and he has from the lord three meals worth 2½ *d.*; and thus the work has a value of 3½ *d.* clear.

And he ought to carry in the autumn beans or oats for two days with one cart and three of his own animals, the price of the work is 12 *d.*; and he has from the lord three meals of the above price for each day, and thus the work is worth 7 *d.* clear.

And he ought to carry wood from the woods of the lord to the manor house for two days in summer with one cart and three of his own animals, the price of the work is 9 *d.*; and he receives from the lord for each day three meals of the above price. And so the work is worth 4 *d.* clear.

And he ought to find one man for two days to cut heath, the price of the work is 4 [*d.*]; and he will have three meals for each day of the above price; and so the lord loses if he receives the work 1 *d.*; and thus that cutting is worth nothing to the work of the lord.

And he ought to carry the heath that he has cut, the price of the work is 5 *d.*; and he receives from the lord three meals of the price of 2½ *d.*; and thus the work is worth 2½ *d.* clear.

And he ought to carry to Battle [Abbey] two times in the summer half a load of grain each time, the price of the work is 4 *d.*; and he will receive in the manor each time one meal worth 2 *d.*; and thus the work is worth 2 *d.* clear.

The sum of the rents, with the price of the chickens is 2 *s.* 4 *d.*; the sum of the value of the work is 2 *s.* 3½ *d.*; owed from the said John per year. . . .

And it must be noted that all the aforesaid villeins may not marry their daughters nor have their sons tonsured, nor can they cut down timber growing on the lands they hold, without the personal approval of the bailiff or servant of the lord, and then for building and no other purpose.

And after the death of any one of the aforesaid villeins the lord will have as a heriot the best animal that he had; if, however, he had no living beast, the lord will have no heriot, as they say.

The sons or daughters of the aforesaid villeins will give to enter the tenement after the death of their ancestors as much as they gave in rent per year.

46

From the Magna Carta

The Magna Carta was a contract between King John of England and his nobles (or "liegemen") in which the king agreed to recognize certain rights and liberties of the nobility. In return the nobles accepted certain obligations to the king. What were some of these rights and obligations? Can you tell from these provisions what some of the nobles' complaints had been? Did the signing of this agreement in 1215 improve the position of the common people, women, or foreigners? What does the document tell you about English society in the early thirteenth century?

Thinking Historically

This is obviously a political document, as it details the mutual obligations of King John and his nobles, the barons. But in addition to political matters, it covers a number of issues that might be considered economic, social, and cultural. Which items would you characterize as falling into one of those categories?

What does the Magna Carta have in common with the other European documents on feudalism and manorialism? What does this commonality tell you about European society in the Middle Ages?

John, by the grace of God, King of England, Lord of Ireland, Duke of Normandy and Aquitaine, and Count of Anjou: To the Archbishops, Bishops, Abbots, Earls, Barons, Justiciaries, Foresters, Sheriffs, Reeves, Ministers, and all Bailiffs and others, his faithful subjects, Greeting. Know ye that in the presence of God, and for the health of Our soul,

"Magna Carta," trans. E. P. Cheney, in D. C. Munro, ed., *Translations and Reprints from the Original Sources of European History,* vol. I, bk. 6 (Philadelphia: University of Pennsylvania Press, 1897), 6–15, passim.

and the souls of Our ancestors and heirs, to the honor of God, and the exaltation of Holy Church, and amendment of Our Kingdom, by the advice of Our reverend Fathers, Stephen, Archbishop of Canterbury, Primate of all England, and Cardinal of the Holy Roman Church; Henry, Archbishop of Dublin; William of London, Peter of Winchester, Jocelin of Bath and Glastonbury, Hugh of Lincoln, Walter of Worcester, William of Coventry, and Benedict of Rochester, Bishops; Master Pandulph, the Pope's subdeacon and familiar; Brother Aymeric, Master of the Knights of the Temple in England; and the noble persons, William Marshal, Earl of Pembroke; William, Earl of Salisbury; William, Earl of Warren; William, Earl of Arundel; Alan de Galloway, Constable of Scotland; Warin Fitz-Gerald, Peter Fitz-Herbert, Hubert de Burgh, Seneschal of Poitou, Hugh de Neville, Matthew Fitz-Herbert, Thomas Basset, Alan Basset, Philip Daubeny, Robert de Roppelay, John Marshal, John Fitz-Hugh, and others, Our liegemen:

1. We have, in the first place, granted to God, and by this Our present Charter confirmed for Us and Our heirs forever — That the English Church shall be free and enjoy her rights in their integrity and her liberties untouched. And that We will this so to be observed appears from the fact that We of Our own free will, before the outbreak of the dissensions between Us and Our barons, granted, confirmed, and procured to be confirmed by Pope Innocent III the freedom of elections, which if considered most important and necessary to the English Church, which Charter We will both keep Ourself and will it to be kept with good faith by Our heirs forever. We have also granted to all the free men of Our kingdom, for Us and Our heirs forever, all the liberties underwritten, to have and to hold to them and their heirs of Us and Our heirs.

2. If any of Our earls, barons, or others who hold of Us in chief by knight's service shall die, and at the time of his death his heir shall be of full age and owe a relief[1] he shall have his inheritance by ancient relief; to wit, the heir or heirs of an earl of an entire earl's barony, £100; the heir or heirs of a baron of an entire barony, £100; the heir or heirs of a knight of an entire knight's fee, 100*s.* at the most; and he that owes less shall give less, according to the ancient custom of fees.

3. If, however, any such heir shall be under age and in ward, he shall, when he comes of age, have his inheritance without relief or fine.

4. The guardian of the land of any heir thus under age shall take therefrom only reasonable issues, customs, and services, without destruction or waste of men or property; and if We shall have committed the wardship of any such land to the sheriff or any other person answerable to Us for the issues thereof, and he commit destruction or waste, We will take an amends from him, and the land shall be com-

[1] A form of tax. [Ed.]

mitted to two lawful and discreet men of that fee, who shall be answerable for the issues to Us or to whomsoever We shall have assigned them. And if We shall give or sell the wardship of any such land to anyone, and he commit destruction or waste upon it, he shall lose the wardship, which shall be committed to two lawful and discreet men of that fee, who shall, in like manner, be answerable unto Us as has been aforesaid.

5. The guardian, so long as he shall have the custody of the land, shall keep up and maintain the houses, parks, fishponds, pools, mills, and other things pertaining thereto, out of the issues of the same, and shall restore the whole to the heir when he comes of age, stocked with ploughs and tillage, according as the season may require and the issues of the land can reasonably bear.

6. Heirs shall be married without loss of station, and the marriage shall be made known to the heir's nearest of kin before it be contracted.

7. A widow, after the death of her husband, shall immediately and without difficulty have her marriage portion and inheritance. She shall not give anything for her marriage portion, dower, or inheritance which she and her husband held on the day of his death, and she may remain in her husband's house for forty days after his death, within which time her dower shall be assigned to her.

8. No widow shall be compelled to marry so long as she has a mind to live without a husband, provided, however, that she give security that she will not marry without Our assent, if she holds of Us, or that of the lord of whom she holds, if she holds of another.

9. Neither We nor Our bailiffs shall seize any land or rent for any debt so long as the debtor's chattels are sufficient to discharge the same; nor shall the debtor's sureties be distrained so long as the debtor is able to pay the debt. If the debtor fails to pay, not having the means to pay, then the sureties shall answer the debt, and, if they desire, they shall hold the debtor's lands and rents until they have received satisfaction of the debt which they have paid for him, unless the debtor can show that he has discharged his obligation to them.

10. If anyone who has borrowed from the Jews any sum of money, great or small, dies before the debt has been paid, the heir shall pay no interest on the debt so long as he remains under age, of whomsoever he may hold. If the debt shall fall into Our hands, We will take only the principal sum named in the bond.

12. No scutage[2] or aid shall be imposed in Our kingdom unless by common counsel thereof, except to ransom Our person, make Our eldest son a knight, and once to marry Our eldest daughter, and for these only a reasonable aid shall be levied. So shall it be with regard to aids from the City of London.

2 A payment in place of a personal service. [Ed.]

13. The City of London shall have all her ancient liberties and free customs, both by land and water. Moreover, We will and grant that all other cities, boroughs, towns, and ports shall have their liberties and free customs.

14. For obtaining the common counsel of the kingdom concerning the assessment of aids (other than in the three cases aforesaid) or of scutage, We will cause to be summoned, severally by Our letters, the archbishops, bishops, abbots, earls, and great barons; We will also cause to be summoned, generally, by Our sheriffs and bailiffs, all those who hold lands directly of Us, to meet on a fixed day, but with at least forty days' notice, and at a fixed place. In all letters of such summons We will explain the cause thereof. The summons being thus made, the business shall proceed on the day appointed, according to the advice of those who shall be present, even though not all the persons summoned have come.

15. We will not in the future grant permission to any man to levy an aid upon his free men, except to ransom his person, make his eldest son a knight, and once to marry his eldest daughter, and on each of these occasions only a reasonable aid shall be levied.

16. No man shall be compelled to perform more service for a knight's fee or other free tenement than is due therefrom.

17. Common Pleas shall not follow Our Court, but shall be held in some certain place.

20. A free man shall be amerced[3] for a small fault only according to the measure thereof, and for a great crime according to its magnitude, saving his position; and in like manner a merchant saving his trade, and a villein[4] saving his tillage, if they should fall under Our mercy. None of these amercements shall be imposed except by the oath of honest men of the neighborhood.

21. Earls and barons shall be amerced only by their peers, and only in proportion to the measure of the offense.

22. No amercement shall be imposed upon a clerk's[5] lay property, except after the manner of the other persons aforesaid, and without regard to the value of his ecclesiastical benefice.

23. No village or person shall be compelled to build bridges over rivers except those bound by ancient custom and law to do so.

28. No constable or other of Our bailiffs shall take corn or other chattels of any man without immediate payment, unless the seller voluntarily consents to postponement of payment.

[3] Fined. [Ed.]
[4] Serf. [Ed.]
[5] Clergyman. [Ed.]

29. No constable shall compel any knight to give money in lieu of castle-guard when the knight is willing to perform it in person or (if reasonable cause prevents him from performing it himself) by some other fit man. Further, if We lead or send him into military service, he shall be quit of castle-guard for the time he shall remain in service by Our command.

30. No sheriff or other of Our bailiffs, or any other man, shall take the horses or carts of any free man for carriage without the owner's consent.

31. Neither We nor Our bailiffs will take another man's wood for Our castles or for any other purpose without the owner's consent.

35. There shall be one measure of wine throughout Our kingdom, and one of ale, and one measure of corn, to wit, the London quarter, and one breadth of dyed cloth, russets, and haberjets[6] to wit, two cells within the selvages. As with measure so shall it also be with weights.

38. In the future no bailiff shall upon his own unsupported accusation put any man to trial without producing credible witnesses to the truth of the accusation.

39. No free man shall be taken, imprisoned, disseised,[7] outlawed, banished, or in any way destroyed, nor will We proceed against or prosecute him, except by the lawful judgment of his peers and by the law of the land.

40. To no one will We sell, to none will We deny or delay, right or justice.

41. All merchants shall have safe conduct to go and come out of and into England, and to stay in and travel through England by land and water for purposes of buying and selling, free of illegal tolls, in accordance with ancient and just customs, except, in time of war, such merchants as are of a country at war with Us. If any such be found in Our dominion at the outbreak of war, they shall be attached, without injury to their persons or goods, until it be known to Us or Our Chief Justiciary how Our merchants are being treated in the country at war with Us, and if Our merchants be safe there, then theirs shall be safe with Us.

42. In the future it shall be lawful (except for a short period in time of war, for the common benefit of the realm) for anyone to leave and return to Our kingdom safely and securely by land and water, saving his fealty to Us. Excepted are those who have been imprisoned or out-

[6] Types of cloth. [Ed.]
[7] Dispossessed. [Ed.]

lawed according to the law of the land, people of the country at war with Us, and merchants, who shall be dealt with as aforesaid.

52. If anyone has been disseised or deprived by Us, without the legal judgment of his peers, of lands, castles, liberties, or rights, We will immediately restore the same, and if any dispute shall arise thereupon, the matter shall be decided by judgment of the twenty-five barons mentioned below in the clause for securing the peace. With regard to all those things, however, of which any man was disseised or deprived, without legal judgment of his peers, by King Henry Our Father or Our Brother King Richard, and which remain in Our warranty, We shall have respite during the term commonly allowed to the Crusaders, except as to those matters on which a plea had arisen, or an inquisition had been taken by Our command, prior to Our taking the Cross. Immediately after Our return from Our pilgrimage, or if by chance We should remain behind from it, We will at once do full justice.

47

From The Koran

The Koran is the founding document of Islamic (or Muslim) civilization. Muslims believe that the Koran is the word of God, revealed to Muhammad, an illiterate caravan trader, beginning around his fortieth year (610 C.E.) and continuing until his death (632). Muhammad had been influenced by the monotheism of Jews and Christians in Arabia, finding their beliefs preferable to the polytheism of most Arab tribes. But the Koran (literally the "recitation" of Muhammad) was understood by the early Muslims (including those who wrote it down in later years) as a fresh revelation from God to the last of his prophets, bringing a conclusion to revelations that had come for thousands of years to prophets that included Abraham, Moses, and Jesus.

The rich, subtle, and evocative Arabic of the Koran is said to be virtually untranslatable. Its accessibility to non-Muslims is made even more difficult by the way in which it is organized: generally later, longer sections first, followed by earlier shorter ones. Nevertheless, some sense of the power and sweep of the book can be inferred.

The Glorious Koran, trans. Muhammad Marmaduke Pickthall (Mecca: Muslim World League, 1977), 27–30, 75–76, 727.

Early sections, from the period before 622 when Muhammad left Mecca for Medina, display the power of the call to worship only God. The first selection, roman numeral C, called "The Coursers" (or "The Chargers") — one of the early Meccan surahs (or chapters) — captures the passion of those years. What appears to be the message of this surah?

While some were converted to Islam by words like these, others, especially among the ruling elite of Mecca, were threatened by them. To preserve the pilgrimage trade at their pagan shrine, the ka'bah in Mecca, the elite of the city conspired to kill Muhammad. But Muhammad and his Meccan followers were saved by a call from members of two feuding tribes in the more northerly city of Medina who had heard Muhammad preach and asked him to come and bring peace. Muhammad's migration to Medina in 622 marks year 1 in the Muslim calendar, the year when the rule of God was instituted on earth.

The surahs that come from this last decade of Muhammad's life reflect the role of the prophet as lawgiver. The selection from "The Cow" (surah II) discusses some of the ways in which a devout Muslim was expected to behave. What are these requirements? What is the impact of such rules?

Finally, the selection from "Women" (surah IV) shows how detailed the instructions of the Koran became as Muhammad administered a city that was to become an empire and a civilization. What kind of ideas about government and politics would likely develop among those who believed Muhammad revealed the words of God?

Thinking Historically

While the Koran is a religious (that is, cultural) product, it contains passages about politics, economics, and society as well as culture. Find passages from the following selection that deal with each of these four aspects of life.

What sort of social life is suggested by surah C? What kind of social life or society is evoked in "The Cow" and "Women"? What accounts for the different images of social life in these surahs? In what ways are either of these societies different from those depicted in the documents from medieval Europe?

Surah C: The Coursers

In the name of Allah, the Beneficent, the Merciful.

1. By the snorting coursers,
2. Striking sparks of fire
3. And scouring to the raid at dawn.
4. Then, therewith, with their trail of dust,
5. Cleaving, as one, the centre (of the foe),
6. Lo! man is an ingrate unto his Lord

7. And lo! he is a witness unto that;

8. And lo! in the love of wealth he is violent.

9. Knoweth he not that, when the contents of the graves are poured forth

10. And the secrets of the breasts are made known,

11. On that day will their Lord be perfectly informed concerning them.

Surah II: The Cow

177. It is not righteousness that ye turn your faces to the East and the West; but righteous is he who believeth in Allah and the Last Day and the angels and the Scripture and the Prophets; and giveth his wealth, for love of Him, to kinsfolk and to orphans and the needy and the wayfarer and to those who ask, and to set slaves free; and observeth proper worship and payeth the poor-due. And those who keep their treaty when they make one, and the patient in tribulation and adversity and time of stress. Such are they who are sincere. Such are the Godfearing.

178. O ye who believe! Retaliation is prescribed for you in the matter of the murdered; the freeman for the freeman, and the slave for the slave, and the female for the female. And for him who is forgiven somewhat by his (injured) brother, prosecution according to usage and payment unto him in kindness. This is an alleviation and a mercy from your Lord. He who transgresseth after this will have a painful doom.

179. And there is life for you in retaliation, O men of understanding, that ye may ward off (evil).

180. It is prescribed for you, when one of you approacheth death, if he leave wealth, that he bequeath unto parents and near relatives in kindness. (This is) a duty for all those who ward off (evil).

181. And whoso changeth (the will) after he hath heard it — the sin thereof is only upon those who change it. Lo! Allah is Hearer, Knower.

182. But he who feareth from a testator some unjust or sinful clause, and maketh peace between the parties, (it shall be) no sin for him. Lo! Allah is Forgiving, Merciful.

183. O ye who believe! Fasting is prescribed for you, even as it was prescribed for those before you, that ye may ward off (evil);

184. (Fast) a certain number of days; and (for) him who is sick among you, or on a journey, (the same) number of other days; and for those who can afford it there is a ransom: the feeding of a man in need — But whoso doth good of his own accord, it is better for him: and that ye fast is better for you if ye did but know —

185. The month of Ramadān in which was revealed the Qur'ān, a guidance for mankind, and clear proofs of the guidance, and the Criterion (of right and wrong). And whosoever of you is present, let him fast

the month, and whosoever of you is sick or on a journey, (let him fast the same) number of other days. Allah desireth for you ease; He desireth not hardship for you; and (He desireth) that ye should complete the period, and that ye should magnify Allah for having guided you, and that peradventure ye may be thankful.

186. And when My servants question thee concerning Me, then surely I am nigh. I answer the prayer of the suppliant when he crieth unto Me. So let them hear My call and let them trust in Me, in order that they may be led aright.

187. It is made lawful for you to go unto your wives on the night of the fast. They are raiment for you and ye are raiment for them. Allah is aware that ye were deceiving yourselves in this respect and He hath turned in mercy toward you and relieved you. So hold intercourse with them and seek that which Allah hath ordained for you, and eat and drink until the white thread becometh distinct to you from the black thread of the dawn. Then strictly observe the fast till nightfall and touch them not, but be at your devotions in the mosques. These are the limits imposed by Allah, so approach them not. Thus Allah expoundeth His revelations to mankind that they may ward off (evil).

188. And eat not up your property among yourselves in vanity, nor seek by it to gain the hearing of the judges that ye may knowingly devour a portion of the property of others wrongfully.

189. They ask thee, (O Muhammad), of new moons. Say: They are fixed seasons for mankind and for the pilgrimage. It is not righteousness that ye go to houses by the backs thereof (as do the idolaters at certain seasons), but the righteous man is he who wardeth off (evil). So go to houses by the gates thereof, and observe your duty to Allah, that ye may be successful.

190. Fight in the way of Allah against those who fight against you, but begin not hostilities. Lo! Allah loveth not aggressors.

191. And slay them wherever ye find them, and drive them out of the places whence they drove you out, for persecution is worse than slaughter. And fight not with them at the Inviolable Place of Worship until they first attack you there, but if they attack you (there) then slay them. Such is the reward of disbelievers.

192. But if they desist, then lo! Allah is Forgiving, Merciful.

193. And fight them until persecution is no more, and religion is for Allah. But if they desist, then let there be no hostility except against wrongdoers.

194. The forbidden month for the forbidden month, and forbidden things in retaliation. And one who attacketh you, attack him in like manner as he attacked you. Observe your duty to Allah, and know that Allah is with those who ward off (evil).

195. Spend your wealth for the cause of Allah, and be not cast by your own hands to ruin; and do good. Lo! Allah loveth the beneficent.

196. Perform the pilgrimage and the visit (to Mecca) for Allah. And if ye are prevented, then send such gifts as can be obtained with ease, and shave not your heads until the gifts have reached their destination. And whoever among you is sick or hath an ailment of the head must pay a ransom of fasting or almsgiving or offering. And when ye are in safety, then whosoever contenteth himself with the Visit for the Pilgrimage (shall give) such gifts as can be had with ease. And whosoever cannot find (such gifts), then a fast of three days, while on the pilgrimage, and of seven when ye have returned; that is, ten in all. That is for him whose folk are not present at the Inviolable Place of Worship. Observe your duty to Allah, and know that Allah is severe in punishment.

197. The pilgrimage is (in) the well-known months, and whoever is minded to perform the pilgrimage therein (let him remember that) there is (to be) no lewdness nor abuse nor angry conversation on the pilgrimage. And whatsoever good ye do Allah knoweth it. So make provision for yourselves (hereafter); for the best provision is to ward off evil. Therefore keep your duty unto Me, O men of understanding.

198. It is no sin for you that ye seek the bounty of your Lord (by trading). But, when ye press on in the multitude from "Arafāt," remember Allah by the sacred monument. Remember Him as He hath guided you, although before ye were of those astray.

199. Then hasten onward from the place whence the multitude hasteneth onward, and ask forgiveness of Allah. Lo! Allah is Forgiving, Merciful.

200. And when ye have completed your devotions, then remember Allah as ye remember your fathers or with a more lively remembrance. But of mankind is he who saith: "Our Lord! Give unto us in the world," and he hath no portion in the Hereafter.

Surah IV: Women

11. Allah chargeth you concerning (the provision for) your children: to the male the equivalent of the portion of two females, and if there be women more than two, then theirs is two-thirds of the inheritance, and if there be one (only) then the half. And to his parents a sixth of the inheritance if he have a son; and if he have no son and his parents are his heirs, then to his mother appertaineth the third; and if he have brethren, then to his mother appertaineth the sixth, after any legacy he may have bequeathed, or debt (hath been paid). Your parent or your children: Ye know not which of them is nearer unto you in usefulness. It is an injunction from Allah. Lo! Allah is Knower, Wise.

12. And unto you belongeth a half of that which your wives leave, if they have no child; but if they have a child then unto you the fourth of that which they leave, after any legacy they may have bequeathed, or

debt (they may have contracted, hath been paid). And unto them belongeth the fourth of that which ye leave if ye have no child, but if ye have a child then the eighth of that which ye leave, after any legacy ye may have bequeathed, or debt (ye may have contracted, hath been paid). And if a man or a woman have a distant heir (having left neither parent nor child), and he (or she) have a brother or a sister (only on the mother's side) then to each of them twain (the brother and the sister) the sixth, and if they be more than two, then they shall be sharers in the third, after any legacy that may have been bequeathed or debt (contracted) not injuring (the heirs by willing away more than a third of the heritage) hath been paid. A commandment from Allah. Allah is Knower, Indulgent.

13. These are the limits (imposed by) Allah. Whoso obeyeth Allah and His messenger, He will make him enter Gardens underneath which rivers flow, where such will dwell for ever. That will be the great success.

14. And whoso disobeyeth Allah and His messenger and transgresseth His limits, He will make him enter Fire, where such will dwell for ever; his will be a shameful doom.

15. As for those of your women who are guilty of lewdness, call to witness four of you against them. And if they testify (to the truth of the allegation) then confine them to the houses until death take them or (until) Allah appoint for them a way (through new legislation).

16. And as for the two of you who are guilty thereof, punish them both. And if they repent and improve, then let them be. Lo! Allah is Relenting, Merciful.

48

Sayings Ascribed to the Prophet

To understand how Muhammad governed and what he preached, Muslims also consult the *hadiths* or "sayings" attributed to the Prophet. While the sayings have nothing like the force of the Koran, the words of God, they provide valuable insight and guidance. What likely effect would the sayings included here have on a devout Muslim?

Al-Muttaqi, *Kanz al'Ummal,* quoted in *Islam from the Prophet Muhammad to the Capture of Constantinople,* ed. and trans. Bernard Lewis, vol. I (New York: Harper, 1974), 150–51.

Thinking Historically

Most of these sayings deal with religion and government. What attitude toward politics do they express? If this selection was all you had to construct a Muslim idea of government, what would it be? How are these political ideas different from those in medieval Europe? What accounts for the differences?

I charge the Caliph[1] after me to fear God, and I commend the community of the Muslims to him, to respect the great among them and have pity on the small, to honor the learned among them, not to strike them and humiliate them, not to oppress them and drive them to unbelief, not to close his doors to them and allow the strong to devour the weak.

The Imams[2] are of Quraysh;[3] the godly among them rulers of the godly, and the wicked among them rulers of the wicked. If Quraysh gives a crop-nosed Ethiopian slave authority over you, hear him and obey him as long as he does not force any of you to choose between his Islam and his neck. And if he does force anyone to choose between his Islam and his neck, let him offer his neck.

Hear and obey, even if a shaggy-headed black slave is appointed over you.

Whosoever shall try to divide my community, strike off his head.

If allegiance is sworn to two Caliphs, kill the other.

He who sees in his ruler something he disapproves should be patient, for if anyone separates himself from the community, even by a span, and dies, he dies the death of a pagan.

Obey your rulers, whatever happens. If their commands accord with the revelation I brought you, they will be rewarded for it, and you will be rewarded for obeying them; if their commands are not in accord with what I brought you, they are responsible and you are absolved. When you meet God, you will say, "Lord God! No evil." And He will say, "No evil!" And you will say, "Lord God! Thou didst send us Prophets, and we obeyed them by Thy leave; and Thou didst appoint over us Caliphs, and we obeyed them by Thy leave; and Thou didst place over us rulers, and we obeyed them for Thy sake." And He will say, "You speak truth. They are responsible, and you are absolved."

[1] Successor to the prophet; supreme authority. [Ed.]

[2] A leader, especially in prayer; clergyman. [Ed.]

[3] An aristocratic trading clan of Mecca; hostile to Muhammad, but after his death regained prominence. That religious leaders come from Quraysh was agreed after victory of Meccan faction in 661. [Ed.]

If you have rulers over you who ordain prayer and the alms tax and the Holy War for God, then God forbids you to revile them and allows you to pray behind them.

If anyone comes out against my community when they are united and seeks to divide them, kill him, whoever he may be.

He who dies without an Imam dies the death of a pagan, and he who throws off his obedience will have no defense on the Day of Judgment.

Do not revile the Sultan, for he is God's shadow on God's earth. Obedience is the duty of the Muslim man, whether he like it or not, as long as he is not ordered to commit a sin. If he is ordered to commit a sin, he does not have to obey.

The nearer a man is to government, the further he is from God; the more followers he has, the more devils; the greater his wealth, the more exacting his reckoning.

He who commends a Sultan in what God condemns has left the religion of God.

49

J. J. SAUNDERS

Civilization of Medieval Islam

In this selection the author, a modern historian, suggests answers to three important questions. First, he asks why the Arab invasions of the seventh century brought about a cultural flowering while the German invasions of Western Europe in the fifth century had the opposite effect. What, in other words, were the causes of this rise of Arabic civilization? Next, he asks about the nature of that civilization. What were its notable features? Finally, he asks about its decline after the thirteenth century. How was such a vigorous civilization overcome by the previously backward West?

What are the author's answers to these questions? Which answers do you find most convincing? Why?

J. J. Saunders, *A History of Medieval Islam* (London: Routledge, 1978).

Thinking Historically

While it is not the author's intention to distinguish political, social, economic, and cultural matters in this essay, he provides enough detail to enable you to discuss each of these categories for Muslim (or, as he would prefer, Arabic) civilization. Write your own characterizations of these four facets for this civilization, then compare them to your characterizations of the politics, society, economics, and culture of medieval Western Europe. Overall, how would you distinguish Muslim or Arabic civilization from Western European in the Middle Ages?

For some centuries (roughly between A.D. 800 and 1200) the lands conquered by the Arabs were the soil from which grew and blossomed one of the most brilliant civilizations in the history of humanity. To give it a suitable name is a matter of some difficulty. It has been variously styled Arab, Muslim, Islamic, and Arabic. The first is clearly a misnomer, implying as it does that this culture was created or dominated by men of Arab race, which was by no means the case; the second and third define it too narrowly in religious terms, whereas many of its most distinguished figures were Christians, Jews or pagans, and not Muslims at all. "Arabic" seems open to the least objection, since it draws attention to the fact that the literature of this particular civilization was written almost wholly in the Arabic language and acquired its characteristic unity largely from this circumstance.

The causes of the rise and fall of civilizations are often hidden from us, and the questions which start to mind are more easily framed than answered. Why were the German invasions of Western Europe in the fifth century followed by a long "dark age" of barbarism and ignorance, while the Arab invasions of the seventh century were followed by a general rise in the cultural level of the countries affected by them? So startling a contrast demands explanation, which must take the form of showing that certain conditions favourable to the growth of the arts and sciences were present in one case and absent in the other.

1. The Arab conquests politically unified a huge segment of the globe from Spain to India, a unity which remained unbroken until the fall of the Omayyads in 750. The disappearance of so many dividing frontiers, above all the one which had so long separated Rome and Persia, was a useful preliminary to the building of a new civilization.

2. As the Arabs overran one country after another, they carried their language with them. But that language possessed a unique status: to every Muslim it was not just one form of human speech among others, but the vehicle through which God had chosen to deliver his final revelation to men. Arabic was "God's tongue," and as such enjoyed a

prestige which Latin and Greek and Hebrew had never known. The Koran could not, must not be translated: the believer must hear and understand and if possible read the divine book in the original, even though Arabic were not his mother tongue. To study, illustrate, and elucidate the text became a pious duty: the earliest branch of science developed by Muslims was Arabic philology, traditionally founded at Basra in the late Omayyad age. The further Islam spread among non-Arabs, the further a knowledge of Arabic spread with it. A century or so after the conquests even Christians, Jews, and Zoroastrians within the Caliphate found it convenient to speak and write Arabic. Thus to political unity was added the widespread use of a common language, which immensely facilitated the exchange of ideas.

3. The first conquests of the Arabs were made in lands which had been the home of settled, urban civilizations for thousands of years; that is, the river valleys of the Nile and the Tigris-Euphrates. The fighting here was relatively brief (Syria was conquered in six or seven years, Egypt and Iraq in two or three), and the physical destruction was light. The native population was akin to the Arabs in race and speech, and stood aside from a struggle which was essentially between the invaders and the Byzantine or Sassanid[1] ruling class. The local officials often stayed at their posts, and administrative continuity, at least at the lower levels, remained unbroken. From motives of policy, the Caliphs cultivated friendly relations with the Jacobite and Nestorian Christians, who constituted the bulk of the people, and who during the long period of Roman rule had learnt a good deal of the science and philosophy of the Greeks. This learning, translated into Syriac, a Semitic tongue closely related to Arabic, was at the disposal of the newcomers, who were impressed by the rich and ancient culture of the region, and it was this region, and not Arabia proper, which was the birthplace of the Arabic civilization.

4. Once invasion and resettlement were over, the lands brought under the sovereignty of the Caliphs enjoyed immunity from serious external attack for three or four centuries. There was plenty of fighting on the frontiers and many internal revolts and disturbances, but no prolonged and ruinous barbarian assaults such as the Latin Christian West had to endure from the Vikings and Magyars. Under the shield of the *Pax Islamica,* which may be compared with the Augustan and Antonine Peace of the early Roman Empire, the arts and sciences rose to a new and flourishing life. Not until about 1050 did this peace begin to break down: Islam was then exposed to a series of attacks from the nomads of the steppes and deserts, culminating in the dreadful Mongol explosion of the thirteenth century.

[1] Persian dynasty ruling just before the Arab invasion. [Ed.]

5. The creation of the vast Arab Empire, besides levelling barriers and abolishing frontiers, brought into existence a great free-trade area, promoted safe and rapid travel, and gave a tremendous stimulus to commerce. During these four centuries (800–1200) international trade was more vigorous than at any time since the heyday of imperial Rome. Merchants from the Caliphate were found in places as far apart as Senegal and Canton. The hoards of Arabic coins dug up in Scandinavia reveal the brisk exchange of goods between Northern Europe and the cities of Iraq and Persia via the great rivers of Russia. The negro lands south of the Sahara were drawn into the stream of world commerce. The ancient Silk Road through the oases of Central Asia which carried the products of China to the West had never been so frequented. Cities expanded, fortunes were made, a wealthy middle-class of traders, shippers, bankers, manufacturers, and professional men came into being, and a rich and sophisticated society gave increasing employment and patronage to scholars, artists, teachers, physicians, and craftsmen.

6. The pursuit of knowledge was quickened by the use of paper and the so-called "Arabic" numerals. Neither originated in the Islamic world, but both were widely employed there by the ninth century. The manufacture of paper from hemp, rags, and tree-bark seems to have been invented in China about A.D. 100, but it remained unknown outside that country until some Chinese prisoners of war skilled in the art were brought to Samarkand in 751. In 793 a paper manufactory was set up in Baghdad; by 900 the commodity was being produced in Egypt, and by 950 in Spain. The Arabic numerals, despite their name, are probably Hindu, and may have reached Islam through the translation of the *Siddhanta,* a Sanskrit astronomical treatise, made by order of the Caliph Mansur in 773. The oldest Muslim documents employing these signs date from 870–890: the zero is represented by a dot, as has always been the case in Arabic. These innovations multiplied books and facilitated calculation, and the rich scientific literature of the next few centuries undoubtedly owes much to them.

Such are of the possible causes of the rise of the Arabic civilization. To attempt a detailed description and analysis of that civilization would be impossible, but certain notable features or peculiarities of it may be considered: —

1. It was not specifically Muslim. Islam provided it with a framework and a universal language, but its only creations which possess a definitely Muslim character are Arabic grammar, law, and theology. All else came from non-Muslim sources, even Arabic poetry and belles-lettres, which were based on a literary tradition going back to pre-Islamic times, the "days of ignorance" of the sixth century.

2. The biggest single influence which helped to shape it was Greek science and philosophy, but this reached it indirectly, chiefly through

the medium of Syriac. Of course, the great days of Hellenism were long over by the time of the Arab conquests: Greek science went out with Ptolemy in the second century, and the noble line of Greek thinkers ended when Justinian closed the schools of Athens in 529. But if nothing new was being created or discovered, the work of preserving and transmitting what had already been accomplished went on among the Byzantine Greeks and their Syriac-speaking pupils in Syria, Egypt, and Iraq, and when the Arabs broke into these lands most of the leading works of Greek medicine and metaphysics had been translated into Syriac by scholars of the Oriental Christian communities. Established in an educated society, the invaders grew ashamed of their ignorance, and the Caliphs encouraged learned Christians and Jews to turn these books into the dominant language of the Empire. This translating went on for some two centuries (800–1000), at the close of which educated Muslims could read the masters of Hellenic thought in Arabic versions of Syriac translations of the Greek originals.

3. As the Syriac-speaking Christians spread through the Islamic world a knowledge of Greek thought, so the Persians introduced to it much of the lore of Sanskrit India. Hindu influences had travelled west in late Sassanid times: the game of chess and Sanskrit medical writings are said to have reached Ctesiphon in the reign of Khusrau Nushirvan. When the Abbasids moved the metropolis of Islam to Iraq, Persian scholars were given every facility to pursue this quest. At the command of Mansur, Fazari translated the *Siddhanta;* Ibn al-Mukaffa turned into Arabic the famous *Fables of Bidpai,* an Indian collection of animal stories which has gone round the world; and the celebrated mathematician al-Khwarizmi, from whose name the European word "algorism" (the old term for arithmetic) was derived, founded the science of algebra (Arabic *al-jabr,* a restoring, literally, setting a bone) on the basis of Hindu mathematical achievement. Translation from Sanskrit into Arabic went on till the time of the great Persian scientist al-Biruni (973–1048), who among numerous learned works left an admirable sociological description of India. The double and simultaneous impact of Greece and India provided a powerful stimulus to the building of the Arabic civilization.

4. The center of Arabic intellectual life was long fixed in Iraq, the ancient home of culture, "a palimpsest (as it has been styled) on which every civilization from the time of the Sumerians had left its trace." A meeting-place of Hellenic and Iranian culture, it had been the heart of the old Persian monarchy and was the seat of the Caliphate from 750 to 1258. Baghdad became a greater Ctesiphon, the capital not simply of a State but of a world civilization. Perhaps in no other region of its size could such an extraordinary variety of belief and speech have been found. Jews and Zoroastrians, Nestorian, Monophysite and Greek Orthodox Christians, Gnostics and Manichaeans, the pagans of Harran,

and the strange baptist sect of the Mandeans, all mingled in the same province. In the Arab camp settlements of Basra and Kufa the Muslims first found leisure to devote themselves to things of the mind: here was inaugurated the study of Arabic philology and Islamic law. In Baghdad the Caliph Ma'mun, the son of a Persian mother, founded and endowed as a centre of research the Bait al-Hikma, or House of Wisdom, which was at once a library, an observatory and a scientific academy. Men of many races and faiths contributed to the fame of Baghdad as a home of scholarship, and Arabic civilization never recovered from the sack of the city by the Mongols in 1258.

5. The culture of medieval Islam was multiracial. Arabs, Syrians, Jews, Persians, Turks, Egyptians, Berbers, Spaniards, all contributed to it. One of its leading philosophers, al-Kindi, was an Arab of the tribe of Kinda (as his name implies); al-Farabi, a Neo-Platonist and commentator on Aristotle, a Turk from Transoxiana; Ibn Sina or Avicenna, perhaps the finest scientific thinker of Islam, a Persian from Bukhara; and Ibn Rushd, best known under his Europeanized name Averroës, a Spanish Moor from Cordova. A remarkable feature of Arabic philosophical literature is that much of it was written by Jews. As the Jewish religion, like the Christian, was a tolerated one among Muslims, Jews were found settled in almost all the great cities of Islam, where they learnt to write Arabic and to share in the vigorous intellectual life around them. In Spain they acted as mediators between the Muslim and Christian Spanish culture, helping Christian scholars to translate Arabic works into Latin and so making them available to the then backward West. Spain was also the birthplace of Maimonides, "the second Moses," perhaps the acutest Jewish thinker before Spinoza, who was born in Cordova in 1135 and died in Cairo in 1204, and whose *Guide for the Perplexed,* a bold attempt to reconcile reason and religious faith, finds readers to this day.

6. By far the biggest share in the construction of the Arabic civilization was taken by the Persians, a people whose recorded history was already more than a thousand years old when the Arabs broke into their land, and who found in their cultural superiority compensation for their political servitude. Persia has been described as "the principal channel irrigating the somewhat arid field of Islam with the rich alluvial flood of ancient culture": Sufism was virtually a Persian creation, and the Persian al-Ghazali was the greatest of Muslim theologians. In secular learning the Persians were predominant. "If knowledge were attached to the ends of the sky, some amongst the Persians would have reached it," was a traditional saying. Among the famous men of the age sprung from this gifted race were Razi (Rhazes), the great physician who first distinguished smallpox from measles; Tabari (died 923), the Arabic Livy, whose *Annals of Apostles and Kings* provided us with our chief source of information on early Muslim history; Ibn Sina, whose

medical writings instructed the world for centuries; Biruni, a many-sided genius whose fame now rests chiefly on his description of medieval India; Omar Khayyám (died 1123), more celebrated in the East for his mathematical achievements than for his poetry; Shahrastani (died 1153), whose *Book of Religion and Sects* is really a pioneering study in comparative religion; Nasir al-Din al-Tusi (died 1274), a distinguished astronomer who collected valuable data at his observatory at Maragha in Azerbaijan; and Rashid al-Din Fadl Allad (died 1318), author of the first world history worthy of that name. If to these scholars and scientists we add the poets (Firdawsi, Sa'di, Rumi, etc.), who shone luster on their country's literature, the picture is even brighter.

7. The core of the scientific studies of medieval Islam was medicine. Socially, the medical profession had always stood high in the East: whereas in the Greco-Roman world doctors were often freed slaves, in Persia and Babylonia they could rise to be the prime ministers of kings. At the time of the Arab conquests the classical medicine of Hippocrates and Galen was being studied by Egyptian Greeks in Alexandria and Nestorian Christians at Jundi-Shapur, in southwest Persia. The Caliphs employed graduates of these schools as their personal physicians: members of one Nestorian family, the Bakht-yashu (a name meaning "happiness of Jesus") served in this capacity at the court of Baghdad for several generations. Nestorian medical professors translated most of Galen and other authorities into Arabic, and by 900 the science of medicine was being assiduously cultivated by Muslims all over Islam. Razi was the first of their faith to acquire world fame through his vast medical encyclopedia, the *Hawi* (best known under its Latin title *Continens*), which was filled with long extracts from Greek and Hindu writers and displayed a knowledge of chemistry most unusual in that age. A similar work by Ibn Sina, the *Canon,* attained even greater celebrity and was treated for centuries as a kind of medical Bible. The branch of medicine most successively investigated was ophthalmology, eye diseases being sadly common in the East, and the *Optics* of Ibn al-Haitham, court physician to the Fatimids in Cairo where he died in 1039, remained the standard authority on its subject till early modern times, being studied with profit by the astronomer Kepler in the seventeenth century. It was through the medical schools that many of the natural sciences found their way into Muslim education, the curricula including instruction in physics, chemistry, and botany as well as in anatomy and pathology, and it was in this field that the Arabic writers made their greatest contribution to human knowledge. They added substantially to the achievement of the Greeks in the theory and art of healing disease; they founded hospitals and invented new drugs, and they filled libraries of books with detailed and accurate clinical observations. Their long superiority is proved by the fact that most of the Arabic works translated into Latin in the twelfth and thirteenth centuries were medical writings

and that these were among the first to be printed at the time of the Renaissance. Razi, Ibn Sina, and Ibn al-Haitham in their Latinized form continued to be "set books" in the medical schools of Europe till as late as the mid-seventeenth century.

8. Like all civilizations, the Arabic was highly selective in its borrowings from outside. Human societies take over only those elements which seem well suited to fill a conscious gap, and disregard those which conflict with their fundamental values; thus in modern times Russia has appropriated the science rather than the humanism of the West, and China has borrowed Marxism and rejected almost all else of European origin. Islam drew extensively on Hindu mathematics and medicine, but took small notice of Hindu philosophy, which being the reflection of a polytheistic society and of belief in the world as *maya* or illusion, was wholly repugnant to the teachings of the Koran. It helped itself to a good deal of Greek (chiefly Aristotelian) logic and metaphysics, in order to clothe its religious doctrines in a form more acceptable to a sophisticated society and enable it to defend them against philosophically trained opponents, but though it knew Aristotle's *Poetics* and *Rhetoric,* it ignored the Greek poets, dramatists, and historians as spokesmen of a pagan past it had no desire to investigate. In architecture it was ready to use Byzantine and Persian models, but painting and sculpture were virtually banned because the Prophet [Mohammed] was alleged to have pronounced representational art a temptation to idolatry. Of classical Latin literature it knew nothing: the only Latin work ever translated into Arabic is said to have been the *History* of Orosius.

That the Arabic culture was merely imitative, that it copied and transmitted what it learnt at secondhand from the Greeks, and lacked the ability to strike out on independent lines of its own, is a judgment no longer accepted. It certainly borrowed freely from the Greeks — so did the West later — but what it built on these foundations was truly original and creative, and one of the great achievements of the human spirit. For more than four hundred years the most fruitful work in mathematics astronomy, botany, chemistry, medicine, history, and geography was produced in the world of Islam by Muslims and Christians, Jews and Zoroastrians, pagans and Manichaeans. Neither the collapse of the Caliphate nor the Isma'ilian schism checked the process, for the local dynasties which sprang up on the ruins of the old Arab Empire competed with one another to attract scholars and artists to their courts, and the possession of a common language far outweighed the loss of political unity. Yet this brilliant culture, which shone so brightly in contrast to the darkness of the Latin West and the stagnation of Byzantium, began to fade from the thirteenth century onwards. Arabic philosophy was dead by 1200, Arabic science by 1500. The nations of Western Europe, once sunk in barbarism, caught up and overtook the peoples of Islam. How did this come about? The question has hardly yet received a complete and satisfactory answer, but some tentative suggestions may be offered: —

1. The collapse of the *Pax Islamica*[2] after about 1050. The end of the long peace was marked by wave after wave of nomadic invasion, the Banu-Hilal in North Africa, the Turkomans and Seljuks in Western Asia, and the mighty Mongol devastations which inflicted such irreparable damage on so many Muslim lands between 1220 and 1260. Cities were sacked and burnt, wealth dissipated, libraries destroyed, and teachers dispersed. The loss to culture in the fall of Baghdad alone is incalculable. The Christian West escaped all this, since after the Northmen and Magyars had been tamed and converted around 1000, it had nothing more to fear from barbarian attack, and the Mongols never got farther west than Hungary and Silesia.

2. The decay of city life and economic prosperity. The Arabic civilization was essentially urban, and its material basis was the vigorous commercial activity which once covered an area extending as far as Scandinavia, China and the Sudan. This activity was much diminished when nomad raids and invasions threatened the security of the caravan routes. From the eleventh century onwards the volume of international trade contracted, urban wealth declined, and social and economic conditions in the Muslim world underwent drastic change. Princes, finding their revenues falling, were obliged to pay their civil and military officers out of the rents and produce of landed estates: hence the growth of the *ikta* system, which has been compared, rather loosely, to Western feudalism. Owing presumably to the prevalence of slavery, which assured a plentiful supply of labor, there was no stimulus to technological progress and invention, which might have provided some compensation for the loss of distant markets. Nor did the cities of Islam ever develop self-governing institutions or combine in defense of their interests like the Lombard League or the Hansa in contemporary Europe: it was not that civic patriotism was wholly lacking (Arabic literature contains many town histories and biographical dictionaries of famous citizens), but that in this society the primary loyalty of a man was to his religious community, and in cities where Muslims, Christians, and Jews lived together in separate quarters, it was not easy for the inhabitants to feel and act as a united body. Thus the middle classes (merchants, traders, shippers, shopkeepers, and craftsmen) had little defense when the economic basis of their position weakened, and the decline of the town was almost certainly related to the falling off of intellectual capacity and output.

[2] *Pax Islamica*, by analogy to the *Pax Romana*, refers to widespread peace created by Muslim societies from Morocco to India.

3. The loss of linguistic and cultural unity. In the days of its widest expansion, Arabic was written and understood wherever Islam prevailed, but its intellectual monopoly was threatened and finally broken by the revival of Persian in the lands east of the Tigris. The fall of the Sassanid Empire reduced the native tongue to the level of Anglo-Saxon in England after the Norman conquest, but under the Abbasids it began to reemerge in an altered form, its vocabulary swollen with Arabic words and the old Pahlawi script replaced by the Arabic. With the rise of native dynasties after the disintegration of the Caliphate, Persia experienced a literary renaissance; the Samanids and Ghaznavids in particular were generous patrons of poets and scholars, and Firdawsi's great epic, the *Shah-nama,* or Book of Kings, finished in 1010, gave the new Persian a position in world literature it has never since lost. Fewer and fewer Persians wrote in Arabic, though the sacred language of the Koran continued to be used for works of theology, law, and devotion. When the Turks entered Islam *en masse* with the Seljuks, it was the Persianized provinces that they first occupied, and it was on Persian officials that they relied for the administration of their Empire. Deeply affected in consequence by Persian culture, the Turks carried it with them westwards into Asia Minor and eastwards into northern India: by contrast, they set little store by Arabic, except for purely religious purposes. The Mongol invasions, the fall of Baghdad and the destruction of the Caliphate dealt a fatal blow to Arabic in eastern Islam, where in the field of secular learning and literature it was steadily overshadowed by Persian and Turkish. Never again was the Muslim world to be dominated by a single language.

4. Probably the biggest factor was the strongly religious character of Islam itself and the absence of a vigorous pre-Islamic secular tradition. Behind Christian Europe lay the science and rationalism of classical Greece: behind Islam lay nothing save the cultural poverty of "the days of ignorance." The Muslims did, as we have seen, borrow a good deal from Greece, but in a limited and indirect fashion: the Greek past never *belonged* to them in the sense in which it did to Christendom, and there was never a joyous acceptance or recovery of it as took place in the West at the time of the Renaissance. The spirit of Islam was not rational in the Greek sense of the term, in that God is beyond reason and his ordering of the universe is to be accepted rather than explained. True knowledge is that of God and his Law, and the Law embraces all human activity: secular learning for its own sake is to be strongly discouraged, and intellectual pursuits are permissible only insofar as they further a deeper piety and understanding of religious truth. Such an attitude was implicit in Islamic thinking from the onset, but it became explicit only at a later stage, largely in consequence of the reaction against the Isma'ilian heresy and of a fuller realization of the dangers to orthodoxy lurking in Greek philosophy. The shift in outlook became noticeable in the Seljuk age. The great Ghazali devoted his life to the defense

of Koranic truth against what he regarded as the insidious encroachments of unbelief. Islamic dogma was linked with Sufi mysticism. Muslim education was geared to the new orthodoxy by the founding of *madrasas,* where the religious sciences alone received intensive study. The Shari'a came to dominate Muslim life as the Torah had dominated post-exilic Judaism. The door was closed against further borrowings from outside: philosophy was repudiated as a danger to the Faith, because it was alleged to deny a personal God, creation *ex nihilo,* and the resurrection of the body. The attempt of Ibn Rushd (Averroës) in Spain to answer Ghazali and defend the pursuit of secular science fell on deaf ears and exposed him to the charge of teaching atheism. How far the reaction went can be seen from the attitude of Ibn Khaldun (1337–1406), often regarded as Islam's profoundest thinker, who dismissed all knowledge unconnected with religion as useless. Plato (he says) admitted that no certainty about God could be attained by the reason: why then waste our time on such futile inquiries? Truth is to be sought only in divine revelation. The profane sciences, which had always operated on the fringe and had never been free from the suspicion of impiety, were largely and quietly dropped as "un-Muslim."

50

ICHISADA MIYAZAKI

The Chinese Civil Service Exam System

The Chinese civil service examination system originated fourteen hundred years ago, making it the first in the world. As a device for ensuring government by the brightest young men, regardless of class or social standing, it may also be viewed as one of the world's earliest democratic systems. It was not perfect. Like democratic systems in the West only two hundred years ago, it excluded women. The system also put enormous pressure on young boys of ambitious families.

This selection consists of two passages from a book by a noted modern Japanese historian of China. The first passage concerns the elaborate early preparations for the exams.

Ichisada Miyazaki, *China's Examination Hell,* trans. Conrad Schirokauer (New York: Weatherhill, 1976), 13–17, 111–16, passim.

What did young boys have to learn? In what ways was their education different from your own? What effects did the examination system have on the goals and values of young people?

Thinking Historically

The Chinese examination system was primarily a political system, a way for the emperor to rule most effectively, employing the most talented administrators. In what sense did this system make China more "democratic" than the political systems of Western Europe or the Muslim world? In what sense was it less so? Did it become more or less democratic over the course of Chinese history? How did its purpose change from the Tang to the Sung dynasty?

Like any political system, the civil service system had a major impact on other aspects of life, social, economic, and cultural. How did it affect Chinese society, families, class differences, boys and girls? What were the economic effects of the system? How did it change Chinese cultural values, ideas, and education?

Judging from this essay and your readings about Western Europe and the Islamic world, what was the single most important difference between Chinese and Western European civilizations? Between Chinese and Muslim civilization?

Preparing for the Examinations

Competition for a chance to take the civil service examinations began, if we may be allowed to exaggerate only a little, even before birth. On the back of many a woman's copper mirror the five-character formula "Five Sons Pass the Examinations" expressed her heart's desire to bear five successful sons. Girls, since they could not take the examinations and become officials but merely ran up dowry expenses, were no asset to a family; a man who had no sons was considered to be childless. People said that thieves warned each other not to enter a household with five or more girls because there would be nothing to steal in it. The luckless parents of girls hoped to make up for such misfortune in the generation of their grandchildren by sending their daughters into marriage equipped with those auspicious mirrors.

Prenatal care began as soon as a woman was known to be pregnant. She had to be very careful then, because her conduct was thought to have an influence on the unborn child, and everything she did had to be right. She had to sit erect, with her seat and pillows arranged in exactly the proper way, to sleep without carelessly pillowing her head on an arm, to abstain from strange foods, and so on. She had to be careful to avoid unpleasant colors, and she spent her leisure listening to poetry and the classics being read aloud. These preparations were thought to lead to the birth of an unusually gifted boy.

If, indeed, a boy was born the whole family rejoiced, but if a girl arrived everyone was dejected. On the third day after her birth it was the custom to place a girl on the floor beneath her bed, and to make her grasp a tile and a pebble so that even then she would begin to form a lifelong habit of submission and an acquaintance with hardship. In contrast, in early times when a boy was born arrows were shot from an exorcising bow in the four directions of the compass and straight up and down. In later times, when literary accomplishments had become more important than the martial arts, this practice was replaced by the custom of scattering coins for servants and others to pick up as gifts. Frequently the words "First-place Graduate" were cast on those coins, to signify the highest dreams of the family and indeed of the entire clan.

It was thought best for a boy to start upon his studies as early as possible. From the very beginning he was instructed almost entirely in the classics, since mathematics could be left to merchants, while science and technology were relegated to the working class. A potential grand official must study the Four Books, the Five Classics, and other Confucian works, and, further, he must know how to compose poems and write essays. For the most part, questions in civil service examinations did not go beyond these areas of competence.

When he was just a little more than three years old, a boy's education began at home, under the supervision of his mother or some other suitable person. Even at this early stage the child's home environment exerted a great effect upon his development. In cultivated families, where books were stacked high against the walls, the baby sitter taught the boy his first characters while playing. As far as possible these were characters written with only a few strokes.

First a character was written in outline with red ink on a single sheet of paper. Then the boy was made to fill it in with black ink. Finally he himself had to write each character. At this stage there was no special need for him to know the meanings of the characters.

After he had learned in this way to hold the brush and to write a number of characters, he usually started on the *Primer of One Thousand Characters*. This is a poem that begins:

Heaven is dark, earth is yellow,
The universe vast and boundless . . .

It consists of a total of two hundred and fifty lines, and since no character is repeated, it provided the student with a foundation of a thousand basic ideograms.

Upon completing the *Primer,* a very bright boy, who could memorize one thing after another without difficulty, would go on to a history text called *Meng Ch'iu (The Beginner's Search)* and then proceed to the Four Books and the Five Classics normally studied in school. If rumors of such a prodigy reached the capital, a special "tough examination" was held, but often such a precocious boy merely served as a plaything for adults and did not accomplish much in later life. Youth examinations were popular during the Sung dynasty, but declined and finally were eliminated when people realized how much harm they did to the boys.

Formal education began at about seven years of age (or eight, counting in Chinese style). Boys from families that could afford the expense were sent to a temple, village, communal, or private school staffed by former officials who had lost their positions, or by old scholars who had repeatedly failed the examinations as the years slipped by. Sons of rich men and powerful officials often were taught at home by a family tutor in an elegant small room located in a detached building, which stood in a courtyard planted with trees and shrubs, in order to create an atmosphere conducive to study.

A class usually consisted of eight or nine students. Instruction centered on the Four Books, beginning with the *Analects,* and the process of learning was almost entirely a matter of sheer memorization. With their books open before them, the students would parrot the teacher, phrase by phrase, as he read out the text. Inattentive students, or those who amused themselves by playing with toys hidden in their sleeves, would be scolded by the teacher or hit on the palms and thighs with his fan-shaped "warning ruler." The high regard for discipline was reflected in the saying, "If education is not strict, it shows that the teacher is lazy."

Students who had learned how to read a passage would return to their seats and review what they had just been taught. After reciting it a hundred times, fifty times while looking at the book and fifty with the book face down, even the least gifted would have memorized it. At first the boys were given twenty to thirty characters a day, but as they became more experienced they memorized one, two, or several hundred each day. In order not to force a student beyond his capacity, a boy who could memorize four hundred characters would be assigned no more than two hundred. Otherwise he might become so distressed as to end by detesting his studies.

Along with the literary curriculum, the boys were taught proper conduct, such as when to use honorific terms, how to bow to superiors and to equals, and so forth — although from a modern point of view their training in deportment may seem somewhat defective, as is suggested by the incident concerning a high-ranking Chinese diplomat in the late Ch'ing dynasty who startled Westerners by blowing his nose with his fingers at a public ceremony.

It was usual for a boy to enter school at the age of eight and to complete the general classical education at fifteen. The heart of the curriculum was the classics. If we count the number of characters in the classics that the boys were required to learn by heart, we get the following figures:

Analects	11,705
Mencius	34,685
Book of Changes	24,107
Book of Documents	25,700
Book of Poetry	39,234
Book of Rites	99,010
Tso Chuan	196,845

The total number of characters a student had to learn, then, was 431,286.

The *Great Learning* and the *Doctrine of the Mean,* which together with the *Analects* and the *Mencius* constitute the Four Books, are not counted separately, since they are included in the *Book of Rites.* And, of course, those were not 431,286 *different* characters: most of the ideographs would have been used many times in the several texts. Even so, the task of having to memorize textual material amounting to more than 400,000 characters is enough to make one reel. They required exactly six years of memorizing, at the rate of two hundred characters a day.

After the students had memorized a book, they read commentaries, which often were several times the length of the original text, and practiced answering questions involving passages selected as examination topics. On top of all this, other classical, historical, and literary works had to be scanned, and some literary works had to be examined carefully, since the students were required to write poems and essays modeled upon them. Anyone not very vigorous mentally might well become sick of it all halfway through the course.

Moreover, the boys were at an age when the urge to play is strongest, and they suffered bitterly when they were confined all day in a classroom as though under detention. Parents and teachers, therefore, supported a lad, urging him on to "become a great man!" From ancient times, many poems were composed on the theme, "If you study while young, you will get ahead." The Sung emperor Chen-tsung wrote such a one:

To enrich your family, no need to buy good land:
Books hold a thousand measures of grain.
For an easy life, no need to build a mansion:
In books are found houses of gold.

Going out, be not vexed at absence of followers:
In books, carriages and horses form a crowd.
Marrying, be not vexed by lack of a good go-between:
In books there are girls and faces of jade.
A boy who wants to become a somebody
Devotes himself to the classics, faces the window, and reads.

In later times this poem was criticized because it tempted students with the promise of beautiful women and riches, but that was the very reason it was effective.

Nonetheless, in all times and places students find shortcuts to learning. Despite repeated official and private injunctions to study the Four Books and Five Classics honestly, rapid-study methods were devised with the sole purpose of preparing candidates for the examinations. Because not very many places in the classics were suitable as subjects for examination questions, similar passages and problems were often repeated. Aware of this, publishers compiled collections of examination answers, and a candidate who, relying on these compilations, guessed successfully during the course of his own examinations could obtain a good rating without having worked very hard. But if he guessed wrong he faced unmitigated disaster because, unprepared, he would have submitted so bad a paper that the officials could only shake their heads and fail him. Reports from perturbed officials caused the government to issue frequent prohibitions of the publication of such collections of model answers, but since it was a profitable business with a steady demand, ways of issuing them surreptitiously were arranged, and time and again the prohibitions rapidly became mere empty formalities.

An Evaluation of the Examination System

Did the examination system serve a useful purpose? . . .

The purpose of instituting the examinations, some fourteen hundred years ago under the Sui rulers, was to strike a blow against government by the hereditary aristocracy, which had prevailed until then, and to establish in its place an imperial autocracy. The period of disunion lasting from the third to the sixth century was the golden age of the Chinese aristocracy: during that time it controlled political offices in central and local governments. . . .

The important point in China, as in Japan, was that the power of the aristocracy seriously constrained the emperor's power to appoint officials. He could not employ men simply on the basis of their ability, since any imperial initiative to depart from the traditional personnel policy evoked a sharp counterattack from the aristocratic officials. This was the situation when the Sui emperor, exploiting the fact that he had reestablished order and that his authority was at its height, ended the power of the aristocracy to become officials merely by virtue of family status. He achieved this revolution when he enacted the examination system (and provided that only its graduates were to be considered qualified to hold government office), kept at hand a reserve of such officials, and made it a rule to use only them to fill vacancies in central and local government as they occurred. This was the origin of the examination system.

The Sui dynasty was soon replaced by the T'ang, which for the most part continued the policies of its predecessor. Actually, as the T'ang was in the process of winning control over China, a new group of aristocrats appeared who hoped to transmit their privileges to their descendants. To deal with this problem the emperor used the examination system and favored its *chin-shih*[1] trying to place them in important posts so that he could run the government as he wished. The consequence was strife between the aristocrats and the *chin-shih,* with the contest gradually turning in favor of the latter. Since those who gained office simply through their parentage were not highly regarded, either by the imperial government or by society at large, career-minded aristocrats, too, seem to have found it necessary to enter officialdom through the examination system. Their acceptance of this hard fact meant a real defeat for the aristocracy.

The T'ang can be regarded as a period of transition from the aristocratic government inherited from the time of the Six Dynasties to the purely bureaucratic government of future regimes. The examination system made a large contribution to what was certainly a great advance for China's society, and in this respect its immense significance in Chinese history cannot be denied. Furthermore, that change was begun fourteen hundred years ago, at about the time when in Europe the feudal system had scarcely been formed. In comparison, the examination system was immeasurably progressive, containing as it did a superb idea the equal of which could not be found anywhere else in the world at that time.

This is not to say that the T'ang examination system was without defects. First, the number of those who passed through it was extremely small. In part this was an inevitable result of the limited diffusion of China's literary culture at a time when printing had not yet become practical and hand-copied books were still both rare and expensive, thus restricting the number of men able to pursue scholarly studies. Furthermore, because the historical and economic roots of the new bureaucratic system were still shallow, matters did not always go smoothly and sometimes there were harsh factional conflicts among officials. The develop-

[1] Highest degree winner. [Ed.]

ment of those conflicts indicates that they were caused by the examination system itself and constituted a second serious defect.

As has been indicated, a master-disciple relationship between the examiner and the men he passed was established, much like that between a political leader and his henchmen, while the men who passed the examination in the same year considered one another as classmates and helped one another forever after. When such combinations became too strong, factions were born.

These two defects of the examination system were eliminated during the Sung regime. For one thing, the number of men who were granted degrees suddenly rose, indicating a similar rise in the number of candidates. This was made possible by the increase in productive power and the consequent accumulation of wealth, which was the underlying reason that Chinese society changed so greatly from the T'ang period to the Sung. A new class appeared in China, comparable to the bourgeoisie in early modern Europe. In China this newly risen class concentrated hard on scholarship, and with the custom of this group, publishers prospered mightily. The classic books of Buddhism and Confucianism were printed; the collected writings of contemporaries and their discourses and essays on current topics were published; and the government issued an official gazette, so that in a sense China entered upon an age of mass communications. As a result learning was so widespread that candidates for the examinations came from virtually every part of the land, and the government could freely pick the best among them to form a reserve of officials.

In the Sung dynasty the system of conducting the examinations every three years was established. Since about three hundred men were selected each time, the government obtained an average of one hundred men a year who were qualified for the highest government positions. Thus the most important positions in government were occupied by *chin-shih,* and no longer were there conflicts between men who differed in their preparatory backgrounds, such as those between *chin-shih* and non–*chin-shih* that had arisen in the T'ang period.

Another improvement made during the Sung period was the establishment of the palace examination as the apex of the normal examination sequence. Under the T'ang emperors the conduct of the examinations was completely entrusted to officials, but this does not mean that emperors neglected them, because they were held by imperial order. It even happened that Empress Wu (r. 684–705) herself conducted the examinations in an attempt to win popularity. . . .

The position of the emperor in the political system changed greatly from T'ang times to Sung. No longer did the emperor consult on matters of high state policy with two or three great ministers deep in the interior of the palace, far removed from actual administrators. Now he was an autocrat, directly supervising all important departments of government and giving instructions about every aspect of government. Even minor matters of personnel needed imperial sanction. Now the emperor resembled the pivot of a fan, without which the various ribs of government would fall apart and be scattered. The creation of the palace examination as the final examination, given directly under the emperor's personal supervision, went hand in hand with this change in his function in the nation's political machinery and was a necessary step in the strengthening of imperial autocracy.

Thus, the examination system changed, along with Chinese society as a whole. Created to meet an essential need, it changed in response to that society's demand. It was most effective in those early stages when, first in the T'ang period, it was used by the emperor to suppress the power of the aristocracy, and then later, in the Sung period, when the cooperation of young officials with the *chin-shih* was essential for the establishment of imperial autocracy. Therefore, in the early Sung years *chin-shih* enjoyed very rapid promotion; this was especially true of the first-place *chin-shih,* not a few of whom rose to the position of chief councilor in fewer than ten years.

51

LIU TSUNG-YUAN

Camel Kuo the Gardener

Liu Tsung-yuan (773–819) was one of the great writers of the T'ang dynasty (618–907). He was especially loved for his scenes of nature, a topic he uses here for an allegory about government. What is the message of the allegory?

Thinking Historically

Are the ideas of government expressed here more like those of Confucius or Lao Tzu? How do you think Liu Tsung-yuan felt about the civil service system? Can we assume that Chinese government was practiced as the author desired, or that it was not?

Liu Tsung-yuan, "Camel Kuo the Gardener," in *Anthology of Chinese Literature,* ed. and trans. Cyril Birch (New York: Grove Press, 1965), 258–59.

In what ways is this view of government different from that of Western European or Muslim societies? In what sense is it more typically Chinese?

Whatever name Camel Kuo may have had to begin with is not known. But he was a hunchback and walked in his bumpy way with his face to the ground, very like a camel, and so that was what the country folk called him. When Camel Kuo heard them he said, "Excellent. Just the right name for me." — And he forthwith discarded his real name and himself adopted "Camel" also.

He lived at Feng-lo, to the west of Ch'ang-an. Camel was a grower of trees by profession; and all the great and wealthy residents of Ch'ang-an who planted trees for their enjoyment or lived off the sale of their fruit would compete for the favour of his services. It was a matter of observation that when Camel Kuo had planted a tree, even though it was uprooted from elsewhere, there was never a one but lived, and grew strong and glossy, and fruited early and abundantly. Other growers, however they spied on him and tried to imitate his methods, never could achieve his success.

Once, when questioned on the point, Camel replied: "I cannot make a tree live for ever or flourish. What I *can* do is comply with the nature of the tree so that it takes the way of its kind. When a tree is planted its roots should have room to breathe, its base should be firmed, the soil it is in should be old, and the fence around it should be close. When you have it this way, then you must neither disturb it nor worry about it, but go away and not come back. If you care for it like this when you plant it, and neglect it like this *after* you have planted it, then its nature will be fulfilled and it will take the way of its kind. And so all *I* do is avoid harming its growth — I have no power to make it grow; I avoid hindering the fruiting — I have no power to bring it forward or make it more abundant.

"With other growers it is not the same. They coil up the roots and they use fresh soil. They firm the base either too much or not enough. Or if they manage to avoid these faults, then they dote too fondly and worry too anxiously. They inspect the tree every morning and cosset it every night; they cannot walk away from it without turning back for another look. The worst of them will even scrape off the bark to see if it is still living, or shake the roots to test whether they are holding fast. And with all this the tree gets further every day from what a tree should be. This is not mothering but smothering, not affection but affliction. This is why they cannot rival my results: what other skill can I claim?"

"Would it be possible to apply this philosophy of yours to the art of government?" asked the questioner.

"My only art is the growing of trees," said Camel Kuo in answer. "Government is not my business. But living here in the country I have seen officials who go to a lot of trouble issuing orders as though they were deeply concerned for the people; yet all they achieve is an increase of misfortune. Morning and evening runners come yelling, 'Orders from the government: plough at once! Sow right away! Harvest inspection! Spin your silk! Weave your cloth! Raise your children! Feed your livestock!' Drums roll for assembly, blocks are struck to summon us. And we the common people miss our meals to receive the officials and still cannot find the time: how then can we expect to prosper our livelihood and find peace in our lives? This is why we are sick and weary; and in this state of affairs I suppose there may be some resemblance to my profession?"

"Wonderful!" was the delighted cry of the man who had questioned him. "The art I sought was of cultivating trees; the art I found was of cultivating men. Let this be passed on as a lesson to all in office!"

52

Rules for the Fan Lineage's Charitable Estate

From the time of the Sung dynasty (960–1279), many wealthy Chinese families formed charitable trusts for their descendants. One of the first men to set up such a trust was Fan Zhongyan (989–1052), an important political official.

This selection presents the rules that Fan set down for the way in which his descendants would share the income from his estate. What activities did the lineage support? What other activities would have been left to individual families? Why would lineages be more common among wealthy than poor families?

Thinking Historically

Lineage was both a social and economic organization. What impact would these lineages have on Chinese social life? Would they

---

Fan Zhongyan, *Fan Wengzheng gong ji,* in *Chinese Civilization: A Sourcebook,* 2nd ed., ed. and trans. Patricia Ebrey (New York: The Free Press, 1993), 155–56.

strengthen or weaken Chinese families? How might they effect Chinese economic life?

How did lineages make Chinese society different from that of Western Europe? Were there similar social institutions in Islamic society? Is there a modern equivalent?

1. One pint of rice per day may be granted for each person whom a branch has certified to be one of its members. (These quantities refer to polished rice. If hulled rice is used, the amount should be increased proportionately.)

2. Children of both sexes over five years of age are counted in the total.

3. Female servants may receive rice if they have borne children by men in the lineage and the children are over fifteen or they themselves are over fifty.

4. One bolt of silk for winter clothing may be granted for each individual, except children between five and ten years of age who may receive half a bolt.

5. Each branch may receive a rice ration for a single slave, but not any silk.

6. Every birth, marriage, death, or other change in the number of lineage members must immediately be recorded.

7. Each branch should make a list of those entitled to grain rations. At the end of the month the manager should examine these requests. He must not make any prior arrangements or exceed the stipulated monthly rations. The manager should also keep his own register in which he records the quantity due each branch based on the number of its members. If the manager spends money wastefully or makes advance payments to anyone, the branches have the authority to require him to pay an indemnity.

8. For the expenses of marrying a daughter, thirty strings of cash may be granted, unless the marriage is a second one, in which case twenty strings may be granted.

9. For the expenses of taking a first wife, twenty strings may be granted (but nothing for a second wife).

10. Lineage members who become officials may receive the regular rice and silk grants and the special grants for weddings and funerals if they are living at home awaiting a post, awaiting selection, or mourning their parents. They may also receive the grants if they leave their families at home while they serve in Sichuan, Gwangdong, or Fujien, or for any other good reason.

11. For the expenses of mourning and funerals in the various branches, if the deceased is a senior member, when mourning begins, a

grant of ten strings of cash may be made, and a further fifteen at the time of the burial. For more junior members, the figures are five and ten strings respectively. In the case of low-ranking members or youths under nineteen, seven strings for both expenses; for those under fifteen, three strings; for those under ten, two strings. No grant should be made for children who die before seven, or slaves or servants.

12. If any relatives through marriage living in the district face dire need or unexpected difficulties, the branches should jointly determine the facts and discuss ways to provide assistance from the income of the charitable estate.

13. A stock of rice should be stored by the charitable estate from year to year. The monthly rations and the grants of silk for winter clothing should start with the tenth month of 1050. Thereafter, during each year with a good harvest, two years' worth of grain rations should be hulled and stored. If a year of dearth occurs, no grants should be made except for the rice rations. Any surplus over and above the two years' reserve should be used first for funeral and mourning expenses, then marriage expenses. If there is still a remainder, winter clothes may be issued. However, if the surplus is not very large, the priorities should be discussed, and the amount available divided up and granted in equitable proportions. If grants cannot be made to all entitled to them, they should be made first to those who have suffered bereavement, next to those with weddings. In cases where more than one death has occurred at the same time, senior members take precedence over junior ones. Where the relative seniority of those concerned is the same, the grant should be made on the basis of which death or burial took place first. If, after paying out the rations and the allowances for marriages and burials, a surplus still remains, it must not be sold off, but hulled and put into storage for use as rations for three or more years. If there is a danger that the stored grain might go bad, it may be sold off and replaced with fresh rice after the autumn harvest. All members of the branches of the lineage will carefully comply with the above rules.

Tenth month, 1050. Academician of the Zizheng Hall, Vice-president of the Board of Rites, and Prefect of Hangzhou, Fan. Sealed.

REFLECTIONS

To pull together and compare some of the characterizations you made from the selections in this chapter, make a chart: Write the names of the three civilizations — European, Islamic, and Chinese — across the top of the page, and the categories social, economic, political, and cultural down the left margin, allowing a quarter page for each. Try to fill in as many of the blocks as you can. You might use more than one characterization for each. For instance, in the box for social aspects of European civilization you would, no doubt, write "feudalism." You might also write "nobles," "monasteries," "fealty and homage," "vassals defend," "sons inherit status." Or your style of observing and characterizing might lead you to such notes as "churches can be landlords," "lots of witnesses," and "they were very formal." All of these descriptions are correct: Just make sure your comments are about society, social behavior, social relationships, social organization, or various social elements — class, family, men and women, population, and age. Repeat this exercise with the other three categories. These are by no means exclusive, but try not to use the same words in describing, say, a social and an economic aspect.

After you have filled in as many of the blanks as you can, you can make comparisons in a number of interesting ways. (You have already done some of this, but here you can be more systematic.) First, compare how one category, say society, is different in Europe and Islam, or Europe and China, or China and Islam. You might, for example, say that European society was less centralized than Chinese or Islamic society or that the extended family was more important in China.

After doing the same for economics, politics, and culture, notice how the four categories of any civilization fit together. How does the type of society in medieval Europe, for instance, "fit" medieval Europe's economy? This interaction is what constitutes a civilization. See if you used a word repetitively in characterizing each of the four aspects of a particular civilization. Then try to categorize the civilization as a whole.

Now you are ready to compare each of these civilizations to another one. These characterizations may be general, or they may be qualified and later modified, but at the very least you now have a general starting point for more in-depth analysis of these three great civilizations in future chapters.

9

Love and Marriage

HISTORICAL CONTEXT

Medieval Societies and Cultures, 1000–1200 C.E.

Love and marriage are two of the many topics in social history, a field of history that covers every aspect of society and social relationships. Marriage is a social institution — perhaps one of the most common — whereas love is an emotion that affects social behavior. Love and marriage are also topics in cultural history. Love has prompted more literature, art, and music than perhaps any other emotion.

This chapter, like the previous one, explores some of the similarities and differences between medieval civilizations, but here we concentrate on love and marriage and broaden our range of focus to include Japanese, Chinese, Islamic, and Western European civilizations.

While it is unlikely that this chapter will lead us to the "essential" components of each civilization, it suggests one significant area in which different traditions have developed; it also says something about similarities among human societies.

THINKING HISTORICALLY

Developing Comparisons from Sources

Throughout this book you have been encouraged to make comparisons, but until now the comparisons have been suggested to you. Either the secondary sources or the introductions to the primary sources have proposed links and connections for you to consider. Chapter 8 took this a step further by asking you to formulate your own characterizations and then to compare them. You might have used words like *feudal* or *decentralized* and *centralized*; *religious* and *secular*; *agricultural*, *pastoral*, and *urban*; *extended* and *nuclear family*; *contractual* and *bureaucratic*; *theocratic* and *democratic*. This chapter asks you to develop your own characterizations and comparisons directly from the primary sources themselves.

Before you begin, note that generating comparative ideas is *not* the same as reaching conclusions; you cannot make accurate generalizations about civilizations based on a few brief readings. Imagine, for instance, that you are a historian a thousand years in the future, and you find the remains of late second millennium civilization. You want to know about the love and marriage customs of the North American people. Imagine what you might conclude if the only document you found was an article about bigamy. Next imagine that the only document available is a Bible schoolbook for children. You would reach very different conclusions — and neither would be completely accurate.

While no single source gives us enough information to reach a conclusion, any source gives us enough information to start thinking, to characterize, to hypothesize, and to theorize. Generating ideas is as important as testing them. So, as you read each of the selections in this chapter, ask yourself how their ideas of love and marriage are different from what you know and what you have read previously. After all, even without reading the first selection, you have some idea of what people today expect of love and marriage. Become aware of the ideas and opinions you already have and hold. Reading the historical selections critically will alert you to how similar or how different your ideas are from those held by people in the past.

53

LI CH'ING-CHAO

A Wife's Collection

In this document written in 1132 as the Northern Sung Empire of China was being overrun by the Chin Tatars, Li Ch'ing-chao tells the story of books and artwork that she and her husband, Chao Te-fu, had collected in their youth. She added this story to the end of her dead husband's monumental study of Chinese epigraphy (writings) called *Records on Metal and Stone.* What does her story tell you

---

Li Ch'ing-chao, "A Wife's Collection," from Stephen Owen, *Remembrances: The Experience of the Past in Classical Chinese Literature* (Cambridge: Harvard University Press, 1986), 80–98.

about the domestic life of a husband and wife in Sung China? How does the significance of their collection change over the course of their lives? What is the point of her story?

Thinking Historically

Because this is the chapter's first selection, you do not yet have another selection on the same topic with which to compare it, but you do have enough knowledge of the subject of love and marriage to consider how similar or different these ideas are from your own.

There are many ways to make such connections. Often, a good place to begin is to note what you like or dislike about the relationship described in the story. You might then ask yourself how your own expectations of love or marriage are similar to or different from those of Li Ch'ing-chao and her husband. Do you think they had a good marriage? Do you think *they* believed they had a good marriage? Do you think they loved each other?

Realizing that you cannot make accurate generalizations from one example, ask yourself how representative this couple was of Chinese families or of Chinese families from a particular class during that time period. Reread selections 50 and 52 for some perspective.

Recognize, too, that comparisons are always in some sense "virtual." Imagine finding a document that doesn't exist: Li Ch'ing-chao's account of her collecting life with her husband written while they were still young — before their personal losses and the fall of the Northern Sung Dynasty. How would this account be different? Why didn't she write such a document? What religious or philosophical view is expressed in the document she did write?

In 1101, in the first year of the Chien-chung Reign, I came as a bride to the Chao household. At that time my father was a division head in the Ministry of Rites, and my father-in-law, later Grand Councilor, was an executive in the Ministry of Personnel. My husband was then twenty-one and a student in the Imperial Academy. In those days both families, the Chaos and the Lis, were not well-to-do and were always frugal. On the first and fifteenth day of every month, my husband would get a short vacation from the Academy: he would "pawn some clothes" for five hundred cash and go to the market at Hsiang-kuo Temple, where he would buy fruit and rubbings of inscriptions. When he brought these home, we would sit facing one another, rolling them out before us, examining and munching. And we thought ourselves persons of the age of Ko-t'ien. . . .[1] When, two years later, he went to take up a post, we

[1] A mythic golden age. [Ed.]

lived on rice and vegetables, dressed in common cloth; but he would search out the most remote spots and out-of-the-way places to fulfill his interest in the world's most ancient writings and unusual characters. When his father, the Grand Councilor, was in office, various friends and relations held positions in the Imperial Libraries; there one might find many ancient poems omitted from the *Book of Songs,* unofficial histories, and writings never before seen, works hidden in walls and recovered from tombs. He would work hard at copying such things, drawing ever more pleasure from the activity, until he was unable to stop himself. Later, if he happened to see a work of painting or calligraphy by some person of ancient or modern times, or unusual vessels of the Three Dynasties of high antiquity, he would still pawn our clothes to buy them. I recall that in the Ch'ung-ning Reign a man came with a painting of peonies by Hsü Hsi and asked twenty thousand cash for it. In those days twenty thousand cash was a hard sum to raise, even for children of the nobility. We kept it with us a few days, and having thought of no plan by which we could purchase it, we returned it. For several days afterward husband and wife faced one another in deep depression.

Later we lived privately at home for ten years, gathering what we could here and there to have enough for food and clothing. Afterward, my husband governed two commanderies in succession, and he used up all his salary on "lead and wooden tablets" [for scholarly work]. Whenever he got a book, we would collate it with other editions and make corrections together, repair it, and label it with the correct title. When he got hold of a piece of calligraphy, a painting, a goblet, or a tripod, we would go over it at our leisure, pointing out faults and flaws, setting for our nightly limit the time it took one candle to burn down. Thus our collection came to surpass all others in fineness of paper and the perfection of the characters.

I happen to have an excellent memory, and every evening after we finished eating, we would sit in the hall called "Return Home" and make tea. Pointing to the heaps of books and histories, we would guess on which line of which page in which chapter of which book a certain passage could be found. Success in guessing determined who got to drink his or her tea first. Whenever I got it right, I would raise the teacup, laughing so hard that the tea would spill in my lap, and I would get up, not having been able to drink anything at all. I would have been glad to grow old in such a world. Thus, even though we were living in anxiety, hardship, and poverty, our wills were not broken.

When the book collection was complete, we set up a library in "Return Home" hall, with huge bookcases where the books were catalogued in sequence. There we put the books. Whenever I wanted to read, I would ask for the key, make a note in the ledger, then take out the books. If one of them was a bit damaged or soiled, it would be our responsibility to repair the spot and copy it out in a neat hand. There was no longer the same ease and casualness as before. This was an attempt to gain convenience which led instead to nervousness and anxiety. I couldn't bear it. And I began to plan how to do away with more than one meat in our meals, how to do away with all finery in my dress; for my hair there were no ornaments of bright pearls or kingfisher feathers; the household had no implements for gilding or embroidery. Whenever we would come upon a history or the work of a major writer, if there was nothing wrong with the printing and no errors in the edition, we would buy it on the spot to have as a second copy. His family had always specialized in *The Book of Changes* and the *Tso chuan,* so the collection of works in those two traditions was most perfect and complete. Books lay ranged on tables and desks, scattered on top of one another on pillows and bedding. This was what took our fancy and what occupied our minds, what drew our eyes and what our spirits inclined to; and our joy was greater than the pleasure others had in dancing girls, dogs, and horses. . . .

In 1126, the first year of the Ching-k'ang Reign, my husband was governing Tse-ch'uan when we heard that the Chin Tartars were moving against the capital. He was in a daze, realizing that all those full trunks and overflowing chests, which he regarded so lovingly and mournfully, would surely soon be his possessions no longer. In the third month of spring in 1127, the first year of the Chien-yen Reign, we hurried south for the funeral of his mother. Since we could not take the overabundance of our possessions with us, we first gave up the bulky printed volumes, the albums of paintings, and the most cumbersome of the vessels. Thus we reduced the size of the collection several times, and still we had fifteen cartloads of books. When we reached Tung-hai, it took a string of boats to ferry them all across the Huai, and again across the Yangtse to Chien-k'ang. In our old mansion in Ch'ing-chou we still had more than ten rooms of books and various items locked away, and we planned to have them all brought by boat the next year. But in the twelfth month Chin forces sacked Ch'ing-chou, and those ten or so rooms I spoke of were all reduced to ashes.

The next autumn, the ninth month of 1128, my husband took charge of Chien-k'ang Prefecture but relinquished the position in the spring of the following year. Again we put everything in boats and went up to Wu-hu and Ku-shu, intending to take up lodging on the River Kan. That summer in the fifth month we had reached Ch'ih-yang. At that point an imperial decree arrived, ordering my husband to take charge of Hu-chou, and before he assumed that office, to proceed to an audience with the Emperor. Therefore he had the household stop at Ch'ih-yang from which he would go off alone to answer the summons. On the thirteenth day of the sixth month he set off to carry out his duty. He had the boats pulled up onto the shore, and he sat there on the bank, in summer clothes with his headband set high on his forehead, his spirit like a tiger's, his eyes gleaming as though they would shoot into a person, while he gazed toward the boats and took his leave. I was in a terrible state of mind. I shouted to him, "If I hear the city is in danger, what should I do?" He answered from afar, his hands on his hips: "Follow the crowd. If you can't do otherwise, abandon the household goods first, then the clothes, then the books and scrolls, then the old bronzes — but carry the sacrificial vessels for the ancestral temple yourself; live or die with them; don't give *them* up." With this he galloped off on his horse.

As he was hurrying on his journey, he suffered sunstroke from the intense heat, and by the time he reached imperial headquarters, he had contracted a malarial fever. At the end of the seventh month I received a letter that he was lying sick. I was much alarmed, considering my husband's excitable nature and how nothing had been able to prevent the illness deteriorating into fever; his temperature might rise even higher, and in that case he would have to take chilled medicines; then the sickness would really be something to be worried about. Thereupon I set out by boat and in one day and night traveled three hundred leagues. At the point when I arrived he was taking large doses of *ch'ai-hu* and yellow *ch'in;* he had a recurring fever with dysentery, and the illness appeared terminal. I was weeping, and in such a desperate situation I could not bring myself to ask him what was to be done after his death. On the eighteenth day of the eighth month he could no longer get up; he took his brush and wrote a poem; when he finished, he passed away, with no thought at all for the future provision of his family. . . .

When the funeral was over I had nowhere to go. His Majesty had already sent the palace ladies elsewhere, and I heard that crossings of the Yangtse were to be prohibited. At the time I still had twenty thousand *chüan* of books, two thousand copies of inscriptions on metal and stone with colophons, table service and mats enough to entertain a hundred guests, along with other possessions equaling those already mentioned. I also grew very sick, to the point that my only vital sign was a rasping breath. The situation was getting more serious every day. I thought of my husband's brother-in-law, an executive in the Ministry of War on garrison duty in Hung-chou, and I dispatched two former employees of my husband to go ahead to my brother-in-law, taking the baggage. That winter in the twelfth month Chin invaders sacked Hung-chou and all was lost. Those books which, as I said, took a string of boats to ferry across the Yangtse were scattered into clouds of smoke. What remained were a few light scrolls and calligraphy pieces; manuscript copies of the collections of Li Po, Tu Fu, Han Yü, and Liu Tsung-yüan; a copy of *A New Account of Tales of the World (Shih-shuo hsin-yü);* a copy of *Discourses on Salt and Iron (Yen-t'ieh lun);* a few dozen rubbings of stone inscriptions from the Han and T'ang; ten or so ancient tripods and cauldrons; a few boxes of Southern T'ang manuscript editions — all of which I happened to have had removed to my chambers to pass the time during my illness — now a solitary pile of leftovers.

Since I could no longer go upriver, and since the movements of the invaders were unfathomable, I went to stay with my younger brother Li Hang, a reviser of edicts. By the time I reached T'ai-chou, the governor of the place had already fled. Proceeding on to Shan through Mu-chou, we left the clothing and linen behind. Hurrying to Yellow Cliff, we hired a boat to take us toward the sea, following the fleeing court. The court halted a while in Chang-an, then we followed the imperial barge on the sea route to Wen-chou and Yüeh-chou. In the twelfth month of the fourth year of the Chien-yen Reign, early in 1131, all the officials of the government were released from their posts. We went to Ch'ü-chou, and then in the third month of spring, now the first year of the Shao-hsing Reign (1131), we returned to Yüeh-chou, and in 1132, back again to Hang-chou.

When my husband had been gravely ill, a certain academician, Chang Fei-ch'ing, had visited him with a jade pot — actually it wasn't really jade but *min,* a stone like jade. I have no idea who started the story, but there was a false rumor that they had been discussing presenting it to the Chin as a tribute gift. I also learned that someone had made formal charges in the matter. I was terrified and dared say nothing, but I took all the bronze vessels and such things in the household and was about to turn them over to the imperial court. But by the time I reached Yüeh-chou, the court had already gone on to Ssu-ming. I didn't dare keep these things in the household any longer, so I sent them along with the manuscript books to Shah. Later, when the imperial army was rounding up defeated enemy troops, I heard that these had all been taken into the household of General Li. That "solitary pile of leftovers" of which I spoke had now been reduced by about fifty or sixty percent. All that remained were six or so baskets of books, painting, ink, and inkstones that I hadn't been able to part with. I always kept these under my bed and opened them only with my own hands.

At K'uai-chi I chose lodging in a cottage belonging to a local named Chung. Suddenly one night someone made off with five of the baskets through a hole in the wall. I was terribly upset and offered a substantial reward to get them back. Two days later Chung Fu-hao next door produced eighteen of the scrolls and asked for a reward. By that I knew the thief was not far away. I tried every means I could, but I still couldn't get hold of the rest. I have now found out that they were all purchased at a low price by the Circuit Fiscal Supervisor, Wu Yüeh. Now seventy or eighty percent of that "solitary pile of leftovers" is gone. I still have a few volumes from three or so sets, none complete, and some very ordinary pieces of calligraphy, but I still treasure them as if I were protecting my own head — how foolish I am!

Nowadays, when I chance to look over these books, it's like meeting old friends. And I recall when my husband was in the hall called "Calm Governance" in Lai-chou: he had first finished binding the volumes, making title slips of rue leaves to keep out insects and tie-ribbons of pale blue silk, binding ten *chüan* into one volume. Every day in the evening when the office clerks would go home, he would do editorial collations on two *chüan* and write a colophon for one inscription. . . .

Of those two thousand items, colophons were written on five hundred and two. It is so sad — today the ink of his writing seems still fresh, yet the trees by his grave have grown to an armspan in girth. . . .

Long ago when the city of Chiang-ling fell, Hsiao Yi, Emperor Yüan of the Liang, did not regret the fall of his kingdom, yet destroyed his books and printings [unwilling to see them fall into the hands of his conquerors]. When his capital Chiang-tu was sacked, Yang Kuang, Emperor Yang of the Sui, wasn't concerned with his own death, only with recovering his books [his spirit overturning the boat in which they were being transported so that he could have his library in the land of the dead]. It must be that the passions of human nature cannot be forgotten, even standing between life and death. Or maybe it is Heaven's will that beings as insignificant as ourselves are not fit to enjoy these superb things. Or it might be that the dead too have consciousness, and they still treasure such things, give them their devoted attention, unwilling to leave them in the world of the living. How hard they are to obtain and how easy to lose!

From the time I was eighteen [two years younger than Lu Chi when he wrote the "Poetic Exposition on Literature"] until now at the age of fifty-two [two years after the age at which Ch'u Po-yu realized the error of his earlier life] — a span of thirty years — how much calamity, how much gain and loss I have witnessed! When there is possession, there must be lack of possession; when there is a gathering together, there must be a dissolution — that is the constant principle of things. Someone loses a bow; someone else happens to find a bow — what's worth noticing in that? The reason why I have so minutely recorded this story from beginning to end is to serve as a warning for scholars and collectors in later generations.

Written this second year of the Shao-hsing Reign (1132), the eighth month, first day.

Li Ch'ing-chao

54

MURASAKI SHIKIBU

From *The Tale of Genji*

The Tale of Genji is, by most measures, the world's first novel. It was written by Murasaki Shikibu, a woman at the Japanese court, probably in the first decade after the year 1000. During the Heian period (794–1185) of Japanese history, women in the Japanese aristocracy differentiated their culture from the Chinese one that had dominated it since the seventh century.

While Japanese men were still using a dated form of Chinese for official documents, women like Lady Murasaki were fashioning the Japanese language into an effective and contemporary medium of communication. As ladies of the court, they also had the experience and leisure for writing intriguing, richly evocative stories.

The Tale of Genji is about Prince Genji — an attractive, talented, and sensitive son of the emperor — and his love interests. This chapter, occurring near the end of the novel, tells of one of Prince Genji's many flirtations. It also reveals much about the culture of the Japanese court. Notice the cultivation of music, dance, and poetry among the court nobility. What, if anything, does this display of sensitivity have to do with ideas of love and marriage? What signs do you see here of the persistence of Chinese culture in Heian Japan?

Also, notice the absence of monogamy in the court. The emperor is married but has taken in turn three consorts: Kokiden, Kiritsubo, and now Fujitsubo. What is the relationship between marriage and sex in this society? What does that tell you about the mores of the time?

Thinking Historically

Comparisons begin with two or more comparable documents or with a search for a similar work. The first approach requires less effort, so let us begin there. If you were asked to compare this selection from Lady Murasaki's *The Tale of Genji* with the previous selection (Li Ch'ing-chao's "A Wife's Collection"), you might make a number of connections. Even before considering the issue of love and marriage, you might note that both pieces were written by women; that one is fictional and the other a memoir; that one is Japanese, the other Chinese; that they were written at about the same time. All of this is fairly

---

Murasaki Shikibu, *The Tale of Genji,* trans. Arthur Waley (1929; reprint, Garden City, NY: Anchor Books, 1955), 201–10.

basic, but you then might go on to compare the role of women in Japanese and Chinese societies or to contrast how the two women think about men or love. A student of literary genres might even be moved to compare memoir and fiction.

Instead of comparing Japanese and Chinese ideas of men and women, ideas of love, or expectations for marriage, you might choose to compare Murasaki's world with your own. But first you would need to determine whether you will examine Japanese and American cultures, aristocratic and democratic societies, the world of a thousand years ago and today, or something else altogether.

Both of these approaches begin by defining the two points of comparison: Murasaki and Li Ch'ing-chao, or Murasaki and you. A more difficult, but more personal way of generating comparative ideas is to ask yourself, after reading Murasaki, what you want to compare and how you might test your idea. In this approach, the motivation is generated by some personal response you have to the reading. For example, in the previous reading you might have been struck by Li Ch'ing-chao's sacrifices or her loyalty and obedience to her husband's wishes. In order to understand why she acted this way, you would need to compare her behavior to that of other women, and your choice of comparison would depend on what you think explains Li Ch'ing-chao's behavior. If, for instance, you think her behavior might be a Confucian characteristic, you might compare her story with that of a woman raised outside the Confucian tradition. You would also need to consider the story of another woman raised in the Confucian tradition to see if she demonstrates the same behavior as Li Ch'ing-chao. No single comparison explains everything, but each comparison adds something to your observations and hypothesis and deepens your understanding.

What strikes you about Murasaki's story? What idea or action prompts your curiosity? How would you phrase your curiosity in a question about the past? In order to begin to answer your question, who or what would you want to compare with someone, something, or some idea in Murasaki's story?

About the twentieth day of the second month the Emperor gave a Chinese banquet under the great cherry-tree of the Southern Court. Both Fujitsubo and the Heir Apparent were to be there. Kokiden, although she knew that the mere presence of the Empress was sufficient to spoil her pleasure, could not bring herself to forgo so delightful an entertainment. After some promise of rain the day turned out magnificent; and in full sunshine, with the birds singing in every tree, the guests (royal princes, noblemen and professional poets alike) were handed the rhyme words which the Emperor had drawn by lot, and set to work to compose their poems. It was with a clear and ringing voice that Genji read out the word "Spring" which he had received as the rhyme-sound of his poem. Next came To no Chujo who, feeling that all eyes were upon him and determined to impress himself favourably on his audience, moved with the greatest possible elegance and grace; and when on receiving his rhyme he announced his name, rank, and titles, he took great pains to speak pleasantly as well as audibly. Many of the other gentlemen were rather nervous and looked quite pale as they came forward, yet they acquitted themselves well enough. But the professional poets, particularly owing to the high standard of accomplishment which the Emperor's and Heir Apparent's lively interest in Chinese poetry had at that time diffused through the Court, were very ill at ease; as they crossed the long space of the garden on their way to receive their rhymes they felt utterly helpless. A simple Chinese verse is surely not much to ask of a professional poet; but they all wore an expression of the deepest gloom. One expects elderly scholars to be somewhat odd in their movements and behaviour, and it was amusing to see the lively concern with which the Emperor watched their various but always uncouth and erratic methods of approaching the Throne. Needless to say a great deal of music had been arranged for. Towards dusk the delightful dance known as the Warbling of Spring Nightingales was performed, and when it was over the Heir Apparent, remembering the Festival of Red Leaves, placed a wreath on Genji's head and pressed him so urgently that it was impossible for him to refuse. Rising to his feet he danced very quietly a fragment of the sleeve-turning passage in the Wave Dance. In a few moments he was seated again, but even into this brief extract from a long dance he managed to import an unrivalled charm and grace. Even his father-in-law who was not in the best of humour with him was deeply moved and found himself wiping away a tear.

"And why have we not seen To no Chujo?" said the Heir Apparent. Whereupon Chujo danced the Park of Willow Flowers, giving a far more complete performance than Genji, for no doubt he knew that he would be called upon and had taken trouble to prepare his dance. It was a great success and the Emperor presented him with a cloak, which everyone said was a most unusual honour. After this the other young noblemen who were present danced in no particular order, but it was now so dark that it was impossible to discriminate between their performances.

Then the poems were opened and read aloud. The reading of Genji's verses was continually interrupted by loud murmurs of applause. Even the professional poets were deeply impressed, and it may well be imagined with what pride the Emperor, to whom at times Genji was a source of consolation and delight, watched him upon such an occasion as this. Fujitsubo, when she allowed herself to glance in his direction, marvelled that even Kokiden could find it in her heart to hate him. "It is because he is fond of me; there can be no other reason," she decided at last, and the verse, "Were I but a common mortal who now am gazing at the beauty of this flower, from its sweet petals not long should I withhold the dew of love," framed itself on her lips, though she dared not utter it aloud.

It was now very late and the banquet was over. The guests had scattered. The Empress and the Heir Apparent had both returned to the Palace — all was still. The moon had risen very bright and clear, and Genji, heated with wine, could not bear to quit so lovely a scene. The people at the Palace were probably all plunged in a heavy sleep. On such a night it was not impossible that some careless person might have left some door unfastened, some shutter unbarred. Cautiously and stealthily he crept towards Fujitsubo's apartments and inspected them. Every bolt was fast. He sighed; here there was evidently nothing to be done. He was passing the loggia of Kokiden's palace when he noted that the shutters of the third arch were not drawn. After the banquet Kokiden herself had gone straight to the Emperor's rooms. There did not seem to be anyone about. A door leading from the loggia into the house was standing open, but he could hear no sound within. "It is under just such circumstances as this that one is apt to drift into compromising situations," thought Genji. Nevertheless he climbed quietly on to the balustrade and peeped. Everyone must be asleep. But no; a very agreeable young voice with an intonation which was certainly not that of any waiting-woman or common person was softly humming the last two lines of the *Oborozuki-yo.*[1] Was not the voice coming towards him? It seemed so, and stretching out his hand he suddenly found that he was grasping a lady's sleeve. "Oh, how you frightened me!" she cried. "Who is it?" "Do not be alarmed," he whispered. "That both of us were not content to miss the beauty of this departing night is proof more clear than the half-clouded moon that we were meant to meet," and as he recited the words he took her gently by the hand and led her into the house, closing the door behind them. Her surprised and puzzled air fascinated him. "There is someone there," she whispered tremulously, pointing to the inner room. "Child," he answered, "I am allowed to go wherever I please and if you send for your friends they will only tell you that I have every right to be here. But if you will stay quietly here . . ." It was Genji. She knew his voice and the discovery somewhat reassured her. She thought his conduct rather strange, but she was determined that he should not think her prudish or stiff. And so because he on his side was still somewhat excited after the doings of

[1] A famous poem by Oye no Chisato (ninth century): "What so lovely as a night when the moon though dimly clouded is never wholly lost to sight!"

the evening, while she was far too young and pliant to offer any serious resistance, he soon got his own way with her.

Suddenly they saw to their discomfiture that dawn was creeping into the sky. She looked, thought Genji, as though many disquieting reflections were crowding into her mind. "Tell me your name" he said. "How can I write you unless you do? Surely this is not going to be our only meeting?" She answered with a poem in which she said that names are of this world only and he would not care to know hers if he were resolved that their love should last till worlds to come. It was a mere quip and Genji, amused at her quickness, answered, "You are quite right. It was a mistake on my part to ask." And he recited the poem: "While still I seek to find on which blade dwells the dew, a great wind shakes the grasses of the level land." "If you did not repent of this meeting," he continued, "you would surely tell me who you are. I do not believe that you want . . ." But here he was interrupted by the noise of people stirring in the next room. There was a great bustle and it was clear that they would soon be starting out to fetch Princess Kokiden back from the palace. There was just time to exchange fans in token of their new friendship before Genji was forced to fly precipitately from the room. In his own apartments he found many of his gentlemen waiting for him. Some were awake, and these nudged one another when he entered the room as though to say, "Will he never cease these disreputable excursions?" But discretion forbad them to show that they had seen him and they all pretended to be fast asleep. Genji too lay down, but he could not rest. He tried to recall the features of the lady with whom he had just spent so agreeable a time. Certainly she must be one of Kokiden's sisters. Perhaps the fifth or sixth daughter, both of whom were still unmarried. The handsomest of them (or so he had always heard) were Prince Sochi's wife and the fourth daughter, the one with whom To no Chujo got on so badly. It would really be rather amusing if it did turn out to be Chujo's wife. The sixth was shortly to be married to the Heir Apparent. How tiresome if it were she! But at present he could think of no way to make sure. She had not behaved at all as though she did not want to see him again. Why then had she refused to give him any chance of communicating with her? In fact he worried about the matter so much and turned it over in his mind with such endless persistency that it soon became evident he had fallen deeply in love with her. Nevertheless no sooner did the recollection of Fujitsubo's serious and reticent demeanour come back to his mind than he realized how incomparably more she meant to him than this light-hearted lady.

That day the after-banquet kept him occupied till late at night. At the Emperor's command he performed on the thirteen-stringed zithern and had an even greater success than with his dancing on the day before. At dawn Fujitsubo retired to the Emperor's rooms. Disappointed in his hope that the lady of last night would somewhere or somehow make her appearance on the scene, he sent for Yoshikiyo and Koremitsu with whom all his secrets were shared and bade them keep watch upon the lady's family. When he returned next day from duty at the Palace they reported that they had just witnessed the departure of several coaches which had been drawn up under shelter in the Courtyard of the Watch. "Among a group of persons who seemed to be the domestic attendants of those for whom the coaches were waiting two gentlemen came threading their way in a great hurry. These we recognized as Shii no Shosho and Uchuben, so there is little doubt that the carriages belonged to Princess Kokiden. For the rest we noted that the ladies were by no means ill-looking and that the whole party drove away in three carriages." Genji's heart beat fast. But he was no nearer than before to finding out which of the sisters it had been. Supposing her father, the Minister of the Right, should hear anything of this, what a to-do there would be! It would indeed mean his absolute ruin. It was a pity that while he was about it he did not stay with her till it was a little lighter. But there it was! He did not know her face, but yet he was determined to recognize her. How? He lay on his bed devising and rejecting endless schemes. Murasaki too must be growing impatient. Days had passed since he had visited her and he remembered with tenderness how low-spirited she became when he was not able to be with her. But in a moment his thoughts had returned to the unknown lady. He still had her fan. It was a folding fan with ribs of hinoki-wood and tassels tied in a splice-knot. One side was covered with silverleaf on which was painted a dim moon, giving the impression of a moon reflected in water. It was a device which he had seen many times before, but it had agreeable associations for him, and continuing the metaphor of the "grass on the moor" which she had used in her poem, he wrote on the fan — "Has mortal man ever puzzled his head with such a question before as to ask where the moon goes to when she leaves the sky at dawn?" And he put the fan safely away. It was on his conscience that he had not for a long while been to the Great Hall; but fearing that Murasaki too might be feeling very unhappy, he first went home to give her her lessons. Every day she was improving not only in looks, but also in amiability of character. The beauty of her disposition was indeed quite out of the common. The idea that so perfect a nature was in his hands, to train and cultivate as he thought best, was very attractive to Genji. It might however have been objected that to receive all her education from a young man is likely to make a girl somewhat forward in her manner.

First there was a great deal to tell about what happened at the Court entertainments of the last few days. Then followed her music lesson, and already it was time to go. "Oh, why must he always go away so soon?" she wondered sadly, but by now she was so used to it that she no longer fretted as she had done a little while ago.

At the Great Hall he could, as usual, scarcely get a word out of Aoi. The moment that he sat idle a thousand doubts and puzzles began to revolve in his mind. He took up his zithern and began to sing:

Not softlier pillowed is my head
That rests by thine, unloving bride,
Than were those jagged stones my bed
Through which the falls of Nuki stride.

At this moment Aoi's father came by and began to discuss the unusual success of the recent festivities. "Old as I am," he said — "and I may say that I have lived to see four illustrious sovereigns occupy the Throne, I have never taken part in a banquet which produced verses so spirited or dancing and music so admirably performed. Talent of every description seems at present to exist in abundance; but it is creditable to those in authority that they knew how to make good use of it. For my part I enjoyed myself so much that had I but been a few years younger I would positively have joined in the dancing!" "No special steps were taken to discover the musicians," answered Genji. "We merely used those who were known to the government in one part of the country and another as capable performers. If I may say so, it was Chujo's Willow Dance that made the deepest impression and is likely always to be remembered as a remarkable performance. But if you, Sir, had indeed honoured us, a new lustre would have been added to my Father's reign." Aoi's brothers now arrived and leaning against the balustrade gave a little concert, their various instruments blending delightfully.

Fugitive as their meeting had been, it had sufficed to plunge the lady whose identity Prince Genji was now seeking to establish into the depths of despair; for in the fourth month she was to become the Heir Apparent's wife. Turmoil filled her brain. Why had not Genji visited her again? He must surely know whose daughter she was. But how should he know which daughter? Besides, her sister Kokiden's house was not a place where, save under very strange circumstances, he was likely to feel at all at his ease. And so she waited in great impatience and distress; but of Genji there was no news.

About the twentieth day of the third month her father, the Minister of the Right, held an archery meeting in which most of the young noblemen and princes were present. It was followed by a wistaria feast. The cherry blossom was for the most part over, but two trees, which the Minister seemed somehow to have persuaded to flower later than all the rest, were still an enchanting sight. He had had his house rebuilt only a short time ago when celebrating the initiation of his granddaughters, the children of Kokiden. It was now a magnificent building and not a thing in it but was of the very latest fashion. He had invited Genji when he had met him at the Palace only a few days before and was extremely annoyed when he did not appear. Feeling that the party would be a failure if Genji did not come, he sent his son Shii no Shosho to fetch him, with the poem: "Were my flowers as those of other gardens never should I have ventured to summon you." Genji was in attendance upon the Emperor and at once showed him the message. "He seems very pleased with himself and his flowers," said His Majesty with a smile; adding, "as he has sent for you like this, I think you had better go. After all, your half-sisters are being brought up at his house, and you ought not to treat him quite as a stranger." He went to his apartments and dressed. It was very late indeed when at last he made his appearance at the party. He was dressed in a cloak of thin Chinese fabric, white outside but lined with yellow. His robe was of a deep wine-red colour with a very long train. The dignity and grace with which he carried this fancifully regal attire in a company where all were dressed in plain official robes were indeed remarkable, and in the end his presence perhaps contributed more to the success of the party than did the fragrance of the Minister's boasted flowers. His entry was followed by some very agreeable music. It was already fairly late when Genji, on the plea that the wine had given him a headache, left his seat and went for a walk. He knew that his two stepsisters, the daughters of Kokiden, were in the inner apartments of the palace. He went to the eastern portico and rested there. It was on this side of the house that the wistaria grew. The wooden blinds were raised and a number of ladies were leaning out of the window to enjoy the blossoms. They had hung bright-coloured robes and shawls over the windowsill just as is done at the time of the New Year dancing and other gala days and were behaving with a freedom of allure which contrasted very oddly with the sober decorum of Fujitsubo's household. "I am feeling rather overpowered by all the noise and bustle of the flower-party," Genji explained. "I am very sorry to disturb my sisters, but I can think of nowhere else to seek refuge . . ." and advancing towards the main door of the women's apartments, he pushed back the curtain with his shoulder. "Refuge indeed!" cried one of the ladies, laughing at him. "You ought to know by now that it is only poor relations who come to seek refuge with the more successful members of their family. What pray have you come to bother us for?" "Impertinent creatures!" he thought, but nevertheless there was something in their manner which convinced him they were persons of some consequence in the house and not, as he at first supposed, mere waiting-women. A scent of costly perfumes pervaded the room; silken skirts rustled in the darkness. There could be little doubt that these were Kokiden's sisters and their friends. Deeply absorbed, as indeed was the whole of his family, in the fashionable gaieties of the moment, they had flouted decorum and posted themselves at the window that they might see what little they could of the banquet which was proceeding outside. Little thinking that his plan could succeed, yet led on by delightful recollections of his previous encounter, he advanced towards them chanting in a careless undertone the song:

At Ishikawa, Ishikawa
A man from Koma [Korea] took my belt away . . .

But for "belt" he substituted "fan" and by this means he sought to discover which of the ladies was his friend. "Why, you have got it wrong! I never heard of *that* Korean," one of them cried. Certainly it was not she. But there was another who though she remained silent seemed to him to be sighing softly to herself. He stole towards the curtain-of-state behind which she was sitting and taking her hand in his at a venture he whispered the poem: "If on this day of shooting my arrow went astray, 'twas that in dim morning twilight only the mark had glimmered in my view." And she, unable any longer to hide that she knew him, answered with the verse: "Had it been with the arrows of the heart that you had shot, though from the moon's slim bow no brightness came, would you have missed your mark?" Yes, it was her voice. He was delighted, and yet . . .

55

SEI SHONAGON

From *The Pillow Book*

Sei Shonagon was a contemporary of Murasaki Shikibu and also served as a lady-in-waiting at the Japanese imperial court one thousand years ago. She is also recognized as one of the great writers of Japanese literature. Murasaki mentions Sei Shonagon in a diary entry:

> **Sei Shonagon has the most extraordinary air of satisfaction. Yet, if we stop to examine those Chinese writings of hers that she so presumptuously scatters about the place, we find that they are full of imperfections. Someone who makes such an effort to be differ-**

The Pillow Book of Sei Shonagon, trans. and ed. Ivan Morris (Baltimore: Penguin, 1971), 39–40, 49–50, 60–62, 135–36, 182–84.

> ent from others is bound to fall in people's esteem, and I can only think that her future will be a hard one. She is a gifted woman, to be sure. Yet, if one gives free rein to one's emotions even under the most inappropriate circumstances, if one has to sample each interesting thing that comes along, people are bound to regard one as frivolous. And how can things turn out well for such a woman?

Whether fair, accurate, or perhaps inspired by competitive jealousy, Murasaki's account is the only primary source of information we have about Sei Shonagon other than *The Pillow Book* itself. Fortunately, *The Pillow Book* makes up for such limited resources. It is full of personal catalogs of things Sei Shonagon finds hateful, depressing, elegant, annoying, squalid, presumptuous, adorable, and "outstandingly splendid," as well as recollections and brief essays.

What can you deduce about the life of Sei Shonagon from these excerpts? What can you deduce about the lives of women-in-waiting in Heian Japan? What does she tell us about her culture's ideas of love and marriage?

Thinking Historically

Comparisons do not have to be based on grand generalizations about the characteristics of civilizations; they can be specific and precise, revealing elements of a particular society or culture at a particular time.

It is a rare and happy stroke of good luck that two major writers lived at the same time, a thousand years ago, revealing in great detail their society and culture in their works. Because the authors were contemporaries, we are able to compare their writings as checks on each other. Such comparison is especially useful for *The Pillow Book* and *The Tale of Genji,* because the latter is fiction and the former is intentionally personal. How do we know, for instance, that a particular idea or activity presented by Murasaki is not completely fictional? How do we know that an idea expressed by Sei Shonagon is solely her own and no one else's? Contrasting one source with another allows us to establish patterns and consistency or a lack thereof. When reading, try to establish the reliability of the author or narrator. For example, show how a detail or aspect of Japanese Heian culture or society that we are not likely to believe in one source becomes more credible because we find it in the other source.

When I make myself imagine what it is like to be one of those women who live at home, faithfully serving their husbands — women who have not a single exciting prospect in life yet who believe that they are perfectly happy — I am filled with scorn. Often they are of quite good birth, yet have had no opportunity to find out what the world is like. I wish they could live for a while in our society, even if it should mean taking service as Attendants, so that they might come to know the delights it has to offer.

I cannot bear men who believe that women serving in the Palace are bound to be frivolous and wicked. Yet I suppose their prejudice is understandable. After all, women at Court do not spend their time hiding modestly behind fans and screens, but walk about, looking openly at people they chance to meet. Yes, they see everyone face to face, not only ladies-in-waiting like themselves, but even Their Imperial Majesties (whose august names I hardly dare mention), High Court Nobles, senior courtiers, and other gentlemen of high rank. In the presence of such exalted personages the women in the Palace are all equally brazen, whether they be the maids of ladies-in-waiting, or the relations of Court ladies who have come to visit them, or house-keepers, or latrine-cleaners, or women who are of no more value than a roof-tile or a pebble. Small wonder that the young men regard them as immodest! Yet are the gentlemen themselves any less so? They are not exactly bashful when it comes to looking at the great people in the Palace. No, everyone at Court is much the same in this respect.

Women who have served in the Palace, but who later get married and live at home, are called Madam and receive the most respectful treatment. To be sure, people often consider that these women, who have displayed their faces to all and sundry during their years at Court, are lacking in feminine grace. How proud they must be, nevertheless, when they are styled Assistant Attendants, or summoned to the Palace for occasional duty, or ordered to serve as Imperial envoys during the Kamo Festival! Even those who stay at home lose nothing by having served at Court. In fact they make very good wives. For example, if they are married to a provincial governor and their daughter is chosen to take part in the Gosechi dances, they do not have to disgrace themselves by acting like provincials and asking other people about procedure. They themselves are well versed in the formalities, which is just as it should be.

. . . A lover who is leaving at dawn announces that he has to find his fan and his paper. 'I know I put them somewhere last night,' he says. Since it is pitch dark, he gropes about the room, bumping into the furniture and muttering, 'Strange! Where on earth can they be?' Finally he discovers the objects. He thrusts the paper into the breast of his robe with a great rustling sound; then he snaps open his fan and busily fans away with it. Only now is he ready to take his leave. What charmless behaviour! 'Hateful' is an understatement.

Equally disagreeable is the man who, when leaving in the middle of the night, takes care to fasten the cord of his headdress. This is quite unnecessary; he could perfectly well put it gently on his head without tying the cord. And why must he spend time adjusting his cloak or hunting costume? Does he really think someone may see him at this time of night and criticize him for not being impeccably dressed?

A good lover will behave as elegantly at dawn as at any other time. He drags himself out of bed with a look of dismay on his face. The lady urges him on: 'Come, my friend, it's getting light. You don't want anyone to find you here.' He gives a deep sigh, as if to say that the night has not been nearly long enough and that it is agony to leave. Once up, he does not instantly pull on his trousers. Instead he comes close to the lady and whispers whatever was left unsaid during the night. Even when he is dressed, he still lingers, vaguely pretending to be fastening his sash.

Presently he raises the lattice, and the two lovers stand together by the side door while he tells her how he dreads the coming day, which will keep them apart; then he slips away. The lady watches him go, and this moment of parting will remain among her most charming memories.

Indeed, one's attachment to a man depends largely on the elegance of his leave-taking. When he jumps out of bed, scurries about the room, tightly fastens his trouser-sash, rolls up the sleeves of his Court cloak, over-robe, or hunting costume, stuffs his belongings into the breast of his robe and then briskly secures the outer sash — one really begins to hate him.

It is so stiflingly hot in the Seventh Month that even at night one keeps all the doors and lattices open. At such times it is delightful to wake up when the moon is shining and to look outside. I enjoy it even when there is no moon. But to wake up at dawn and see a pale sliver of a moon in the sky — well, I need hardly say how perfect that is.

I like to see a bright new straw mat that has just been spread out on a well-polished floor. The best place for one's three-foot curtain of state[1] is in the front of the room near the veranda. It is pointless to put it in the rear of the room, as it is most unlikely that anyone will peer in from that direction.

It is dawn and a woman is lying in bed after her lover has taken his leave. She is covered up to her head with a light mauve robe that has a lining of dark violet; the colour of both the outside and the lining is fresh and glossy. The woman, who appears to be asleep, wears an unlined orange robe and a dark crimson skirt of stiff silk whose cords hang loosely by her side, as if they have been left untied. Her thick

[1] A curtain to protect women from prying eyes. A three-foot horizontal bar would normally be placed near the veranda approximately four feet above the floor with five widths of curtain. [Ed.]

tresses tumble over each other in cascades, and one can imagine how long her hair must be when it falls freely down her back.

Nearby another woman's lover is making his way home in the misty dawn. He is wearing loose violet trousers, an orange hunting costume, so lightly coloured that one can hardly tell whether it has been dyed or not, a white robe of stiff silk, and a scarlet robe of glossy, beaten silk. His clothes, which are damp from the mist, hang loosely about him. From the dishevelment of his side locks one can tell how negligently he must have tucked his hair into his black lacquered headdress when he got up. He wants to return and write his next-morning letter before the dew on the morning glories has had time to vanish; but the path seems endless, and to divert himself he hums 'The sprouts in the flax fields'.

As he walks along, he passes a house with an open lattice. He is on his way to report for official duty, but cannot help stopping to lift up the blind and peep into the room. It amuses him to think that a man has probably been spending the night here and has only recently got up to leave, just as happened to himself. Perhaps that man too had felt the charm of the dew.

Looking round the room, he notices near the woman's pillow an open fan with a magnolia frame and purple paper; and at the foot of her curtain of state he sees some narrow strips of Michinoku paper and also some other paper of a faded colour, either orange-red or maple.

The woman senses that someone is watching her and, looking up from under her bedclothes, sees a gentleman leaning against the wall by the threshold, a smile on his face. She can tell at once that he is the sort of man with whom she need feel no reserve. All the same, she does not want to enter into any familiar relations with him, and she is annoyed that he should have seen her asleep.

'Well, well, Madam,' says the man, leaning forward so that the upper part of his body comes behind her curtains, 'what a long nap you're having after your morning adieu! You really are a lie-abed!'

'You call me that, Sir,' she replied, 'only because you're annoyed at having had to get up before the dew had time to settle.'

Their conversation may be commonplace, yet I find there is something delightful about the scene.

Now the gentleman leans further forward and, using his own fan, tries to get hold of the fan by the woman's pillow. Fearing his closeness, she moves further back into her curtain enclosure, her heart pounding. The gentleman picks up the magnolia fan and, while examining it, says in a slightly bitter tone, 'How standoffish you are!'

But now it is growing light; there is a sound of people's voices, and it looks as if the sun will soon be up. Only a short while ago this same man was hurrying home to write his next-morning letter before the mists had time to clear. Alas, how easily his intentions have been forgotten!

While all this is afoot, the woman's original lover has been busy with his own next-morning letter, and now, quite unexpectedly, the messenger arrives at her house. The letter is attached to a spray of bush-clover, still damp with dew, and the paper gives off a delicious aroma of incense. Because of the new visitor, however, the woman's servants cannot deliver it to her.

Finally it becomes unseemly for the gentleman to stay any longer. As he goes, he is amused to think that a similar scene may be taking place in the house he left earlier that morning.

On the last day of the Second Month, when there was a strong wind, a dark grey sky, and a little snow, a man from the Office of Grounds came to the Black Door and asked to speak to me. He then approached and gave me a note which he said was from Kintō, the Imperial Adviser. It consisted of a sheet of pocket-paper on which was written,

And for a moment in my heart
I feel that spring has come.

The words were most appropriate for the weather; but what concerned me was that I was bound to produce the opening lines. I asked the messenger which gentlemen were present, and he gave me their names. They were all the type of men to put me on my mettle; but it was Kintō's presence among them that made me most reluctant to give a commonplace answer. I felt very alone and wished that I could show the note to Her Majesty and discuss my predicament; but I knew that she was lying down with the Emperor.

The man from the Office of Grounds urged me to hurry; and I realized that if, in addition to bungling my reply, I was slow about it, I should really disgrace myself. 'It can't be helped,' I thought and, trembling with emotion, wrote the following lines:

As though pretending to be blooms
The snowflakes scatter in the wintry sky.

I handed my poem to the messenger and anxiously wondered how Kintō and the others would receive it. If their verdict was unfavourable I would rather not hear it, I thought as I eagerly awaited the news.

It turned out that the Captain of the Middle Palace Guards (who at that time held the rank of Middle Captain in the Inner Palace Guards) was present when my answer arrived, and he told me that Toshikata, the Imperial Adviser, gave the following judgement: 'After this she deserves to be appointed to the Palace Attendants' Office.'

When a woman lives alone, her house should be extremely dilapidated, the mud wall should be falling to pieces, and if there is a pond, it should be overgrown with water-plants. It is not essential that the garden be covered with sage-brush; but weeds should be growing through the sand in patches, for this gives the place a poignantly desolate look.

I greatly dislike a woman's house when it is clear that she has scurried about with a knowing look on her face, arranging everything just as it should be, and when the gate is kept tightly shut.

When a Court lady is on leave from the Palace, it is pleasant if she can stay with her parents. While she is there, people are always coming and going, there is a lot of noisy conversation in the back rooms, and the clatter of horses' hoofs resounds outside. Yet she is in no danger of being criticized.

Things are very different if she is staying in someone else's house. Let us suppose that a man comes to visit the lady, either openly or in secret. He stands by the front gate and says to her, 'I did not know you were at home, else I should certainly have called on you before. When will you return to Court?' If it is a man she has set her heart on, the lady cannot possibly leave him standing outside and she opens the front door for him.

Then, to her great annoyance, she hears the owner of the house, who has evidently decided that there is too much noise and that it is dangerous to leave the door unbolted so late at night. 'Has the outer gate been closed?' he asks the porter. 'No, Sir,' says the latter in a disgruntled tone. 'There's still a visitor in the house.' 'Well, be sure to close it as soon as he's left. There have been a lot of burglaries recently.' This is especially irking for the lady since the man who is with her can hear everything. Meanwhile the servants are constantly peeping in to see whether the guest is getting ready to leave — much to the amusement of the attendants who have accompanied him on his visit. Then the attendants start imitating the owner's voice. Oh, what a scolding there would be if he heard them!

Sometimes the lady will receive visits from a man who does not show any tender feelings for her in either his looks or his words. Presumably he must care for her; else why would he continue his visits night after night? Nevertheless the man may turn out to be quite harmless and will leave her saying, 'It's really getting late. And I suppose it *is* rather dangerous to keep the gate open at this hour.'

One can tell if a man really loves one, because he will insist on staying all night however much one may urge him to leave. Time after time the night watchman has made his rounds, and now he exclaims in a very audible voice, 'Good heavens! The dawn has come' (as if it were so surprising) 'and someone's gone and left the gate wide open all night. Such carelessness!' Then he securely bolts the gate, though it is now light and there is no need for such precautions. How unpleasant it all is!

Yes, things are a great deal better when one is staying with one's own parents. Parents-in-law, however, are the most awkward of all, since one is always worrying about what they are going to think. I imagine that it must also be difficult to stay with an elder brother.

What I really like is a house where no one cares about the gate either in the middle of the night or at dawn, and where one is free to meet one's visitor, whether he be an Imperial Prince or a gentleman from the Palace. In the winter one can stay awake together all night with the lattices wide open. When the time comes for him to leave, one has the pleasure of watching him playing upon his flute as he goes; if a bright moon is still hanging in the sky, it is a particular delight. After he has disappeared, one does not go to bed at once, but stays up, discussing the visitor with one's companions, and exchanging poems; then gradually one falls asleep.

56

OMAR KHAYYÁM

From *The Rubáiyát*

We move now from Chinese and Japanese cultures to Islamic culture, about a hundred years later — or nine hundred years ago. Islamic or Arabic culture, during this period and since, spans a territory larger than Chinese and Japanese cultures. Local traditions of converted Berbers[1] in Morocco were very different from those of Arabs in Arabia, Iraqis in Baghdad, or mountain tribes in Afghanistan, yet all of these regional cultures were united by the Arabic language and the Islamic faith. To acquire ancient traditions as rich as those of ancient Mesopotamia, Egypt, and India and to mold them into a single culture was an astounding feat of assimilation. Persian culture, which was particularly vibrant, converted to Islam and to the Arabic language. Between 750 and 1000, as the seat of the Abbasid Caliphate,[2] Persia

[1] Indigenous people of North Africa before the Arab conquest in the seventh century.

[2] The ruling government of all Muslims. The Abbasid Caliphate ruled from 749–1258, though after 833 its authority was challenged.

Omar Khayyám, *Rubáiyát of Omar Khayyám,* trans. Edward FitzGerald (New York: St. Martin's Press, 1983), 53, 54, 56–60, 62, 66–67, 70, 74, 76, 84, 87, 90–95, 104.

recentered the Muslim world at Baghdad and gave it new strength and splendor.

Omar Khayyám was a Persian scientist and mathematician who lived at the end of the eleventh and the beginning of the twelfth century. These verses, attributed to Khayyám but communicated to most of the English-speaking world through this 1859 translation by Edward FitzGerald, reflect the sophisticated, cosmopolitan world of Islam around 1100. What do you learn about Islamic society and culture from these verses? What do you learn about ideas of love and marriage in the medieval Muslim world?

Thinking Historically

While verses from this work have graced greeting cards and filled the pages of inspirational books, their deeper meanings are complex. They derive from a tradition of Islam, particularly strong in Persia, called Sufism. Sufis are Muslim mystics, seers, who strive to recognize God's presence in everything. The love professed in these verses is the love of God; the "Thee" and "Thy" refer to God.

Muslim Sufis are, of course, not the only people to speak of the love of God. After reading this selection, try to think of a document in your own cultural tradition that expresses similar ideas of religious love. If you want to determine if such ideas are universal (found in all cultures), general (found in many cultures), or unusual (found in few cultures), where will you look for comparable documents? You have already read many religious selections in this volume. Do any of them help you understand how common or unusual this document is?

I

Wake! For the Sun, who scatter'd into flight
The Stars before him from the Field of Night,
   Drives Night along with them from Heav'n, and strikes
The Sultán's Turret with a Shaft of Light.

II

Before the phantom of False morning died,
Methought a Voice within the Tavern cried,
   "When all the Temple is prepared within,
Why nods the drowsy Worshipper outside?"

IV

Now the New Year reviving old Desires,
The thoughtful Soul to Solitude retires,
  Where the White Hand of Moses on the Bough
Puts out, and Jesus from the Ground suspires.

VII

Come, fill the Cup, and in the fire of Spring
Your Winter-garment of Repentance fling:
  The Bird of Time has but a little way
To flutter — and the Bird is on the Wing.

VIII

Whether at Naishápúr or Babylon,
Whether the Cup with sweet or bitter run,
  The Wine of Life keeps oozing drop by drop,
The Leaves of Life keep falling one by one.

IX

Each Morn a thousand Roses brings, you say;
Yes, but where leaves the Rose of Yesterday?
  And this first Summer month that brings the Rose
Shall take Jamshýd and Kaikobád away.

XI

With me along the strip of Herbage strown
That just divides the desert from the sown,
  Where name of Slave and Sultán is forgot —
And Peace to Mahmúd on his golden Throne!

XII

A Book of Verses underneath the Bough,
A Jug of Wine, a Loaf of Bread — and Thou
  Beside me singing in the Wilderness —
Oh, Wilderness were Paradise enow!

XIII

Some for the Glories of This World; and some
Sigh for the Prophet's Paradise to come;
   Ah, take the Cash, and let the Credit go,
Nor heed the rumble of a distant Drum!

XVI

The Worldly Hope men set their Hearts upon
Turns Ashes — or it prospers; and anon,
   Like Snow upon the Desert's dusty Face,
Lighting a little hour or two — is gone.

XVII

Think, in this batter'd Caravanserai
Whose Portals are alternate Night and Day,
   How Sultán after Sultán with his Pomp
Abode his destined Hour, and went his way.

XXIV

Ah, make the most of what we yet may spend,
Before we too into the Dust descend;
   Dust into Dust, and under Dust to lie
Sans Wine, sans Song, sans Singer, and — sans End!

XXV

Alike lot those who for TO-DAY prepare,
And those that after some TO-MORROW stare,
   A Muezzín from the Tower of Darkness cries
"Fools! your Reward is neither Here nor There."

XXXII

There was the Door to which I found no Key;
There was the Veil through which I might not see:
   Some little talk awhile of ME and THEE
There was — and then no more of THEE and ME.

XXXVII

For I remember stopping by the way
To watch a Potter thumping his wet Clay:
   And with its all-obliterated Tongue
It murmur'd — "Gently, Brother, gently, pray!"

XXXVIII

And has not such a Story from of Old
Down Man's successive generations roll'd
   Of such a clod of saturated Earth
Cast by the Maker into Human mould?

XLII

And if the Wine you drink, the Lip you press
End in what All begins and ends in — Yes;
   Think then you are TO-DAY what YESTERDAY
You were — TO-MORROW you shall not be less.

LV

You know, my Friends, with what a brave Carouse
I made a Second Marriage in my house;
   Divorced old barren Reason from my Bed
And took the Daughter of the Vine to Spouse.

LX

The mighty Mahmúd, Allah-breathing Lord
That all the misbelieving and black Horde
   Of Fears and Sorrows that infest the Soul
Scatters before him with his whirlwind Sword.

LXIV

Strange, is it not? that of the myriads who
Before us pass'd the door of Darkness through,
   Not one returns to tell us of the Road,
Which to discover we must travel too.

LXVI

I sent my Soul through the Invisible,
Some letter of that After-life to spell:
   And by and by my Soul return'd to me,
And answer'd "I Myself am Heav'n and Hell."

LXVII

Heav'n but the Vision of fulfill'd Desire,
And Hell the Shadow from a Soul on fire,
   Cast on the Darkness into which Ourselves,
So late emerged from, shall so soon expire.

LXIX

But helpless Pieces of the Game He plays
Upon this Chequer-board of Nights and Days;
   Hither and thither moves, and checks, and slays,
And one by one back in the Closet lays.

LXXI

The Moving Finger writes; and, having writ,
Moves on: nor all your Piety nor Wit
   Shall lure it back to cancel half a Line,
Nor all your Tears wash out a Word of it.

LXXIII

With Earth's first Clay They did the Last Man knead;
And there of the Last Harvest sow'd the Seed:
   And the first Morning of Creation wrote
What the Last Dawn of Reckoning shall read.

LXXXVII

Whereat some one of the loquacious Lot —
I think a Súfi pipkin — waxing hot —
   "All this of Pot and Potter — Tell me then,
Who is the Potter, pray, and who the Pot?"

57

ANDREAS CAPELLANUS

From *The Art of Courtly Love*

Andreas Capellanus (Andreas the Chaplain) compiled this guide to a new idea and practice of love in Europe at some point between 1174 and 1186. Scholars have traced the notion that romantic love is ennobling to the love poetry that European knights brought to southern France after the Crusades. The roots of that poetry sung by the troubadours in France likely derived from Sufi poems of religious love. While courtly love, or romantic love, was expressed between men and women, it still served something like a religious purpose. What was that purpose? What does this love have to do with marriage? What does it have to do with sex?

Thinking Historically

You might compare the idea of courtly love with the idea of love in other societies, as expressed in other selections. Did the Japanese and Chinese espouse this idea of passionate love? The similarities and differences between European courtly love and the social rituals of the Heian court are particularly interesting. What might account for the similar stylized attention to coupling in such apparently different societies?

You might also compare the idea of courtly love with present-day notions of love. In what ways are our ideas of love similar to or derived from the tradition of courtly love? In what ways are our culture's idea of love different from these? A survey of the love themes in contemporary American popular culture (e.g., movies, television series, soap operas) as points of comparison might be interesting.

Introduction to the Treatise on Love

We must first consider what love is, whence it gets its name, what the effect of love is, between what persons love may exist, how it may be acquired, retained, increased, decreased, and ended, what are the signs

Andreas Capellanus, *The Art of Courtly Love,* trans. John J. Parry (New York: Columbia University Press, 1990), 28–32, 159–86.

that one's love is returned, and what one of the lovers ought to do if the other is unfaithful.

What Love Is

Love is a certain inborn suffering derived from the sight of and excessive meditation upon the beauty of the opposite sex, which causes each one to wish above all things the embraces of the other and by common desire to carry out all of love's precepts in the other's embrace.

That love is suffering is easy to see, for before the love becomes equally balanced on both sides there is no torment greater, since the lover is always in fear that his love may not gain its desire and that he is wasting his efforts. He fears, too, that rumors of it may get abroad, and he fears everything that might harm it in any way, for before things are perfected a slight disturbance often spoils them. If he is a poor man, he also fears that the woman may scorn his poverty; if he is ugly, he fears that she may despise his lack of beauty or may give her love to a more handsome man; if he is rich, he fears that his parsimony in the past may stand in his way. To tell the truth, no one can number the fears of one single lover. This kind of love, then, is a suffering which is felt by only one of the persons and may be called "single love." But even after both are in love the fears that arise are just as great, for each of the lovers fears that what he has acquired with so much effort may be lost through the effort of someone else, which is certainly much worse for a man than if, having no hope, he sees that his efforts are accomplishing nothing, for it is worse to lose the things you are seeking than to be deprived of a gain you merely hope for. The lover fears, too, that he may offend his loved one in some way; indeed he fears so many things that it would be difficult to tell them.

That this suffering is inborn I shall show you clearly, because if you will look at the truth and distinguish carefully you will see that it does not arise out of any action; only from the reflection of the mind upon what it sees does this suffering come. For when a man sees some woman fit for love and shaped according to his taste, he begins at once to lust after her in his heart; then the more he thinks about her the more he burns with love, until he comes to a fuller meditation. Presently he begins to think about the fashioning of the woman and to differentiate her limbs, to think about what she does, and to pry into the secrets of her body, and he desires to put each part of it to the fullest use. Then after he has come to this complete meditation, love cannot hold the reins, but he proceeds at once to action; straightway he strives to get a helper to find an intermediary. He begins to plan how he may find favor with her, and he begins to seek a place and a time opportune for talking; he looks upon a brief hour as a very long year, because he cannot do anything fast enough to suit his eager mind. It is well known that many things happen to him in this manner. This inborn suffering comes, therefore, from seeing and meditating. Not every kind of meditation can be the cause of love, an excessive one is required; for a restrained thought does not, as a rule, return to the mind, and so love cannot arise from it.

Between What Persons Love May Exist

Now, in love you should note first of all that love cannot exist except between persons of opposite sexes. Between two men or two women love can find no place, for we see that two persons of the same sex are not at all fitted for giving each other the exchanges of love or for practicing the acts natural to it. Whatever nature forbids, love is ashamed to accept.

What the Effect of Love Is

Now it is the effect of love that a true lover cannot be degraded with any avarice. Love causes a rough and uncouth man to be distinguished for his handsomeness; it can endow a man even of the humblest birth with nobility of character; it blesses the proud with humility; and the man in love becomes accustomed to performing many services gracefully for everyone. O what a wonderful thing is love, which makes a man shine with so many virtues and teaches everyone, no matter who he is, so many good traits of character! There is another thing about love that we should not praise in few words: it adorns a man, so to speak, with the virtue of chastity, because he who shines with the light of one love can hardly think of embracing another woman, even a beautiful one. For when he thinks deeply of his beloved the sight of any other woman seems to his mind rough and rude.

If One of the Lovers Is Unfaithful to the Other

If one of the lovers should be unfaithful to the other, and the offender is the man, and he has an eye to a new love affair, he renders himself wholly unworthy of his former love, and she ought to deprive him completely of her embraces.

But what if he should be unfaithful to his beloved — not with the idea of finding a new love, but because he has been driven to it by an irresistible passion for another woman? What, for instance, if chance should present to him an unknown woman in a convenient place or what if at a time when Venus is urging him on to that which I am talking about he should meet with a little strumpet or somebody's servant girl? Should he, just because he played with her in the grass, lose the love of his beloved? We can say without fear of contradiction that just for this a lover is not considered unworthy of the love of his beloved unless he indulges in so many excesses with a number of women that we may conclude that he is overpassionate. But if whenever he becomes acquainted with a woman he pesters her to gain his end, or if he attains his object as a result of his efforts, then rightly he does deserve to be deprived of his former love, because there is strong presumption that he has acted in this way with an eye toward a new one, especially where he has strayed with a woman of the nobility or otherwise of an honorable estate.

I know that once when I sought advice I got the answer that a true lover can never desire a new love unless he knows that for some definite and sufficient reason the old love is dead; we know from our own experience that this rule is very true. We have fallen in love with a woman of the most admirable character, although we have never had, or hope to have, any fruit of this love. For we are compelled to pine away for love of a woman of such lofty station that we dare not say one word about it, nor dare we throw ourself upon her mercy, and so at length we are forced to find our body shipwrecked. But although rashly and without foresight we have fallen into such great waves in this tempest, still we cannot think about a new love or look for any other way to free ourself.

But since you are making a special study of the subject of love, you may well ask whether a man can have a pure love for one woman and a mixed or common love with another. We will show you, by an unanswerable argument, that no one can feel affection for two women in this fashion. For although pure love and mixed love may seem to be very different things, if you will look at the matter properly you will see that pure love, so far as its substance goes, is the same as mixed love and comes from the same feeling of the heart. The substance of the love is the same in each case, and only the manner and form of loving are different, as this illustration will make clear to you. Sometimes we see a man with a desire to drink his wine unmixed, and at another time his appetite prompts him to drink only water or wine and water mixed; although his appetite manifests itself differently, the substance of it is the same and unchanged. So likewise when two people have long been united by pure love and afterwards desire to practice mixed love, the substance of the love remains the same in them, although the manner and form and the way of practicing it are different.

Various Decisions in Love Cases

Now then, let us come to various decisions in cases of love:

I. A certain knight loved his lady beyond all measure and enjoyed her full embrace, but she did not love him with equal ardor. He sought to leave her, but she, desiring to retain him in his former status, opposed his wish. In this affair the Countess of Champagne gave this response: "It is considered very unseemly for a woman to seek to be loved and yet to refuse to love. It is silly for anybody disrespectfully to ask of others what she herself wholly refuses to give to others."

II. A certain man asked the Lady Ermengarde of Narbonne to make clear where there was the greater affection — between lovers or between married people. The lady gave him a logical answer. She said: "We consider that marital affection and the true love of lovers are wholly different and arise from entirely different sources, and so the ambiguous nature of the word prevents the comparison of the things and we have to place them in different classes. Comparisons of more or less are not valid when things are grouped together under an ambiguous heading and the comparison is made in regard to that ambiguous term. It is no true comparison to say that a name is simpler than a body or that the outline of a speech is better arranged than the delivery."

III. The same man asked the same lady this question. A certain woman had been married, but was now separated from her husband by a divorce, and her former husband sought eagerly for her love. In this case the lady replied: "If any two people have been married and afterwards separate in any way, we consider love between them wholly wicked."

IV. A certain knight was in love with a woman who had given her love to another man, but he got from her this much hope of her love — that if it should ever happen that she lost the love of her beloved, then without a doubt her love would go to this man. A little while after this the woman married her lover. The other knight then demanded that she give him the fruit of the hope she had granted him, but this she absolutely refused to do, saying that she had not lost the love of her lover. In this affair the Queen gave her decision as follows: "We dare not oppose the opinion of the Countess of Champagne, who ruled that love can exert no power between husband and wife. Therefore we recommend that the lady should grant the love she has promised."

V. The Queen was also asked which was preferable: the love of a young man or of one advanced in years. She answered this question with wonderful subtlety by saying, "We distinguish between a good and a better love by the man's knowledge and his character and his praiseworthy manners, not by his age. But as regards that natural instinct of passion, young men are usually more eager to gratify it with older women than with young ones of their own age; those who are older prefer to receive the embraces and kisses of young women rather than of the older ones. But on the other hand a woman whether young or somewhat older likes the embraces and solaces of young men better than those of older ones. The explanation of this fact seems to be a physiological one. . . ."

The Rules of Love

Let us come now to the rules of love, and I shall try to present to you very briefly those rules which the King of Love[1] is said to have proclaimed with his own mouth and to have given in writing to all lovers. . . .

I. Marriage is no real excuse for not loving.
II. He who is not jealous cannot love.
III. No one can be bound by a double love.
IV. It is well known that love is always increasing or decreasing.
V. That which a lover takes against the will of his beloved has no relish.
VI. Boys do not love until they arrive at the age of maturity.
VII. When one lover dies, a widowhood of two years is required of the survivor.
VIII. No one should be deprived of love without the very best of reasons.
IX. No one can love unless he is impelled by the persuasion of love.
X. Love is always a stranger in the home of avarice.
XI. It is not proper to love any woman whom one should be ashamed to seek to marry.
XII. A true lover does not desire to embrace in love anyone except his beloved.
XIII. When made public love rarely endures.
XIV. The easy attainment of love makes it of little value; difficulty of attainment makes it prized.
XV. Every lover regularly turns pale in the presence of his beloved.
XVI. When a lover suddenly catches sight of his beloved his heart palpitates.
XVII. A new love puts to flight an old one.
XVIII. Good character alone makes any man worthy of love.
XIX. If love diminishes, it quickly fails and rarely revives.
XX. A man in love is always apprehensive.
XXI. Real jealousy always increases the feeling of love.
XXII. Jealousy, and therefore love, are increased when one suspects his beloved.
XXIII. He whom the thought of love vexes, eats and sleeps very little.
XXIV. Every act of a lover ends in the thought of his beloved.
XXV. A true lover considers nothing good except what he thinks will please his beloved.
XXVI. Love can deny nothing to love.
XXVII. A lover can never have enough of the solaces of his beloved.

[1] King Arthur of Britain. [Ed.]

XXVIII. A slight presumption causes a lover to suspect his beloved.
XXIX. A man who is vexed by too much passion usually does not love.
XXX. A true lover is constantly and without intermission possessed by the thought of his beloved.
XXXI. Nothing forbids one woman being loved by two men or one man by two women.

REFLECTIONS

There are numerous ways to reflect on the selections in this chapter. Each reading bears the weight of an enormous body of literature — some of which is impressive and interesting, and some of which you may be eager to go on to read and explore. Li Ch'ing-chao's memoir is taken from a delightful study of memory in China by Steven Owen called *Remembrances: Experience of the Past in Classical Chinese Literature.* If one wanted to study the relationship between memoir and history or (as might be the case for Murasaki) between memoir and fiction, this would be the place to start.

Ivan J. Morris explores, in a compelling style, the literature of Heian Japan in *The World of the Shining Prince.* There is also an abundance of literature on the European courtly love tradition, beginning with Denis de Rougemont's *Love and Death in the Western World.* The classics include *Tristan and Iseult, Le Roman de la Rose* (*Romance of the Rose*) by Guillaume de Lorris, and *Lancelot* by Chretien De Troyes.

The words *love* and *marriage* — it should be clear by now — were paired within the last two hundred years of Western European culture. Andreas and the proponents of courtly love explicitly reject any connection between love and marriage, and other selections in this chapter simply ignore the issue. Why do you suppose this is the case?

To the extent to which you discover similar notions of love and marriage in the civilizations studied here, it would be interesting to determine whether the similarity is related to a broader similarity in society or culture. For instance, historians have sometimes pointed out similarities between European and Japanese feudalism. (As these readings suggest, early Heian society [before 1000] was still fairly centralized; feudal decentralization came later). All feudal societies have been called "patriarchal," meaning they were dominated by men. Is that something that feudal societies share? Does that have any bearing on the otherwise diverse attitudes toward love and marriage? In what ways do the ideas and institutions concerning love and marriage contribute to or perpetuate a patriarchal society?

10

The First Crusade

HISTORICAL CONTEXT

Muslims, Christians, and Jews during the First Crusade, 1095–1099 C.E.

The Crusades were an important chapter in the religious and military history — or more broadly, the cultural and political history — of both European and Islamic civilizations. In 1095 the Crusades began with Pope Urban II's call for Christian knights to rout the new Muslim occupiers of Jerusalem and the surrounding Holy Land. Some historians have suggested that the Pope was also concerned with pacifying European society by channeling into foreign wars the private armies of knights who, when not fighting each other, preyed on Christian peasants.

The Crusades brought large numbers of European Christians and Muslims into contact with each other in a struggle and dialogue that would last for centuries. With the Crusades, Byzantine civilization began to crumble, and European Christians were set against Orthodox Christians and Jews as well as Muslims.

THINKING HISTORICALLY

Analyzing and Writing Narrative

When most people think of history, they think of narrative — the story itself. It is what the average person has come to expect from historians, not social science chapters on subjects like love and marriage — we will try to make amends.

Narrative settles on specific details — one at a time — neither indiscriminately nor as examples of general laws, but usually chronologically, as they happen, woven in a chain of cause and effect. The "truth" of narrative is different from that of social science, which aspires to generality. The social scientist writes, "Holy wars among states are a dime a dozen." The narrative historian immerses us in the specific details of the battle: "The Duke's trumpets sounded, the shimmering line swayed forward, the long lances came down to point at the foe, their pennons shadowing the ground before them." A good narrative has the appeal of a good story: It places the reader on the scene, enables us to feel the drama of the moment, to experience what happened as it happened.

In this chapter you will read a number of brief narratives about the Crusades. You will analyze each narrative in order to understand how it works, and then you will be encouraged to write your own.

58

AMIN MAALOUF

From *The Crusades Through Arab Eyes*

Amin Maalouf is a modern writer and journalist. In this selection from the beginning of his history of Arab (or Muslim) responses to the Crusades, he evokes the initial shock Muslims must have felt when Jerusalem was captured by the Crusaders. It is a story not just of Christianity and Islam, because by 1095 there were two centers of Christianity and two armies of Islam.

The schism of 1054 separated Roman and Greek Christianity over points of doctrine and the relative authority of the Roman Pope and the Greek Patriarch, but both leaders shared concerns about the spread of Islam. Specifically, the Muslim Seljuk Turks had successfully conquered much of what used to be the Byzantine Empire, in what is today Turkey and Syria. Interestingly, the Turks did not conquer the Abbassid caliphate, which had ruled the Muslim world from Baghdad since 750; rather, they left it a shadow of itself, out of respect for its traditional authority and in appreciation of its current weakness. There were, then, two Muslim civilizations, the original Arabic that after 750 had integrated Persian elements in Baghdad, and

---

Amin Maalouf, *The Crusades Through Arab Eyes* (New York: Schocken Books, 1985), xiii–xvi, 3–10.

the nomadic Turks who now ruled cities of diverse populations in Turkey and Syria.

What, according to the author, was the attitude of Alexius, the Byzantine emperor, to the invasion of the largely French force of European Christians? Did he ask for their help or fear their intervention?

What was the attitude of the Abbassid caliphate at Baghdad to the European conquest of Jerusalem in 1099? Why wasn't Kilij Arslan, the Seljuk Sultan, prepared for what was to happen?

Follow the events described in this selection on a map. How far are the distances that the Europeans traveled? How far did Abū Sa'ad al-Harawi travel from Jerusalem to Baghdad to Damascus?

Thinking Historically

A historical narrative is generally written in the third person (that is, He did this; she did that), as this selection is. It allows the historian to distance himself as story teller and to be "objective." After all, this is not the historian's personal story. Nevertheless, even an objective historian must choose a subject and a point of view from which to describe it. The subject of this narrative is the Arab (or Muslim) perspective of the Crusades. Would it be possible to write about this subject from a European or Christian point of view? How does the author help us see events as Muslims might have? How does this approach enlist our sympathy for the Muslim side?

Drama is another powerful narrative device. How does the use of drama engage the reader? In this selection, does drama enlist the reader's sympathy for the Muslim side?

Here, the author's narrative is not straightforward and chronological. On a time line, mark how the story progresses from beginning to middle to end. What effect does the change in time have?

Baghdad, August 1099.

Wearing no turban, his head shaved as a sign of mourning, the venerable *qādī*[1] Abū Sa'ad al-Harawi burst with a loud cry into the spacious *dīwān*[2] of the caliph al-Mustazhir Billāh, a throng of companions, young and old, trailing in his wake. Noisily assenting to his every word, they, like him, offered the chilling spectacle of long beards and shaven skulls. A few of the court dignitaries tried to calm him, but al-Harawi swept them aside with brusque disdain, strode resolutely to the centre of the hall, and then, with the searing eloquence of a seasoned

[1] Judge. [Ed.]
[2] Court. [Ed.]

preacher declaiming from his pulpit, proceeded to lecture all those present, without regard to rank.

'How dare you slumber in the shade of complacent safety', he began, 'leading lives as frivolous as garden flowers, while your brothers in Syria have no dwelling place save the saddles of camels and the bellies of vultures? Blood has been spilled! Beautiful young girls have been shamed, and must now hide their sweet faces in their hands! Shall the valorous Arabs resign themselves to insult, and the valiant Persians accept dishonour?'

'It was a speech that brought tears to many an eye and moved men's hearts', the Arab chroniclers would later write. The entire audience broke out in wails and lamentations. But al-Harawi had not come to elicit sobs.

'Man's meanest weapon', he shouted, 'is to shed tears when rapiers stir the coals of war.'

If he had made this arduous trip from Damascus to Baghdad, three long summer weeks under the merciless sun of the Syrian desert, it was not to plead for pity but to alert Islam's highest authorities to the calamity that had just befallen the faithful, and to implore them to intervene without delay to halt the carnage. 'Never have the Muslims been so humiliated', al-Harawi repeated, 'never have their lands been so savagely devastated.' All the people travelling with him had fled from towns sacked by the invaders; among them were some of the few survivors of Jerusalem. He had brought them along so that they could relate, in their own words, the tragedy they had suffered just one month earlier.

The Franj[3] had taken the holy city on Friday, the twenty-second day of the month of Sha'bān, in the year of the Hegira 492, or 15 July 1099, after a forty-day siege. The exiles still trembled when they spoke of the fall of the city: they stared into space as though they could still see the fair-haired and heavily armoured warriors spilling through the streets, swords in hand, slaughtering men, women, and children, plundering houses, sacking mosques.

Two days later, when the killing stopped, not a single Muslim was left alive within the city walls. Some had taken advantage of the chaos to slip away, escaping through gates battered down by the attackers. Thousands of others lay in pools of blood on the doorsteps of their homes or alongside the mosques. Among them were many *imāms*,[4] *'ulamā'*,[5] and Sufi ascetics who had forsaken their countries of origin for a life of pious retreat in these holy places. The last survivors were

[3] French. [Ed.]
[4] Readers. [Ed.]
[5] Scholars. [Ed.]

forced to perform the worst tasks: to heave the bodies of their own relatives, to dump them in vacant, unmarked lots, and then to set them alight, before being themselves massacred or sold into slavery.

The fate of the Jews of Jerusalem was no less atrocious. During the first hours of battle, some participated in the defence of their quarter, situated on the northern edge of the city. But when that part of the city walls overhanging their homes collapsed and the blond knights began to pour through the streets, the Jews panicked. Re-enacting an immemorial rite, the entire community gathered in the main synagogue to pray. The Franj barricaded all the exits and stacked all the bundles of wood they could find in a ring around the building. The temple was then put to the torch. Those who managed to escape were massacred in the neighbouring alleyways. The rest were burned alive.

A few days after the tragedy, the first refugees from Palestine arrived in Damascus, carrying with them, with infinite care, the Koran of 'Uthmān, one of the oldest existing copies of the holy book. Soon afterwards the survivors of Jerusalem duly approached the Syrian capital. When they glimpsed the distant outlines of the three minarets of the Umayyad mosque looming up from its square courtyard, they unrolled their prayer rugs and bowed to give thanks to the Almighty for having thus prolonged their lives, which they had thought were over. Abu Sa'ad al-Harawi, grand *qādī* of Damascus, welcomed the refugees with kindness. This magistrate, of Afghan origin, was the city's most respected personality, and he offered the Palestinians both advice and comfort. He told them that a Muslim need not be ashamed of being forced to flee from his home. Was not Islam's first refugee the Prophet Muhammad himself, who had to leave Mecca, his native city, whose population was hostile to him, to seek refuge in Medina, where the new religion had been more warmly received? And was it not from his place of exile that he launched the holy war, the *jihād*, to free his country of idolatry? The refugees must therefore consider themselves *mujāhidīn*, soldiers of the holy war, so highly honoured in Islam that the *hijra*, the Prophet's 'emigration', was chosen as the starting point of the Muslim calendar.

Indeed, for many believers, exile is a duty in the event of occupation. The great traveller Ibn Jubayr, an Arab of Spain who visited Palestine nearly a century after the beginning of the Frankish invasion, was to be shocked when he found that some Muslims, 'slaves to their love for their native land', were willing to accept life in occupied territory.

'There is no excuse before God,' he would say, 'for a Muslim to remain in a city of unbelief, unless he be merely passing through. In the land of Islam he finds shelter from the discomforts and evils to which he is subjected in the countries of the Christians, as, for example, when he hears disgusting words spoken about the Prophet, particularly by the most besotted, or finds it impossible to cleanse himself properly, or has to live among pigs and so many other illicit things. Beware! Beware of entering their lands! You must seek God's pardon and mercy for such an error. One of the horrors that strikes any inhabitant of the Christian countries is the spectacle of Muslim prisoners tottering in irons, condemned to hard labour and treated as slaves, as well as the sight of Muslim captives bearing iron chains round their legs. Hearts break at the sight of them, but they have no use for pity.'

Although excessive from a doctrinal standpoint, Ibn Jubayr's words nevertheless accurately reflect the attitude of the thousands of refugees from Palestine and northern Syria who gathered in Damascus in that July of 1099. While they were sick at heart at having been forced to abandon their homes, they were determined never to return until the occupiers had departed for ever, and they resolved to awaken the consciences of their brothers in all the lands of Islam.

Why else would they have followed al-Harawi to Baghdad? Was it not to the caliph, the Prophet's successor, that Muslims must turn in their hour of need? Was it not to the prince of the faithful that they should address their complaints and their tales of woe?

In Baghdad, however, the refugees' disappointment was to be as great as their hopes had been high. The caliph al-Mustazhir Billāh began by expressing his profound sympathy and compassion. Then he ordered seven exalted dignitaries to conduct an inquiry into these troublesome events. It is perhaps superfluous to add that nothing was ever heard from that committee of wise men.

The sack of Jerusalem, starting point of a millennial hostility between Islam and the West, aroused no immediate sensation. It would be nearly half a century before the Arab East would mobilize against the invader, before the call to *jihād* issued by the *qādī* of Damascus in the caliph's *dīwān* would be celebrated in commemoration of the first solemn act of resistance.

At the start of the invasion, few Arabs were as perspicacious as al-Harawi in weighing the scope of the threat from the West. Some adapted all too rapidly to the new situation. Most, bitter but resigned, sought merely to survive. Some observed more or less lucidly, trying to understand these events, as unexpected as they were novel. The most touching of these was the Damascene chronicler Ibn al-Qalānisi, a young scholar born of a family of notables. A witness to the story from the outset, he was twenty-three when the Franj arrived in the East in 1096, and he assiduously and regularly recorded all the events of which he had some knowledge. His chronicle faithfully recounts, in a fairly detached manner, the advance of the invaders as seen from his native city.

For him it all began during those anxious days when the first rumours drifted into Damascus.

The Franj Arrive

> In that year, news began to trickle in about the appearance of Franj troops, coming down from the Sea of Marmara in an innumerable multitude. People took fright. This information was confirmed by King Kilij Arslan, whose territory was closest to these Franj.

The King Kilij Arslan whom Ibn al-Qalānisi mentions here was not yet seventeen when the invaders arrived. The first Muslim leader to be informed of their approach, this young Turkish sultan with the slightly slanting eyes would be the first to inflict a defeat upon them — but also the first to be routed by the formidable knights.

In July 1096 Kilij Arslan learned that an enormous throng of Franj was en route to Constantinople. He immediately feared the worst. Naturally, he had no idea as to the real aims of these people, but in his view nothing good could come of their arrival in the Orient.

The sultanate under his rule covered much of Asia Minor, a territory the Turks had only recently taken from the Greeks. Kilij Arslan's father, Süleymān, was the first Turk to secure possession of this land, which many centuries later would come to be called Turkey. In Nicaea, the capital of this young Muslim state, Byzantine churches were still more numerous than Muslim mosques. Although the city's garrison was made up of Turkish cavalry, the majority of the population was Greek, and Kilij Arslan had few illusions about his subjects' true sentiments: as far as they were concerned, he would never be other than a barbarian chieftain. The only sovereign they recognized — the man whose name, spoken in a low whisper, was murmured in all their prayers — was the basileus Alexius Comnenus, 'Emperor of the Romans'. Alexius was in fact the emperor of the Greeks, who proclaimed themselves the inheritors of the Roman empire. The Arabs, indeed, recognized them as such, for in the eleventh century — as in the twentieth — they designated the Greeks by the term Rūm, or 'Romans'. The domain conquered from the Greek empire by Kilij Arslan's father was even called the Sultanate of the Rūm.

Alexius was one of the most prestigious figures of the Orient at the time. Kilij Arslan was genuinely fascinated by this short-statured quinquagenarian,[6] always decked in gold and in rich blue robes, with his carefully tended beard, elegant manners, and eyes sparkling with malice. Alexius reigned in Constantinople, fabled Byzantium, situated less

[6] Fifty-year-old man. [Ed.]

than three days' march from Nicaea. This proximity aroused conflicting emotions in the mind of the young sultan. Like all nomadic warriors, he dreamed of conquest and pillage, and was not displeased to find the legendary riches of Byzantium so close at hand. At the same time he felt threatened: he knew that Alexius had never abandoned his dream of retaking Nicaea, not only because the city had always been Greek, but also and more importantly because the presence of Turkish warriors such a short distance from Constantinople represented a permanent threat to the security of the empire.

Although the Byzantine army, torn by years of internal crisis, would have been unable to undertake a war of reconquest on its own, it was no secret that Alexius could always seek the aid of foreign auxiliaries. The Byzantines had never hesitated to resort to the services of Western knights. Many Franj, from heavily armoured mercenaries to pilgrims en route to Palestine, had visited the Orient, and by 1096 they were by no means unknown to the Muslims. Some twenty years earlier — Kilij Arslan had not yet been born, but the older emirs[7] in his army had told him the story — one of these fair-haired adventurers, a man named Roussel of Bailleul, had succeeded in founding an autonomous state in Asia Minor and had even marched on Constantinople. The panicky Byzantines had had no choice but to appeal to Kilij Arslan's father, who could hardly believe his ears when a special envoy from the basileus implored him to rush to their aid. The Turkish cavalry converged on Constantinople and managed to defeat Roussel; Süleymān received handsome compensation in the form of gold, horses, and land.

The Byzantines had been suspicious of the Franj ever since, but the imperial armies, short of experienced soldiers, had no choice but to recruit mercenaries, and not only Franj: many Turkish warriors also fought under the banners of the Christian empire. It was precisely from his congeners enrolled in the Byzantine army that Kilij Arslan learned, in July 1096, that thousands of Franj were approaching Constantinople. He was perplexed by the picture painted by his informants. These Occidentals bore scant resemblance to the mercenaries to whom the Turks were accustomed. Although their number included several hundred knights and a significant number of foot-soldiers, there were also thousands of women, children, and old people in rags. They had the air of some wretched tribe evicted from their lands by an invader. It was also reported that they all wore strips of cloth in the shape of a cross, sewn onto the backs of their garments.

The young sultan, who doubtless found it difficult to assess the danger, asked his agents to be especially vigilant and to keep him informed of the exploits of these new invaders. He had the fortifications

[7] Military commanders. [Ed.]

of his capital inspected as a precaution. The walls of Nicaea, more than a *farsakh* (six thousand metres) in length, were topped by 240 turrets. South-west of the city, the placid waters of the Ascanian Lake offered excellent natural protection.

Nevertheless by early August the serious nature of the threat had become clear. Escorted by Byzantine ships, the Franj crossed the Bosporus and, despite a blazing summer sun, advanced along the coast. Wherever they passed, they were heard to proclaim that they had come to exterminate the Muslims, although they were also seen to plunder many a Greek church on their way. Their chief was said to be a hermit by the name of Peter. Informants estimated that there were several tens of thousands of them in all, but no one would hazard a guess as to where they were headed. It seemed that Basileus Alexius had decided to settle them in Civitot, a camp that had earlier been equipped for other mercenaries, less than a day's march from Nicaea.

The sultan's palace was awash with agitation. While the Turkish cavalry stood ready to mount their chargers at a moment's notice, there was a constant flow of spies and scouts, reporting the smallest movements of the Franj. It transpired that every morning hordes several thousand strong left camp to forage the surrounding countryside: farms were plundered or set alight before the rabble returned to Civitot, where their various clans squabbled over the spoils of their raids. None of this was surprising to the sultan's soldiers, and their master saw no reason for particular concern. The routine continued for an entire month.

One day, however, toward the middle of September, there was a sudden change in the behaviour of the Franj. Probably because they were unable to squeeze anything more out of the immediate neighbourhood, they had reportedly set out in the direction of Nicaea. They passed through several villages, all of them Christian, and commandeered the harvests, which had just been gathered, mercilessly massacring those peasants who tried to resist. Young children were even said to have been burned alive.

Kilij Arslan found himself taken unawares. By the time the news of these events reached him, the attackers were already at the walls of his capital, and before sunset the citizens could see the smoke rising from the first fires. The sultan quickly dispatched a cavalry patrol to confront the Franj. Hopelessly outnumbered, the Turks were cut to pieces. A few bloodied survivors limped back into Nicaea. Sensing that his prestige was threatened, Kilij Arslan would have liked to join the battle immediately, but the emirs of his army dissuaded him. It would soon be night, and the Franj were already hastily falling back to their camp. Revenge would have to wait.

But not for long. Apparently emboldened by their success, the Occidentals decided to try again two weeks later. This time the son of

Süleymān was alerted in time, and he followed their advance step by step. A Frankish company, including some knights but consisting mainly of thousands of tattered pillagers, set out apparently for Nicaea. But then, circling around the town, they turned east and took the fortress of Xerigordon by surprise.

The young sultan decided to act. At the head of his men, he rode briskly towards the small stronghold, where the drunken Franj, celebrating their victory, had no way of knowing that their fate was already sealed, for Xerigordon was a trap. As the soldiers of Kilij Arslan well knew (but the inexperienced foreigners had yet to discover), its water supplies lay outside and rather far from the walls. The Turks quickly sealed off access to the water. Now they had only to take up positions around the fortress and sit and wait. Thirst would do the fighting in their stead.

An atrocious torment began for the besieged Franj. They went so far as to drink the blood of their mounts and their own urine. They were seen looking desperately up into the sky, hoping for a few drops of rain in those early October days. In vain. At the end of the week, the leader of the expedition, a knight named Reynald, agreed to capitulate provided his life would be spared. Kilij Arslan, who had demanded that the Franj publicly renounce their religion, was somewhat taken aback when Reynald declared his readiness not only to convert to Islam but even to fight at the side of the Turks against his own companions. Several of his friends, who had acceded to the same demands, were sent in captivity to various cities of Syria or central Asia. The rest were put to the sword.

The young sultan was proud of his exploit, but he kept a cool head. After according his men a respite for the traditional sharing out of the spoils, he called them to order the following day. The Franj had admittedly lost nearly six thousand men, but six times that number still remained, and the time to dispose of them was now or never. Kilij Arslan decided to attempt a ruse. He sent two Greek spies to the Civitot camp to report that Reynald's men were in an excellent position, and that they had succeeded in taking Nicaea itself, whose riches they had no intention of sharing with their coreligionists. In the meantime, the Turkish army would lay a gigantic ambush.

As expected, the carefully propagated rumours aroused turmoil in the camp of Civitot. A mob gathered, shouting insults against Reynald and his men; it was decided to proceed without delay to share in the pillage of Nicaea. But all at once, no one really knows how, an escapee from the Xerigordon expedition arrived, divulging the truth about his companions' fate. Kilij Arslan's spies thought that they had failed in their mission, for the wisest among the Franj counselled caution. Once the first moment of consternation had passed, however, excitement soared anew. The mob bustled and shouted: they were ready to set out in a trice, no longer to join in pillage, but 'to avenge the martyrs.' Those who hesitated were dismissed as cowards. The most enraged voices carried the day, and the time of departure was set for the following morning. The sultan's spies, whose ruse had been exposed but its objective attained, had triumphed after all. They sent word to their master to prepare for battle.

At dawn on 21 October 1096 the Occidentals left their camp. Kilij Arslan, who had spent the night in the hills near Civitot, was not far away. His men were in position, well hidden. From his vantage point, he could see all along the column of Franj, who were raising great clouds of dust. Several hundred knights, most of them without their armour, marched at the head of the procession, followed by a disordered throng of foot-soldiers. They had been marching for less than an hour when the sultan heard their approaching clamour. The sun, rising at his back, shone directly into the eyes of the Franj. Holding his breath, he signalled his emirs to get ready. The fateful moment had arrived. A barely perceptible gesture, a few orders whispered here and there, and the Turkish archers were slowly bending their bows: a thousand arrows suddenly shot forth with a single protracted whistle. Most of the knights fell within the first few minutes. Then the foot-soldiers were decimated in their turn.

By the time the hand-to-hand combat was joined, the Franj were already routed. Those in the rear ran for their camp, where the non-combatants were barely awake. An aged priest was celebrating morning mass, the women were preparing food. The arrival of the fugitives, with the Turks in hot pursuit, struck terror throughout the camp. The Franj fled in all directions. Those who tried to reach the neighbouring woods were soon captured. Others, in an inspired move, barricaded themselves in an unused fortress that had the additional advantage of lying alongside the sea. Unwilling to take futile risks, the sultan decided not to lay a siege. The Byzantine fleet, rapidly alerted, sailed in to pick up the Franj. Two or three thousand men escaped in this manner. Peter the Hermit, who had been in Constantinople for several days, was also saved. But his partisans were not so lucky. The youngest women were kidnapped by the sultan's horsemen and distributed to the emirs or sold in the slave markets. Several young boys suffered a similar fate. The rest of the Franj, probably nearly twenty thousand of them, were exterminated.

Kilij Arslan was jubilant. He had annihilated the Frankish army, in spite of its formidable reputation, while suffering only insignificant losses among his own troops. Gazing upon the immense booty amassed at his feet, he basked in the most sublime triumph of his life.

And yet, rarely in history has a victory proved so costly to those who had won it.

Intoxicated by his success, Kilij Arslan pointedly ignored the information that came through the following winter about the arrival of fresh groups of Franj in Constantinople. As far as he was concerned — and even the wisest of his emirs did not dissent — there was no reason for disquiet. If other mercenaries of Alexius dared to cross the Bosporus, they would be cut to pieces like those who had come before them. The sultan felt that it was time to return to the major preoccupations of the hour — in other words, to the merciless struggle he had long been waging against the other Turkish princes, his neighbours. It was there, and nowhere else, that his fate and that of his realm would be decided. The clashes with the Rūm or with their foreign Franj auxiliaries would never be more than an interlude.

The young sultan was well placed to feel certain about this. Was it not during one of these interminable battles among chiefs that his father, Süleymān, had laid down his life in 1086? Kilij Arslan was then barely seven years old, and he was to have succeeded his father under the regency of several faithful emirs. But he had been kept from power and taken to Persia under the pretext that his life was in danger. There he was kept: adulated, smothered in respect, waited on by a small army of attentive slaves, but closely watched, and strictly prevented from visiting his realm. His hosts — in other words, his jailers — were none other than the members of his own clan, the Seljuks.

If there was one name known to everyone in the eleventh century, from the borders of China to the distant land of the Franj, it was theirs. Within a few years of their arrival in the Middle East from central Asia, the Seljuk Turks, with their thousands of nomadic horsemen sporting long braided hair, had seized control of the entire region, from Afghanistan to the Mediterranean. Since 1055 the caliph of Baghdad, successor of the Prophet and inheritor of the renowned 'Abbasid empire, had been no more than a docile puppet in their hands. From Isfahan to Damascus, from Nicaea to Jerusalem, it was their emirs who laid down the law. For the first time in three centuries, the entire Muslim East was united under the authority of a single dynasty which proclaimed its determination to restore the past glory of Islam. The Rūm, who were crushed by the Seljuks in 1071, would never rise again. The largest of their provinces, Asia Minor, had been invaded, and their capital itself was no longer secure. Their emperors, including Alexius himself, dispatched one delegation after another to the pope in Rome, the supreme commander of the West, imploring him to declare holy war against this resurgence of Islam.

59

ANNA COMNENA

From *The Alexiad*

Anna Comnena was the daughter of Emperor Alexius (r. 1081–1118) of Byzantium, who was mentioned in the previous selection. Threatened on three sides — by the Seljuk Turks to the east, the Norman Kingdom of southern Italy to the west, and rebellions to the north — Alexius appealed for aid to Pope Urban II of Rome in 1095. He expected a mercenary army, but because the Pope saw a chance to send a massive force against Muslim occupiers of Jerusalem as well as against those threatening Istanbul, Alexius instead received an uncontrollable ragtag force of Christians and Crusaders that included his Norman enemies, led by Bohemond.

Princess Anna, the emperor's daughter, recalled the story of the first Crusader's appearance in Byzantium some forty years later in her history called, after her father, *The Alexiad.* In what ways was the Byzantine attitude toward the Franks similar to the Muslim? In what respects was it different? Did Alexius fear the Franks more than he feared the Turks?

Thinking Historically

Anna Comnena's story of the Frankish invasion of Byzantium, especially Nicaea, is told in great detail as is the modern Arab account given in the preceding selection. Despite their differing points of view, on what do the two narratives agree? Construct your own narrative, using both of these sources, to tell the story of the Franks' attack on Nicaea. From whose viewpoint will you write and why?

Before he had enjoyed even a short rest, he heard a report of the approach of innumerable Frankish armies. Now he dreaded their arrival for he knew their irresistible manner of attack, their unstable and mobile character and all the peculiar natural and concomitant characteristics which the Frank retains throughout; and he also knew that they were always agape for money, and seemed to disregard their truces readily for any reason that cropped up. For he had always heard this

Anna Comnena, *The Alexiad of the Princess Anna Comnena,* trans. Elizabeth A. S. Dawes (London: Routledge & Kegan Paul Ltd., 1967), 247–52. Reprinted in William H. McNeill and Schuyler O. Houser, *Medieval Europe* (Oxford University Press, 1971), 135–40.

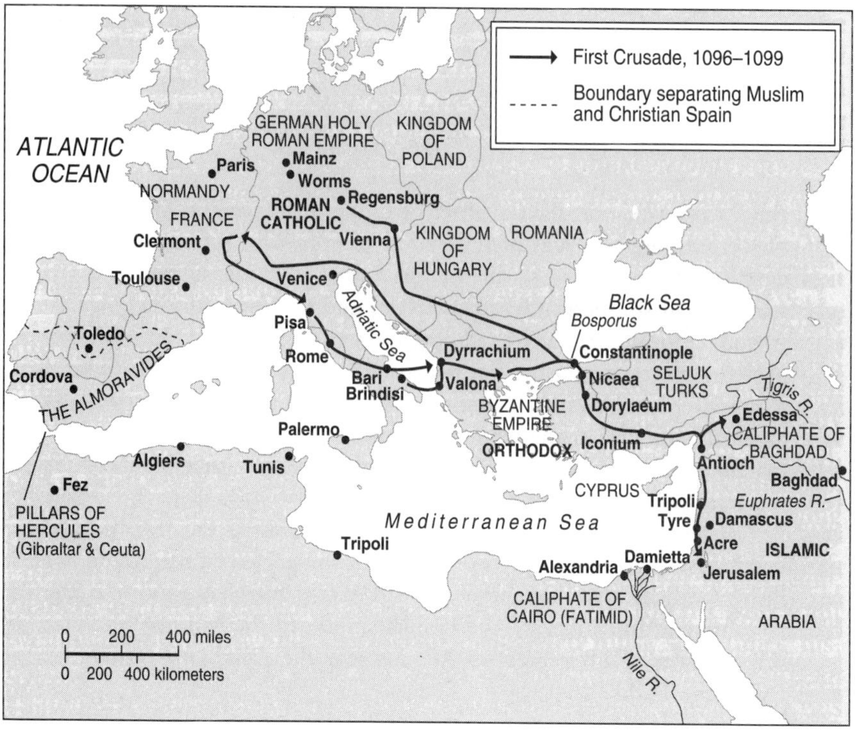

Figure 1. Map of Crusader routes.

reported of them, and found it very true. However, he did not lose heart, but prepared himself in every way so that, when the occasion called, he would be ready for battle. And indeed the actual facts were far greater and more terrible than rumour made them. For the whole of the West and all the barbarian tribes which dwell between the further side of the Adriatic and the pillars of Heracles, had all migrated in a body and were marching into Asia through the intervening Europe, and were making the journey with all their household. The reason of this upheaval was more or less the following. A certain Frank, Peter by name, nicknamed Cucupeter, had gone to worship at the Holy Sepulchre and after suffering many things at the hands of the Turks and Saracens who were ravaging Asia, he got back to his own country with difficulty. But he was angry at having failed in his object, and wanted to undertake the same journey again. However, he saw that he ought not to make the journey to the Holy Sepulchre alone again, lest worse things befall him, so he worked out a cunning plan. This was to preach in all the Latin countries that "the voice of God bids me announce to all the Counts in France" that they should all leave their homes and set out to worship at the Holy Sepulchre, and to endeavour wholeheartedly with hand and mind to deliver Jerusalem from the hand of Hagarenes.[1] And he really succeeded. For after inspiring the souls of all with this quasi-divine command he contrived to assemble the Franks from all sides, one after the other, with arms, horses and all the other paraphernalia of war. And they were all so zealous and eager that every highroad was full of them. And those Frankish soldiers were accompanied by an unarmed host more numerous than the sand or the stars, carrying palms and crosses on their shoulders, women and children, too, came away from their countries and the sight of them was like many rivers streaming from all sides, and they were advancing towards us through Dacia generally with all their hosts. Now the coming of these many peoples was preceded by a locust which did not touch the wheat, but made a terrible attack on the vines. This was really a presage as the diviners of the time interpreted it, and meant that this enormous Frankish army would, when it came, refrain from interference in Christian affairs, but fall very heavily upon the barbarian Ishmaelites who were slaves to drunkenness, wine, and Dionysus.[2] For this race is under the sway of Dionysus and Eros,[3] rushes headlong into all kind of sexual intercourse, and is not circumcised either in the flesh or in their passions. It is nothing but a slave, nay triply enslaved, to the ills wrought by Aphrodite. For this reason they worship and adore Astarte and Ashtaroth[4] too and value above all the image of the moon, and the golden figure of Hobar[5] in their country. Now in these symbols Christianity was taken to be the corn because of its wineless and very nutritive qualities; in this manner the diviners interpreted the vines and the wheat. However let the matter of the prophecy rest.

The incidents of the barbarians' approach followed in the order I have described, and persons of intelligence could feel that they were witnessing a strange occurrence. The arrival of these multitudes did not take place at the same time nor by the same road (for how indeed could such masses starting from different places have crossed the straits of Lombardy all together?). Some first, some next, others after them and thus successively all accomplished the transit, and then marched through the Continent. Each army was preceded, as we said, by an unspeakable number of locusts; and all who saw this more than once recognized them as forerunners of the Frankish armies. When the first of them began crossing the straits of Lombardy sporadically the Emperor

1 Saracens, who were considered "children of Hagar" (cf. Gen. 16). [Ed.]

2 Anna's account of the beliefs of the Muslims was highly biased. Muhammad forbade his followers to drink intoxicating liquors.

3 Dionysus was the Greek god associated with wine and revelry; Eros was the patron of lovers, and son of Aphrodite, goddess of love.

4 Names of the Semitic goddess of fertility.

5 I.e., Hathor, the Egyptian goddess of love, usually depicted with the head of a cow. (N.B. Idol worship was strictly forbidden by Islamic law.)

summoned certain leaders of the Roman forces, and sent them to the parts of Dyrrachium and Valona[6] with instructions to offer a courteous welcome to the Franks who had crossed, and to collect abundant supplies from all the countries along their route; then to follow and watch them covertly all the time, and if they saw them making any foraging-excursions, they were to come out from under cover and check them by light skirmishing. These captains were accompanied by some men who knew the Latin tongue, so that they might settle any disputes that arose between them.

Let me, however, give an account of this subject more clearly and in due order. According to universal rumour Godfrey,[7] who sold his country, was the first to start on the appointed road; this man was very rich and very proud of his bravery, courage and conspicuous lineage; for every Frank is anxious to outdo the others. And such an upheaval of both men and women took place then as had never occurred within human memory, the simpler-minded were urged on by the real desire of worshipping at our Lord's Sepulchre, and visiting the sacred places; but the more astute, especially men like Bohemund and those of like mind, had another secret reason, namely, the hope that while on their travels they might by some means be able to seize the capital itself, looking upon this as a kind of corollary. And Bohemund disturbed the minds of many nobler men by thus cherishing his old grudge against the Emperor. Meanwhile Peter, after he had delivered his message, crossed the straits of Lombardy before anybody else with eighty thousand men on foot, and one hundred thousand on horseback, and reached the capital by way of Hungary.[8] For the Frankish race, as one may conjecture, is always very hotheaded and eager, but when once it has espoused a cause, it is uncontrollable.

The Emperor, knowing what Peter had suffered before from the Turks, advised him to wait for the arrival of the other Counts, but Peter would not listen for he trusted the multitude of his followers, so he crossed and pitched his camp near a small town called Helenopolis.[9] After him followed the Normans numbering ten thousand, who separated themselves from the rest of the army and devastated the country round Nicaea, and behaved most cruelly to all. For they dismembered some of the children and fixed others on wooden spits and roasted them at the fire, and on persons advanced in age they inflicted every kind of torture. But when the inhabitants of Nicaea became aware of

[6] Ports on the Adriatic, directly opposite the heel of Italy in modern Albania.

[7] Godfrey of Bouillon, the duke of Lower Lorraine (c. 1060–1100). To raise money for the Crusade, he sold two of his estates, and pledged his castle at Bouillon to the bishop of Liège.

[8] Peter's contingent probably numbered about twenty thousand including noncombatants.

[9] I.e., Peter moved his forces across the Bosphorus and into Asia Minor.

these doings, they threw open their gates and marched out upon them, and after a violent conflict had taken place they had to dash back inside their citadel as the Normans fought so bravely. And thus the latter recovered all the booty and returned to Helenopolis. Then a dispute arose between them and the others who had not gone out with them, as is usual in such cases, for the minds of those who stayed behind were aflame with envy, and thus caused a skirmish after which the headstrong Normans drew apart again, marched to Xerigordus[10] and took it by assault. When the Sultan[11] heard what had happened, he dispatched Elchanes[12] against them with a substantial force. He came, and recaptured Xerigordus and sacrificed some of the Normans to the sword, and took others captive, at the same time laid plans to catch those who had remained behind with Cucupeter. He placed ambushes in suitable spots so that any coming from the camp in the direction of Nicaea would fall into them unexpectedly and be killed. Besides this, as he knew the Franks' love of money, he sent for two active-minded men and ordered them to go to Cucupeter's camp and proclaim there that the Normans had gained possession of Nicaea, and were now dividing everything in it. When this report was circulated among Peter's followers, it upset them terribly. Directly [When] they heard the words "partition" and "money" they started in a disorderly crowd along the road to Nicaea, all but unmindful of their military experience and the discipline which is essential for those starting out to battle. For, as I remarked above, the Latin race is always very fond of money, but more especially when it is bent on raiding a country; it then loses its reason and gets beyond control. As they journeyed neither in ranks nor in squadrons, they fell foul of the Turkish ambuscades near the river Dracon and perished miserably. And such a large number of Franks and Normans were the victims of the Ishmaelite sword, that when they piled up the corpses of the slaughtered men which were lying on either side they formed, I say, not a very large hill or mound or a peak, but a high mountain as it were, of very considerable depth and breadth — so great was the pyramid of bones. And later men of the same tribe as the slaughtered barbarians built a wall and used the bones of the dead to fill the interstices as if they were pebbles, and thus made the city their tomb in a way. This fortified city is still standing today with its walls built of a mixture of stones and bones. When they had all in this way fallen a prey to the sword, Peter alone with a few others escaped and reentered Helenopolis,[13] and the Turks who wanted to capture him, set fresh ambushes for him. But when the Emperor received reliable information of all this,

10 A castle held by the Turks.

11 Qilij Arslan I, ruled 1092–1106.

12 An important Turkish military commander.

13 According to other accounts of the battle, Peter was in Constantinople at the time.

and the terrible massacre, he was very worried lest Peter should have been captured. He therefore summoned Constantine Catacalon Euphorbenus (who has already been mentioned many times in this history), and gave him a large force which was embarked on ships of war and sent him across the straits to Peter's succour. Directly the Turks saw him land they fled. Constantine, without the slightest delay, picked up Peter and his followers, who were but few, and brought them safe and sound to the Emperor. On the Emperor's reminding him of his original thoughtlessness and saying that it was due to his not having obeyed his, the Emperor's, advice that he had incurred such disasters, Peter, being a haughty Latin, would not admit that he himself was the cause of the trouble, but said it was the others who did not listen to him, but followed their own will, and he denounced them as robbers and plunderers who, for that reason, were not allowed by the Saviour to worship at His Holy Sepulchre. Others of the Latins, such as Bohemund and men of like mind, who had long cherished a desire for the Roman Empire, and wished to win it for themselves, found a pretext in Peter's preaching, as I have said, deceived the more single-minded, caused this great upheaval and were selling their own estates under the pretence that they were marching against the Turks to redeem the Holy Sepulchre.

60

WILLIAM OF TYRE

Peter the Hermit

William of Tyre (c. 1130–1185) was probably born of Frankish parents in Latin-occupied Palestine,[1] in the city of Jerusalem or Tyre. He was educated in Europe by Latin priests and returned to the Diocese of Tyre to serve in the Church. At the request of the Latin King of Jerusalem, William researched and wrote a history of the Crusades, from which this selection is excerpted.

[1]Latin refers to Roman church, the language of which was Latin, as opposed to Greek in the Orthodox church.

William of Tyre, "Peter the Hermit," in D. C. Munro, ed., *Translation and Reprints from the Original Sources of European History*, 4th ed., vol. I, bk. 2 (New York: AMS Press, Inc., 1971), 20–22.

William's is the first Roman Christian account in this chapter. He tells the story of Peter the Hermit to explain the origin of the Crusades. Why, according to this story, did Peter want Roman Christians to retake Jerusalem? How did he help initiate the First Crusade?

Thinking Historically

In what ways is William's story about Peter different from Anna Comnena's narrative? Write your own story of Peter's role, drawing information from both sources. How will you decide what facts to include? How will you choose between divergent interpretations? Is your account "objective"?

A certain priest named Peter, from the kingdom of the Franks and the bishopric of Amiens, a hermit both in deed and name, led by the same ardor, arrived at Jerusalem. He was small in stature and his external appearance contemptible, but greater valor ruled in his slight frame. For he was sharp witted, his glance was bright and captivating, and he spoke with ease and eloquence. Having paid the tax which was exacted from all Christians who wished to enter, he went into the city and was entertained by a trusty man who was also a confessor of Christ. He diligently questioned his host, as he was a zealous man, and learned more fully from him not only the existing perils, but also the persecutions which their ancestors had suffered long before. And if in what he heard any details were lacking, he completed the account from the witness of his own eyes. For remaining in the city and visiting the churches he learned more fully the truth of what had been told to him by others.

Hearing also that the Patriarch of the city was a devout and God-fearing man, he wished to confer with him and to learn more fully from him the truth concerning some matters. Accordingly he went to him, and having been presented by a trustworthy man, both he and the Patriarch mutually enjoyed their conferences.

The name of the Patriarch was Simeon. As he learned from Peter's conversation that the latter was prudent, able and eloquent, and a man of great experience, he began to disclose to him more confidentially all the evils which the people of God had suffered while dwelling in Jerusalem.

To whom Peter relied: "You may be assured, holy father, that if the Roman church and the princes of the West should learn from a zealous and a reliable witness the calamities which you suffer, there is not the slightest doubt that they would hasten to remedy the evil, both by words and deeds. Write then zealously both to the lord Pope and the

Roman church and to the kings and princes of the West, and confirm your letter by the authority of your seal. I, truly, for the sake of the salvation of my soul, do not hesitate to undertake this task. And I am prepared under God's guidance to visit them all, to exhort them all, zealously to inform them of the greatness of your sufferings and to urge them to hasten to your relief."

Of a truth, Thou art great, O Lord our God, and to thy mercy there is no end! Of a truth, blessed Jesus, those who trust in Thee shall not be brought to confusion! How did this poor pilgrim, destitute of all resources and far from his native land, have so great confidence that he dared to undertake an enterprise so much beyond his strength and to hope to accomplish his vow, unless it was that he turned all his thoughts to Thee, his protector, and filled with charity, pitying the misfortunes of his brethren, loving his neighbor as himself, he was content to fulfill the law? Strength is a vain thing, but charity overcometh. What his brethren prescribed might appear difficult and even impossible, but the love of God and of his neighbor rendered it easy for him, for love is strong as death. Faith which worketh by love availeth with Thee, and the good deeds near Thee do not remain without fruit. Accordingly Thou didst not permit Thy servant long to remain in doubt. Thou didst manifest Thyself to him. Thou didst fortify him by Thy revelation that he might not hesitate, and breathing into him Thy hidden spirit, Thou madest him arise with greater strength to accomplish the work of charity.

Therefore, after performing the usual prayers, taking leave of the lord Patriarch and receiving his blessing, he went to the sea-coast. There he found a vessel belonging to some merchants who were preparing to cross to Apulia. He went on board, and after a successful journey arrived at Bari. Thence he proceeded to Rome, and found the lord Pope Urban in the vicinity. He presented the letters of the Patriarch and of the Christians who dwelt at Jerusalem, and showed their misery and the abominations which the unclean races wrought in the holy places. Thus faithfully and prudently he performed the commission entrusted to him.

61

ROBERT THE MONK

Pope Urban II's Call to the First Crusade

Pope Urban's call for a crusade at the Council of Clermont in France in 1095 is reported in four histories of the period. This selection, taken from Robert the Monk's *History of the Crusade to Jerusalem*, is similar to the other three accounts, so we can consider it fairly representative.

Judging from this account, was Pope Urban's appeal prompted by Peter the Hermit, Emperor Alexius, or both? Historians have suggested that Pope Urban II's speech was carefully planned and orchestrated. Do you see any signs of this? What obstacles did Pope Urban II envision to his call? How did he try to surmount these obstacles?

Thinking Historically

In what ways does a recounted speech have a different feeling than a narrative account about action? Does a recounted speech take the drama out of the narrative account or the story line out of the narrative? How does Robert the Monk avoid this difficulty?

If you were to compose your own narrative history of the Crusades, would you include Pope Urban II's speech? If so, where would you place the speech in your narrative?

In the year of our Lord's Incarnation one thousand and ninety-five, a great council was convened within the bounds of Gaul, in Auvergne, in the city which is called Clermont. Over this Pope Urban II presided, with the Roman bishops and cardinals. This council was a famous one on account of the concourse of both French and German bishops, and of princes as well. Having arranged the matters relating to the Church, the lord Pope went forth into a certain spacious plain, for no building was large enough to hold all the people. The Pope then, with sweet and persuasive eloquence, addressed those present in words something like the following, saying:

"Oh, race of Franks, race beyond the mountains,[1] race beloved and chosen by God (as is clear from many of your works), set apart from all

[1] The Alps. [Ed.]

Robert the Monk, "Pope Urban II's Call to the 1st Crusade," in *A Sourcebook of Mediaeval History*, ed. Frederic Austin Ogg (New York: American Book Company, 1907), 284–88.

other nations by the situation of your country, as well as by your Catholic faith and the honor you render to the holy Church: to you our discourse is addressed, and for you our exhortations are intended. We wish you to know what a serious matter has led us to your country, for it is the imminent peril threatening you and all the faithful that has brought us hither.

"From the confines of Jerusalem and from the city of Constantinople a grievous report has gone forth and has been brought repeatedly to our ears; namely, that a race from the kingdom of the Persians, an accursed race, a race wholly alienated from God, 'a generation that set not their heart aright, and whose spirit was not steadfast with God,'[2] has violently invaded the lands of those Christians and has depopulated them by pillage and fire. They have led away a part of the captives into their own country, and a part they have killed by cruel tortures. They have either destroyed the churches of God or appropriated them for the rites of their own religion. They destroy the altars, after having defiled them with their uncleanness. . . . The kingdom of the Greeks[3] is now dismembered by them and has been deprived of territory so vast in extent that it could not be traversed in two months' time.

"On whom, therefore, rests the labor of avenging these wrongs and of recovering this territory, if not upon you — you, upon whom, above all other nations, God has conferred remarkable glory in arms, great courage, bodily activity, and strength to humble the heads of those who resist you? Let the deeds of your ancestors encourage you and incite your minds to manly achievements — the glory and greatness of King Charlemagne and of his son Louis,[4] and of your other monarchs, who have destroyed the kingdoms of the Turks and have extended the sway of the holy Church over lands previously pagan. Let the holy sepulcher of our Lord and Saviour, which is possessed by the unclean nations especially arouse you, and the holy places which are now treated with ignominy and irreverently polluted with the filth of the unclean. Oh most valiant soldiers and descendants of invincible ancestors, do not degenerate, but recall the valor of your ancestors.

"But if you are hindered by love of children, parents, or wife, remember what the Lord says in the Gospel, 'He that loveth father or mother more than me is not worthy of me.'[5] 'Every one that hath forsaken houses, or brethren, or sisters, or father, or mother, or wife, or children, or lands, for my name's sake, shall receive an hundred-fold, and shall inherit everlasting life.'[6] Let none of your possessions restrain you, nor anxiety for your family affairs. For this land which you in-

[2] Ps. 78:8. [Ed.]
[3] The Eastern Empire. [Ed.]
[4] The Pious. [Ed.]
[5] Matt. 10:37. [Ed.]
[6] Matt. 19:29. [Ed.]

habit, shut in on all sides by the seas and surrounded by the mountain peaks, is too narrow for your large population; nor does it abound in wealth; and it furnishes scarcely food enough for its cultivators. Hence it is that you murder and devour one another, that you wage war, and that very many among you perish in civil strife.

"Let hatred, therefore, depart from among you; let your quarrels end; let wars cease; and let all dissensions and controversies slumber. Enter upon the road of the Holy Sepulcher; wrest that land from the wicked race, and subject it to yourselves. That land which, as the Scripture says, 'floweth with milk and honey'[7] was given by God into the power of the children of Israel. Jerusalem center of the earth; the land is fruitful above all others, like another paradise of delights. This spot the Redeemer of mankind has made illustrious by His advent, has beautified by His sojourn, has consecrated by His passion, has redeemed by His death, has glorified by His burial.

"This royal city, however, situated at the center of the earth, is now held captive by the enemies of Christ and is subjected, by those who do not know God, to the worship of the heathen. She seeks, therefore, and desires to be liberated, and ceases not to implore you to come to her aid. From you especially she asks succor, because, as we have already said, God has conferred upon you, above all other nations, great glory in arms. Accordingly, undertake this journey eagerly for the remission of your sins, with the assurance of the reward of imperishable glory in the kingdom of heaven."

When Pope Urban had skillfully said these and very many similar things, he so centered in one purpose the desires of all who were present that all cried out, "It is the will of God! It is the will of God!" When the venerable Roman pontiff heard that, with eyes uplifted to heaven, he gave thanks to God and, commanding silence with his hand, said:

"Most beloved brethren, today is manifest in you what the Lord says in the Gospel, 'Where two or three are gathered together in my name, there am I in the midst of them.'[8] For unless God had been present in your spirits, all of you would not have uttered the same cry; since, although the cry issued from numerous mouths, yet the origin of the cry was one. Therefore I say to you that God, who implanted this in your breasts, has drawn it forth from you. Let that, then, be your war cry in battle, because it is given to you by God. When an armed attack is made upon the enemy, let this one cry be raised by all the soldiers of God: 'It is the will of God! It is the will of God!'

"And we neither command nor advise that the old or feeble, or those incapable of bearing arms, undertake this journey. Nor ought

[7] Num. 13:27. [Ed.]
[8] Matt. 18:20. [Ed.]

women to set out at all without their husbands, or brothers, or legal guardians. For such are more of a hindrance than aid, more of a burden than an advantage. Let the rich aid the needy; and according to their wealth let them take with them experienced soldiers. The priests and other clerks,[9] whether secular or regular, are not to go without the consent of their bishop; for this journey would profit them nothing if they went without permission. Also, it is not fitting that laymen should enter upon the pilgrimage without the blessing of their priests.

"Whoever, therefore, shall decide upon this holy pilgrimage, and shall make his vow to God to that effect, and shall offer himself to Him for sacrifice, as a living victim, holy and acceptable to God, shall wear the sign of the cross of the Lord on his forehead or on his breast. When he shall return from his journey, having fulfilled his vow, let him place the cross on his back between his shoulders. Thus shall ye, indeed, by this twofold action, fulfill the precept of the Lord, as He commands in the Gospel, 'He that taketh not his cross, and followeth after me, is not worthy of me.'"[10]

[9] Clergy. [Ed.]
[10] Luke 14:27. [Ed.]

62

Chronicle of Solomon bar Simson

Solomon bar Simson (who is known only from this Chronicle) provides the most complete of the Hebrew chronicles of the First Crusade. He takes up the story after Pope Urban II's appeal. Franks and Germans have organized their armies of knights, suppliers, aides, and followers, and have set off for Jerusalem by way of Constantinople. Why did these Crusaders stop at Mainz and other German cities to murder Jews?

Thinking Historically

This narrative introduces a fourth point of view to the story of the Crusades. In what ways is a European Jewish view of the Crusades different from a Muslim, Byzantine, or Frankish view?

"Chronicle of Solomon bar Simson," in *The Jews and the Crusaders: The Hebrew Chronicles of the First and Second Crusades*, ed. and trans. Shlomo Eidelberg (Madison: The University of Wisconsin Press, 1977), 21–26.

This narrative, like some of those in previous selections, includes quotations of speeches. How can you tell that some of these quotations do not contain the exact words that were spoken?

Solomon bar Simson's narrative contains another element that, while absent from modern histories, is found in other narratives of the Crusades and is especially pronounced here. This is not just a narrative of human action and intention, but it interprets divine action and intention as well. Why is this narrative strategy necessary for this author? If you were writing a narrative of the Crusades today, would you want to tell both of these stories, or only the human one? Why?

I will now recount the event of this persecution in other martyred communities as well — the extent to which they clung to the Lord, God of their fathers, bearing witness to His Oneness to their last breath.

In the year four thousand eight hundred and fifty-six, the year one thousand twenty-eight of our exile, in the eleventh year of the cycle Ranu, the year in which we anticipated salvation and solace, in accordance with the prophecy of Jeremiah: "Sing with gladness for Jacob, and shout at the head of the nations," etc. — this year turned instead to sorrow and groaning, weeping and outcry. Inflicted upon the Jewish People were the many evils related in all the admonitions; those enumerated in Scripture as well as those unwritten were visited upon us.

At this time arrogant people, a people of strange speech, a nation bitter and impetuous, Frenchmen and Germans, set out for the Holy City, which had been desecrated by barbaric nations, there to seek their house of idolatry and banish the Ishmaelites and other denizens of the land and conquer the land for themselves. They decorated themselves prominently with their signs, placing a profane symbol — a horizontal line over a vertical one — on the vestments of every man and woman whose heart yearned to go on the stray path to the grave of their Messiah. Their ranks swelled until the number of men, women, and children exceeded a locust horde covering the earth; of them it was said: "The locusts have no king [yet go they forth all of them by bands]." Now it came to pass that as they passed through the towns where Jews dwelled, they said to one another: "Look now, we are going a long way to seek out the profane shrine and to avenge ourselves on the Ishmaelites, when here, in our very midst, are the Jews — they whose forefathers murdered and crucified him for no reason. Let us first avenge ourselves on them and exterminate them from among the nations so that the name of Israel will no longer be remembered, or let them adopt our faith and acknowledge the offspring of promiscuity."

When the Jewish communities became aware of their intentions, they resorted to the custom of our ancestors, repentance, prayer, and charity. The hands of the Holy Nation turned faint at this time, their hearts melted, and their strength flagged. They hid in their innermost rooms to escape the swirling sword. They subjected themselves to great endurance, abstaining from food and drink for three consecutive days and nights, and then fasting many days from sunrise to sunset, until their skin was shriveled and dry as wood upon their bones. And they cried out loudly and bitterly to God.

But their Father did not answer them; He obstructed their prayers, concealing Himself in a cloud through which their prayers could not pass, and He abhorred their tent, and He removed them out of His sight — all of this having been decreed by Him to take place "in the day when I visit"; and this was the generation that had been chosen by Him to be His portion, for they had the strength and the fortitude to stand in His Sanctuary, and fulfill His word, and sanctify His Great Name in His world. It is of such as these that King David said: "Bless the Lord, ye angels of His, ye almighty in strength, that fulfil His word," etc.

That year, Passover fell on Thursday, and the New Moon of the following month, Iyar, fell on Friday and the Sabbath. On the eighth day of Iyar, on the Sabbath, the foe attacked the community of Speyer and murdered eleven holy souls who sanctified their Creator on the holy Sabbath and refused to defile themselves by adopting the faith of their foe. There was a distinguished, pious woman there who slaughtered herself in sanctification of God's Name. She was the first among all the communities of those who were slaughtered. The remainder were saved by the local bishop without defilement [i.e., baptism], as described above.

On the twenty-third of Iyar they attacked the community of Worms.[1] The community was then divided into two groups; some remained in their homes and others fled to the local bishop seeking refuge. Those who remained in their homes were set upon by the steppe-wolves who pillaged men, women, and infants, children and old people. They pulled down the stairways and destroyed the houses, looting and plundering; and they took the Torah Scroll, trampled it in the mud, and tore and burned it. The enemy devoured the children of Israel with open maw.

Seven days later, on the New Moon of Sivan — the very day on which the Children of Israel arrived at Mount Sinai to receive the Torah — those Jews who were still in the court of the bishop were subjected to great anguish. The enemy dealt them the same cruelty as the first group and put them to the sword. The Jews, inspired by the valor

[1] Town in the Holy Roman Empire (now Germany). [Ed.]

of their brethren, similarly chose to be slain in order to sanctify the Name before the eyes of all, and exposed their throats for their heads to be severed for the glory of the Creator. There were also those who took their own lives, thus fulfilling the verse: "The mother was dashed in pieces with her children." Fathers fell upon their sons, being slaughtered upon one another, and they slew one another — each man his kin, his wife and children; bridegrooms slew their betrothed, and merciful women their only children. They all accepted the divine decree wholeheartedly and, as they yielded up their souls to the Creator, cried out: "Hear, O Israel, the Lord is our God, the Lord is One." The enemy stripped them naked, dragged them along, and then cast them off, sparing only a small number whom they forcibly baptized in their profane waters. The number of those slain during the two days was approximately eight hundred — and they were all buried naked. It is of these that the Prophet Jeremiah lamented: "They that were brought up in scarlet embrace dunghills." I have already cited their names above. May God remember them for good.

When the saints, the pious ones of the Most High, the holy community of Mainz, whose merit served as shield and protection for all the communities and whose fame had spread throughout the many provinces, heard that some of the community of Speyer had been slain and that the community of Worms had been attacked a second time, and that the sword would soon reach them, their hands became faint and their hearts melted and became as water. They cried out to the Lord with all their hearts, saying: "O Lord, God of Israel, will You completely annihilate the remnant of Israel? Where are all your wonders which our forefathers related to us, saying: 'Did You not bring us up from Egypt and from Babylonia and rescue us on numerous occasions?' How, then, have You now forsaken and abandoned us, O Lord, giving us over into the hands of evil Edom so that they may destroy us? Do not remove Yourself from us, for adversity is almost upon us and there is no one to aid us."

The leaders of the Jews gathered together and discussed various ways of saving themselves. They said: "Let us elect elders so that we may know how to act, for we are consumed by this great evil." The elders decided to ransom the community by generously giving of their money and bribing the various princes and deputies and bishops and governors. Then, the community leaders who were respected by the local bishop approached him and his officers and servants to negotiate this matter. They asked: "What shall we do about the news we have received regarding the slaughter of our brethren in Speyer and Worms?" They [the Gentiles] replied: "Heed our advice and bring all your money into our treasury. You, your wives, and your children, and all your belongings shall come into the courtyard of the bishop until the hordes have passed by. Thus will you be saved from the errant ones."

Actually, they gave this advice so as to herd us together and hold us like fish that are caught in an evil net, and then to turn us over to the enemy, while taking our money. This is what actually happened in the end, and "the outcome is proof of the intentions." The bishop assembled his ministers and courtiers — mighty ministers, the noblest in the land — for the purpose of helping us; for at first it had been his desire to save us with all his might, since we had given him and his ministers and servants a large bribe in return for their promise to help us. Ultimately, however, all the bribes and entreaties were of no avail to protect us on the day of wrath and misfortune.

It was at this time that Duke Godfrey [of Bouillon], may his bones be ground to dust, arose in the hardness of his spirit, driven by a spirit of wantonness to go with those journeying to the profane shrine, vowing to go on this journey only after avenging the blood of the crucified one by shedding Jewish blood and completely eradicating any trace of those bearing the name "Jew," thus assuaging his own burning wrath. To be sure, there arose someone to repair the breach — a God-fearing man who had been bound to the most holy of altars — called Rabbi Kalonymos, the *Parnass* of the community of Mainz. He dispatched a messenger to King Henry in the kingdom of Pula, where the king had been dwelling during the past nine years, and related all that had happened.

The king was enraged and dispatched letters to all the ministers, bishops, and governors of all the provinces of his realm, as well as to Duke Godfrey, containing words of greeting and commanding them to do no bodily harm to the Jews and to provide them with help and refuge. The evil duke then swore that he had never intended to do them harm. The Jews of Cologne nevertheless bribed him with five hundred *zekukim* of silver, as did the Jews of Mainz. The duke assured them of his support and promised them peace.

However, God, the maker of peace, turned aside and averted His eyes from His people, and consigned them to the sword. No prophet, seer, or man of wise heart was able to comprehend how the sin of the people infinite in number was deemed so great as to cause the destruction of so many lives in the various Jewish communities. The martyrs endured the extreme penalty normally inflicted only upon one guilty of murder. Yet, it must be stated with certainty that God is a righteous judge, and we are to blame.

Then the evil waters prevailed. The enemy unjustly accused them of evil acts they did not do, declaring: "You are the children of those who killed our object of veneration, hanging him on a tree, and he himself had said: 'There will yet come a day when my children will come and avenge my blood.' We are his children and it is therefore obligatory for us to avenge him since you are the ones who rebel and disbelieve in him. Your God has never been at peace with you. Although He intended to deal kindly with you, you have conducted yourselves improperly before Him. God has forgotten you and is no longer desirous of you since you are a stubborn nation. Instead, He has departed from you and has taken us for His portion, casting His radiance upon us."

When we heard these words, our hearts trembled and moved out of their places. We were dumb with silence, abiding in darkness, like those long dead, waiting for the Lord to look forth and behold from heaven.

And Satan — the Pope of evil Rome — also came and proclaimed to all the nations believing in that stock of adultery — these are the stock of Seir[2] — that they should assemble and ascend to Jerusalem so as to conquer the city, and journey to the tomb of the superstition whom they call their god. Satan came and mingled with the nations, and they gathered as one man to fulfill the command, coming in great numbers like the grains of sand upon the seashore, the noise of them clamorous as a whirlwind and a storm. When the drops of the bucket had assembled, they took evil counsel against the people of the Lord and said: "Why should we concern ourselves with going to war against the Ishmaelites dwelling about Jerusalem, when in our midst is a people who disrespect our god — indeed, their ancestors are those who crucified him. Why should we let them live and tolerate their dwelling among us? Let us commence by using our swords against them and then proceed upon our stray path."

The heart of the people of our God grew faint and their spirit flagged, for many sore injuries had been inflicted upon them and they had been smitten repeatedly. They now came supplicating to God and fasting, and their hearts melted within them. But the Lord did as He declared, for we had sinned before Him, and He forsook the sanctuary of Shiloh — the Temple-in-Miniature — which He had placed among His people who dwelt in the midst of alien nations. His wrath was kindled and He drew the sword against them, until they remained but as the flagstaff upon the mountaintop and as the ensign on the hill, and He gave over His nation into captivity and trampled them underfoot. See, O Lord, and consider to whom Thou hast done thus: to Israel, a nation despised and pillaged, Your chosen portion! Why have You uplifted the shield of its enemies, and why have they gained in strength? Let all hear, for I cry out in anguish; the ears of all that hear me shall be seared: How has the staff of might been broken, the rod of glory — the sainted community comparable to fine gold, the community of Mainz! It was caused by the Lord to test those that fear Him, to have them endure the yoke of His pure fear. . . .

[2] An enemy of ancient Israel.

63

COUNT STEPHEN OF BLOIS

Letter from Antioch

The backbone of the Crusades were the armies whose services Alexius and Pope Urban II requested from about ten nobles. Count Stephen of Blois was one such noble. In 1096 before he departed, he made a gift to the Abbey of Marmoutier so that, in his words, "God, at the intercession of St. Martin and his monks, might pardon me for whatever I have done wrong and lead me on the journey out of my homeland and bring me back healthy and safe, and watch over my wife Adela and our children."

What seem to be the circumstances of this letter from Antioch? In what ways has the crusade been a success for Stephen of Blois? How is his account of the battle of Nicaea different from others you have read? What apparently motivated the Crusaders in their travels through lands held by Turks?

Thinking Historically

Narratives are not found only in histories or chronicles. Every day, we tell stories to each other to explain what has happened in our lives. In this selection, Stephen of Blois, on the First Crusade in Antioch (northern Syria), uses narrative to tell his wife about the Crusaders' struggles and journey through Turkey into Syria. He provides a useful summary that you can follow easily on a map. While he doesn't tell a divine narrative explicitly, there is certainly one implicit in his letter. How would you explain and summarize this divine narrative?

In what ways is a letter different from a history? What elements of this letter would you want to include if you were writing a narrative of the Crusades?

Count Stephen to Adele, his sweetest and most amiable wife, to his dear children, and to all his vassals of all ranks — his greeting and blessing.

You may be very sure, dearest, that the messenger whom I sent to give you pleasure, left me before Antioch safe and unharmed, and through God's grace in the greatest prosperity. And already at that

---

Count Stephen of Blois, "Letter from Antioch," in D. C. Munro, ed., *Translations and Reprints from the Original Sources of European History,* 4th ed., vol. I, bk. 4 (New York: AMS Press, Inc., 1971), 5–7.

time, together with all the chosen army of Christ, endowed with great valor by Him, we had been continuously advancing for twenty-three weeks toward the home of our Lord Jesus. You may know for certain, my beloved, that of gold, silver and many other kind of riches I now have twice as much as your love had assigned to me when I left you. For all our princes, with the common consent of the whole army, against my own wishes, have made me up to the present time the leader, chief and director of their whole expedition.

You have certainly heard that after the capture of the city of Nicaea we fought a great battle with the perfidious Turks and by God's aid conquered them. Next we conquered for the Lord all Romania and afterwards Cappadocia. And we learned that there was a certain Turkish prince Assam, dwelling in Cappadocia; thither we directed our course. All his castles we conquered by force and compelled him to flee to a certain very strong castle situated on a high rock. We also gave the land of that Assam to one of our chiefs and in order that he might conquer the above-mentioned Assam, we left there with him many soldiers of Christ. Thence, continually following the wicked Turks, we drove them through the midst of Armenia, as far as the great river Euphrates. Having left all their baggage and beasts of burden on the bank, they fled across the river into Arabia.

The bolder of the Turkish soldiers, indeed, entering Syria, hastened by forced marches night and day, in order to be able to enter the royal city of Antioch before our approach. The whole army of God learning this gave due praise and thanks to the omnipotent Lord. Hastening with great joy to the aforesaid chief city of Antioch, we besieged it and very often had many conflicts there with the Turks; and seven times with the citizens of Antioch and with the innumerable troops coming to its aid, whom we rushed to meet, we fought with the fiercest courage, under the leadership of Christ. And in all these seven battles, by the aid of the Lord God, we conquered and most assuredly killed an innumerable host of them. In those battles, indeed, and in very many attacks made upon the city, many of our brethren and followers were killed and their souls were borne to the joys of paradise.

We found the city of Antioch very extensive, fortified with incredible strength and almost impregnable. In addition, more than 5,000 bold Turkish soldiers had entered the city, not counting the Saracens, Publicans, Arabs, Turcopolitans, Syrians, Armenians and other different races of whom an infinite multitude had gathered together there. In fighting against these enemies of God and of our own we have, by God's grace, endured many sufferings and innumerable evils up to the present time. Many also have already exhausted all their resources in this very holy passion. Very many of our Franks, indeed, would have met a temporal death from starvation, if the clemency of God and our money had not succoured them. Before the above-mentioned city of Antioch indeed, throughout the whole winter we suffered for our Lord Christ from excessive cold and enormous torrents of rain. What some say about the impossibility of bearing the heat of the sun throughout Syria is untrue, for the winter there is very similar to our winter in the west.

When truly Caspian [Bagi Seian], the emir of Antioch — that is, prince and lord — perceived that he was hard pressed by us, he sent his son Sensodolo [Chems Eddaulah] by name, to the prince who holds Jerusalem, and to the prince of Calep, Rodoam [Rodoanus], and to Docap [Deccacus Ibn Toutousch], prince of Damascus. He also sent into Arabia to Bolianuth and to Carathania to Hamelnuth. These five emirs with 12,000 picked Turkish horsemen suddenly came to aid the inhabitants of Antioch. We, indeed, ignorant of all this, had sent many of our soldiers away to the cities and fortresses. For there are one hundred and sixty-five cities and fortresses throughout Syria which are in our power. But a little before they reached the city, we attacked them at three leagues' distance with 700 soldiers, on a certain plain near the "Iron Bridge." God, however, fought for us, His faithful, against them. For on that day, fighting in the strength that God gives, we conquered them and killed an innumerable multitude — God continually fighting for us — and we also carried back to the army more than two hundred of their heads, in order that the people might rejoice on that account. The emperor of Babylon also sent Saracen messengers to our army with letters, and through these he established peace and concord with us. . . .

64

RAYMOND OF ST. GILES, COUNT OF TOULOUSE

The Capture of Jerusalem by the Crusaders

The author of this letter or proclamation was the secular military leader chosen by Pope Urban II to lead the crusade. By the time of the capture of Jerusalem in 1099, he was certainly — with the Norman Bohemond and a couple other nobles — among the top four military leaders. How does he account for their capture of Jerusalem? How would you explain it? Compare Raymond's description of the event

---

Raymond of St. Giles, Count of Toulouse, "The Capture of Jerusalem by the Crusaders," in D. C. Munro, ed., *Translations and Reprints from the Original Sources of European History*, 4th ed., vol. I, bk. 4 (New York: AMC Press, Inc., 1971) 8–12.

with that of Abū Sa'ad al-Harawi in selection 58. Compare their treatments of the Abbassid caliph (Babylonian emperor).

Thinking Historically

Using this and the other selections in this chapter that you find relevant, write your own brief narrative of the First Crusade. First, you need to decide when you want to begin your story, what major events you want to include, and what point of view you want to adopt. You are, of course, severely limited by the documents included here. If you were to do a more complete narrative, what other things would you want to know? What sort of documents might help you learn these things?

To lord Paschal, pope of the Roman church, to all the bishops, and to the whole Christian people, from the archbishop of Pisa, duke Godfrey, now, by the grace of God, defender of the church of the Holy Sepulchre, Raymond, count of St. Giles, and the whole army of God, which is in the land of Israel, greeting.

Multiply your supplications and prayers in the sight of God with joy and thanksgiving, since God has manifested His mercy in fulfilling by our hands what He had promised in ancient times. For after the capture of Nicaea, the whole army, made up of more than three hundred thousand soldiers, departed thence. And, although this army was so great that it could have in a single day covered all Romania and drunk up all the rivers and eaten up all the growing things, yet the Lord conducted them amid so great abundance that a ram was sold for a penny and an ox for twelve pennies or less. Moreover, although the princes and kings of the Saracens rose up against us, yet, by God's will, they were easily conquered and overcome. Because, indeed, some were puffed up by these successes, God opposed to us Antioch, impregnable to human strength. And there He detained us for nine months and so humbled us in the siege that there were scarcely a hundred good horses in our whole army. God opened to us the abundance of His blessing and mercy and led us into the city, and delivered the Turks and all of their possessions into our power.

Inasmuch as we thought that these had been acquired by our own strength and did not worthily magnify God who had done this, we were beset by so great a multitude of Turks that no one dared to venture forth at any point from the city. Moreover, hunger so weakened us that some could scarcely refrain from eating human flesh. It would be tedious to narrate all the miseries which we suffered in that city. But God looked down upon His people whom He had so long chastised and mercifully consoled them. Therefore, He at first revealed to us, as a recompense for our tribulation and as a pledge of victory, His lance which had lain hidden since the days of the apostles. Next, He so fortified the hearts of the men, that they who from sickness or hunger had been unable to walk, now were endued with strength to seize their weapons and manfully to fight against the enemy.

After we had triumphed over the enemy, as our army was wasting away at Antioch from sickness and weariness and was especially hindered by the dissensions among the leaders, we proceeded into Syria, stormed Barra and Marra, cities of the Saracens, and captured the fortresses in that country. And while we were delaying there, there was so great a famine in the army that the Christian people now ate the putrid bodies of the Saracens. Finally, by the divine admonition, we entered into the interior of Hispania, and the most bountiful, merciful and victorious hand of the omnipotent Father was with us. For the cities and fortresses of the country through which we were proceeding sent ambassadors to us with many gifts and offered to aid us and to surrender their walled places. But because our army was not large and it was the unanimous wish to hasten to Jerusalem, we accepted their pledges and made them tributaries. One of the cities forsooth, which was on the sea-coast, had more men than there were in our whole army. And when those at Antioch and Laodicea and Archas heard how the hand of the Lord was with us, many from the army who had remained in those cities followed us to Tyre. Therefore, with the Lord's companionship and aid, we proceeded thus as far as Jerusalem.

And after the army had suffered greatly in the siege, especially on account of the lack of water, a council was held and the bishops and princes ordered that all with bare feet should march around the walls of the city, in order that He who entered it humbly in our behalf might be moved by our humility to open it to us and to exercise judgment upon His enemies. God was appeased by this humility and on the eighth day after the humiliation He delivered the city and His enemies to us. It was the day indeed on which the primitive church was driven thence, and on which the festival of the dispersion of the apostles is celebrated. And if you desire to know what was done with the enemy who were found there, know that in Solomon's Porch and in his temple our men rode in the blood of the Saracens up to the knees of their horses.

Then, when we were considering who ought to hold the city, and some moved by love for their country and kinsmen wished to return home, it was announced to us that the king of Babylon had come to Ascalon with an innumerable multitude of soldiers. His purpose was, as he said, to lead the Franks, who were in Jerusalem, into captivity, and to take Antioch by storm. But God had determined otherwise in regard to us.

Therefore, when we learned that the army of the Babylonians was at Ascalon, we went down to meet them, leaving our baggage and the sick in Jerusalem with a garrison. When our army was in sight of the enemy, upon our knees we invoked the aid of the Lord, that He who in our other adversities had strengthened the Christian faith, might in the present battle break the strength of the Saracens and of the devil and extend the kingdom of the church of Christ from sea to sea, over the whole world. There was no delay; God was present when we cried for His aid, and furnished us with so great boldness, that one who saw us rush upon the enemy would have taken us for a herd of deer hastening to quench their thirst in running water. It was wonderful, indeed, since there were in our army not more than 5,000 horsemen and 15,000 foot-soldiers, and there were probably in the enemy's army 100,000 horsemen and 400,000 foot-soldiers. Then God appeared wonderful to His servants. For before we engaged in fighting, by our very onset alone, He turned this multitude in flight and scattered all their weapons, so that if they wished afterwards to attack us, they did not have the weapons in which they trusted. There can be no question how great the spoils were, since the treasures of the king of Babylon were captured. More than 100,000 Moors perished there by the sword. Moreover, their panic was so great that about 2,000 were suffocated at the gate of the city. Those who perished in the sea were innumerable. Many were entangled in the thickets. The whole world was certainly fighting for us, and if many of ours had not been detained in plundering the camp, few of the great multitude of the enemy would have been able to escape from the battle.

And although it may be tedious, the following must not be omitted: On the day preceding the battle the army captured many thousands of camels, oxen and sheep. By the command of the princes these were divided among the people. When we advanced to battle, wonderful to relate, the camels formed in many squadrons and the sheep and oxen did the same. Moreover, these animals accompanied us, halting when we halted, advancing when we advanced, and charging when we charged. The clouds protected us from the heat of the sun and cooled us.

Accordingly, after celebrating the victory, the army returned to Jerusalem. Duke Godfrey remained there; the count of St. Giles, Robert, count of Normandy, and Robert, count of Flanders, returned to Laodicea. There they found the fleet belonging to the Pisans and to Bohemond. After the archbishop of Pisa had established peace between Bohemond and our leaders, Raymond prepared to return to Jerusalem for the sake of God and his brethren.

Therefore, we call upon you of the Catholic Church of Christ and of the whole Latin church to exult in the so admirable bravery and devotion of your brethren, in the so glorious and very desirable retribution of the omnipotent God, and in the so devoutedly hoped-for remission of all our sins through the grace of God. And we pray that He may make you — namely, all bishops, clerks and monks who are leading devout lives, and all the laity — to sit down at the right hand of God, who liveth and reigneth God for ever and ever. And we ask and beseech you in the name of our Lord Jesus, who has ever been with us and aided us and freed us from all our tribulations, to be mindful of your brethren who return to you, by doing them kindnesses and by paying their debts, in order that God may recompense you and absolve you from all your sins and grant you a share in all the blessings which either we or they have deserved in the sight of the Lord. Amen.

REFLECTIONS

You have had some flexibility in deciding when you wanted to begin your narrative, but you were limited by the sources in choosing an ending point. The chapter's sources ended with the capture of Jerusalem by the Christians in 1099, thereby limiting your narrative to the First Crusade and ending with a Latin victory. But with additional sources, we could have continued the story another two years to end with the defeat of a third wave of crusaders by the Turks. How would your narrative have been different with that ending?

The First Crusade (1095–1102) only marks the beginning of a protracted conflict between Christians and Muslims that continued until, perhaps, the eighteenth century. In the Holy Land there were crusades in 1107–1108, 1120–1125, 1128–1129, and 1139–1140. Another in 1147–1149 was called the Second Crusade. Meanwhile, the conquest of Muslims in Spain, which had been equated with the crusade by Pope Urban II, continued, as did frequent crusades into Eastern Europe. The establishment of Latin kingdoms in Palestine could not be maintained without continual reinforcements, and they were vulnerable to Muslim attack. In 1187 Saladin reconquered most of Palestine, including Jerusalem, for the Muslims, a trauma for the Christians that led to the Third Crusade (1189–1192) and German Crusade (1197–1198) by which Christians retook settlements on the coast. Popular enthusiasm continued in the Children's Crusade (1212) and the Crusade of the Shepherds (1251). The armies of the Fourth Crusade (1202–1204) were diverted to Constantinople which they sacked in 1204 and the conquest of Greece. A Fifth Crusade (1217–1229) recovered Jerusalem, which was retaken by the Muslims in 1244, leading to crusades initiated by King Louis IX of France. Other crusading armies invaded Egypt, Tunisia, Muslim Spain, northwest Africa, southern France, Poland, Latvia, Germany, Russia, the Mongols, Finland, Bosnia, and Italy, against papal enemies and Eastern Orthodox Christians as well as Muslims. Recent histories of the Crusades have ended their narratives in 1521, 1560, 1588, and 1798, according to Jonathan Riley-Smith who ends the recent *Oxford Illustrated History of the Crusades* with images of the crusades in twentieth century wars. Does the imagery of the Crusades still animate our wars?

11

Technology, Ecology, and Science

HISTORICAL CONTEXT

Europe, Asia, and Africa, 500-1500 C.E.

Everyone knows that the world has changed drastically since the Middle Ages. And, most people would agree that the most important and far-reaching changes have occurred in the fields of technology, ecology, and science. Global population has grown ten-fold. The world has become a single ecological unit where microbes, migrants, and money travel everywhere at jet speed. In most parts of the world, average life expectancy has doubled; cities have mushroomed, replacing farm and pasture. Machines have replaced the labor of humans and animals. Powers that were only imagined in the Middle Ages — elixirs to cure disease, energy to harness rivers, machines that would fly — are now commonplace. Other aspects of life — among them religion, political behavior, music, and art — have also evolved, but even these were affected significantly by advances in modern science and technology.

Precisely what change or changes occurred? When did the cycle of change begin and what caused it? These are the questions we will examine in this chapter. You will read two substantial answers, the first and last selections in the chapter. Lynn White Jr. defines the transformation to modernity in largely technological and ecological terms. He recognizes secondary cultural causes as well. Lynda Shaffer, on the other hand, discusses technological and scientific changes as spreading through contact and trade.

These two explanations of long-term change differ most markedly in how they explain the roots of the transformation. White, a historian of medieval European technology, focuses on the role of medieval European religion: Christianity. Shaffer, a world historian, underscores the role of India and South Asia.

THINKING HISTORICALLY

Recognizing and Explaining Major Changes

Most narrative or story-based histories, the subject of Chapter 10, recount details in an active voice as they unfold, making for an engaging account, dramatic tension, and for the listener or reader, a sense of participation in the events of the past. What narratives often lack, in consequence, is perspective: They typically fail to question the past. In general, narrative history engages and entertains more than interpretive or synthetic history. Thus, it appeals to popular audiences (and is easily transformed into film). While anyone likes a good story, professional historians usually begin with questions about the past that they want answered. Their research involves defining a manageable problem, analyzing the relevant factors, gathering data, setting up a test case or a way of checking their results, and then coming up with an answer. While the answer is usually presented as a report on the research, or as an argument for a new interpretation, it may have a narrative element. But the pieces of the narrative are chosen for their bearing on the argument or interpretation, not for their drama or emotional engagement.

While the desire by professional historians to ask manageable questions (i.e., questions that can be answered) narrows the focus of much historical work (so that it is sometimes said that each provides a "building block" to a larger truth), the larger questions about historical change must also be addressed.

In this chapter we study how two historians recognize, report, and explain major changes in technology, ecology, and science. In one sense, their work might still be called narrative: You will notice, for instance, how both historians discuss their subjects chronologically. But, because the time spans discussed are so expansive, their accounts lack the human scale that would allow us to feel empathy for individual participants, a cornerstone of narrative technique.

Using Pictorial Evidence

As well, this chapter introduces a second historical skill or habit of mind: interpreting pictorial evidence. Pictures from the past are primary sources as are writings from the past. Once you have learned how to "read" pictures as evidence, you will be able to glean important pieces of information from them and better understand each historian's interpretation.

65

LYNN WHITE JR.

The Historical Roots of Our Ecological Crisis

This classic essay first appeared in the magazine *Science* in 1967 and has since been reprinted and commented on many times. What do you think of White's linkage of ecological crisis and Christianity?

Thinking Historically

What is the central observation that leads White to this inquiry? What is the major change that White sets out to explain? What is the causal explanation he offers for this change? Notice the range of materials he draws on to offer evidence for his explanation. Which pieces of evidence do you find most compelling or convincing? Which do you find least compelling or convincing? Why?

We will discuss pictorial primary sources as evidence in later selections. As you read this selection, consider what sorts of pictures (from the Middle Ages) you would like to have in order to evaluate White's argument.

Finally, notice the difference in writing style between this historical account and the narrative stories of the previous chapter. How would you describe the differences between them?

A conversation with Aldous Huxley[1] not infrequently put one at the receiving end of an unforgettable monologue. About a year before his lamented death he was discoursing on a favorite topic: man's unnatural treatment of nature and its sad results. To illustrate his point he told how, during the previous summer, he had returned to a little valley in England where he had spent many happy months as a child. Once it had been composed of delightful grassy glades; now it was becoming overgrown with unsightly brush because the rabbits that formerly kept such growth under control had largely succumbed to a disease, myxomatosis, that was deliberately introduced by the local farmers to reduce

1 Aldous Huxley (1894–1963), British author of novels, short stories, travel books, biography, and essays. Best known for *Brave New World* (1932). [Ed.]

Lynn White Jr., "The Historical Roots of Our Ecologic Crisis," *Science* 155 (March 1967): 1203–07.

the rabbits' destruction of crops. Being something of a Philistine,[2] I could be silent no longer, even in the interests of great rhetoric. I interrupted to point out that the rabbit itself had been brought as a domestic animal to England in 1176, presumably to improve the protein diet of the peasantry.

All forms of life modify their contexts. The most spectacular and benign instance is doubtless the coral polyp. By serving its own ends, it has created a vast undersea world favorable to thousands of other kinds of animals and plants. Ever since man became a numerous species he has affected his environment notably. The hypothesis that his fire-drive[3] method of hunting created the world's great grasslands and helped to exterminate the monster mammals of the Pleistocene from much of the globe is plausible, if not proved. For six millennia at least, the banks of the lower Nile have been a human artifact rather than the swampy African jungle which nature, apart from man, would have made it. The Aswan Dam, flooding five thousand square miles, is only the latest stage in a long process. In many regions terracing or irrigation, overgrazing, and the cutting of forests by Romans to build ships to fight Carthaginians or by Crusaders to solve the logistics problems of their expeditions have profoundly changed some ecologies. Observation that the French landscape falls into two basic types, the open fields of the north and the *bocage*[4] of the south and west, inspired Marc Bloch to undertake his classic study of medieval agricultural methods. Quite unintentionally, changes in human ways often affect nonhuman nature. It has been noted, for example, that the advent of the automobile eliminated huge flocks of sparrows that once fed on the horse manure littering every street.

The history of ecologic change is still so rudimentary that we know little about what really happened, or what the results were. The extinction of the European aurochs[5] as late as 1627 would seem to have been a simple case of overenthusiastic hunting. On more intricate matters it often is impossible to find solid information. For a thousand years or more the Frisians and Hollanders have been pushing back the North Sea, and the process is culminating in our own time in the reclamation

[2] An anti-intellectual (though obviously White is not; he was only impatient with Huxley's pedantry). [Ed.]

[3] Paleolithic hunters used fires to drive animals to their deaths. [Ed.]

[4] Full of groves or woodlands. Marc Bloch reasoned that the open fields north of the Loire River in France must have been plowed by teams of oxen and heavy plows because of the hard soil. In the south farmers could use scratch plows on the softer soil and therefore did not clear large fields, preserving more woodlands. [Ed.]

[5] A now extinct European wild ox believed to be the ancestor of European domestic cattle. [Ed.]

of the Zuider Zee.[6] What, if any, species of animals, birds, fish, shore life, or plants have died out in the process? In their epic combat with Neptune have the Netherlanders overlooked ecological values in such a way that the quality of human life in the Netherlands has suffered? I cannot discover that the questions have ever been asked, much less answered.

People, then, have often been a dynamic element in their own environment, but in the present state of historical scholarship we usually do not know exactly when, where, or with what effects man-induced changes came. As we enter the last third of the twentieth century, however, concern for the problem of ecologic backlash is mounting feverishly. Natural science, conceived as the effort to understand the nature of things, had flourished in several eras and among several peoples. Similarly there had been an age-old accumulation of technological skills, sometimes growing rapidly, sometimes slowly. But it was not until about four generations ago that Western Europe and North America arranged a marriage between science and technology, a union of the theoretical and the empirical approaches to our natural environment. The emergence in widespread practice of the Baconian creed that scientific knowledge means technological power over nature can scarcely be dated before about 1850, save in the chemical industries, where it is anticipated in the eighteenth century. Its acceptance as a normal pattern of action may mark the greatest event in human history since the invention of agriculture, and perhaps in nonhuman terrestrial history as well.

Almost at once the new situation forced the crystallization of the novel concept of ecology; indeed, the word *ecology* first appeared in the English language in 1873. Today, less than a century later, the impact of our race upon the environment has so increased in force that it has changed in essence. When the first cannons were fired, in the early fourteenth century, they affected ecology by sending workers scrambling to the forests and mountains for more potash, sulfur, iron ore, and charcoal, with some resulting erosion and deforestation. Hydrogen bombs are of a different order: A war fought with them might alter the genetics of all life on this planet. By 1285 London had a smog problem arising from the burning of soft coal, but our present combustion of fossil fuels threatens to change the chemistry of the globe's atmosphere as a whole, with consequences which we are only beginning to guess. With the population explosion, the carcinoma of planless urbanism, the now geological deposits of sewage and garbage, surely no creature other than man has ever managed to foul its nest in such short order.

There are many calls to action, but specific proposals, however worthy as individual items, seem too partial, palliative, negative: Ban

[6] Once a Dutch lake, it was joined to the North Sea by a flood in the thirteenth century but has since been reclaimed by the building of a dam. [Ed.]

the bomb, tear down the billboards, give the Hindus contraceptives and tell them to eat their sacred cows. The simplest solution to any suspect change is, of course, to stop it, or, better yet, to revert to a romanticized past: Make those ugly gasoline stations look like Anne Hathaway's cottage or (in the Far West) like ghost-town saloons. The "wilderness area" mentality invariably advocates deep-freezing an ecology, whether San Gimignano or the High Sierra, as it was before the first Kleenex was dropped. But neither atavism nor prettification will cope with the ecologic crisis of our time.

What shall we do? No one yet knows. Unless we think about fundamentals, our specific measures may produce new backlashes more serious than those they are designed to remedy.

As a beginning we should try to clarify our thinking by looking, in some historical depth, at the presuppositions that underlie modern technology and science. Science was traditionally aristocratic, speculative, intellectual in intent; technology was lower-class, empirical, action-oriented. The quite sudden fusion of these two, toward the middle of the nineteenth century, is surely related to the slightly prior and contemporary democratic revolutions which, by reducing social barriers, tended to assert a functional unity of brain and hand. Our ecologic crisis is the product of an emerging, entirely novel, democratic culture. The issue is whether a democratized world can survive its own implications. Presumably we cannot unless we rethink our axioms.

The Western Traditions of Technology and Science

One thing is so certain that it seems stupid to verbalize it: Both modern technology and modern science are distinctively *Occidental.* Our technology has absorbed elements from all over the world, notably from China; yet everywhere today, whether in Japan or in Nigeria, successful technology is Western. Our science is the heir to all the sciences of the past, especially perhaps to the work of the great Islamic scientists of the Middle Ages, who so often outdid the ancient Greeks in skill and perspicacity: al-Rāzī in medicine, for example; or ibn-al-Haytham in optics; or Omar Khayyám in mathematics. Indeed, not a few works of such geniuses seem to have vanished in the original Arabic and to survive only in medieval Latin translations that helped to lay the foundations for later Western developments. Today, around the globe, all significant science is Western in style and method, whatever the pigmentation or language of the scientists.

A second pair of facts is less well recognized because they result from quite recent historical scholarship. The leadership of the West, both in technology and in science, is far older than the so-called Scientific Revolution of the seventeenth century or the so-called Industrial

Revolution of the eighteenth century. These terms are in fact outmoded and obscure the true nature of what they try to describe — significant stages in two long and separate developments. By A.D. 1000 at the latest — and perhaps, feebly, as much as two hundred years earlier — the West began to apply water power to industrial processes other than milling grain. This was followed in the late twelfth century by the harnessing of wind power. From simple beginnings, but with remarkable consistency of style, the West rapidly expanded its skills in the development of power machinery, labor-saving devices, and automation. Those who doubt should contemplate that most monumental achievement in the history of automation: the weight-driven mechanical clock, which appeared in two forms in the early fourteenth century. Not in craftsmanship but in basic technological capacity, the Latin West of the later Middle Ages far outstripped its elaborate, sophisticated, and esthetically magnificent sister cultures, Byzantium and Islam. In 1444 a great Greek ecclesiastic, Bessarion, who had gone to Italy, wrote a letter to a prince in Greece. He is amazed by the superiority of Western ships, arms, textiles, glass. But above all he is astonished by the spectacle of waterwheels sawing timbers and pumping the bellows of blast furnaces. Clearly, he had seen nothing of the sort in the Near East.

By the end of the fifteenth century the technological superiority of Europe was such that its small, mutually hostile nations could spill out over all the rest of the world, conquering, looting, and colonizing. The symbol of this technological superiority is the fact that Portugal, one of the weakest states of the Occident, was able to become, and to remain for a century, mistress of the East Indies. And we must remember that the technology of Vasco da Gama and Albuquerque was built by pure empiricism, drawing remarkably little support or inspiration from science.

In the present-day vernacular understanding, modern science is supposed to have begun in 1543, when both Copernicus and Vesalius published their great works. It is no derogation of their accomplishments, however, to point out that such structures as the *Fabrica*[7] and the *De revolutionibus*[8] do not appear overnight. The distinctive Western tradition of science, in fact, began in the late eleventh century with a massive movement of translation of Arabic and Greek scientific works into Latin. A few notable books — Theophrastus, for example — escaped the West's avid new appetite for science, but within less than two hundred years ef-

[7] *De Humani Corporis Fabrica* (1543), an illustrated work on human anatomy based on dissections, was produced by Andreas Vesalius (1514–1564), a Flemish anatomist, at the University of Padua in Italy. [Ed.]

[8] *De revolutionibus orbium coelestium* (1543; On the Revolutions of Heavenly Bodies) was published by Nicolas Copernicus (1473–1543); it showed the sun as the center of a system around which the Earth revolved. [Ed.]

fectively the entire corpus of Greek and Muslim science was available in Latin, and was being eagerly read and criticized in the new European universities. Out of criticism arose new observation, speculation, and increasing distrust of ancient authorities. By the late thirteenth century Europe had seized global scientific leadership from the faltering hands of Islam. It would be as absurd to deny the profound originality of Newton, Galileo, or Copernicus as to deny that of the fourteenth century scholastic scientists like Buridan or Oresme on whose work they built. Before the eleventh century, science scarcely existed in the Latin West, even in Roman times. From the eleventh century onward, the scientific sector of Occidental culture has increased in a steady crescendo.

Since both our technological and our scientific movements got their start, acquired their character, and achieved world dominance in the Middle Ages, it would seem that we cannot understand their nature or their present impact upon ecology without examining fundamental medieval assumptions and developments.

Medieval View of Man and Nature

Until recently, agriculture has been the chief occupation even in "advanced" societies; hence, any change in methods of tillage has much importance. Early plows, drawn by two oxen, did not normally turn the sod but merely scratched it. Thus, cross-plowing was needed and fields tended to be squarish. In the fairly light soils and semiarid climates of the Near East and Mediterranean, this worked well. But such a plow was inappropriate to the wet climate and often sticky soils of northern Europe. By the latter part of the seventh century after Christ, however, following obscure beginnings, certain northern peasants were using an entirely new kind of plow, equipped with a vertical knife to cut the line of the furrow, a horizontal share to slice under the sod, and a moldboard to turn it over. The friction of this plow with the soil was so great that it normally required not two but eight oxen. It attacked the land with such violence that cross-plowing was not needed, and fields tended to be shaped in long strips.

In the days of the scratch-plow, fields were distributed generally in units capable of supporting a single family. Subsistence farming was the presupposition. But no peasant owned eight oxen: to use the new and more efficient plow, peasants pooled their oxen to form large plow-teams, originally receiving (it would appear) plowed strips in proportion to their contribution. Thus, distribution of land was based no longer on the needs of a family but, rather, on the capacity of a power machine to till the earth. Man's relation to the soil was profoundly changed. Formerly man had been part of nature; now he was the exploiter of nature. Nowhere else in the world did farmers develop any analogous agricultural implement. Is it coincidence that modern technology, with its ruthlessness toward nature, has so largely been produced by descendants of these peasants of northern Europe?

This same exploitive attitude appears slightly before A.D. 830 in Western illustrated calendars. In older calendars the months were shown as passive personifications. The new Frankish calendars, which set the style for the Middle Ages, are very different: They show men coercing the world around them — plowing, harvesting, chopping trees, butchering pigs. Man and nature are two things, and man is master.

These novelties seem to be in harmony with larger intellectual patterns. What people do about their ecology depends on what they think about themselves in relation to things around them. Human ecology is deeply conditioned by beliefs about our nature and destiny — that is, by religion. To Western eyes this is very evident in, say, India or Ceylon. It is equally true of ourselves and of our medieval ancestors.

The victory of Christianity over paganism was the greatest psychic revolution in the history of our culture. It has become fashionable today to say that, for better or worse, we live in "the post-Christian age." Certainly the forms of our thinking and language have largely ceased to be Christian, but to my eye the substance often remains amazingly akin to that of the past. Our daily habits of action, for example, are dominated by an implicit faith in perpetual progress which was unknown either to Greco-Roman antiquity or to the Orient. It is rooted in, and is indefensible apart from, Judeo-Christian teleology.[9] The fact that Communists share it merely helps to show what can be demonstrated on many other grounds: that Marxism, like Islam, is a Judeo-Christian heresy. We continue today to live, as we have lived for about seventeen hundred years, very largely in a context of Christian axioms.

What did Christianity tell people about their relations with the environment?

While many of the world's mythologies provide stories of creation, Greco-Roman mythology was singularly incoherent in this respect. Like Aristotle, the intellectuals of the ancient West denied that the visible world had had a beginning. Indeed, the idea of a beginning was impossible in the framework of their cyclical notion of time. In sharp contrast, Christianity inherited from Judaism not only a concept of time as nonrepetitive and linear but also a striking story of creation. By gradual stages a loving and all-powerful God had created light and

[9] The Biblical idea that God's purpose is revealed in his creation, that human history can be seen as the result of God's intentions. [Ed.]

darkness, the heavenly bodies, the earth and all its plants, animals, birds, and fishes. Finally, God had created Adam and, as an afterthought, Eve to keep man from being lonely. Man named all the animals, thus establishing his dominance over them. God planned all of this explicitly for man's benefit and rule: No item in the physical creation had any purpose save to serve man's purposes. And, although man's body is made of clay, he is not simply part of nature: He is made in God's image.

Especially in its Western form, Christianity is the most anthropocentric religion the world has seen. As early as the second century both Tertullian and Saint Irenaeus of Lyons were insisting that when God shaped Adam he was foreshadowing the image of the incarnate Christ, the Second Adam. Man shares, in great measure, God's transcendence of nature. Christianity, in absolute contrast to ancient paganism and Asia's religions (except, perhaps, Zoroastrianism), not only established a dualism of man and nature but also insisted that it is God's will that man exploit nature for his proper ends.

At the level of the common people this worked out in an interesting way. In Antiquity every tree, every spring, every stream, every hill had its own *genius loci,* its guardian spirit. These spirits were accessible to men, but were very unlike men; centaurs, fauns, and mermaids show their ambivalence. Before one cut a tree, mined a mountain, or dammed a brook, it was important to placate the spirit in charge of that particular situation, and to keep it placated. By destroying pagan animism, Christianity made it possible to exploit nature in a mood of indifference to the feelings of natural objects.

It is often said that for animism the Church substituted the cult of saints. True; but the cult of saints is functionally quite different from animism. The saint is not *in* natural objects; he may have special shrines, but his citizenship is in heaven. Moreover, a saint is entirely a man; he can be approached in human terms. In addition to saints, Christianity of course also had angels and demons inherited from Judaism and perhaps, at one remove, from Zoroastrianism. But these were all as mobile as the saints themselves. The spirits *in* natural objects, which formerly had protected nature from man, evaporated. Man's effective monopoly on spirit in this world was confirmed, and the old inhibitions to the exploitation of nature crumbled.

When one speaks in such sweeping terms, a note of caution is in order. Christianity is a complex faith, and its consequences differ in differing contexts. What I have said may well apply to the medieval West, where in fact technology made spectacular advances. But the Greek East, a highly civilized realm of equal Christian devotion, seems to have produced no marked technological innovation after the late seventh century, when Greek fire was invented. The key to the contrast may perhaps be found in a difference in the tonality of piety and thought which students of comparative theology find between the Greek and the Latin Churches. The Greeks believed that sin was intellectual blindness, and that salvation was found in illumination, orthodoxy — that is, clear thinking. The Latins, on the other hand, felt that sin was moral evil, and that salvation was to be found in right conduct. Eastern theology has been intellectualist. Western theology has been voluntarist. The Greek saint contemplates; the Western saint acts. The implications of Christianity for the conquest of nature would emerge more easily in the Western atmosphere.

The Christian dogma of creation, which is found in the first clause of all the Creeds, has another meaning for our comprehension of today's ecologic crisis. By revelation, God had given man the Bible, the Book of Scripture. But since God had made nature, nature also must reveal the divine mentality. The religious study of nature for the better understanding of God was known as natural theology. In the early Church, and always in the Greek East, nature was conceived primarily as a symbolic system through which God speaks to men: The ant is a sermon to sluggards; rising flames are the symbol of the soul's aspiration. This view of nature was essentially artistic rather than scientific. While Byzantium preserved and copied great numbers of ancient Greek scientific texts, science as we conceive it could scarcely flourish in such an ambience.

However, in the Latin West by the early thirteenth century natural theology was following a very different bent. It was ceasing to be the decoding of the physical symbols of God's communication with man and was becoming the effort to understand God's mind by discovering how his creation operates. The rainbow was no longer simply a symbol of hope first sent to Noah after the Deluge: Robert Grosseteste, Friar Roger Bacon, and Theodoric of Freiberg produced startlingly sophisticated work on the optics of the rainbow, but they did it as a venture in religious understanding. From the thirteenth century onward, up to and including Leibnitz and Newton, every major scientist, in effect, explained his motivations in religious terms. Indeed, if Galileo had not been so expert an amateur theologian he would have got into far less trouble: The professionals resented his intrusion. And Newton seems to have regarded himself more as a theologian than as a scientist. It was not until the late eighteenth century that the hypothesis of God became unnecessary to many scientists.

It is often hard for the historian to judge, when men explain why they are doing what they want to do, whether they are offering real reasons or merely culturally acceptable reasons. The consistency with which scientists during the long formative centuries of Western science said that the task and the reward of the scientist was "to think God's thoughts after him" leads one to believe that this was their real motivation. If so, then modern Western science was cast in a matrix of Christian theology. The dynamism of religious devotion, shaped by the Judeo-Christian dogma of creation, gave it impetus.

An Alternative Christian View

We would seem to be headed toward conclusions unpalatable to many Christians. Since both *science* and *technology* are blessed words in our contemporary vocabulary, some may be happy at the notions, first, that, viewed historically, modern science is an extrapolation of natural theology and, second, that modern technology is at least partly to be explained as an Occidental, voluntarist realization of the Christian dogma of man's transcendence of, and rightful mastery over, nature. But, as we now recognize, somewhat over a century ago science and technology — hitherto quite separate activities — joined to give mankind powers which, to judge by many of the ecologic effects, are out of control. If so, Christianity bears a huge burden of guilt.

I personally doubt that disastrous ecologic backlash can be avoided simply by applying to our problems more science and more technology. Our science and technology have grown out of Christian attitudes toward man's relation to nature which are almost universally held not only by Christians and neo-Christians but also by those who fondly regard themselves as post-Christians. Despite Copernicus, all the cosmos rotates around our little globe. Despite Darwin, we are *not,* in our hearts, part of the natural process. We are superior to nature, contemptuous of it, willing to use it for our slightest whim. The newly elected Governor of California, like myself a churchman but less troubled than I, spoke for the Christian tradition when he said (as is alleged), "when you've seen one redwood tree, you've seen them all." To a Christian a tree can be no more than a physical fact. The whole concept of the sacred grove is alien to Christianity and to the ethos of the West. For nearly two millennia Christian missionaries have been chopping down sacred groves, which are idolatrous because they assume spirit in nature.

What we do about ecology depends on our ideas of the man-nature relationship. More science and more technology are not going to get us out of the present ecologic crisis until we find a new religion, or rethink our old one. The beatniks, who are the basic revolutionaries of our time, show a sound instinct in their affinity for Zen Buddhism, which conceives of the man-nature relationship as very nearly the mirror image of the Christian view. Zen, however, is as deeply conditioned by Asian history as Christianity is by the experience of the West, and I am dubious of its viability among us.

Possibly we should ponder the greatest radical in Christian history since Christ: Saint Francis of Assisi. The prime miracle of Saint Francis is the fact that he did not end at the stake, as many of his left-wing followers did. He was so clearly heretical that a General of the Franciscan Order, Saint Bonaventura, a great and perceptive Christian, tried to suppress the early accounts of Franciscanism. The key to an understanding of Francis is his belief in the virtue of humility — not merely for the individual but for man as a species. Francis tried to depose man from his monarchy over creation and set up a democracy of all God's creatures. With him the ant is no longer simply a homily for the lazy, flames a sign of the thrust of the soul toward union with God; now they are Brother Ant and Sister Fire, praising the Creator in their own ways as Brother Man does in his.

Later commentators have said that Francis preached to the birds as a rebuke to men who would not listen. The records do not read so: He urged the little birds to praise God, and in spiritual ecstasy they flapped their wings and chirped rejoicing. Legends of saints, especially the Irish saints, had long told of their dealings with animals but always, I believe, to show their human dominance over creatures. With Francis it is different. The land around Gubbio in the Apennines was being ravaged by a fierce wolf. Saint Francis, says the legend, talked to the wolf and persuaded him of the error of his ways. The wolf repented, died in the odor of sanctity, and was buried in consecrated ground.

What Sir Steven Ruciman calls "the Franciscan doctrine of the animal soul" was quickly stamped out. Quite possibly it was in part inspired, consciously or unconsciously, by the belief in reincarnation held by the Cathar heretics who at that time teemed in Italy and southern France, and who presumably had got it originally from India. It is significant that at just the same moment, about 1200, traces of metempsychosis are found also in western Judaism, in the Provençal *Cabbala.* But Francis held neither to transmigration of souls nor to pantheism. His view of nature and of man rested on a unique sort of pan-psychism of all things animate and inanimate, designed for the glorification of their transcendent Creator, who, in the ultimate gesture of cosmic humility, assumed flesh, lay helpless in a manger, and hung dying on a scaffold.

I am not suggesting that many contemporary Americans who are concerned about our ecologic crisis will be either able or willing to counsel with wolves or exhort birds. However, the present increasing disruption of the global environment is the product of a dynamic technology and science which were originating in the Western medieval world against which Saint Francis was rebelling in so original a way. Their growth cannot be understood historically apart from distinctive attitudes toward nature which are deeply grounded in Christian dogma. The fact that most people do not think of these attitudes as

Christian is irrelevant. No new set of basic values has been accepted in our society to displace those of Christianity. Hence we shall continue to have a worsening ecologic crisis until we reject the Christian axiom that nature has no reason for existence save to serve man.

The greatest spiritual revolutionary in Western history, Saint Francis, proposed what he thought was an alternative Christian view of nature and man's relation to it: He tried to substitute the idea of the equality of all creatures, including man, for the idea of man's limitless rule of creation. He failed. Both our present science and our present technology are so tinctured with orthodox Christian arrogance toward nature that no solution for our ecologic crisis can be expected from them alone. Since the roots of our trouble are so largely religious, the remedy must also be essentially religious, whether we call it that or not. We must rethink and refeel our nature and destiny. The profoundly religious, but heretical, sense of the primitive Franciscans for the spiritual autonomy of all parts of nature may point a direction. I propose Francis as a patron saint for ecologists.

66

Life of Boniface: Converting the Hessians

This story about the Christian missionary Boniface was told in the *Life of Boniface,* written between 754 and 768, by Willibald, one of his students. The Hessians, previously converted to Christianity, had reverted to paganism, and Boniface traveled from England to Germany to reconvert them. Hessians were Saxons (in what is today Germany). They were widely regarded by the early Christian missionaries to Germany as a difficult people to convert. Boniface's success became a guide for future missions. What does this account tell us about the nature of Hessian paganism? What does Boniface do to reconvert them to Christianity? What, if anything, does the story tell us about Christianity?

The Anglo-Saxon Missionaries in Germany, trans. C. H. Talbot (London: Sheed and Ward, 1954), 45–46.

Thinking Historically

This is the first of a series of short primary sources that you will be asked to relate to the previous selection by Lynn White Jr. How does it relate to White's article? Does it support his argument? Can a single piece like this ever prove an argument like White's, or can it only illustrate it?

In what ways does a written primary source like this differ from a graphic image (say, a line drawing or a painting) from the same period? Imagine that you are a monk in the eighth century and are asked to create a picture from this story. What sort of image would you choose? Why? Would such an image be more or less useful as evidence for or against White's thesis? Would it matter if the artist was an eyewitness to the event or not? Why?

Now many of the Hessians who at that time had acknowledged the Catholic faith were confirmed by the grace of the Holy Spirit and received the laying-on of hands. But others, not yet strong in the spirit, refused to accept the pure teachings of the Church in their entirety. Moreover, some continued secretly, others openly, to offer sacrifices to trees and springs, to inspect the entrails of victims; some practised divination, legerdemain[1] and incantations; some turned their attention to auguries, auspices and other sacrificial rites; whilst others, of a more reasonable character, forsook all the profane practices of heathenism and committed none of these crimes. With the counsel and advice of the latter persons, Boniface in their presence attempted to cut down, at a place called Gaesmere, . . . a certain oak of extraordinary size called by the pagans of olden times the Oak of Jupiter. Taking his courage in his hands (for a great crowd of pagans stood by watching and bitterly cursing in their hearts the enemy of the gods), he cut the first notch. But when he had made a superficial cut, suddenly the oak's vast bulk, shaken by a mighty blast of wind from above, crashed to the ground shivering its topmost branches into fragments in its fall. As if by the express will of God (for the brethren present had done nothing to cause it) the oak burst asunder into four parts, each part having a trunk of equal length. At the sight of this extraordinary spectacle the heathens who had been cursing ceased to revile and began, on the contrary, to believe and bless the Lord. Thereupon the holy bishop took counsel with the brethren, built an oratory from the timber of the oak and dedicated it to St. Peter the Apostle. He then set out on a journey to

[1] Sleight of hand.

Thuringia, having accomplished by the help of God all the things we have already mentioned. Arrived there, he addressed the elders and the chiefs of the people, calling on them to put aside their blind ignorance and to return to the Christian religion which they had formerly embraced . . .

67

Image from a Cistercian Manuscript, Twelfth Century

Monk Chopping Tree

This image of a monk chopping down a tree while his lay servant prunes the branches is from a manuscript of the Cistercian order of monks, from the twelfth century. The Cistercians, more than other orders, spoke out in favor of conserving forest resources, but they also celebrated manual labor. Does this image indicate that the monks were in favor of forest clearance?

Thinking Historically

Does this image lend support to White's argument in selection 65? Why or why not? As a single piece of historical evidence, is it more or less persuasive than the previous written source on Boniface? Would the impact be greater if written and visual evidence were combined? If there were many such images, would visual evidence like this convince you of White's argument? Would it be more convincing if almost all European images of trees showed someone chopping them down and virtually no Chinese tree images showed that? In other words, how much visual evidence would convince you of White's interpretation?

Image from a Cistercian manuscript, 12th c., monk chopping tree (Dijon, Bibliothèque municipale, MS 173), duplicated in *Cambridge Illustrated History of the Middle Ages,* Robert Fossier, ed. (Cambridge: Cambridge University Press, 1997), 72.

Figure 2. Twelfth-century manuscript.

68

Image from a Calendar, Fifteenth Century

This French calendar scene for March is from the early fifteenth century. What sorts of activities does it show? How does it relate specifically to White's argument about the changing images of European calendars? (See p. 355.) The top half of the calendar shows a zodiac. In what ways are these images of nature different from those in the bottom half?

Thinking Historically

What technologies are shown here? Were any of these technologies particularly recent or European? Does this image merely illustrate White's argument, or does it support it to some extent? What other visual evidence would you want to see in order to be persuaded by White's argument?

From *Les trés riches heures du duc de Berry,* Giraudon, Musée de Condé.

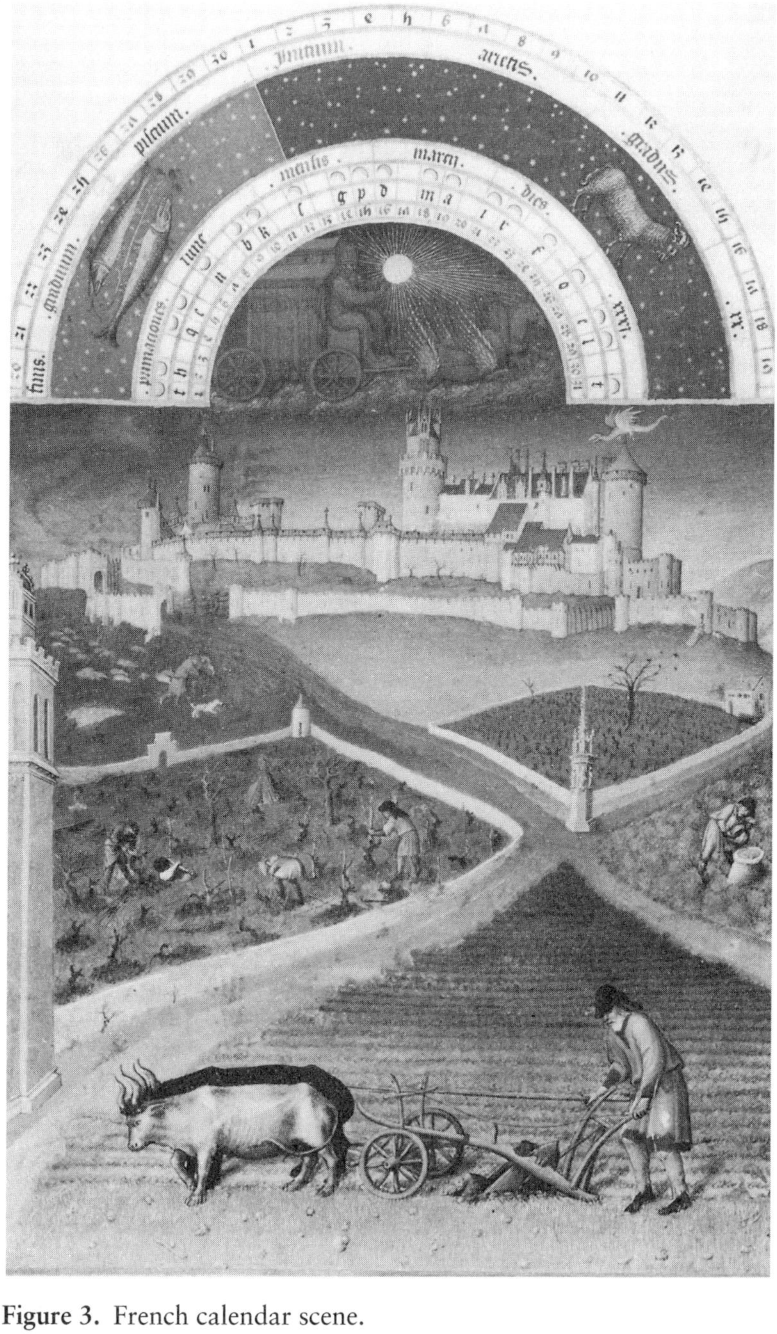

Figure 3. French calendar scene.

69

FAN KUAN

Image of a Chinese Landscape

Travelers amid Mountains and Streams

Landscape was both a common and noble subject for Chinese painters. This painting is by Fan Kuan (c. 990–1020). What signs of human habitation can you see? What, if anything, does that suggest to you about Chinese art and culture?

Thinking Historically

Does the popularity and prestige of this kind of landscape painting in China lend support to White's thesis? Does this sort of painting together with naturalist philosophies like Taoism persuade us of White's thesis? Does the relative absence of this sort of painting from Europe lend credence to White's argument?

Fan Kuan, *Travellers amid Mountains and Streams,* National Palace Museum, Taiwan, People's Republic of China; from *Cambridge Illustrated History of China,* Patricia Buckley Ebrey, ed. (Cambridge: Cambridge University Press, 1996), 162.

Figure 4. *Travelers amid Mountains and Streams.*

70

WEN ZHENGMING

Image of Chinese Nature to Depict Human Strength

Nature Depicts Human Strength

Wen Zhengming (1470–1559), a scholar-official at the age of eighty, drew this image of a cypress tree and rock to depict strength. The poem he wrote, shown in the upper left, reads:

> Weighed down by snow, oppressed by frost, with the passing of years and months its branches become twisted and its crown bent down, yet its strength remains majestic.

How does the image fit the poem? Does the poem make the image more understandable? How is this a particularly Chinese image and poem? Is there a European equivalent of this?

Thinking Historically

Here, nature is not just a landscape but an allegory for human strength. Does this suggest even greater human subordination to nature than the previous painting? If so, how? Is the image alone more or less convincing evidence of White's thesis than the poem by itself?

Finally, what can you say about pictorial sources as evidence for historical ideas or interpretations?

Nelson-Atkins Museum of Art, Kansas City, Missouri (Purchase: Nelson Trust), 46–48.

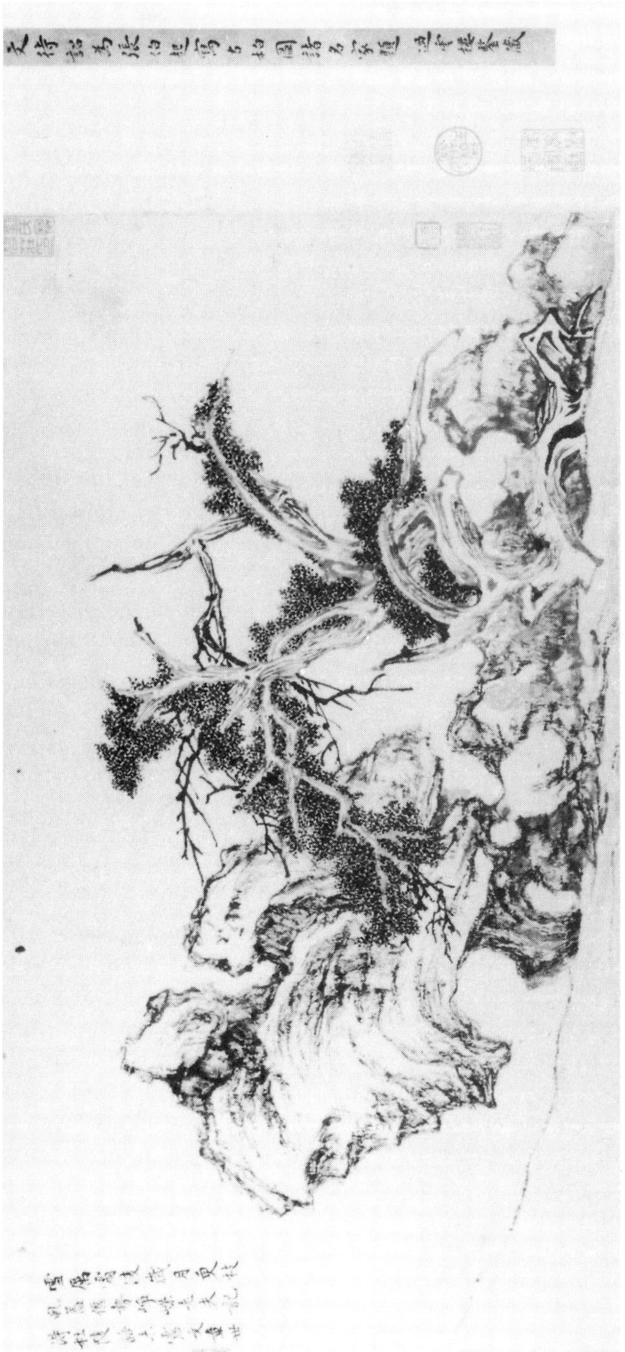

Figure 5. Old cypress tree and rock.

71

LYNDA SHAFFER

Southernization

The author of this selection began her career as an historian of China, but she is currently a world historian, having published books on Native American, Southeast Asian, and Chinese history. How does Shaffer's global perspective inform her idea of "southernization"? What do you think of her argument? How does her argument differ from that of Lynn White Jr.? Who do you find more convincing, and why?

Thinking Historically

Is the change that Shaffer describes the same as the one White addresses? Are the two authors trying to explain the same thing? In what ways are their explanations at odds with each other? Can they both be right?

Does Shaffer's argument challenge or invalidate the pictorial evidence offered in the preceding selections? Are there parts of Shaffer's argument that the pictorial evidence would support?

The term *southernization* is a new one. It is used here to refer to a multifaceted process that began in Southern Asia and spread from there to various other places around the globe. The process included so many interrelated strands of development that it is impossible to do more here than sketch out the general outlines of a few of them. Among the most important that will be omitted from this discussion are the metallurgical, the medical, and the literary. Those included are the development of mathematics; the production and marketing of subtropical or tropical spices; the pioneering of new trade routes; the cultivation, processing, and marketing of southern crops such as sugar and cotton; and the development of various related technologies.

The term *southernization* is meant to be analogous to *westernization*. Westernization refers to certain developments that first occurred in western Europe. Those developments changed Europe and eventually spread to other places and changed them as well. In the same way, southernization changed Southern Asia and later spread to other areas, which then underwent a process of change.

Lynda Shaffer, "Southernization," *Journal of World History* 5 (Spring 1994): 1–21.

Southernization was well under way in Southern Asia by the fifth century C.E., during the reign of India's Gupta kings (320–535 C.E.). It was by that time already spreading to China. In the eighth century various elements characteristic of southernization began spreading through the lands of the Muslim caliphates. Both in China and in the lands of the caliphate, the process led to dramatic changes, and by the year 1200 it was beginning to have an impact on the Christian Mediterranean. One could argue that within the Northern Hemisphere, by this time the process of southernization had created an eastern hemisphere characterized by a rich south and a north that was poor in comparison. And one might even go so far as to suggest that in Europe and its colonies, the process of southernization laid the foundation for westernization.

The Indian Beginning

Southernization was the result of developments that took place in many parts of southern Asia, both on the Indian subcontinent and in Southeast Asia. By the time of the Gupta kings, several of its constituent parts already had a long history in India. Perhaps the oldest strand in the process was the cultivation of cotton and the production of cotton textiles for export. Cotton was first domesticated in the Indus River valley some time between 2300 and 1760 B.C.E., and by the second millennium B.C.E., the Indians had begun to develop sophisticated dyeing techniques. During these early millennia Indus River valley merchants are known to have lived in Mesopotamia, where they sold cotton textiles.

In the first century C.E. Egypt became an important overseas market for Indian cottons. By the next century there was a strong demand for these textiles both in the Mediterranean and in East Africa, and by the fifth century they were being traded in Southeast Asia. The Indian textile trade continued to grow throughout the next millennium. Even after the arrival of European ships in Asian ports at the turn of the sixteenth century, it continued unscathed. According to one textile expert, "India virtually clothed the world" by the mid-eighteenth century. The subcontinent's position was not undermined until Britain's Industrial Revolution, when steam engines began to power the production of cotton textiles.

Another strand in the process of southernization, the search for new sources of bullion, can be traced back in India to the end of the Mauryan Empire (321–185 B.C.E.). During Mauryan rule Siberia had been India's main source of gold, but nomadic disturbances in Central Asia disrupted the traffic between Siberia and India at about the time that the Mauryans fell. Indian sailors then began to travel to the Malay peninsula and the islands of Indonesia in search of an alternative source, which they most likely "discovered" with the help of local peoples who knew the sites. (This is generally the case with bullion discoveries, including those made by Arabs and Europeans.) What the Indians (and others later on) did do was introduce this gold to international trade routes.

The Indians' search for gold may also have led them to the shores of Africa. Although its interpretation is controversial, some archaeological evidence suggests the existence of Indian influence on parts of East Africa as early as 300 C.E. There is also one report that gold was being sought in East Africa by Ethiopian merchants, who were among India's most important trading partners.

The sixth-century Byzantine geographer Cosmas Indicopleustes described Ethiopian merchants who went to some location inland from the East African coast to obtain gold. "Every other year they would sail far to the south, then march inland, and in return for various made-up articles they would come back laden with ingots of gold." The fact that the expeditions left every other year suggests that it took two years to get to their destination and return. If so, their destination, even at this early date, may have been Zimbabwe. The wind patterns are such that sailors who ride the monsoon south as far as Kilwa can catch the return monsoon to the Red Sea area within the same year. But if they go beyond Kilwa to the Zambezi River, from which they might go inland to Zimbabwe, they cannot return until the following year.

Indian voyages on the Indian Ocean were part of a more general development, more or less contemporary with the Mauryan Empire, in which sailors of various nationalities began to knit together the shores of the "Southern Ocean," a Chinese term referring to all the waters from the South China Sea to the eastern coast of Africa. During this period there is no doubt that the most intrepid sailors were the Malays, peoples who lived in what is now Malaysia, Indonesia, the southeastern coast of Vietnam, and the Philippines.

Sometime before 300 B.C.E. Malay sailors began to ride the monsoons, the seasonal winds that blow off the continent of Asia in the colder months and onto its shores in the warmer months. Chinese records indicate that by the third century B.C.E. "Kunlun" sailors, the Chinese term for the Malay seamen, were sailing north to the southern coasts of China. They may also have been sailing east to India, through the straits now called Malacca and Sunda. If so they may have been the first to establish contact between India and Southeast Asia.

Malay sailors had reached the eastern coast of Africa at least by the first century B.C.E., if not earlier. Their presence in East African waters is testified to by the peoples of Madagascar, who still speak a Malayo-Polynesian language. Some evidence also suggests that Malay sailors had settled in the Red Sea area. Indeed, it appears that they were the first to develop a long-distance trade in a southern spice. In the last centuries B.C.E., if not earlier, Malay sailors were delivering cinnamon from South China Sea ports to East Africa and the Red Sea.

By about 400 C.E. Malay sailors could be found two-thirds of the way around the world, from Easter Island to East Africa. They rode the monsoons without a compass, out of sight of land, and often at latitudes below the equator where the northern pole star cannot be seen. They navigated by the wind and the stars, by cloud formations, the color of the water, and swell and wave patterns on the ocean's surface. They could discern the presence of an island some thirty miles from its shores by noting the behavior of birds, the animal and plant life in the water, and the swell and wave patterns. Given their manner of sailing, their most likely route to Africa and the Red Sea would have been by way of the island clusters, the Maldives, the Chagos, the Seychelles, and the Comoros.

Malay ships used balance lug sails, which were square in shape and mounted so that they could pivot. This made it possible for sailors to tack against the wind, that is, to sail into the wind by going diagonally against it, first one way and then the other. Due to the way the sails were mounted, they appeared somewhat triangular in shape, and thus the Malays' balance lug sail may well be the prototype of the triangular lateen, which can also be used to tack against the wind. The latter was invented by both the Polynesians to the Malays' east and by the Arabs to their west, both of whom had ample opportunity to see the Malays' ships in action.

It appears that the pepper trade developed after the cinnamon trade. In the first century C.E. southern India began supplying the Mediterranean with large quantities of pepper. Thereafter, Indian merchants could be found living on the island of Socotra, near the mouth of the Red Sea, and Greek-speaking sailors, including the anonymous author of the *Periplus of the Erythraean Sea,* could be found sailing in the Red Sea and riding the monsoons from there to India.

Indian traders and shippers and Malay sailors were also responsible for opening up an all-sea route to China. The traders' desire for silk drew them out into dangerous waters in search of a more direct way to its source. By the second century C.E. Indian merchants could make the trip by sea, but the route was slow, and it took at least two years to make a round trip. Merchants leaving from India's eastern coast rounded the shores of the Bay of Bengal. When they came to the Isthmus of Kra, the narrowest part of the Malay peninsula, the ships were unloaded, and the goods were portaged across to the Gulf of Thailand. The cargo was then reloaded on ships that rounded the gulf until they reached Funan, a kingdom on what is now the Kampuchea-Vietnam border. There they had to wait for the winds to shift, before embarking upon a ship that rode the monsoon to China.

Some time before 400 C.E. travelers began to use a new all-sea route to China, a route that went around the Malay peninsula and thus avoided the Isthmus of Kra portage. The ships left from Sri Lanka and sailed before the monsoon, far from any coasts, through either the Strait of Malacca or the Strait of Sunda into the Java Sea. After waiting in the Java Sea port for the winds to shift, they rode the monsoon to southern China. The most likely developers of this route were Malay sailors, since the new stopover ports were located within their territories.

Not until the latter part of the fourth century, at about the same time as the new all-sea route began to direct commercial traffic through the Java Sea, did the fine spices — cloves, nutmeg, and mace — begin to assume importance on international markets. These rare and expensive spices came from the Moluccas, several island groups about a thousand miles east of Java. Cloves were produced on about five minuscule islands off the western coast of Halmahera; nutmeg and mace came from only a few of the Banda Islands, some ten islands with a total area of seventeen square miles, located in the middle of the Banda Sea. Until 1621 these Moluccan islands were the only places in the world able to produce cloves, nutmeg, and mace in commercial quantities. The Moluccan producers themselves brought their spices to the international markets of the Java Sea ports and created the market for them.

It was also during the time of the Gupta kings, around 350 C.E., that the Indians discovered how to crystallize sugar. There is considerable disagreement about where sugar was first domesticated. Some believe that the plant was native to New Guinea and domesticated there, and others argue that it was domesticated by Southeast Asian peoples living in what is now southern China. In any case, sugar cultivation spread to the Indian subcontinent. Sugar, however, did not become an important item of trade until the Indians discovered how to turn sugarcane juice into granulated crystals that could be easily stored and transported. This was a momentous development, and it may have been encouraged by Indian sailing, for sugar and clarified butter (ghee) were among the dietary mainstays of Indian sailors.

The Indians also laid the foundation for modern mathematics during the time of the Guptas. Western numerals, which the Europeans called Arabic since they acquired them from the Arabs, actually come from India. (The Arabs call them Hindi numbers.) The most significant feature of the Indian system was the invention of the zero as a number concept. The oldest extant treatise that uses the zero in the modern way is a mathematical appendix attached to Aryabhata's text on astronomy, which is dated 499 C.E.

The Indian zero made the place-value system of writing numbers superior to all others. Without it, the use of this system, base ten or otherwise, was fraught with difficulties and did not seem any better than alternative systems. With the zero the Indians were able to perform calculations rapidly and accurately, to perform much more complicated calculations, and to discern mathematical relationships more aptly. These numerals and the mathematics that the Indians developed with them are now universal — just one indication of the global significance of southernization.

As a result of these developments India acquired a reputation as a place of marvels, a reputation that was maintained for many centuries after the Gupta dynasty fell. As late as the ninth century Amr ibn Bahr al Jahiz (c. 776–868), one of the most influential writers of Arabic, had the following to say about India:

> As regards the Indians, they are among the leaders in astronomy, mathematics — in particular, they have Indian numerals — and medicine; they alone possess the secrets of the latter, and use them to practice some remarkable forms of treatment. They have the art of carving statues and painted figures. They possess the game of chess, which is the noblest of games and requires more judgment and intelligence than any other. They make Kedah swords, and excel in their use. They have splendid music. . . . They possess a script capable of expressing the sounds of all languages, as well as many numerals. They have a great deal of poetry, many long treatises, and a deep understanding of philosophy and letters; the book *Kalila wa-Dimna* originated with them. They are intelligent and courageous. . . . Their sound judgment and sensible habits led them to invent pins, cork, toothpicks, the drape of clothes, and the dyeing of hair. They are handsome, attractive, and forbearing; their women are proverbial; and their country produces the matchless Indian aloes which are supplied to kings. They were the originators of the science of *fikr,* by which a poison can be counteracted after it has been used, and of astronomical reckoning, subsequently adopted by the rest of the world. When Adam descended from Paradise, it was to their land that he made his way.

The Southernization of China

These Southern Asian developments began to have a significant impact on China after 350 C.E. The Han dynasty had fallen in 221 C.E., and for more than 350 years thereafter China was ruled by an ever-changing collection of regional kingdoms. During these centuries Buddhism became increasingly important in China, Buddhist monasteries spread throughout the disunited realm, and cultural exchange between India and China grew accordingly. By 581, when the Sui dynasty reunited the empire, processes associated with southernization had already had a major impact on China. The influence of southernization continued during the T'ang (618–906) and Sung (960–1279) dynasties. One might even go so far as to suggest that the process of southernization underlay the revolutionary social, political, economic, and technological developments of the T'ang and Sung.

The Chinese reformed their mathematics, incorporating the advantages of the Indian system, even though they did not adopt the Indian numerals at that time. They then went on to develop an advanced mathematics, which was flourishing by the time of the Sung dynasty. Cotton and indigo became well established, giving rise to the blue-black peasant garb that is still omnipresent in China. Also in the Sung period the Chinese first developed cotton canvas, which they used to make a more efficient sail for ocean-going ships.

Although sugar had long been grown in some parts of southern China it did not become an important crop in this region until the process of southernization was well under way. The process also introduced new varieties of rice. The most important of these was what the Chinese called Champa rice, since it came to China from Champa, a Malay kingdom located on what is now the southeastern coast of Vietnam. Champa rice was a drought-resistant, early ripening variety that made it possible to extend cultivation up well-watered hillsides, thereby doubling the area of rice cultivation in China. . . .

In Southern China the further development of rice production brought significant changes in the landscape. Before the introduction of Champa rice, rice cultivation had been confined to lowlands, deltas, basins, and river valleys. Once Champa rice was introduced and rice cultivation spread up the hillsides, the Chinese began systematic terracing and made use of sophisticated techniques of water control on mountain slopes. Between the mid-eighth and the early twelfth century the population of southern China tripled, and the total Chinese population doubled. According to Sung dynasty household registration figures for 1102 and 1110 — figures that Sung dynasty specialists have shown to be reliable — there were 100 million people in China by the first decade of the twelfth century.

Before the process of southernization, northern China had always been predominant, intellectually, socially, and politically. The imperial center of gravity was clearly in the north, and the southern part of China was perceived as a frontier area. But southernization changed this situation dramatically. By 600, southern China was well on its way to becoming the most prosperous and most commercial part of the empire. The most telling evidence for this is the construction of the Grand Canal, which was completed around 610, during the Sui dynasty. Even though the rulers of the Sui had managed to put the pieces of the empire back together in 581 and rule the whole of China again from a single northern capital, they were dependent on the new southern crops. Thus it is no coincidence that this dynasty felt the need to build a canal that could deliver southern rice to northern cities.

The T'ang dynasty, when Buddhist influence in China was especially strong, saw two exceedingly important technological innovations — the invention of printing and gunpowder. These developments may also be linked to southernization. Printing seems to have developed within the walls of Buddhist monasteries between 700 and 750, and subtropical Sichuan was one of the earliest centers of the art. The invention of gunpowder in China by Taoist alchemists in the ninth century may also be related to the linkages between India and China created by Buddhism. In 644 an Indian monk identified soils in China that contained saltpeter and demonstrated the purple flame that results from its ignition. As early as 919 C.E. gunpowder was used as an igniter in a flamethrower, and the tenth century also saw the use of flaming arrows, rockets, and bombs thrown by catapults. The earliest evidence of a cannon or bombard (1127) has been found in Sichuan, quite near the Tibetan border, across the Himalayas from India.

By the time of the Sung the Chinese also had perfected the "south-pointing needle," otherwise known as the compass. Various prototypes of the compass had existed in China from the third century B.C.E., but the new version developed during the Sung was particularly well suited for navigation. Soon Chinese mariners were using the south-pointing needle on the oceans, publishing "needle charts" for the benefit of sea captains, and following "needle routes" on the Southern Ocean.

Once the Chinese had the compass they, like Columbus, set out to find a direct route to the spice markets of Java and ultimately to the Spice Islands in the Moluccas. Unlike Columbus, they found them. They did not bump into an obstacle, now known as the Western Hemisphere, on their way, since it was not located between China and the Spice Islands. If it had been so situated, the Chinese would have found it some 500 years before Columbus.

Cities on China's southern coasts became centers of overseas commerce. Silk remained an important export, and by the T'ang dynasty it had been joined by a true porcelain, which was developed in China sometime before 400 C.E. China and its East Asian neighbors had a monopoly on the manufacture of true porcelain until the early eighteenth century. Many attempts were made to imitate it, and some of the resulting imitations were economically and stylistically important. China's southern ports were also exporting to Southeast Asia large quantities of ordinary consumer goods, including iron hardware, such as needles, scissors, and cooking pots. Although iron manufacturing was concentrated in the north, the large quantity of goods produced was a direct result of the size of the market in southern China and overseas. Until the British Industrial Revolution of the eighteenth century, no other place ever equaled the iron production of Sung China.

The Muslim Caliphates

In the seventh century C.E., Arab cavalries, recently converted to the new religion of Islam, conquered eastern and southern Mediterranean shores that had been Byzantine (and Christian), as well as the Sassanian empire (Zoroastrian) in what is now Iraq and Iran. In the eighth century they went on to conquer Spain and Turko-Iranian areas of Central Asia, as well as northwestern India. Once established on the Indian frontier, they became acquainted with many of the elements of southernization.

The Arabs were responsible for the spread of many important crops, developed or improved in India, to the Middle East, North Africa, and Islamic Spain. Among the most important were sugar, cotton, and citrus fruits. Although sugarcane and cotton cultivation may have spread to Iraq and Ethiopia before the Arab conquests, only after the establishment of the caliphates did these southern crops have a major impact throughout the Middle East and North Africa.

The Arabs were the first to import large numbers of enslaved Africans in order to produce sugar. Fields in the vicinity of Basra, at the northern end of the Persian Gulf, were the most important sugar-producing areas within the caliphates, but before this land could be used, it had to be desalinated. To accomplish this task, the Arabs imported East African (Zanj) slaves. This African community remained in the area, where they worked as agricultural laborers. The famous writer al Jahiz, whose essay on India was quoted earlier, was a descendant of Zanj slaves. In 869, one year after his death, the Zanj slaves in Iraq rebelled. It took the caliphate fifteen years of hard fighting to defeat them, and thereafter Muslim owners rarely used slaves for purposes that would require their concentration in large numbers.

The Arabs were responsible for moving sugarcane cultivation and sugar manufacturing westward from southern Iraq into other relatively arid lands. Growers had to adapt the plant to new conditions, and they had to develop more efficient irrigation technologies. By 1000 or so sugarcane had become an important crop in the Yemen; in Arabian oases; in irrigated areas of Syria, Lebanon, Palestine, Egypt, and the Mahgrib; in Spain; and on Mediterranean islands controlled by Muslims. By the tenth century cotton also had become a major crop in the lands of the caliphate, from Iran and Central Asia to Spain and the Mediterranean islands. Cotton industries sprang up wherever the plant was cultivated, producing for both local and distant markets. . . .

Under Arab auspices, Indian mathematics followed the same routes as the crops. Al-Kharazmi (c. 780–847) introduced Indian mathematics to the Arabic-reading world in his *Treatise on Calculation with the Hindu Numerals,* written around 825. Mathematicians within the caliphates then could draw upon the Indian tradition, as well as the Greek and Persian. On this foundation Muslim scientists of many nationalities, including al-Battani (d. 929), who came from the northern reaches of the Mesopotamian plain, and the Persian Omar Khayyám (d. 1123), made remarkable advances in both algebra and trigonometry.

The Arab conquests also led to an increase in long-distance commerce and the "discovery" of new sources of bullion. Soon after the Abbasid caliphate established its capital at Baghdad, the caliph al-Mansur (r. 745–75) reportedly remarked, "This is the Tigris; there is no obstacle between us and China; everything on the sea can come to us." By this time Arab ships were plying the maritime routes from the Persian Gulf to China, and they soon outnumbered all others using these routes. By the ninth century they had acquired the compass (in China, most likely), and they may well have been the first to use it for marine navigation, since the Chinese do not seem to have used it for this purpose until after the tenth century.

. . . Thus it was that the Arabs "pioneered" or improved an existing long-distance route across the Sahara, an ocean of sand rather than water. Routes across this desert had always existed, and trade and other contacts between West Africa and the Mediterranean date back at least to the Phoenician period. Still, the numbers of people and animals crossing this great ocean of sand were limited until the eighth century when Arabs, desiring to go directly to the source of the gold, prompted an expansion of trade across the Sahara. Also during the eighth century Abdul al-Rahman, an Arab ruler of Morocco, sponsored the construction of wells on the trans-Saharan route from Sijilmasa to Wadidara to facilitate this traffic. This Arab "discovery" of West African gold eventually doubled the amount of gold in international circulation. East Africa, too, became a source of gold for the Arabs. By the tenth century Kilwa had become an important source of Zimbabwean gold.

Developments After 1200: The Mongolian Conquest and the Southernization of the European Mediterranean

By 1200 the process of southernization had created a prosperous south from China to the Muslim Mediterranean. Although mathematics, the pioneering of new ocean routes, and "discoveries" of bullion are not inextricably connected to locations within forty degrees of the equator, several crucial elements in the process of southernization were closely linked to latitude. Cotton generally does not grow above the fortieth parallel. Sugar, cinnamon, and pepper are tropical or subtropical crops, and the fine spices will grow only on particular tropical islands. Thus for many centuries the more southern parts of Asia and the Muslim Mediterranean enjoyed the profits that these developments brought, while locations that were too far north to grow these southern crops were unable to participate in such lucrative agricultural enterprises.

The process of southernization reached its zenith after 1200, in large part because of the tumultuous events of the thirteenth century. During that century in both hemispheres there were major transformations in the distribution of power, wealth, and prestige. In the Western Hemisphere several great powers went down. Cahokia (near East St. Louis, Illinois), which for three centuries had been the largest and most influential of the Mississippian mound-building centers, declined after 1200, and in Mexico Toltec power collapsed. In the Mediterranean the prestige of the Byzantine empire was destroyed when Venetians seized its capital in 1204. From 1212 to 1270 the Christians conquered southern Spain, except for Granada. In West Africa, Ghana fell to Sosso, and so did Mali, one of Ghana's allies. But by about 1230 Mali, in the process of seeking its own revenge, had created an empire even larger than Ghana's. At the same time Zimbabwe was also becoming a major power in southern Africa.

The grandest conquerors of the thirteenth century were the Central Asians. Turkish invaders established the Delhi sultanate in India. Mongolian cavalries devastated Baghdad, the seat of the Abbasid caliphate since the eighth century, and they captured Kiev, further weakening Byzantium. By the end of the century they had captured China, Korea, and parts of mainland Southeast Asia as well.

Because the Mongols were pagans at the time of their conquests, the western Europeans cheered them on as they laid waste to one after another Muslim center of power in the Middle East. The Mongols were stopped only when they encountered the Mamluks of Egypt at Damascus. In East Asia and Southeast Asia only the Japanese and the Javanese were able to defeat them. The victors in Java went on to found Majapahit, whose power and prestige then spread through maritime Southeast Asia.

Both hemispheres were reorganized profoundly during this turmoil. Many places that had flourished were toppled, and power gravitated to new locales. In the Eastern Hemisphere the Central Asian conquerors had done great damage to traditional southern centers just about everywhere, except in Africa, southern China, southern India, and maritime Southeast Asia. At the same time the Mongols' control of overland routes between Europe and Asia in the thirteenth and early fourteenth centuries fostered unprecedented contacts between Europeans and peoples from those areas that had long been southernized. Marco Polo's long sojourn in Yüan Dynasty China is just one example of such interaction.

Under the Mongols overland trade routes in Asia shifted north and converged on the Black Sea. After the Genoese helped the Byzantines to retake Constantinople from the Venetians in 1261, the Genoese were granted special privileges of trade in the Black Sea. Italy then became directly linked to the Mongolian routes. Genoese traders were among the first and were certainly the most numerous to open up trade with the Mongolian states in southern Russia and Iran. In the words of one Western historian, in their Black Sea colonies they "admitted to citizenship" people of many nationalities, including those of "strange background and questionable belief," and they "wound up christening children of the best ancestry with such uncanny names as Saladin, Hethum, or Hulugu."

Such contacts contributed to the southernization of the Christian Mediterranean during this period of Mongolian hegemony. Although European conquerors sometimes had taken over sugar and cotton lands in the Middle East during the Crusades, not until some time after 1200 did the European-held Mediterranean islands become important exporters. Also after 1200 Indian mathematics began to have a significant impact in Europe. Before that time a few western European scholars had become acquainted with Indian numerals in Spain, where the works of al-Kharazmi, al-Battani, and other mathematicians had been translated into Latin. Nevertheless, Indian numerals and mathematics did not become important in western Europe until the thirteenth century after the book *Liber abaci* (1202), written by Leonardo Fibonacci of Pisa (c. 1170–1250), introduced them to the commercial centers of Italy. Leonardo had grown up in North Africa (in what is now Bejala, Algeria), where his father, consul over the Pisan merchants in that port, had sent him to study calculation with an Arab master.

In the seventeenth century, when Francis Bacon observed the "force and virtue and consequences of discoveries," he singled out three technologies in particular that "have changed the whole face and state of things throughout the world." These were all Chinese inventions — the compass, printing, and gunpowder. All three were first acquired by Europeans during this time of hemispheric reorganization.

It was most likely the Arabs who introduced the compass to Mediterranean waters, either at the end of the twelfth or in the thirteenth century. Block printing, gunpowder, and cannon appeared first in Italy in the fourteenth century, apparently after making a single great leap from Mongolian-held regions of East Asia to Italy. How this great leap was accomplished is not known, but the most likely scenario is one suggested by Lynn White Jr., in an article concerning how various other Southern (rather than Eastern) Asian technologies reached western Europe at about this time. He thought it most likely that they were introduced by "Tatar" slaves, Lama Buddhists from the frontiers of China whom the Genoese purchased in Black Sea marts and delivered to Italy.

By 1450 when this trade reached its peak, there were thousands of these Asian slaves in every major Italian city.

Yet another consequence of the increased traffic and communication on the more northern trade routes traversing the Eurasian steppe was the transmission of the bubonic plague from China to the Black Sea. The plague had broken out first in China in 1331, and apparently rats and lice infected with the disease rode westward in the saddlebags of Mongolian post messengers, horsemen who were capable of traveling one hundred miles per day. By 1346 it had reached a Black Sea port, whence it made its way to the Middle East and Europe.

During the latter part of the fourteenth century the unity of the Mongolian empire began to disintegrate, and new regional powers began to emerge in its wake. Throughout much of Asia the chief beneficiaries of imperial disintegration were Turkic or Turko-Mongolian powers of the Muslim faith. The importance of Islam in Africa was also growing at this time, and the peoples of Southeast Asia, from the Malay peninsula to the southern Philippines, were converting to the faith.

Indeed, the world's most obvious dynamic in the centuries before Columbus was the expansion of the Islamic faith. Under Turkish auspices Islam was even spreading into eastern Europe, a development marked by the Ottoman conquest of Constantinople in 1453. This traumatic event lent a special urgency to Iberian expansion. The Iberians came to see themselves as the chosen defenders of Christendom. Ever since the twelfth century, while Christian Byzantium had been losing Anatolia and parts of southeastern Europe to Islam, they had been retaking the Iberian peninsula for Christendom.

One way to weaken the Ottomans and Islam was to go around the North African Muslims and find a new oceanic route to the source of West African gold. Before the Portuguese efforts, sailing routes had never developed off the western shore of Africa, since the winds there blow in the same direction all year long, from north to south. (Earlier European sailors could have gone to West Africa, but they would not have been able to return home.)

The Portuguese success would have been impossible without the Chinese compass, Arabic tables indicating the declination of the noonday sun at various latitudes, and the lateen sail, which was also an Arab innovation. The Portuguese caravels were of mixed, or multiple, ancestry, with a traditional Atlantic hull and a rigging that combined the traditional Atlantic square sail with the lateen sail of Southern Ocean provenance. With the lateen sail the Portuguese could tack against the wind for the trip homeward.

The new route to West Africa led to Portugal's rounding of Africa and direct participation in Southern Ocean trade. While making the voyages to West Africa, European sailors learned the wind patterns and ocean currents west of Africa, knowledge that made the Columbian voyages possible. The Portuguese moved the sugarcane plant from Sicily to Madeira, in the Atlantic, and they found new sources of gold, first in West Africa and then in East Africa. Given that there was little demand in Southern Ocean ports for European trade goods, they would not have been able to sustain their Asian trade without this African gold.

The Rise of Europe's North

The rise of the north, or more precisely, the rise of Europe's northwest, began with the appropriation of those elements of southernization that were not confined by geography. In the wake of their southern European neighbors, they became partially southernized, but they could not engage in all aspects of the process due to their distance from the equator. Full southernization and the wealth that we now associate with northwestern Europe came about only after their outright seizure of tropical and subtropical territories and their rounding of Africa and participation in Southern Ocean trade. . . .

Even though the significance of indigenous developments in the rise of northwestern Europe should not be minimized, it should be emphasized that many of the most important causes of the rise of the West are not to be found within the bounds of Europe. Rather, they are the result of the transformation of western Europe's relationships with other regions of the Eastern Hemisphere. Europe began its rise only after the thirteenth-century reorganization of the Eastern Hemisphere facilitated its southernization, and Europe's northwest did not rise until it too was reaping the profits of southernization. Thus the rise of the North Atlantic powers should not be oversimplified so that it appears to be an isolated and solely European phenomenon, with roots that spread no farther afield than Greece. Rather, it should be portrayed as one part of a hemisphere-wide process, in which a northwestern Europe ran to catch up with a more developed south — a race not completed until the eighteenth century.

REFLECTIONS

The differing approaches to explaining the roots of modernity, represented in this chapter by White and Shaffer, reflect generational differences between the historians. White, whose training before 1960 emphasized the homogeneity and importance of Western Civilization (largely Europe and North America), represents an earlier generation of historians; Shaffer became an historian more recently in a world made both smaller by transportation and communication technologies and more knowable by the amount of research in the last few decades.

This difference in approach is, in part, the legacy of different wars. The idea of "Western Civilization" developed after World War I — first in American universities — as a way to explain and understand the new leadership role of the United States in an Atlantic alliance. (The first version of the civilization course, "War Aims," was taught at Columbia University in 1919.) Western civilization was the standard introduction to history for most college students from the 1930s to the 1960s.

The Cold War that developed between the United States (allied with Europe) and the Soviet Union (now Russia) after World War II prompted studies of specific areas and "non-Western" studies at universities in the United States. America's assumption of global leadership, combined with an influx of students and citizens from a new group of Asian and Latin American immigrants, brought to the fore interest in and knowledge of the histories of Asia, Africa, and Latin America. These areas of the world were virtually omitted from history, geography, and other courses in the United States prior to 1960.

The differences between the selections by White and Shaffer might be attributed to new knowledge. Today, world history is something that can be readily understood and taught. We can recognize global connections that simply were not obvious even thirty years ago thanks to satellite photos, coordinated research, instantaneous global communication, and the fading of national boundaries.

This new awareness has led some world historians to dismiss a "Western Civilization" approach as dated and Eurocentric. E. L. Jones, for example, in *Recurring Growth* (Oxford, 1988) criticizes the great economist John Maynard Keynes for having "a 'Western Civ' conception of history." He adds: "There was no room in it for the profound changes being made in China nor for the evidence of a progressive drift of ideas from China right across Eurasia, until at length they were embodied in the techniques of the red-haired barbarians of Europe." In the same book, Jones is expressly critical of White's thesis as a manifestation of this approach:

> The assumption that there is something preternaturally malign about Christian attitudes toward nature is an aberrant opinion of the 1960s and 1970s. It has more to do with the self-abnegation of Western intellectuals than with real historical differences between cultures or religions. The evidence tends to be philosophical statements in the Christian literature rather than comparative data on how Christian and other societies actually treated the environment (pp. 60–61).

What do you make of this criticism? Does Jones overreact? Has the pendulum swung too far in rejecting European origins of modern science and the industrial revolution?

Our discussion of images was fairly elementary and inconclusive, but this might be a good time to reflect on the historical value of images of all kinds. Do you think that in research, for instance, you would find photographs more useful than paintings or drawings? Why? Of course, there were no photographs until the middle of the nineteenth century, but European painters of the Renaissance and seventeenth-century scientific revolution often painted with mirror-like naturalism. The Dutch painter Jan Vermeer (1632–1675) would often use a camera obscura (a darkened room-sized box with a small hole facing the subject that let in light and cast a reversed image of the subject on the back wall of the box), so the picture could be practically traced. Would a Vermeer be as useful historically as a photograph? Is it significant that Vermeer sought a mirror image and Wen Zhengming did not?

12

"Barbarians" and Mongols

HISTORICAL CONTEXT

Mongol Eurasia, 1200–1350 C.E.

The ancient Greeks called any people who did not speak Greek "Barbarians." For the Greeks, this term was both descriptive (foreign languages sounded to the Greeks like "barbar") and critical (foreigners were not Greek). In time, the term *barbarian* was applied with increasing criticism by the settled peoples of the Mediterranean to all of the nomadic peoples who came out of the enormous stretch of grasslands or steppe that stretched from eastern Europe to northern China. Periodic migrations or invasions of these nomads into the settled societies of China, India, and the Mediterranean fueled the stories and myths of their prowess and brutality. Successive waves of these barbarians were blamed for the fall of the Roman Empire, the Han dynasty, and (as we saw in Chapter 10) the Seljuk invasions of the Byzantine Empire and Muslim caliphate.

The Mongol[1] invasions of the thirteenth century were simply another stage in the conflict between the pastoral people of the great Eurasian steppe and the settled people of farms and cities. But this time there was a difference. In previous eras, population or grazing pressures forced one group of people to bump another, setting off chain reactions of expansion that eventually reached the great cities of China, the Middle East, India, and the Mediterranean. The Mongols organized a massive confederacy of peoples that, at least for a few generations, united the entire steppe under a single ruler, systematically conquered settlements from China to Europe, and ruled the largest empire the world had ever known.

[1] The term "Mongol" generally refers to the peoples of Mongolia in central Asia, whose language is Mongolian.

Our question in this chapter is, who were the Mongols? While we pay some attention to the history of other nomadic peoples from the Eurasian grasslands, our primary concern is not a comparison of the Mongols with other peoples. Rather, we examine how the Mongols were viewed by other people and how they viewed themselves. Perhaps somewhere between these two accounts, we will discover who and what they were.

THINKING HISTORICALLY

Making Moral Judgments about History

While not all outside observers and non-Mongol historians have been critical of the Mongols, the Mongols were widely condemned in their heyday (1206–1348) and have been since. And yet, as their defenders are quick to point out, there are reasons to question the objectivity of all of this bad press. Initial criticism of course came from the settled, literate, wealthy, urban societies that the Mongols conquered. These city observers and historians were not good losers. Try to imagine, if you were conquered, how you would write about your conqueror. Would you be biased? Would you be right?

The role of moral or ethical judgments in history is a thorny issue. For the most part, historians believe they should not let their own sense of what is right and wrong intrude on the way they describe and explain the past. This may remain an elusive goal, but it is especially difficult to achieve when the historian believes that the facts demonstrate that one side was the aggressor, the other the victim. Even if we try to be objective, the language we use tends to be full of moral judgment, explicitly or implicitly. Do we call it a migration or an invasion? Do we speak of the dead or the slaughtered? And even if the historian is able to find a neutral vocabulary, there are some who would say that she should not. Perhaps outrageous acts require outrage, and their import is dulled by bland description. These are some of the questions you will consider as you read these selections. What role does moral judgment play in a particular description or interpretation? What role should it play? Can historians be morally neutral? Should they be? Does the audience matter? Do the Mongols and their subjects need the same or different histories?

72

GREGORY GUZMAN

Were the Barbarians a Negative or Positive Factor in Ancient and Medieval History?

Gregory Guzman is a modern world historian, specializing in the Middle Ages and the Mongols. In this essay he sets the treatment of Mongol history within the context of "barbarian history."

How did the horse shape life on the steppe? How effective were these pastoralists as rulers of settled societies? What were the achievements of the pastoral nomads, including the Mongols?

Thinking Historically

Why, according to Guzman, have most histories of the barbarians made them look bad? Have city people or historians let their own judgments block an appreciation of the achievements of pastoralists in general and the Mongols in particular?

According to the general surveys of ancient and medieval history found in most textbooks, barbarian peoples and/or primitive savages repeatedly invaded the early Eurasian civilized centers in Europe, the Middle East, India, and China. All accounts of the early history of these four civilizations contain recurrent references to attacks by such familiar and famous barbarians as the Hittites, Hyksos, Kassites, Aryans, Scythians, Sarmatians, Hsiung-nu, Huns, Germans, Turks, and Mongols, and they also record the absorption and assimilation of these Inner Asian barbarian hordes into the respective cultures and lifestyles of the more advanced coastal civilizations. The early sources generally equate the barbarians with chaos and destruction. The barbarians are presented as evil and despicable intruders, associated only with burning, pillaging, and slaughtering, while the civilized peoples are portrayed as the good and righteous forces of stability, order, and progress.

But it must be remembered that most of these early sources are not objective; they are blatantly one-sided, biased accounts written by

---

Gregory Guzman, "Were the Barbarians a Negative or Positive Factor in Ancient and Medieval History?" *The Historian* L (August 1988): 558–72.

members of the civilized societies. Thus, throughout recorded history, barbarians have consistently received bad press — bad PR to use the modern terminology. By definition, barbarians were illiterate, and thus they could not write their own version of events. All written records covering barbarian-civilized interaction came from the civilized peoples at war with the barbarians — often the sedentary peoples recently defeated and overwhelmed by those same barbarians. Irritated and angered coastal historians tended to record and emphasize only the negative aspects of their recent interaction with the barbarians. The following quotations clearly illustrate the tendency of the authors to condemn and denigrate the way their barbarian opponents looked and to associate them with the devil and evil, rather than to report with objectivity what actually happened.

> The Roman historian Ammianus Marcellinus, whose description is distorted by hatred and fear, described the barbarians as "two-footed beasts, seemingly chained to their horses from which they take their meat and drink, never touching a plough and having no houses."
>
> While living in Jerusalem, St. Jerome also left a vivid description of the Huns who " . . . filled the whole earth with slaughter and panic alike as they flittered hither and thither on their swift horses. . . . They were at hand everywhere before they were expected; by their speed they outstripped rumor, and they took pity neither upon religion nor rank nor age nor wailing childhood. Those who had just begun to live were compelled to die. . . ."

Such reports obviously made the barbarians look bad, while their nomadic habits and practices, which differed from those of the sedentary coastal peoples, were clearly portrayed as inferior and less advanced: the incarnation of evil itself. These horror-filled and biased descriptions were not the accounts of weak and defenseless peoples. Rather, they were written by the citizens of the most advanced and powerful states and empires in Europe, the Middle East, India, and China. The individual barbarian tribes were, nevertheless, able to attack and invade these strong and well-organized civilized states with relative impunity — pillaging and killing almost at will.

Several important questions, not addressed by the ancient and medieval historians, need to be answered here. Who were these barbarians? Why and how did they manage to repeatedly defeat and overwhelm so easily the wealthiest and most advanced civilizations of the day? And why were they so vehemently condemned and hated in recorded history, if these barbarian Davids were able to consistently defeat such mighty Goliath civilized centers? Since the rich and populous civilized states enjoyed tremendous advantages in the confrontations, why have the barbarians so often been denied the popular role of the underdog?

In the process of answering those questions, this study would like to suggest that maybe the barbarians were not really the "bad guys." While they may not deserve to be called the "good guys," they made a much more positive contribution to human civilization than presented in the grossly distorted written sources. The barbarians deserve much more credit than they have been given, for they created a complex pastoral lifestyle as an alternative to sedentary agriculture, and in that achievement they were not subhuman savages only out to loot, pillage, and destroy. As this study will show, the barbarians played a much more positive and constructive role in the development and diffusion of early human history than that with which they are usually credited.

Before proceeding further, it is necessary to identify these much-maligned barbarians and describe how their way of life and their basic practices differed from those of the sedentary coastal peoples in order to better evaluate the barbarian role and its impact on the history of humanity.

In terms of identity, the barbarians were the steppe nomads of Inner Asia or Central Eurasia. This area represents one of the toughest and most inhospitable places in the world in which to survive. The climate of the interior of the large Eurasian landmass is not moderated by the distant seas, resulting in extremes of climate, of hot and cold, wet and dry. It is an area of ice, forest, desert, and mountains — with bitter winds, dust, and poor soil. Unlike the coastal regions with their dependable moisture and warmth, the soil of Inner Asia was too cold, poor, and dry for agriculture; thus the sedentary urban lifestyle of the coastal civilized centers was not an option in the Eurasian heartland. The people living there had to be tough to endure such a hostile environment, where they constantly fought both nature and other people for survival.

Due to necessity, the people of Inner Asia were nomads, wandering in search of food and pasture, and they became herdsmen, shepherds, and warriors. These steppe nomads, the barbarians of recorded history, were frequently nothing more than migrants looking for new homes; these people needed little encouragement to seek safety, security, and better living conditions in the warm, rich, and fertile coastal civilization centers. Thus the steppe barbarians were not always savage marauders coming only to loot and pillage. Many of the so-called barbarian invaders constituted a surplus population which harsh Inner Asia could not support, or they represented whole tribes being pushed out of their ancestral homeland by stronger tribes behind them. At any rate, these repeated waves of nomadic peoples leaving the steppes soon encountered the coastal civilizations.

These Inner Asian barbarians were more or less harmless outsiders until the horse dramatically changed their lifestyle on the vast steppes. They adopted the pastoral system as the best way of providing for basic needs. The natural pasture provided by the steppe grassland proved ideal for grazing large herds and flocks of animals. Soon their whole life revolved around their animals; they became shepherds, herders, and keepers of beasts. . . .

The dominant feature of this emerging barbarian pastoralism was its mounted nature; it was essentially a horse culture by 1000 B.C. At first small horses were kept only for food and milk, but bigger horses eventually led to riding. Once an accomplished fact, mounted practices dramatically changed the lifestyle of the barbarian steppe peoples. Horseback riding made the tending of scattered herds faster and less tiring, and it enlarged the size of herds while increasing the range of pastoral movement. It also made possible, when necessary, the total migration of entire tribes and clans. Mastery of the horse reduced the vast expanses of steppe pasturage to more manageable proportions. Steppe nomads moved twice a year between traditional winter and summer pastures; the spring and fall were spent moving between the necessary grazing grounds. All peoples and possessions moved with regularity; the nomads became used to living in the saddle, so to speak.

The horse thus became the center of pastoral life on the steppes. The barbarian nomads could literally live off their animals which provided meat, milk, and hides for clothing, coverings, boots, etc. Tools and weapons were made from the bones and sinews, and dried dung was used as fuel. The barbarians ate, sold, negotiated, slept, and took care of body functions in the saddle as indicated in the following quotations: "From their horses, by day and night every one of that nation buys and sells, eats and drinks, and bowed over the narrow neck of the animal relaxes in a sleep so deep as to be accompanied by many dreams." "All the time they let themselves be carried by their horses. In that way they fight wars, participate in banquets, attend public and private business. On their back, they move, stand still, carry on trade, and converse." These mounted practices led to the emergence of the centaur motif in Middle Eastern art, as the civilized people tended to view the horse and rider as one inseparable unit.

Military action also became an integral part of nomadic steppe life. Warfare was simply cavalry action by the pastoral herdsmen who served as soldiers for the duration of the conflict. Steppe military service differed little from the normal, on-the-move pastoral life. Large-scale steppe alliances were hard to organize and even harder to hold together among the independent nomads. Such temporary alliances, called hordes, rose swiftly to great strength and power, but they usually declined and disintegrated just as quickly.

At any rate, these barbarian nomads were tough and hardy warriors. The horse gave them speed and mobility over both the light and heavily armed infantry of the civilized centers, but for this speed and mobility the barbarians gave up any type of defensive armor. They learned to guide their horses with their knees, since both arms needed to be free for the bow and arrow, their primary offensive weapon. By 1000 B.C. the compound bow was in common use by barbarians. This shorter bow could be handled with ease from horseback, and arrows could be shot up to three hundred yards with accuracy. As steppe hunters, all barbarians made excellent archers.

Early civilized armies had no cavalry. The famous Macedonian phalanx and the formidable Roman legions contained only light and heavily armed infantry. At first these brave foot soldiers had no tactical maneuvers to face and contain a barbarian cavalry charge. Even more devastating was the storm of arrows raining down upon them long before they could engage in the traditional hand-to-hand combat. The formidable steppe cavalry thus subjected civilized defenses to continuous pressure. Every nomad with a horse and bow was a potential frontline soldier who was tough, resourceful, and ferocious, whereas only a small percentage of the civilized population was equipped and trained for war. The nomadic lifestyle and the speed of the horse eliminated the need for expensive and heavy metal armor and its accompanying technological skills. Cavalry tactics gave an initial military advantage to the barbarians and the mounted horsemen won most of the early battles. The best defense against barbarian cavalry was an insurmountable obstacle, a wall. Ten- to twenty-foot-high walls of dirt, wood, or stone were built around cities and along some frontiers, i.e., the Great Wall of China. The old statement that Rome fell because China built a wall may not be such a simple overstatement after all.

Since they had the military advantage of cavalry tactics, the steppe nomads attacked and conquered various coastal civilizations with regularity. In a typical conquest, the victorious barbarians were the new military/political rulers. These new rulers possessed strengths obvious to all. The barbarians had vigorous and dynamic leadership; good, able, and charismatic leadership had been needed to organize the independent nomads into an effective horde in the first place. The new rulers had the complete loyalty of their followers; their group identity based on common blood and ancestors resulted in an intense personal and individual allegiance and commitment.

The first century after the initial conquest was usually an era of dynamic leadership, good government, and economic prosperity, as nomadic strengths mixed with the local advances and practices of that civilization. The new ruling family was often a fusion of the best of both sides as the barbarian victors married into the previous ruling dynasty. This brought forth an age of powerful and successful rulers, and produced an era of energetic leadership, good government, low taxes, agricultural revival, and peace. . . .

After this early period of revitalized and dynamic rule, slow decline usually set in. Royal vigor and ability sank as the rulers became soft, both mentally and physically. Without physical exercise and self-discipline, the rulers became overindulgent, instantly acquiring everything they wanted — excessive amounts of food or drink, harems, puppets, and yes-men as advisers. At the same time court rivalries and internal divisiveness began to emerge once the strong unity required for the conquest was no longer needed. A rivalry that often arose was between the ruler and various groups of his followers — his military, his bureaucracy, his harem (especially the queen mothers), his conquered subjects, and his old nomadic supporters. His steppe horsemen began to give first loyalty to their new family land rather than to their individual leader who was now weak, impaired, and soft. Such internal rivalries weakened the central government and led to chaos and civil wars. Thus, a civilized center was ripe for the next series of invasions and conquest by the next group of unified, tough, and well-led barbarians who would, in turn, be assimilated and absorbed in this process of ongoing revitalization of stagnant civilizations.

Despite the usual negative view and definition of barbarians provided by the sedentary civilized peoples, the steppe nomads had developed a complex pastoral and nomadic society. They were tough and hardy horsemen whose cavalry tactics gave them the military advantage for several centuries. The barbarians used this advantage, and their periodic attacks on civilization centers caused destruction, sometimes severe destruction. But the barbarian role in mankind's history was not always negative. The barbarians can and should be viewed as representing a dynamic and vital element in human history for they periodically revived many stagnating coastal civilizations. Many of these sedentary centers flourished, growing rich and powerful. In the process they also became conservative, settled into a fixed routine. Preferring the status quo, they tended to use old answers and ways to face new problems and issues, and as a consequence they lost the vitality and flexibility required for healthy and progressive growth.

The barbarians were active and dynamic. In their conquests of civilized centers, they frequently destroyed and eliminated the old and outdated and preserved and passed on only the good and useful elements. Sometimes, the mounted invaders also introduced new ideas and practices. Some of these new barbarian innovations (horseback riding, archery, trousers, and boots, etc.) fused with the good and useful practices of the sedentary peoples. Old and new practices and processes merged, and provided viable alternatives to the old, outdated civilized ways which had failed or outlived their usefulness. This fusion brought forth dynamic creativity and development. The ongoing encounters with barbarian strangers inevitably fostered innovation and progress in the civilized centers — due to their need to adjust in order to survive....

It can be argued that barbarians also played a positive role in the spread and diffusion of civilization itself. The four major Eurasian civilization centers were separated from each other by deserts, mountains, and the vast expanses of the steppe heartland of Inner Asia. In its early stages each civilization was somewhat isolated from the others. Overland trade and contact was possible only through the barbarian steppe highway which stretched over five thousand miles across Eurasia, from Hungary to Manchuria. There was little early sea contact between the four sedentary centers, as naval travel was longer and more dangerous than the overland routes.

Thus the steppe barbarians were the chief agency through which the ideas and practices of one civilization were spread to another before 1500 A.D. According to [historian] William H. McNeill, there was much conceptual diffusion carried along the steppe highway by the barbarians. Writing originated in the ancient Middle East. The concept, not the form, of writing then spread eastward from the Middle East, as the Indian and Chinese forms and characters were significantly different than Middle Eastern cuneiform. The making and use of bronze and chariots also spread from the Middle East to Europe, India, and China. Chariots were introduced to China, on the eastern end of the steppe highway, a few centuries after their appearance in the Middle East. Needless to say, this type of early cultural diffusion is difficult to document with any degree of certainty, but enough evidence exists to make it highly probable, even if not scientifically provable.

The late medieval period provides even more examples of cultural diffusion via the movement of barbarians along the Inner Asian steppe highway. The great Eurasian *Pax Mongolica* opened the way for much cultural cross-fertilization in the late-thirteenth and early-fourteenth centuries. Chinese inventions like gunpowder and printing made their way to the Middle East and Europe in this period. Records show that Chinese artillerymen accompanied the Mongol armies into the Middle East. Papal envoys like John of Plano Carpini and William of Rubruck traveled to the Mongol capital of Karakorum in the 1240s and 1250s. In the 1280s, Marco Polo brought with him from Kublai Khan's court in China a Mongol princess to be the bride of the Mongol Khan of Persia....

This cultural interaction and exchange between Eurasian coastal civilizations ended with the collapse of the Mongol Khanates in Persia and China in the mid-fourteenth century. The barbarian Mongols, therefore, provided the last period of great cultural cross-fertilization before the modern age.

Historical evidence that exists enables one to argue that the barbarian nomads played an active and positive role in the history of mankind. The barbarian invaders revitalized stagnant and decaying civilizations and were responsible for a certain amount of cultural diffusion between emerging ancient and medieval civilizations. The traditional portrayal of barbarians as mere marauders and destroyers is misleading and incorrect. Unfortunately this is the usual role they are given when historians center their study of the past narrowly on the civilized centers and the biased written sources produced by those peoples. All too often historians tend to adopt and reflect the biases and values of their subjects under study, and thus continue to denigrate and condemn all barbarians without objectively evaluating their real contributions to human development. The study of the steppe nomads, the barbarians, is just as valid a topic for historical analysis as the traditional study of coastal sedentary civilizations. Only by knowing and understanding the pastoral barbarian can historians accurately evaluate the constant interaction between the two lifestyles and come to understand the full picture of humanity's early growth and development in the ancient and medieval periods of Eurasian history.

73

DAVID MORGAN

From *The Mongols*

In this selection, another modern historian of the Mongols examines the military aspects of Mongol society. Judging from the reading, would you consider the Mongols a military or a warrior society? What accounts for their success at conquest and governing? Why is it difficult to determine the size of Mongol armies? What were the limitations of Mongol expansion?

Thinking Historically

Underline the language in this selection that you would classify as moral or judgmental. What other phrasing or words might Morgan have used? Does Morgan's writing suggest or support a particular moral judgment about the Mongols? How would you characterize

David Morgan, *The Mongols* (Oxford: Blackwell, 1986), 73–94, passim.

that judgment? How is Morgan's opinion and interpretation of the Mongols similar to or different from that of Guzman's in the preceding selection?

The immediate effects of Chingiz Khān's[1] conquests, seen from the point of view of those who bore the brunt of them, were undeniably catastrophic, though this has not prevented some modern historians from arguing that the destruction and loss of life have been greatly exaggerated. But one should not be distracted by admiration for the later achievements of Qubilai in China, or by respect for the attempts of Ghazan to put matters right in Persia, from recognising that the Mongol conquests were a disaster on a grand and unparalleled scale. North China was subjected to a series of destructive campaigns over a period of twenty-five years. According to one oft-repeated if possibly apocryphal story, the Mongols seriously considered wiping out the whole population of the former Chin Empire so as to turn the land over to pasture: They were only dissuaded when their Khitan adviser Yeh-lü Ch'u-ts'ai pointed out to them how much income in taxation they could expect to extract from an unmassacred Chinese people. To the west, Transoxania and more particularly eastern Persia had to endure something that must have seemed to approximate very nearly to attempted genocide.

Contemporary historians were unanimous when they wrote about the horrors that accompanied the Mongol invasion of the Khwārazm-shāh's empire. Ibn al-Athīr . . . is perhaps the best known and the most vivid of them. Jūzjānī wrote a similar account in his Delhi sanctuary. Jalāl al-Dīn's secretary, Nasawī, who accompanied that last of the Khwārazm-shāhs in his campaigns and wanderings, conveys much the same impression, as do such sources as the local history of Harāt, Sayfī's *Ta'rīkh-nāma-i Harāt*. The figures that these writers quote for the numbers of people massacred are beyond belief. Sayfī tells us that 1,600,000 were killed at the sack of Harāt, and 1,747,000 at Nīshāpūr. Jūzjānī puts the Harāt death toll even higher, at 2,400,000.

What are we to make of such figures? One difficulty is that no one has a clear idea of what size the population of a great Islamic city may have been in the early thirteenth century. It does not seem likely, however, that Khurāsān possessed so many cities with more inhabitants than the Sung Chinese capital, Hang-chou, which as we saw is esti-

[1] The Mongol sound for Great Khan has been spelled a number of different ways, using the Latin alphabet: Chingiz Khān (as here), Chinggis or Chingis Khan, Jenghiz Khan, and Genghis Khan. [Ed.]

mated at about one million people. Moreover, not enough Islamic archaeology has been comprehensively undertaken to enable us to estimate population from the remains now on or under the ground. . . .

It is possible, indeed likely, that the great walled cities of Khurāsān had to find room at the last minute for large numbers of refugees from the countryside. This may be part of the explanation for the chroniclers' huge numbers. But it is no more a total solution than the glib assertion that "chroniclers always exaggerate." Very similar chroniclers reported the Saljūq invasions of the eleventh century, and if they indulged in exaggeration of its (admittedly much lesser) horrors, that exaggeration was kept within strict limits. On the other hand, the sorts of figures just quoted cannot be reproduced as though they were reliable statistics. Even if our chroniclers had been present at the massacres, how would they have been in a position to calculate the numbers involved? It seems more reasonable to regard these figures not as statistical information but as evidence of the state of mind created by the character of the Mongol invasion. The shock induced by the scale of the catastrophe had no precedent: hence these enormous figures. This must imply that the death and destruction which produced that shock had no precedent either. . . .

The Mongol Army

The Mongol Empire was the creation of military conquest, and it was military supremacy that sustained it. There may have been truth in the old Chinese saw that Yeh-lü Ch'u-ts'ai is said to have repeated to the Great Khān Ögedei: that although the empire had been conquered on horseback, it could not be ruled from horseback. But without the Mongol army, no amount of efficient administration would have kept the Mongol Empire in being. The army must therefore be regarded as the basic and most essential of imperial institutions.

The nature of nomadic society on the steppe was such that to speak of the Mongol army is really no more than to speak of the Mongol people in one of its natural aspects. For the whole of life was a process of military training. The same techniques that were necessary for survival in a herding and hunting environment were, with very little adaptation, those used in warfare.

This was particularly true of hunting. The Mongols mounted an annual expedition for the acquisition of meat to tide them through the hard Mongolian winter. This took the form of a *nerge,* a vast ring of hunters, which gradually contracted, driving the game before it. Any hunter who allowed an animal to escape from the ring, or who killed one before the appointed time, was punished. At the end the khān would loose the first arrow, and the slaughter would commence. A few "emaciated stragglers" would ultimately be spared. Juwaynī remarks that "war — with its killing, counting of the slain, and sparing of the survivors — is after the same fashion, and indeed analogous in every detail." . . .

Mongols learned to ride very young indeed; and a Mongol who could ride was a potential soldier. All male Mongol adults below the age of sixty were liable for military service. There was no such thing as a civilian. Juwaynī says that the Mongol army "is a peasantry in the dress of an army, of which, in time of need, all, from small to great, from those of high rank to those of low estate, are swordsmen, archers, or spearmen." The Mongol rulers therefore had available to them a cavalry force which could be speedily mobilised, was highly trained, and consisted in theory — and even to some extent in practice — of the entire adult male population.

Can this be part of the explanation of the enormous size — if we are to believe our sources — of the Mongol armies? It must certainly have been of great significance that the Mongols could mobilise so much greater a proportion of their manpower than was possible in the sedentary states that they invaded. Other explanations have been offered. Marco Polo took the view that more men were to hand because of the Asiatic custom of polygamy. According to him the result of this was that more children would be born than under a monogamous system — a somewhat dubious proposition if the ratio between the sexes was more or less equal. More plausibly it might be pointed out that the very manoeuvrability of the Mongol forces would incline their enemies to overestimate the numbers involved. The Mongols themselves were not above employing tricks to suggest that they were present in overwhelming strength. Each Mongol went on campaign with a string of several horses. The number quoted varies, but something of the order of five horses per man would seem not to have been unusual. The mounting of dummies on spare horses, a device sometimes used, could have the effect, on the battlefield, of multiplying the apparent size of the army and increasing the terror in the hearts of the enemy soldiers.

It is probably impossible to arrive at a really accurate estimate of the size of the Mongol army. The two most valuable figures in the sources are those that can be extracted from the *Secret History* and from the *Altan Debter,* via Rashīd al-Dīn. Both sources offer a detailed breakdown of the Mongol military formations at their respective dates, and it is possible that the totals may have some relation to reality. The *Secret History*'s figures refer to the army at the time of the *quriltai*[2] of

[2] An assembly of Mongol princes or tribal leaders; the *quriltai* of 1206 elected or acclaimed Temujin (sometimes written as Temuchin) as Chingiz Khān and set on a plan to conquer China. [Ed.]

1206, and seem to suggest an army of around 105,000 men. Rashīd al-Dīn is concerned with the forces inherited by Chingiz Khān's sons at his death in 1227. According to him the size of the army in Mongolia proper was 129,000 men.

Chroniclers writing from outside the Mongol Empire tend to quote much higher figures. Jūzjānī variously reports Chingiz Khān's army that attacked the Khwārazm-shāh as being 700,000 or 800,000 strong. The Mamlūk fourteenth-century writer al-'Umarī estimated the number of soldiers on the registers of the Ilkhanate in his day at 200,000 to 300,000. He says that an army from the Golden Horde that invaded Transoxania around the end of the thirteenth century consisted of 250,000 men, each having not only five horses but also two slaves, a weapon wagon, and thirty head of sheep and goats.

It does not seem likely that such figures should be treated literally, though it is only fair to point out that some scholars think that they should. If Chingiz Khān's army in around 1220 was indeed 800,000 strong, and if for the sake of argument al-'Umari's remarks are taken as representing some kind of norm, then theoretically some four million horses, to say nothing of twenty-four million sheep and goats, may have been on the move through Transoxania and Khurāsān. The Mongols certainly developed considerable expertise in solving logistical problems, as Juwaynī's account of the elaborate arrangements made by Hülegü for the supply of his army shows. But however efficient the sturdy Mongol horse may have been at feeding itself in the most unpromising circumstances, it is hard to believe that eastern Persia could have sustained an influx of animals on anything remotely approaching this scale. . . . It is the character rather than the size of the Mongol army that is crucial.

The best-known fact about the Mongols' military administration is that they organised their forces according to a decimal system, with units of ten, one hundred, one thousand, and ten thousand. Of these the *tümen* of ten thousand was the major fighting unit, but the individual Mongol trooper would probably identify most readily with his thousand. This may be illustrated in the name "Hazāra," that of a people of central Afghanistan, Persian-speaking but with a very Mongolian look about it, and which is thought to descend from Mongol military settlers. *Hazāra* is Persian for one thousand. . . .

Although the succession to the Mongol Great Khanate and to the various successor khanates was contested frequently and more often than not bloodily, there is one very striking fact about such contests: No candidates appear to have been considered except for properly authenticated descendants of Chingiz Khān. There was no attempt to set up an alternative ruling house of, say, Kerait or Tatar origin. This is presumably to be explained partly in terms of the almost sacred prestige that accrued to the house of the founder of the empire. But it may be suspected that there was more to it than this, and that Chingiz Khān's radical reconstruction of the old tribal pattern in Mongolia provides the main explanation.

Chingiz Khān reorganised the whole Turko-Mongolian manpower of Mongolia into his new decimal military structure. Old tribal identities were not wholly ignored, and tribes which had been allies of the rising Chingiz retained at least some of their integrity as groupings: Hence there were Önggüt and Qonggirat thousand formations. But the "enemy" tribes — Tatars, Merkits, Keraits, Naimans and so forth — were broken up, and such of their men as had not been killed during the process of tribal unification were distributed among other units. So there were no Kerait *tümens* in existence that might have posed a threat to Mongol and Chingizid supremacy. Instead, Chingiz seems to have created what might be described as an artificial tribal system, in which old tribal loyalties were superseded by loyalty to the individual soldier's new military unit. Beyond that the Mongol royal house became the ultimate focus of obedience and allegiance.

Over and above the ordinary fighting formations, Chingiz Khān created an imperial guard (*keshig*). Its nucleus was his original and most faithful followers, the *nökers* of his early days of struggle. As time passed its functions multiplied, as did its numbers. By 1206 it was ten thousand strong. It was recruited across tribal boundaries, and membership was regarded as a supreme honour. The enlistment of highborn guards from all the tribes of Mongolia enabled Chingiz to treat his imperial guard corps as a useful form of honourable hostage taking. The guard in effect constituted Chingiz's household too, and as such provided the machinery and personnel through which the empire was administered in its early stages. Any trooper in the imperial guard took precedence, if necessary, even over a commander of a thousand in the army proper. The imperial guard formed the nursery of the new empire's ruling class.

Originally the Mongol soldier received no pay other than booty, which was divided up according to fixed principles. Military service was not regarded as a job. Indeed, the Mongol soldiers themselves paid contributions in kind, called *qūbchūr*, to their commanders for such purposes as the maintenance of poor or disabled troopers. However, this did not prove to be a workable system once the empire had ceased its rapid expansion and when plunder was no longer so readily available. Ultimately the Mongol troops in China were salaried, at least so far as the officers were concerned; and they were able to pass on their military offices to their heirs. In Persia the reforming Ilkhān Ghazan, after trying out various methods of providing for the Mongols' needs, attempted to meet the problem by utilising a traditional Persian device, the *iqṭā*ʿ, whereby the soldiers were allotted assignments of agricultural land, receiving the produce in lieu of salary.

In the first instance a cavalry force, the army consisted essentially of light cavalry archers, using the standard compound bow of the steppes, which was made of layers of horn and sinew on a wooden frame. This bow required a pull much stiffer than the English longbow, even though it was fired from horseback. It had impressive range and power of penetration. It was a very long time indeed before the hand gun could match the compound bow in range, penetration, or rate of fire; we should be wary of assuming that the invention of gunpowder immediately made the steppe archer obsolete. The Tatar archers of the Crimea were still campaigning successfully in eastern Europe in the seventeenth century. In addition to their light cavalry the Mongols also used some armoured heavy cavalry, equipped with lances. Both the Chinese and the Middle Easterners provided units of siege engineers.

It would not have been possible to conquer such enormous areas if the Mongol army proper had alone been available. From very early days, Chinese troops were used in large numbers, and the Sung Empire, with its vast walled cities, its numerous waterways, and its rice paddy fields, could hardly have been taken by any number of cavalry manoeuvres. Chinese forces were used mainly as infantry and as garrison troops once the conquest was completed. In Persia, similarly, native Persian troops were utilised for garrison duty and to guard passes. Ghazan is said to have organised them decimally.

A further use of non-Mongols was as a rather disagreeable tactical device. When prisoners were taken at the fall of a city they were compelled to undertake dangerous siege works, or were driven in front of the Mongol assault troops at the storming of the next city. The expectation was that the defenders would be reluctant to slaughter their own compatriots, or at least that casualties among the Mongols themselves would be minimised. Other tactics included encirclement (after the pattern of the hunt); the use of surprise, especially through appearing by an unexpected (sometimes a supposedly impossible) route; the efficient synchronisation of forces that were far apart; the ancient steppe device of the feigned flight, which could usually be counted on to work; and terror. Unlike many other Asiatic conquerors the Mongols did not generally indulge in wanton cruelty as such. Countless thousands of innocent people were killed, but normally this was done as quickly and efficiently as possible, without the use of torture.

Chingiz's principle seems to have been much the same as President Truman's over Hiroshima and Nagasaki. The apparent rationale was that if the population of one city was subjected to a frightful massacre, the next city would be more likely to surrender without resistance, thus avoiding unnecessary Mongol casualties. The morality of this approach to warfare is no doubt open to discussion, but there can be no disputing that it worked. The Mongols' policy was that any city which surrendered without fighting would be spared, but that those who caused the Mongol army to suffer casualties could expect no mercy. The Mongols usually kept their word, and the message, to judge from the number of cities that did surrender on demand, seems speedily to have spread. . . .

74

From *The Secret History of the Mongols*

This Mongol account records the early years of Mongol expansion under Chingis Khan, the founder of the empire. Born Temujin in 1155 or 1167, the young son of a minor tribal chieftain attracted the support of Mongol princes in the years between 1187 and 1206 through a series of decisive military victories over other tribes and competing Mongol claimants to the title of Great Khan.

The Mongols were illiterate before the time of Chingis Khan, who adopted the script of the Uighurs, one of the more literate peoples of the steppe. Thus the *Secret History* was written in Mongolian with Uighur letters. The only version that has survived is a fourteenth-century Chinese translation (in which Chinese characters were used phonetically, to represent Uighur sounds for Mongol words). The author is unknown, but the book provides detailed accounts of the early years of Temujin and ends with the reign of his son and successor, Ogodai, in 1228 — only a year after his father's death.

Because so much about the Mongols was written by their literate enemies, *The Secret History* is an invaluable resource: It is clearly an "insider's" account of the early years of Mongol expansion. While it includes mythic elements — it begins with the augury of the birth of a blue wolf to introduce Chingis Khan — *The Secret History* is, without doubt, an authentic representation of a Mongol point of view.

In this selection, you will read four passages. The first describes a meeting in about 1187 of several tribal leaders who agree that the twenty-year-old Temujin should become Great Khan (Chingis Khan).

Adapted by K. Reilly from R. P. Lister, *Genghis Khan* (New York: Barnes & Noble, 1993), 99–100, 136–39, 166–76, 191–93. While this volume is a retelling of the almost indecipherable *The Secret History of the Mongols* in Lister's own words, the selections that follow simplify without contextualizing or explaining the original work. More scholarly editions, trans. and ed. Francis Woodman Cleaves (Cambridge: Harvard University Press, 1982) and Paul Kahn (San Francisco: North Point Press, 1984) are less accessible.

What do these tribal leaders expect to gain from this alliance under Temujin? What do they offer in return?

The second passage deals with an early Mongol victory in 1202 over the neighboring Tatars, a tribe that Europeans often confused with the Mongols. How merciful or harsh does Chingis Khan seem? The defeat of the Tatars leads directly to a story of two sisters. What does this story tell you about Mongol customs?

The third passage recounts the story of an important Mongol victory over the Naiman in 1204. What does this section tell you about the sources of Mongol military strength?

The fourth passage concerns Temujin's brother, Kasar, and his mother, Hoelun. What does this scene suggest about the power of women in Mongol society?

How does this "insider's" view of the Mongols provide unique information or a perspective that would be unattainable from non-Mongols?

Thinking Historically

What moral values does this selection reveal? From what you can tell from this source, do the Mongols seem to think of themselves as "moral" people? Does the author-historian seem interested in describing what happened objectively, or in presenting an unblemished, sanitized view?

In what ways does this written Mongol history make you more sympathetic to the Mongols? Notice that the "Mongols Conquer the Naiman" passage begins with a Naiman account of the Mongols. How fair does the Mongol author seem to be toward the Naiman? Would this be a good source for understanding the Naiman? Do you think the Mongol authors described the Naiman more accurately than Chinese or Europeans described the Mongols?

The Choosing of the Khan

. . . A general council of all the chieftains was called, and the three most notable men among them, Prince Altan, Khuchar, and Sacha Beki, came forward. They addressed Temujin formally, in the following manner:

We will make you Khan; you shall ride at our head, against our foes.
We will throw ourselves like lightning on your enemies;
We will bring you their finest women and girls, their rich tents like palaces.
From all the peoples and nations we will bring you the fair girls and the high-stepping horses;

When you hunt wild beasts, we will drive them towards you; we will encircle them, pressing hard at their heels.

If on the day of battle we disobey you,
Take our flocks from us, our women and children, and cast our worthless heads on the steppe.
If in times of peace we disobey you,
Part us from our men and our servants, our wives and our sons;
Abandon us and cast us out, masterless, on the forsaken earth. . . .

Mongol Conquest of Tatars

. . . Temujin came up against the Tatars at Dalan Namurgas, on the Khalkha, east of Buir Nor, and defeated them in battle. They fell back; the Mongol armies pursued them, slaying and capturing them in large numbers.

The princes, Altan, Khuchar, and Daritai, were less assiduous in the pursuit. Finding a great number of animals roaming the steppes in the absence of their Tatar owners, they followed the usual custom of rounding them up, and collecting anything that took their fancy in the abandoned Tatar camps.

Temujin, having issued a clear order [against looting], could not tolerate their disobedience. He detached portions of his army, placed them under the command of Jebe and Khubilai, and sent them off after the disobedient princes, with orders to take away from them everything they had captured. The outcome was what might have been expected. Prince Altan and Khuchar, retiring in haste with as much of their booty as they could take with them, departed from their allegiance to him. They re-established themselves as independent chieftains, entering into such arrangements with Ong Khan, Jamukha, and other rulers as seemed desirable.

Daritai, however, seeing a little more clearly than the others, submitted to having his booty taken away from him.

Owing to his determined pursuit of the Tatars, Temujin found that he had a very considerable number of Tatar prisoners. They were kept under guard in the Mongol camp, and for the most part they were not greatly perturbed by their situation. Some of the chieftains might expect to be executed, but the lesser men had a reasonable hope of surviving. Some might have to serve as warriors under the Mongols, or even be enslaved, but a slave of talents could always hope to become a warrior again.

Temujin held a council to decide what to do with them. It was a great matter, and nobody was present at this council but his own family. The Khan's intention [was] to wipe out his enemies on a large scale. . . .

Belgutai had . . . made friends among the Tatar prisoners. One of these was Yeke Charan, the principal Tatar leader. . . . When Yeke Charan asked him what decision the family council had come to, Belgutai did not hesitate to tell him.

"We agreed to measure you against the linchpin,"[1] he said.

Yeke Charan told his fellow prisoners of the Khan's decision. Having nothing to lose, they rose up against their guards and fought their way out of the camp, taking with them what weapons they could seize. They gathered themselves together on a hilltop in a tight formation of fierce warriors. Men who are going to be killed whatever happens, and know it, fight well. The destruction of the Tatars, which was in due course accomplished, cost many Mongol lives.

Temujin was remarkably lenient towards Belgutai.

"Because Belgutai revealed the decision of the family council," he said, "Our army suffered great losses. From now on, Belgutai will take no part in the council. While it is being held, he will remain outside, keeping order in the camp, and he will sit in judgment during that time over the quarrelsome, the thieves, and the liars. When the council is finished and the wine is all drunk, then Belgutai can come in."

He ordered at the same time that Daritai should be banned from the family councils, for disobeying his *yasakh*.[2]

The Khan acquired a new woman from among these Tatars. She was Yesugen, the daughter of the chieftain Yeke Charan. He found her pleasing, and treated her with favour. Yesugen was wise enough not to quarrel unduly with fate, which had ungently disposed of her father, but provided her with some measure of fortune herself.

While they were still in the Tatar country, she said to Temujin: "The Khan, showing favour towards me, takes care of me well and provides me with goods and servants. But I have an elder sister, Yesui, who would please the Khan even more than I. She is married; Yeke Charan acquired a son-in-law, who came to live with her. But at present, in this dispersion of the people, I do not know where they have gone."

Temujin . . . [said]:

"If your elder sister is even more beautiful than you are, I will send men in search of her. But if she comes, will you give up your place to her?"

"If the Khan pleases, as soon as I see my elder sister, I will give up my place to her."

[1] This was a not unknown procedure, though it had never been applied on quite such a vast scale. Prisoners were led past the wheel of a wagon. Those who were taller than the linchpin were beheaded; the children, who were smaller, survived to be taken into the Mongol armies when they grew up.

[2] Order, law.

Temujin gave the order that Yesui must be searched for; and the warriors found her hiding in the forest, with the son-in-law who had been given to her. The husband fled, but the lady Yesui was brought in.

Yesugen, as soon as she saw her elder sister, rose, made her sit on the seat she had lately occupied, and herself took a seat lower down. . . .

One day the Khan was sitting outside the tent, drinking with some friends. He sat between the lady Yesui and the lady Yesugen; and he heard the lady Yesui suddenly catch her breath. Temujin said nothing to her; but after reflecting for a time he called the princes Bo'orchu and Mukhali to him and said: "Have all the people here divide themselves up into their clans. If any find a man with them who is not of their clan, let them set him aside."

When the people were arranged, clan by clan, a young man, good-looking and alert, was standing apart from all the clansmen. When they asked him who he was, he replied: "I am the son-in-law of Yeke Charan the Tatar, to whom was given his daughter Yesui. When we were surprised by the enemy, I was frightened, and escaped; then I came here, telling myself that it would be safe here. In the middle of so many people, how should I be recognised as a stranger?"

When these words were reported to the Khan, he said: "He was already an enemy; he is now a masterless man. What has he come to spy on us for? We have measured people of his kind against the linchpin of a wagon wheel. There is no need for any further investigation. Take him out of my sight."

They cut the young man's head off immediately. . . .

Mongols Conquer the Naiman

When the news was brought to Tayang Khan that someone claiming to be Ong Khan had been slain at the Neikun watercourse, his mother, Gurbesu, said: "Ong Khan was the great Khan of former days. Bring his head here! If it is really he, we will sacrifice to him."

She sent a message to Khorisu, commanding him to cut the head off and bring it in. When it was brought to her, she recognised it as that of Ong Khan. She placed it on a white cloth, and her daughter-in-law carried out the appropriate rites. . . . A wine-feast was held and stringed instruments were played. Gurbesu, taking up a drinking-bowl, made an offering to the head of Ong Khan.

When the sacrifice was made to it, the head grinned.

"He laughs!" Tayang Khan cried. Overcome by religious awe, he flung the head on the floor and trampled on it until it was mangled beyond recognition.

The great general Kokse'u Sabrakh was present at these ceremonies, and observed them without enthusiasm. It was he who had been the only Naiman general to offer resistance to Temujin and Ong Khan on their expedition against Tayang Khan's brother Buyiruk.

"First of all," he remarked, "you cut off the head of a dead ruler, and then you trample it into the dust. What kind of behaviour is this? Listen to the baying of those dogs: It has an evil sound. The Khan your father, Inancha Bilgei, once said: 'My wife is young, and I, her husband, am old. Only the power of prayer has enabled me to beget my son, this same Tayang. But will my son, born a weakling, be able to guard and hold fast my common and evil-minded people?'

"Now the baying of the dogs seems to announce that some disaster is at hand. The rule of our queen, Gurbesu, is firm; but you, my Khan, Torlukh Tayang, are weak. It is truly said of you that you have no thought for anything but the two activities of hawking and driving game, and no capacity for anything but these."

Tayang Khan was accustomed to the disrespect of his powerful general, but he was stung into making a rash decision.

"There are a few Mongols in the east. From the earliest days this old and great Ong Khan feared them, with their quivers; now they have made war on him and driven him to death. No doubt they would like to be rulers themselves. There are indeed in Heaven two shining lights, the sun and the moon, and both can exist there; but how can there be two rulers here on earth? Let us go and gather those Mongols in."

His mother Gurbesu said: "Why should we start making trouble with them? The Mongols have a bad smell; they wear black clothes. They are far away, out there; let them stay there. Though it is true," she added, "that we could have the daughters of their chieftains brought here; when we had washed their hands and feet, they could milk our cows and sheep for us."

Tayang Khan said: "What is there so terrible about them? Let us go to these Mongols and take away their quivers."

"What big words you are speaking," Kokse'u Sabrakh said. "Is Tayang Khan the right man for it? Let us keep the peace."

Despite these warnings, Tayang Khan decided to attack the Mongols. It was a justifiable decision; his armies were stronger, but time was on Temujin's side. Tayang sought allies, sending a messenger to Alakhu Shidigichuri of the Onggut, in the south, the guardians of the ramparts between Qashin and the Khingan. "I am told that there are a few Mongols in the east," he said. "Be my right hand! I will ride against them from here, and we will take their quivers away from them."

[Alakhu Shidigichuri's] reply was brief: "I cannot be your right hand." He in his turn sent a message to Temujin. "Tayang Khan of the Naiman wants to come and take away your quivers. He sent to me and asked me to be his right hand. I refused. I make you aware of this, so that when he comes your quivers will not be taken away."[3]

When he received Alakhu's message Temujin, having wintered near Guralgu, was holding one of his . . . roundups of game on the camel-steppes of Tulkinche'ut, in the east. The beasts had been encircled by the clansmen and warriors; the chieftains were gathered together, about to begin the great hunt.

"What shall we do now?" some of them said to each other. "Our horses are lean at this season."

. . . The snow had only lately left the steppe; the horses had found nothing to graze on during these recent months. Their ribs stuck out and they lacked strength.

The Khan's youngest brother, Temuga, spoke up. . . .

"How can that serve as an excuse," he said, "that the horses are lean? My horses are quite fat enough. How can we stay sitting here, when we receive a message like that?"

Prince Belgutai spoke. . . .

"If a man allows his quivers to be taken away during his lifetime, what kind of an existence does he have? For a man who is born a man, it is a good enough end to be slain by another man, and lie on the steppe with his quiver and bow beside him. The Naiman make fine speeches, with their many men and their great kingdom. But suppose, having heard their fine speeches, we ride against them, would it be so difficult to take their quivers away from them? We must mount and ride; it is the only thing to do."

Temujin was wholly disposed to agree with these sentiments. He broke off the hunt, set the army in motion, and camped near Ornu'u on the Khalkha. Here he paused for a time while he carried out a swift reorganisation of the army. A count was held of the people; they were divided up into thousands, hundreds, and tens, and commanders of these units were appointed. Also at this time he chose his personal bodyguards, the seventy day-guards and eighty night-guards. . . .

Having reorganised the army, he marched away from the mountainside of Ornu'u on the Khalkha, and took the way of war against the Naiman.

The spring of the Year of the Rat [1204] was by now well advanced. During this westward march came the Day of the Red Disc, the sixteenth day of the first moon of summer. On this day, the moon being at the full, the Khan caused the great yak's-tail banner to be consecrated, letting it be sprinkled with fermented mare's milk, with the proper observances.

[3] Temujin, grateful for this warning, sent him five hundred horses and a thousand sheep. His friendship with Alakhu was valuable to him at a later time.

They continued the march up the Kerulen, with Jebe and Khubilai in the van. When they came on to the Saari steppes, they met with the first scouts of the Naiman. There were a few skirmishes between the Naiman and Mongol scouts; in one of these, a Mongol scout was captured, a man riding a grey horse with a worn saddle. The Naiman studied this horse with critical eyes, and thought little of it. "The Mongols' horses are inordinately lean," they said to each other.

The Mongol army rode out on to the Saari steppes, and began to deploy themselves for the forthcoming battle. . . . Dodai Cherbi, one of the newly appointed captains, put a proposal before the Khan.

"We are short in numbers compared to the enemy; besides this, we are exhausted after the long march, our horses in particular. It would be a good idea to settle in this camp, so that our horses can graze on the steppe, until they have had as much to eat as they need. Meanwhile, we can deceive the enemy by making puppets and lighting innumerable fires. For every man, we will make at least one puppet, and we will burn fires in five places. It is said that the Naiman people are very numerous, but it is rumoured also that their king is a weakling, who has never left his tents. If we keep them in a state of uncertainty about our numbers, with our puppets and our fires, our geldings can stuff themselves till they are fat."

The suggestion pleased Temujin, who had the order passed on to the soldiers to light fires immediately. Puppets were constructed and placed all over the steppe, some sitting or lying by the fires, some of them even mounted on horses.

At night, the watchers of the Naiman saw, from the flanks of the mountain, fires twinkling all over the steppe. They said to each other: "Did they not say that the Mongols were very few? Yet they have more fires than there are stars in Heaven."

Having previously sent to Tayang Khan news of the lean grey horse with the shabby saddle, they now sent him the message: "The warriors of the Mongols are camped out all over the Saari steppes. They seem to grow more numerous every day; their fires outnumber the stars."

When this news was brought to him from the scouts, Tayang Khan was at the watercourse of Khachir. He sent a message to his son Guchuluk.

"I am told that the geldings of the Mongols are lean, but the Mongols are, it seems, numerous. Once we start fighting them, it will be difficult to draw back. They are such hard warriors that when several men at once come up against one of them, he does not move an eyelid; even if he is wounded, so that the black blood flows out, he does not flinch. I do not know whether it is a good thing to come up against such men.

"I suggest that we should assemble our people and lead them back to the west, across the Altai; and all the time, during this retreat, we will fight off the Mongols as dogs do, by running in on them from either side as they advance. Our geldings are too fat; in this march we shall make them lean and fit. But the Mongols' lean geldings will be brought to such a state of exhaustion they will vomit in the Mongols' faces."

On receiving this message, Guchuluk Khan, who was more warlike than his father, said: "That woman Tayang has lost all his courage, to speak such words. Where does this great multitude of Mongols come from? Most of the Mongols are with Jamukha, who is here with us. Tayang speaks like this because fear has overcome him. He has never been farther from his tent than his pregnant wife goes to urinate. He has never dared to go so far as the inner pastures where the knee-high calves are kept." So he expressed himself on the subject of his father, in the most injurious and wounding terms.

When he heard these words, Tayang Khan said: "I hope the pride of this powerful Guchuluk will not weaken on the day when the clash of arms is heard and the slaughter begins. Because once we are committed to battle against the foe, it will be hard to disengage again."

Khorisu Beki, a general who commanded under Tayang Khan, said: "Your father, Inancha Bilgei, never showed the back of a man or the haunch of a horse to opponents who were just as worthy as these. How can you lose your courage so early in the day? We would have done better to summon your mother Gurbesu to command over us. It is a pity that Kokse'u Sabrakh has grown too old to lead us. Our army's discipline has become lax. For the Mongols, their hour has come. It is finished! Tayang, you have failed us." He belted on his quiver and galloped off.

Tayang Khan grew angry. "All men must die," he said. "Their bodies must suffer. It is the same for all men. Let us fight, then."

So, having created doubt and dismay, and lost the support of some of his best leaders, he decided to give battle. He broke away from the watercourse of Khachir, marched down the Tamir, crossed the Orkhon and skirted the eastern flanks of the mountain Nakhu. When they came to Chakirma'ut, Temujin's scouts caught sight of them and brought back the message: "The Naiman are coming!"

The Battle of Chakirma'ut

When the news was brought to Temujin he said: "Sometimes too many men are just as big a handicap as too few."

Then he issued his general battle orders. "We will march in the order 'thick grass,' take up positions in the 'lake' battle order, and fight in the

[4] These were the names of various tactical disciplines in which he had drilled his army.

manner called 'gimlet.'"[4] He gave Kasar the command of the main army, and appointed Prince Otchigin to the command of the reserve horses, a special formation of great importance in Mongol warfare.

The Naiman, having advanced as far as Chakirma'ut, drew themselves up in a defensive position on the foothills of Nakhu, with the mountain behind them. . . . The Mongols forced their scouts back on to the forward lines, and then their forward lines back on to the main army, and drove tightly knit formations of horsemen again and again into the Naiman ranks. The Naiman, pressed back on themselves, could do nothing but retreat gradually up the mountain. Many of their men . . . hardly had the chance to fight at all, but were cut down in an immobile mass of men as soon as the Mongols reached them.

Tayang Khan, with his advisers, also retreated up the mountain as the day advanced. From the successive spurs to which they climbed, each one higher than the last, they could see the whole of this dreadful disaster as it took place below them.

Jamukha was with Tayang Khan. . . .

"Who are those people over there," Tayang Khan asked him, "who throw my warriors back as if they were sheep frightened by a wolf, who come huddling back to the sheepfold?"

Jamukha said: "My *anda*[5] Temujin has four hounds whom he brought up on human flesh, and kept in chains. They have brows of copper, snouts like chisels, tongues like bradawls, hearts of iron, and tails that cut like swords. They can live on dew, and ride like the wind. On the day of battle they eat the flesh of men. You see how, being set loose, they come forward slavering for joy. Those two are Jebe and Khubilai; those two are Jelmei and Subetai. That is who those four hounds are."

He pointed out to him also the Uru'ut and the Mangqut, who, as Tayang Khan remarked, seemed to bound like foals set loose in the morning, when, after their dams have suckled them, they frisk around her on the steppe. "They hunt down men who carry lances and swords," he said. "Having struck them down, they slay them, and rob them of all they possess. How joyful and boisterous they look, as they ride forward!"

"Who is it coming up there in the rear," Tayang Khan asked him, "who swoops down on our troops like a ravening falcon?"

"That is my *anda* Temujin. His entire body is made of sounding copper; there is no gap through which even a bodkin could penetrate. There he is, you see him? He advances like an eagle about to seize his prey. You said formerly that if you once set eyes on the Mongols you

[5] Sworn brother, blood brother, declared ally.

would not leave so much of them as the skin of a lamb's foot. What do you think of them now?"

By this time the chieftains were standing on a high spur. Below them, the great army of the Naiman, Jamukha's men with them, were retreating in confusion, fighting desperately as the Mongols hemmed them in.

"Who is that other chieftain," Tayang asked Jamukha, "who draws ever nearer us, in a dense crowd of men?"

"Mother Hoelun brought up one of her own sons on human flesh. He is nine feet tall; he eats a three-year-old cow every day. If he swallows an armed man whole, it makes no difference to his appetite. When he is roused to anger, and lets fly with one of his *angqu'a* [forked] arrows, it will go through ten or twenty men. His normal range is a thousand yards; when he draws his bow to its fullest extent, he shoots over eighteen hundred yards. He is mortal, but he is not like other mortals; he is more than a match for the serpents of Guralgu. He is called Kasar."

They were climbing high up the mountain now, to regroup below its summit. Tayang Khan saw a new figure among the Mongols.

"Who is that coming up from the rear?" he asked Jamukha.

"That is the youngest son of Mother Hoelun. He is called Otchigin [Odeigin] the Phlegmatic. He is one of those people who go to bed early and get up late. But when he is behind the army, with the reserves, he does not linger; he never comes too late to the battle lines."

"We will climb to the peak of the mountain," Tayang Khan said.

Jamukha, seeing that the battle was lost, slipped away to the rear and descended the mountain, with a small body of men. One of these he sent to Temujin with a message. "Say this to my *anda*. Tayang Khan, terrified by what I have told him, has completely lost his senses. He has retreated up the mountain as far as he can. He could be killed by one harsh word. Let my *anda* take note of this: They have climbed to the top of the mountain, and are in no state to defend themselves any more. I myself have left the Naiman."

Since the evening was drawing on, Temujin commanded his troops in the forefront of the attack to draw back. Bodies of men were sent forward on the wings, east and west, to encircle the summit of Mount Nakhu. There they stood to arms during the night. During the night, the Naiman army tried to break out of the encircling ring. Bodies of horsemen plunged down the mountainside in desperate charges; many fell and were trampled to death, the others were slain. In the first light they were seen lying about the mountain in droves, like fallen trees. Few were left defending the peak; they put up little resistance to the force sent up against them.

It is said that Tayang Khan, suddenly gaining courage when it was too late to be of any use to him, tried to fight his way out through the encircling army. When captured he was gravely wounded, and he died not long afterwards. His son Guchuluk Khan, though, was still at liberty; he tried to dig himself in on the Tamir, but was driven out of his entrenchments and took to flight with his attendants. . . .

After the battle of Chakirma'ut the Mongol clansmen who had been with Jamukha came over to Temujin. There were men of the Khadagin, the Salji'ut, the Durben, the Taijut, and the Onggirat amongst them.[6]

The mother of Tayang Khan, Gurbesu, was brought to him.

"Did you not say that the Mongols smelt badly?" he asked her. "If that is so, why have you come here?" He took her into his tents to serve him. . . .

Temujin, His Brother Kasar, and Their Mother Hoelun

. . . The seven sons of the thoughtful Father Munglik, the seven young princes of the Qongqotadai . . . having had some argument with Kasar . . . surrounded him and not only treated him with disrespect, but handled him roughly.

Kasar, aggrieved, went to complain to Temujin, expecting to be granted permission to take his revenge on the Qongqotadai; but Temujin had grown suspicious of his powerful brother, and heard him without sympathy. Kasar went away to sulk in his own tents.

Temujin himself stood in awe of Teb Tenggeri. Having fulfilled so many earthly ambitions, he was greatly concerned at this time, and during his later years, with the meaning of life, and the relation between men and the higher powers of Heaven.

Teb Tenggeri [the shaman] sought an audience with the Khan, and said to him: "The ruler of Heaven has sent me a prophecy, saying: 'At one time, Temujin shall have the realm in his hand; at another time, Kasar.' Who can say what will happen if you do not forestall Kasar in his ambition?"

[6] Among those captured on the mountaintop, the Mongols found an attendant of Tayang Khan who was no warrior, but in the absence of weapons carried at his belt a peculiar device whose purpose no one could readily understand. He was brought before the Khan, who questioned him at length. It appeared that he was an Uighur, by the name of Tatatonga, and what he carried was the seal of Tayang Khan, which he had hoped to deliver over to Guchuluk. Temujin approved of the Uighur's loyal attitude to his late rulers, and took both the man and the seal into his service.

It was this same Tatatonga who, by the command of the Khan, devised a form of letters which could be used for writing down the Mongol speech; the letters which were used thirty-six years later, under the great Khan Ogodai, to write down the history of the Mongols, at the seven domed hills on the Kerulen.

Temujin went with a bodyguard that night to ride to Kasar's tents. Kuchu and Kokochu, the first two boys, now men, that he had given to Hoelun, went to her and told her that the Khan had ridden to arrest Kasar.

Though it was nighttime, Hoelun had a white camel harnessed to a black covered wagon, and drove after the Khan to Kasar's tents.

She arrived there at sunrise. Temujin had had Kasar bound, and had taken away his cap and girdle, as a sign of his disgrace; he was about to try him. When Hoelun came storming into the camp, he trembled before her. She herself, in her rage, got down from the wagon, loosed Kasar's bonds, and gave him back his cap and belt.

She sat down with her legs folded under her, pulled out her ample breasts from her dress, spread them out on her knees and said: "Do you see these? They are the breasts from which you sucked. You, who, as the proverb says, gnawed your own afterbirth, tore your own umbilical cord!

"What has Kasar done? When I nursed you, Temujin, you drained one of my breasts. Khaji'un and Otchigin together could only drain one of them. Kasar, though, drained them both, and gave me peace. He emptied my breasts, and I was free!

"My cunning Temujin received the gift of the spirit. Kasar received strength, and skill in shooting with the bow. He brought under your dominion those who sought to escape from it; he shot down those who sought to flee. Now, when your enemies have been brought to their end, you wish to look on Kasar no more."

Temujin said: "When my mother is angered against me, I am terrified. I am ashamed of myself. Let us go back to the camp."

They returned to the tents, and peace was made. But the Khan was still full of mistrust. Without letting Hoelun know of it, he took away many of Kasar's men, leaving him with a diminished retinue of only fourteen hundred followers. When Hoelun came to know of this, she took it so much to heart that her strength failed, and age and death came rapidly down on her. . . .

75

JOHN OF PLANO CARPINI

From History of the Mongols

Chingis Khan united the tribes of the steppe and conquered northern China, capturing Peking by 1215. He then turned his armies against the West, conquering the tribes of Turkestan and the Khorezmian Empire, the great Muslim power of central Asia, by 1222. The following year he chased Khorezmian troops into northern India, while sending an army around the Caspian Sea into Russia. In 1226, he turned again to the East, subduing and destroying the kingdom of Tibet before he died in 1227. One historian, Christopher Dawson, summarizes the career of Chingis Khan this way:

> In spite of the primitive means at his disposal, it is possible that [Chingis Khan] succeeded in destroying a larger portion of the human race than any modern expert in total warfare. Within a dozen years from the opening of his campaign against China, the Mongol armies had reached the Pacific, the Indus, and the Black Sea, and had destroyed many of the great cities in India. For Europe especially, the shock was overwhelming.

European fears intensified in 1237 as the principal Mongol armies under Batu Khan systematically destroyed one Russian city after another. In April 1241, one Mongol army destroyed a combined force of Polish and German armies, while another defeated the Hungarian army and threatened Austria. Only the death and funeral of Ogedai (r. 1229–41), the second Great Khan, provided relief, because Batu Khan returned to Mongolia for the funeral, leaving his troops at their headquarters in Russia.

At the time no one could have known that future Mongol pressure would be brought against the Muslim Middle East rather than the Christian West. Pope Innocent IV sent a mission to the Mongols in 1245, trying to accomplish such a shift and to learn as much as possible about Mongol intentions. For this important task, he sent two Franciscan monks — one of whom was John of Plano Carpini — with two letters addressed to the Emperor of the Tartars (a compounded error that changed the Tatars, the Mongols' enemy, into the denizens

---

John of Plano Carpini, "History of the Mongols," in *Mission to Asia: Narratives and Letters of the Franciscan Missionaries in Mongolia and China in the Thirteenth and Fourteenth Centuries*, trans. a nun of Stanbrook Abbey, ed. Christopher Dawson (1955; reprint, New York: Harper & Row, 1966), 60–69.

of Tartarus, or Hell). In May, the barefoot sixty-five-year-old Friar John reached Batu's camp on the Volga River, from which he was relayed to Mongolia by five fresh horses a day in order to reach the capital at Karakorum in time for the installation of the third Great Khan, Guyuk (r. 1246–48) in July and August.

In this selection from his *History of the Mongols,* John writes of his arrival in Mongolia for the installation of Guyuk (here written as Cuyuk). In what ways does John's account change or expand your understanding of the Mongols? Was John a good observer? In what ways does he compensate for his ignorance (as an outside observer) of Mongol society and culture? In what ways does he remain a victim of his outsider status?

Thinking Historically

What explicit moral judgments does John make about the Mongols? What moral judgments does he merely assume? Does his account change your own opinion of the Mongols? If so, how? Is your own moral judgment of the Mongols important to you? How is it related to your historical understanding?

. . . On our arrival Cuyuc had us given a tent and provisions, such as it is the custom for the Tartars to give, but they treated us better than other envoys. Nevertheless we were not invited to visit him for he had not yet been elected, nor did he yet concern himself with the government. The translation of the Lord Pope's letter, however, and the things I had said had been sent to him by Bati. After we had stayed there for five or six days he sent us to his mother where the solemn court was assembling. By the time we got there a large pavilion had already been put up made of white velvet, and in my opinion it was so big that more than two thousand men could have got into it. Around it had been erected a wooden palisade, on which various designs were painted. On the second or third day we went with the Tartars who had been appointed to look after us and there all the chiefs were assembled and each one was riding with his followers among the hills and over the plains round about.

On the first day they were all clothed in white velvet, on the second in red — that day Cuyuc came to the tent — on the third day they were all in blue velvet, and on the fourth in the finest brocade. In the palisade round the pavilion were two large gates, through one of which the Emperor alone had the right to enter and there were no guards placed at it although it was open, for no one dare enter or leave by it; through the other gate all those who were granted admittance entered and there were guards there with swords and bows and arrows. If anyone approached the tent beyond the fixed limits, he was beaten if caught; if he ran away he was shot at, but with arrows however which had no heads. The horses were, I suppose, two arrow-flights away. The chiefs went about everywhere armed and accompanied by a number of their men, but none, unless their group of ten was complete, could go as far as the horses; indeed those who attempted to do so were severely beaten. There were many of them who had, as far as I could judge, about twenty marks' worth of gold on their bits, breastplates, saddles, and cruppers. The chiefs held their conference inside the tent and, so I believe, conducted the election. All the other people however were a long way away outside the aforementioned palisade. There they remained until almost midday and then they began to drink mare's milk and they drank until the evening, so much that it was amazing to see. We were invited inside and they gave us mead as we would not take mare's milk. They did this to show us great honour, but they kept on plying us with drinks to such an extent that we could not possibly stand it, not being used to it, so we gave them to understand that it was disagreeable to us and they left off pressing us.

Outside were Duke Jerozlaus of Susdal in Russia and several chiefs of the Kitayans and Solangi, also two sons of the King of Georgia, the ambassador of the Caliph of Baghdad, who was a Sultan, and more than ten other Sultans of the Saracens, so I believe and so we were told by the stewards. There were more than four thousand envoys there, counting those who were carrying tribute, those who were bringing gifts, the Sultans and other chiefs who were coming to submit to them, those summoned by the Tartars and the governors of territories. All these were put together outside the palisade and they were given drinks at the same time, but when we were outside with them we and Duke Jerozlaus were always given the best places. I think, if I remember rightly, that we had been there a good four weeks when, as I believe, the election took place; the result however was not made public at that time; the chief ground for my supposition was that whenever Cuyuc left the tent they sang before him and as long as he remained outside they dipped to him beautiful rods on the top of which was scarlet wool, which they did not do for any of the other chiefs. They call this court the Sira Orda.

Leaving there we rode all together for three or four leagues to another place, where on a pleasant plain near a river among the mountains another tent had been set up, which is called by them the Golden Orda, it was here that Cuyuc was to be enthroned on the feast of the Assumption of Our Lady. . . .

At that place we were summoned into the presence of the Emperor, and Chingay the protonotary wrote down our names and the names of those who had sent us, also the names of the chief of the Solangi and of others, and then calling out in a loud voice he recited them before the Emperor and all the chiefs. When this was finished each one of us genuflected four times on the left knee and they warned us not to touch the lower part of the threshold. After we had been most thoroughly searched for knives and they had found nothing at all, we entered by a door on the east side, for no one dare enter from the west with the sole exception of the Emperor or, if it is a chief's tent, the chief; those of lower rank do not pay much attention to such things. This was the first time since Cuyuc had been made Emperor that we had entered his tent in his presence. He also received all the envoys in that place, but very few entered his tent.

So many gifts were bestowed by the envoys there that it was marvellous to behold — gifts of silk, samite, velvet, brocade, girdles of silk threaded with gold, choice furs, and other presents. The Emperor was also given a sunshade or little awning such as is carried over his head, and it was all decorated with precious stones. . . .

Leaving there we went to another place where a wonderful tent had been set up all of red velvet, and this had been given by the Kitayans; there also we were taken inside. Whenever we went in we were given mead and wine to drink, and cooked meat was offered us if we wished to have it. A lofty platform of boards had been erected, on which the Emperor's throne was placed. The throne, which was of ivory, was wonderfully carved and there was also gold on it, and precious stones, if I remember rightly, and pearls. Steps led up to it and it was rounded behind. Benches were also placed round the throne, and here the ladies sat in their seats on the left; nobody, however, sat on the right, but the chiefs were on benches in the middle and the rest of the people sat beyond them. Every day a great crowd of ladies came.

The three tents of which I have spoken were very large. The Emperor's wives however had other tents of white felt, which were quite big and beautiful. At that place they separated, the Emperor's mother going in one direction and the Emperor in another to administer justice. The mistress of the Emperor had been arrested; she had murdered his father with poison at the time when their army was in Hungary and as a result the army in these parts retreated. Judgment was passed on her along with a number of others and they were put to death. . . .

After the death of Jerozlaus, if I remember the time correctly, our Tartars took us to the Emperor. When he heard from them that we had come to him he ordered us to go back to his mother, the reason being that he wished on the following day to raise his banner against the whole of the Western world — we were told this definitely by men who knew . . . — and he wanted us to be kept in ignorance of this. On our return we stayed for a few days, then we went back to him again and remained with him for a good month, enduring such hunger and thirst that we could scarcely keep alive, for the food provided for four was barely sufficient for one, moreover, we were unable to find anything to buy, for the market was a very long way off. If the Lord had not sent us a certain Russian, by name Cosmas, a goldsmith and a great favourite of the Emperor, who supported us to some extent, we would, I believe, have died, unless the Lord had helped us in some other way.

Before the enthronement Cosmas showed us the Emperor's throne which he himself had made and his seal which he had fashioned, and he also told us what the inscription was on the seal. We picked up many other bits of private information about the Emperor from men who had come with other chiefs, a number of Russians and Hungarians knowing Latin and French, and Russian clerics and others, who had been among the Tartars, some for thirty years, through wars and other happenings, and who knew all about them, for they knew the language and had lived with them continually some twenty years, others ten, some more, some less. With the help of these men we were able to gain a thorough knowledge of everything. They told us about everything willingly and sometimes without being asked, for they knew what we wanted.

After this the Emperor sent for us, and through Chingay his protonotary told us to write down what we had to say and our business, and give it to him, We did this and wrote out for him all that we said earlier to Bati. . . . A few days passed by; then he had us summoned again and told us through Kadac, the procurator of the whole empire, in the presence of Bala and Chingay his protonotaries and many other scribes, to say all we had to say: We did this willingly and gladly. Our interpreter on this as on the previous occasion was Temer, a knight of Jerozlaus': and there were also present a cleric who was with him and another cleric who was with the Emperor. On this occasion we were asked if there were any people with the Lord Pope who understood the writing of the Russians or Saracens or even of the Tartars. We gave answer that we used neither the Ruthenian nor Saracen writing; there were however Saracens in the country but they were a long way from the Lord Pope; but we said that it seemed to us that the most expedient course would be for them to write in Tartar and translate it for us, and we would write it down carefully in our own script and we would take both the letter and the translation to the Lord Pope. Thereupon they left us to go to the Emperor.

On St. Martin's day we were again summoned, and Kadac, Chingay, and Bala, the aforementioned secretaries, came to us and translated the letter for us word by word. When we had written it in Latin, they had it translated so that they might hear a phrase at a time, for they wanted to know if we had made a mistake in any word. When both letters were written, they made us read it once and a second time in case we had left out anything, and they said to us: "See that you clearly understand everything, for it would be inconvenient if you did not understand everything, seeing you have to travel to such far-distant lands." When we replied "We understand everything clearly," they wrote the letter once again in Saracenic, in case anyone should be found in those parts who could read it, if the Lord Pope so wished.

It is the custom for the Emperor of the Tartars never to speak to a foreigner, however important he may be, except through an intermediary, and he listens and gives his answer, also through the intermediary. Whenever his subjects have any business to bring before Kadac, or while they are listening to the Emperor's reply, they stay on their knees until the end of the conversation, however important they may be. It is not possible nor indeed is it the custom for anyone to say anything about any matter after the Emperor has declared his decision. This Emperor not only has a procurator and protonotaries and secretaries, but all officials for dealing with both public and private matters, except that he has no advocates, for everything is settled according to the decision of the Emperor without the turmoil of legal trials. The other princes of the Tartars do the same in those matters concerning them.

The present Emperor may be forty or forty-five years old or more; he is of medium height, very intelligent, and extremely shrewd, and most serious and grave in his manner. He is never seen to laugh for a slight cause nor to indulge in any frivolity, so we were told by the Christians who are constantly with him. The Christians of his household also told us that they firmly believed he was about to become a Christian, and they have clear evidence of this, for he maintains Christian clerics and provides them with supplies of Christian things; in addition he always has a chapel before his chief tent and they sing openly and in public and beat the board for services after the Greek fashion like other Christians, however big a crowd of Tartars or other men be there. The other chiefs do not behave like this.

According to our Tartars the Emperor proposed sending ambassadors with us, to accompany us. I think, however, that they wanted us to request him to do this, for one of our Tartars, the eldest, advised us to make this petition. But since it did not seem good to us that they should come, we told him it was not for us to do the asking, but if the Emperor by his own desire should send them, we would by the help of God conduct them safely. There were several reasons why it did not seem expedient to us that they should come. In the first place we were afraid lest, seeing the dissensions and wars which are rife among us, they might be all the more encouraged to attack us. The second reason was that we feared that their real purpose might be to spy out the land. The third reason was that we were apprehensive that they might be killed, for our people are for the most part arrogant and proud. When at the request of the Cardinal, who is legate in Germany, the servants with us went to him wearing Tartar costume, they were very nearly stoned by the Germans on the way and obliged to take off the costume.

Now it is the custom of the Tartars never to make peace with men who kill their envoys, until they have taken vengeance on them.

The fourth reason is that we were afraid they might be taken from us by force, as happened on one occasion to a Saracen prince, who is still in captivity if he has not died. The fifth reason is that no good purpose would be served by their coming, since they would have no other mandate or authority than that of taking to the Lord Pope and to the other princes the letters which we had; and we believed that this might have harmful consequences. For these reasons we were not in favour of their coming.

Two days later, that is to say on the feast of St. Brice [November 13th], they gave us a permit to depart and a letter sealed with the Emperor's seal, and sent us to the Emperor's mother. She gave each of us a fox-skin cloak, which had the fur outside and was lined inside, and a length of velvet; our Tartars stole a good yard from each of the pieces of velvet and from the piece given to our servant they stole more than half. This did not escape our notice, but we preferred not to make a fuss about it.

We then set out on the return journey. . . .

76

GUYUK KHAN

Letter to Pope Innocent IV

This is the letter to Pope Innocent IV that John of Plano Carpini refers to in the previous selection. This version of the letter comes from a brief narrative of the same trip by John's Polish companion, Brother Benedict the Pole. What is Guyuk Khan's message? Judging from this letter and the previous selection, what is the religion of the Mongols, and what is the status of Christianity among the Mongols?

From "Narrative of Brother Benedict the Pole," in *Mission to Asia: Narratives and Letters of the Franciscan Missionaries in Mongolia and China in the Thirteenth and Fourteenth Centuries,* trans. by a nun of Stanbrook Abbey and ed. Christopher Dawson (1955; reprint, New York: Harper & Row, 1966), 83–84.

Thinking Historically

How would you describe the moral tone of Guyuk's letter? In what ways is Guyuk's moral tone different from or similar to John's tone in the previous selection? Do moral issues prevent either Guyuk or Pope Innocent IV from understanding each other?

The Strength of God, the Emperor of All Men, to the Great Pope, Authentic and True Letters

Having taken counsel for making peace with us, You Pope and all Christians have sent an envoy to us, as we have heard from him and as your letters declare. Wherefore, if you wish to have peace with us, You Pope and all kings and potentates, in no way delay to come to me to make terms of peace and then you shall hear alike our answer and our will. The contents of your letters stated that we ought to be baptized and become Christians. To this we answer briefly that we do not understand in what way we ought to do this. To the rest of the contents of your letters, viz: that you wonder at so great a slaughter of men, especially of Christians and in particular Poles, Moravians, and Hungarians, we reply likewise that this also we do not understand. However, lest we may seem to pass it over in silence altogether, we give you this for our answer.

Because they did not obey the word of God and the command of Chingis Chan and the Chan, but took council to slay our envoys, therefore God ordered us to destroy them and gave them up into our hands. For otherwise if God had not done this, what could man do to man? But you men of the West believe that you alone are Christians and despise others. But how can you know to whom God deigns to confer His grace? But we worshipping God have destroyed the whole earth from the East to the West in the power of God. And if this were not the power of God, what could men have done? Therefore if you accept peace and are willing to surrender your fortresses to us, You Pope and Christian princes, in no way delay coming to me to conclude peace and then we shall know that you wish to have peace with us. But if you should not believe our letters and the command of God nor hearken to our counsel then we shall know for certain that you wish to have war. After that we do not know what will happen: God alone knows.

Chingis Chan, first Emperor, second Ochoday Chan, third Cuiuch Chan.

77

From The Journey of William of Rubrick

William of Rubrick, who is known only from this account of his travels to Mongolia eight years after John of Plano Carpini, was a younger man than John, probably a native of Flanders, and also a Franciscan friar.

In two main respects, William's mission was different from John's: First, in addition to having information about the earlier mission, William — as a resident of the Crusaders' city of Acre — was more in touch with Asia, more knowledgeable about the Mongols, and was able to have his letters of introduction translated into Persian and Syrian. Second, his mission was more religious than political, despite the fact that he went in the service of King Louis IX of France (called St. Louis) and not the Pope. The Crusading King Louis had learned that Batu Khan's son was a Christian, so he sent William to establish relations with Mongol Christians. William's journey proceeded much like John's, beginning with an overland trip to Batu Khan's camp on the Volga and then long days of horse relays to the Mongolian capital of Karakorum where he met Monke (r. 1251–59) (here written as Mangu), the fourth Great Khan.

In this selection, William has arrived at the palace of Monke where a goldsmith named Master William of Paris has completed an unusual work of sculpture. Notice the number of Europeans and other foreigners at the court of Monke. Unlike the envoys mentioned in Selection 76, many of these foreigners were people captured by the Mongols. How have they adapted to Mongol rule?

William is interested, as John was, in Mongol religion. Notice William's conflicted attitude toward Nestorian Christianity, an Eastern Christianity that was practiced by, among others, much of the Kerait tribe — a source of intermarriage for the Mongols. Many Kerait wives of Mongol princes exerted great influence on their husbands and sons.

Thinking Historically

What sorts of moral struggles does William experience in the court of the Great Khan? Compare William's attitude toward the Nestorian Christians with Monke's. How do the moral and religious commit-

---

From "The Journey of William of Rubrick," in *Mission to Asia: Narratives and Letters of the Franciscan Missionaries in Mongolia and China in the Thirteenth and Fourteenth Centuries,* trans. a nun of Stanbrook Abbey, ed. Christopher Dawson (1955; reprint, New York: Harper & Row, 1966), 175–78.

ments of these two men affect their behavior? How do William's moral and religious attitudes affect his account? Would William's history have been more accurate if he had no moral or religious ideas of his own ?

At Caracorum, Mangu has a large orda[1] close by the city walls; it is surrounded by a brick wall as are our priories of monks. There is a large palace there in which he holds his drinking festival twice in the year, once round about Easter when he passes by that way and once in the summer on his return. The second is the more important for on that occasion there assemble at his court all the nobles anywhere within a two months' journey; and then he bestows on them garments and presents and displays his great glory. There are many other buildings there, long like barns, and in these are stored his provisions and treasures.

At the entrance to this palace, seeing it would have been unseemly to put skins of milk and other drinks there, Master William of Paris has made for him a large silver tree, at the foot of which are four silver lions each having a pipe and all belching forth white mares' milk. Inside the trunk four pipes lead up to the top of the tree and the ends of the pipes are bent downward and over each of them is a gilded serpent, the tail of which twines round the trunk of the tree. One of these pipes pours out wine, another caracosmos, that is the refined milk of mares, another *boal,* which is a honey drink, and another rice mead, which is called *terracina.* Each of these has its silver basin ready to receive it at the foot of the tree between the other four pipes. At the very top he fashioned an angel holding a trumpet; underneath the tree he made a crypt in which a man can be secreted, and a pipe goes up to the angel through the middle of the heart of the tree. At first he had made bellows but they did not give enough wind. Outside the palace there is a chamber in which the drinks are stored, and servants stand there ready to pour them out when they hear the angel sounding the trumpet. The tree has branches, leaves, and fruit of silver.

And so when the drinks are getting low the chief butler calls out to the angel to sound his trumpet. Then, hearing this, the man who is hidden in the crypt blows the pipe going up to the angel with all his strength, and the angel, placing the trumpet to his mouth, sounds it very loudly. When the servants in the chamber hear this each one of them pours out his drink into its proper pipe, and the pipes pour them

[1] A tent-palace compound.

out from above and below into the basins prepared for this, and then the cup-bearers draw the drinks and carry them round the palace to the men and women.

The palace is like a church with a middle nave and two side aisles beyond two rows of pillars, and there are three doors on the south side; inside before the middle door stands the tree, and the Chan himself sits at the northern end high up so that he can be seen by everyone; and there are two stairways leading up to him, and the man bringing him his cup goes up by the one and comes down by the other. The space in the middle between the tree and the steps up to him is empty, and there the cup-bearer stands and also envoys who are bringing gifts. The Chan sits up there like a god. On his right-hand side, that is to the west, are the men, on the left the women, for the palace extends from the north southward. To the south, next to the pillars on the right, are rows of seats raised up like a balcony, on which sit his son and brothers. It is the same on the left where his wives and daughters sit. Only one wife sits up there beside him; she however is not as high up as he is.

When the Chan heard that the work was finished he gave orders to the master to place it in position and get it in working order, and he himself about Passion Sunday went ahead with the small dwellings leaving the large ones behind. The monk and we followed him and he sent us another bottle of wine. He journeyed through mountainous districts, and there was a strong wind and severe cold and a heavy fall of snow. Consequently about midnight the Chan sent to the monk and us asking us to pray to God to lessen the cold and the wind, for all the animals accompanying them were in danger, especially because at that season they were with young and bringing forth. Thereupon the monk sent him some incense, bidding him put it on the coals as an offering to God. I do not know if he did this, but the storm, which had lasted for two days and was already entering on its third, did abate.

On Palm Sunday we were near Caracorum. At dawn we blessed branches of willow, which as yet bore no sign of buds, and about three o'clock we entered the city, the cross raised on high with the banner, and passing the Saracen quarters, where the bazaar and market are, we went to the church. The Nestorians came to meet us in procession. On entering the church we found them ready to celebrate Mass; when this had been celebrated they all received Holy Communion and asked me if I wished to communicate. I replied that I had had a drink and it is not lawful to receive the Sacrament except fasting.

Mass having been said, it was now evening and Master William took us with great joy to his lodging to have supper with him. His wife, who was born in Hungary, was the daughter of a man from Lorraine and she knew French and Coman well. We also came across another man there, Basil by name, the son of an Englishman, who had been born in Hungary and knew the same languages. After supper they accompanied us with great rejoicing to our hut, which the Tartars had set up for us in a square near the church along with the monk's oratory.

The following day the Chan entered his palace and the monk and I and the priests went to him. My companion was not allowed to go because he had trodden on the threshold. I deliberated a great deal about my own case, what I ought to do, whether to go or not to go, and, fearing to give scandal by dissociating myself from the other Christians, and seeing that it pleased the Chan, and fearing lest the good I was hoping to be able to bring about might be hindered, I decided to go even though it meant that I should witness their acts of sorcery and idolatry. And there I did nothing but pray aloud for the whole Church and also for the Chan that God would direct him into the way of eternal salvation.

And so we made our entrance into that orda, which is very well laid out and in summer they convey streams of water in all directions to irrigate it. We next entered the palace, which was full of men and women, and we stood before the Chan having at our backs the tree I have mentioned which together with its basins occupied a large part of the palace; the priests brought two little blessed cakes of bread and fruit on a dish which they presented to the Chan after they had pronounced a blessing, and a butler took them to him as he sat there in a place very high and lifted up. He immediately began to eat one of the cakes and sent the other to his son and his younger brother, who is being brought up by a Nestorian and knows the Gospel, and he also sent for my Bible so that he could look at it. After the priests the monk said his prayer, and I after the monk. Then the Chan promised that the following day he would come to the church, which is quite large and beautiful, and the roof above is all covered with silk interwoven with gold. The following day he went on his way, sending a message of excuse to the priests saying he dared not come to the church for he had learned that the dead were carried there. . . .

78

Images from Rashīd al-Dīn Fadl Allah

Mongol Cavalry in Pursuit
Mongols Taking Prisoners

The great hope held by Roman Catholics in Europe, that the Mongols would convert to Roman Catholicism and accept the pope as patriarch, was not fulfilled, despite the influence of Nestorian Christians in Central Asia. Instead, as the Mongol Empire began to fragment after the reign of Monke, different Mongol dynasties absorbed the religious ethos of the societies they dominated. For instance, in the Middle Eastern Islamic world, the Ilkanate (Mongol Kingdom of Persia and Iraq) became Muslim.

Rashīd al-Dīn Fadl Allah, a Persian historian of Muslim faith and statesman for the Mongols, was chief minister under the Ilkanate of Ghazan (r. 1295–1304). The illustrations in this selection were made for his *Jāmi al-tawārīkh*, a "Collection of Histories" of peoples known to the Mongols — a kind of world history of the time.

As Persians, Rashīd al-Dīn's ancestors had felt the fury of Mongol invasion and destruction. As a Muslim official for a Muslim Mongol ruler, Rashīd al-Dīn experienced the regime from the inside. Do these images show you an insider's or outsider's view of the Mongols?

One illustration shows Mongols with prisoners. Does this appear to be a particularly brutal way of handling captives? The other illustration shows Mongols in battle. The artist imagines both sides in Mongol armour, so we are unable to tell which side is which. It shows us, however, the wide range of weapons that were available to Mongol cavalry. How many of these can you name?

Thinking Historically

Do these images express or support any particular moral attitude toward the Mongols? Would you call them pro-Mongol or anti-Mongol? Why? Rashīd al-Dīn's history includes many images of Mongols at peace — at court and with wives and family — as well as at war. Mongols would have thought of themselves in both ways too. Do the two war images shown here make the Mongols seem more warlike? Do the two travelers' accounts of the Mongol court included in this chapter make them seem less warlike? Why or why not?

Mongol Cavalry in Hot Pursuit (Istanbul: Topkapi Palace Library), MS. H. 1653 fol. 165. *The Mongol Captives Led Away* (West Berlin: *Staats-bibliothek Preussischer Kulturbesitz*), MS. Diez A, fol. 7.

Figure 6. Mongol cavalry in pursuit.

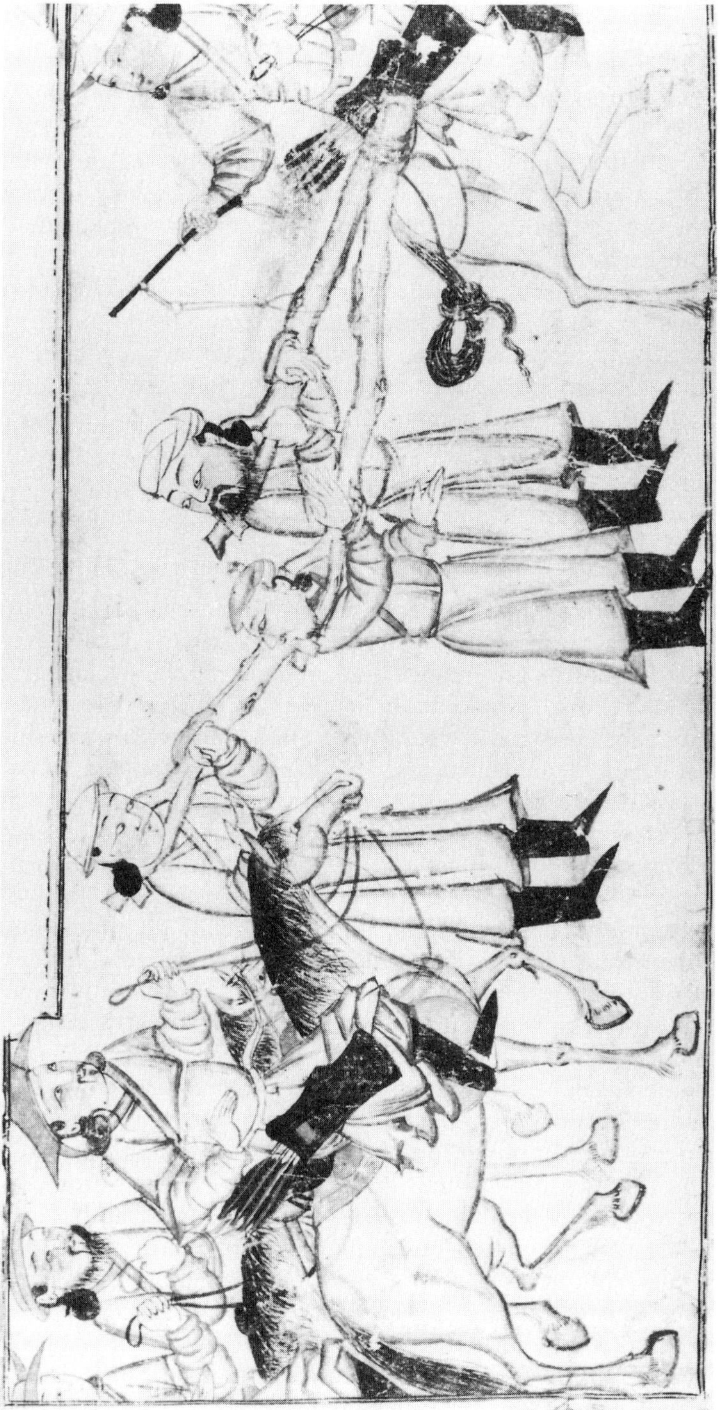

Figure 7. Mongols taking prisoners.

REFLECTIONS

The great Chinese artist Cheng Ssu-hsaio (1241–1318) continued to paint his delicate Chinese orchids in the years after the Mongol defeat of the Sung dynasty, under the alien rule of Khubilai Khan (r. 1260–94), the fifth Great Khan and the founder of the Mongol Yuan Dynasty of China. But when Cheng was asked why he always painted the orchids without earth around their roots, he replied that the earth had been stolen by the barbarians.

Just as it would be a mistake to see a fifth generation Mongol ruler like Khubilai as a barbarian, it would also be a mistake to assume that Cheng's hardened resistance remained the norm. In fact, a younger generation of artists found opportunity and even freedom in Khubilai's China. Khubilai appointed some of the most famous Chinese painters of his era to positions of government — Ministries of War, Public Works, Justice, Personnel, Imperial Sacrifices — actively recruiting the bright young men, artists and intellectuals, for his government. While some painters catered to the Mongol elite's inclination for paintings of horses, others relished the wider range of subjects allowed by a regime free of highly cultivated prejudices.

If conquest invariably brings charges of barbarism, it also eventually turns to issues of governance and administration. Administrators need officials. Though Khubilai abolished the Chinese civil service examination system because it would have forced him to rely on Chinese officials, the Chinese language, and an educational system based on the Chinese classics, he actively sought ways of governing that were neither too Chinese nor too Mongolian. Typically, he promulgated a Chinese alphabet that was based on Tibetan, hoping that its phonetic symbols would make communication easier and less classical. Many of his achievements were unintended. While his officials continued to use Chinese characters and the Uighur script, the Yüan dynasty witnessed a flowering of literary culture, including theater and novels. For some, no doubt, the wind from the steppe blew away the dust and cobwebs that had accumulated for too long.

Our judgment of the Mongols depends to a great extent on the period of Mongol history we consider. But while it is easy to condemn the initial conquests and praise the later enlightened governance, two considerations come to mind: First, in the great sweep of history, many "barbarians" became benign, even indulgent, administrators. Second, the Mongols were not unique in making that transition.

This raises an interesting moral question: Namely, what is the relation between historical memory and forgiveness? In recent years, we have pondered this when commemorating the fiftieth anniversary of World War II, the five-hundredth anniversary of the European settlement of the Americas, and the history of slavery.

At some point, it seems, former "barbarians" should be judged in terms of what they have become rather than what they once were. Even if forgiveness is not possible or desirable, old wounds fester, and the better course is to move forward with hope.

On the other hand, as Cheng's orchids remind us, people need to remember the past in order not to repeat it. Judgments about the past set guidelines, norms for the future.

Have you ever had an experience in your own life when you felt memory was a moral act? Was there ever a time when you thought it was better to forget? Does forgiveness require forgetting?

13

Cities: Contrast and Convergence

HISTORICAL CONTEXT

European, Chinese, and Islamic Cities, 900–1500 C.E.

During the last five thousand years, cities have grown and multiplied, the world becoming increasingly urbanized. There have been interruptions in this process, however: the period of the Mongol invasions in the first half of the thirteenth century and the era of the Black Death, a plague that wiped out urban populations in the middle of the fourteenth century, for instance. But, by and large, the general course of world history has promoted the rise and expansion of cities and of urban over rural populations.

In this chapter, we ask what this increasing urbanization meant for those who lived in the cities and for those who did not. We compare cities in various parts of the world between 1200 and 1500, although not necessarily during the same time period. We will study primary and secondary sources, and you will be asked to note the ways in which these cities are similar and different.

THINKING HISTORICALLY

Evaluating Alternate Theses

As you compare and contrast various cities in this chapter, you will consider two alternate theses (or perhaps, more broadly, two different approaches) to understanding the history of cities. The first thesis considers the differences or contrasting characteristics between cities to be more important and more telling than similarities. Sometimes the contrast is cultural, as if cities are microcosms of their particular cultures.

In this view, Paris is an extreme version of "Frenchness" — more a magnification of its own culture than a sister city to New York. Defining what a culture is can be difficult, though. Is Cairo extremely Egyptian, or is it Arab, Muslim, or Middle Eastern? Is Calcutta a distillation of things Indian? Or, is it more Bengal, South Asian, or Hindu? Cultural characterizations are always disputable, but clearly cities do concentrate local cultural tendencies. They produce newspapers, gather writers and artists, and serve as cultural hothouses.

The alternative approach might be called "convergence" or coming together. Cities have a way of assimilating people, so regardless of local variations in culture or traditions, we are able to identify universal commonalities. For instance, city inhabitants are less concerned with the immediate tasks of growing food and are more devoted to such secondary activities as trade, arts and crafts, and government. As well, all cities must find ways of dealing with population density, the close contact of strangers, and protecting concentrated stores of wealth. This idea seems especially convincing in light of today's modern globalization: City people the world over seem to imitate each other, communicate with each other, and share more of the same values than they do with people in the more rural areas of their countries.

In addition, we might compare and contrast types of cities: rich versus poor, big versus small, inland versus port, administrative versus commercial, and capital versus lesser cities, for instance.

Supplementing Written Sources with Maps

This chapter also explores the use of maps as aides to understanding cities and for making comparisons between types of cities. Maps help us determine where a city is situated, but also help us see how environments are shaped. Sometimes the shape of a place tells us much about the inhabitants' lives. When we look at a map of a city, for example, we can see how distinct the city is from the countryside, whether it is landlocked or has access to waterways, how ordered or chaotic the streets and neighborhoods are, how unified or segmented city districts are. You might begin your study of maps by looking at a map of a city near you, or by imagining a map of your own city. What would such a graphic representation tell you about peoples' actual lives?

79

Charter of Henry I for London, 1130–1133

In the last century types of cities have been distinguished by historians and sociologists who have recognized that European cities in the late Middle Ages were relatively independent of rulers and other cities due to charters of freedom. Town and city charters were frequently drawn up between European lords, princes, and kings, on the one hand, and the inhabitants, owners, or burghers, on the other. These charters, which were granted to the town for a fee, brought needed income to the lord or ruler while ensuring the ruler access to an active class of artisans, merchants, specialists, and luxury providers.

In this charter, for London, England, what does the king give to the townspeople? What powers does the king retain? What seem to have been the main concerns of the townspeople and king that are settled here?

Thinking Historically

Does this charter reflect King Henry's strength or his weakness? Why would this sort of arrangement be more likely to develop in a feudal society like Europe than it would in a Mongol or Chinese empire?

Henry, by the grace of God, king of the English, to the archbishop of Canterbury, and to the bishops and abbots, and earls and barons and justices and sheriffs, and to all his liegemen, both French and English, of the whole of England, greeting. Know that I have granted to my citizens of London that they shall hold Middlesex at "farm" for three hundred pounds "by tale" for themselves and their heirs from me and my heirs, so that the citizens shall appoint as sheriff from themselves whomsoever they may choose, and shall appoint from among themselves as justice whomsoever they choose to look after the pleas of my crown and the pleadings which arise in connexion with them. No other shall be justice over the same men of London. And the citizens shall not plead outside the walls of the city in respect of any plea; and they shall

---

Charter of Henry I for London (1130–1133), from *English Historical Documents,* vol. II., ed. David C. Douglas and George W. Greenaway (London: Eyre and Spottiswoode, Ltd., 1955), 945–46.

be quit of scot and of Danegeld[1] and the murder-fine. Nor shall any of them be compelled to offer trial by battle. And if any one of the citizens shall be impleaded in respect of the pleas of the crown, let him prove himself to be a man of London by an oath which shall be judged in the city. Let no one be billeted within the walls of the city, either of my household, or by the force of anyone else. And let all the men of London and their property be quit and free from toll and passage and lestage[2] and from all other customs throughout all England and at the seaports. And let the churches and barons and citizens hold and have well and in peace their sokes,[3] with all their customs, so that those who dwell in these sokes shall pay no customs except to him who possesses the soke, or to the steward whom he has placed there. And a man of London shall not be fined at mercy except according to his "were," that is to say, up to one hundred shillings: This applies to an offence which can be punished by a fine. And there shall no longer be "miskenning"[4] in the hustings court,[5] nor in the folk-moot,[6] nor in other pleas within the city. And the hustings court shall sit once a week, to wit, on Monday. I will cause my citizens to have their lands and pledges and debts within the city and outside it. And in respect of the lands about which they make claim to me, I will do them right according to the law of the city. And if anyone has taken toll or custom from the citizens of London, then the citizens of London may take from the borough or village where toll or custom has been levied as much as the man of London gave for toll, and more also may be taken for a penalty. And let all debtors to the citizens of London discharge their debts, or prove in London that they do not owe them; and if they refuse either to pay, or to come and make such proof, then the citizens to whom the debts are due may take pledges within the city either from the borough or from the village or from the county in which the debtor lives. And the citizens shall have their hunting chases, as well and fully as had their predecessors, to wit, in Chiltern and Middlesex and Surrey.

1 A medieval land tax, originally levied to buy off raiding Danes (literally, "Dane's money"). First levied in England in 868, but generally discontinued in the twelfth century. [Ed.]

2 Sometimes "lastage": a toll payable by traders attending fairs and markets. [Ed.]

3 A right of local jurisdiction. [Ed.]

4 A verbal error in making a formal oath. [Ed.]

5 King's court or court of king's representatives. [Ed.]

6 A general assembly of the people. [Ed.]

80

GREGORIO DATI

Corporations and Community in Florence

This is an account of the Italian city of Florence and its inhabitants from 1380 to 1405. While family identity was primary, residents of Florence were also members of many corporate organizations that served to channel their loyalty to the larger urban community. Among these were guilds and parish churches, as well as political, welfare, and religious organizations. On public holidays like the feast day of St. John the Baptist, the patron saint of Florence, these various groups would come together in a display of communal solidarity that was often more fraternal than the deliberations in the political arena. What seems to motivate people to participate in public acts and parades in Florence?

Thinking Historically

Would a chartered city be more or less likely than a city run by a king to hold these sorts of festivities? In what ways would you expect the politics of Florence to be similar to and different from those of London? What is the relationship between public participation in festivals and public participation in politics?

When springtime comes and the whole world rejoices, every Florentine begins to think about organizing a magnificent celebration on the feast day of St. John the Baptist [June 24]. . . . For two months in advance, everyone is planning marriage feasts or other celebrations in honor of the day. There are preparations for the horse races, the costumes of the retinues, the flags, and the trumpets; there are the pennants and the wax candles and other things which the subject territories offer to the Commune. Messengers are sent to obtain provisions for the banquets, and horses come from everywhere to run in the races. The whole city is engaged in preparing for the feast, and the spirits of the young people and the women [are animated] by these preparations. . . .

Gregorio Dati, "*Istoria di Firenze dall'anno MCCCLXXX all'anno MCCCCV*" (History of Florence from 1380 to 1405) (Florence, 1735), in *The Society of Renaissance Florence*, ed. and trans. Gene Brucker (New York: Harper & Row, 1971), 75–78.

Everyone is filled with gaiety; there are dances and concerts and songfests and tournaments and other joyous activities. Up to the eve of the holiday, no one thinks about anything else.

Early on the morning of the day before the holiday, each guild has a display outside of its shops of its fine wares, its ornaments, and jewels. There are cloths of gold and silk sufficient to adorn ten kingdoms. . . . Then at the third hour, there is a solemn procession of clerics, priests, monks, and friars, and there are so many [religious] orders, and so many relics of saints, that the procession seems endless. [It is a manifestation] of great devotion, on account of the marvelous richness of the adornments . . . and clothing of gold and silk with embroidered figures. There are many confraternities of men who assemble at the place where their meetings are held, dressed as angels, and with musical instruments of every kind and marvelous singing. They stage the most beautiful representations of the saints, and of those relics in whose honor they perform. They leave from S. Maria del Fiore [the cathedral] and march through the city and then return.

Then, after midday, when the heat has abated before sunset, all of the citizens assemble under [the banner of] their district, of which there are sixteen. Each goes in the procession in turn, the first, then the second, and so on with one district following the other, and in each group the citizens march two by two, with the oldest and most distinguished at the head, and proceeding down to the young men in rich garments. They march to the church of St. John [the Baptistery] to offer, one by one, a wax candle weighing one pound. . . . The walls along the streets through which they pass are all decorated, and there are . . . benches on which are seated young ladies and girls dressed in silk and adorned with jewels, pearls, and precious stones. This procession continues until sunset, and after each citizen has made his offering, he returns home with his wife to prepare for the next morning.

Whoever goes to the Piazza della Signoria on the morning of St. John's Day witnesses a magnificent, marvelous, and triumphant sight, which the mind can scarcely grasp. Around the great piazza are a hundred towers which appear to be made of gold. Some were brought on carts and others by porters. . . . [These towers] are made of wood, paper, and wax [and decorated] with gold, colored paints, and with figures. . . . Next to the rostrum of the palace [of the Signoria] are standards . . . which belong to the most important towns which are subject to the Commune: Pisa, Arezzo, Pistoia, Volterra, Cortona, Lucignano. . . .

First to present their offering, in the morning, are the captains of the Parte Guelfa, together with all of the knights, lords, ambassadors, and foreign knights. They are accompanied by a large number of the most honorable citizens, and before them, riding on a charger covered with a cloth . . . is one of their pages carrying a banner with the insignia of the Parte Guelfa. Then there follow the above-mentioned standards, each one carried by men on horseback . . . and they all go to make their offerings at the Baptistery. And these standards are given as tribute by the districts which have been acquired by the Commune of Florence. . . . The wax candles, which have the appearance of golden towers, are the tribute of the regions which in most ancient times were subject to the Florentines. In order of dignity, they are brought, one by one, to be offered to St. John, and on the following day, they are hung inside the church and there they remain for the entire year until the next feast day. . . . Then come . . . an infinite number of large wax candles, some weighing one hundred pounds and others fifty, some more and some less . . . carried by the residents of the villages [in the *contado*[1]] which offer them. . . .

Then the lord priors and their colleges come to make their offerings, accompanied by their rectors, that is, the podestà, the captain [of the *popolo*[2]], and the executor. . . . And after the lord [priors] come those who are participating in the horse race, and they are followed by the Flemings and the residents of Brabant who are weavers of woolen cloth in Florence. Then there are offerings by twelve prisoners who, as an act of mercy, have been released from prison . . . in honor of St. John, and these are poor people. . . . After all of these offerings have been made, men and women return home to dine. . . .

81

MARCO POLO

From *The Travels of Marco Polo*

According to *The Travels of Marco Polo,* by the time the Venetian merchant had come to Hangchow (which he calls Kinsay) he had been to Karakorum, the Mongol capital; Peking; Changan, the T'ang dynasty capital; and a number of other cities in China (which he calls Manzi); other parts of Asia; and, of course, his native Venice. Why

[1] Countryside. [Ed.]
[2] People. [Ed.]

Marco Polo, *The Travels of Marco Polo,* the Complete Yule-Currier ed., vol. 2 (New York: Dover, 1993), 185–93, 200–06.

does he say that this city is the "finest and noblest of the world"? How does his description support that characterization?

Thinking Historically

In what ways does the Hangchow that emerges from this document resemble London or Florence? In what ways was Hangchow significantly different? Using the theories of contrast and convergence suggested in the introduction to this chapter, how would you account for those similarities or differences?

When you have left the city of Changan and have travelled for three days through a splendid country, passing a number of towns and villages, you arrive at the most noble city of Kinsay, a name which is as much as to say in our tongue "The City of Heaven," as I told you before.

And since we have got thither I will enter into particulars about its magnificence; and these are well worth the telling, for the city is beyond dispute the finest and the noblest in the world. In this we shall speak according to the written statement which the Queen of this Realm sent to Bayan the conqueror of the country for transmission to the Great Kaan, in order that he might be aware of the surpassing grandeur of the city and might be moved to save it from destruction or injury. I will tell you all the truth as it was set down in that document. For truth it was, as the said Messer Marco Polo at a later date was able to witness with his own eyes. And now we shall rehearse those particulars.

First and foremost, then, the document stated the city of Kinsay to be so great that it hath an hundred miles of compass. And there are in it twelve thousand bridges of stone,[1] for the most part so lofty that a great fleet could pass beneath them. And let no man marvel that there are so many bridges, for you see the whole city stands as it were in the water and surrounded by water, so that a great many bridges are required to give free passage about it. [And though the bridges be so high, the approaches are so well contrived that carts and horses do cross them.]

The document aforesaid also went on to state that there were in this city twelve guilds of the different crafts, and that each guild had twelve thousand houses in the occupation of its workmen. Each of these houses contains at least twelve men, whilst some contain twenty and some forty, — not that these are all masters, but inclusive of the journeymen who work under the masters. And yet all these craftsmen

[1] Generally assumed to be an exaggeration; one thousand would have been a lot. [Ed.]

had full occupation, for many other cities of the kingdom are supplied from this city with what they require.

The document aforesaid also stated that the number and wealth of the merchants, and the amount of goods that passed through their hands, was so enormous that no man could form a just estimate thereof. And I should have told you with regard to those masters of the different crafts who are at the head of such houses as I have mentioned, that neither they nor their wives ever touch a piece of work with their own hands, but live as nicely and delicately as if they were kings and queens. The wives indeed are most dainty and angelical creatures! Moreover it was an ordinance laid down by the King that every man should follow his father's business and no other, no matter if he possessed 100,000 bezants.[2]

Inside the city there is a Lake which has a compass of some thirty miles:[3] and all round it are erected beautiful palaces and mansions, of the richest and most exquisite structure that you can imagine, belonging to the nobles of the city. There are also on its shores many abbeys and churches of the Idolaters. In the middle of the Lake are two Islands, on each of which stands a rich, beautiful and spacious edifice, furnished in such style as to seem fit for the palace of an Emperor. And when any one of the citizens desired to hold a marriage feast, or to give any other entertainment, it used to be done at one of these palaces. And everything would be found there ready to order, such as silver plate, trenchers, and dishes [napkins and tablecloths], and whatever else was needful. The King made this provision for the gratification of his people, and the place was open to every one who desired to give an entertainment. . . .

The people are Idolaters; and since they were conquered by the Great Kaan they use paper money. [Both men and women are fair and comely, and for the most part clothe themselves in silk, so vast is the supply of that material, both from the whole district of Kinsay, and from the imports by traders from other provinces.] And you must know they eat every kind of flesh, even that of dogs and other unclean beasts, which nothing would induce a Christian to eat.

Since the Great Kaan occupied the city he has ordained that each of the twelve thousand bridges should be provided with a guard of ten men, in case of any disturbance, or of any being so rash as to plot treason or insurrection against him. [Each guard is provided with a hollow

[2] A gold coin struck at Byzantium (or Constantinople) and used throughout Europe from the ninth century. [Ed.]

[3] The circumference of the lake was more probably 30 li. A li was about a third of a mile, but it was sometimes used to mean a hundredth of a day's march. The entire circumference of the city could not have been more than 100 li. [Ed.]

instrument of wood and with a metal basin, and with a timekeeper to enable them to know the hour of the day or night. . . .

Part of the watch patrols the quarter, to see if any light or fire is burning after the lawful hours; if they find any they mark the door, and in the morning the owner is summoned before the magistrates, and unless he can plead a good excuse he is punished. Also if they find any one going about the streets at unlawful hours they arrest him, and in the morning they bring him before the magistrates. Likewise if in the daytime they find any poor cripple unable to work for his livelihood, they take him to one of the hospitals, of which there are many, founded by the ancient kings, and endowed with great revenues. Or if he be capable of work they oblige him to take up some trade. If they see that any house has caught fire they immediately beat upon that wooden instrument to give the alarm, and this brings together the watchmen from the other bridges to help to extinguish it, and to save the goods of the merchants or others, either by removing them to the towers above mentioned, or by putting them in boats and transporting them to the islands in the lake. For no citizen dares leave his house at night, or to come near the fire; only those who own the property, and those watchmen who flock to help, of whom there shall come one or two thousand at the least.] . . .

The Kaan watches this city with especial diligence because it forms the head of all Manzi;[4] and because he has an immense revenue from the duties levied on the transactions of trade therein, the amount of which is such that no one would credit it on mere hearsay.

All the streets of the city are paved with stone or brick, as indeed are all the highways throughout Manzi, so that you ride and travel in every direction without inconvenience. Were it not for this pavement you could not do so, for the country is very low and flat, and after rain 'tis deep in mire and water. [But as the Great Kaan's couriers could not gallop their horses over the pavement, the side of the road is left unpaved for their convenience. The pavement of the main street of the city also is laid out in two parallel ways of ten paces in width on either side, leaving a space in the middle laid with fine gravel, under which are vaulted drains which convey the rain water into the canals; and thus the road is kept ever dry.]

You must know also that the city of Kinsay has some three thousand baths, the water of which is supplied by springs. They are hot baths, and the people take great delight in them, frequenting them several times a month, for they are very cleanly in their persons. They are the finest and largest baths in the world; large enough for one hundred persons to bathe together.

[4] China. [Ed.]

And the Ocean Sea comes within twenty-five miles of the city at a place called Ganfu, where there is a town and an excellent haven, with a vast amount of shipping which is engaged in the traffic to and from India and other foreign parts, exporting and importing many kinds of wares, by which the city benefits. And a great river flows from the city of Kinsay to that sea-haven, by which vessels can come up to the city itself. This river extends also to other places further inland.

Know also that the Great Kaan hath distributed the territory of Manzi into nine parts, which he hath constituted into nine kingdoms. To each of these kingdoms a king is appointed who is subordinate to the Great Kaan, and every year renders the accounts of his kingdom to the fiscal office at the capital. This city of Kinsay is the seat of one of these kings, who rules over one hundred forty great and wealthy cities. For in the whole of this vast country of Manzi there are more than twelve hundred great and wealthy cities, without counting the towns and villages, which are in great numbers. And you may receive it for certain that in each of those twelve hundred cities the Great Kaan has a garrison, and that the smallest of such garrisons musters one thousand men; whilst there are some of ten thousand, twenty thousand and thirty thousand; so that the total number of troops is something scarcely calculable. The troops forming these garrisons are not all Tartars. Many are from the province of Cathay, and good soldiers too. But you must not suppose they are by any means all of them cavalry; a very large proportion of them are foot soldiers, according to the special requirements of each city. And all of them belong to the army of the Great Kaan.

I repeat that everything appertaining to this city is on so vast a scale, and the Great Kaan's yearly revenues therefrom are so immense, that it is not easy even to put it in writing, and it seems past belief to one who merely hears it told. But I *will* write it down for you.

First, however, I must mention another thing. The people of this country have a custom, that as soon as a child is born they write down the day and hour and the planet and sign under which its birth has taken place; so that every one among them knows the day of his birth. And when any one intends a journey he goes to the astrologers, and gives the particulars of his nativity in order to learn whether he shall have good luck or no. Sometimes they will say *no,* and in that case the journey is put off till such day as the astrologer may recommend. These astrologers are very skilful at their business, and often their words come to pass, so the people have great faith in them.

They burn the bodies of the dead. And when any one dies the friends and relations make a great mourning for the deceased, and clothe themselves in hempen garments, and follow the corpse playing on a variety of instruments and singing hymns to their idols. And when they come to the burning place, they take representations of things cut out of parchment, such as caparisoned horses, male and female slaves, camels, armour suits of cloth of gold (and money), in great quantities, and these things they put on the fire along with the corpse, so that they are all burnt with it. And they tell you that the dead man shall have all these slaves and animals of which the effigies are burnt, alive in flesh and blood, and the money in gold, at his disposal in the next world; and that the instruments which they have caused to be played at his funeral, and the idol hymns that have been chaunted, shall also be produced again to welcome him in the next world; and that the idols themselves will come to do him honour.

Furthermore there exists in this city the palace of the king who fled, him who was Emperor of Manzi, and that is the greatest palace in the world, as I shall tell you more particularly. For you must know its demesne[5] hath a compass of ten miles, all enclosed with lofty battlemented walls; and inside the walls are the finest and most delectable gardens upon earth, and filled too with the finest fruits. There are numerous fountains in it also, and lakes full of fish. In the middle is the palace itself, a great and splendid building. It contains twenty great and handsome halls, one of which is more spacious than the rest, and affords room for a vast multitude to dine. It is all painted in gold, with many histories and representations of beasts and birds, of knights and dames, and many marvellous things. It forms a really magnificent spectacle, for over all the walls and all the ceiling you see nothing but paintings in gold. And besides these halls the palace contains one thousand large and handsome chambers, all painted in gold and divers colours.

Moreover, I must tell you that in this city there are 160 *tomans*[6] of fires, or in other words 160 *tomans* of houses. Now I should tell you that the *toman* is 10,000, so that you can reckon the total as altogether 1,600,000 houses, among which are a great number of rich palaces. There is one church only, belonging to the Nestorian Christians.

There is another thing I must tell you. It is the custom for every burgess of this city, and in fact for every description of person in it, to write over his door his own name, the name of his wife, and those of his children, his slaves, and all the inmates of his house, and also the number of animals that he keeps. And if any one dies in the house then the name of that person is erased, and if any child is born its name is added. So in this way the sovereign is able to know exactly the population of the city. And this is the practice also throughout all Manzi and Cathay.

And I must tell you that every hosteler who keeps an hostel for travellers is bound to register their names and surnames, as well as the day and month of their arrival and departure. And thus the sovereign

[5] Size. [Ed.]
[6] A *toman* is a Mongol measurement of ten thousand. [Ed.]

hath the means of knowing, whenever it pleases him, who come and go throughout his dominions. And certes this is a wise order and a provident. . . .

[The position of the city is such that it has on one side a lake of fresh and exquisitely clear water (already spoken of), and on the other a very large river. The waters of the latter fill a number of canals of all sizes which run through the different quarters of the city, carry away all impurities, and then enter the Lake; whence they issue again and flow to the Ocean, thus producing a most excellent atmosphere. By means of these channels, as well as by the streets, you can go all about the city. Both streets and canals are so wide and spacious that carts on the one and boats on the other can readily pass to and fro, conveying necessary supplies to the inhabitants.

At the opposite side the city is shut in by a channel, perhaps forty miles in length, very wide, and full of water derived from the river aforesaid, which was made by the ancient kings of the country in order to relieve the river when flooding its banks. This serves also as a defence to the city, and the earth dug from it has been thrown inward, forming a kind of mound enclosing the city.

In this part are the ten principal markets, though besides these there are a vast number of others in the different parts of the town. The former are all squares of half a mile to the side, and along their front passes the main street, which is forty paces in width, and runs straight from end to end of the city, crossing many bridges of easy and commodious approach. At every four miles of its length comes one of those great squares of two miles (as we have mentioned) in compass. So also parallel to this great street, but at the back of the marketplaces, there runs a very large canal, on the bank of which toward the squares are built great houses of stone, in which the merchants from India and other foreign parts store their wares, to be handy for the markets. In each of the squares is held a market three days in the week, frequented by forty thousand or fifty thousand persons, who bring thither for sale every possible necessary of life, so that there is always an ample supply of every kind of meat and game, as of roebuck, red-deer, fallow-deer, hares, rabbits, partridges, pheasants, francolins, quails, fowls, capons, and of ducks and geese an infinite quantity; for so many are bred on the Lake that for a Venice groat of silver you can have a couple of geese and two couple of ducks. Then there are the shambles where the larger animals are slaughtered, such as calves, beeves, kids, and lambs, the flesh of which is eaten by the rich and the great dignitaries.

Those markets make a daily display of every kind of vegetables and fruits; and among the latter there are in particular certain pears of enormous size, weighing as much as ten pounds apiece, and the pulp of which is white and fragrant like a confection; besides peaches in their season both yellow and white, of every delicate flavour.

Neither grapes nor wine are produced there, but very good raisins are brought from abroad, and wine likewise. The natives, however, do not much care about wine, being used to that kind of their own made from rice and spices. From the Ocean Sea also come daily supplies of fish in great quantity, brought twenty-five miles up the river, and there is also great store of fish from the lake, which is the constant resort of fishermen, who have no other business. Their fish is of sundry kinds, changing with the season; and, owing to the impurities of the city which pass into the lake, it is remarkably fat and savoury. Any one who should see the supply of fish in the market would suppose it impossible that such a quantity could ever be sold; and yet in a few hours the whole shall be cleared away; so great is the number of inhabitants who are accustomed to delicate living. Indeed they eat fish and flesh at the same meal.

All the ten marketplaces are encompassed by lofty houses, and below these are shops where all sorts of crafts are carried on, and all sorts of wares are on sale, including spices and jewels and pearls. Some of these shops are entirely devoted to the sale of wine made from rice and spices, which is constantly made fresh, and is sold very cheap.

Certain of the streets are occupied by the women of the town, who are in such a number that I dare not say what it is. They are found not only in the vicinity of the marketplaces, where usually a quarter is assigned to them, but all over the city. They exhibit themselves splendidly attired and abundantly perfumed, in finely garnished houses, with trains of waiting-women. These women are extremely accomplished in all the arts of allurement, and readily adapt their conversation to all sorts of persons, insomuch that strangers who have once tasted their attractions seem to get bewitched, and are so taken with their blandishments and their fascinating ways that they never can get these out of their heads. Hence it comes to pass that when they return home they say they have been to Kinsay or the City of Heaven, and their only desire is to get back thither as soon as possible.

Other streets are occupied by the Physicians, and by the Astrologers, who are also teachers of reading and writing; and an infinity of other professions have their places round about those squares. In each of the squares there are two great palaces facing one another, in which are established the officers appointed by the King to decide differences arising between merchants, or other inhabitants of the quarter. It is the daily duty of these officers to see that the guards are at their posts on the neighbouring bridges, and to punish them at their discretion if they are absent. . . .

The natives of the city are men of peaceful character, both from education and from the example of their kings, whose disposition was the same. They know nothing of handling arms, and keep none in their houses. You hear of no feuds or noisy quarrels or dissensions of any kind among them. Both in their commercial dealings and in their manufactures they are thoroughly honest and truthful, and there is such a degree of good will and neighbourly attachment among both men and women that you would take the people who live in the same street to be all one family.

And this familiar intimacy is free from all jealousy or suspicion of the conduct of their women. These they treat with the greatest respect, and a man who should presume to make loose proposals to a married woman would be regarded as an infamous rascal. They also treat the foreigners who visit them for the sake of trade with great cordiality, and entertain them in the most winning manner, affording them every help and advice on their business. But on the other hand they hate to see soldiers, and not least those of the Great Kaan's garrisons, regarding them as the cause of their having lost their native kings and lords.

82

IRA M. LAPIDUS

Muslim Cities and Islamic Societies

Map of Cairo, 1441
Map of Baghdad, 770–950 C.E.
Map of Florence, Twelfth–Fourteenth Century
Illustration of Florence, 1470

The author of this selection is a modern historian of Islam. In this excerpt, he asks what is distinctive about the cities of the Muslim Middle East. He questions the role of cities in shaping Muslim civilization, and he compares the cities of medieval Islam, especially Cairo and Baghdad, with European cities.

Ira M. Lapidus, "Muslim Cities and Islamic Societies," in *Middle Eastern Cities,* ed. Ira M. Lapidus (Berkeley and Los Angeles: University of California Press, 1969), 60–67, 73–74. Map of Cairo from Janet Abu-Lughod, *Cairo: A Thousand and One Years of the City Victorious* (Princeton: Princeton University Press, 1971), facing p. 47. Map of Baghdad, A.H. 150–300, from Guy Le Strange, *Baghdad des Abbasiads* (Oxford: Oxford University Press, 1924), 47. Map of Florence from Daniel Waley, *The Italian City Republics* (New York: McGraw-Hill, 1969), 36. Illustration of Florence from Howard Saalman, *Medieval Cities* (New York: George Braziller, 1968), Instituto Geografico Militare, Florence.

What does Lapidus mean when he says that Muslim cities were not "geographically defined communities" or that they had no "internal unity"? Were cities important to Islam? In what sense were Muslim cities "double cities" or "multiple cities"? Why did they consist of these different segments? How were Muslim cities similar to or different from the surrounding countryside?

Thinking Historically

Which of the approaches to comparing cities described in the introduction to this chapter does Lapidus endorse? What is the significance of the difference he draws between Muslim and European cities?

The maps of Cairo and Baghdad are included here to help you visualize these cities. Lapidus writes about how Cairo was actually a series of successive cities: Fustat, Askar, Qatai (Katai), Kahira, and the Citadel. Locate these cities on the map.

When the Arabs conquered Egypt in 641, they set up an administrative capital at the Roman site of Babylon (near the bottom of the map). A mosque to the north became the center of the city of Fustat, the most important city in Egypt until it was burned to the ground in 750. The new dynasty, the Abbasid, constructed a new fortified city called el Askar ("The Military Quarter"). Al Quatai (Al Katai) was built by a governor who declared his independence from the Abbasids in 868. When the Fatimids invaded from North Africa in 969, they built their capital on the unoccupied northern plain, calling it Al Kahira (Cairo). After Crusader attacks and another burning of Fustat, Saladin came from Syria to administer Egypt and built both the Citadel, a fortified city within the city, and a wall that surrounded the Citadel, Al Katai, and Al Kahira (see the Mameluke Cairo wall on the map). Notice also how the silting of the Nile River permitted the westward expansion of the city and the doubling of its size.

Lapidus also discusses Baghdad, the capital of the Abbasid caliphate (after 750). Notice on the map how "the round city" sits as a walled fortress in the midst of other districts. Can you tell from the map what the "round city" was? What was its function? Is this what Lapidus means by a "double city"?

Finally, a map and an engraving of Florence is included here for comparison. Notice that Florence also has a history in which its size and shape changed. How was its history different from Cairo's? Notice that all three cities have walls. How does the function of the walls differ in each city? Notice that all three cities have rivers running through them as well. Does this construct what Lapidus calls a "double city," or does he mean something else? What do these maps tell you about different types of cities?

. . . As opposed to the ancient *polis* or medieval European commune, there were no geographically defined communities in the Muslim world. Though tentative, this model of social organization suggests that we reconsider the meaning of cities in Islamic societies. If Muslim communities were not exclusively urban communities (even though cities, being large settlements, were naturally crucial foci of social life), how shall we understand the view widely held among scholars of Islam that Muslim cities were opposed to the countrysides? How may we reconcile our conception of social organization with the equally widespread idea that Muslim cities were of crucial religious significance for Muslim societies? Can we hold simultaneously that Muslim social groupings were not urban bodies and that Muslim cities had a distinctive social, geographical, and religious reality? Obviously this is a complex problem for which I have no comprehensive solution. Nonetheless, we might re-examine the geographical and religious aspects of the usual conception of Muslim cities, for upon close examination both these conceptions will have to be modified in ways which suggest new directions for interpreting the meaning of cities in Muslim civilization.

At one level the fact that Muslim cities had no internal unity has long been evident. Yet this mystique of cities has nonetheless inspired efforts to define a characteristic social quality for Muslim cities. One justification for the persistent feeling that Muslim cities must form a social world of their own stems from the contrast between city and country. The image of the walled town standing in relief against a shapeless countryside has long inspired scholarly quests for that decisive property which unifies Muslim towns. The image, however, is misleading. When examined closely, the geography and ecology of Muslim cities in relation to the surrounding countrysides proves to be exceedingly complex. In fact, in many situations, no *absolute* distinction between urban and rural habitats may be drawn. This may seem contradictory, and heretical to the stereotype of the Muslim city as isolated from and opposed to the countryside. Nonetheless, just as both environments were knit together by elements of social organization, so in certain cases did they interpenetrate or resemble each other in some geographical and ecological aspects. To define precisely what is meant demands fuller consideration of the physical form of Muslim cities and regional geographies.

In the Muslim world of our period, larger settlements such as metropolitan centers, provincial or regional capitals, smaller market towns and even some large villages were not generally distinct entities, but most often composites of lesser units. Settlements of all types, from the largest metropolises to the smallest towns and villages, were clusters of distinct physical and social units.

The great capital cities, Baghdad and Cairo — homes of cosmopolitan populations, creative sources of Muslim culture, centers of imperial administration and international trade — were unique in size but not atypical in form. Cities such as Baghdad and Cairo, with populations estimated at 200,000 or 300,000 — vastly larger than any which had existed previously in the Middle East, and several orders of magnitude bigger than their contemporaries — were not single cities but composites of cities. Both developed by the juxtaposition of a succession of palace centers and military encampments, each of which grew into a settlement having the size and characteristics of a separate city. Baghdad, the Madīnāt al-Salām, surrounded by al-Ḥarbiyya on the north and commercial al-Karkh on the south, faced similar districts, such as al-Ruṣāfa across the Tigris, and thus repeated the configuration of Sassanian Madā'in — a city of cities. Cairo, similarly, took shape as a set of adjacent administrative, military, and commercial centers, sometimes separated by open spaces. The most important founding, al-Qāhira in 969 A.D., was neither the first nor the last major extension of metropolitan Cairo. Al-Fusṭāṭ al-'Askar, and al-Qatā'i' preceded it, and subsequently Saladin's citadel and the new districts built around it extended the metropolitan complex into new areas.

Lesser cities were similarly composed. Twin cities or double cities made up of wholly distinct physical entities, often separated by open space, were common in the medieval Muslim world. Isfahan and Raqqa, among others, were double cities which slowly grew together across the spaces which separated them. In Egypt and Iraq, many cities and towns were divided into two sectors by canals or rivers, each of which might have separate mosques and bazaars. There were different types of double cities — those composed of fortresses and their suburbs, and those formed whenever suburbs grew in size and facilities to equal the original settlement. Iranian cities generally were composed of several units — a citadel, the city proper, and its suburbs — each surrounded by its own walls.

There are several reasons for the existence of such double cities. Many developed naturally in densely populated areas, especially where waterways or fortified places formed likely foci for adjacent settlements. More dramatically, double cities were created by the Arab conquerors and late Muslim regimes. New suburbs and quarters were frequently developed to settle conquering armies or the ethnic allies of new dynasties in the vicinity of existing city centers. The Arab conquerors of the Middle East not only founded new garrison cities, but also took over parts of established cities or created new suburbs. Later regimes adopted the same policy. Most dramatic was the founding of royal suburbs which housed a ruler's household, administration, and military forces. Baghdad and Cairo were creations of this sort. . . .

Moreover, these double multiple cities were also internally divided into separate quarters. In Baghdad and Cairo, each city within the metropolitan complex was subdivided into suburbs, quarters, wards, streets, and markets. Lesser cities and towns were also composed of distinct quarters, which were sometimes separated by walls and gates and sometimes merely by the hostile feelings of the community. Such quarters had various origins. Some were vestiges of the circumstances of city foundings. In the cities founded as bedouin encampments, the populace was settled into tribal quarters which, as in the case of Basra, Kufa, Cairo, and other cities, retained the characteristics created by the earliest divisions. Similarly, cities founded by the enclosure of a number of villages or by the establishment of a market serving several settlements, might long retain open spaces between the districts and later, though grown into a solid mass, continue to harbor the original settlements as quarters of the city. Muslim Kazvin was formed in this way, as were Qum, Merv, Kazarun, and possibly Bukhara. Most important were the social divisions within city populations which necessitated the creation of separate quarters.

In the formation of such settlements, no absolute distinctions were made between urban and rural elements, or to put it another way, among quarters, suburbs, and adjacent villages. Cities often had an agricultural component. Walled suburbs were often used for gardening and other forms of agriculture, and the outlying villages could be regarded as quarters or suburbs of the city proper. In addition, the fabric of Muslim settlements allowed for gardens and agriculture inside the city proper, either in open spaces or in garden lots attached to townhouses. Many cities, especially in Iran, were also surrounded by gardens and fields owned and or worked by people who lived in the cities. Thus, the populations of these composite settlements included not only a skilled and sophisticated bourgeoisie of administrators, scholars, merchants, and craftsmen, but also many people who differed little in their attitudes, mores, and manner of life from rural people. Besides agriculturalists, migrants fleeing rural hardship or looking for temporary work came to the cities. Many villagers or nomads settled there permanently, forming quarters or suburbs of their own, while others fell into an unassimilated mass of lumpen-proletarians. Among the middle and upper classes were found nomadic chieftains and people who came from village families to study in the *madrasas*[1] and schools of the capitals. Though the rural upper classes were more likely to absorb city manners than the lower classes, not all city people shared an urban way of life.

Conversely, in many areas, villages or rural settlements differed less from towns or urban settlements than one might think. Places called villages by the geographers (presumably because of their relatively

[1] Muslim college. [Ed.]

small size, agricultural orientation, and limited facilities) very often had pronounced urban features. In the frontier regions of Khurasan where no substantial towns existed, villages were fortified to provide local security. More commonly, villages were sites of periodic markets and fairs. Others were caravan stations equipped with *khāns*[2] or *ribāṭs*[3] for travellers and sometimes permanent shops and bazaars. Villages were also centers of cloth manufacturing. Premodern industry, as evidenced by the "putting-out" system of European manufacturers, was not necessarily concentrated in towns, but was entrusted to villages or peasants who earned their off-season income by spinning, weaving, and related activities. Neither were villages necessarily deprived of the spiritual facilities of towns. Some villages were sites of Sufi convents. Others had mosques, particularly Friday mosques, even though these are supposedly the distinguishing feature of town life. Many places called villages, which had mosques and markets, served the same functions as local marketing towns. In fact, though not in terminology, no distinction can be made between them. In Egypt, places called villages were sometimes the *chef-lieu,* residences of a governor or *qāḍī*, though elsewhere this seems to have been true only when towns decreased in size but retained their former jurisdictions. In short, these so-called villages had a full complement of urban facilities — baths, markets, and mosques.

Concomitantly, villages with varied activities had differentiated populations. Not only peasants, but landowners, "*ulamā*,"[4] merchants, and artisans were also part of village populations. In Egypt, Khwarezm, the oasis of Damascus, and Bukhara, landowning families who were part of the cities' bourgeoisie resided in the villages. Villages were also the home of *qāḍīs*, preachers, *imāms*,[5] scholars and holy men. They were resorts for townspeople, and in some special cases, as at Hormuz, merchants traded in the city but lived in the suburban villages. . . .

Thus, many "cities" had rural components and villages had "urban" features or were in fact small towns in all but name. In some regions no hard-and-fast distinction between urban and rural habitats may be formulated. They form a continuum of geographical and ecological traits. To understand all the realities of geographical structure in the Muslim world, we should eschew the urban-rural dichotomy and avoid using "city" and "village" as absolute categories. . . .

Despite the temptations of "common sense" and the pressure of historical and cultural ideologies, we can no longer think of Muslim

[2] A caravansary (i.e., a place where caravans would stop for food and rest). [Ed.]

[3] Residence for warriors and mystics. [Ed.]

[4] Scholars of Islam. [Ed.]

[5] Supreme leader of Muslim community. [Ed.]

cities as unique, bounded, or self-contained entities. From the study of social organization we find that none of the characteristic social bodies of Muslim society — the quarter, the fraternity, the religious community, and the state — were specifically urban forms of organization. Nor were any of the groups identified with cities *qua* physical settlements. Muslim populations were organized into groups which formed subcommunities within city spaces and super-communities of religion or state which extended beyond any single city space. Cities, in this view, were simply the geographical locus of groups whose membership and activities were either smaller than or larger than themselves. Cities were nodules of population woven into the fabric of a larger society — places which concentrated persons and activities, facilitated the organization of populations which cut across their own space, and helped them to resolve their relations to one another. Cities were physical entities but not unified social bodies defined by characteristically Muslim qualities.

Moreover, Muslim cities were no more isolated as physical bodies than as social bodies from the larger world in which they were embedded. Muslim settlements formed geographical and ecological, as well as social composites including territories and populations which were neither exclusively urban nor exclusively rural, but a combination of the two. The integration of villages, quarters, suburbs, and towns into larger geographical units provided a physical context for the kind of social pattern we have described. Furthermore, the role of the *jāmi'*[6] in Muslim religious life seems entirely consistent with the actualities of social and geographical organization. From this point of view we should not speak of "Muslim cities," but of settlements in the Middle East harboring a certain kind of Muslim society. If these hypotheses are well founded, we may begin to supersede our interest in cities as a crucial topic of historical, sociological, and cultural investigations by a more differentiated conception of the relationships between social structures, geographical forms, and religious meanings.

[6] Mosque for Friday prayers. [Ed.]

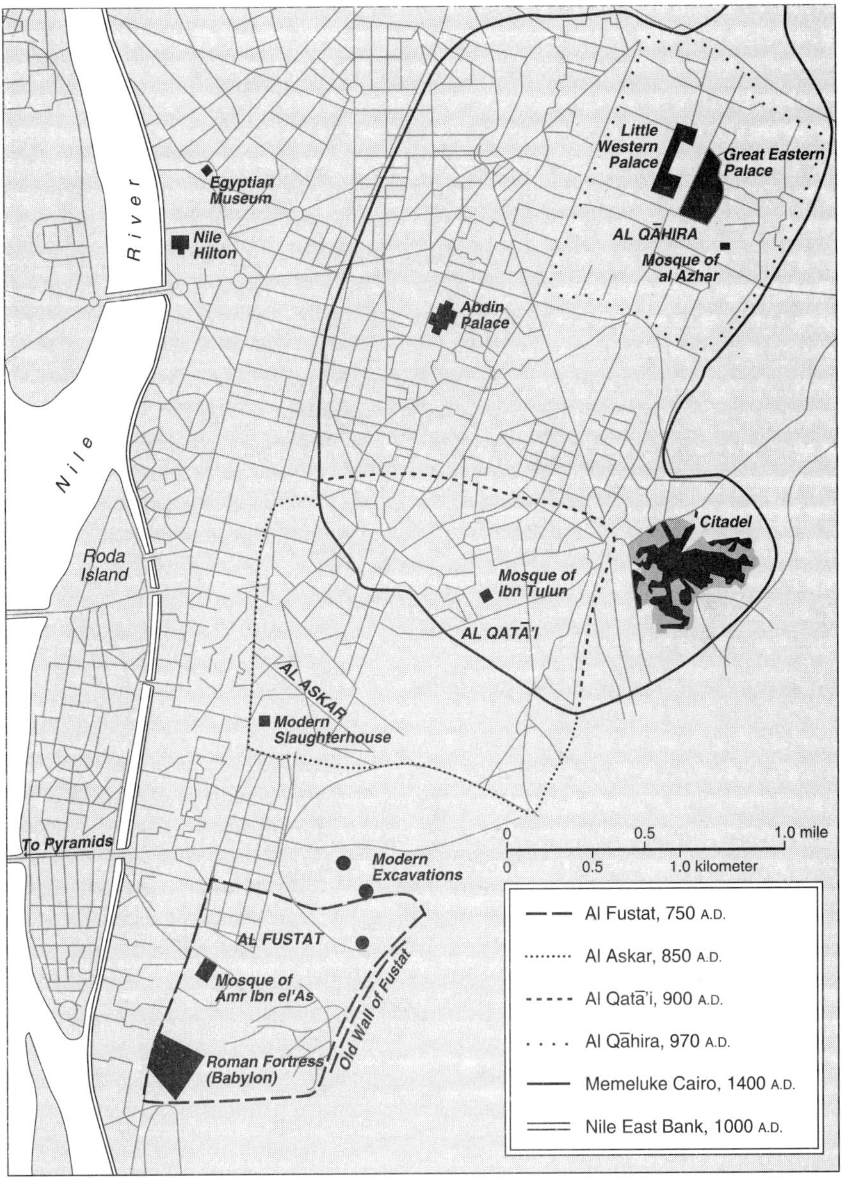

Figure 8. Map of Cairo, 1441.

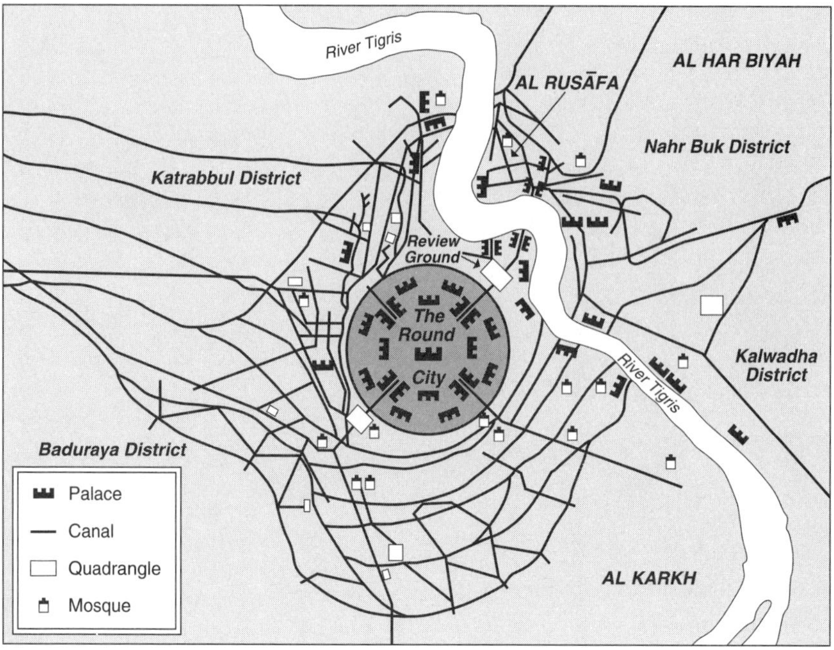

Figure 9. Map of Baghdad, 770–950 C.E.

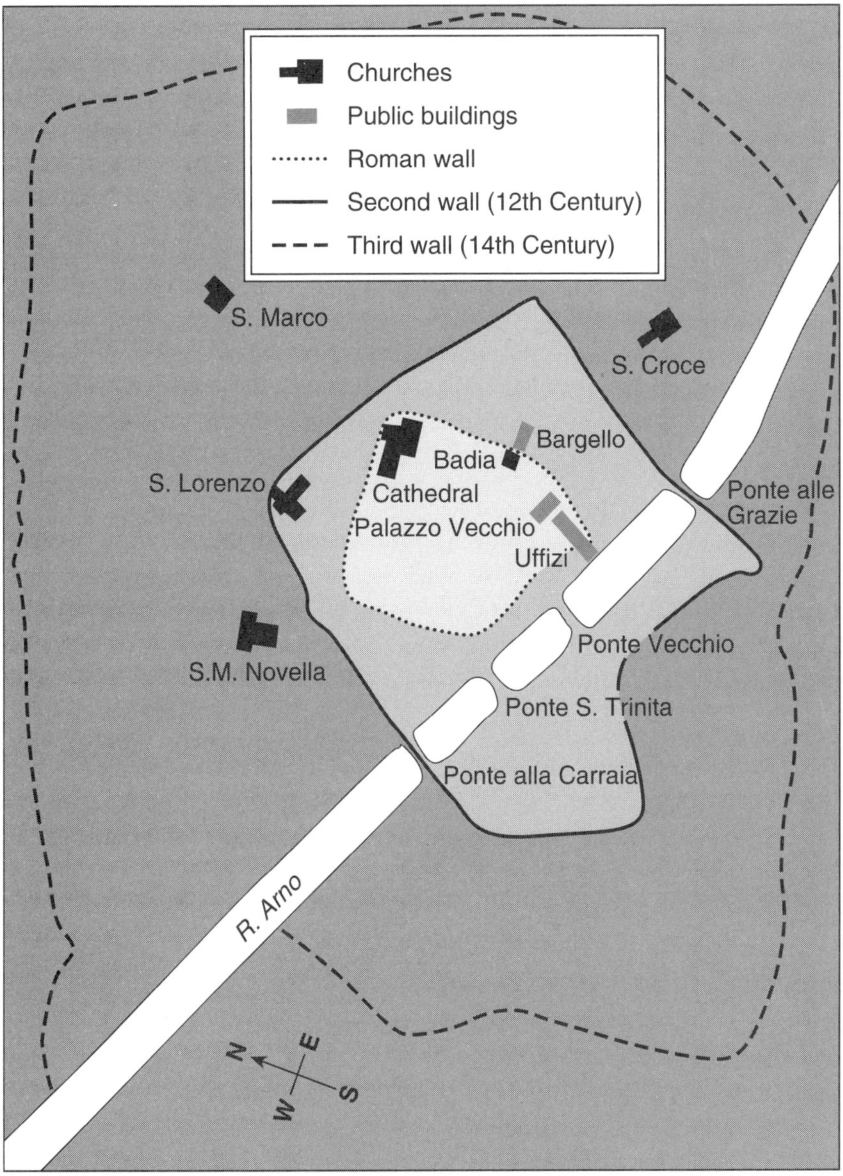

Figure 10. Map of Florence, twelfth–fourteenth century.

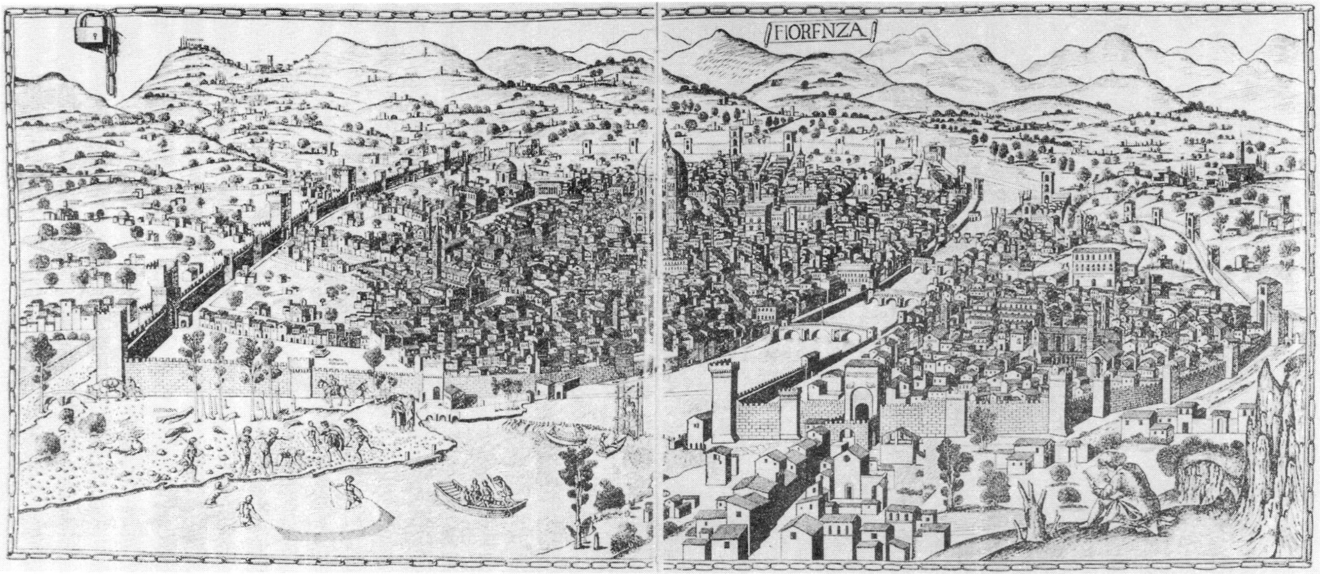

Figure 11. Illustration of Florence, 1470.

83

S. D. GOTIEN

Cairo: An Islamic City in Light of the Geniza

The author of this selection provides an especially detailed picture of medieval Cairo due to an unusual find of documents. "The Geniza" refers to a treasure trove of documents maintained by a Jewish synagogue in Cairo from the tenth to thirteenth centuries. Because it was considered sacrilegious for Jews to destroy the word of God or the word "God," the synagogue maintained a room where all written records could be deposited. Since anything might contain a word that should not be destroyed, virtually anything that had writing on it was brought to the synagogue for safe deposit. The Geniza contains correspondence, legal documents, receipts, inventories, prescriptions, and notes — written in Hebrew characters in the Arabic language — and offers a rare opportunity to review virtually everything a community wrote over a long period of time. It is an extremely valuable resource that can answer most questions about medieval society in Cairo.

In this selection, S. D. Gotien studies the documents for the insight they provide into city life in Cairo. What do the Geniza documents tell us about city life in Cairo? What possible inferences can we draw from the author's first sentence? What meaning does he draw? What would it have been like to live in medieval Cairo?

Thinking Historically

In what ways would life in medieval Cairo have been similar to or different from life in Florence? Which theses of medieval city life described in the chapter introduction, convergence or contrast, does Gotien's essay support? How is the rare mention of government buildings supporting evidence for this interpretation? What other characteristics of Cairo, mentioned here, support this interpretation?

. . . It is astounding how rarely government buildings are mentioned in the Geniza documents. There were the local police stations and prisons, as well as the offices where one received the licenses occasionally

---

S. D. Gotien, "Cairo: An Islamic City in Light of the Geniza," in *Middle Eastern Cities*, ed. Ira M. Lapidus (Berkeley and Los Angeles: University of California Press, 1969), 90–95.

needed, but even these are seldom referred to. The Mint and the Exchange are frequently referred to, but at least the latter was only semipublic in character, since the persons working there were not on the government payroll. Taxes were normally collected by tax farmers. Thus there was little direct contact between the government and the populace and consequently not much need for public buildings. The imperial palace and its barracks formed a city by itself, occasionally mentioned in Ayyūbid times, but almost never in the Fāṭimid period.

Government, although not conspicuous by many public buildings, was present in the city in many other ways. A city was governed by a military commander called *amīr,* who was assisted by the *wālī* or superintendent of the police. Smaller towns had only a *wālī* and no *amīr.* Very powerful, sometimes more powerful than the *amīr,* was the *qāḍī,* or judge, who had administrative duties in addition to his substantial judicial functions. The chief *qāḍī* often held other functions such as the control of the taxes or of a port, as we read with regard to Alexandria or Tyre. The city was divided into small administrative units called *rab'* (which is not the classical *rub',* meaning quarter, but instead designates an area, or rather a compound). Each *rab'* had a superintendent called *ṣāḥib rab'* (pronounced rub'), very often referred to in the Geniza papers. In addition to regular and mounted police there were plain clothesmen, or secret service men, called *aṣḥāb al-khabar,* "informants" who formed a government agency independent even of the *qāḍī,* a state of affairs for which there seem to exist parallels in more modern times.

An ancient source tells us that the vizier[1] al-Ma'mūn, mentioned above, instructed the two superintendents of the police of Fusṭāṭ and Cairo, respectively, to draw up exact lists of the inhabitants showing their occupations and other circumstances and to permit no one to move from one house to another without notification of the police. This is described as an extraordinary measure aimed at locating any would-be assassins who might have been sent to the Egyptian capital by the Bāṭiniyya, an Ismā'īlī group using murder as a political weapon. Such lists, probably with fewer details, no doubt were in regular use for the needs of taxation. In a letter from Sicily, either from its capital Palermo or from Mazara on its southwestern tip, the writer, an immigrant from Tunisia around 1063, informs his business friend in Egypt that he is going to buy a house and that he has already registered for the purpose in the *qānūn* (Greek *canon*) which must have designated an official list of inhabitants. With regard to non-Muslims, a differentiation was made between permanent residents and newcomers. Whether the same practice existed with respect to Muslims is not evident from the Geniza papers.

[1] Prime minister. [Ed.]

What were the dues that a town dweller had to pay to the government in his capacity as the inhabitant of a city, and what were the benefits that he derived from such payments? By right of conquest, the ground on which Fusṭāṭ stood belonged to the Muslims, that is, to the government (the same was the case in many other Islamic cities), and a ground rent, called *ḥikr,* had to be paid for each building. A great many deeds of sale, gift, and rent refer to this imposition. . . .

Besides the ground rent, every month a *ḥarāsa,* or "due for protection," had to be paid to the government. The protection was partly in the hands of a police force, partly in those of the superintendents of the compounds, and partly was entrusted to nightwatchmen, usually referred to as *ṭawwāfūn,* literally, "those that make the round," but known also by other designations. As we learn expressly from a Geniza source, the nightwatchmen, like the regular police, were appointed by the government (and not by a municipality or local body which did not exist). The amounts of the *ḥarāsa* in the communal accounts cannot be related to the value of the properties for which they were paid, but it is evident that they were moderate.

In a responsum written around 1165, Rabbi Maimon, the father of Moses Maimonides, states that the markets of Fusṭāṭ used to remain open during the nights, in contrast of course to what the writer was accustomed from having lived in other Islamic cities. In Fusṭāṭ, too, this had not been always the case. In a description of the festival of Epiphany from the year 941 in which all parts of the population took part, it is mentioned as exceptional that the streets were not closed during that particular night.

Sanitation must have been another great concern of the government, for the items "removal of rubbish" (called "throwing out of dust") and "cleaning of pipes" appear with great regularity in the monthly accounts preserved in the Geniza. One gets the impression that these hygienic measures were not left to the discretion of each individual proprietor of a house. The clay tubes bringing water (for washing purposes) to a house and those connecting it with a cesspool constantly needed clearing, and there are also many references to their construction. The amounts paid for both operations were considerable. The Geniza has preserved an autograph note by Maimonides permitting a beadle to spend a certain sum on "throwing out of dust" (presumably from a synagogue). This may serve as an illustration for the fact that landlords may have found the payment of these dues not always easy.

In this context we may also draw attention to the new insights gained through the study of the documents from the Geniza about the social life of Cairo. Massignon had asserted, and he was followed by many, that the life-unit in the Islamic city was the professional corporation, the guilds of the merchants, artisans, and scholars which had professional, as well as social and religious functions. No one would deny that this was true to a large extent for the sixteenth through the nineteenth centuries. However, there is not a shred of evidence that this was true for the ninth through the thirteenth centuries. . . .

The term "guild" designates a medieval union of craftsmen or traders which supervised the work of its members in order to uphold standards, and made arrangements for the education of apprentices and their initiation into the union. The guild protected its members against competition, and in Christian countries was closely connected with religion.

Scrutinizing the records of the Cairo Geniza or the Muslim handbooks of market supervision contemporary with them, one looks in vain for an Arabic equivalent of the term "guild." There was no such word because there was no such institution. The supervision of the quality of the artisans' work was in the hands of the state police, which availed itself of the services of trustworthy and expert assistants.

Regarding apprenticeship and admission to a profession, no formalities and no rigid rules are to be discovered in our sources. Parents were expected to have their sons learn a craft and to pay for their instruction, and the Geniza has preserved several contracts to this effect.

The protection of the local industries from the competition of newcomers and outsiders is richly documented by the Geniza records, but nowhere do we hear about a professional corporation fulfilling this task. It was the Jewish local community, the central Jewish authorities, the state police, or influential notables, Muslim and Jewish, who were active in these matters.

As to the religious aspect of professional corporation, the associations of artisans and traders in imperial Rome, or at least a part of them, bore a religious character and were often connected with the local cult of the town from which the founders of an association had originated. Similarly, the Christian guilds of the late Middle Ages had their patron saints and special rites. The fourteenth century was the heyday of Muslim corporations, especially in Anatolia (the present day Turkey), which adopted the doctrines and ceremonies of Muslim mystic brotherhoods. One looks in vain for similar combinations of artisanship and religious cult in the period and the countries under discussion. On the other hand, we find partnerships of Muslims and Jews both in workshops and in mercantile undertakings, for free partnerships were the normal form of industrial cooperation, and were common as well in commercial ventures. The classical Islamic city was a free enterprise society, the very opposite of a community organized in rigid guilds and tight professional corporations.

Further, we have stated before that no formal citizenship existed. The question is, however, how far did people feel a personal attachment to their native towns. "Homesickness," says Professor Gibb in his translation of the famous traveler Ibn Baṭṭūṭa "was hardly to be expected in a society so cosmopolitan as that of medieval Islam." Indeed the extent of travel and migration reflected in the Geniza is astounding. No less remarkable, however, is the frequency of expressions of longing for one's native city and the wish to return to it, as well as the fervor with which compatriots stuck together when they were abroad. On the other hand, I cannot find much of neighborhood factionalism or professional *esprit de corps,* both of which were so prominent in the later Middle Ages. Under an ever more oppressive military feudalism and government-regimented economy, life became miserable and insecure, and people looked for protection and assistance in their immediate neighborhood. In an earlier period, in a free-enterprise, competitive society, there was no place for such factionalism. A man felt himself to be the son of a city which provided him with the security, the economic possibilities, and the spiritual amenities which he needed.

84

ROSS E. DUNN

From *The Adventures of Ibn Battuta*

Map of Delhi Sultanate, 1325–1351
Map of Delhi, Fourteenth Century

In this selection, a modern historian recounts the story of Ibn Battuta's travels to the Indian city of Delhi in 1334. Ibn Battuta was a Muslim from Morocco — the westernmost Islamic society — who, as Ross Dunn relates, was welcomed as an official in Muslim India. What does this account tell you about how Delhi was governed?

Ross E. Dunn, *The Adventures of Ibn Battuta: A Muslim Traveler of the Fourteenth Century* (Berkeley: University of California Press, 1986), 196–200. Map of Delhi Sultanate under Muhammad Tughluq in *Atlas and Survey of South Asian History,* ed. Karl J. Schmidt (Armonk, NY: M. E. Sharpe, 1995), 41. Map of Delhi from Faiz Habib, in *Delhi Through the Ages,* ed. R. E. Frykenberg (Delhi: Oxford University Press, 1993), frontispiece.

Why was this inexperienced foreigner able to get an important job as a judge in a city he did not know, thousands of miles from his own, where the language of administration was Persian rather than Arabic and the tradition of Koranic law different from that of North Africa?

Thinking Historically

What does this story tell you about the Islamic city? Could something like this have happened in a European or a Chinese city? Which of the ideas about cities discussed in the chapter introduction does this selection support? How?

This selection also contains two maps. The first is a map of India under the Delhi Sultanate at its farthest extent, under Muhammad Tughluq (r. 1325–51), the sultan that Ibn Battuta met in 1334. The strongest sultan in the previous dynasty, the Khaljis (1290–1320) was Alauddin, who had extended his control only as far as the Tapi River in the central plain called the Deccan. How does that fact help explain Muhammad Tughluq's attempt to move the capital from Delhi? What does this map suggest about the success of that move?

The second map is of Delhi in the fourteenth century. It is called "Cities of Delhi" because it shows distinct urban areas, separated by villages and open spaces. The earliest of these cities is called Old Delhi, the site of the earlier Hindu fortress, Kil'a Ray Pithora, which had been conquered in 1192. The Muslims used the building's stone for their own fortress and mosque, the Quwwat al-Islam (mentioned in the text) and the Qutb Minar (on the map). Notice the distance between Old Delhi and the Yamuna River. In the 1260s an invasion cut off the water supply from the river to the Muslim tanks that had been built near the city, so the next settlement was established at Ghayaspur and a walled palace city erected at Kilokri in the 1280s, followed by the construction of the New City in the 1290s; the Sultan was suspicious of the loyalty of the citizens of Old Delhi. Under Mongol attack, Sultan Alauddin moved to higher ground and built a fortress capital at Siri and new markets in Old Delhi. The founder of the new Tughluq dynasty in 1320 built a new fortified capital east of Old Delhi at Tughluqabad, with the Hall of a Thousand Pillars where Ibn Battuta met the Sultan Muhammad Tughluq. The Sultan walled in the expanding population of Siri and Old Delhi, naming the territory Jahanpanah. The next ruler, Firuz Tughluq (r. 1351–88) built Firuzabad farther north while Old Delhi began to decay. How do each of these stages of Delhi reflect the needs of a conqueror? Which other cities does Delhi resemble in layout? What accounts for that similarity?

Ibn Battuta's first impression of Delhi might be clearer to us if he did not describe it in one part of the *Rihla* as "a vast and magnificent city . . . the largest city in India, nay rather the largest of all the cities of Islam in the East" and in another part as "empty and unpopulated save for a few inhabitants." The contradiction probably reflects the *'ulama's* disapproval, which Ibn Battuta shared, of Sultan Muhammad's decision in 1327 to move them to Daulatabad, his new capital in the dreary Deccan. Over about two years large numbers of officials, courtiers, and artisans did relocate. When Ibn Battuta arrived some time in the spring of 1334, part of the intelligentsia was still in Daulatabad. When he tells us the city was "empty and unpopulated," he was probably thinking only of the people that mattered, like a bored social climber at a crowded cocktail party who recalls that "nobody was there." In fact the large lower-class Hindu population of Delhi likely never went anywhere, excepting servants and employees of the state. Indeed about the same time that the sultan imposed his Daulatabad policy he also started building Jahanpanah, his new walled urban complex and palace a few miles northeast of old Delhi. Moreover, by the early 1330s he was giving up his dream of a capital in the center of his empire and permitting groups of unhappy exiles to return north if they wished. There seems little doubt that the city Ibn Battuta saw was in fact the largest in India and growing rapidly to serve the insatiable needs of the governing class.

When he arrived there, the sultan was absent in the Doab region southeast of Delhi. A tax revolt had erupted among the much-burdened peasantry, and Muhammad had been obliged to lead an army out from the capital to crush it. Nevertheless Ibn Battuta and his party went immediately to the new palace in Jahanpanah. There, in the huge wooden-roofed audience chamber called the Hall of a Thousand Pillars (Hazar Sutun), they paid their respects to Khwaja Jahan, the sultan's vizier. They also presented gifts at the palace residence of al-Makhdumah Jahan (the sultan's blind mother), ate a ceremonial meal, and accepted silk robes and other token gratuities befitting their status. At a second audience on the following day the vizier gave Ibn Battuta two thousand silver dinars to "wash his head," a symbolic gift of welcome proportioned in amount to the visitor's importance. A comfortably furnished house awaited him and his personal retinue in Kil'a Ray Pithora, the ancient Delhi of sandstone buildings and narrow streets clustered around the Quwwat al-Islam and its lofty minaret. In this house he would live during the next several years, passing many hours, we may presume, in the courts and domed arcades of the great mosque.

Until Muhammad Tughluq returned to Delhi, Ibn Battuta had no official appointment. However, the sultan was receiving regular reports on all the foreigners arriving in the capital in his absence. He sent orders to the vizier to give the new man, who had not yet lifted a finger in service to the state, an annual stipend of five thousand silver dinars to be paid from the revenue of two and a half villages located about sixteen miles north of the city. It was customary for state officials, army officers, and special honorees of the sultan to be paid regular allowances from taxes on crops produced in peasant villages rather than directly from the royal treasury. In the areas of North India where the authority of the sultanate was firm, the thousands of rural hamlets were registered, grouped in units of one hundred, and administered at the local level by petty Hindu or Muslim functionaries under the authority of the provincial governors. Grants of revenue from these villages could be awarded, withdrawn, or transferred at the pleasure of the sultan, and they carried no hereditary rights. The grantee did not have to live on his estate (and normally did not) nor take responsibility for the governing of its inhabitants, a task the state assumed directly. The poor farmers who toiled to produce this income had, of course, nothing to say about these arrangements.

Unknown *faqih*[1] that he was, Ibn Battuta's initial emolument did not amount to much by comparison with the revenue estates of the established elite. Nonetheless, while awaiting the emperor's return during the late spring of 1334, he took the trouble to ride out to the North Indian plain to inspect his two and a half villages. The Hindu country folk inhabiting these wretched clusters of mud wall and thatch held no fascination for him. He says nothing in the *Rihla* about the look of the hamlets or their residents, and he probably never bothered to visit them more than once.

Then on 8 June word came that Muhammad Tughluq was camped at a castle just seven miles from the city. On the vizier's orders, Ibn Battuta and the other newcomers went immediately out to the fort to greet the ruler with their gifts of obeisance. In order of their professional eminence each suppliant entered the audience room and was presented to the Master of the World, a tall, robust, white-skinned man seated, his legs tucked beneath him, on a gold-plated throne. This was the critical moment, for the emperor's first reaction to a man could mean the difference between future riches and total, immediate ostracism from the royal court.

> I approached the sultan, who took my hand and shook it, and continuing to hold it addressed me most affably, saying in Persian, "This is a blessing; your arrival is blessed; be at ease, I shall be compassionate to you and give you such favors that your fellow-countrymen will hear of it and come to join you." Then he asked me where I came from and I said to him, "From the land of the Maghrib." . . . Every time he said

[1] Scholar of Islamic law; jurist. [Ed.]

> any encouraging word to me I kissed his hand, until I had kissed it seven times, and after he had given me a robe of honor I withdrew.

Thus Ibn Battuta jumped the first hurdle into the circle of privilege. The next day he joined the triumphal entry into Delhi, a spectacular cavalcade of festooned elephants and cavalry, Hindu infantry columns, and singing girls. Muhammad Tughluq, the crusher of insurgent peasants, was now the benefactor to his people in the most extravagant tradition of a Hindu king:

> On some of the elephants there were mounted small military catapults, and when the sultan came near the city parcels of gold and silver coins mixed together were thrown from these machines. The men on foot in front of the sultan and the other persons present scrambled for the money, and they kept on scattering it until the procession reached the palace.

Shortly after these events two court officials paid a visit to Ibn Battuta and some of his associates to tell them the emperor was ready to make appointments to various government and religious posts: ministers, secretaries, commanders, judges, and *madrasa*[2] teachers. "Everyone was silent at first," Ibn Battuta remembers, "for what they were wanting was to gain riches and return to their countries." He for one was ready to come forward, declaring that he was descended from a long line of legal scholars and that he would be pleased to serve in some juridical capacity.

Forthwith he and several other notables were led to the Hall of a Thousand Pillars, where Sultan Muhammad awarded him the important office of *qadi* of Delhi. The emperor controlled all appointments to the judiciary, which constituted a branch of government separate from the political administration. Ibn Battuta would serve under the *qadi al-qudat,* or Chief Judge of the realm. Moreover, in a city as large as Delhi he was probably only one of several judges holding comparable positions. His compensation was to be two villages in addition to the ones he already had, carrying a total annual salary of twelve thousand silver dinars. He also received twelve thousand dinars in cash as an advance bonus, a horse with saddle and bridle, and yet another robe of honor. Such an income was not nearly as large as that of other, more prominent appointees. The average Hindu family, however, lived on about five dinars a month; a soldier in the royal army was paid nineteen and a half. Compared to ordinary folk of Hindustan, the obscure Moroccan *faqih* was about to become a very rich man.

[2] College of law and religion. [Ed.]

After several years of enjoying the favor of numerous kings and princes purely on the strength of his social status, earnest piety, and bright personality, Ibn Battuta was now walking into circumstances far more promising than anything he had known before. Muhammad Tughluq's policy was to pack his government with foreign professionals on whose personal loyalty he thought he could rely. Alien origin had become a more important criterion for office than distinction and experience. Only such circumstances can explain this stranger from the Far West of Islam being handed a magistracy whose responsibilities should have put him way out of his depth. Since leaving Morocco, he had spent hardly any time in sustained study of the law, excepting his brief sojourn in Damascus and his months in Mecca. He had had virtually no experience as a jurisconsult or sitting judge. Persian was the language of administrative and legal affairs in the sultanate, yet he did not, as he pointed out to his new master, speak it well at all. He also admitted that, as Maghribi, he was trained in the Maliki *madhhab,* whereas almost all *shari'a* decisions in India were founded on the Hanafi school. Very few people from Maliki countries lived in India, so there could hardly be much work to do. The sultan dismissed all these objections and appointed two Persian-speaking Hanafi scholars to serve as his "substitutes." Their job was presumably to do the day-to-day work of hearing cases of religious infraction or civil disputes among Muslims, the normal responsibilities of a *qadi.* "They will be guided by your advice," the emperor charged his new magistrate, "and you will be the one who signs all the documents." . . .

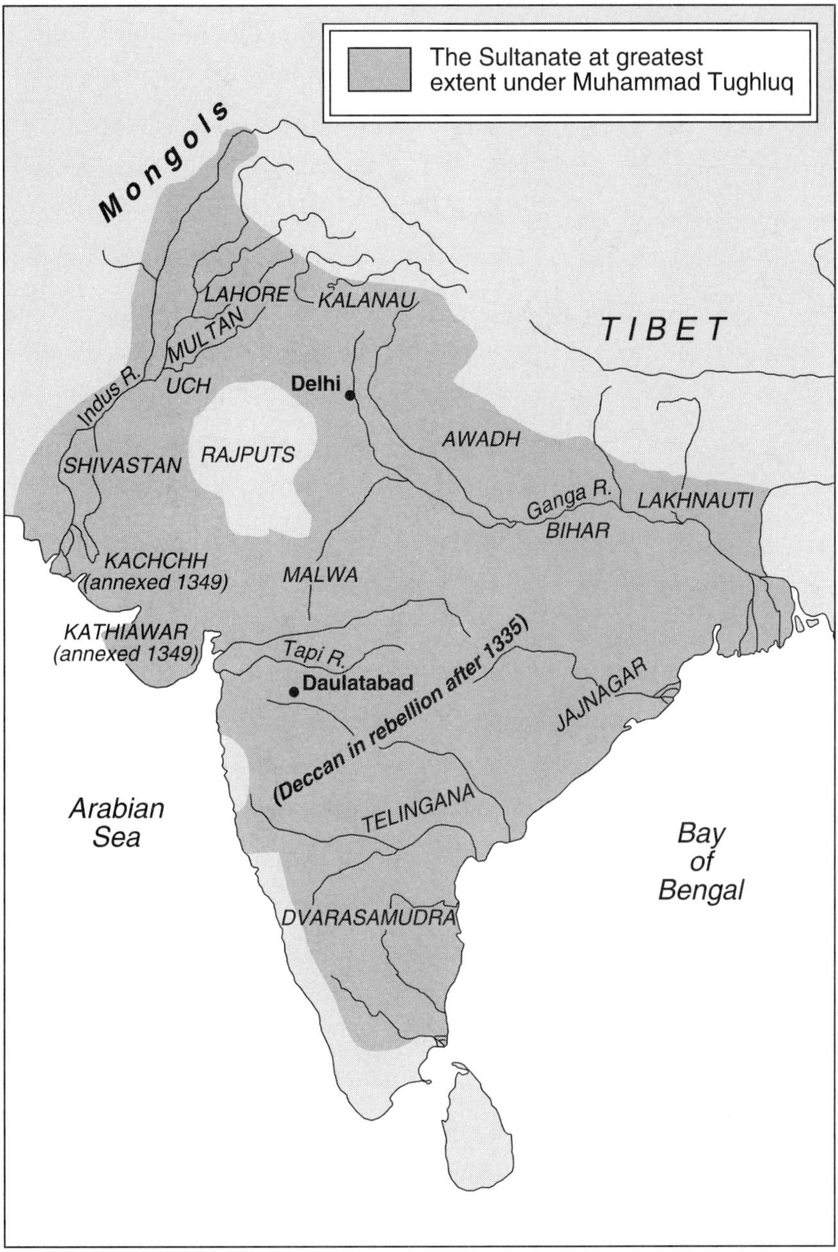

Figure 12. Map of Delhi Sultanate, 1325–1351.

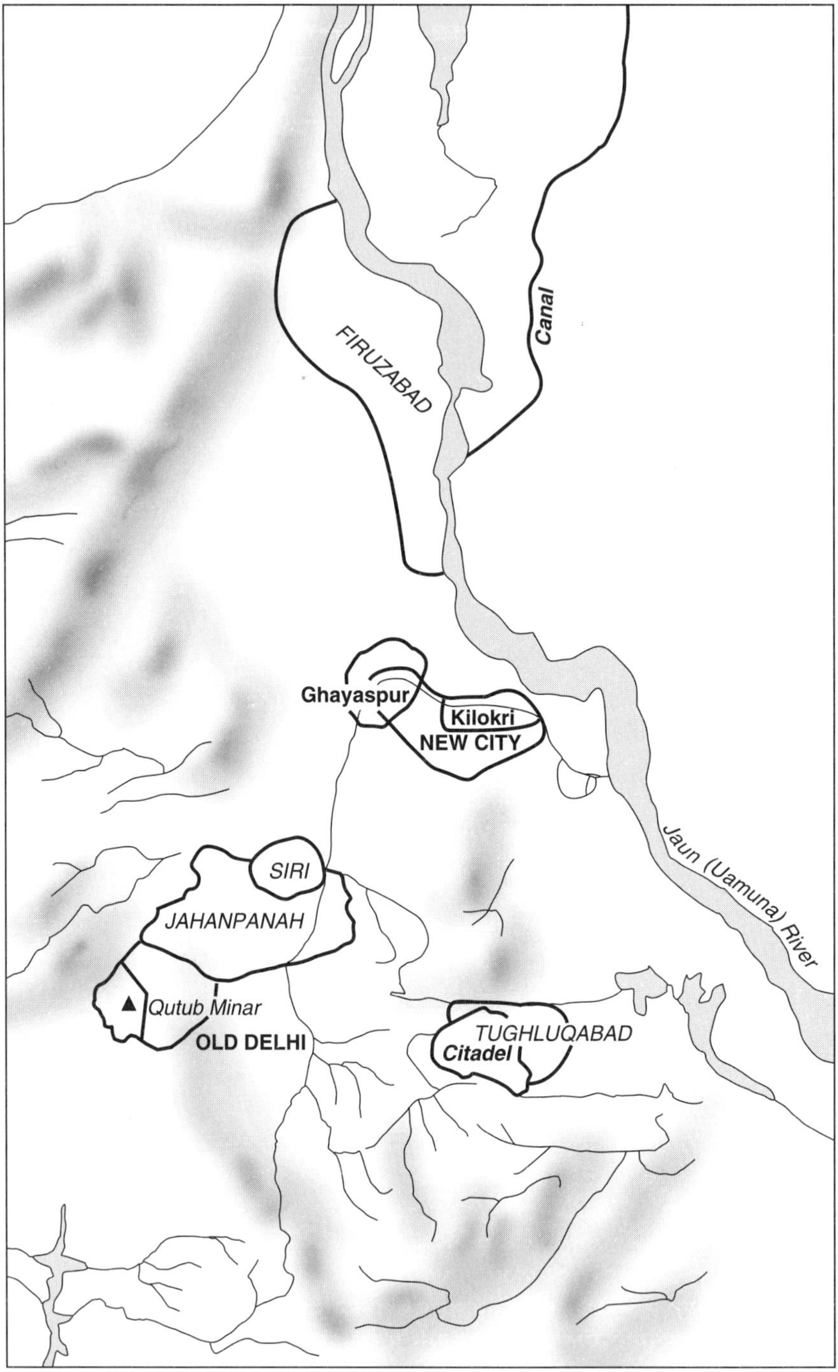

Figure 13. Map of Delhi, fourteenth century.

85

AL OMARI

Mali in the Fourteenth Century

The world of Islam extended across the Indian Ocean and the Sahara desert. In 1324 while making a pilgrimage to Mecca, the king of Mali, Mansa Musa, stopped in Cairo. The presence of his five-hundred member entourage, each carrying a four-pound staff of gold, was vividly recalled by Cairenes for years after his departure. One of those witnesses was the sultan's welcoming official, who here tells the historian Al Omari about that memorable visit. Al Omari also writes about Mansa Musa's Mali and its capital city, Niane.

Why was Mansa Musa reluctant to see the Sultan of Egypt? Why did the price of gold decline after Mansa Musa's visit to Egypt? Who were the pagans, and why did the king of Mali not convert them? What was the importance of the horse to Mali?

Thinking Historically

In what ways was Cairo a different kind of city from Mansa Musa's Niane? Sociologists distinguish between administrative capital cities that are usually large and contain a bureaucracy and "regal" ceremonial cities that are marked more by importance than size. Which of these would you call Niane?

Traveling through Cairo

During my first journey to Cairo and sojourn there I heard talk of the arrival of the Sultan Musa [*Mansa* Musa, emperor of Mali], and I found the Cairenes very glad to talk of the large expenditures of those people. I questioned the Emir Abu'l 'Abbas Ahmed ben Abi'l Haki, el Mehmendar, who spoke of the sultan's noble appearance, dignity, and trustworthiness. "When I went out to greet him in the name of the glorious Sultan el Malik en Nasir [of Egypt]," he told me, "he gave me the warmest of welcomes and treated me with the most careful politeness. But he would talk to me only through an interpreter [that is, his spokesman or linguist], although he could speak perfect Arabic. He carried his imperial treasure in many pieces of gold, worked or otherwise.

Al Omari, "Mali in the Fourteenth Century," in *The African Past,* trans. and ed. Basil Davidson (Boston: Atlantic, Little Brown, 1964), 75–79.

"I suggested that he should go up to the palace and meet the Sultan [of Egypt]. But he refused, saying: 'I came for the pilgrimage, and for nothing else, and I do not wish to mix up my pilgrimage with anything else.' He argued about this. However, I well understood that the meeting was repugnant to him because he was loath to kiss the ground [before the Sultan] or to kiss his hand. I went on insisting, and he went on making excuses. But imperial protocol obliged me to present him, and I did not leave him until he had agreed. When he came into the Sultan's presence we asked him to kiss the ground. But he refused and continued to refuse, saying: 'However can this be?' Then a wise man of his suite whispered several words to him that I could not understand. 'Very well,' he thereupon declared, 'I will prostrate myself before Allah who created me and brought me into the world.' Having done so he moved toward the Sultan. The latter rose for a moment to welcome him and asked him to sit beside him; then they had a long conversation. After Sultan Musa had left the palace the Sultan of Cairo sent him gifts of clothing for himself, his courtiers, and all those who were with him; saddled and bridled horses for himself and his chief officers . . .

"When the time of pilgrimage arrived, [the Sultan of Egypt] sent him a large quantity of drachmas, baggage camels, and choice riding camels with saddles and harness. [The Sultan of Egypt] caused abundant quantities of foodstuffs to be bought for his suite and his followers, established posting-stations for the feeding of the animals, and gave to the emirs of the pilgrimage a written order to look after and respect [the Emperor of Mali]. When the latter returned it was I who went to greet him and settle him into his quarters . . ."

"This man," el Mehmendar also told me, "spread upon Cairo the flood of his generosity: There was no person, officer of the [Cairo] court or holder of any office of the [Cairo] sultanate who did not receive a sum in gold from him. The people of Cairo earned incalculable sums from him, whether by buying and selling or by gifts. So much gold was current in Cairo that it ruined the value of money." . . .

Let me add [continues Omari] that gold in Egypt had enjoyed a high rate of exchange up to the moment of their arrival. The gold *mitqal* that year had not fallen below twenty-five drachmas. But from that day [of their arrival] onward, its value dwindled; the exchange was ruined, and even now it has not recovered. The *mitqal* scarcely touches twenty-two drachmas. That is how it has been for twelve years from that time, because of the great amounts of gold they brought to Egypt and spent there.

The Empire of Mali

The king of this country is known to the people of Egypt as the king of Tekrur [roughly, inland Senegal]; but he himself becomes indignant when he is called thus, since Tekrur is only one of the countries of his empire. The title he prefers is that of lord of Mali, the largest of his states; it is the name by which he is most known. He is the most important of the Muslim Negro kings; his land is the largest, his army the most numerous; he is the king who is the most powerful, the richest, the most fortunate, the most feared by his enemies, and the most able to do good to those around him.

His kingdom consists of the lands of Gana, Zagun, Tirakka, Tekrur, Bambugu, Zarquatabana, Darmura, Zara, Kabora, Bara-guri, Gao-gao. The inhabitants of Gao-gao are of the tribes of Yarten. The region of Mali is that where the residence of the king is situated [in] the town of Niane, and all the other regions are dependent on it; it has the official name of Mali because it is the capital of this kingdom which also includes towns, villages, and centers of population to the number of fourteen.

The honorable and truthful Sheikh Abu Sa'id Otman ed Dukkali, who has lived in the town of Niane for thirty-five years and traveled throughout the kingdom, has told me that this is square in shape, being four months [of travel] in length and at least as much in breadth. . . .

The sultan of this country has sway over the land of the "desert of native gold," whence they bring him gold every year. The inhabitants of that land are savage pagans whom the sultan would subject to him if he wished. But the sovereigns of this kingdom have learned by experience that whenever one of them has conquered one of these gold towns, established Islam there, and sounded the call to prayer, the harvest of gold dwindles and falls to nothing, meanwhile it grows and expands in neighboring pagan countries. When experience had confirmed them in this observation, they left the gold country in the hands of its pagan inhabitants, and contented themselves with assuring their obedience and paying tribute.

Reception at Court

The sultan of this kingdom presides in his palace on a great balcony called *bembe*, where he has a great seat of ebony that is like a throne fit for a large and tall person: On either side it is flanked by elephant tusks turned toward each other. His arms stand near him, being all of gold, saber, lance, quiver, bow and arrows. He wears wide trousers made of about twenty pieces [of stuff] of a kind which he alone may wear. Behind him there stand about a score of Turkish or other pages which are bought for him in Cairo. One of them, at his left, holds a silk umbrella surmounted by a dome and a bird of gold: The bird has the figure of a falcon. His officers are seated in a circle about him, in two rows, one to the right and one to the left; beyond them sit the chief commanders of his cavalry. In front of him there is a person who never leaves him and who is his executioner; also another who serves as intermediary [that is, official spokesman] between the sovereign and his subjects, and who is named the herald. In front of them again, there are drummers. Others dance before their sovereign, who enjoys this, and make him laugh. Two banners are spread behind him. Before him they keep two saddled and bridled horses in case he should wish to ride.

The Importance of Horses

Arab horses are brought for sale to the kings of this country, who spend considerable sums in this way. Their army numbers one hundred thousand men, of whom there are about ten thousand horse-mounted cavalry: The others are infantry, having neither horses nor any other mounts. They have camels in this country but do not know the art of riding them with a saddle . . .

The officers of this king, his soldiers, and his guard receive gifts of land and presents. Some among the greatest of them receive as much as fifty thousand *mitqals* of gold a year, besides which the king provides them with horses and clothing. He is much concerned with giving them fine garments and making his cities into capitals.

Royal Bureaucracy

It is one of their customs that whenever someone charged with a certain task of important affair reports to the king, the latter questions him on everything that has happened from the time of his departure to the time of his return, and in great detail. Legal cases and appeals also go up to the sovereign who examines them himself. Generally he writes nothing; but gives his orders, most of the time, orally. He has *qadis,* secretaries, offices.

REFLECTIONS

In the debate between cities as contrasting and converging worlds, this chapter has emphasized the case for contrasting types, focusing on the differences between European autonomous and communal cities and Chinese and Muslim administrative ones. Now might be a good time to qualify those judgments.

First, we should not assume that autonomous or communal cities were limited to Europe. Rather, they were a product of a feudal, or politically weak and decentralized society, where urban populations were able to bargain for special privileges. We could find similar examples of urban autonomy among, for example, Japanese port cities during the Japanese feudal era of the fourteenth to sixteenth centuries. One of these, Sakai, was called the Venice of Japan. Sakai's wealthy commercial elite — whose prosperity resulted from commerce in textiles, lacquer ware, metal castings, rice, and lumber — staffed and ran their own municipal governments. The Japanese cities of Nara and Amagasaki also used commercial prosperity to gain political independence. Not until after 1600 and the re-centralization of Japan under the Tokugawa administration were these independent cities brought to heel. In many ways, Tokugawa developments paralleled those of Europe, where centralized states also subordinated the independence of commercial cities after 1700.

Second, the absence of a movement for urban autonomy in Islamic and Chinese cities — important as it was in the time and places discussed in this chapter — was not universal. Chinese cities before the Mongol Yüan dynasty, especially in the earlier Sung dynasty, had developed an extremely prosperous commercial class. And while it is true that they did not gain (or seek) urban independence, they were content to exercise sufficient influence on the local representatives of the emperor. No appointed mayor could think lightly of ignoring the advice of the many Chinese guilds (one of the more important forces for self-government in Europe) or of the uniquely Chinese class of civil-service exam graduates, active and retired. Chinese merchants did not create democratic voting councils to govern their cities. Most distrusted the judgments of the uneducated people. But governors always sought the wisdom and advice of the well educated, and the urban elite always got their way.

Third, while medieval Muslim cities encouraged little urban autonomy or identity, a prosperous class of merchants — always at the core of Islam — were nourished by more enlightened sultans and emirs. The Turkish historian Halil Inalcik writes that it was "the deliberate policy" of the Ottoman government, as it founded its successive capitals at Bursa in 1326, Edirne in 1402, and Istanbul in 1453, to create commercial and industrial centers, and that it consequently used every means — from tax exemptions to force — to attract and settle merchants and artisans in the new capitals. With the same end in view, Mehmed II encouraged the Jews of Europe to migrate to his new capital at Istanbul as they were being expelled from Spain and Portugal.

Fourth, there are many forces of convergence in the history of urbanization that the selections in this chapter have not addressed. Almost all of our sources celebrate the magnificence and magnification of urban, as opposed to rural or village, life. Each city is the largest or richest of its kind; the authors of these sources, especially the visitors, are overwhelmed.

Are there certain pressures that all cities exert? If so, what are they? In Chapters 2 and 3, you read about ancient cities. Did those cities have certain tendencies that continued in Medieval cities? Chapter 2, for example, asked if ancient cities created patriarchies. Did medieval urbanization continue this trend? The cities, after all, were the places where men came together. Patriarchs must protect their wives and daughters in cities. In China, foot-binding, which crippled women's feet and restricted their movement, developed in the cities of the T'ang and Sung. While Berber and Muslim women traveled freely in the countryside, cities exposed them to the glances of men who were strangers, so they had to be veiled. No doubt cities provided opportunities as well as patriarchal traps for women, but it is likely that the opportunities came at considerable cost.

Finally, we have limited our survey in the interest of coherence to a few great societies — European, Chinese, and Muslim. We said little of Africa and nothing of the Americas. The Americas will be the subject of the next chapter, and we will begin with a survey of one of its great cities, the Aztec capital of Mexico. While we will read about the Americas for other purposes, think about cities as well: Broaden the range of your knowledge to encompass more of the world.

14

The Spanish Conquest of Mexico

HISTORICAL CONTEXT

The Spanish Conquest of Mexico and "the Indies," 1500–1550 C.E.

That so many people in Mexico, the West Indies, and South America today speak Spanish is somewhat fortuitous. Christopher Columbus was a sailor from Genoa who traveled for the Portuguese in the 1480s. He tried to convince the Portuguese king to finance a voyage (based on a Florentine map and the miscalculations of the Venetian traveler Marco Polo) that located the spice-rich Indies as being closer to the West than to the East. The Portuguese king declined, because he knew that sailing around Africa was shorter, as the Portuguese navigator Vasco da Gama did in 1497. However, because Spain (which, but for the recent union of Ferdinand of Aragon and Isabella of Castile, barely existed) supported Columbus, and because of its expansionary fervor as Ferdinand and Isabella expelled the Jews and conquered the Muslims, and because the royal couple could draw funds from the Jewish financiers who worked with their palace treasurer, Columbus would eventually "discover America" for Spain. During four voyages, Columbus claimed a number of Caribbean Islands and points on the coast from modern Nicaragua to Venezuela, settled Spaniards on Hispaniola, and laid the groundwork for one of the largest empires in world history. All the while, in perhaps one of the most productive blunders ever, Columbus believed he was near China and Japan, in the realm of the Great Khan, whom Marco Polo had met and who actually had died hundreds of years earlier.

Fortuitous or not, Spain rapidly established, in Santo Domingo on Hispaniola, an imperial administration that sought out every opportunity to trade and profit, to conquer and convert — all for God and gold.

In many ways, Spain's expansionism was a continuation of the Crusades — the next step after the defeat of Granada, the last Muslim stronghold on the Iberian Peninsula in 1492. Its consequences, however, would create a new world that was more unified than Columbus ever could have imagined.

The conquest of Mexico was the first financially successful strike for the Spanish. On the Caribbean islands, the Spanish failed to find the gold, spices, or fabled cities Columbus had imagined. The chief economic advantage of the islands was land, which the Spanish claimed with due ceremony, and Indian labor, which they seized without hesitation. The land remained but the Indians died off, requiring the Spanish to look further afield for new opportunities. Then came the discovery of Mexico. Mexico provided opportunities beyond the Spaniards' wildest dreams, but the conquest had consequences that even today are profound and tragic.

While in retrospect it is easy for historians to see how the Spanish experience in the Indies and Mexico bore certain similarities to other colonial endeavors (e.g., Crusader states in Jerusalem, earlier Muslim expansion), the experience for those involved was one of continual shock and surprise. Little could be expected of a world not previously known to exist.

Observe what the Spanish and Indians see and think of each other in this far-reaching encounter. What were each group's motives, their strategies, their successes and failures? What drove the Spanish in their conquest, especially because they were on foreign ground? What, ultimately, do you think these two peoples understood of each other?

THINKING HISTORICALLY

Understanding How and Why Events Are Reinterpreted

Not only are there two sides to every story, but the context of the story changes over time. In this chapter, we examine the encounter between the Spanish and the Indians of Mexico when it occurred, as it was understood within a generation or two of the conquest, and as it is interpreted by present-day historians at the end of the twentieth century. Our goal here is to understand how and why an event — particularly such a consequential event about which much is known — is remembered and reinterpreted, and then remembered and reinterpreted once again. What, this chapter asks, is the relationship between the truth of the past and each generation's need to ask its own questions and develop its own understanding?

86

BERNAL DÍAZ

From *The Conquest of New Spain*

Bernal Díaz del Castillo was born in Spain in 1492, the year Columbus sailed to America. After participating in two explorations of the Mexican coast, Díaz joined the expedition of Hernán Cortés in 1519. He wrote this history of the conquest much later, in his seventies, and he died around 1580, a municipal official with a small estate in Guatemala.

The conquest of Mexico did not automatically follow from the first Spanish settlements in the West Indies (first in Santo Domingo, Hispaniola, and then Cuba). The Spanish crown had given permission for trade and exploration, not colonization. But the fortune-seeking peasant-soldiers whose fathers had fought to rid Spain of Muslims and Jews were not easily dissuaded from conquering their own lands and gaining their own populations of dependent Indians. Hernán Cortés, of minor noble descent and a failed student at the University of Salamanca, at the age of nineteen sailed to the Indies, where he enjoyed a sizeable estate on the island of Hispaniola. When he heard stories of Montezuma's gold from an Indian woman who had been given to him in tribute, he determined to find the fabled capital of the Aztec Empire, Tenochtitlán (modern Mexico City). Cortés gathered more than five hundred amateur soldiers, eleven ships, sixteen horses, and several pieces of artillery, sailed across the Caribbean and Gulf of Mexico to a settlement he christened Veracruz, and then began the long march from the coast up to the high central plateau of Mexico.

The Aztecs were new to central Mexico, arriving from the North American desert only about two hundred years before the Spanish, around 1325. They settled on an island in the middle of the large lake on the central plain, shunned by the peoples of other cities who considered themselves more sophisticated and cultured than the newcomers. In less than two hundred years, this band of uncouth foreigners established dominion over almost all the other city-states of Mexico, by 1500 ruling an empire that stretched as far south as Guatemala and as far east as the Mayan lands of the Yucatan Peninsula.

Aztec power relied on a combination of old and new religious ideas and a military system that conquered through terrorism. The older religious traditions that the Aztecs adopted were those of the classical

---

Bernal Díaz, *The Conquest of New Spain*, trans. J. M. Cohen (London: Penguin Books), 220–45. Map of Mexico City, published with the Second Letter of Hernán Cortés, in *Praeclara Ferdinandi Cortesii De Nova Maris Oceani Hispanica Narratio* (Nuremberg, 1524).

Toltec culture, at the center of which stood the god Quetzalcoatl — the feathered serpent, god of creation and brotherhood. The nurturing forces of Quetzalcoatl continued in Aztec society in a system of universal and obligatory education and in festivals dedicated to life, creativity, and procreation. But the Aztecs also celebrated a god they had brought with them from the north, Huitzilopochtli — a warrior god, primed for death and sacrifice.

Huitzilopochtli (rendered as Huichilobos in this selection) was given dominant status in the Aztec pantheon by Tlacaelel, an adviser to Montezuma's predecessor, Itzcoatl (r. 1428–1440). Tlacaelel envisioned Huitzilopochtli as a force for building a powerful Aztec Empire. Drawing on the god's need for human sacrifice — a need not unknown among the religions of central Mexico (or Christians) — Tlacaelel built altars to Huitzilopochtli at Tenochtitlán, Cholula, and other sites. According to the tenets of the religion, the war god required a neverending supply of human hearts, which compelled Aztec armies to seek out sacrificial victims in ever more remote sections of Central America, necessarily creating an endless supply of enemies for the Aztecs. Among these, the Tlaxcalans — whom the Aztecs left independent so they could be conquered at will for war captives — proved to be an eager ally of Cortés and the Spanish. Other Mexican peoples eagerly joined the Spanish-Tlaxcalan alliance.

The eclipse of Quetzalcoatl by Huitzilopochtli was never complete. In 1519, people still remembered the stories of Quetzalcoatl's departure. He had been given a mirror by his enemies. When he looked into it, he saw that his image was like his creation — and thus might be subject to the same mortality. Despondent, he left his people, promising to return on a fixed day in the future, Ce Acatl, the Day of the Reed.

As that day approached in 1519, the Aztec seers recorded various unnatural disturbances: fires streaked across the sky; the waters of the lake around Tenochtitlán boiled with rage; and a woman was heard crying for people to leave the city. In addition, an unusual gray bird was found in the nets of fishermen — a bird with a mirror in its head; in the mirror Montezuma could see strange people coming forward quickly over a distant plain. When Montezuma was informed of the two great towers (ships) that moved over the waters, when he heard of the white-faced fishermen sitting on giant deer (horses), he knew Quetzalcoatl had returned.

With the help of his Indian captive and companion, Doña Marina, called La Malinche by some of the Indians (Montezuma thus sometimes calls Cortés "Lord Malinche" in the selection), Cortés was able to communicate with the Tlaxcalans and other Indians who were frustrated with Aztec domination. On his march toward Tenochtitlán, Cortés stopped to join forces with the Tlaxcalans, perhaps cementing the relationship and demonstrating his resolve with a brutal massacre of the people of Cholula, an Aztec ally and arch enemy of the Tlaxcalans. By the time Cortés arrived at Tenochtitlán, Montezuma knew of the defeat of his allies at Cholula.

This selection from Bernal Díaz begins with the Spanish entry into Tenochtitlán. What impresses Díaz, and presumably other Spanish conquistadors, about the Mexican capital city? What parts of the city most attract his attention? What conclusions does he draw about Mexican (or Aztec) civilization? Does he think Spanish civilization is equal, inferior, or superior to that of Mexico?

Map of Tenochtitlán (Mexico City) from Cortés's Letter

Notice the map of Tenochtitlán included here. This map was drawn as part of a letter that Cortés wrote to the Spanish king, though this rendition was the engraving made for the published edition in Nuremberg in 1524. You can trace the route of Cortés from the southern city of Iztalpalapa up the causeway to Tenochtitlán. Notice that the central square within the main temple (see Figure 14) is at the center of the city. Notice also the number of other cities shown on the map. This map was a popular introduction to Mexico for readers in Europe. What does a map like this tell Europeans who believe that cities are the mark of a civilized people? The Latin inscription on the central square that shows both the great temple (called Teocali) and Montezuma's palace reads, "A temple where human sacrifice was carried out." Beneath the great temple stands a headless figure, and heads with hair are shown on racks both under the figure and to the left of the great temple. What message does this imagery convey about Aztec civilization?

Thinking Historically

In this chapter we examine the ways in which the encounter between Spaniards and Mexicans has been understood and debated over the centuries. What does the history of Díaz tell you about the ways in which Spaniards and Aztecs viewed each other in 1519? Díaz, of course, is a Spanish conquistador, but does he, intentionally or not, help us understand the Aztec view of this encounter?

Díaz gives us a dramatic account of the meeting of Cortés and Montezuma. What do you think each is thinking and feeling? Do you detect any signs of tension in their elaborate greetings? Why are both behaving so politely? What do they want from each other?

Notice how the initial hospitality turns tense. What causes this? Is either side more to blame for what happens next? Was conflict inevitable? Could the encounter have ended in some sort of peaceful resolution?

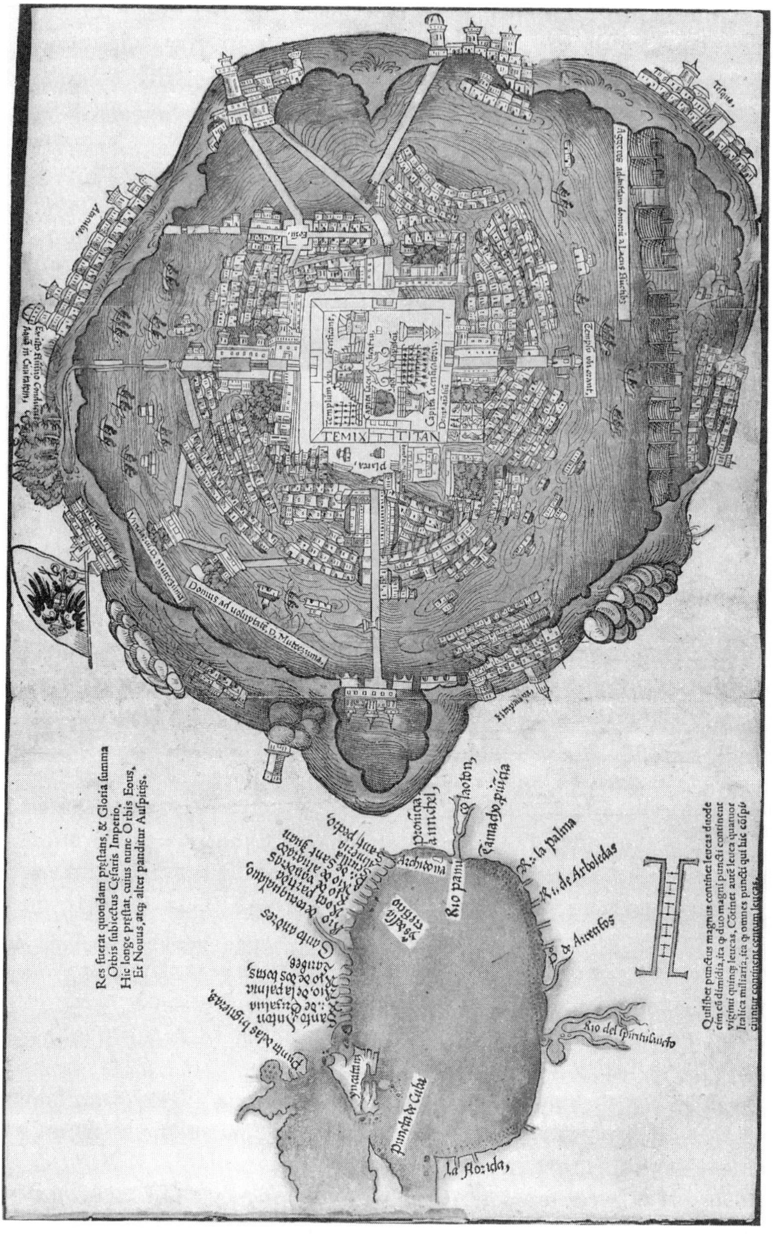

Figure 14. Map of Tenochtitlán (Mexico City).

Cortés's map can also be studied for clues about Spanish and Mexican perceptions of each other. The map renders the main causeways, streets, and canals with a fair degree of accuracy. The houses, however, are European rather than Mexican, as is the monumental

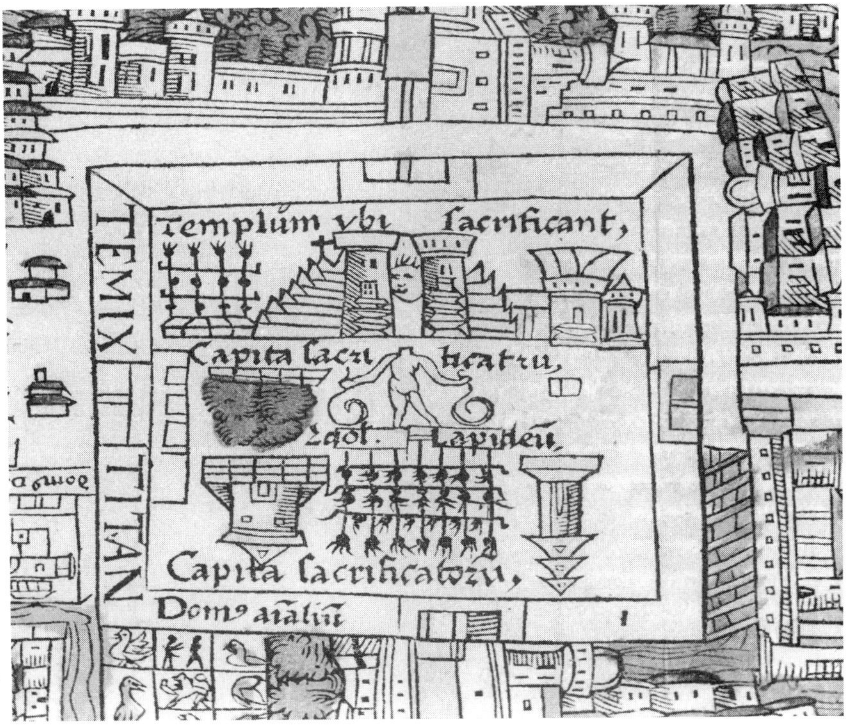

Figure 15. Detail of Central Square.

architecture. Only the inset with the Teocali temple shows us Aztec pyramid architecture and that, too, is surrounded by European-style towers and palaces, one of which would be Montezuma's palace. Why does the artist turn Mexican dwellings into European ones? Why does he translate the pyramid towers, except for Teocali, into European-style towers? Why, in short, does the artist prefer European icons for house, temple, and palace, instead of images that show what these buildings actually looked like? Is it possible that Tenochtitlán looked too foreign for Spanish eyes? Might European icons have made the city more Spanish?

When Cortes saw, heard, and was told that the great Montezuma was approaching, he dismounted from his horse, and when he came near to Montezuma each bowed deeply to the other. Montezuma welcomed our Captain, and Cortes, speaking through Doña Marina, answered by wishing him very good health. Cortes, I think, offered Montezuma his right hand, but Montezuma refused it and extended his own. Then

Cortes brought out a necklace which he had been holding. It was made of those elaborately worked and coloured glass beads called *margaritas* . . . and was strung on a gold cord and dipped in musk to give it a good odour. This he hung round the great Montezuma's neck, and as he did so attempted to embrace him. But the great princes who stood round Montezuma grasped Cortes's arm to prevent him, for they considered this an indignity.

Then Cortes told Montezuma that it rejoiced his heart to have seen such a great prince, and that he took his coming in person to receive him and the repeated favours he had done him as a high honour. After this Montezuma made him another complimentary speech, and ordered two of his nephews who were supporting him, the lords of Texcoco and Coyoacan, to go with us and show us our quarters. Montezuma returned to the city with the other two kinsmen of his escort, the lords of Cuitlahuac and Tacuba; and all those grand companies of *Caciques*[1] and dignitaries who had come with him returned also in his train. And as they accompanied their lord we observe them marching with their eyes downcast so that they should not see him, and keeping close to the wall as they followed him with great reverence. Thus space was made for us to enter the streets of Mexico without being pressed by the crowd.

Who could now count the multitude of men, women, and boys in the streets, on the rooftops, and in canoes on the waterways, who had come out to see us? It was a wonderful sight and, as I write, it all comes before my eyes as if it had happened only yesterday.

They led us to our quarters, which were in some large houses capable of accommodating us all and had formerly belonged to the great Montezuma's father, who was called Axayacatl. Here Montezuma now kept the great shrines of his gods, and a secret chamber containing gold bars and jewels. This was the treasure he had inherited from his father, which he never touched. Perhaps their reason for lodging us here was that, since they called us *Teules*[2] and considered us as such, they wished to have us near their idols. In any case they took us to this place, where there were many great halls, and a dais hung with the cloth of their country for our Captain, and matting beds with canopies over them for each of us.

On our arrival we entered the large court, where the great Montezuma was awaiting our Captain. Taking him by the hand, the prince led him to his apartment in the hall where he was to lodge, which was very richly furnished in their manner. Montezuma had ready for him a very rich necklace, made of golden crabs, a marvellous piece of work, which he hung round Cortes's neck. His captains were greatly astonished at this sign of honour.

After this ceremony, for which Cortes thanked him through our interpreters, Montezuma said: "Malinche, you and your brothers are in

[1] Chiefs. [Ed.]
[2] Gods. [Ed.]

your own house. Rest awhile." He then returned to his palace, which was not far off.

We divided our lodgings by companies, and placed our artillery in a convenient spot. Then the order we were to keep was clearly explained to us, and we were warned to be very much on the alert, both the horsemen and the rest of us soldiers. We then ate a sumptuous dinner which they had prepared for us in their native style.

So, with luck on our side, we boldly entered the city of Tenochtitlán or Mexico on 8 November in the year of our Lord 1519.

The Stay in Mexico

When the great Montezuma had dined and was told that our Captain and all of us had finished our meal some time ago, he came to our quarters in the grandest state with a great number of princes, all of them his kinsmen. On being told of his approach, Cortes came into the middle of the hall to receive him. Montezuma then took him by the hand, and they brought chairs made in their fashion and very richly decorated in various ways with gold. Montezuma requested our Captain to sit down, and both of them sat, each on his own chair.

Then Montezuma began a very good speech, saying that he was delighted to have such valiant gentlemen as Cortes and the rest of us in his house and his kingdom. That two years ago he had received news of a Captain who had come to Champoton, and that last year also he had received a report of another Captain who had come with four ships. Each time he had wished to see them, and now that he had us with him he was not only at our service but would share all that he possessed with us. He ended by saying that we must truly be the men about whom his ancestors had long ago prophesied, saying that they would come from the direction of the sunrise to rule over these lands, and that he was confirmed in this belief by the valour with which we had fought at Champoton and Tabasco and against the Tlascalans, for lifelike pictures of these battles had been brought to him.

Cortes replied through our interpreters that we did not know how to repay the daily favours we received from him, and that indeed we did come from the direction of the sunrise, and were vassals and servants of a great king called the Emperor Charles, who was ruler over many great princes. Having heard news of Montezuma and what a great prince he was, the Emperor, he said, had sent us to this country to visit him, and to beg them to become Christians, like our Emperor and all of us, so that his soul and those of all his vassals might be saved. Cortes promised to explain to him later how this could be, and how we worship the one true God and who He is, also many other good things which he had already communicated to his ambassadors Tendile, Pitalpitoque, and Quintalbor.

The great Montezuma had some fine gold jewels of various shapes in readiness which he gave to Cortes after this conversation. And to each of our captains he presented small gold objects and three loads of cloaks of rich feather work; and to us soldiers he gave two loads of cloaks each, all with a princely air. For in every way he was like a great prince. After the distribution of presents, he asked Cortes if we were all brothers and vassals of our great Emperor; and Cortes answered that we were brothers in love and friendship, persons of great distinction, and servants of our great king and lord. Further polite speeches passed between Montezuma and Cortes, but as this was the first time he had visited us and we did not want to tire him, the conversation ended.

Montezuma had ordered his stewards to provide us with everything we needed for our way of living: maize, grindstones, women to make our bread, fowls, fruit, and plenty of fodder for the horses. He then took leave of us all with the greatest courtesy, and we accompanied him to the street. However, Cortes ordered us not to go far from our quarters for the present until we knew better what conduct to observe.

Next day Cortes decided to go to Montezuma's palace. But first he sent to know whether the prince was busy and to inform him of our coming. He took four captains with him: Pedro de Alvarado, Juan Velazquez de Leon, Diego de Ordaz, and Gonzalo de Sandoval, and five of us soldiers.

When Montezuma was informed of our coming, he advanced into the middle of the hall to receive us, closely surrounded by his nephews, for no other chiefs were allowed to enter his palace or communicate with him except upon important business. Cortes and Montezuma exchanged bows, and clasped hands. Then Montezuma led Cortes to his own dais, and setting him down on his right, called for more seats, on which he ordered us all to sit also.

Cortes began to make a speech through our interpreters, saying that we were all now rested, and that in coming to see and speak with such a great prince we had fulfilled the purpose of our voyage and the orders of our lord the King. The principal things he had come to say on behalf of our Lord God had already been communicated to Montezuma through his three ambassadors,[3] on that occasion in the sandhills when he did us the favour of sending us the golden moon and sun. We had then told him that we were Christians and worshipped one God alone, named Jesus Christ, who had suffered His passion and death to save us; and that what they worshipped as gods were not gods but devils, which were evil things, and if they were ugly to look at, their deeds were uglier. But he had proved to them how evil and ineffectual their gods were, as both the prince and his people would observe in the

[3] A meeting on the coast of the Gulf of Mexico with Montezuma's ambassadors on the prior Easter Sunday (1519). [Ed.]

course of time, since, where we had put up crosses such as their ambassadors had seen, they had been too frightened to appear before them.

The favour he now begged of the great Montezuma was that he should listen to the words he now wished to speak. Then he very carefully expounded the creation of the world, how we are all brothers, the children of one mother and father called Adam and Eve; and how such a brother as our great Emperor, grieving for the perdition of so many souls as their idols were leading to hell, where they burnt in living flame, had sent us to tell him this, so that he might put a stop to it, and so that they might give up the worship of idols and make no more human sacrifices — for all men are brothers — and commit no more robbery or sodomy. He also promised that in the course of time the King would send some men who lead holy lives among us, much better than our own, to explain this more fully, for we had only come to give them warning. Therefore he begged Montezuma to do as he was asked.

As Montezuma seemed about to reply, Cortes broke off his speech, saying to those of us who were with him: "Since this is only the first attempt, we have now done our duty."

"My lord Malinche," Montezuma replied, "these arguments of yours have been familiar to me for some time. I understand what you said to my ambassadors on the sandhills about the three gods and the cross, also what you preached in the various towns through which you passed. We have given you no answer, since we have worshipped our own gods here from the beginning and know them to be good. No doubt yours are good also, but do not trouble to tell us any more about them at present. Regarding the creation of the world, we have held the same belief for many ages, and for this reason are certain that you are those who our ancestors predicted would come from the direction of the sunrise. As for your great King, I am in his debt and will give him of what I possess. For, as I have already said, two years ago I had news of the Captains who came in ships, by the road that you came, and said they were servants of this great king of yours. I should like to know if you are all the same people."

Cortes answered that we were all brothers and servants of the Emperor, and that they had come to discover a route and explore the seas and ports, so that when they knew them well we could follow, as we had done. Montezuma was referring to the expeditions of Francisco Hernandez de Cordoba and of Grijalva, the first voyages of discovery. He said that ever since that time he had wanted to invite some of these men to visit the cities of his kingdom, where he would receive them and do them honour, and that now his gods had fulfilled his desire, for we were in his house, which we might call our own. Here we might rest and enjoy ourselves, for we should receive good treatment. If on other occasions he had sent to forbid our entrance into his city, it was not of his own free will, but because his vassals were afraid. For they told him we shot out flashes of lightning, and killed many Indians with our horses, and that we were angry *Teules,* and other such childish stories. But now that he had seen us, he knew that we were of flesh and blood and very intelligent, also very brave. Therefore he had a far greater esteem for us than these reports had given him, and would share with us what he had.

We all thanked him heartily for his . . . good will, and Montezuma replied with a laugh, because in his princely manner he spoke very gaily: "Malinche, I know that these people of Tlascala with whom you are so friendly have told you that I am a sort of god or *Teule,* and keep nothing in any of my houses that is not made of silver and gold and precious stones. But I know very well that you are too intelligent to believe this and will take it as a joke. See now, Malinche, my body is made of flesh and blood like yours, and my houses and palaces are of stone, wood, and plaster. It is true that I am a great king, and have inherited the riches of my ancestors, but the lies and nonsense you have heard of us are not true. You must take them as a joke, as I take the story of your thunders and lightnings."

Cortes answered also with a laugh that enemies always speak evil and tell lies about the people they hate, but he knew he could not hope to find a more magnificent prince in that land, and there was good reason why his fame should have reached our Emperor. . . .

The great Montezuma was about forty years old, of good height, well proportioned, spare and slight, and not very dark, though of the usual Indian complexion. He did not wear his hair long but just over his ears, and he had a short black beard, well-shaped and thin. His face was rather long and cheerful, he had fine eyes, and in his appearance and manner could express geniality or, when necessary, a serious composure. He was very neat and clean, and took a bath every afternoon. He had many women as his mistresses, the daughters of chieftains, but two legitimate wives who were *Caciques* in their own right, and when he had intercourse with any of them it was so secret that only some of his servants knew of it. He was quite free from sodomy. The clothes he wore one day he did not wear again till three or four days later. He had a guard of two hundred chieftains lodged in rooms beside his own, only some of whom were permitted to speak to him. When they entered his presence they were compelled to take off their rich cloaks and put on others of little value. They had to be clean and walk barefoot, with their eyes downcast, for they were not allowed to look him in the face, and as they approached they had to make three obeisances, saying as they did so, "Lord, my lord, my great lord!" Then, when they had said what they had come to say, he would dismiss them with a few words. They did not turn their backs on him as they went out, but kept their faces toward him and their eyes downcast, only turning round when they had left the room. Another thing I noticed was that when other great chiefs came from distant lands about disputes or on business, they too had to take off their shoes and put on poor cloaks before entering Montezuma's apartments; and they were not allowed to enter the palace immediately but had to linger for a while near the door, since to enter hurriedly was considered disrespectful. . . .

Montezuma had two houses stocked with every sort of weapon; many of them were richly adorned with gold and precious stones. There were shields large and small, and a sort of broadsword, and two-handed swords set with flint blades that cut much better than our swords, and lances longer than ours, with five-foot blades consisting of many knives. Even when these are driven at a buckler or a shield they are not deflected. In fact they cut like razors, and the Indians can shave their heads with them. They had very good bows and arrows, and double and single-pointed javelins as well as their throwing-sticks and many slings and round stones shaped by hand, and another sort of shield that can be rolled up when they are not fighting, so that it does not get in the way, but which can be opened when they need it in battle and covers their bodies from head to foot. There was also a great deal of cotton armour richly worked on the outside with different coloured feathers, which they used as devices and distinguishing marks, and they had casques and helmets made of wood and bone which were also highly decorated with feathers on the outside. They had other arms of different kinds which I will not mention through fear of prolixity, and workmen skilled in the manufacture of such things, and stewards who were in charge of these arms. . . .

I have already described the manner of their sacrifices. They strike open the wretched Indian's chest with flint knives and hastily tear out the palpitating heart which, with the blood, they present to the idols in whose name they have performed the sacrifice. Then they cut off the arms, thighs, and head, eating the arms and thighs at their ceremonial banquets. The head they hang up on a beam, and the body of the sacrificed man is not eaten but given to the beasts of prey. They also had many vipers in this accursed house, and poisonous snakes which have something that sounds like a bell in their tails. These, which are the deadliest snakes of all, they kept in jars and great pottery vessels full of feathers, in which they laid their eggs and reared their young. They were fed on the bodies of sacrificed Indians and the flesh of the dogs that they bred. We know for certain, too, that when they drove us out of Mexico and killed over eight hundred and fifty of our soldiers, they fed those beasts and snakes on their bodies for many days, as I shall relate in due course. These snakes and wild beasts were dedicated to their fierce idols, and kept them company. As for the horrible noise when the lions and tigers roared, and the jackals and foxes howled, and the serpents hissed, it was so appalling that one seemed to be in hell.

I must now speak of the skilled workmen whom Montezuma employed in all the crafts they practised, beginning with the jewellers and workers in silver and gold and various kinds of hollowed objects, which excited the admiration of our great silversmiths at home. Many of the best of them lived in a town called Atzcapotzalco, three miles from Mexico. There were other skilled craftsmen who worked with precious stones and *chalchihuites,* and specialists in feather-work, and very fine painters and carvers. We can form some judgment of what they did then from what we can see of their work today. . . .

Let us go on to the women, the weavers and sempstresses, who made such a huge quantity of fine robes with very elaborate feather designs. These things were generally brought from some towns in the province of Cotaxtla, which is on the north coast, quite near San Juan de Ulua. In Montezuma's own palaces very fine cloths were woven by those chieftains' daughters whom he kept as mistresses; and the daughters of other dignitaries, who lived in a kind of retirement like nuns in some houses close to the great *cue*[4] of Huichilobos, wore robes entirely of feather-work. Out of devotion for that god and a female deity who was said to preside over marriage, their fathers would place them in religious retirement until they found husbands. They would then take them out to be married.

Now to speak of the great number of performers whom Montezuma kept to entertain him. There were dancers and stilt-walkers, and some who seemed to fly as they leapt through the air, and men rather like clowns to make him laugh. There was a whole quarter full of these people who had no other occupation. He had as many workmen as he needed, too — stonecutters, masons, and carpenters — to keep his houses in repair.

We must not forget the gardens with their many varieties of flowers and sweet-scented trees planted in order, and their ponds and tanks of fresh water into which a stream flowed at one end and out of which it flowed at the other, and the baths he had there, and the variety of small birds that nested in the branches, and the medicinal and useful herbs that grew there. His gardens were a wonderful sight, and required many gardeners to take care of them. Everything was built of stone and plastered; baths and walks and closets and rooms like summerhouses where they danced and sang. There was so much to see in these gardens, as everywhere else, that we could not tire of contemplating his great riches and the large number of skilled Indians employed in the many crafts they practised. . . .

We carried our weapons, as was our custom, both by night and day. Indeed, Montezuma was so used to our visiting him armed that he did not think it strange. I say this because our Captain and those of us

[4] Pyramid or temple. [Ed.]

who had horses went to Tlatelolco mounted, and the majority of our men were fully equipped. On reaching the marketplace, escorted by the many *Caciques* whom Montezuma had assigned to us, we were astounded at the great number of people and the quantities of merchandise, and at the orderliness and good arrangements that prevailed, for we had never seen such a thing before. The chieftains who accompanied us pointed everything out. Every kind of merchandise was kept separate and had its fixed place marked for it.

Let us begin with the dealers in gold, silver, and precious stones, feathers, cloaks, and embroidered goods, and male and female slaves who are also sold there. They bring as many slaves to be sold in that market as the Portuguese bring Negroes from Guinea. Some are brought there attached to long poles by means of collars round their necks to prevent them from escaping, but others are left loose. Next there were those who sold coarser cloth, and cotton goods and fabrics made of twisted thread, and there were chocolate merchants with their chocolate. In this way you could see every kind of merchandise to be found anywhere in New Spain, laid out in the same way as goods are laid out in my own district of Medina del Campo, a centre for fairs, where each line of stalls has its own particular sort. So it was in this great market. There were those who sold sisal cloth and ropes and the sandals they wear on their feet, which are made from the same plant. All these were kept in one part of the market, in the place assigned to them, and in another part were skins of tigers and lions, otters, jackals, and deer, badgers, mountain cats, and other wild animals, some tanned and some untanned, and other classes of merchandise.

There were sellers of kidney beans and sage and other vegetables and herbs in another place, and in yet another they were selling fowls, and birds with great dewlaps,[5] also rabbits, hares, deer, young ducks, little dogs, and other such creatures. Then there were the fruiterers; and the women who sold cooked food, flour and honey cake, and tripe, had their part of the market. Then came pottery of all kinds, from big water jars to little jugs, displayed in its own place, also honey, honey paste, and other sweets like nougat. Elsewhere they sold timber too, boards, cradles, beams, blocks, and benches, all in a quarter of their own.

Then there were the sellers of pitch-pine for torches, and other things of that kind, and I must also mention, with all apologies, that they sold many canoe loads of human excrement, which they kept in the creeks near the market. This was for the manufacture of salt and the curing of skins, which they say cannot be done without it. I know that many gentlemen will laugh at this, but I assure them it is true. I may add that on all the roads they have shelters made of reeds or straw

[5] Turkeys.

or grass so that they can retire when they wish to do so, and purge their bowels unseen by passersby, and also in order that their excrement shall not be lost.

But why waste so many words on the goods in their great market? If I describe everything in detail I shall never be done. . . .

Now let us leave the market . . . and come to the courts and enclosures in which their great *cue* stood. Before reaching it you passed through a series of large courts, bigger I think than the Plaza at Salamanca. These courts were surrounded by a double masonry wall and paved, like the whole place, with very large smooth white flagstones. Where these stones were absent everything was whitened and polished, indeed the whole place was so clean that there was not a straw or a grain of dust to be found there.

When we arrived near the great temple and before we had climbed a single step, the great Montezuma sent six *papas* and two chieftains down from the top, where he was making his sacrifices, to escort our Captain; and as he climbed the steps, of which there were one hundred and fourteen, they tried to take him by the arms to help him up in the same way as they helped Montezuma, thinking he might be tired, but he would not let them near him.

The top of the *cue* formed an open square on which stood something like a platform, and it was here that the great stones stood on which they placed the poor Indians for sacrifice. Here also was a massive image like a dragon, and other hideous figures, and a great deal of blood that had been spilled that day. Emerging in the company of two *papas* from the shrine which houses his accursed images, Montezuma made a deep bow to us all and said: "My lord Malinche, you must be tired after climbing this great *cue* of ours." And Cortes replied that none of us was ever exhausted by anything. Then Montezuma took him by the hand, and told him to look at his great city and all the other cities standing in the water, and the many others on the land round the lake; and he said that if Cortes had not had a good view of the great marketplace he could see it better from where he now was. So we stood there looking, because that huge accursed *cue* stood so high that it dominated everything. We saw the three causeways that led into Mexico: the causeway of Iztapalapa by which we had entered four days before, and that of Tacuba along which we were afterward to flee on the night of our great defeat, when the new prince Cuitlahuac drove us out of the city (as I shall tell in due course), and that of Tepeaquilla.[6] We saw the fresh water which came from Chapultepec to supply the city, and the bridges that were constructed at intervals on the causeways so that the water could flow in and out from one part of the lake to an-

[6] Guadalupe.

other. We saw a great number of canoes, some coming with provisions and others returning with cargo and merchandise; and we saw too that one could not pass from one house to another of that great city and the other cities that were built on the water except over wooden drawbridges or by canoe. We saw *cues* and shrines in these cities that looked like gleaming white towers and castles: a marvellous sight. All the houses had flat roofs, and on the causeways were other small towers and shrines built like fortresses.

Having examined and considered all that we had seen, we turned back to the great market and the swarm of people buying and selling. The mere murmur of their voices talking was loud enough to be heard more than three miles away. Some of our soldiers who had been in many parts of the world, in Constantinople, in Rome, and all over Italy, said that they had never seen a market so well laid out, so large, so orderly, and so full of people. . . .

Our Captain said to Montezuma, through our interpreters, with something like a laugh: "Lord Montezuma, I cannot imagine how a prince as great and wise as your Majesty can have failed to realize that these idols of yours are not gods but evil things, the proper name for which is devils. But so that I may prove this to you, and make it clear to all your *papas,* grant me one favour. Allow us to erect a cross here on the top of this tower, and let us divide off a part of this sanctuary where your Huichilobos and Tezcatlipoca stand, as a place where we can put an image of Our Lady" — which image Montezuma had already seen — "and then you will see, by the fear that your idols have of her, how grievously they have deceived you."

Montezuma, however, replied in some temper (and the two *papas* beside him showed real anger): "Lord Malinche, if I had known that you were going to utter these insults I should not have shown you my gods. We hold them to be very good. They give us health and rain and crops and weather, and all the victories we desire. So we are bound to worship them and sacrifice to them, and I beg you to say nothing more against them."

On hearing this and seeing Montezuma's fury, our Captain said no more on the subject but observed cheerfully: "It is time for your Majesty and ourselves to depart." Montezuma replied that this was so, but that he had to pray and offer certain sacrifices on account of the great *tatacul* — that is to say sin — which he had committed in allowing us to climb his great *cue* and in being instrumental in letting us see his gods and in the dishonour we had done them by our abuse. Therefore before he left he must pray and worship. . . .

It being our habit to examine and inquire into everything, when we were all assembled in our lodging and considering which was the best place for an altar, two of our men, one of whom was the carpenter Alonso Yañez, called attention to some marks on one of the walls which showed that there had once been a door, though it had been well plastered up and painted. Now as we had heard that Montezuma kept his father's treasure in this building, we immediately suspected that it must be in this room, which had been closed up only a few days before. Yañez made the suggestion to Juan Velazquez de Leon and Francisco de Lugo, both relatives of mine, to whom he had attached himself as a servant; and they mentioned the matter to Cortes. So the door was secretly opened, and Cortes went in first with certain captains. When they saw the quantity of golden objects — jewels and plates and ingots — which lay in that chamber they were quite transported. They did not know what to think of such riches. The news soon spread to the other captains and soldiers, and very secretly we all went in to see. The sight of all that wealth dumbfounded me. Being only a youth at the time and never having seen such riches before, I felt certain that there could not be a store like it in the whole world. We unanimously decided that we could not think of touching a particle of it, and that the stones should immediately be replaced in the doorway, which should be blocked again and cemented just as we had found it. We resolved also that not a word should be said about this until times changed, for fear Montezuma might hear of our discovery.

Let us leave this subject of the treasure and tell how four of our most valiant captains took Cortes aside in the church, with a dozen soldiers who were in his trust and confidence, myself among them, and asked him to consider the net or trap in which we were caught, to look at the great strength of the city and observe the causeways and bridges, and remember the warnings we had received in every town we had passed through that Huichilobos had counselled Montezuma to let us into the city and kill us there. We reminded him that the hearts of men are very fickle, especially among the Indians, and begged him not to trust the good will and affection that Montezuma was showing us, because from one hour to another it might change. If he should take it into his head to attack us, we said, the stoppage of our supplies of food and water, or the raising of any of the bridges, would render us helpless. Then, considering the vast army of warriors he possessed, we should be incapable of attacking or defending ourselves. And since all the houses stood in the water, how could our Tlascalan allies come in to help us? We asked him to think over all that we had said, for if we wanted to preserve our lives we must seize Montezuma immediately, without even a day's delay. We pointed out that all the gold Montezuma had given us, and all that we had seen in the treasury of his father Axayacatl, and all the food we ate was turning to poison in our bodies, for we could not sleep by night or day or take any rest while these thoughts were in our minds. If any of our soldiers gave him less drastic advice, we concluded, they would be senseless beasts charmed by the gold and incapable of looking death in the eye.

When he had heard our opinion, Cortes answered: "Do not imagine, gentlemen, that I am asleep or that I do not share your anxiety.

You must have seen that I do. But what strength have we got for so bold a course as to take this great lord in his own palace, surrounded as he is by warriors and guards? What scheme or trick can we devise to prevent him from summoning his soldiers to attack us at once?"

Our captains (Juan Velazquez de Leon, Diego de Ordaz, Gonzalo de Sandoval, and Pedro de Alvarado) replied that Montezuma must be got out of his palace by smooth words and brought to our quarters. Once there, he must be told that he must remain as a prisoner, and that if he called out or made any disturbance he would pay for it with his life. If Cortes was unwilling to take this course at once, they begged him for permission to do it themselves. With two very dangerous alternatives before us, the better and more profitable thing, they said, would be to seize Montezuma rather than wait for him to attack us. Once he did so, what chance would we have? Some of us soldiers also remarked that Montezuma's stewards who brought us our food seemed to be growing insolent, and did not serve us as politely as they had at first. Two of our Tlascalan allies had, moreover, secretly observed to Jeronimo de Aguilar that for the last two days the Mexicans had appeared less well disposed to us. We spent a good hour discussing whether or not to take Montezuma prisoner, and how it should be done. But our final advice, that at all costs we should take him prisoner, was approved by our Captain, and we then left the matter till next day. All night we prayed God to direct events in the interests of His holy service. . . .

87

From *The Broken Spears: The Aztec Account of the Conquest of Mexico*

This Aztec account of the encounter between the Spanish and Indians of Mexico was written some years after the events described. Spanish Christian monks helped a postconquest generation of Aztec Nahuatl speakers translate the illustrated manuscripts of the conquest period. According to this account, how did Montezuma (Motecuhzoma in this account) respond to Cortés? Was Montezuma's attitude toward the Spanish shared by other Aztecs? How reliable is this account, do

---

The Broken Spears: The Aztec Account of the Conquest of Mexico, ed. Miquel Leon-Portilla (Boston: Beacon Press, 1990), 64–76.

you think, in describing Montezuma's thoughts, motives, and behavior?

Thinking Historically

How does the Aztec account of the conquest differ from that of the Spanish, written by Díaz? Does the Aztec account contradict the Spanish account in some areas? If so, how? To the extent to which there are contradictions, how will you decide which account to believe and accept?

In some areas, the Aztec account is merely different from that of Díaz. For one thing, it tells us about a later period. Can you trust the Aztec account? What sort of confirmation might you look for? Overall, how different is the Aztec account from that of Díaz?

Speeches of Motecuhzoma and Cortes

When Motecuhzoma had given necklaces to each one, Cortes asked him: "Are you Motecuhzoma? Are you the king? Is it true that you are the king Motecuhzoma?"

And the king said: "Yes, I am Motecuhzoma." Then he stood up to welcome Cortes; he came forward, bowed his head low and addressed him in these words: "Our lord, you are weary. The journey has tired you, but now you have arrived on the earth. You have come to your city, Mexico. You have come here to sit on your throne, to sit under its canopy.

"The kings who have gone before, your representatives, guarded it and preserved it for your coming. The kings Itzcoatl, Motecuhzoma the Elder, Axayacatl, Tizoc, and Ahuitzol ruled for you in the City of Mexico. The people were protected by their swords and sheltered by their shields.

"Do the kings know the destiny of those they left behind, their posterity? If only they are watching! If only they can see what I see!

"No, it is not a dream. I am not walking in my sleep. I am not seeing you in my dreams. . . . I have seen you at last! I have met you face to face! I was in agony for five days, for ten days, with my eyes fixed on the Region of the Mystery. And now you have come out of the clouds and mists to sit on your throne again.

"This was foretold by the kings who governed your city, and now it has taken place. You have come back to us; you have come down from the sky. Rest now, and take possession of your royal houses. Welcome to your land, my lords!"

When Motecuhzoma had finished, La Malinche translated his address into Spanish so that the Captain could understand it. Cortes replied in his strange and savage tongue, speaking first to La Malinche: "Tell Motecuhzoma that we are his friends. There is nothing to fear.

We have wanted to see him for a long time, and now we have seen his face and heard his words. Tell him that we love him well and that our hearts are contented."

Then he said to Motecuhzoma: "We have come to your house in Mexico as friends. There is nothing to fear."

La Malinche translated this speech and the Spaniards grasped Motecuhzoma's hands and patted his back to show their affection for him. . . .

The Spaniards Take Possession of the City

When the Spaniards entered the Royal House, they placed Motecuhzoma under guard and kept him under their vigilance. They also placed a guard over Itzcuauhtzin, but the other lords were permitted to depart.

Then the Spaniards fired one of their cannons, and this caused great confusion in the city. The people scattered in every direction; they fled without rhyme or reason; they ran off as if they were being pursued. It was as if they had eaten the mushrooms that confuse the mind, or had seen some dreadful apparition. They were all overcome by terror, as if their hearts had fainted. And when night fell, the panic spread through the city and their fears would not let them sleep.

In the morning the Spaniards told Motecuhzoma what they needed in the way of supplies: tortillas, fried chickens, hens' eggs, pure water, firewood, and charcoal. Also: large, clean cooking pots; water jars; pitchers; dishes; and other pottery. Motecuhzoma ordered that it be sent to them. The chiefs who received this order were angry with the king and no longer revered or respected him. But they furnished the Spaniards with all the provisions they needed — food, beverages and water, and fodder for the horses.

The Spaniards Reveal Their Greed

When the Spaniards were installed in the palace, they asked Motecuhzoma about the city's resources and reserves and about the warriors' ensigns and shields. They questioned him closely and then demanded gold.

Motecuhzoma guided them to it. They surrounded him and crowded close with their weapons. He walked in the center, while they formed a circle around him.

When they arrived at the treasure house called Teucalco, the riches of gold and feathers were brought out to them: ornaments made of quetzal feathers, richly worked shields, disks of gold, the necklaces of the idols, gold nose plugs, gold greaves, and bracelets, and crowns.

The Spaniards immediately stripped the feathers from the gold shields and ensigns. They gathered all the gold into a great mound and set fire to everything else, regardless of its value. Then they melted down the gold into ingots. As for the precious green stones, they took only the best of them; the rest were snatched up by the Tlaxcaltecas. The Spaniards searched through the whole treasure house, questioning and quarreling, and seized every object they thought was beautiful.

The Seizure of Motecuhzoma's Treasures

Next they went to Motecuhzoma's storehouse, in the place called Totocalco [Place of the Palace of the Birds],[1] where his personal treasures were kept. The Spaniards grinned like little beasts and patted each other with delight.

When they entered the hall of treasures, it was as if they had arrived in Paradise. They searched everywhere and coveted everything; they were slaves to their own greed. All of Motecuhzoma's possessions were brought out: fine bracelets, necklaces with large stones, ankle rings with little gold bells, the royal crowns and all the royal finery — everything that belonged to the king and was reserved to him only. They seized these treasures as if they were their own, as if this plunder were merely a stroke of good luck. And when they had taken all the gold, they heaped up everything else in the middle of the patio.

La Malinche called the nobles together. She climbed up to the palace roof and cried: "Mexicanos, come forward! The Spaniards need your help! Bring them food and pure water. They are tired and hungry; they are almost fainting from exhaustion! Why do you not come forward? Are you angry with them?"

The Mexicans were too frightened to approach. They were crushed by terror and would not risk coming forward. They shied away as if the Spaniards were wild beasts, as if the hour were midnight on the blackest night of the year. Yet they did not abandon the Spaniards to hunger and thirst. They brought them whatever they needed, but shook with fear as they did so. They delivered the supplies to the Spaniards with trembling hands, then turned and hurried away. . . .

The Statue of Huitzilopochtli

On the evening before the fiesta of Toxcatl, the celebrants began to model a statue of Huitzilopochtli. They gave it such a human appearance that it seemed the body of a living man. Yet they made the statue

[1] The zoological garden attached to the royal palaces.

with nothing but a paste made of the ground seeds of the chicalote, which they shaped over an armature of sticks.

When the statue was finished, they dressed it in rich feathers, and they painted crossbars over and under its eyes. They also clipped on its earrings of turquoise mosaic; these were in the shape of serpents, with gold rings hanging from them. Its nose plug, in the shape of an arrow, was made of gold and was inlaid with fine stones.

They placed the magic headdress of hummingbird feathers on its head. They also adorned it with an *anecuyotl,* which was a belt made of feathers, with a cone at the back. Then they hung around its neck an ornament of yellow parrot feathers, fringed like the locks of a young boy. Over this they put its nettle-leaf cape, which was painted black and decorated with five clusters of eagle feathers. . . .

The Beginning of the Fiesta

Early the next morning, the statue's face was uncovered by those who had been chosen for that ceremony. They gathered in front of the idol in single file and offered it gifts of food, such as round seedcakes or perhaps human flesh. But they did not carry it up to its temple on top of the pyramid.

All the young warriors were eager for the fiesta to begin. They had sworn to dance and sing with all their hearts, so that the Spaniards would marvel at the beauty of the rituals.

The procession began, and the celebrants filed into the temple patio to dance the Dance of the Serpent. When they were all together in the patio, the songs and the dance began. Those who had fasted for twenty days and those who had fasted for a year were in command of the others; they kept the dancers in file with their pine wands. (If anyone wished to urinate, he did not stop dancing, but simply opened his clothing at the hips and separated his clusters of heron feathers.)

If anyone disobeyed the leaders or was not in his proper place they struck him on the hips and shoulders. Then they drove him out of the patio, beating him and shoving him from behind. They pushed him so hard that he sprawled to the ground, and they dragged him outside by the ears. No one dared to say a word about this punishment, for those who had fasted during the year were feared and venerated; they had earned the exclusive title "Brothers of Huitzilopochtli."

The great captains, the bravest warriors, danced at the head of the files to guide the others. The youths followed at a slight distance. Some of the youths wore their hair gathered into large locks, a sign that they had never taken any captives. Others carried their headdresses on their shoulders; they had taken captives, but only with help.

Then came the recruits, who were called "the young warriors." They had each captured an enemy or two. The others called to them:

"Come, comrades, show us how brave you are! Dance with all your hearts!"

The Spaniards Attack the Celebrants

At this moment in the fiesta, when the dance was loveliest and when song was linked to song, the Spaniards were seized with an urge to kill the celebrants. They all ran forward, armed as if for battle. They closed the entrances and passageways, all the gates of the patio: the Eagle Gate in the lesser palace, the Gate of the Canestalk and the Gate of the Serpent of Mirrors. They posted guards so that no one could escape, and then rushed into the Sacred Patio to slaughter the celebrants. They came on foot, carrying their swords and their wooden or metal shields.

They ran in among the dancers, forcing their way to the place where the drums were played. They attacked the man who was drumming and cut off his arms. Then they cut off his head, and it rolled across the floor.

They attacked all the celebrants, stabbing them, spearing them, striking them with their swords. They attacked some of them from behind, and these fell instantly to the ground with their entrails hanging out. Others they beheaded: they cut off their heads, or split their heads to pieces.

They struck others in the shoulders, and their arms were torn from their bodies. They wounded some in the thigh and some in the calf. They slashed others in the abdomen, and their entrails all spilled to the ground. Some attempted to run away, but their intestines dragged as they ran; they seemed to tangle their feet in their own entrails. No matter how they tried to save themselves, they could find no escape.

Some attempted to force their way out, but the Spaniards murdered them at the gates. Others climbed the walls, but they could not save themselves. Those who ran into the communal houses were safe there for a while; so were those who lay down among the victims and pretended to be dead. But if they stood up again, the Spaniards saw them and killed them.

The blood of the warriors flowed like water and gathered into pools. The pools widened, and the stench of blood and entrails filled the air. The Spaniards ran into the communal houses to kill those who were hiding. They ran everywhere and searched everywhere; they invaded every room, hunting and killing.

88

BARTOLOMÉ DE LAS CASAS

From *The History of the Indies*

Spanish and Aztec chroniclers presented different views of the Spanish conquest of Mexico, but they did not engage in historical debate. History was among the spoils that went to the victor.

Still, as Spanish dominion in the Americas extended throughout the Caribbean and Mexico, spilling over into the Inca Empire in Peru, voices were raised that questioned not only the Spanish treatment of Mexicans, but their treatment of conquered peoples throughout the New World. Often these voices belonged to members of the Spanish clergy living in the Americas.

One of the most effective of these critics was Bartolomé de Las Casas (1474–1566). Las Casas was nineteen years old when he witnessed Columbus's triumphal return to Spain in 1493 and twenty-eight when he sailed to Hispaniola in 1502. As a Spaniard, he was entitled to and received an *encomienda,* a grant from the king of all the Indians within a village or territory. In return for their protection and instruction in Christian doctrine, the encomienda holder received indian labor. As he learned in Hispaniola and during his participation in the conquest of Cuba between 1511 and 1515, this arrangement was, in most cases, a system of indifferent slavery. In 1515 Las Casas renounced his *encomienda* and sailed for Spain to speak out against the brutal treatment of the Indians in the Indies. It was a cause to which he dedicated the rest of his life, becoming a Dominican priest in 1524 and returning to Mexico.

This selection from Las Casas's personal and passionate *History of the Indies* — written between 1527 and 1564 and left unfinished at his death — recounts an episode of the conquest of Cuba and a Christmas sermon delivered by a Dominican priest Fray Antonio de Montesinos, in Hispaniola in 1511. How was the Spanish conquest of Caribbean islands like Hispaniola and Cuba different from their conquest of Mexico? What accounts for these differences? What was the impact of the Catholic Church in Spain's colonization of the Americas? How typical do you think Fray Antonio de Montesinos was?

Bartolomé de Las Casas, from *The History of the Indies,* in *Bartolomé de Las Casas: A Selection of His Writings,* ed. and trans. George Sanderlin (New York: Knopf, 1971), 61–66, 80–85. Reproduced in *The Borzoi Anthology of Latin American Literature,* vol. I, ed. Emir Rodgriguez Monegal (New York: Knopf, 1987), 24–30.

Thinking Historically

Las Casas's history offers a revealing insight into the debates that were going on among settlers in the first decades of Spanish colonization. In addition to pointing out the role an independent clergy could sometimes play, this selection lays bare the economic interests underlying an emerging debate. What kind of people were these settlers? What was the basis of their disagreements about Indian slavery? What sorts of objections did the colonialists of Hispaniola have to the appeal of Fray Antonio de Montesinos?

The controversy over Spanish treatment of the Indians came to a head in 1550 when King Charles commanded Las Casas and one of his chief opponents, Juan Ginés de Sepúlveda, to come to the city of Valadoid and debate the issue of Spanish responsibility to the Indians in the colonies.

Sepúlveda (1490–1573) — a scholar who had translated Aristotle — like the ancient Greek philosopher believed in a hierarchy of natural superiors and inferiors and considered the benefits of slavery to the inferiors: "It is with perfect right that the Spanish dominate these barbarians of the New World . . . who are so inferior to the Spanish in prudence, intelligence, virtue, and humanity, as children are to adults, as women to men, that I am tempted to say that there is between us both as much difference as between . . . monkeys and men."[1] For Sepúlveda, the rightness of enslavement could be seen in the conquest itself and in the different characters of Montezuma and Cortés:

> Informed of the arrival of Cortés and of his victories and of his intention to come to Mexico under pretext of a conference, Montezuma sought all possible means to divert him from his plan. Failing in this, terrorized and filled with fear, he received him in the city with about three hundred Spaniards. Cortés, for his part, after taking possession of the city, held the people's cowardice, ineptitude, and rudeness in such contempt that he not only compelled the king and his principal subjects, through terror, to receive the yoke and rule of the king of Spain, but also imprisoned King Montezuma himself, because of his suspicion that a plot was afoot to kill some Spaniards in a certain province. This he could do because of the stupor and inertia of the people, who were indifferent to the situation and preoccupied with other things than the taking up of arms to liberate their king. And thus Cortés, though aided by such a small number of Spanish and so few na-

[1] Adapted by Kevin Reilly from Juan Ginés de Sepúlveda, *Democrates Secundus, or the Treatise on the Just Causes of War Against the Indians* (1547) in Charles Gibson, ed., *The Spanish Tradition in America* (New York: Harper & Row, 1968), 113.

tives, was able to hold them, oppressed and fearful at the beginning, for many days. They were so immense a multitude that he seemed entirely lacking not only in prudence but in common sense. Could there be a better or clearer testimony of the superiority that some men have over others in talent, skill, strength of spirit, and virtue? Is it not proof that the Mexicans are slaves by nature?

Drawing on this selection from Las Casas and your previous readings on the conquest, write a reply to Sepúlveda that Las Casas might have delivered. How might your own reply to Sepúlveda differ from that which Las Casas would have delivered in 1550?

The Spaniards entered the province of Camagüey, which is large and densely populated . . . and when they reached the villages, the inhabitants had prepared as well as they could cassava bread from their food; what they called *guaminiquinajes* from their hunting; and also fish, if they had caught any.

Immediately upon arriving at a village, the cleric Casas would have all the little children band together; taking two or three Spaniards to help him, along with some sagacious Indians of this island of Hispaniola, whom he had brought with him, and a certain servant of his, he would baptize the children he found in the village. He did this throughout the island . . . and there were many for whom God provided holy baptism because He had predestined them to glory. God provided it at a fitting time, for none or almost none of those children remained alive after a few months. . . .

When the Spaniards arrived at a village and found the Indians at peace in their houses, they did not fail to injure and scandalize them. Not content with what the Indians freely gave, they took their wretched subsistence from them, and some, going further, chased after their wives and daughters, for this is and always has been the Spaniards' common custom in these Indies. Because of this and at the urging of the said father, Captain Narváez ordered that after the father had separated all the inhabitants of the village in half the houses, leaving the other half empty for the Spaniards' lodging, no one should dare go to the Indians' section. For this purpose, the father would go ahead with three or four men and reach a village early; by the time the Spaniards came, he had already gathered the Indians in one part and cleared the other.

Thus, because the Indians saw that the father did things for them, defending and comforting them, and also baptizing their children, in which affairs he seemed to have more command and authority than others, he received much respect and credit throughout the island among the Indians. Further, they honored him as they did their priests, magicians, prophets, or physicians, who were all one and the same.

Because of this . . . it became unnecessary to go ahead of the Spaniards. He had only to send an Indian with an old piece of paper on a stick, informing them through the messenger that those letters said thus and so. That is, that they should all be calm, that no one should absent himself because he would do them no harm, that they should have food prepared for the Christians and their children ready for baptism, or that they should gather in one part of the village, and anything else that it seemed good to counsel them — and that if they did not carry these things out, the father would be angry, which was the greatest threat that could be sent them. . . .

They [Spaniards] arrived at the town of Caonao in the evening. Here they found many people, who had prepared a great deal of food consisting of cassava bread and fish, because they had a large river close by and also were near the sea. In a little square were two thousand Indians, all squatting because they have this custom, all staring, frightened, at the mares. Nearby was a large *bohio,* or large house, in which were more than five hundred other Indians, close-packed and fearful, who did not dare come out.

When some of the domestic Indians the Spaniards were taking with them as servants (who were more than one thousand souls . . .) wished to enter the large house, the Cuban Indians had chickens ready and said to them: "Take these — do not enter here." For they already knew that the Indians who served the Spaniards were not apt to perform any other deeds than those of their masters.

There was a custom among the Spaniards that one person, appointed by the captain, should be in charge of distributing to each Spaniard the food and other things the Indians gave. And while the captain was thus on his mare and the others mounted on theirs, and the father himself was observing how the bread and fish were distributed, a Spaniard, in whom the devil is thought to have clothed himself, suddenly drew his sword. Then the whole hundred drew theirs and began to rip open the bellies, to cut and kill those lambs — men, women, children, and old folk, all of whom were seated, off guard and frightened, watching the mares and the Spaniards. And within two credos, not a man of all of them there remains alive.

The Spaniards enter the large house nearby, for this was happening at its door, and in the same way, with cuts and stabs, begin to kill as many as they found there, so that a stream of blood was running, as if a great number of cows had perished. Some of the Indians who could make haste climbed up the poles and woodwork of the house to the top, and thus escaped.

The cleric had withdrawn shortly before this massacre to where another small square of the town was formed, near where they had lodged him. This was in a large house where all the Spaniards also had to stay, and here about forty of the Indians who had carried the Spaniards' baggage from the provinces farther back were stretched out on the ground, resting. And five Spaniards chanced to be with the cleric. When these heard the blows of the swords and knew that the Spaniards were killing the Indians — without seeing anything, because there were certain houses between — they put hands to their swords and are about to kill the forty Indians . . . to pay them their commission.

The cleric, moved to wrath, opposes and rebukes them harshly to prevent them, and having some respect for him, they stopped what they were going to do, so the forty were left alive. The five go to kill where the others were killing. And as the cleric had been detained in hindering the slaying of the forty carriers, when he went he found a heap of dead, which the Spaniards had made among the Indians, which was certainly a horrible sight.

When Narváez, the captain, saw him he said: "How does your Honor like what these our Spaniards have done?"

Seeing so many cut to pieces before him, and very upset at such a cruel event, the cleric replied: "That I commend you and them to the devil!"

The heedless Narváez remained, still watching the slaughter as it took place, without speaking, acting, or moving any more than if he had been marble. For if he had wished, being on horseback and with a lance in his hands, he could have prevented the Spaniards from killing even ten persons.

Then the cleric leaves him, and goes elsewhere through some groves seeking Spaniards to stop them from killing. For they were passing through the groves looking for someone to kill, sparing neither boy, child, woman, nor old person. And they did more, in that certain Spaniards went to the road to the river, which was nearby. Then all the Indians who had escaped with wounds, stabs, and cuts — all who could flee to throw themselves into the river to save themselves — met with the Spaniards who finished them.

Another outrage occurred which should not be left untold, so that the deeds of our Christians in these regions may be observed. When the cleric entered the large house where I said there were about five hundred souls — or whatever the number, which was great — and saw with horror the dead there and those who had escaped above by the poles or woodwork, he said to them:

"No more, no more. Do not be afraid. There will be no more, there will be no more."

With this assurance, believing that it would be thus, an Indian descended, a well-disposed young man of twenty-five or thirty years, weeping. And as the cleric did not rest but went everywhere to stop the killing, the cleric then left the house. And just as the young man came down, a Spaniard who was there drew a cutlass or half sword and gives him a cut through the loins, so that his intestines fall out. . . .

The Indian, moaning, takes his intestines in his hands and comes fleeing out of the house. He encounters the cleric . . . and the cleric tells him some things about the faith, as much as the time and anguish permitted, explaining to him that if he wished to be baptized he would go to heaven to live with God. The sad one, weeping and showing pain as if he were burning in flames, said yes, and with this the cleric baptized him. He then fell dead on the ground. . . .

Of all that has been said, I am a witness. I was present and saw it; and I omit many other particulars in order to shorten the account.

"Are Not the Indians Men?"

When Sunday and the hour to preach arrived . . . Father Fray Antonio de Montesinos ascended the pulpit and took as the text and foundation of his sermon, which he carried written out and signed by the other friars: "I am the voice of one crying in the desert." After he completed his introduction and said something concerning the subject of Advent, he began to emphasize the aridity in the desert of Spanish consciences in this island, and the ignorance in which they lived; also, in what danger of eternal damnation they were, from taking no notice of the grave sins in which, with such apathy, they were immersed and dying.

Then he returns to his text, speaking thus: "I have ascended here to cause you to know those sins, I who am the voice of Christ in the desert of this island. Therefore it is fitting that you listen to this voice, not with careless attention, but with all your heart and senses. For this voice will be the strangest you ever heard, the harshest and hardest, most fearful and most dangerous you ever thought to hear."

This voice cried out for some time, with very combative and terrible words, so that it made their flesh tremble, and they seemed already standing before the divine judgment. Then, in a grand manner, the voice . . . declared what it was, or what that divine inspiration consisted of: "This voice," he said, "declares that you are all in mortal sin, and live and die in it, because of the cruelty and tyranny you practice among these innocent peoples.

"Tell me, by what right or justice do you hold these Indians in such a cruel and horrible servitude? On what authority have you waged such detestable wars against these peoples, who dwelt quietly and peacefully on their own land? Wars in which you have destroyed such infinite numbers of them by homicides and slaughters never before heard of?

Why do you keep them so oppressed and exhausted, without giving them enough to eat or curing them of the sicknesses they incur from the excessive labor you give them, and they die, or rather, you kill them, in order to extract and acquire gold every day?

"And what care do you take that they should be instructed in religion, so that they may know their God and creator, may be baptized, may hear Mass, and may keep Sundays and feast days? Are these not men? Do they not have rational souls? Are you not bound to love them as you love yourselves? Don't you understand this? Don't you feel this? Why are you sleeping in such a profound and lethargic slumber? Be assured that in your present state you can no more be saved than the Moors or Turks, who lack the faith of Jesus Christ and do not desire it."

In brief, the voice explained what it had emphasized before in such a way that it left them astonished — many numb as if without feeling, others more hardened than before, some somewhat penitent, but none, as I afterward understood, converted.

When the sermon was concluded, Antonio de Montesinos descended from the pulpit with his head not at all low, for he was not a man who would want to show fear — as he felt none — if he displeased his hearers by doing and saying what seemed fitting to him, according to God. With his companion he goes to his thatch house where, perhaps, they had nothing to eat but cabbage broth without olive oil, as sometimes happened. But after he departed, the church remains full of murmurs so that, as I believe, they scarcely permitted the mass to be finished. . . .

Seeing how little God's servants feared all kinds of threats made against them, the officials softened, beseeching them to reconsider the matter and, having carefully done so, to emend what had been said in another sermon — this to satisfy the community, which had been, and was, greatly scandalized. At last . . . in order to rid themselves of the officials and to put an end to their frivolous importunities, the fathers conceded that at a seasonable time it would be thus: the same Father Fray Antonio de Montesinos would return to preach the next Sunday and would go back to the subject and say what seemed best to him about it, and, as much as possible, would try to satisfy them and explain everything he had said. This having been agreed upon, the officials departed, happy in this hope.

They then proclaimed, or some of them did, that they had left with an agreement with the vicar and the others that on the following Sunday that friar would retract everything he had said. And to hear this second sermon no invitations were needed, for there was not a person in the whole city who was not found in the church on that day. . . .

When the hour for the sermon came, after Antonio de Montesinos ascended the pulpit, the text given as the basis of his retraction was a saying from Job, Chapter 36, which commences: "I will go back over my knowledge from the beginning, and I will prove that my discourse is without falsehood." That is, "I will go back to rehearse from the beginning my knowledge and the truths which I preached to you last Sunday, and I will show that those words of mine which embittered you are true."

Upon hearing this text of his, the most clear-sighted saw immediately where he was going to end, and it was misery enough to allow him to go on from there. He began to . . . corroborate with more arguments and texts what he had affirmed before, that those oppressed and exhausted peoples were held unjustly and tyrannically. He repeated his understanding that the Spaniards could certainly not be saved in the state they were in, and that therefore they should in time heal themselves. He made them know that the friars would not confess a man of them, any more than they would confess highway robbers, and that the Spaniards might proclaim and write that to whomever they wished in Castile. In all this, the friars considered it certain that they were serving God and doing the king no small favor.

After the sermon was finished, Antonio de Montesinos went to his house. And all the people in the church remained agitated, grumbling, and much angrier at the friars than before, finding themselves defrauded of their vain and wicked hope that what had been said would be unsaid — as if, after the friar made his retraction, the law of God which they disobeyed by oppressing and exterminating these peoples would be changed.

89

CARLOS FUENTES

From *The Buried Mirror*

In this selection from a recent history of Mexico, Carlos Fuentes, one of Mexico's great writers, explores some of the connections between Mexico and Spain and between the past and present. In the first part of this selection, "The Indies Are Being Destroyed!" Fuentes recalls Father Antonio and Las Casas. In what ways did Las Casas serve the interests of the Spanish monarchy as opposed to "feudal pretension"?

Carlos Fuentes, from *The Buried Mirror* (Boston: Houghton Mifflin, 1992), 130–35, 144–47.

Was the *encomienda* system a continuation or revival of European feudalism? Why would the crown want to leave the conquistadors and their descendants in legal ambiguity regarding their holdings?

Fuentes also discusses the development of the Black Legend — the "legend," spread especially by Protestant Northern European powers, that Catholic Spanish colonialism was "blackest" or most brutal of all. Las Casas was often blamed for providing ammunition for the Black Legend. Do you think this is a fair charge? Often, published images like those of Theodor de Bry, which other European publishers used to illustrate Las Casas's text, were more instrumental than words in spreading the Black Legend. How would the images (see Figures 16, 17, and 18) spread the idea that Spanish colonialism was the most brutal? What does Fuentes say about criticisms of Spanish colonialism? How is his judgment different from that of Las Casas?

In the second part of the selection, "Father and Mother," Fuentes examines the religious impact of the Spanish conquest of Mexico. What, according to Fuentes, was that impact? Was it what Las Casas would have wanted?

Thinking Historically

Fuentes says in the second part of this selection that after the conquest Las Casas saw hope for Mexicans in "denunciation" — denouncing the injustices, the atrocities, slavery, and exploitation. What do you think Fuentes thinks about denunciation as a path to hope today, almost five hundred years later? How does Fuentes's approach to the Spanish conquest differ from Las Casas's? How would you characterize his approach, and how does it provide hope for Mexicans?

"The Indies Are Being Destroyed!"

This was the cry of Father Bartolomé de Las Casas, who picked up Father Montesinos's Christmas sermon of 1511 and his question about the Indians: "Are these not men? Have they not rational souls?" — "the first cry for justice in the Americas," wrote the modern Dominican writer Pedro Henríquez Ureña.

Bartolomé de Las Casas was a slave owner in Cuba who renounced his holdings and joined the Dominicans in 1524, accusing the conquistadors of "endless crimes and offenses against the Indians who were the king's subjects. "Over a period of fifty years, from the moment he forsook his *encomienda* in 1515 to his death in 1566, Father Las Casas denounced the "destruction of the Indies" by the conquistadors, accusing them of "the torts and offenses that they do to the kings of Castile, destroying their kingdoms . . . in the Indies." He went so far as to praise the Indians for the religiosity that they displayed, even if they were pagans. Had not the Greeks, the Romans, and the Hebrews been idolaters too? And had this pagan religiosity excluded them from the human race, or rather, nicely predisposed them for conversion?

Las Casas denied the rights of conquest, especially the institution of the *encomienda,* which he considered "more unjust and cruel than Pharaoh's oppression of the Jews," and which deprived "both masters and subjects of their freedom and of their lives." These modern ideas on the master-slave relationship, along with Las Casas's principal demands, were incorporated into the Laws of the Indies in 1542. The *encomienda* was legally abolished, although it remained, disguised as *repartimientos,* or provisional allotments of Indian laborers, as a self-perpetuating fact within the real economic system in the New World. The Crown went on combatting it, substituting administrative systems and royalist controls for it, refusing the conquistadors and their descendants property rights to their lands, and endlessly postponing decisions that would grant them feudal domination, titles of nobility, or hereditary rights.

In this sense, it can be said, with all due respect to Father Bartolomé de Las Casas, that he was the Crown's most useful tool in attacking feudal pretensions while defending humanitarian values. But in the final analysis, this struggle left a wide margin for the de facto powers of the conquistadors while preserving the eminent domain of Spanish royalty. The conquistadors and their descendants were purposely left by the Crown in the legal light of usurpers. But the Laws of the Indies, it was said, were like a spider's web, which caught only the smaller criminals and let the big ones get off scot free.

Many sixteenth-century testimonies depict the actual brutality of the *encomienda* and its even more severe form, work in the mine (*la mita*). In his marvelous line drawings of the life of Peru before and after the conquest, Guamán Poma de Ayala, a descendant of the Inca nobility, depicted the absolute impunity of the *encomendero* and his henchmen. The drawings of Theodor de Bry, which accompanied the best-selling volume by Father Las Casas, *The Destruction of the Indies,* fathered the so-called Black Legend of a brutal, sanguinary, and sadistic Spain, torturing and killing wherever she went — in tacit contrast, no doubt, to the lily-white colonialists from France, England, and the Netherlands. Yet while the latter piously disguised their own cruelties and inhumanities, they never did what Spain permitted. A debate on the nature of the conquered peoples and the rights of conquest raged through the Hispanic world for a full century, becoming the first full-fledged modern debate on human rights. This was hardly anything that the other colonial powers worried about.

There were even notes of humor in the debate, from both the Indian and the Spanish sides. During the conquest of Chile, the Araucanian chieftain Caupolicán was impaled by the conquistadors, yet as he was dying, he said, "I wish I had invaded and conquered Spain." The

Figure 16. Indians mining silver.

same idea, from the other side of the water, was expressed by a defender of human rights just as important as Las Casas, Father Francisco de Vitoria. A Jesuit teaching at Salamanca in 1539, he asked his students if they would like to see Spaniards treated by Indians in Spain the way Spaniards treated Indians in America. Discovery and conquest, he said, gave Spain no more right to American territory than the Indians would have if they discovered and conquered Spain. No doubt the same thing could have been said of the English colonization of North America. But what Father Vitoria did in his books and teachings was to internationalize the problem of power over the colonies and of the human rights of the conquered peoples. He attempted to set down rules limiting colonial power through international law, then called *jus gentium,* or the rights of people. His nemesis was the aforementioned Juan Ginés de Sepúlveda, who accused the Indians of cannibalism and human sacrifice in a society not very different from a colony of ants. As the Indians were presocial, they could legitimately be conquered by "civil men" from Europe, and all their goods could be put to civilized use, argued Sepúlveda. But were not the Spaniards, Vitoria argued right back, also guilty of crimes against nature? Were not all European nations culpable of acts of destruction and war? If this was so, no one had the moral right to conquer the Indians. . . .

Figure 17. Three Native Americans.

Father and Mother

Whether the conquest was right or wrong, the church knew that its primary mission was to evangelize. Its missionaries met a population torn between the desire to revolt and the desire to find protection. The church offered the latter as abundantly as it could. Many Indian groups, including the Coras in Mexico, the Quechuas in Peru, and the Araucanians in Chile, resisted the Spanish for a long time. Others thronged to the church, asking for baptism in the streets and roads. The Franciscan priest Toribio de Benavente, who arrived in Mexico in 1524, was called Motolinia by the Indians, which means "the poor and humble one." He wrote, "Many come to be baptized, not only on Sundays or feast days, but even on weekdays, children and adults, healthy and sick, and from all the regions; and when the friars travel, the Indians come out to the roads with their children in their arms, and with their sick on their backs, and even decrepit old people come out, demanding to be baptized. . . . And as they go to baptism, some pray, others complain, others implore on their knees, others lift their arms, moaning and twisting, and others receive it crying and sighing."

Motolinia affirmed that in this way, fifteen years after the fall of the Aztecs in 1521, "more than four million souls had been baptized."

Even if this is church propaganda, the fact remains that the formal events of Catholicism, from baptism to death rites, became a permanent fixture of popular life throughout Spanish America, and that church architecture displayed a practical imagination in uniting two vital factors of the new societies of the Americas: the need for a sense of parenthood, a father and mother, and the need for a protective physical space where the old gods might be admitted in disguise, behind the altars of the new gods.

Most mestizos did not know their fathers. They knew only their Indian mothers, the common-law wives of the Spanish. Miscegenation was certainly the rule in the Iberian colonies, as opposed to racial purity and puritanical hypocrisy in the English colonies. But this did not soften the sensation of orphanhood that many offspring of Spaniards and Indian women must have felt. La Malinche had a child by Cortés, who recognized him and had him baptized Martín. Cortés had another son, also named Martín, by his not yet strangled wife, Catalina Juárez. In time the brothers met, and in 1565 staged the first rebellion of Mexican Creole and mestizo nationalism against Spanish rule. The legitimation of the bastard, the identification of the orphan, became one of the

Figure 18. Indians retaliating.

central, if at times unspoken, problems of Latin American culture. It was dealt with by the Spaniards through religious and legal means.

The flight of the gods, who had abandoned their people; the destruction of the temples; the razing of the cities; the wholesale pillage and destruction of Indian culture; the devastation of the Indian economy by the mine and the *encomienda;* plus the almost paralyzing sense of amazement, of sheer wonder at what had happened — where was hope to be found? The subjugated Indians could hardly see a glimmer anywhere. How were despair and insurrection to be avoided? This was the question raised by the humanists of the colonies, but also by their wiser (and wilier) politicians. One answer had been Las Casas's denunciation. But it was truly the second viceroy and first archbishop of Mexico City, Juan de Zumárraga, who found the lasting solution: Give a mother to the orphaned children of the New World.

In early December 1531, on Tepeyac Hill near Mexico City, a site previously dedicated to the worship of the Aztec goddess Tonantzin, the Virgin of Guadalupe appeared, bearing roses in winter and choosing a lowly *tameme,* or Indian bearer, Juan Diego, as the object of her love and recognition. In one fabulous stroke, the Spanish authorities transformed the Indian people from children of violated women to children of the pure Virgin. From Babylon to Bethlehem, in one flash of political genius, whore became virgin and Malinche became Guadalupe. Nothing has proved as consoling, unifying, and worthy of fierce respect since then as the figure of the Virgin of Guadalupe in Mexico, the Virgin of La Caridad del Cobre in Cuba, and the Virgin of Coromoto in Venezuela. The conquered people now had a mother.

They also found a father. Mexico imposed on Cortés the mask of Quetzalcoatl. Cortés refused it and instead imposed on Mexico the mask of Christ. Ever since, it has been impossible to know who is worshipped at the baroque altars of Puebla, Oaxaca, and Tlaxcala: Christ or Quetzalcoatl? In a universe accustomed to seeing men sacrificed to the gods, nothing amazed the Indians more than the sight of a god who had sacrificed himself to men. It was the redemption of humankind by Christ that fascinated and really defeated the Indians of the New World. The true return of the gods was the arrival of Christ. Christ was the recovered memory that in the beginning it *was* the gods who sacrificed themselves for the benefit of humankind. This misty memory, engulfed by the somber human sacrifices ordained by Aztec power, was now rescued by the Christian church. The result was flagrant syncretism, the blending of Christian and aboriginal faiths, one of the cultural foundations of the Spanish American world.

Yet a striking fact remains: All the Mexican Christs are dead, or at the very least in agony. Whether in Calvary, on the cross, or laid out in a glass bier, the Christ that one sees in Mexico's village churches is bleeding, prostrate, and lonely. By contrast, the Virgin, as in Spain, is surrounded by perpetual glory, celebration, flowers, and processions. And the decor itself, the great baroque architecture of Latin America, is both a celebration of the new religion and a risky celebration of the survival of the old one.

The marvelous chapel at Tonantzintla near Cholula is one of the most startling confirmations of syncretism as the dynamic basis of post-conquest culture. What happened here happened throughout Latin America. The Indian artisans were given engravings of the saints and other religious motifs by the Christian evangelizers and asked to reproduce them inside the churches. But the artisans and masons of the temples had something more than a copy in mind. They wished to celebrate their old gods as well as the new ones, but they had to mask this intention by blending a praise of nature with a praise of heaven and making them indistinguishable. Tonantzintla is in effect a re-creation of the Indian paradise. White and gold, it overflows with plenty as all the fruits and the flowers of the tropics climb up to its dome, a dream of infinite abundance. Religious syncretism triumphed as, somehow, the conquerors were conquered.

In Tonantzintla, the Indians depicted themselves as innocent angels on the way to heaven, while the Spanish conquistadors were shown as ferocious, fork-tongued, bearded devils. Paradise can be regained after all.

90

ALFRED CROSBY

From *The Columbian Exchange*

The modern historian Alfred Crosby takes us back to Aztec Mexico, even if the names and dates at first do not seem familiar. Why, according to Crosby, were the Spanish able to conquer the Aztecs? What were the major consequences of the conquest? What would have most surprised Lord Ahuitzotl if he could have returned one hundred years later?

Alfred W. Crosby, "The Biological Metamorphosis of the Americas," in *Germs, Seeds, and Animals: Studies in Ecological History* ed. Alfred W. Crosby (Armonk: M. E. Sharpe, 1994), 45–49, 60.

Thinking Historically

What is the meaning of the Spanish conquest for this modern historian? Is his interpretation better, more modern, or merely different from the earlier interpretations you have read? To what extent are his interpretations merely a result of asking different questions? Are his questions "modern" ones that could not have been asked in the sixteenth century?

Chimalpahin Cuauhlehuanitzin, one of our best sources of information on Mexico in the years immediately before and after the Spanish conquest, was an Indian historian whom the invaders trained in the reading and writing of the Roman alphabet in the sixteenth century. His writings (in Nahuatl) inform us that the year 13-Flint before the invasion was a grim one in the Valley of Mexico. There was sickness, hunger, and an eclipse of the sun; an eruption of some sort between the volcanoes Iztaccíhuatl and Popocatépetl; "and many ferocious beasts devoured the children." But 13-Flint, Chimalpahin makes clear, was an exception in what was an era of triumph for the Aztecs. They, who within recorded memory had been wanderers from the savage north, now exacted tributes of food, gold, quetzal feathers, and human hearts from vassal states all the way from the remote dry lands from which they had emerged to the rain forests of the south and east. The stiff-necked Tarascos, at the cost of perennial war, retained their independence, as did — precariously — the anciently civilized Mayas, and there were a few others who survived in the chinks of the Aztec Empire. Otherwise, central Mexico lay under the hegemony of the Aztecs.

Lord Ahuitzotl, who was ruler of the Aztecs in 13-Flint, used the legions and wealth under his command to improve and adorn his capital, the incomparable Tenochtitlán. He built a new aqueduct to bring fresh water to its scores of thousands of inhabitants. He rebuilt and reconsecrated the gigantic temple to the Aztec tribal deities, Huitzilopochtli and Tezcatlipoca. He did not — how could he have? — see in the strange events of 13-Flint portents of the end of his empire and of his world.

A decade later, in 10-Rabbit, his nephew Motecuhzoma Xocoyotzin, known to us as Montezuma, succeeded him as leader of the Aztecs. Montezuma's subjects numbered in the millions, and, so far as he or they knew, the empire had no equal in power and riches under the sky. Montezuma made plans to rebuild the great temple once more, higher and more extravagantly than any of his predecessors.

Reports drifted in from the eastern coast of pale, hairy visitors in boats "like towers or small mountains." There were only a few of them, and invaders traditionally came from the north, as had the Aztecs themselves, not from the east and never from the sea. Gods, however, might come from the sea.

The Onslaught

In the year 1-Reed the visitors came to invade and to stay forever. The invaders proved to be humans, not gods, but they were incomprehensibly alien and powerful. . . .

Most hideous of all the invaders' allies was a pestilence, a *hueyzahuatl,* that swept all the land immediately after the Aztecs, quickened by atrocities, turned on the invaders, killing half of them as they fought their way out of Tenochtitlán. The pestilence spared the invaders but was a thing of agony, disfigurement, and death for the peoples of Mexico. There was no defense against it nor cure for it. Bernardino de Sahagún learned how it struck in the month of Tepeilhuitl and

> spread over the people as great destruction. Some it quite covered on all parts — their faces, their heads, their breasts, and so on. There was a great havoc. Very many died of it. They could not walk; they only lay in their resting places and beds. They could not move; they could not stir; they could not change position, nor lie on one side; nor face down, nor on their backs. And if they stirred, much did they cry out. Great was its destruction. Covered, mantled with pustules, very many people died of them.

One-third, one-half — no one knows how many — of the Aztecs and the other peoples of Mexico died. . . .

The invaders' chief, Hernán Cortés, ordered that stones from the temple of which Lord Ahuitzotl had been so proud should be gathered up, and that a Christian cathedral should be made of them in the center of what had become, by his victory, Mexico City. The vanquished learned that the ominous year 13-Flint was more properly designated as the year 1492 of a deity both more imperialistic and more merciful than Huitzilopochtli or Tezcatlipoca, and that Tenochtitlán had fallen in the year 1521, not 3-House.

The fall of Tenochtitlán in the year 3-House was the worst discrete event in the Aztecs' history. Worse, however, was this: 3-House was the beginning of the most tragic century of their history. Their civilization suffered massive amputations and survived at the root only by accepting alien graftings in the branch, as the conquistadores and the friars replaced their ancient noble and priestly classes. There were advantages that came with the defeat: an alphabet, a more supple instrument for expression than their own logo-syllabic system of writing; the true arch to replace the corbel; tools with an iron edge that did not shatter like an obsidian edge when it struck the rock hidden in the leaves. But the magnitude of the change, good and bad, was almost greater than the mind could encompass or the heart endure. The metamorphosis was more than political or religious or intellectual or technological; it was biological. The biota of Mexico — its *life* — and, in time, that of the entire Western Hemisphere changed.

The Change

If Lord Ahuitzotl had returned to Mexico (now New Spain) a hundred years after 13-Flint he would have found much the same as in his lifetime. He would have recognized the profiles of the mountains, all the wild birds, and most of the plants. The basic and holy food of his people was still maize. But he would have been stunned by the sight of plants and creatures he had never seen or dreamed of during his days on earth. Alien plants grew alongside the old plants in Mexico, and its 1592 fauna, in its large animals, was as different from that of 1492 as the native fauna of Zimbabwe is from that of Spain.

The invaders had brought in wheat and other Eurasian and African grains; peach, pear, orange, and lemon trees; chick-peas, grape vines, melons, onions, radishes, and much more. A Spanish nobleman come to America could require his *indios* to furnish his table with the foods of his ancestors. Along with the Old World crops had come Old World weeds. European clover was by now so common that the Aztecs had a word of their own for it. They called it Castilian *ocoxochitl,* naming it after a low native plant that also prefers shade and moisture.

Of all the new sights of 1592 — the cathedrals, the fields of wheat, wheeled vehicles, brigantines with sails and lounging sailors on Lake Texcoco where there had once been only canoes and sweating paddlers — nothing could have amazed Ahuitzotl more than the new animals: pigs, sheep, goats, burros, and others. Now there were cattle everywhere, and ranches with more than a hundred thousand each in the north. Now there were thousands upon thousands of horses, and they were available to any European (and, despite the law, the Indian, too) with a few coins or the skill to rope them. The horsemanship of the Mexican *vaquero* was already legendary on both sides of the Atlantic.

During Lord Ahuitzotl's lifetime the best way to move four hundred ears of maize in Mexico was on the bent back of a man, and the fastest means to deliver a message was by a runner. Now the bent man loaded four thousand ears onto a wheeled wagon pulled by a burro, and the messenger vaulted onto a horse and set off at several times the fastest pace of the fastest sprinter.

But Lord Ahuitzotl was an Aztec, an *indio,* and what would have put a catch in his breath a century after 13-Flint was not so much the new animals, for all their number, but his own kind of people, in their meager number. War, brutality, hunger, social and family disarray, loss of farmland to the invading humans and their flocks, and exploitation in general had taken their toll, but disease was the worst enemy. The *hueyzahuatl* of 1520–21, like the fall of Tenochtitlán, may have been the worst of its kind, but, more important, it was the beginning of a series of pestilential onslaughts. The worst of the worst of the times of *cocoliztli* were 1545–48, a time of bleeding from the nose and eyes, and 1576–81, when, again, many bled from the nose and windrows of Indians fell, but few Spaniards. If Lord Ahuitzotl had returned a century after his death, he would have found one for every ten or even twenty *indios* who had lived in his time.

Some of the survivors were *mestizos,* children of European men and Indian women. The mestizo, with his Indian skin and Visigothic eyes, proffering a cup of cocoa, a mixture of *chocolatl* and Old World sugar; the wild Chichimec on his Berber mare; the Zapotec herder with his sheep; the Aztec, perhaps the last of the line of Ahuitzotl, receiving the final rites of the Christian faith as he slipped into the terminal coma of an infection newly arrived from Seville — in so many ways New Spain was *new,* a combination, crossing, and concoction of entities that had never before existed on the same continent. . . .

And on and on to the present day. Alaska's and Canada's most remote Eskimos and Indians and South America's last tribes of hunter-gatherers and horticulturists have been decimated by tuberculosis, measles, and influenza within living memory. In 1990 the Yanomamö of the borderland of Brazil and Venezuela were decreasing rapidly under the attack not only or even primarily of the encroaching gold miners, but of malaria, influenza, measles, and chicken pox. The best ally of the invaders continues to be disease. . . .

Native Americans often object to the name "New World," a European term for the lands of the Western Hemisphere. They point out that those lands were familiar to them long before Christopher Columbus was born, and their argument is one the rest of us owe respectful consideration. But we all are justified in the use of the title for the Americas since 1492. Until Columbus found his way across the Atlantic, the biota of the two sets of continents on either side were markedly different, the products of what, through time, had usually been divergent evolution. Since then the biota of both, most undeniably of the Americas, have in significant part been the product of revolution, that is, the abrupt addition and explosive propagation of exotic species from the lands on the other side of the waters that Columbus crossed in 1492. The great Genovese navigated, administered, crusaded, enslaved, but above all he mixed, mingled, jumbled, and homogenized the biota of our planet.

REFLECTIONS

Truth and change are concepts we sometimes have difficulty reconciling. If something is true, how can it change? How can new truths replace old truths without making the old truths false? These are questions that are even more perplexing when it comes to historical writing, because history is the study of the past. It would seem that because the past does not change, a new interpretation of it would simply supercede the older one, and, yet, this is not necessarily so.

Las Casas's *The History of the Indies,* with its grand comparative sweep and its great political mission, could not have been written in the heat of battle. We might say that it is a wonder that it was written at all, and a wonder that it found an audience — especially a Spanish audience — and a king, who were willing to listen, read, and debate the issues it raised. The Protestant Reformation might have ensured its publication by Spain's enemies, but, as Fuentes observes, the Spanish debate over Indian rights was unique in Europe. It was also a debate that the Spanish could not have held before 1550. The language of the initial contact, in Díaz's and the Aztec accounts, was wonder, surprise, revulsion, fear, remorse perhaps, but not self-analysis, cultural criticism, or political reform. The year 1550 was, in fact, too early for tolerance or equality. Slavery did not end in European colonies for another three hundred years. It took three hundred years to build a consensus around the rights of life, liberty, and property — a consensus nourished by history books perceived as moral tales, stories of outrageous acts in the tradition of Las Casas.

Good guys and bad guys were out of style at the end of the twentieth century. Historians in former colonies that have been self-governing for generations or centuries find no benefit in blaming the colonizers or in feeling victimized. What is needed for renewal are stories that highlight old abilities and new hopes. In a world of hyphenated identities, five hundred years after the beginning of a "new race" in Mexico, what is needed is no race, no division. Fuentes looks for a Mexico that is both Spanish and Indian, Christian and pagan, beyond blame and schism. Like many of today's historians of the Spanish conquest, Fuentes emphasizes the continuity between preconquest and postconquest Mexican culture, Malinche and Guadalupe, Quetzalcoatl and Christ. Does the desire for solidarity make for a history that is less true? Or is it more true because it answers questions that are relevant to peoples' needs today?

Alfred Crosby is a founder of ecological history in the United States, probably one of the most rapidly developing subfields in the discipline. Like world history, it is an approach to the past that answers recent questions and concerns. Much of our knowledge of species, microbes, and climate comes from a postsatellite age. If postsatellite ecological history glosses over heroes and villains (as postmodern history forsakes morals and heroics for irony and nuance), every generation gets what it needs. Old narrative styles do not disappear.

One of the most popular history books of the nineteenth century was William H. Prescott's *History of the Conquest of Mexico* (1843), which was essentially a retelling of Bernal Díaz's *The Conquest of New Spain,* with all of the drama, heroism, and excitement of the original. More recent is the popular *Conquest: Montezuma, Cortés, and the Fall of Old Mexico* (1993) by Hugh Thomas — the big narrative has not gone out of style.

In types of history, like everything else, our age tries to "have it all." In one sense we can: Bookstores — new, used, and virtual — offer abundant possibilities. It's a free country: People can read whatever they want. But when writing a history, a common goal is to get it right. Readers who have less than infinite time want something that is accurate, informed, truthful. On all such levels, historians must make choices. Even if we only want to tell a story, we must choose whose story to tell. Reading the accounts by Díaz and the Aztec account and Alfred Crosby reminds us that observations of the same event are as unique as the individual who communicates them; indeed, the tellings may seem to record different events altogether.

One of the most useful lessons history teaches us, then, is the partiality of any interpretation and, by inference, the possibility of so many other interpretations. Perhaps that realization will allow us to tolerate the eccentric, grow from disagreements, and expand our own possibilities, asking our own questions, yielding our own answers. And if we can do that without losing sight of the obdurate, unchanging reality of the past, we will have learned to think historically.

(*Continued from p. ii*)

Anonymous excerpt from *The Bhagavad-Gita,* translated by Barbara Stoler Miller. Copyright © 1986 by Barbara Stoler Miller. Reprinted with the permission of Bantam Books, a division of Bantam Doubleday Dell Publishing Group, Inc.

Anonymous, excerpt from *The Epic of Gilgamesh,* translated by N. K. Sandars. Copyright © 1972 by N. K. Sandars. Reprinted with the permission of Penguin Books, Ltd.

Anonymous, excerpt from *Nihongi: Chronicles of Japan from the Earliest Times,* Volume 2, translated by W. G. Aston. Copyright © 1956 by W. G. Aston. Reprinted with the permission of Unwin Hyman/HarperCollins Publishers, Ltd.

Anonymous, excerpt from "The Rig-Veda" in *Sources of Indian Tradition,* Second Edition, edited and revised by Ainslie T. Embree. Copyright © 1988 by Columbia University Press. Reprinted with the permission of the publishers.

Anonymous, excerpt from "Svetasvatara Upanishad" from *The Upanishads: Breath of the Eternal,* translated by Swami Prabhavananda and Frederick Manchester. Copyright © 1948, 1957 by The Vedanta Society of Southern California. Reprinted with permission.

Anonymous, excerpt from "The Upanishads" [Brihad Aranyaka, IV: 4: 5–6] from *The Thirteen Principle Upanishads,* edited and translated by R. E. Hume. Copyright © 1954 by R. E. Hume. Reprinted with the permission of Oxford University Press, New Delhi.

Anonymous, excerpt from "The Upanishads" [Chandyoga V:10: 7] from *The Hindu Tradition: Readings in Oriental Thought,* edited by Ainslie T. Embree. Copyright © 1966 and renewed 1994 by Random House, Inc. Reprinted with the permission of the publishers.

Anonymous, "Setne Khamwas and Naneferkaptah" from Miriam Lichtheim, *Ancient Egyptian Literature: Volume III, The Late Period.* Copyright © 1980 by The Regents of the University of California. Reprinted with the permission of the University of California Press.

Aristotle, excerpt from "The Athenian Constitution" from *Aristotle, Politics and the Athenian Constitution,* translated by John Warrington. Copyright © 1959 by John Warrington. Reprinted with the permission of David Campbell Publishers, Ltd.

Aṣṭasāhasrikā Prajñāpāramitā, 22.402–403 and Pañcaviṃśatisāhasrikā Prajñāpāramitā, from William Theodore de Bary (editor), *The Buddhist Tradition in India, China, and Japan.* Copyright © 1969 and renewed 1998 by William Theodore de Bary. Reprinted with the permission of Random House, Inc.

"Aztec Account of the Conquest" from *The Broken Spears: The Aztec Account of the Conquest of Mexico* by Miguel Leon-Portilla, translated by Lysander Kemp. Copyright © 1962 by Beacon Press. Reprinted with the permission of the publisher.

Elise Boulding, "Women and the Agricultural Revolution" from *The Underside of History: A View of Women Through Time* (Boulder: Westview Press, 1976). Copyright © 1976 by Elise Boulding. Reprinted with the permission of the author.

Andreas Capellanus, excerpt from *The Art of Courtly Love,* translated by John J. Parry. Copyright © 1990 by Columbia University Press. Reprinted with the permission of the publisher.

Celsus, "On Christians," translated by H. Chadwick, as quoted in Ramsay MacMullen, *Christianizing the Roman Empire A.D. 100–400*. Copyright © 1984 by Yale University. Reprinted with the permission of Yale University Press.

Chia Yi, "Rhymeprose on an Owl" (excerpt), translated by John Robert Hightower, from Cyril Birch, ed., *An Anthology of Chinese Literature: From Early Times to the Fourteenth Century*. Copyright © 1965 by Grove Press, Inc. Reprinted with the permission of Grove/Atlantic, Inc.

"Chronicle of Simon bar Simson" from Shlomo Eidelberg (editor and translator), *The Jews and the Crusaders: The Hebrew Chronicles of the First and Second Crusades* (Madison: The University of Wisconsin Press, 1977). Copyright © 1977. Reprinted with the permission of Shlomo Eidelberg.

Cicero, "Against Verres" (II, 5) from *On Government*, translated by Michael Grant. Copyright © 1993 by Michael Grant. Reprinted with the permission of Penguin Books, Ltd.

Anna Comnena, excerpt from *The Alexiad of Princess Anna Comnena*, translated by Elizabeth A. S. Dawes. Reprinted with the permission of Barnes and Noble Books, Totowa, New Jersey, 07512.

Confucius, excerpts from *The Analects of Confucius*, translated by Arthur Waley. Copyright © 1958 by Arthur Waley. Reprinted with the permission of George Allen & Unwin and HarperCollins UK.

"Converting the Hessians" from Willibard's *Life of Boniface*, from *The Anglo-Saxon Missionaries in Germany*, translated by C. H. Talbot. Copyright © 1945. Reprinted with the permission of Sheed & Ward, Ltd.

Alfred Crosby, "The Columbian Exchange" from *Germs, Seeds, and Animals*. Copyright © 1994. Reprinted with the permission of M. E. Sharpe, Inc., Armonk, NY 10504.

Gregorio Dati, "Corporations and Community in Florence" from Gene Brucker, ed. and trans., *The Society of Renaissance Florence* (New York: Harper & Row, Publishers, 1971). Copyright © 1971. Reprinted with the permission of The Renaissance Society of America.

William Theodore de Bary (editor), "Buddhism and Caste" from *The Buddhist Tradition in India, China and Japan*. Copyright © 1969 and renewed 1998 by William Theodore de Bary. Reprinted with the permission of Random House, Inc.

Bernal Diaz, excerpt from *The Conquest of New Spain*, translated by J. M. Cohen. Copyright © 1963 by J. M. Cohen. Reprinted with the permission of Penguin Books, Ltd.

Ross E. Dunn, excerpt from *The Adventures of Ibn Battuta*. Copyright © 1986 by The Regents of the University of California. Reprinted with the permission of The University of California Press.

Patricia Buckley Ebrey, "The Creation of the Bureaucratic Empire" from *The Cambridge Illustrated History of China*. Copyright © 1996. Reprinted with the permission of Cambridge University Press.

The Koran, excerpts from *The Qur'an: Selections from the Noble Reading*, Third Edition, translated by T. B. Irving (Cedar Rapids: Mother Mosque Foundation, 1991). Copyright © 1991 by T. B. Irving. Reprinted with the permission of the author.

Brenda Fowler, "Find Suggests Weaving Preceded Settled Life" from *The New York Times* (May 9, 1995). Copyright © 1995 by The New York Times Company. Reprinted with the permission of *The New York Times*.

Carlos Fuentes, excerpt from *The Buried Mirror: Reflections on Spain and the New World.* Copyright © 1992 by Carlos Fuentes. Reprinted with the permission of the Houghton Mifflin Company. All rights reserved.

Jacques Gernet, "Street Life in Hangchow" from *Daily Life in China: On the Eve of the Mongol Invasion, 1250–1276,* translated by H. M. Wright (New York: Macmillan Publishing Company, 1962). Copyright © 1959 by Hachette. English translation copyright © 1962 by George Allen & Unwin, Ltd. Reprinted with the permission of Georges Borchardt, Inc.

S. D. Gotien, "Cairo: An Islamic City in Light of the Geniza" from Ira M. Lapidus, ed., *Middle Eastern Cities.* Copyright © 1969 by the Regents of the University of California. Reprinted with the permission of the University of California Press.

Gregory Guzman, "Were the Barbarians a Negative or Positive Factor in Ancient and Medieval History?" from *The Historian* L. (August 1988). Copyright © 1988. Reprinted with the permission of the author.

Hung-ming chi, excerpt from "Taishō daizōkyō," [LII, 1–7], quoted in William Theodore de Bary (editor), *The Buddhist Tradition in India, China, and Japan.* Copyright © 1969 and renewed 1998 by William Theodore de Bary. Reprinted with the permission of Random House, Inc.

John of Plano Carpini, excerpt from *History of the Mongols,* Guyuk Khan, "Letter to Pope Innocent IV" from "Narrative of Brother Benedict the Pole," and excerpt from *The Journey of William of Rubrick* from *Mission to Asia: Narratives and Letters of the Franciscan Missionaries in Mongolia and China in the Thirteenth and Fourteenth Centuries,* trans. by a nun of Stanbrook Abbey, edited by Christopher Dawson. Copyright © 1955. Reprinted with the permission of Sheed & Ward, Ltd.

James Kritzeck, "The Koran: Scripture and Literature" from *Anthology of Islamic Literature.* Copyright © 1964 by James Kritzeck. Reprinted with the permission of Henry Holt and Company, Inc.

Lao Tzu, excerpts from *The Way and Its Power: A Study of the Tao Te Ching,* translated by Arthur Waley (London: George Allen & Unwin, 1934). Copyright © 1934 by Arthur Waley. Reprinted with the permission of the Estate of Arthur Waley.

Ira M. Lapidus, "Muslim Cities and Islamic Societies" from Ira M. Lapidus, ed., *Middle Eastern Cities.* Copyright © 1969 by the Regents of the University of California. Reprinted with the permission of the University of California Press.

Bartolomé Las Casas, from *The History of the Indies,* translated and edited by Andree Collard. Copyright © 1971 by Alfred A. Knopf, Inc. Reprinted with the permission of the publishers.

Gerda Lerner, "The Urban Revolution: Origins of Patriarchy" from *The Creation of Patriarchy.* Copyright © 1986 by Gerda Lerner. Reprinted with the permission of Oxford University Press, Inc.

Letter of Paul to the Galatians 1:1–2:20, 6:11–18 and the Acts of the Apostles 15–19 from *The New English Bible.* Copyright © 1961, 1970 by Oxford University Press and Cambridge University Press. Reprinted with permission.

Li Ch'ing-chao, "A Wife's Collection" from Stephen Owen, *Remembrances: The Experience of the Past in Classical Chinese Literature* (Cambridge, Mass.: Harvard University Press, 1986). Copyright © 1986 by the President and Fellows of Harvard College. Reprinted with the permission of the translator.

Liu Tsung-yuan, "Camel Kuo the Gardener" from Cyril Birch, ed., *An Anthology of Chinese Literature: From Early Times to the Fourteenth Century.* Copyright © 1965 by Grove Press, Inc. Reprinted with the permission of Grove/Atlantic, Inc.

Amin Maalouf, excerpt from *The Crusades Through Arab Eyes,* translated by Jon Rothschild. Copyright © 1984 by Saqi Books. Reprinted with the permission of Al Saqi Books, London, England.

Mary Kilbourne Matossian, "From Hominids to Human Beings" from *Shaping World History: Breakthroughs in Ecology, Technology, Science, and Politics.* Copyright © 1997 by M. E. Sharpe, Inc. Reprinted with the permission of M. E. Sharpe, Inc., Armonk, NY 10504.

William H. McNeill, "Greek and Indian Civilization" from *A World History,* Second Edition. Copyright © 1971 by Oxford University Press. Reprinted with the permission of the author.

Ichisada Miyazaki, "The Chinese Civil Service Exam System" from *China's Examination Hell,* translated by Conrad Schirokauer. Reprinted with permission of the publishers, Weatherhill, Inc.

David Morgan, from *The Mongols.* Copyright © 1986 by David Morgan. Reprinted with the permission of Basil Blackwell.

Al Omari, "Mali in the Fourteenth Century" from Basil Davidson, ed., *The African Past: Chronicles from Antiquity to Modern Times* (Boston: Little, Brown and Company, 1964), pp. 75–79. Copyright © 1964 by Basil Davidson. Reprinted with the permission of Curtis Brown, Ltd.

Pliny, "Pliny consults the Emperor Trajan" [Letters 10: 96–97] from *Pliny Secundus: Letters and Panegyricus,* Volume II, translated by Betty Radice. Copyright © 1969 by the President and Fellows of Harvard College, Reprinted with the permission of Harvard University Press.

Plutarch, "Cicero" from *Fall of the Roman Empire,* translated by Rex Warner. Copyright © 1958 by Rex Warner, renewed 1986 by Frances C. Warner. Reprinted with the permission of Penguin Books, Ltd.

Marco Polo, excerpt from *Marco Polo: The Travels,* translated by Ronald Latham. Copyright © 1958 by Ronald Latham. Reprinted with the permission of Penguin Books, Ltd.

Nicholas Purcell, "Rome: The Arts of Government" in John Boardman, Jasper Griffin and Oswyn Murray, *The Oxford History of the Classical World: The Roman World.* Copyright © 1988 by Oxford University Press. Reprinted with the permission of the publishers.

Kevin Reilly, "Cities and Civilization" from *The West and the World: A History of Civilization,* Second Edition. Copyright © 1989 by Kevin Reilly. Reprinted with the permission of HarperCollins Publishers, Inc.

"Rules for the Fan Lineage's Charitable Estate" from Patricia Buckley Ebrey (editor and translator), *Chinese Civilization: A Sourcebook,* Second Edition. Copyright © 1993 by Patricia Buckley Ebrey. Reprinted with the permission of The Free Press, a division of Simon & Schuster.

Carl Sagan, excerpt from *The Dragons of Eden: Speculations on the Origins of Human Intelligence.* Copyright © 1977 by Carl Sagan. Reprinted with the permission of the Estate of Carl Sagan, c/o Janklow & Nesbit, New York.

J. J. Saunders, excerpt from "The Civilization of Medieval Islam" from *A History of Medieval Islam.* Copyright © 1978. Reprinted with the permission of Routledge UK.

Lynda Shaffer, "Southernization" from *Journal of World History* 5, no. 1 (Spring 1994).

Lady Murasaki Shikibu, excerpt from *The Tale of the Genji,* translated by Arthur Waley.

Magna Carta, excerpt from the Magna Carta, translated by A. E. Dick Howard.

Sei Shonagon, excerpt from *The Pillow Book of Sei Shonagon,* translated and edited by Ivan Morris.

Marjorie Shostak, "Memories of a !Kung Girlhood" from *Nisa: The Life and Words of a !Kung Woman.*

Sima Qian, "The Annals of Qin" and "The Builder of the Great Wall" from *Historical Records,* translated by Raymond Dawson.

Suetonius, "Augustus" from *The Twelve Caesars,* translated by Robert Graves, revised by Michael Grant.

John Noble Wilford, "The Seeds of History: A Find in Mexico" from *The New York Times* (May 9, 1997).

John Noble Wilford, "Three Fossil Discoveries Clarify the Murky Origins of Life" from *The New York Times* (October 31, 1995).

Lynn White Jr., "The Historical Roots of Our Ecological Crisis" from *Science,* 155, no. 3767 (March 10, 1967).

ILLUSTRATIONS

Figure 1. "The Eastern Mediterranean at the Time of the First Crusade." From *Medieval Europe* by William H. McNeill and Schuyler O. Houser, (New York: Oxford University Press, 1971), p. 120. Reprinted by permission of William H. McNeill.

Figure 2. "Image from Cistercian Manuscript, 12th Century, Monk Chopping Down Tree." Courtesy of Tresorier Principal Municipal – Dijon.

Figure 3. Limbourg Brothers. Month of March: Ploughing the field. In the background the Lurignan Castle. From the *Tres Riches Heures du Duc de Berry.* Courtesy of Musee Conde, Chantilly, France.

Figure 4. *Travellers amid Mountains and Streams* by Fan K'uan, Sung Dynasty. Courtesy of National Palace Museum, Taipei, Taiwan, Republic of China.

Figure 5. Old Cypress and Rock. Drawing by Wen Zhenming, 1550. Courtesy of THE NELSON-ATKINS MUSEUM OF ART, KANSAS CITY, MISSOURI (Purchase: Nelson Trust).

Figure 6. "The Mongol cavalry in hot pursuit." From a manuscript of Rashid al-Din's *Jami al-rawarikh.* Topkapi Palace Library, Istanbul, Turkey.

Figure 7. "The Mongols' captives led away." From a manuscript of Rashid al-Din's *Jami al-rawarikh.* Courtesy of Staatsbibliothek zu Berlin Preussicher Kulturbesitz Orientabteilung.

Figure 8. "Ravaisse's Boundary Approximations (based on Makrizi, 1441) in relation to modern Cairo." From Abu-Lughod, J. L., *Cairo: A Thousand and One Years of the City Victorious.* Copyright 1971 by Princeton University Press. Reprinted by permission of Princeton University Press.

Figure 10. "Florence: the expanding city walls." From *The Italian City Republics* by Daniel Waley (New York: McGraw-Hill, 1969), p. 36. Adapted and reprinted by permission of The Orion Publishing Group, Ltd., London, England.

Figure 11. "City view of Florence, 1482," by Lucantonio degli Uberti. Courtesy of Kupferstichkabinett, Staatliche Museen zu Berlin – Preubischer Kulturbesitz.

Figure 12. "Map of Delhi Sultanate under Muhammad Tughluq." From Karl J. Schmidt, *Atlas and Survey of South Asian History,* 1995, p. 41. Reprinted by permission from M.E. Sharpe, Inc., Armonk, NY 10504.

Figure 13. "Map of Delhi, 14th century, 1325–51." Courtesy of Oxford University Press, New Delhi.

Figure 14. "Map of Mexico City, published with the Second Letter of Hernan Cortes, in *Praeclara Ferdinandi Cortesii De Nova Maris Oceani Hispanica Narratio.*" Courtesy of Edward E. Ayer, The Newberry Library, Chicago.

Figure 15. "Detail of Central Square." Courtesy of Edward E. Ayer, The Newberry Library, Chicago.

Figure 16. "Indians Mining Silver" by Theodore de Bary. Courtesy of Lauros-Giraudon Photographie, Paris, France.

Figure 17. "Three Native Americans" by Theodore de Bary. Courtesy of Lauros-Giraudon Photographie, Paris, France.

Figure 18. "Indians Retaliating" by Theodore de Bary. Courtesy of Lauros-Giraudon Photographie, Paris, France.